Shoveler

THE LONG ROAD
TO GRAFTON

A Genealogy
of
Thomas Eastman Shoveller

The Long Road To Grafton: A Genealogy of Thomas Eastman Shoveller
by Dr. Tracy Rockwell (1955)

Volume 6
of the Rockwell Genealogies

First Published in Australia in 2022
by Pegasus Publishing (A)
PO Box 980, Edgecliff, NSW, 2027

Orders: pegasuspublishing@iinet.net.au
www.pegasuspublishing.com.au

Copyright © Pegasus Publishing
An Ashnong Pty Ltd Company

A CIP catalogue record for this book is available from the National Library of Australia.

ISBN: 978-1-925909-08-1

Printed and sold on Demand through:
Pegasus Publishing   -   www.pegasuspublishing.square.site
Ingram Lightning Source   -   www.ingramspark.com

Volumes In The Series - 'The Rockwell Genealogies':

Front Cover: 'South bend of the Clarence River, NSW,' taken from South Grafton looking west to Susan Island, photo by Dr Tracy P. Rockwell (2021).

OPPOSITE: Thomas Eastman Shoveller journeyed from San Francisco in the "Eclair", a vessel that would have resembled this small 50 ton schooner, eventually arriving in Sydney on the 23rd September 1851.

THE LONG ROAD TO GRAFTON

A Genealogy of Thomas Eastman Shoveller

Volume 6 of the Rockwell Genealogies

By
Dr Tracy Rockwell

Pegasus Publishing

CONTENTS & PLATES

LIST OF PEDIGREE CHARTS...

LIST OF MAPS...

LIST OF DESCENDANTS & FAMILIES...

▲ 'A Family Tree', by Norman Rockwell (1959).

DEDICATION

This genealogy is dedicated to the memory of Thomas Eastman Shoveller and his wife Susan Hann, who through great courage and strength of character as pioneers survived the many difficulties of early Australian life during the mid to late 19th century. A toast to their determination...

"To the land we live in... and the land we left behind."

Giraldus Cambrensus, Welsh Chronicler (1146-1223)

PREFACE

This story is exciting in its own right, but the Rockwell Genealogies are essentially one long book, and it could have been longer still. However, for ease of reading, I have divided the manuscript into a number of volumes, otherwise it would be impossible to publish one single volume light enough to read in bed. So expansive and illuminating has been the research that one volume has been published for each of my great-great grandparents, where there is sufficient evidence; one volume for my great grandparents and grandparents together; and one final volume for my parents, which I feel would be both a respectful and honourable tribute to the presence of these ancestors upon this earth.

In recording these stories my task was threefold: to reveal what could be found of the life and times of our illustrious and honoured ancestors; to reproduce the 'old life' without either sentimentality or caricature; and to preserve pedigrees, stories, verses and traditions that otherwise might be hopelessly lost. Within these pages I hope to have stored such flotsam and jetsam as could be rescued from the waters of oblivion.

While it is encouraging to read that even great historians have insights that resemble our own, a major persuasion in undertaking this detailed work was to preserve my own genealogical research accumulated across some 40 years of investigations. The publication of the 'Rockwell Genealogies' in an organised and interesting fashion, rather than filing away an indecipherable and ragged assemblage of notes, diagrams, tables and images is self-evident, particularly for those that come after. My greatest fear is in presenting too much material, as "a wealth of information creates a poverty of attention." However, genealogy is not a precise undertaking and while evidence for some branches and ancestors has been voluminous, little or no evidence whatsoever has been revealed for other branches of the family.

My initial goal was to discover 'how our forebears came to reside in Australia,' which I originally envisioned would encompass one or two volumes. With Australia being such a young country, I felt compelled to understand 'how, when and why our ancestors could possibly end up so far away from their places of birth?' Researching and documenting the various family members not only identified and revealed how and where they lived, it also recognised the sacrifices they experienced and the contributions they made, without which, few of us would be here today.

As the research broadened and evolved, more distant antecedents from the old countries were increasingly identified, and it became both worthwhile and necessary to also examine the lives of more distant relatives. To understand further, I have made recent efforts to visit as many of the towns, cities, regions and countries of my ancestors as possible. As such, it has to date been a thrill to connect with, and walk in the footsteps of these forebears as "they are now like little ghosts, forever ebbing slowly away from us."

This volume explores the genealogy of Thomas Eastman Shoveller (1827-1908), who emigrated from his native England to forge a new life as a pioneer in what became the township of Grafton in northern New South Wales. The manuscript covers the hereditary and ancestral families of Shoveller, Bignell, Eastman and Sabine in detail, and examines the significant lives of his known forebears.

Tracy Rockwell

Dip. Teach; BSc; MSc; PhD

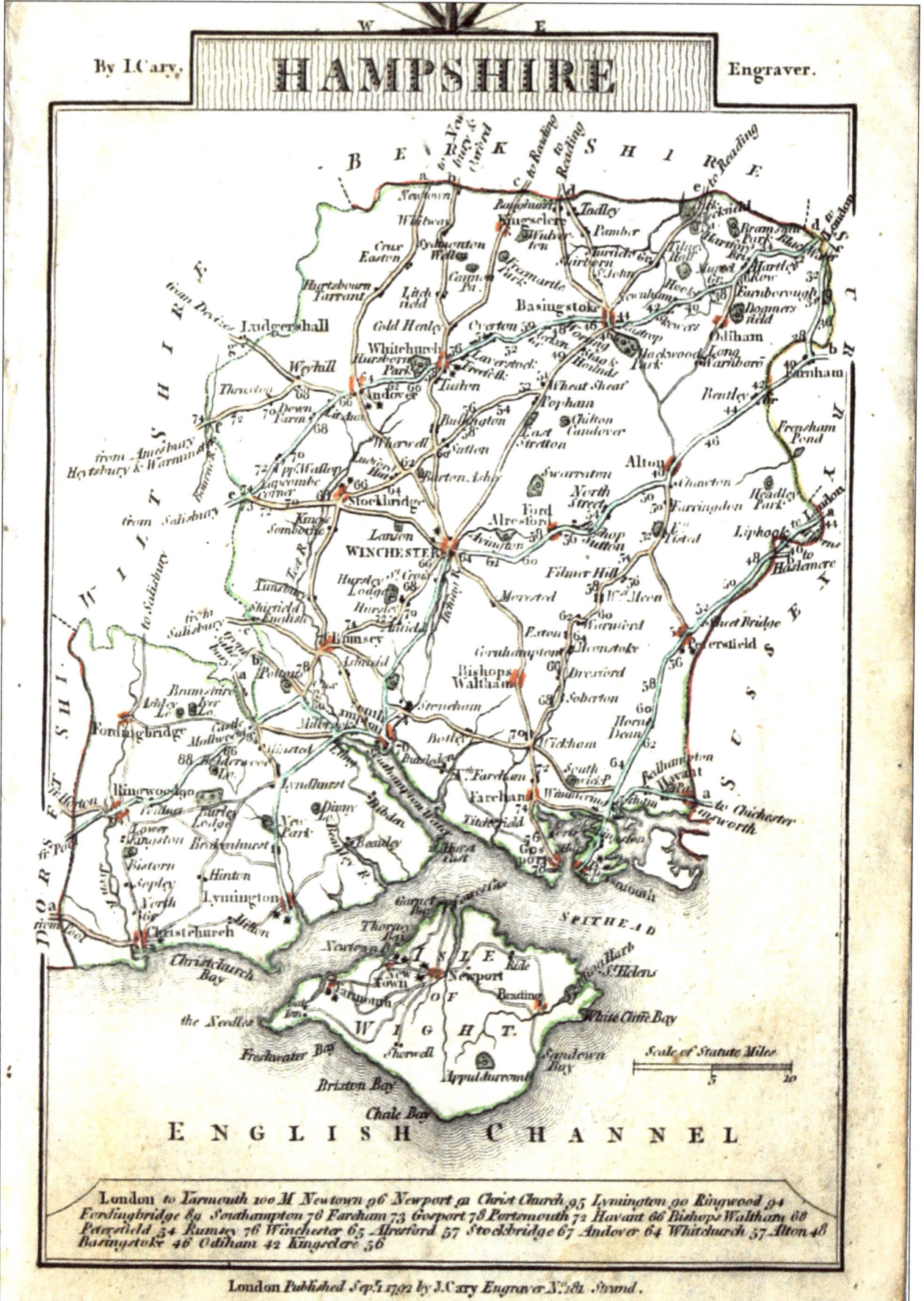

By I. Cary.

HAMPSHIRE

Engraver.

ENGLISH CHANNEL

London to Yarmouth 100 M Newtown 96 Newport 91 Christ Church 95 Lymington 90 Ringwood 94
Fordingbridge 89 Southampton 76 Fareham 73 Gosport 78 Portsmouth 72 Havant 66 Bishops Waltham 68
Petersfield 54 Rumsey 76 Winchester 65 Alresford 57 Stockbridge 67 Andover 64 Whitchurch 57 Alton 48
Basingstoke 46 Odiham 42 Kingsclere 56

London Published Sep.1 1792 by J. Cary Engraver N.181 Strand.

▲ *The earliest known Shoveller ancestors were found in the city of Portsmouth. ABOVE: Cary's 1792 map of the County of Hampshire.*

ACKNOWLEDGEMENTS

This book has been a pleasure to write, and I hope it is also a pleasure to read. A number of people and organisations have helped me write it, yet it would be impossible to acknowledge the assistance of each and every contributer. Of notable mention however, are the staff at the Clarence River Historical Society, who pointed me in the right direction at the start of my research in the early days from 1980. Of invaluable support was the Society of Australian Genealogists in Sydney, the Mitchell and State Libraries of New South Wales, the Port of Yamba Historical Society, the National Library of Australia and their online Trove digital newspaper and photography facilities.

Online websites and resources have also been extraordinarily helpful in researching content for this publication and my sincere thanks goes to the NSW Govt Registry of Births, Deaths and Marriages and the State Archives of NSW. In the old country, I am thankful to the Titchfield History Society, Hampshire; Portsmouth Public Library; Oxford University Archives; Cambridge University Archives; the Goldsmiths Company, London; The National Archives; British History Online, and Hampshire Archives and Local Studies at Hampshire County Council. International websites were also consulted including the International Genealogical Index (aka IGI or Family Search), Ancestry, as well as Wikitree and Wikipedia, which have all been invaluable sources of information.

ABBREVIATIONS & SYMBOLS

The following abbreviations and symbols have been used to summarise the historical information throughout the text, and a legend is provided below to help make sense of the various systems and codes used in the production of this book. If not indicated herein, it should be noted that in the case of baptisms, marriages and burials, the source is to be understood to be the parish register of the church where the ceremony took place.

One final note, is that the following pages are interspersed with escutcheons that are a representation of the various known ancestral families of Thomas Eastman Shoveller (1827-1908). However, these are mostly included to delineate the family groups and as such do not, for the most part, represent any particular grant of arms or official blazon.

Legend of Abbreviations & Symbols

C&RE	Clarence & Richmond Examiner.	bc.	born circa.
CF	Copyright free image.	bp.	baptised.
GS	Government Servant (convict).	c.	circa [*Latin*], about.
IGI	International Genealogical Index.	d.	died.
MM	Maternal Maternal.	dc.	died circa.
MP	Maternal Paternal.	d.s.p.	decessit sine prole [*Latin*], died
NA	National Arch. of England & Wales.		without issue.
PM	Paternal Maternal.	dspm.	descessit sine prole mascula [*Latin*];
PP	Paternal Paternal.		died without male issue.
PRO	Public Record Office, London.	dv.	divorced
SSD	Sands Sydney Directory.	d.v.p.	decessit vitae patre [*Latin*], died in
SMH	Sydney Morning Herald.		father's lifetime.
UV	Unverified.	fl.	flourished.
TES	Thomas Eastman Shoveller.	m.	married.
▲	Served in Australian Military Forces	mc.	married circa.
*	died before adulthood.	r.	reigned.
b.	born.	s.	succeeded

INTRODUCTION

As any family historian will tell you, genealogy is an addictive pastime, with the ever-present thrill of discovering ones ancestors, or connecting to some great icon, aristocrat or even royalty. My passion for this amazing pastime developed into a keen interest from the early 1980s, when I was working with QANTAS as an international flight steward. During stays in London while flying the QF1 route, I would often spend my three layover days trawling through documents at Somerset House and the Public Record Office in search of long lost relatives.

Genealogy can be an immensely rewarding and exacting pastime, but is also frustrating by nature of the fact that it is constantly evolving. I've often made the mistake of thinking that every possible facet had been uncovered about an ancestor, only to be surprised by some new piece of evidence, and so the research goes on, and on. Where information has come to light, the 'Rockwell Genealogies' examines the ancestry of each of the great-great grandparents of the author. The information is presented sequentially from paternal to maternal ancestors, examining the known strands of information by relevant family root and branch. I would however, gladly welcome feedback and corrections that genealogists or family members may wish to contribute.

What makes genealogy difficult is investigating common names in heavily populated places eg. trying to find a Smith or a Brown in New York would be next to impossible. Conversely, the task becomes easier when dealing with uncommon names, especially where there are fewer people, as possible linkages can be more readily presumed and proven. In researching our ancestors I was mostly fortunate in locating families that more often than not, had quite distinctive surnames, and resided for the most part in smaller towns and villages. The world wide web too, has brought about a revolution in genealogy, as we can today immediately research what years ago would have taken weeks and months.

In the former British colonies and America, few think it necessary to belong to a titled or landed family in order to have a pedigree worth recording. On the contrary, descent from anyone, esquire or artisan from colonial times is a source of pride; nor are these descendants diffident about their ancestors of any period, so long as they were honest people. Naturally, the knowledge or hope of distinguished ancestry is an additional stimulant.

By definition, the old right of succession belonging to a firstborn child was known as 'primogeniture', which benefitted families by preventing the subdivision of family estates. Primogeniture lessened the pressure today's families have to equally sub-divide property granted to beneficiaries. Historically however, younger sons of the nobility or the landed gentry across Europe had little or no prospect of inheriting property, and it was common for them to seek careers in the church, in military service by purchasing commissions, or in government.

But all of this was of no use without first being able to identify people. Surnames became necessary when governments introduced personal taxation. In England this was known as the 'Poll Tax.' Throughout the centuries, surnames in every country have continued to 'develop' often leading to astonishing variants of the original spellings. The early recording of births, deaths and marriages in England was voluntarily undertaken by the clergy of various local parish churches. Many of these original records have been copied into the International Genealogical Index (IGI aka 'Family Search') and are now directly accessible through the internet.

However, the increasingly poor state of English parish registration led to numerous attempts to shore up the system in the eighteenth and early nineteenth centuries. The Marriage Act of 1753 attempted to prevent 'clandestine' marriages by imposing a standard form of entry for marriages, which had to be signed by both parties and witnessed. Additionally, except in the case of Jews, Quakers and Catholics, legal marriages had to be carried out according to the rites of the Church of England. Sir George Rose's Parochial Registers Act of 1812 laid down that all events had to be entered on standard entries in bound volumes. It also declared that the church registers of 'non-conformists' were not admissible in court as evidence of births, marriages and deaths. Only those maintained by the clergy of the Church of England could be presented in court as legal documents. This caused considerable hardship for non-conformists and Catholics. As a result, a number of proposals were presented to Parliament to set up a centralised registry for recording vital events in the 1820s, but none came to fruition.

Eventually, increasing concern that the poor registration of baptisms, marriages and burials undermined property rights, by making it difficult to establish lines of descent, coupled with the complaints of non-conformists, led to the establishment in 1833 of a Parliamentary Select Committee on Parochial Registration. This committee took evidence on the state of the parochial system of registration, and made proposals that were eventually incorporated into the 1836 Registration and Marriage Acts. In addition, the government wanted to collect information on infant mortality, fertility and literacy to bring about improvements in health and social welfare. The medical establishment advocated these changes because there was a rapidly growing population in the northern towns, caused by the Industrial Revolution. Severe overcrowding resulted and links between poor living conditions and short life expectancy were then becoming known.

The answer was the establishment of a civil registration system. It was hoped that improved registration of vital events would protect property rights through the more accurate recording of lines of descent. Civil registration also removed the need for non-conformists to rely upon the Church of England for registration, and provide medical data for research. As a result, legislation was passed in 1836 that ordered the civil registration of births, marriages and deaths in England and Wales, which took effect from the 1st July 1837. An office was set up in London and the Department of Registrar Generals was established. Indeed, our ancestor John Shoveller LLD (*see Chapter 14*) received letters patent from King William IV, as one of the commissioners that enquired into and made recommendations for the introduction of national registers for the recording of births, marriages and deaths across England and Wales.

England and Wales were subsequently divided into 619 registration districts (623 from 1851), each under the supervision of a Superintendent Registrar. The districts were based on the recently introduced poor law unions. The registration districts were further divided into sub-districts (possibly two or more), each under the charge of Registrars who were locally appointed. Compulsory registration of births, deaths and marriages were susequently introduced into Scotland (1854), Australia (1856) and Ireland (1864), and although not all events were rigorously registered, this same system continues today.

"Time is a sort of river of passing events, and strong is its current; no sooner is a thing brought to sight than it is swept by and another takes its place, and this too will be swept away."

Marcus Aurelius, Roman Emporer

The town and harbour at Portsmouth with a view of His Majestys fleet at Spithead, possibly painted by Louis Gerard Scotin, c.1755.

THE ROCKWELL GENEALOGIES

Pedigree Chart 1 - The Ancestors & Descendants of Robert & Octavia Rockwell of Naremburn, NSW

Rockwell Branch
(Paternal Paternal)

Unknown — Unknown   Unknown — Unknown

Unknown   Unknown

Augustus Rockwell (UV)   Frances Austin (UV)

m.Unknown

Volume 1

William Henry Rockwell
c.1859-1932
b. London, ENG

Bantin / Barrett Branch
(Paternal Maternal)

Henry Bantin c.1802-1854 b. London, ENG — Mary Drewe ▲ 1805-1868 b. Colyton, ENG

George Barrett c.1801-1845 b. ?, ENG — Mary Avenell ▲ 1801-1869 b. Puttenham, ENG

m.1825, Colyton, Devon   m.1831, Puttenham, Surrey

Robert Bantin 1836-1884 b. London, ENG — Mary Barrett 1833-1906 b. Puttenham, ENG

m.1855, London, ENG

Volume 2

Elizabeth Bantin
1866-1955
b. Glebe, NSW

O'Sullivan / Frawley Branch
(Maternal Paternal)

Thadeus O'Sullivan ▲ 1800-1877 b. Rathmore, IRE — Zenobia E. Mahony ▲ 1800-1873 b. Tralee, IRE

John Frawley# ▲ c.1816-1901 b. Limerick, IRE — Mary Ann McGarry# ▲ c.1813-1889 b. Limerick, IRE

m.1823, Killarney, co. Kerry   m.1840, Wollongong, NSW

Volume 3   Volume 5

James Mahony O'Sullivan c.1837-1891 b. Coomb Cottage, IRE — Ellen Frawley 1842-1909 b. Wariguberra, NSW

m.1869, Sydney, NSW

Volume 4

Humphrey Joseph O'Sullivan
1871-1905
b. Fish River Creek, NSW

Shoveller / Hann Branch
(Maternal Maternal)

John Shoveller ▲ 1789-1847 b. Poole, ENG — Elizabeth Eastman ▲ 1785-1852 b. Portsmouth, ENG

John Hann# ▲ c.1800-1857 b. East Stour, ENG — Mary Ann Thompson# ▲ 1816-1882 b. London, ENG

m.1812, Portsea, Hampshire   m.1855, Parramatta, NSW

Volume 6   Volume 7

Thomas Eastman Shoveller 1827-1908 b. Warnford, ENG — Susan Hann 1840-1919 b. Clarence River, NSW

m.1856, Grafton, NSW

Lenore Shoveller
1866-1945
b. Grafton, NSW

Volume 8

Robert Archibald Rockwell
1904-1966
b. Glebe, NSW

m.1901, Sydney, NSW

================

m.1926, Glebe, NSW

Octavia Corelli O'Sullivan
1902-1976
b. Leichhardt, NSW

m.1900, Sydney, NSW

Joy Corelli Rockwell
1927-2018
b. Naremburn, NSW
m.1966
William Hyde
1925-2000

1. Robert William Hyde
1967-2016

Robert Hunter Rockwell
1929-1984
b. Naremburn, NSW
m.1954
Betty Jean Wardle
1935-1996

Volume 12

1. Tracy Paul Rockwell
1955
2. Robert Wayne Rockwell
1959-1963
3. Sandra Kay Rockwell
1964

Elwood Lorraine Rockwell
1933-1987
b. Naremburn, NSW
d.s.p.

Lindsay Archibald Rockwell
1937
b. Naremburn, NSW
m.1957
Lynette Ellen Watson
1939-2006

1. Rhonda Janine Rockwell
1960
2. Glen Lindsay Rockwell
1962

Ronie Malcolm Rockwell
1943-2000
b. Naremburn, NSW

1m.1961
Coral J. Stretton
c.1943-1981

2m.1981
Cheryl Pooley
1945-2013

1. Brett Anthony Rockwell
1961
2. Mark Malcolm Rockwell
1962
3.Paul Steven Rockwell
1965

1. Samuel Joshua Rockwell
1974
2. Jessica Molly Rockwell
1977

Janet Lenore Rockwell
1946
b. Naremburn, NSW

1m.1965
Roland Whiting
c.1945-1982

2m.1981
Gordon Carr
3m.1987
Ilya Sippen

1. Michelle Lena Whiting
1965
2. Stephen Hunter Whiting
1968
3. Adam Roger Whiting
1971

Legend: ☐ Born England ☐ Born Ireland ☐ Born Australia (UV) Unverified # Convict

▲The Rockwell Genealogies spans 12 separate volumes and includes the ancestors and descendants of Robert Archibald Rockwell & Octavia Corelli O'Sullivan, featuring the 'Bantin/Barrett' branch (#2), the 'Mahony's of Dunloe' (#3), the 'O'Sullivan/Mahony' branch (#4), the 'Frawley/McGarry' branch (#5), the 'Shoveller/Eastman' branch (#6), the 'Hann/Thompson' branch (#7) and the 'Rockwell/O'Sullivan' great grandparents & grandparents (#8). NOTE: Volume 1 is reserved for the 'Rockwell' branch if evidence ever emerges. Volumes not listed above detail the ancestors and descendants of William Wallace Wardle & Mary Agnes Cummings, which feature the 'Cummins/Sheehan' branch (#9), the 'McDonald/Harvey' branch (#10) and the 'Wardle/Cummings' great grandparents & grandparents (#11). The final volume records the life of 'Robert & Betty Rockwell' (#12), which in total pays tribute to the presence of these ancestors upon this earth.

Chapter One

THE SHOVELLER ANCESTORS
(Paternal paternal antecedents of Thomas Eastman Shoveller)

The Pacific was the last of the oceans to be explored, a vast area of water dotted with islands, the least known, yet the most romantic. On Tuesday the 23rd September 1851, out of that great ocean appeared an inconspicous vessel called the "Eclair," which entered Port Jackson and sailed slowly up Sydney Harbour, before dropping anchor in Neutral Bay and reporting to the port authorities. In addition to the crew and the master, Mr. F. J. Peppercorn, the small 50 ton schooner had sailed all the way from San Francisco via Honolulu and the Isle of Pines with just four passengers on board. One of those lucky few was 24 year old Thomas Eastman Shoveller, who was destined to become a pioneer of the Northern Rivers region of NSW, and the developing settlement of Grafton.

Following his fathers death in 1847, 21 year old Thomas embarked from London on an amazing voyage throughout the Pacific before his 1851 arrival in Sydney. From there he gradually travelled north to Grafton, where he settled, married and produced a family. As a pioneer he was the first chairman of the town, and lived to become one of its oldest residents.

The history that follows is a genealogical journey through the ancestry of Thomas Eastman Shoveller and the families that contributed to his creation. The work methodically explores each of his hereditary branches, highlights significant individuals and describes what is known to date of his forebears as well as the life, love and descendants of Thomas Eastman Shoveller himself.

The process described in this book is a narrative history and it tells some of the greatest

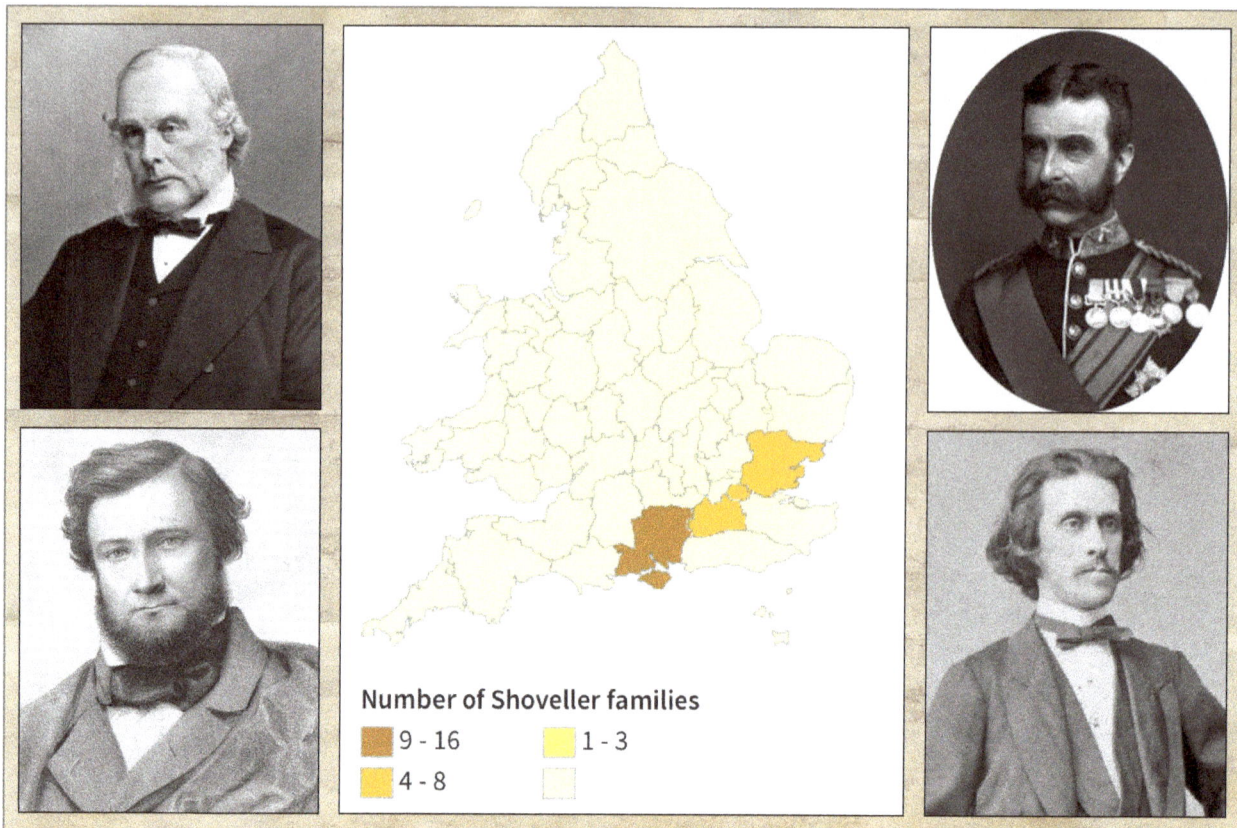

Number of Shoveller families

■ 9 - 16   □ 1 - 3
■ 4 - 8   □

▲ Sadly, no photograph of Thomas Eastman Shoveller has been found, but notable people that shared his 1827 year of birth were... TOP (Left): Joseph Lister (1827-1912), a British surgeon, medical scientist, experimental pathologist and a pioneer of antiseptic surgery and preventative medicine. (Centre): Map of the distribution and density of Shoveller families across England and Wales in 1891 (Ancestry). (Right): Frederic Thesiger (1827-1905), 2nd Baron Chelmsford, GCB, GCVO, a British Army officer who rose to prominence during the Anglo-Zulu War, when an expeditionary force under his command suffered a decisive defeat and the loss of 1500 British soldiers at the hands of a Zulu force at the Battle of Isandlwana in 1879, which was followed by the heroic defence of 'Rorke's Drift'. ABOVE (Left): Peter Lalor (1827-1889), an Irish-Australian rebel, and later politician who rose to fame for his leading role in the 'Eureka Rebellion', an event identified with the 'birth of democracy' in Australia. (Right): Josef Strauss (1827-1870) was an Austrian composer, with talents as an artist, painter, poet, dramatist, singer and inventor.

stories of these families, which mostly took place between the age of enlightenment about 1750, and the 1st World War. But this is also a book written to entertain, and it spans great events such as the industrial revolution, the French revolution, the Napoleonic era, as well as the Victorian and Edwardian periods. But what better way to begin than with an understanding of how, when and where the intriguing surname of Shoveller was derived.

The Surname Of Shoveller

This story commences with an investigation into the unique surname of Shoveller. This interesting surname may have arisen from two possible sources. It likely developed from Anglo-Saxon origin, as a nickname for someone with broad shoulders, or some peculiarity of the shoulders, from the Olde English pre 7th century word "sculdor," meaning shoulder. There is also a possibility however, that the surname was a variant of "Shouler," which is a metonymic occupational name for a maker or seller of shovels, or for someone who regularly used a shovel in his work, from the Olde English element "scofl," and Middle English "schovel," derivatives of "scufan," which means to push or shove.

The surname from the former source first appears in the early 12th century, while other early examples of the surname include: Robert Schuldre (Norfolk, 1275); William le Schovelere (Oxford, 1301); Simon Shulder (Sussex, 1327); and Nicholas Shouler, Schoveler (Essex, 1366). In the modern idiom the variants of the name include Shouler, Showler, Shoulders and Shoveller.

The first recorded instance of the family name was that of Ran Sculdur, which dates from about 1100 in the "Old English Bynames of Devon," during the reign of King Henry I, otherwise known as "The Lion of Justice," (1100-1135).[1] Years later, Mary Shoulder, daughter of John Shoulder, was christened on 27th November 1594 at St. Margaret's, Westminster in London, while Margaret Shoulder married Stephen Mount on 17th September 1638 at St. Dunstan's, Stepney in London.

The 1891 England and Wales Census recorded relatively few Shoveller families across England, with family groups emanating mostly from the counties of Essex, London, Surrey and Hampshire, the latter accounting for more than half of the population of this uncommon surname at that time.[2]

Shovellers of Cranbury Park[3]

So where do the Shoveller ancestors fit into the English landscape? Records reveal that they were quintessentially English, with at least one family of Hampshire Shovellers being aristocrats that once occupied a stately home called Cranbury Park, situated in the parish of Hursley, near Winchester, England. Cranbury was originally an important hamlet of Hursley, with many distinct farms and cottages, but now the name belongs only to Cranbury House and Park.[4] It was formerly the home of Sir Isaac Newton (1643-1727) and was later home to the Chamberlayne family, whose descendants now own and occupy the house and surrounding farmland. The current magnificent Cranbury Park house was constructed in the year 1780 to the designs of noted architect George Dance the younger. These days the house and park are not generally open to the public, although open days are occasionally held.

Although no link to any later relatives has been found, the first recorded tenant of Cranbury Park was a Mr. Shoveller, who surrendered it to Roger Coram before 1580.[5] Coram rented Cranbury at £17.2s per annum from the Lord of the Manor of Merdon, Sir Thomas Clarke.[6] At this time, an incident was recorded of a dispute between Coram and Clarke regarding the rights of the tenants and the Lord of the Manor: 'It seems that when the tenants were called on to perform work in hedging, reaping, or hay-making upon the

▲Although it has since been rebuilt, an early branch of the Shoveller family resided at stately Cranbury Park in Hampshire, during the 1500s.

lands of the lord of the manor, in lieu of money rent he was bound to feed them through the day, and generally to conclude with a merry-making. So, no doubt, it had been in the good old days of the bishops and the much loved and lamented John Bowland, but harder times came with Sir Thomas Clarke, when it required the interference of Mr. Coram of Cranbury to secure them even an eatable meal. No doubt such stout English resistance saved the days of compulsory labour from becoming a burden intolerable as in France.'[7]

> "...upon a haydobyn-day (320 or 340 reapers) the cart brought a-field for them a hogs-head of porridge, which stunk and had worms swimming in it. The reapers refused to work without better provisions. Mr. Coram of Cranbury would not suffer them to work. Mr. Pye, Sir Thomas Clarke's steward, and Coram drew their daggers and rode at each other through the wheat. At last Lady Clarke promised to dress for them two or three hogs of bacon."

> From "Reformation Times', by Charlotte M. Yonge [8]

The Shoveller Ancestors

Despite the fact that the Shoveller surname is relatively uncommon, ancestors of that name have been difficult to trace much earlier than about the mid to late 18th century. However, it appears that two distinct lines of the family developed around the early 1700s, one centering around Canterbury in Kent, and the other establishing themselves in Hampshire, mostly around the town of Portsmouth. Although both branches presumably came from an as yet unknown common ancestor, some movement of the families obviously occurred.

Whilst a few early references to Shovellers occasionally appear in records, they are random and infrequent. Two exceptions were a marriage recorded on the 24th October 1586 between Edward Shoveler and the widow Elizabeth Robynson, and a Mary Shoveler who was buried in Streatham, Sussex on the 24th September 1592. But whilst tantalising hints of Shovellers occupying grand houses such as Cranbury Park exist,[9] relatively few records have been found much earlier than the 1730s. Therefore, research on 'Ancestry'

▲ French prizes brought into Portsmouth Harbour after Lord Richard Howe's victory in the naval Battle of Ushant, otherwise known as the Glorious First of June, during the French Revolutionary Wars, 1794. Illustration by Thomas Rowlandson.

▲ *The grand appearance of High Street, Portsmouth, masked the squalor of other parts of the town, c.1842.*

and on the 'Family Search' database has been concentrated more towards the Shovellers of Hampshire, and mostly concern ancestors that resided in the vicinity of Portsea and Portsmouth.

Portsea & Portsmouth[10]

"The area of Portsea was once called Portsmouth Common. Until the end of the 17th century the town of Portsea was just farmland, and the township of Portsmouth consisted of just the area now called Old Portsmouth. North of this was a large inlet from the sea where a dam was built across it, and as the tide came in, the water was allowed through the dam. When the tide turned, the dam was closed and the trapped water was only allowed out under a watermill. This created power to grind grain into flour for the townspeople and the structure was called a sea mill. It is remembered today in Portsmouth by the street named 'Sea Mill Gardens.'

In 1495 King Henry VII commenced building the dockyard. At first it stood on its own, separated from Portsmouth by fields, but throughout the 16th and 17th centuries the dockyard grew much larger, until in 1663 the dockyard and the navy had to use the quay at the Camber. In that year a special wharf was constructed for the navy and the dockyard to use, which they called the 'Gunwharfe'.

The first houses in Portsea were built around St George's Square at the end of the 17th century. Number 90 still stands and was built about 1690 for a wealthy merchant.

The visit of Queen Anne to Portsmouth in 1711 was commemorated by the naming of Queen Street, and Prince George Street. Union Street was named after the act of Union in 1707, which joined England and Scotland. In the 19th century, Union Street was the thoroughfare where most of Portsmouth's lawyers resided. Hanover Street got its name because of the Georges (George I, George II and George III), who were all kings of Hanover in Germany as well as England, sometimes called the Hanoverian kings. North Street was probably not given its name because it lies in the north of Portsea, but rather after Lord North, who was prime minister in the 18th century. Hawke Street was named after Admiral

▲ *Print of merchant and Royal Navy ships at Portsmouth Harbour, circa 1780.*

Edward Hawke (1705-1781). There used to be an Orange Street named after William of Orange, which was changed to King Street. Marlborough Row, which is now in the dockyard, was named after the Duke of Marlborough who won several battles against the French at the beginning of the 18th century. Cumberland Street was probably named after the Duke of Cumberland, and some streets in Portsea were named after Inns for example, Clock Street, Sun Street and Three Tuns Street. There also used to be a Half Moon Street as its name plate is still on the side of a pub.

'The Hard' was derived from a slipway where men dumped clay in the sea at low tide then rolled it until it became hard. In the 19th century 'The Hard' was also known as the Devil's Acre. By 1900 there were 13 pubs along The Hard. Bonfire Corner probably got its name because dockyard workers burned rubbish there, and an alley in Portsea was even called 'Squeeze-Gut Alley' because it was so narrow.

The area soon outgrew Old Portsmouth and by 1792 its name was changed from Portsmouth Common to Portsea. By 1801 Portsea had a population of about 25,000 while Old Portsmouth had only about 7,000. However it was not until the 1770's that the walls around Old Portsmouth were extended to include Portsea. In 1764 a body of men called 'The Improvement Commissioners' was formed with powers to pave and clean the streets of Portsea. They also granted a contract to a man called a scavenger who arrived with a cart and rang a bell. As almost all rubbish was organic in those days, he was allowed to collect and sell it off as fertiliser.

In the 18th century, Portsmouth Cathedral was only a parish church. People who lived in Portsea were part of the parish of St Mary's Church in Fratton to the east of the town. But the dockyard workers grew tired of walking to church and decided to build their own, with St George's Church being erected in 1754. Two other Anglican churches were built in Portsea including St John's in Prince George Street in 1789, and Holy Trinity, which was built in the early 19th century in North Street, but both of these were destroyed by bombing during World War II.

In 1755 the Beneficial Society was formed as a friendly society providing help in times

Last Will & Testament of Thomas Shoveller, Shipwright of Portsea
Drafted - 3rd April 1778 & Proved 13 Feb 1796

Translation

"This is the last will and Testament of me **Thomas Shoveller** of the Parish of Portsea in the County of Southampton, Shipwright made whilst in health and ????? disposing mind & memory and understanding in manner following (that is to say) I Give and Bequeath all and singular my Household Goods and furniture of household plates linen and china and also all and singular other my estate as well swear as personal as I shall be in any manner interested in or entitled unto at the time of my death. To my beloved wife for ?? and during the term of her natural life or during such time as she shall continue my widow and unmarried and from and immediately after the final determination of either of the above terms. It is my will purpose and ????? that my Executor herein after named shall dispose of the whole of my said effects for the most monies that may be gotten for the same and after that in necessary expenditures for the maintenance of my children to divide the remainder share and share alike amongst them as they shall respectively attain the age of twenty one years and if any die or none of them show ????? die up before be due or they shall obtain the said age of twenty one years _____ as aforesaid then the part of his her or them so dying shall go and be divided among the survivors and I do hereby appoint my brother **John Shoveller** Executor of this my will and constitute him in the fullest manner Guardian to my several children during their minority. I also desire on ????? ?? ????? effects be taken by him as soon as conveniently may be after my decease and I do hereby revoke all former Wills by me at any time heretofore made. In witness whereof I the said Testator **Thomas Shoveller** have to this my last Will and Testament set my hand and seal this third day of April in the year of our Lord one thousand seven hundred and seventy eight - **Thos. Shoveller**, Witness - Signed, Sealed, Published and Declared by the said **Thomas Shoveller** as and for his last Will and Testament in the presence of us who at his request in his presence and in the presence of each other have heretofore submitted our names as witnesses - **Benjamin Cromwell, John Chessell, ? Davies**

On the thirteenth day of February in the year of our Lord one thousand seven hundred and ninety six Administration with the will annexed of all and singular the goods chattels and credits of Thomas Shoveller late of Ports(mouth/ea) in the county of Southampton, and carpenter of **His Majesty's Ship "Veteran"** in the West Indies. Probate was granted to **Ann Shoveller** widow ??? ?? and the ????? ????? for life or widowhood named in the said will having been first sworn by commission duly to administer **John Shoveller** the brother of the deceased and the sole executor named in the said will having first witnessed the execution thereof."

- -

NOTE: **Thomas Shoveller** (?-1796) was a ship's carpenter aboard **"HMS Veteran,"** a 64-gun third rate ship of the line of the Royal Navy, launched on 14 August 1787 at East Cowes. "HMS Veteren" was designed by Sir Edward Hunt, and was the only ship built to her draught. In 1801, "HMS Veteran" was present at the Battle of Copenhagen, as part of Admiral Sir Hyde Parker's reserve fleet. She was broken up in 1816.[17]

▲TOP: The will of Thomas Shoveller Jr., RN (likely brother of John Shoveller, see chapter 2) - proved on the 13th February 1796 with translation (England & Wales, Prerogative Court of Canterbury Wills, 1384-1858 [PROB 11: Will Registers (1796-1798), Piece 12`71: Harris, Quire No 49-97, 1796]). ABOVE: "HMS Captain" (1787-1813, 74 guns) was a sister ship to "HMS Veteran" (1787-1816), in which Thomas Shoveller Jr. worked as a ship's carpenter.

of sickness and provided funerals, and it also ran a school for poor children. In the 18th century, and for long afterwards, the dockyard was the main employer in Portsea. Men worked from 6am to 6pm with half an hour off for breakfast and one and a half hours for lunch. Men were not permitted to smoke or light fires in the dockyard, but were allowed to take home 'chips' of wood, some of which were so large that carpenters ended up making furniture like beds from 'wood chips.'

In 1775 an observer wrote that from "a barren, desolate heath, Portsea is now a very populous, genteel town, exceeding Portsmouth itself in the number of its inhabitants and edifices." By 1820 the Improvement Commissioners decided to introduce gas street lighting. They were not very generous however, as the streetlights were not lit if there was a full moon nor on the two nights before and after. The Commissioners felt that on those nights you didn't really need streetlights. Treadgolds Ironmongery opened about 1820 and is now a museum and Kent Street School opened in 1873. Portsmouth Harbour Railway Station was built in 1876. By the late 19th century, a military hospital was constructed in Lion Terrace, but closed at the beginning of the 20th century. In 1908 another military hospital was built to replace it on the slopes of Portsdown Hill, which eventually became 'Queen Alexandra's Hospital.'

The first council houses in Portsmouth were built in Portsea after a horrid slum called 'Whites Row' was demolished in 1911. By 1912 council houses were built with the new street being named after Admiral Curzon Howe. In 1923 a woman was murdered in Blossom Alley on the site of Blossom Square. People were shocked not just by the murder, but by the terrible conditions the woman endured. She lived in a 'house' consisting of two tiny rooms, one above the other, joined by a ladder. There was no hall, the front and only door opened

A time honoured custom of Portsmouth locals was to welcome and farewell their Royal Navy ships, as in this painting of "HMS Asia" leaving Portsmouth Harbour, painted by William Adolphus Knell (1830, oil painting).

1.1 Descendants of Thomas Shoveller Sr. & Mary Benson

Thomas SHOVELLER Sr. (c.1710-?), a blacksmith married on the 16th November 1735 at St. Mary's Church, Alverstoke to Mary Benson (c.1712-c.1808), with issue:

1. William Shoveller (c.1735-?), *a shipwright, married on 10 Nov 1860 to Elizabeth Hall, but his baptism and death details are unknown, with issue:*

1.1 Francis SHOVELLER (1764-?), apprenticed as a caulker, married on 30 May 1790 at Gosport to Susannah Wood, issue unknown?

1.2 Thomas SHOVELLER (1766-1849), married on 17 Nov. 1805 at Portsea to Ann Paffard (?-?), with issue:
a. James Thomas SHOVELLER (1806-1885), married 7 Sep 1830 at Alverstoke to Louisa Baker, with issue:
b. Ann Shoveller (1808-1808)*
c. Eliza Shoveller ?

1.3 Elizabeth Shoveller (1769-?), unknown?

1.4 Daniel SHOVELLER (1775-?), soldier in the 62nd Regt of Foot, received a pension in 1818, unmarried?

2. Mary Shoveller (1736<1808), *details for the baptism, marriage, issue or death of Mary Shoveller are unknown.*

3. John Shoveller (c.1737-1798), *was a shipchandler and ropemaker in Portsea. He married on the 13 July 1755 at Wymering, Hampshire to a woman named Mary (surname unknown, c.1738-1818).[18] The date of their wedding places John and Mary's birth dates around the late 1730s, but baptism dates are unknown. They produced the following issue:*

3.1 Mary Shoveller (1756-c.1737)
3.2 Elizabeth Shoveller (1757-1760)*
3.3 John SHOVELLER (1760-1851)
3.4 Elizabeth Shoveller (1762-1763)*
3.5 William SHOVELLER (1764-1832)
3.6 Elizabeth Shoveller (1766-1782)*
3.7 Thomas SHOVELLER (1769-1782)*
3.8 Ann Shoveller (1783-1783)*
3.9 Charlotte Shoveller (?-1784)*
3.10 Harriet Shoveller (1786-1786)*

4. Thomas Shoveller Jr., RN (c.1738-1796), *married to Ann, but his baptism and issue are unclear. He drafted his Will in 1778 and died in 1796, naming his brother John Shoveller as executor.*

5. Richard Shoveller (c.1740-1740)*, *died as an infant, with no details of baptism.*

* Died before adulthood - d.s.p.
(Some names not listed in the index).

Hampshire, England, Allegations for Marriage Licences, 1689-1837
Hampshire Allegations for Marriage Licences Vol 2

IN THE REGISTRY OF THE BISHOP OF WINCHESTER.   203

SHOVELLER, ——, of Fareham, postman, 21, b., & Ann Slade, of the s., 21, sp., at F., 3 Oct., 1784.

SHOVELLER, John, of Portsmouth, rope-maker, 21, b., & Susannah Horsey, of Portsea, 21, sp., at Portsea, 4 Feb., 1783. Joseph Horsey, of Portsea, minister of the gospel, bondsman.

SHOVELLER, John, of Portsea, coal merchant, a minor, with c. of his f., John Shoveller, of Portsea, ropemaker, & Mary Barfoot, of the s., w., at P., 29 Jan., 1789.

SHOVELLER, John, of Portsea, gent., 21, b., & Elizabeth Eastman, of the s., 21, sp., at P., 24 March, 1812. William Shoveller, of the s., gent., bondsman.

SHOVELLER, Thomas, of Portsea, blacksmith, & Mary Benson, of the s., sp., at Alverstoke, 16 Nov., 1735.

SHOVELLER, Thomas, of Portsea, joiner, 21, b., & Ann Paffard, of Portsmouth, 21, sp., at Portsea, 17 Nov., 1805.

SHOVELLER, William, of Poole, co. Dorset, 21, b., & Mary Bignell, of Warnford, 20, with c. of her f., John Bignell, at W., 3 Jan., 1789.

SHOVELLER, William, of Portsea, shipwright, w., & Frances Hall, of the s., w., at P., 31 Aug., 1796.

▲TOP: The likely descendants of Thomas Shoveller & Mary Benson of Portsea, Hampshire. ABOVE: Shoveller marriages (Registry of the Bishop of Winchester. Hampshire Allegations for Marriage Licences, England, Vol 2).

onto a little courtyard. Five houses shared taps with only three outside toilets. In the 1920s and 30s dreadful slums in Portsea were demolished and a number of these were replaced by council flats in Cumberland Street.

During World War II Portsea was heavily bombed and many houses were destroyed. The whole area was redeveloped in the 1950s, '60s and early '70s with Queen Street being widened. During the 20th century a major employer in Portsea was Brickwoods Brewery, which was sold to Whitbreads in 1974 and the brewery had closed completely by 1983. However, since the beginning of the 21st century Portsea has again experienced rapid development."[11] For a more detailed history of Portsmouth (*see Appendix A*).

Thomas Shoveller & Mary Benson

It is probable but not certain, that the earliest traceable Shoveller ancestors in Hampshire were Thomas Shoveller (c.1710-?), a blacksmith who married on the 16th November 1735 at Alverstoke to the spinster Mary Benson (c.1712-c.1808),[12] from which they produced offspring. Although no birth, baptism, death or burial information has come to light, it is likely that this Thomas and Mary Shoveller produced up to five children *(see 1.1 Descendants of Thomas Shoveller Sr. & Mary Benson)*. The place name 'Alverstoke' was most likely derived from a corruption of the name 'Alwara', an Anglo-Saxon lady of the manor, and 'Stoke', a settlement on the area of Alverstoke.[13] Alverstoke was mentioned in the Domesday Book as Alwarestock.[14]

Although not specifically stated on the parish registration, it is likely that the marriage of Thomas and Mary occurred at Alverstoke's St Mary's Church, which dates back to as early as 1122. The ancient church and what was known locally as Alverstoke village lay within half a mile of the shore of Stokes Bay and near the head of a creek, which extended

a mile westward from Portsmouth Harbour. In 1724 the roof of St. Mary's Church was raised and in 1737, about the same time as their wedding, a gallery was built at the west end.[15] Up until the early 19th century the parish extended about 4.5 miles from North to South and 2.5 miles from east to west. It was bounded on the east by Portsmouth Harbour, on the south by the Solent and on the west mainly by the parish of Rowner. On the north it adjoined Fareham and Titchfield parishes and was once a large agricultural area containing the villages of Alverstoke and Gosport.

Regrettably, a number of Shoveller marriages in Hampshire remain unlinked, although they likely stem from Shoveller brothers or cousins that lived a generation or two prior to Thomas Shoveller the blacksmith.

"HMS Maria Anna", "HMS Earl of Chatham" and "HMS Achilles" off Portsmouth, by Thomas Luny (1759–1837), c.1780.

It is probable but not certain, that the earliest traceable Shoveller ancestors in Hampshire were Thomas Shoveller Sr. (c.1710-?), a blacksmith who married on the 16th November 1735 at Alverstoke to the spinster Mary Benson (c.1712-c.1808). ▲(LEFT & RIGHT): The blacksmith was an essential service and trade across the Tudor, Stuart and Georgian periods.

It is by John Shoveller (c.1737-1798), the likely third child of Thomas Shoveller Sr. and Mary Benson, that this genealogy descends. The next chapter examines the known life and events of this John Shoveller, who has been identified as the progenitor of the Shoveller family in Hampshire, and the earliest verifiable ancestor of Thomas Eastman Shoveller, who emigrated to Australia and Grafton, New South Wales (NSW) in 1851.[16]

References

1. Surname DB - Shoveller [https://www.surnamedb.com/Surname/Shoveller].

2. Ancestry - Shoveller Family History [https://www.ancestry.co.uk/name-origin?surname=shoveller].

3. Wikipedia - Cranbury Park [https://en.wikipedia.org/wiki/Cranbury_Park].

4. Page, William (1908). "Parishes – Hursley: Cranbury," A History of the County of Hampshire: Volume 3. [www.british-history.ac.uk]. Retrieved 23 September 2009.

5. Ibid.

6. Yonge, Charlotte M. (1898). "Reformation Times," John Keble's Parishes: Chapter 3. [www.online-literature.com]. Retrieved 23 September 2009.

7. Ibid.

8. Ibid.

9. Wikipedia - Cranbury Park, op. cit.

10. Lambert, Tim (2021). 'A History of Portsea & Portsmouth' [https://localhistories.org/a-history-of-portsea/].

11. Ibid.

12. Thomas Shoveller & Mary Benson - Marriage held on the 16th Nov. 1735 at Alverstoke, Hampshire (Registry of the Bishop of Winchester. Hampshire Allegations for Marriage Licences, England, Vol 2).

13. "The Place Names of Gosport" Archived 3 December 2013 at the Wayback Machine, Unofficial portrayals by Philip Eley, Hantsweb

14. Gosport Borough Council - "A History of Gosport," 31 July 2007.

15. Church of England - St Mary's Alverstoke, Diocese of Portsmouth [https://stmarysalverstoke.org.uk].

16. John Shoveller & Mary (unknown) - Marriage held on the 13th July 1755 at Wymering, Hampshire (England, Select Marriages, 1538–1973).

17. Lavery, Brian (2003). 'The Ship of the Line - Vol 1: The development of the battlefleet 1650-1850.' Conway Maritime Press, p.182. [ISBN 0-85177-252-8].

18. John Shoveller & Mary (unknown) - Marriage held on the 13th July 1755 at Wymering, op. cit.

Chapter Two

JOHN & MARY SHOVELLER

(Paternal paternal great grandparents of Thomas Eastman Shoveller)

During the 17th and 18th centuries, Portsmouth expanded rapidly with new docks and warehouses, and in 1704 a church was built and dedicated to St Anne. Rows of houses were erected inside the dockyard for senior officers who needed to be close to their work, and a naval academy for training naval officers was opened in 1733.

People began to build north of the town near the dockyard on an area known as the Common, with the first houses being erected there about 1690. However, by the late 1700s the town of Portsmouth had reached bursting point, and at the start of the 18th century workmen grew tired of trudging the long distance from Old Portsmouth to work each day, so they erected their homes on farmland outside the dockyard. But this new development alarmed the governor who feared that houses built too near the workyards and warehouses could potentially provide cover for invading enemy troops. As the dockyard had its own guns, in 1703 he threatened to fire his cannons at any newly erected structures. The standoff was only resolved when Prince George, the husband of Queen Anne visited Portsmouth and the dockyard workers appealed directly to him. By 1704 the Queen granted permission for the townsfolk to build houses near the dockyard and a new suburb called 'Portsmouth Common' was developed, which in 1792 changed its name to Portsea.

John & Mary Shoveller

At the time of his marriage in 1735, whether Thomas and Mary Shoveller were residents of Alverstoke or Portsea is unclear, but working as a blacksmith, his skills were in high demand as it was an essential trade at that time.[1] If they hadn't already moved to Portsmouth, it was only a ferry ride away and although the relationship is foggy, it is likely that their children, including their first born son John Shoveller, all grew up in Portsmouth.

Although we know little of his early life, John Shoveller (c.1737-1798), no doubt spent his childhood and most of his youth in and around Portsmouth, England's premier maritime hub of that time. Along with Woolwich, Deptford, Chatham and Plymouth, Portsmouth was one of the main Royal Navy bases and dockyards throughout English history, with King Richard I ordering construction of the first dock on the site in 1194. But Portsmouth also became a hub for the Honourable East India Company (HEIC), as well as being a key international trading port.

By the mid 1750s John Shoveller had come of age and he married on the 13th of July 1755 at Wymering, just 2.5 miles north of the town.[2] At that time, Wymering was a residential satellite of the city of Portsmouth, but was located on the mainland rather than on Portsea Island. It was one of the estates held by Hampshire's biggest landowner Edward the Confessor immediately prior to the Norman conquest and was mentioned in the Domesday Book.[3]

John Shoveller's wedding most likely occurred at the ancient St. Peter and St. Paul Church, in Wymering, which dates from about 1125 and as such is one of the oldest churches in the

▲TOP (Left): St Peter & St Paul Church at Wymering, Hampshire, the wedding venue of John & Mary Shoveller in 1755. (Right): The interior of St Peter & St Paul Church at Wymering, Hampshire. ABOVE: The ropery at Chatham. Rope was essential in sailing ships and the standard length for a British naval rope was 1,000 feet (300m). A Royal Navy ship of the line such as "HMS Victory" required an astounding 31 miles (50 km) of rope.

Portsmouth area. John's bride was a woman recorded only by her christian name of Mary (1725-1818),[4] with later evidence revealing that she was almost 30 years of age at the time.[5]

Shoveller & Parmeter

At a relatively young age, but with a savvy outlook on life, John Shoveller was quick to realise the maritime business potential of Portsmouth and he worked himself up as a rope-maker, before commencing a ships chandlery business in partnership with William Parmeter. The premier British port for naval, passenger and mercantile shipping proved to be a superb location as it rapidly developed into the principal sea-going hub of the British Empire.

Surrounded by slipways they located their partnership of Shoveller & Parmeter in the heart of the maritime precinct in East Street, on Portsmouth Point where they established a 'rope-walk', a centre for making rope, but also conducted auctions and dealt in coal, while offering a myriad of merchant goods and services through their ships chandlery.

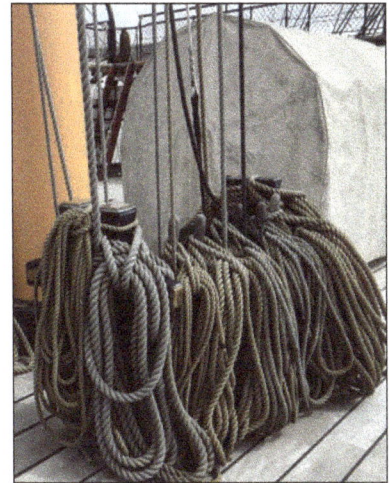

▲ TOP (Left): Loading ships cannon off the Gunwharfe at Portsmouth Point c.1800, just 100m from John Shoveller's 'ropewalk', painted by Dominic Serres (1722–1793). (Right): The working of pre-20th century ships required multitudes of rope in all shapes and sizes. ABOVE: Interior of a ropewalk at the Plymouth Cordage Company, exactly as carried on by rope makers Shoveller & Parmeter at East Street, Portsmouth Point from about 1770 to the 1820s.

Timeline for the City of Portsmouth

1180 - Jean de Gisors founds a town at Portsmouth.
1185 - A parish church is built.
1194 - King Edward I grants Portsmouth a charter (a document giving the townspeople certain rights).
1212 - The Domus Dei (House of God) is built.
1338 - The French burn Portsmouth.
1369 - The French burn Portsmouth again.
1377 - The French attack Portsmouth again.
1380 - The French burn Portsmouth for the last time. Afterward, a wooden wall is built around the town.
c.1418 - The Round Tower is built.
1450 - Adam Moleyns, Bishop of Chichester lynched in Portsmouth.
1494 - The Square Tower is built.
1495 - King Henry VII founds Portsmouth Dockyard.
1522 - A great chain of iron is built across Portsmouth Harbour.
1527 - King Henry VIII extends the Dockyard.
1540 - King Henry VIII closes the Domus Dei.
1544 - Southsea Castle is built.
1545 - The "Mary Rose" sinks in an engagement with the French.
1563 - Portsmouth has a population of around 2,000, but 300 are killed by an outbreak of plague.
1625 - Plague strikes Portsmouth again.
1628 - The Duke of Buckingham is assassinated by John Felton in Portsmouth.
1642 - Parliamentary soldiers capture Southsea Castle then Portsmouth.
1663 - A new wharf, called the 'Gunwharfe' is built for the navy and Dockyard.
1667-85 - The fortifications around Portsmouth are rebuilt.
1670 - The population of Portsmouth is about 3,500.
1704 - St Anne's Church is built in the Dockyard. Dockyard workers are given permission to build houses on the Common by the Dockyard and a new suburb (Portsea) grows.
1733 - A man leaves money in his will to found Portsmouth Grammar School.
1764 - A body of men is formed in Portsea with the power to pave and clean the streets.
1768 - A similar body is formed in Old Portsmouth.
1787 - The "First Fleet" departs for Botany Bay.
1789 - The "HMS Bounty" under William Bligh, departs fo Tahiti.
1801 - The "HMS Investigator" under Matthew Flinders departs for Sydney.
1805 - Admiral Lord Nelson departs Portsmouth for the last time in "HMS Victory."

1806 - Isambard Kingdom Brunel is born in Portsmouth.
1809 - A new suburb begins at Southsea.
1812 - Charles Dickens is born in Portsmouth.
1820 - Gas street lights are installed in Portsea. Old Portsmouth follows in 1823.
1836 - The first modern police force is formed in Portsmouth.
1840 - Horse drawn buses start to run in Portsmouth.
1847 - The railway reaches Portsmouth.
1849 - The first modern hospital in Portsmouth opens.
1857 - The streets of Southsea are paved, lit and cleaned for the first time.
1861 - Clarence Pier is built.
1865 - Horse drawn trams begin running in Portsmouth.
1865-70 - Portsmouth council builds sewers.
1879 - St James Hospital opens.
1883 - The first public library in Portsmouth opens.
1885 - A Telephone Exchange opens.
1898 - St Mary's Hospital opens.
1901-03 - Trams were converted to electricity.
1910 - Robert Falcon Scott's "Terra Nova" departs for Antartica.
1911 - The first council houses in Portsmouth are built in Curzon Howe Road.
1919 - The first motor buses begin running.
1920 - The boundaries of Portsmouth are extended to include Cosham.
1922 - The corporation purchases Southsea Common.
1928 - The Cumberland House opens as a museum and art gallery.
1932 - The boundaries of Portsmouth are extended to include Drayton and Farlington.
1934-36 - Highbury estate is built.
1936 - The last tram runs in Portsmouth.
1939-45 - 930 people are killed by bombs during WWII.
1946 - The council begins building a new estate at Paulsgrove.
1955 - A survey shows that 7,000 houses in Portsmouth are unfit for human habitation. In the 1960s and early 1970s, large areas of the city are rebuilt.
1982 - The "Mary Rose" is raised.
1984 - The D Day Museum opens.
1987 - "HMS Warrior" arrives at Portsmouth.
1989 - The Cascades Shopping Centre opens in Portsmouth.
2001 - A new shopping centre opens at Gunwharfe.
2005 - The Spinnaker Tower opens in Portsmouth.

▲ A timeline of important events in the history of Portsmouth, Hampshire, from 'A History of Portsea & Portsmouth' (2021), by Tim Lambert.

Their ropewalk had to have been perhaps 1200' long and was a covered narrow structure where long strands of mostly natural fibre like manila hemp were laid before being twisted into rope. Due to the length of some ropewalks, workers used wheeled carts and later bicycles to get from one end to the other. Many ropewalks were in the open air, while others were covered only by flimsy roofs. Ropewalks historically were harsh sweatshops and frequently caught fire, as hemp dust ignited easily and burnt fiercely, but rope was an essential component of all sailing ships. The standard length of a British Naval rope was 1,000 feet (300 m), and a sailing ship such as "HMS Victory" required an incredible 31 miles (50 km) of rope.[6]

John Shoveller's partner William Parmeter was from Alverstoke, and he married on the 10th May 1785 at Alverstoke to Elizabeth Wallace, a widow of Portsmouth Common. Their son John Parmeter of Portsea, later inherited his fathers interest in Shoveller & Parmeter, and married himself on the 4th November 1804 at Portsea to Olivia-Ann Griffin.[7]

The Shoveller & Parmeter ropewalk and ships chandlery was situated on the 'Poynt', outside the city walls of Old Portsmouth, which at one period had over 40 Ale Houses and taverns where now only three remain. Also known as Spice Island, the Point was the haunt of fisherman, sailors and smugglers and a very lively area, while Bath Square was traditionally where the local people came to bathe. By situating their business in the advantageous position of being able to supply both Royal Navy and merchant marine requirements, trade quickly increased and by 1778, Shoveller & Parmeter Ropemakers was valued at £1200 according to a 'Sun Fire Insurance Policy.'[8]

During this time Portsmouth also served as a staging post for the Honourable East India Company, the Royal Navy as well as the British Army, which was engaged in the Seven Years War against France (1756-1763), the American Revolution (1765-1783), the French Revolution 1st Phase (1792-1802) and the Irish Rebellion (1798).

Many significant expeditions also departed from Portsmouth for various destinations around the world, including to New South Wales. Amongst this throng of adventurers was the 11 ship First Fleet under the command of Captain Arthur Philip, which departed in May 1787 for Botany Bay; "HMS Bounty" under the command of Lt. William Bligh, which departed in December 1787 for Tahiti; and "HMS Investigator" under Commander Matthew Flinders, which departed from Portsmouth on the 18th July 1801 to circumnavigate the great southern continent (*see Timeline for the City of Portsmouth*).

At this same time the slave trade was in full swing and wasn't officially prohibited in Britain until the Slave Abolition Act of 1833. To receive the incoming human and non-human cargo, goods and supplies, effect repairs to ships and then re-supply out-going vessels with goods and services required a massive logistical effort, and Portsmouth's waterfront was constantly active. One particular problem was finding sufficient numbers of sailors to man the ships of both the Royal Navy and the maritime fleets, which had to be helped from time to time by the vigorous use of the 'press' gangs.

Impressment

Impressment, colloquially called 'the press or the 'press gang', referred to the act of abducting and subjugating men into a military or naval force by compulsion, with or without notice. Navies of several nations used forced recruitment by various means, but the massive

▲ *Waterside activity at Portsmouth Point in 1780, by Thomas Rowlandson (1757-1827). Also known as Spice Island, the 'Poynt' was a lively area and became the haunt of fisherman, sailors and smugglers.*

THE ROYAL DOCK-YARD

This view was taken in May 1790, from abreast of the Common Hard, looking up the Harbour.

"*This yard in 1650, was of little note, compared to its present greatness, at that time there was no Mast house, nor drydock, nor above 100 Shipwrights, and but one team of horses, but so vast has been its increase, that at the present time, there is upwards of 900 Shipwrights, and to include other Artificers and Laborers, it may be supposed nearly 2000 Men, are employed, and from the Magnitude of its Storehouses,*

T PORTSMOUTH

masthouse, Rope Yard and docks, it may be considered the first of the Royal Arsenals, for equipping large Ships of War, but no more can be said of its consequence, than to remind that at this present day of Oct' 1st 1790, there is riding at Anchor in its Roadstead (Spithead) the grandest Naval Armament that ever prest the Ocean, or that ever was equipped by any single Nation in the World. Publish'd Nov' 1: 1790. by J & J. Boydell, Cheapside & at the Shakspeare Gallery, Pall Mall, London."

size of the Royal Navy in the 'age of sail' meant impressment was most commonly associated with Britain. This method of recruitment was regularly used by the Royal Navy in wartime, beginning in 1664 and during the 18th and early 19th centuries as a means of crewing warships, although legal sanction for the practice goes back to the time of King Edward I. The Royal Navy impressed many merchant sailors, as well as some sailors from other nations. People liable to impressment were "eligible men of seafaring habits between the ages of 18 and 55 years." Non-seamen were sometimes impressed as well, although rarely.

▲ TOP: Watercolour of Portsmouth Point in 2016, by Tracy Rockwell. ABOVE (Left): The "Charlotte", and "Lady Penrhyn" (left) ride at anchor in Portsmouth Harbour, prior to the departure of the First Fleet for Botany Bay (May 1787). (Right): The Dolphin Hotel, reputed to be Portsmouth's oldest ale house.

BIRTH OF AUSTRALIA

UNVEILED BY
HER MAJESTY THE QUEEN
13TH MAY 1987

On 13th May 1787, a fleet of eleven ships under the
command of Captain Arthur Phillip RN,
set sail from Portsmouth's naval anchorage at Spithead.
On board were the first of those sentenced to
transportation to the recently charted coast of
New South Wales.
Captain Phillip was commissioned to establish a penal colony
and to assume the role of Governor.
The First Fleet arrived at Sydney Cove on
26th January 1788
- the birth of modern Australia.

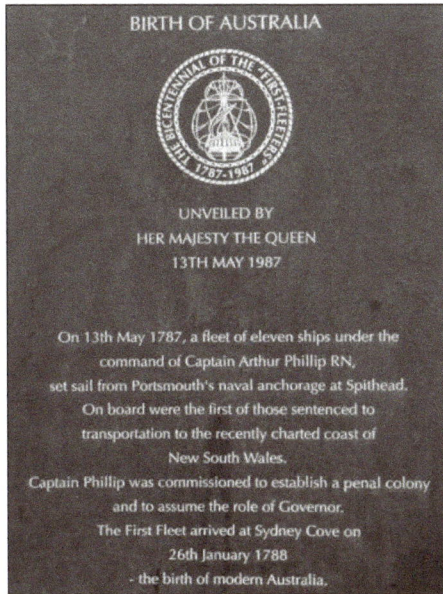

▲ TOP (Left): "HMS Bounty" sailed from Portsmouth for Tahiti in December 1787. (Centre): Portsmouth plaque commemorating the bi-centenary of the departure of the First Fleet in May 1787, and the subsequent 'Birth of Australia.' (Right): "HMS Victory" has been resident in Portsmouth both before, and ever since the Battle of Trafalgar in October 1805. ABOVE: British caricature drawing of a press gang in action, c.1780.

Impressment was essentially a Royal Navy practice, reflecting the size of the British fleet and its substantial demands for manpower, although there were also many volunteers for naval service. The work for individual sailors was less than on merchant ships as the size of naval crews was determined by the number needed to man the guns, which was around four times the number of crew required to sail the ship. Also the food supplied by the navy was plentiful and of much better quality by the standards of the day. At the time of the Battle of Trafalgar in October 1805, over half the Royal Navy's 120,000 sailors were pressed men.

The townships of Portsmouth and Portsea in the 18th and early 19th centuries were places of mixed reputation with a variety of residents coming from every social class. Officers

Last Will & Testament of John Shoveller, Merchant of Portsea
Drafted - March 1798 & Proved 14 Aug 1798

Translation

This is the last will and Testament of one **John Shoveller** of the parish of Portsea in the county of Southampton, Gentleman hereby recommend my soul to God and dispose of all my worldly estate and effects both real and in personal manner following (that is to say) all in singular, my messuages ??? tenements then ??? ??? real estate whereof or wherein I have any disposing power and give and devise unto my dear and loving wife **Mary Shoveller** and her assigns for and during the term of her natural life and from and immediately after her decease I give and devise unto my son **John Shoveller** his heirs executors administrators and assigns respectively part of my said real estate that is to say all that messuages tenements dwelling house now occupied by him situate on the north side of East Street on the point of Portsmouth in the said county with the storehouse adjoining thereto and also all that other storehouse called ??? House ??? the said last mentioned storehouse with the Appurts to the said premises respectively belonging And also all my moiety estate right title and ??? of and to all that ropewalk with the aforesaid workhouses and ??? stables thereunto belonging and also the supplies and utensils of trade of and belonging to the said ropewalk the same being situate ??? Hyde Park ??? in the parish of Portsea aforesaid and wherein my said son and **John Parmeter** carry on business and ??? ??? and to the use of my said son **John Shoveller** his heirs executors admons and assigns respectively for such the state term and terms of right and ??? and I may have varying at the time of my said deceased subject to my said wife the state for life as aforesaid I also give and revise onto my son **William Shoveller** his executors admons and assigns other part of my said real property are namely all that storehouse called the old store storehouse and also the boatyard adjoining with the Appurto the same respectively belonging situate also on the north side of the East Street aforesaid and contiguous to the before mentioned storehouses given to my said son **John Shoveller** between home and my said son **William Shoveller** I ??? the ??? and the road or passage ??? from East Street to ??? aforesaid ??? store house shall be jointly held and enjoyed and also by and between there respective executors headlines ??? to band ??? a science during their several estates my several messuages tenements and dwelling houses with their band ??? of there at hotel ??? seven tournaments then Number situated in the street aforesaid and now in this several occupations of Little ??? ??? **Robert Purcell, William ???, Thomas Boulin?, John Purcell** and their undertenants to hold unto and to the use of my said son **William Shoveller** his executors admits and assigns for and during the residue of the terms I have therein and which shall be unexpired at the time of the decease of my said wife I also give and devise the residue of my said real property being all that my freehold messuages tenements dwelling house wherein I now live situate in the Surry street in the parish of Portsea aforesaid unto my said son **William Shoveller** to hold the same now and immediately after the decease of my said wife unto him my said son **William Shoveller** his heirs and assigns for ever I also give unto my said wife all and singular household goods and furniture plate linen pictures and China and all such ready money as I shall have in my said dwelling house at the time of my decease and which shall be then due unto me for interest money dividends in the funds rents of houses and other my real property to and for her own proper use by and benefit All the rest residue and remains of my personal estate and effects of every degree and denomination whatsoever that shall be possessed of interests in or any way entitled unto at the time of my decease after payment of my just debts funeral expenses and the costs of proving this my will I give and bequeath unto my executors hereunto named ??? ??? to pay the dividends interest or proceed thereof from time to time and the same shell become due and be survived by them unto my said wife **Mary Shoveller** for and during the term of her natural life and from and immediately after her decease I get and bequeath the dividends or interest of £2700 sterling as vested in my name in the three cent ??? unto my daughter **Mary the wife of Robert Bowyer** for and during the time of her natural life and from and immediately after her decease I give the said £2700 sterling and all interest which shall be then due for the same unto all and every her child or children to be equally divided between them if more than one share and share alike and if she shall have no children or child at the time of her decease then I give the said £2700 sterling unto all and every the child and children of them my said sons **John Shoveller** and **William Shoveller** which shall be living at the decease of my said daughter to be equally divided between them share and share alike and in case of the death of any or either of said children of them my said sons before their shares shall become payable, then I give the proportions of such of them so dying on to the survivors awesome five I also give unto my said son **John Shoveller** the sum of £800 sterling to and for his own use and benefit I also give unto my said son **William Shoveller** the sum of £400 sterling now listed in my ??? in the five per cent to and for his own use and benefit and I ???? aid last mentioned ??? to my said sons respectively to be paid with all convenient speed after the decease of my said wife and the surplus of the rich and you of my said personal estate (if any) I give after the decease of my said wife onto my said sons **John Shoveller** and **William Shoveller** to be equally divided between them and I do hereby nominate and appoint my friend **John Bignell** of Warnford in the said county Southampton and my said son **John Shoveller** executors of this my will and I do hereby revoke all former wills by me made and witness whereof I have hereunto set my hand and seal this 1?th day of March 1798 - **John Shoveller**- signed sealed published and declared by the said **John Shoveller** the ??? testator and for his last will and Testament upon the say of the ??? in the presence of ?? who in his presence and at his request have subscribed our names as witnesses - **John Parmeter, Susanna Apsey, R. Callaway**

This will was proven at London the 14th day of August in the year of Our Lord 1798 before the **Right Honourable Sir William Wynn**, Knight, Doctor of Laws, Master Keeper of Arms, Commissionary of the Prerogative Court of Canterbury carefully constituted by the oaths of **John Bignell** and **John Shoveller** the son of the deceased and the executors named in said will to whom administration of all and singular the goods and chattels and effects of the said deceased ??? grants having been first sworn dusty to administer (by Commission).

▲ *The will of John Shoveller - proved on the 14th August 1798 (England & Wales, Prerogative Court of Canterbury Wills, 1384-1858 [Prob 11- Will Registers, 1796-1798, Piece 1311, Walpole, Quire No.527-569, 1798]).*

and common sailors, gentlemen and petty thieves, respectable wives and fallen women were all to be found in both towns. Portsmouth had its famous High Street, considered by some to be one of the finest thoroughfares outside London, while the nearby Point had loads of brothels and beerhouses. These two aspects of the towns coexisted uneasily, with friction created by events like the annual Free Mart Fair. The fortifications of the two towns meant that buildings were crammed in, creating a geography of narrow streets, squalid dwellings and filth-ridden alleys behind the genteel main streets.

When Dr George Pinckard visited Portsmouth in 1795 he described it as "crowded with a class of low and abandoned beings, who seem to have declared open war against every habit of common decency and decorum." Portsmouth did have its growing middle class, but a large proportion of inhabitants were extremely poor. Houses were badly built, with older homes allowing damp in through dilapidated cellars and newer buildings being quickly and shoddily erected. Malnutrition and lack of clothing were persistent problems, and the annual death rate of children under five was well above the national average.

Last Will & Testament of Mary Shoveller, of Portsea
Drafted - 20 Oct 1804 & Proved 5 May 1818

Translation

This is the last will and Testament of me **Mary Shoveller** of Portsea widow, whereby I give unto the Poor ??? of the Church in Meeting House Alley Portsea the sum of £5.40 and ???

I give unto my daughter **Mary Bowyer** you're all mine wearing apparel and £100 I also give unto my grand daughter **Susanna Ellis** and to my grandson **John Shoveller** the children of my son **John Shoveller** £50 each and also give unto my grand daughter **Mary Shoveller** and my grand daughter **Jane Shoveller** children of my son **William Shoveller** £50 each and all that remains of my estate I give equally between my three children and my daughter **Mary Bowyer** my son **John Shoveller** and my son **William Shoveller** and I do appoint the **Mr John Parmeter** of Portsea and my said son **John Shoveller** as executors of this my will in witness whereof I have hereunto set my hand and seal this 20th day of October 1804 - **Mary Shoveller** - ??? ??? and ??? this is the last will and Testament of **Mary Shoveller** in the presence of us and of each other - **S. Horsey, John Miller.**

Proved at London 5th May 1818 before the worshipful **Samuel ???, Parson**, Doctor of Laws and Surrogate by the oath of the **Rev. John Shoveller** the son and one of the executors to whom Admon was granted in having been first sworn duly as administer. Power ??? as **John Parmeter** the other executor.

▲ The will of Mary Shoveller - proved on the 5th May 1818 (England & Wales, Prerogative Court of Canterbury Wills, 1384-1858 [Prob 11- Will Registers, 1815-1818, Piece 1606, Cresswell, Quire No.209-258, 1818]).

There were many other hazards and dangers for the residents of Portsmouth and Portsea at this time, with the twin towns attracting a fair deal of criminal activity. Pickpocketing, for example, was particularly common with many reports being published in the Hampshire Telegraph of this kind of theft.[9]

The Death of John & Mary Shoveller

After a fortunate life, John Shoveller retired from his business around 1795, and drafted his last will and testament in mid March of 1798. The document verifies the name of his wife as Mary Shoveller, and reveals that they produced three surviving children in Mary Shoveller the wife of Robert Bowyer, Rev. John Shoveller Sr. and William Shoveller.[10] Fortunately, John and Mary Shoveller both lived to experience the birth of all ten of their grandchildren.

John Shoveller passed from this life at his home in Surrey Street shortly after the birth of his tenth grandchild Elizabeth, and he was buried on the 8th June 1798 at Portsea, Hampshire.[11,12] His will was proved on the 14th August 1798 in London under the auspices of the Right Honourable Sir William Wynne, Judge of the Prerogative Court of Canterbury.[13]

John's wife Mary Shoveller lived on for another 20 years, to the ripe old age of perhaps 93, which was recorded in a number of newspaper notices announcing her death on the 7th January 1818, while she was staying with her son John and family, at Poole, Dorset.[14] She too recorded a concise will of her own in 1804, which was proved just after her death on the 5th May 1818.[15]

After John Shovellers demise in 1798, the ropemaking and ships chandlery business

▲ The Royal Navy ship of the line "HMS Foudroyant" is seen here leading the French ship of the line "Pégase" into Portsmouth Harbour after capturing her during the Battle of Ushant in 1782, painted by Dominic Serres.

Shoveller & Parmeter

NEWCASTLE COALS.
TO be SOLD by Tho. Naters, at Mr. Parsons's Coal Wharf, on Portsmouth Point, the lower End of East-street, opposite the Town Quay, any Quantity or single Chaldrons of South-Moor or Tanfield-Moor Coals, on board two Ships lying in Portsmouth Harbour, at 24s. per Chaldron. All Orders for Coals shall be duly attended to, by applying to Mr. John Shoveller, at the above Wharf, or the said Tho. Naters, at Mr. John Whitmells, in Union-street on the Common, who has Loadings of Windsors and Simpsons; Pontops, South-Moor, Tanfield-Moor, and Long Benton Coals, to sell to any Merchant within the Wight, from 180 to 300 Chaldrons each Ship.
☞ All Letters duly answered.
The Public may depend on being constantly supplied with the best Coals, on reasonable Terms.
Portsmouth, March 9, 1775.

PORTSMOUTH.
TO be SOLD by AUCTION, By Mr. M. MARCH, Jun.
On Friday, the 12th day of July instant, at three o'clock in the afternoon, at the Crown-inn, Portsmouth,
Upwards of 500 QUARTERS of FINE WHEAT. For the conveniency of purchasers it will be put up in lots of; and 10 quarters each.——After the sale of the Wheat, will be sold, 18 PIPES of choice old VIDONA WINE, samples of which will be produced at the time of sale.
The wheat is lying in the stores of Mr. Shoveller, East-street, Portsmouth-point; and may be viewed three days preceding the sale, by applying to Mr. A. Moody, of Portsmouth, of whom catalogues may be had, and also at the auctioneer's, in Gosport.

PORTSMOUTH.
TO be SOLD by AUCTION, on Monday the 24th of March, 1794, at Mr. W. Moore's Coal Exchange, on the Point, Portsmouth, between the hours of six and eight in the evening,
The good SLOOP TRYALL, built at Itchenor in Sussex, in the year 1784; measures about 96 tons; will carry 140 tons to sea; is well found and fit for sea.
An inventory may be seen by applying to Mr. John Shoveller, on the Point, Portsmouth; or Mr. John Battershell, at Gosport; or Captain James Stride, on-board the said Sloop, lying in Portsmouth harbour.

Deaths of John & Mary Shoveller

This week died, Mr. Shoveller, a rope-maker on the Point, but had retired from business a short time since.

DEATHS.
At Newhouse, near Stroud, Gloucestershire, S. Wathen, esq. a magistrate.—Mr. R. Gedge, the much respected editor and proprietor of the Bury and Norwich Post.—In his 69th year, M. W. Hall, esq. barrister-at-law, in the Temple.—At St. James's Palace, in his 100th year, Mr. J. Eldred, page to his Majesty and previously to George the second.—At Ashburton, in her 84th year, Mrs. Mary Dunning, sister of the late and aunt of the present Lord Ashburton.—At Poole, Dorset, in her 93d year, Mrs. Shoveller, mother of the Rev. John Shoveller, of that place.—In her 17th year, the young-

POOLE, Jan. 7.—Died, greatly regretted by a numerous circle, Mrs. Shoveller, relict of the late Mr. Shoveller, of Portsmouth, merchant, and mother of the Rev. John Shoveller of this place, in the 93d year of her age. She retained the exercise of her mental faculties in their full vigour, together with a very cheerful disposition, to the end of her pious pilgrimage, and has now left a sincerely mourning family to join (we doubt not) the songs of Saints and Angels in a world of ineffable bliss.

Died, on Wednesday morning, greatly regretted by an extensive circle of friends, in the 93d year of her age, Mrs. Shoveller, relict of the late Mr. Shoveller, of Portsmouth, Merchant, and mother of the Rev. John Shoveller, of Poole: she retained the exercise of her mental faculties in their full vigour: —A cheerfulness of disposition, which never forsook her, and a resignation to the will of her Heavenly Father, through her whole life, but especially in the hour of death, were among the most conspicuous evidences & ornaments of her genuine Christian character.

▲LEFT COLUMN: 1-Advertisement for coal at John Shoveller's wharf on Portsmouth Point (Hampshire Chronicle, 13 March 1775, p.3); 2-Advertisement for trading wheat by John Shoveller (Hampshire Chronicle, 8 July 1793, p.3); 3-Advertisement for auctioning the sloop "Tryall" (Hampshire Chronicle, 24 March 1794, p.2). RIGHT COLUMN: 1-Death notice for John Shoveller (Hampshire Chronicle, 9 June 1798, p.4); 2-Death notice for Mary Shoveller (Oxford Uni & City Herald, 17th Jan.1818); 3-Death notice for Mary Shoveller (Salisbury and Winchester Journal, 12th Jan. 1818); 4-Death notice for Mary Shoveller (Hampshire Telegraph, 12th Jan. 1818, p.4).

was bequeathed to his first born son Rev. John Shoveller Sr., who was recorded as being involved at the East Street, Portsmouth premises from 1798 until at least 1827. However, while the business continued throughout this period, some of its premises were occasionally leased out to tenants.

John and Mary Shoveller managed to produce a family of ten children born from 1756 to 1786, although they paid the heavy and painful price of following seven of their infants to the grave. Just three of their offspring were fortunate enough to survive into adulthood, although these three in turn managed to introduce three rather distinguished individuals to join the Shoveller family through marriage, and their unique stories are the subject of the next chapter.

References

1. Thomas Shoveller & Mary Benson - Marriage held on the16th Nov. 1735 at Alverstoke, Hampshire (Registry of the Bishop of Winchester. Hampshire Allegations for Marriage Licences, England, Vol 2).

2. John Shoveller & Mary (unknown) - Marriage, 13th July 1755 at Wymering, Hampshire (England, Select Marriages, 1538–1973).

3. Addison, Sir William (1978). 'Understanding English Place-names,' Pavilion Books [ISBN 0 7134 0295 4].

4. John Shoveller & Mary (unknown), op. cit.

5. Mary Shoveller - Death notices (Oxford Uni & City Herald, 17th Jan.1818; Salisbury and Winchester Journal, 12th Jan. 1818; Hampshire Telegraph, 12th Jan. 1818, p.4).

6. Wikipedia - Ropewalk [https://en.wikipedia.org/wiki/Ropewalk].

7. Familypedia - Parmeter [https://familypedia.fandom.com/wiki/Hampshire/bdm]).

8. Sun Insurance Policy (1778). #398242 for Shoveller & Parmeter [1 264 08\10\79 BN].

9. Hantsphere - 'Portsmouth and its people 1800-1850' [http://www.hantsphere.org.uk/portsmouth-and-its-people-1800-1850].

10. John Shoveller - Will, Proved 14th August 1798 (England & Wales, Prerogative Court of Canterbury Wills, 1384-1858 [Prob 11- Will Registers, 1796-1798, Piece 1311, Walpole, Quire No.527-569, 1798]).

11. John Shoveller - Death notice (Hampshire Chronicle, 9 June 1798, p.4).

12. John Shoveller -Burial held on the 8th June 1798 at Portsea, Hampshire (England Deaths & Burials, 1538-1991).

13. John Shoveller - Will, Proved 14th August 1798, op. cit.

14. Mary Shoveller - Death notices, op. cit.

15. Mary Shoveller - Will, Proved 5th May 1818 (England & Wales, Prerogative Court of Canterbury Wills, 1384-1858 [Prob 11- Will Registers, 1815-1818, Piece 1606, Cresswell, Quire No.209-258, 1818]).

Chapter Three

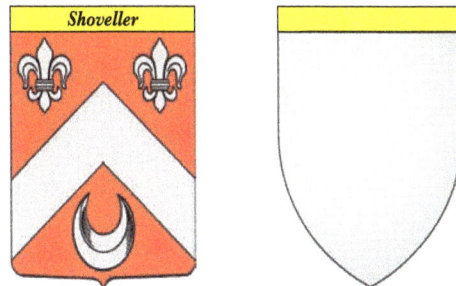

THE DESCENDANTS OF
JOHN & MARY SHOVELLER

At the beginning of the 19th century, maritime activity in southern England was focused on the two principal townships of Portsmouth and Portsea. Hemmed in by strong fortifications, these two towns could only be developed so much before virtually no space remained for erecting more structures. The overcrowding inevitably led to the development of land outside the walls with Landport and Southsea being the key areas where subsequent expansion took place.

Portsmouth and Portsea were particularly dominated by the existence of the dockyard and the Royal Navy. The military presence produced the fortification of Portsmouth, with major works beginning in 1770 and concluding in 1809. Britain was at war with France during much of this time, and there had been a long tradition of cross channel attacks. However, the occupation by the military was not always of benefit to the townspeople as naval requirements were normally met internally, with the Admiralty following a policy of self sufficiency. Most metal and woodwork tasks were carried out by naval employees, and smiths and rope makers were employed up to as late as 1850. Even when dress became an important and leading industrial commodity, it was focused more on the needs of naval and military officers and their families rather than the general populace.

As a result of the vast influence of the navy, these towns saw an influx of a great

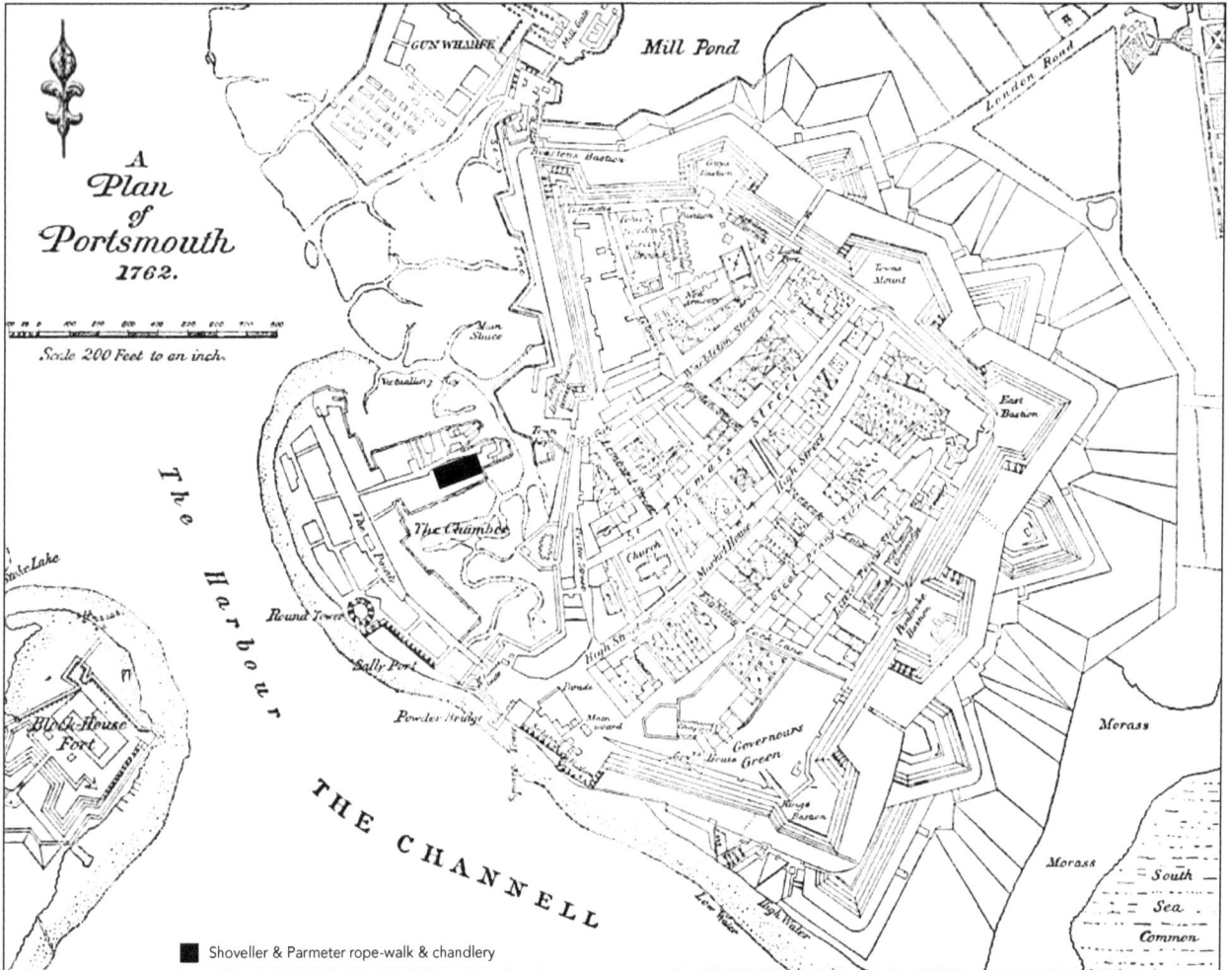

■ Shoveller & Parmeter rope-walk & chandlery

▲ *1762 Plan of Portsmouth, showing the elaborate defensive bastions, the Gunwharfe, the Round Tower erected in 1418, and the location of the Shoveller & Parmeter rope-walk on Portsmouth Point.*

social diaspora from differing classes and socio-economic backgrounds. Officers, sailors, merchants, entertainers and tradespeople across all classes mixed together in the confines of Portsmouth and Portsea. Throughout much of this time, the local economy was strongly dependent on war for its prosperity with workforces dropping off significantly after the war against France ended in 1815.[1]

In and amongst the global socio-political events that drove the Portsmouth economy, John Shoveller rose from obscurity to become a maritime merchant of some significance, and with his wife Mary, they managed to produce a family of some ten children. Tragically however, through pox, disease and illness, they experienced the heavy and painful trial of following seven of these to the grave. The unlucky seven were three Elizabeths (1757, 1762 & 1766), a Thomas (1769), and an Ann, Charlotte and Harriet.[2] However, three were fortunate enough to survive into adulthood, and as a result they introduced three more rather distinguished individuals to join the family through marriage, which over time blossomed with the birth of ten grandchildren.

Descendants of John & Mary Shoveller

Evidence reveals that John and Mary Shoveller began a family the year following their 1755 wedding, with the birth of their daughter Mary. Notably, all the Shoveller children were baptised and buried at St. Mary's at Kingston, the Portsea Church. It was the mother

SHOVELLER, John, of Portsmouth, rope-maker, 21, b., & Susannah Horsey, of Portsea, 21, sp., at Portsea, 4 Feb., 1783. Joseph Horsey, of Portsea, minister of the gospel, bondsman.

▲TOP: An 1820's drawing of St Mary's Church in Portsea, England. ABOVE: Marriage registration for Rev. John Shoveller Sr. to Susannah Horsey on 4th Feb 1783 in Portsea. ◄A well weathered entry door of the new St Mary's Church, Portsmouth, which was completed in 1889 and replaced the original structure. ▶ABOVE: Marriage registration for Susannah Shoveller to Mr. William Ellis (Hampshire Telegraph, 7th Nov. 1803). BELOW: Marriage for a Mr [Thomas] Shoveller to Miss [Ann] Paffard. The Mr. Paffard was Joseph Paffard (1794-1861), who wed Elizabeth Shoveller (1783-1826), a likely Shoveller cousin (Hampshire Telegraph, 25th Nov 1805, p.3).

MARRIAGES.----On Wednesday, W. Silver, Esq. of Bedford-street, London, to Miss Clarke, daughter of William Clarke, Esq. of Newport. On Tuesday, Mr. W. Ellis, jun. of Portsea, to Miss Shoveller, daughter of Mr. Shoveller, of this town. On Thursday, Mr. Bradshaw, Master in

On Sunday was married, Mr. Shoveller, of Portsea, to Miss Paffard, of this town. On Wednesday, Mr. Paffard, of this place, to Miss Shoveller, of Portsea, sister of Mr. Shoveller.

church for much of Portsea Island, and the parish included the town of Portsmouth.

St Mary's was established about 1180, but was not formally separated from the settlement until the 14th Century. Although the present building dates only from 1889, there has been a church on the same site since at least 1164. About that time Baldwin of Portsea (de Portesia) gave the church to Southwick Priory, with all its lands, tithes, offerings and everything else belonging to it. It was here that John and Mary Shoveller brought their children to be guided by the principles and doctrines of the Church of England, with the following descendants evolving from their union (*see Pedigree Chart 2*).

1. Mary Shoveller (1756-c.1837)

The first of John and Mary Shoveller's children was Mary Shoveller, who was baptised on the 25th April 1756 at St. Mary's

▲Drawing of the interior of St Mary's Church in Portsea, where a tower was added during Tudor times, and the lowly roof unusually featured dormer windows.

BOWYER, ROBERT (1758–1834), miniature painter, seems to have been at an early
date known to Smart, the miniature painter,
and is supposed by Redgrave to have been
Smart's pupil. He exhibited miniatures and
paintings at the Royal Academy occasionally
between 1783 and 1828; was appointed
painter in water-colours to the king, and
miniature painter to the queen; and received much fashionable patronage. In 1792
he issued a prospectus giving details of a
plan for an edition of Hume's 'History of
England,' with continuation to date, to be
'superbly embellished.' West, Smirke, Loutherbourg, and other leading artists of the
day furnished historical pictures specially to
be engraved for this work, which contains
besides a number of engravings of portraits,
medals, and antiquities. It was issued in
parts, and by 1806 five unwieldy folios were
published, reaching to the year 1888; the continuation was never issued, as a loss of 30,000l.
is asserted to have been already incurred.
Bowyer also published 'An Impartial Narrative of Events from 1816 to 1823,' London,
1823. He died at his house at Byfleet,
Surrey, 4 June 1834.

[Cat. Brit. Mus. Lib.; Cat. R. A.; Gent.
Mag. August 1834, p. 221; Redgrave's Dict. of
Artists (1878).]   W. H–N.

▲LEFT: The school chosen by John Shoveller for his children was likely to have been Portsmouth Grammar School, the entrance of which can be seen above.
RIGHT: Listing for Robert Bowyer in the UK Dictionary of National Biography, Vol 2, 1834.

Church, Portsea, and likely due to her fathers business acumen, experienced a privileged life as a young lady.[3] In 1732, William Smith, a former Mayor of Portsmouth and previously the garrison physician, had bequeathed his estate to Christ Church, Oxford. His will contained instructions to build a new school and 'The Portsmouth Grammar School' was opened in Penny Street in 1750, although despite its founder's intentions, it later became a fee-paying school. Mary most likely attended the Portsmouth Grammar School from which she would have received a first class formal education.[4]

Mary married in her 21st year on the 14th July 1777 at St. Thomas Church, Portsmouth, Hampshire to a younger gentleman named Robert (1758-1834), the son of Amos Bowyer and Betty Ann Lockett of Portsea.[5] Robert Bowyer was to become a highly commended and respected British miniature painter and publisher, and in the year following their wedding, the Bowyers produced a daughter in Harriet Bowyer (1777-c.1796).

Robert Bowyer Esq. (1758-1834)

Robert Bowyer was born two years after his future wife, the son of Amos Bowyer and Betty Ann Lockett,[6] and was baptised on the 18th June 1758 at Portsmouth. He was also probably educated at Portsmouth Grammar School and was to become a highly regarded British miniature painter and publisher between 1783 and 1828. Robert exhibited thirty-two portraits at the Royal Academy and when the miniaturist of King George III, Jeremiah Meyer died in 1789, Bowyer was appointed in his place.[7] This was an unusual appointment given Bowyer's religious nonconformity, as he was a lifelong Baptist, but perhaps an example of how surprisingly pluralistic the Georgian era had become. These opportunities presented Bowyer with access to the aristocracy and the nations royalty, many of whom were extraordinarily influential people. An in-depth biography of Robert Bowyer was published in 2016 (see Appendix B).[8]

During his life, Robert Bowyer enjoyed a distinguished career as a painter of miniature portraits for an eminent clientele, which included King George III, King George IV and King William IV.[9] Other famous subjects included the Dukes of Clarence and of York, John

Montagu 4th Earl Sandwich, John Russell 1st Earl Russell, Charles Fox the famous M.P., Admiral Lord Nelson and many other British admirals, generals and politicians.[10,11]

Bowyer received a good deal of favourable patronage from the gentry, an aristocratic circles. His portrait of Sir Edward Hughes "was described as a wonderful performance, and the Prince of Wales said it was one of the best miniatures he ever beheld."[12]

The high quality of English engravings in the late 18th century encouraged the publication of ornately illustrated editions of major works, and Bowyer's fame as an artist was supplemented by his labours as a publisher of lavishly illustrated works.[13] Bowyer opened a historic gallery in Schomberg House at 82 Pall Mall in the 1790s, and also fashioned a career as a dealer in art prints and as a publisher of fine books. He was also an

On the 4th inst. aged 76, Robert Bowyer, Esq. of Byfleet Lodge, Surrey, Portrait Painter in water colours to his Majesty, and publisher of the embellished History of England, and various other splendid works of art.

▲Self-portrait of Robert Bowyer of almost half-length, turned to the right, eyes to front, wearing jacket with cravat, c.1795-1800 (Graphite, with watercolour, from The British Museum). INSET: Robert Bowyer - Death notice (The Belfast Newsletter, 17 June 1834, p.3).

The Art of Robert Bowyer [72]

Robert Bowyer (18 June 1758 - 4 June 1834) was a British miniature painter and publisher, born in Portsmouth the son of Amos Bowyer and Betty Ann Lockett of Portsea. His first job was as a clerk to a merchant in Portsmouth and then London. Two different accounts of his career shift to becoming a painter survive. The first claims that he had decided to voyage to America, and before leaving wanted to obtain a portrait of himself for his fiancée, Mary Shoveller. Unable to afford to commission one, he painted one himself and eventually gave up the idea of going to America and became a miniaturist. The second account claims that he was simply looking for a job and decided to paint. In any event Bowyer married Mary Shoveller on the 14th July 1777, becoming a son-in-law to John Shoveller, and the couple produced a daughter, Harriet in 1778.

Bowyer probably began to train with the miniature painter John Smart in the late 1770s and exhibited his first works at the Society of Artists in 1782, and at the Royal Academy in 1783. Bowyer had a successful career, painting the John Henry Manners 5th Duke Rutland, James Cecil Marchioness of Salisbury, and Admiral Lord Nelson. On 4th March 1789, following the death of Jeremiah Meyer, Bowyer was appointed 'Miniature Painter in Ordinary' to the King.

In the 1790s, Bowyer became a print publisher, beginning with his own works. However, his two major endeavours were an illustrated edition of the Bible, and David Hume's 'The History of England'. Bowyer's Bible, begun in 1791 and finished in 1795, included 32 engravings by James Fittler after 'Old Master' paintings. Bowyer also bought prints in France that he incorporated into a later edition of "Bowyer's Bible", he had an agent purchase even more during the Napoleonic wars. These were added to Thomas Macklin's illustrated edition of the Bible, extending it to 45 volumes.

Bowyer displayed the paintings he commissioned for Hume's work in a 'Historic Gallery', cited in the Schomberg House building at 82 Pall Mall. The idea of placing the original pictures for the illustrated edition on display followed the examples of the Boydell Shakespeare Gallery, Thomas Macklin's Gallery of the Poets, and Henry Fuseli's Milton Gallery, all of which operated in Pall Mall at around the same time. Benjamin West and others contributed a total of 60 works to the Historic Gallery. By 1806, Bowyer had printed five folios, covering the years back to 1688, but high costs then prevented him from completing the work. Bowyer lost as much as £30,000 on the project and in 1805, to recoup some of these costs, he followed John Boydell's route in applying to Parliament for permission to hold a lottery for the gallery contents. Even after receiving approval for the lottery, it took Bowyer a further year to ensure that two paintings by Robert Smirke and 18 engravings were completed whereby the sale could proceed.

Due to his relationship with Smart, Bowyer also published a series of engravings regarding India. In 1794 for example, he published 'Picturesque Views', with a 'Descriptive History of the Country of Tipoo Sultan' after drawings by Robert Home and in 1797 'Oriental Scenery: Twenty-Four Views in Hindoostan' after drawings by Thomas Daniell.

In 1796, the Bowyers' only daughter died aged 18 and Robert wrote to Warren Hastings that he feared his wife might die as well. Three years later, however, the couple adopted Catherine Andras (1767-1839), an orphaned wax modeller from Bristol. During the Peace of Amiens, the Bowyers and Andras went to Paris as members of the Baptist Missionary Society and helped form the French Evangelical Society. Bowyer became increasingly active in religious causes later in his life, for example by establishing a Sunday School. He even bought a public house, demolished it, and built a chapel in its place near his place of business. In addition to religious activities, Bowyer turned back to miniature portrait painting at the end of his life when King George IV and others sat for him.

Bowyer's last years were plagued by financial difficulties and his home suffered a significant fire. He died on 4th June 1834 when Mary Parkes, a maid and shop assistant, inherited the business. Mary Bowyer died about two years prior to the death of Catherine Andras, who willed the estate to a Shoveller niece Mary Stratten, the wife of the Rev. Thomas Stratten.

◀Portraits of Admiral Horatio Nelson & Vice-Admiral, and Sir Thomas L. Frederick, by renowned portraitist, Robert Bowyer. ▼Portraits of Robert & Mary (nee Shoveller) Bowyer, painted by John Opie.

THE BOWYER BIBLE AND CABINET.

VALUE THREE THOUSAND ONE HUNDRED GUINEAS;

THE HIGHEST PORTION IN MRS MARY PARKES'S LAST GRAND CLUB SUBSCRIPTION.

SHARES ONE GUINEA EACH

▲CLOCKWISE (from top left): Engravings painted or published by Robert Bowyer of: King George III; King George IV; King William IV: Prime Minister William Pitt; Charles James Fox; The 'Bowyer Bible'; Arthur Wellesley, 1st Duke of Wellington & Vice Admiral Cuthbert Collingwood, 1st Baron Collingwood (centre).

Mr. and Mrs. Whitbread, with a large party, were yesterday at the Historic Gallery to see that very curious production of art the Model of the ever to be lamented Nelson. The composition of which this Model is made so exactly to resemble nature that it is with truth described as a perfect fac simile.——It has met with such decided approbation by

the family of the departed Hero, that they have with great liberality presented Miss Andras, the artist, with the whole of the cloaths in which the model appears, and which was often worn by the gallant Nelson. His Lordship had given Miss Andras several sittings previous to his last departure from London, to go on board the Victory.

▲ TOP (Left): Relief of Admiral Lord Nelson modeled in wax by Catherine Andras about 1806 (V&A Museum, London). (Right): Label on the back of the wax model of Nelson, 1806 (V&A Museum, London). MID (Left): Byfleet Lodge, known as the Clock House, at Byfleet, Surrey, the home of Mary (nee Shoveller), Robert Bowyer, and their adopted daughter Catherine Andras until 1839. (Right): The ornate Billiards room at Byfleet Lodge, Surrey. ABOVE: The newspaper notice announcing the unveiling of Lord Nelson's Wax Model by Catherine Andras (Morning Post, 24 May 1806).

avid supporter of the Anti-Slavery movement.[14] As a publisher, his two major endeavours were an illustrated edition of the Bible, a colossal undertaking that became known as the 'Bowyer Bible,' now housed in the Bolton Museum, and David Hume's 'History of England.' Bowyer travelled widely and was evidently in Paris during the brief peace of 1802, where he obtained personal permission from Napoleon to engage in his research and collect prints for his illustrated magnum opus. The family treasured the following autographed letter received from 'Boney' himself:

"Let Mr. Boywer [sic.] refer this matter to the French Consul Mr. Otto, and if he sees no objection, let a passport be granted to Mr. Bowyer's agent."

Napoleon Bonaparte [15]

Catherine Andras (1767-1839)

Tragically, the only child of Robert and Mary Bowyer was Harriet, who passed away on the 4th August 1796, at just 18 years of age, and was buried on the 6th August at Portsea.[16,17] Some three years later, the Bowyers befriended a young woman of slightly older age to their deceased daughter, an orphaned wax modeller from Bristol named Catherine Andras (1767-1839).[18] She had travelled to London seeking to have some wax models engraved by Bowyer, who instantly recognised her talent. Bowyer and his wife Mary Shoveller, obviously connected with this young woman on a deeper level as they soon adopted Catherine as a daughter.

Catherine exhibited in the capital from 1799 onwards and amongst the many subjects of her pink-wax low relief carved portraits was the founder of Methodism John Wesley, and the Polish General Tadeusz Kosciuszko, but it was her commission in 1800 to model the five-year-old Princess Charlotte, probably obtained through Bowyer's royal connections, that likely brought her to prominence. Other subjects in Andras's long career included Charles James Fox, William Pitt the Younger, the Duke of Wellington, Sir Walter Scott and Hannah More.[19]

By 1802 Catherine Andras had become wax modeller to Queen Charlotte and in the same year was awarded 'The Larger Silver Pallet' by the Society for the Encouragement of Arts, Manufactures and Commerce for her model of Princess Charlotte, and for a portrait of Admiral Lord Nelson. The latter commission probably also came through Bowyer, who had himself been commissioned to paint a miniature of the naval hero. Andras supplied the wax effigy of Nelson, which was used at his funeral and is now exhibited in Westminster Abbey.[20] Sitting simultaneously for Andras and Bowyer, Lord Nelson is said to have quipped that he "was not used to being attacked in that manner starboard and larboard at the same time."[21] In 1806, Bowyer wrote a contemporary account of a conversation he had with Lady Hamilton, Nelson's mistress, concerning Catherine's ability, who remarked:

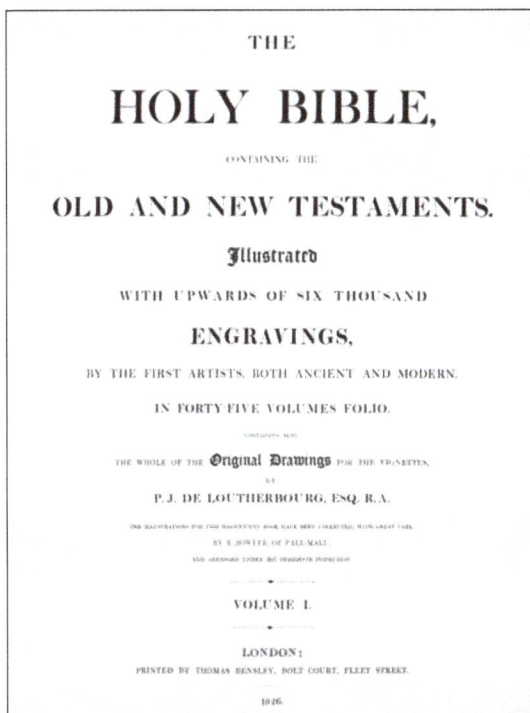

THE

HOLY BIBLE,

CONTAINING THE

OLD AND NEW TESTAMENTS.

Illustrated

WITH UPWARDS OF SIX THOUSAND

ENGRAVINGS,

BY THE FIRST ARTISTS, BOTH ANCIENT AND MODERN.

IN FORTY-FIVE VOLUMES FOLIO.

THE WHOLE OF THE Original Drawings FOR THE VIGNETTES,

BY

P. J. DE LOUTHERBOURG, ESQ. R.A.

VOLUME I.

LONDON:

PRINTED BY THOMAS BENSLEY, BOLT COURT, FLEET STREET.

1826.

▲LEFT: Title page of Robert Bowyer's 1826, 45 volume illustrated bible. RIGHT: The Bowyer illustrated bible is housed today in its originally designed cabinet at the Bolton Museum, in Bolton, Lancashire.

> To R. Bowyer, Esq.
>
> Feb. 14, 1798
>
> Not a day has hurried by, since I parted with my dear friends in Pall Mall, but they have been in my affectionate remembrance; but not being able to speak with any satisfaction respecting our dear child, I have withheld myself from imparting new anxieties to bosoms already alive to painful sensibility.
>
> At length, however, a gracious God puts it in my power to say, that there is hope.[76] After languishing between life and death for many days, she now seems to amend. We flatter ourselves that she has passed the crisis, and will yet be restored to our arms; but parental fears forbid too strong a confidence. It may be that our most merciful God saw that the shock of a sudden removal would be too strong for the tender feelings of a mother; and so by degrees, prepares for the stroke which must fall at last. However, she is in the best hands, and we are, I hope, preparing for submission to whatever may be the blessed will of God.
>
> I was brought home in safety, and feel myself in much better health in consequence of my journey. Oh that it may be all consecrated to my Redeemer's praise!
>
> Happy should I be, if I could oftener enjoy your friendly society; but we must wait for the full accomplishment of our social wishes till we come to that better world for which divine grace is preparing us. There our best, our brightest hopes, and there our warmest affections must be found. Could we have all we want below, we should be reluctant to ascend, when Jesus calls us home. No, this is not our rest; it is polluted with sin, and dashed with sorrow: but though our pains in themselves are evil, yet our God turns the curse into a blessing, and makes all that we meet with accomplish our good.
>
> What better can I wish, my friends, than the humble place of Mary, or the happy rest of John! Faith can enjoy them both, till actually we fall at the Saviour's feet, and lean upon his bosom, when we see him as he is.
>
> Oh the delights, the heavenly joys,
> The glories of the place,
> Where Jesus sheds the brightest beams
> Of his o'erflowing grace![77]
>
> *Andrew Fuller*

▲ *Rev. Andrew Fuller writing to Robert Bowyer re his daughter Harriet in 1798 (Belcher, J. (1824) 'The Complete Works of the Rev. Andrew Fuller,' Vol.1, London).*

"she shewed me the inclosed Wax Profile which She declares is the most striking likeness that has been taken, & much more so than our little drawing or print by Mr Da Costa. On asking Lady H: in what features the model so closely resembled Lord Nelson as she had declared; she said, "in the direction & form of the nose, mouth and chin, that the general carriage of the body was exactly his, and that altogether the likeness was so great it was impossible for anybody who had known him to doubt about or mistake it'."

Lady Hamilton, c.1806 [22]

Robert Bowyer made his brother-in-law Rev. John Shoveller Sr., the executor of his will in 1830, and died four years later on the 4th June 1834 aged seventy-six, at Golden Square, near Piccadilly in London.[23] Considering the vast sum of £300,000 he claimed to have expended in the cause of British art, he died a comparatively poor man.[24] Although his will spoke of giving all to his wife and £1,000 to 'my friend' Catherine Andras, the probate granted was for only £1,000. Mary Bowyer passed away sometime prior to the preparation of Catherine Andras' will in November 1837, who died herself in early 1839. Catherine bequeathed the household treasures to Mary's niece, Mary Stratten (nee Shoveller), the wife of the Rev. Thomas Stratten.[25]

Although Robert and Mary Bowyer's grand residence was formerly known as Byfleet Lodge, it was later called 'Clock House,' and is situated at the junction of the High Road and Church Road in Byfleet. The property once had another tower, and was built on the site of Byfleet Cottage, which for many years provided charity housing. Robert Bowyer was a lifelong active member of the Baptist church and became a minister himself in later life.[26] "The story of Robert Bowyer is a reminder that many of those who spent years in the pew have a life worthy of recall from comparative oblivion."[27]

2. Elizabeth Shoveller (1757-1760)

In 1757, as soon as she recovered from her first birth, Mary Shoveller was pregnant again. The second child of John and Mary Shoveller was baptised Elizabeth on the 4th December 1757 at St. Mary's Church, Portsea, but she passed away in 1760.[28] The little girl was just three years old and was buried with dignity in St Mary's churchyard, Portsea.

3. Rev. John Shoveller (1760-1851)

John Shoveller, the third child and eldest son of John and Mary Shoveller, was baptised on the 6th April 1760, at St. Mary's Church, Portsea.[29] His birth would have relieved some of the sadness felt earlier that year when young Elizabeth died. Like his older sister Mary, John was well educated and likely followed in his sisters footsteps at Portsmouth Grammar School. Although he was apprenticed in his teens as a 'caulker',[30] and groomed by his father to take over the successful ropewalk and ships chandlery in East Street, Portsmouth, young John was attracted by the light of the Baptist faith. Indeed, he grew up to become heavily involved in the Baptist movement, and it is perhaps illuminating to understand how that denomination, and the non-conformist movement became so influential in Portsea.

The Baptist Church At Meeting House Alley, Portsea

The persons who formed the first Baptist church at Portsea originally left from a church at Alverstoke, near Gosport in 1704. However, having tried unsuccessfully to attract a

Shoveller & Parmeter - Ropemakers & Chandlers

▲Following his father's death in 1798, his son Rev. John Shoveller Sr., took over the rope-making business at Portsmouth as evidenced by these notices. LEFT COLUMN: 1-Advertisement for Stolen Horse (Salisbury & Winchester Journal, 18 May 1801, p.1); 2-John Shoveller - Property Auction (Hampshire Telegraph, 11 July 1803); 3-Rope Theft (Hampshire Chronicle, 26 Dec 1808, p.3). CENTRE COLUMN: 1-Shoveller & Parmeter, Rope-Makers (Hampshire Chronicle, 18 April 1808, p.1); 2-Bankruptcy Auction Sale by Mr. Shoveller (Hampshire Chronicle, 25 June 1810, p.2). RIGHT COLUMN: 1-Mr. Shoveller - Auction (Hampshire Telegraph, 25 March 1811); 2-1827 Shoveller & Parmeter - Auction (Hampshire Telegraph, 26 March 1827); 3-Mr. [John] Parmeter - Death notice in 1827 (Hampshire Telegraph, 2 Apr 1827), which finalised the partnership and likely brought the enterprise to an end.

► Elizabeth Shoveller - Baptism held on the 24 Oct 1783, at Meeting House Alley Baptist Church, Portsea, Hampshire (England & Wales, Non-Conformist and Non-Parochial Registers, 1567-1936).

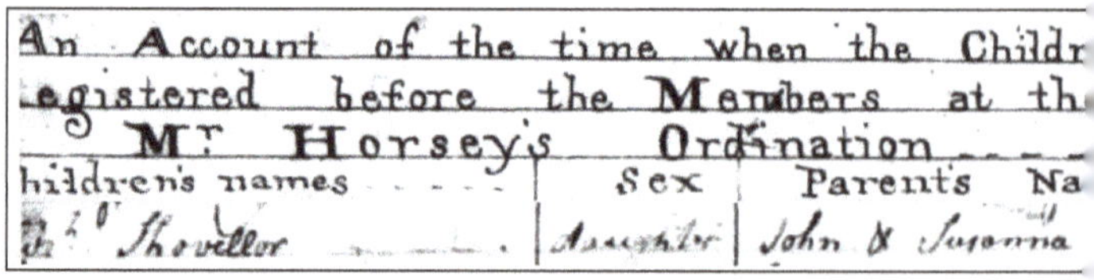

minister, years later they wrote... "perceiving the disappointments of providence with regard to 'foreign ministers', they began to look among themselves for assistance, and having gifted brethren who were members of the church, they called upon John Lacey to undertake carrying on the public ministry." Mr. Lacey accepted the call, and after solemn prayer and fasting was ordained their pastor in the year 1733, when they enlarged their meeting-house at an expense of £180.[31]

By the time Queen Anne died in 1714, the Baptists were so much persecuted that Lacey had not sufficient fortitude to bear the reproaches and sneers to which he was exposed for going to meeting, so that for two years he attended St Mary's parish church at Kingston, going with the prayer book under his arm. At the end of that time his conscience so distressed him on account of his having left the Dissenters, that he returned to the congregation in Meeting-house Alley, Portsmouth, and never after left. It is not known at what time his conversion took place, but he did not join the church until after his 1728 marriage. With several others, he was baptized in a pond in front of a farm-house at Eastney, in the island of Portsea, by the light of lanterns. The Baptists at that period were so greatly annoyed that they baptized at night, chiefly in the pond above mentioned, and at other times in the moat round the Portsmouth walls.[32]

Mr. Lacey accompanied a Mr. Meredith to solicit subscriptions from his own people towards a new place of worship and a new meeting house was built in Orange Street, which could accommodate some 2500 persons. There was no Episcopal chapel at that time, and Mr. Lacey used to say pleasantly, "Well, let them build as many places as they will, ours will always be the mother church." Mr. Lacey was pastor of the

An Account of the time when the Childr registered before the Members at th Mr Horsey's Ordination

hildren's names	Sex	Parents Na
Eliz.th Shoveller	Daughter	John & Susanna

Rev. John Shoveller Jr. (1796-1831)

MARRIED—Saturday se'nnight, at Clifton, Mr. George Richardson, of Cotham, to Miss Jane Whitchurch, of King's-parade.—Monday, at Holt, by the Rev. E.B. Lye, Mr.Rumsey, of this city, to Miss Ferris, of Holt, Wilts.—Monday se'nnight, Mr. Robert Rawlings, perfumer, of Clifton, to Miss Horton, daughter of the late Mr. Horton, apothecary, of Bath—Mr. A. Snell, tailor, Bridewell-lane, to Miss Maria Hollandish.—On Tuesday last, by the Rev. J. Townsend, at Taunton St. Mary Magdalene, the Rev. John Shoveller, of Melksham, Wilts, to Eliza, youngest daughter of the Rev. R. Horsey, of Taunton.—

On Wednesday, Eliza, wife of the Rev. John Shoveller, Baptist Minister, Bridgnorth.

At Bridgnorth, aged 30, Eliza, wife of the Rev. J. Shoveller, jun. and daughter of the Rev. R. Horsey, of Wellington, Somerset.

MARRIED.
Last week, at St. Sidwell's church, Exeter, the Rev. John Shoveller, of Penzance, Baptist Minister, to Miss Dorothy Toms, of St. Sidwell's.

Died, on Monday the 10th inst. at Henley on Thames, Mrs. Shoveller, the beloved wife of the Rev. John Shoveller, jun. Her loss is sincerely regretted by a numerous circle of relatives and friends.

At Henley, in her 23d year, Dorothea, wife of the Rev. John Shoveller, Baptist Minister, late of Penzance.—On Monday

Died, on the 12th Dec. last, at Kingston, in the Island of Jamaica, after four days' illness, the Rev. John Shoveller (son of the Rev. John Shoveller, of Portsea). Missionary and Pastor of the Baptist Church in that City.—His zealous and enlightened labours for the conversion of souls proved eminently successful; while, by his pious, amiable, and friendly demeanour, he secured for himself the esteem of Christians of every denomination. His pall was supported by three Clergymen of the Established Church with three Wesleyan Ministers, and Ministers of his own and other denominations followed his remains as mourners to the grave. The attendance of a deeply affected crowd of more than three thousand persons marked how extensively his loss is felt by those for whose spiritual benefit he was found faithful unto death.

DIED.—On the 6th December, at Kingston, Jamaica, the Rev. John Shoveller, Baptist Missionary, formerly of Henley-on-Thames.—On the 21st Feb. at Compton, William.

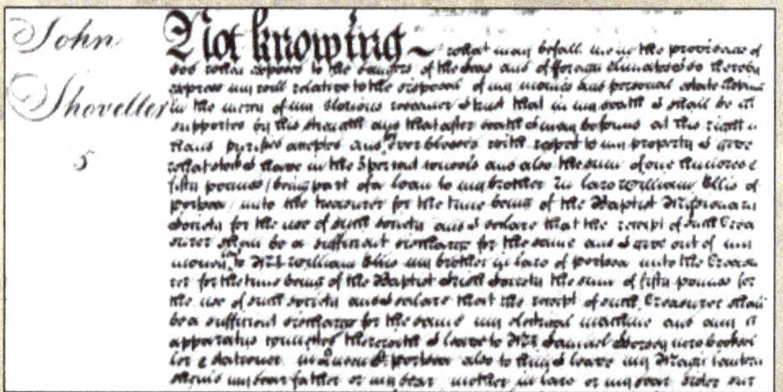

John Shoveller [handwritten will text, largely illegible]

▲ 1-Marriage notice for Rev. John Shoveller Jr. & Eliza Horsey (Bristol Mirror, 17 April 1819); 2-Death notice for Eliza Shoveller (nee Horsey) - (Staffordshire Advertiser, 20 May 1826); 3-1st wife Eliza Shoveller (hee Horsey) - Death notice (Hampshire Chronicle, 29 May 1826); 4-Marriage notice for Rev. John Shoveller Jr. & Dorothy Toms (Royal Cornwall Gazette, 18 April 1829); 5-2nd wife, Dorothea Toms - Death notice (Hampshire Telegraph, 17 Jan 1831); 6-Death notice for Dorothea Shoveller (nee Toms, Oxford Journal, 22 January 1831); 7- Obituary for Rev. John Shoveller Jr. (Hampshire Telegraph, 27th Feb 1832 p.4); 8- Death notice for Rev. John Shoveller Jr. (Reading Mercury, 5th March 1832); 9-Last will & testament for Rev. John Shoveller Jr.

the Members of this Church were born.

Monthly Church Meetings since

May 15ᵗ 1702.

when born 39	when died
Octo 24. 1703	

Rev. Joseph Horsey (1737-1802)

Portrait of Rev. Joseph Horsey, half-length, dressed in a dark frockcoat over his waistcoat with a powdered bobwig, c.1785.

Memoir of the late Rev. Joseph Horsey, of Portsea. By John Shoveller. *With Mr. Horsey's last Farewell Address to his Church, a short time previous to his Decease. Also the Funeral Sermon, delivered at the Interment, by Daniel Miall; to which is added, an Elegy, by Mrs. Saffrey, Portsea. 80 pp. 2s. sewed.*

THESE memoirs, we are informed, were not intended to exhibit to the world a character of any considerable celebrity in the circles of literature and science; but chiefly to gratify the wishes of many friends; and to hand down to posterity an example worthy of imitation. Mr. Horsey is here represented as a man of singular piety, superiority of intellect, and eminent benevolence. As a preacher, his talents were highly esteemed, and his labours rendered useful to many. We are not favoured with any abstracts of Mr. Horsey's manuscripts in these memoirs, as it was his particular request, a short time previous to his decease, that they should all be destroyed. The substance of his last address to his people, however, was taken down at the time it was delivered, and is annexed to these memoirs. — The retrospect he takes of his ministration among his people, may be considered as both ingenious and instructive. " It is now," says he, " twenty years ago since I was set apart to the pastoral office over this church; during which time, many important events have taken place respecting you. — One hundred of our members have died and left the church militant, we hope, to join the church triumphant. This teaches us the uncertainty of life with all its enjoyments, and urges the necessity of great seriousness, and an actual readiness for our great change, from a conviction that we shall very soon be called to follow them. Thirty of our brethren and sisters have been dismissed to other churches; by which we are taught, that here we have no continuing city; that it is altogether uncertain where our lot will be cast, and how we shall be situated in the present world. But, the most painful of all to relate is, that thirty-eight of our members, who once made a great profession of attachment to Christ and his cause, have been separated from us on account of sin. This calls upon us to be exceedingly circumspect in our walk and conversation before the world; and to be always on our watch against the very appearance of evil; as well as to be very earnest in prayer to him who is able to keep us from falling; that by his power we may be kept, through faith, unto eternal salvation."

" Mr. Miall, in his sermon, bears an honourable testimony of Mr. H., who was " a man, that well supported the Christian character; who constantly filled up his public station as a minister and a Christian; and who, in his temper, was particularly amiable and affectionate." " Twenty-eight years (says Mr. Miall) I have stood in connection with him as a minister, and in all that time, scarcely heard an angry word; and rarely did the sun go down upon his wrath." As Mr. Horsey's life was marked with prudence, generosity, and piety, so in his death, he manifested a mind resigned, placid, and most devoutly occupied. He died Sept. 4, 1802, aged 65 years.

'Memoir of the late Rev. Joseph Horsey', by the Rev. John Shoveller Sr. (1802), from 'The Evangelical Magazine for 1803,' London.

church nearly fifty years, but he died on 13th April 1781, within a few weeks of reaching eighty-one years of age.[33]

Meanwhile, Mr. Joseph Horsey had become an assistant to Mr. Lacey, and after his death, was invited to the pastoral office by a large majority, and ordained on the 15th May 1782.[34] Joseph Horsey was born at Crewkerne, in Somersetshire, and being apprenticed at Gosport led to his becoming a member of the church at Portsea. He possessed very acceptable talents, and was much esteemed both as a christian and a minister. He laboured in connexion with his assistant, Mr. Daniel Miall, with much success until 1801, when he himself was rendered incapable by a stroke of paralysis, and died on the 4th September 1802.[35]

In growing up in Portsmouth, John Shoveller attended the Baptist congregation in Portsmouth Common, later called Meeting House Alley under John Lacey. But his fervour for God was undoubtedly propagated by the influence of the Rev. Joseph Horsey, who replaced John Lacey as the Baptist minister at Portsea from 1782 to 1802.

Indeed, John Shoveller likely met his future wife at meetings of the Baptist brethren, as he subsequently married Susannah Horsey, on the 4th February 1783, which for legal purposes was conducted at St. Mary's Church, Portsea.[36] Susannah (1759-1816), and her younger sister Elizabeth Horsey (1762-1798), the first wife of the Rev. John Saffery (1762-1825), were both daughters of the Rev. Joseph Horsey and Susannah Todd. Following the death of Rev. Joseph Horsey

Mr. **Shoveller** writing of him, says, " Mr. Horsey's character still lives in the recollection of many, and in the praise of the churches ; for the urbanity of his disposition, for his skill in the word of righteousness, and for the faithful discharge of his ministerial duties both at home and abroad ; for he was well known and greatly esteemed, both in the Metropolis and the Western parts of the Kingdom.

▲ *Rev. John Shoveller Sr.'s description of the Rev. Joseph Horsey (in Ridoutt, F. (Ed.), 1888). 'The Early Baptist History of Portsmouth - And the Formation of the Churches in the Town.' Printed at Landport, G. Chamberlain, 120pp).*

Documents of Rev. John Shoveller Sr.(1760-1851)

On Sunday was married, Mr. Shoveller, of Portsea, to Miss Paffard, of this town. On Wednesday, Mr. Paffard, of this place, to Miss Shoveller, of Portsea, sister of Mr. Shoveller.

STOLEN on Thursday night last, from a Meadow in the vicinity of Portsmouth.—An aged BAY HORSE, about fifteen hands high, with his ears cropped close, and short tail; he has been used both with a saddle and for draught—He evinces considerable spirit, particularly when h [] t by the heel. "If such a horse should be offered for sale, it is desired he may be stopped, and information sent to Mr. John Shoveller, Portsmouth; or to the printer of this paper; and Ten Guineas reward will be paid on conviction of the offender or offenders. [] June [], 1810.

POOLE.
To Timber and Coal Merchants, Builders, &c.
TO be SOLD by PRIVATE CONTRACT,—All that desirable Piece or Parcel of GROUND, situate at the back of the Bull's Head Inn, in High-street, Poole, and lately used by Messrs. Mottley, Son, and Ellis, as a timber and slab yard; together with three TENEMENTS, adjoining thereto, in Leg-lane. This Estate, in the very centre of the town, is well worthy the attention of any person wanting room in the vicinity of the Quay.   [7410
References (post-paid) may be made to Mottley, Son, and Ellis, Portsea. or to the Rev. John Shoveller, Poole.

ISLE OF WIGHT.
TO be SOLD by AUCTION, by Messrs TUCKER & PITTS, at the Bugle Inn, Newport, on Wednesday the 15th day of September, 1813, at three o'clock in the afternoon;—
Lot 1.—All that substantial and convenient FREE-HOLD DWELLING-HOUSE, and large, GARDEN, situate in the Parish of Carisbrooke, near the West end of the town of Newport, now in the occupation of the Rev. Mr. Shoveller, and comprising a large dining parlour, breakfast ditto, large kitchen, cellar, and other convenient offices, four good bed-chambers, three attic rooms, with good closets. The situation is well adapted for a Tanner, Fell-monger's Yard, or any other business requiring a supply of water, being bounded on the North by a constant stream.

POOLE.
To Timber and Coal Merchants, Builders, &c.
TO be SOLD by PRIVATE CONTRACT,—All that desirable Piece or Parcel of GROUND, situate at the back of the Bull's Head Inn, in High-street, Poole, and lately used by Messrs. Mottley, Son, and Ellis, as a timber and slab yard; together with three TENEMENTS, adjoining thereto, in Leg-lane. This Estate, in the very centre of the town, is well worthy the attention of any person wanting room in the vicinity of the Quay.   [7410
References (post-paid) may be made to Mottley, Son, and Ellis, Portsea. or to the Rev. John Shoveller, Poole.

To Timber Merchants, Coal Merchants, Builders, &c.
TO be SOLD by AUCTION, by Mr. BRISTOWE, at the Old Antelope Inn, Poole, on Thursday, July 15th, 1819, at three o'clock, in one Lot,—All that most desirable ESTATE, lately used as a TIMBER YARD, adjoining the Passage leading through the Bull-Head-Yard into High-street; together with the TENEMENTS connected with the said Estate; the whole forming confessedly the most eligible site of disposal Land in the whole Town of Poole—For particulars apply to Messrs. Mottley and Ellis, Portsea; to the Rev. Mr. Shoveller, Hill-street; or to the Broker, Poole.

TO THE RIGHT WORSHIPFUL THE MAYOR OF PORTSMOUTH.
SIR,
WE, the undersigned, request you will, at an early period, call a PUBLIC MEETING of the Inhabitants of the Borough, to take into consideration the propriety of PETITIONING PARLIAMENT for the entire and speedy ABOLITION OF NEGRO SLAVERY in every part of his Majesty's Dominions. PORTSMOUTH, October 8th, 1830.

FEMALE PENITENTIARY, SPRING-STREET, LANDPORT.
WANTED, for the above Establishment, a LAUNDRESS, who fully understands her business; she must be a Woman of decided piety, and produce proper testimonials as to character and ability. Apply to Mrs. Shoveller, Marlborough Row, Portsea.

The funds for the purchase or building of suitable Premises for the Female Penitentiary, in this neighbourhood, in lieu of the House now rented for that purpose, are, we are happy to remark, rapidly progressing, and we doubt not will soon realize the sum required. We have been favored with the sight of a letter, addressed to the Secretary of the Building Committee, (Rev. J. Shoveller,) from which we with pleasure make the following extract:—
SIR,—I have to request that you will inform the Members of the Committee for Building or Purchasing a House for a Penitentiary for Portsmouth, that I have this day received a cheque for 200l. from a gentleman, with the following instruction:—"That provided a House be either built or purchased, for the purpose of a Penitentiary, on or before the 1st of January, 1839, I am to pay 200l. towards the Building Fund; but in case the House is not obtained by that time, the said sum of 200l. is to be differently applied." The donor's name I am not a liberty to disclose. He requests me to add, that he trusts you will follow up your declaration made at the Public Meeting, that the House shall be suitably built in a healthy situation.

Tea Meeting.—On Thursday evening last, a very large and respectable tea meeting, amounting to between four and five hundred persons, was held at the Queen's Rooms, Mill-dam, in aid of the fund for re-building Meeting-House Alley Chapel. The assembly were informed by the pastor of the Church, the Rev. C. Room, of the reasons which had induced the religious community he represented, to reconstruct their edifice; by this step, they were apprized that, beside adequate school accommodation, and a public entrance in Kent-street, a considerable addition would be made to the number of pews, and a wise economy would be observed. After the devotional services, which were efficiently sustained by the Rev. Mr. Dawson, of Staines, the Rev. T. Tilly, and the Rev. C. Cakebread, several speeches were delivered. The Rev. Mr. Shoveller, having alluded to the antiquity of the Church (founded about the year 1704), indulged the meeting with interesting reminiscences of the period when the site of the fabric was styled "Portsmouth Common," and when instead of being surrounded with buildings as at present, hardly a house was to be seen, but he had rambled with boyish delight among the heath-flowers, and the wild briar, which everywhere abounded. The Rev.

MRS. SHOVELLER, Died, February the 7th, 1816, AGED 56 YEARS.

MRS. SHOVELLER, wife of the Rev. John Shoveller, of Poole, in the county of Dorset, was the eldest daughter of the late Rev. Joseph Horsey, who, for many VOL. VIII.   2 N

years, fulfilled the duties of the pastoral office, over the Baptist church at Portsea. The memory of this man of God will be ever dear to those who were acquainted with him. As a man, he was remarkable for his amiableness of disposition; so much so, that, wherever he was known,

On Wednesday last died, Mrs. Shoveller, aged 56 years, wife of the Rev. John Shoveller, of Poole, and daughter of the late Rev. Joseph Horsey. Whilst on a visit to her friends in this place, she was summoned to ascend to a sublime state of society, to experience, through eternal ages, purer joys, and friendships more refined. Her loss will be long and deeply deplored by an extensive circle, as the virtues which adorn every relation of life were, in her character eminently illustrated.

City or Borough of Portsmouth						83 Enumeration Schedule
Parish or Township of Portsea						

PLACE	HOUSES	NAMES of each Person who abode therein the preceding Night	AGE and SEX	PROFESSION, TRADE, EMPLOYMENT, or of INDEPENDENT MEANS	Where Born	
Marlborough Row		Robert do	5		Y.	
		Emily do	3		Y.	
		Maria do	m		Y.	
do	1	John Shoveller	80		N.	
		Sarah do	60		N.	
		Elizabeth do	20	F[]		

Shoveller Rev. John, 17 Marlborough row, Portsea

DEATHS.
On the 20th inst., at Portsea, Sarah, relict of the Rev. John Shoveller, in the 94th year of her age.

MARRIAGES solemnized in the Parish of _____ in the County of _____ in the Year 1826

John Shoveller, Widower of the Parish of Portsea in the County of Hants
and Sarah Hook Spinster of this Parish
were married in this Church by Licence with Consent of
this thirteenth Day of July in the Year One thousand eight hundred and twenty Six
By me [] Seale Curate of []
This Marriage was solemnized between us { John Shoveller, Sarah Hook
In the Presence of { Chris Hook, [] Hook, Andrew Hook
No. 499.

156	WILLS. 1870.
SHOVELLER Sarah. Effects under £5,000.	6 August. The Will of Sarah Shoveller late of Portsea in the County of Southampton Widow deceased who died 20 July 1870 at Marlborough-row Portsea aforesaid was proved at Winchester by the oaths of Eliza Hook of Portsea aforesaid Spinster the Niece and Charles Townsend Hook of Snodland near Maidstone in the County of Kent Paper Manufacturer the Nephew the Executors.

▲LEFT COLUMN: 1-Miss [Elizabeth] Shoveller & Mr. Joseph Paffard - Marriage (Hampshire Telegraph, 25 Nov 1805); 2-Stolen Bay Horse (Salisbury & Winchester Journal, 18 June 1810, p.1); 3-Rev. John Shoveller Sr - Poole Property For Sale (Hampshire Telegraph, 10 Feb 1817); 4-Funds for a Female Penitentiary (Hampshire Telegraph, 15th Jan 1838, p.4); 5-Death notice for Mrs (Susannah Horsey) Shoveller (Hampshire Chronicle, 12 Feb 1816); 6-Death notice for Mrs (Susannah Horsey). 7-Marriage Registration for Rev. John Shoveller Sr. & Sarah Hook, at Melksham, 13th July 1826. TOP CENTRE COLUMN: 1-Auction of Rev. John Shoveller Sr's home on the Isle of Wight (Hampshire Telegraph, 13 Sept 1813, p.1); 2-Land Auction at Poole (Hampshire Telegraph, 10 Feb 1817, p.3). RIGHT COLUMN: 1-Rev. Mr. Shoveller - Estate Auction in Poole (Hampshire Telegraph, 12 July 1819); 2-Rev. John Shoveller - Support for Abolition of Slavery (Hampshire Telegraph, 11 Oct 1830); 3-Mrs Shoveller - Laundress Required (Hampshire Telegraph, 4 June 1832); 4-Re-building fund for Meeting House Alley Chapel (Hampshire Telegraph, 21st Sept 1844, p.4); 5-1841 Census listing for John & Sarah Shoveller at Portsea (England and Wales Census); 6-1844 Pigot's Directory listing for Rev. John Shoveller Sr. at 17 Marlborough Row, Portsea; 7- Death notice for Sarah Shoveller (Hampshire Advertiser, 27 July 1870); 8-Probate notice for Sarah Shoveller (1870).

in 1802, Rev. John Shoveller Sr. published his 'Memoirs of the Late Rev. Joseph Horsey, of Portsea, with Mr. Horsey's last farewell address to this Church, a short time previous to his decease.'[37]

After 11 years working as a caulker, ropemaker, painter, glazier and coal merchant at his fathers business in Portsmouth, Rev. John Shoveller Sr. removed to London. By 1791, he was residing in Upper Newman Street where he commenced work as a copper-plate printer, creating prints for most of the portraits that appeared in the early volumes of the Evangelical Magazine. At this time he became acquainted with most of the Baptist and evangelical Calvinist Anglican ministers in London, including John Newton, who penned the now eternal hymn 'Amazing Grace.' During their tenure in London from 1791 to 1796, the Shovellers worshiped at the Baptist congregation in Eagle Street, under the ministry of the Rev. William Smith, though as his 'memoir' points out, due to travelling distances they often worshipped at the Tottenham Court Chapel, which was founded by George Whitefield.[38]

Rev. John Shoveller Sr. returned to Portsea in September 1796, reuniting with Rev. Horsey's congregation, who was being assisted at that time by Daniel Miall and a young

John Newton (1725-1807)[73]

John Newton grew up without any particular religious conviction, but his life's path was formed by a variety of twists and coincidences, that were often put into motion by other's reactions to what they took as his recalcitrant insubordination. He was pressed (conscripted) into service in the Royal Navy, and after leaving the service, became involved in the Atlantic slave trade. In 1748, a violent storm battered his vessel off the coast of County Donegal, Ireland, so severely that he called out to God for mercy. This moment marked his spiritual conversion, but he continued slave trading until 1754 or 1755, when he ended his seafaring altogether. Newton then began studying Christian theology and later became an abolitionist, and an associate of the Rev. John Shoveller Sr..

With words written from personal experience, John Newton, was responsible for writing the universal and immensely popular Christian hymn 'Amazing Grace,' which was first published in 1779, and is now used both for religious and secular purposes.[74]

Rev. John Saffery (1763-1825)[75]

Was an active supporter of the Baptist Missionary Society and popular hymn writer, Saffery served as pastor of the Baptist church at Brown Street, Salisbury from 1790 to 1825, succeeding Henry Phillips (1720-1789). He was originally from Portsea. His first wife was Elizabeth Horsey, daughter of Rev. Joseph Horsey, Baptist minister at Portsea. After her death in 1798, he married the following year to Maria Grace Andrews (1772-1858), poet, novelist and hymn writer. Saffery was succeeded at Brown Street by his son, Philip as pastor of the Baptist church in Salisbury, serving from 1826 to 1836. Philip attended Bristol Baptist Academy from 1818-20, and ministered at Hastings after leaving Salisbury before joining the Baptist church at Waltham Abbey in the 1840s. See G. A. Moore and R. J. Huckle, Salisbury Baptist Church 1655-2000 (Salisbury: n.p., 2000) 21-27; Brian Talbot, "John Saffery (1763-1825)," ed. Haykin, in The British Particular Baptists, 3:43-83; DEB.

Letter from... John Saffery, Northampton, to John Shoveller, London

23rd August 1795 (a)

My Dear Bror & Sister

I am much obliged by your affecte note which I recd Saturday on a whole sheet of paper. Am glad to hear you are all with our dear Father well (b) – thro' mercy it is thus with me except feeling rather more ye effects of yesterdays exercises yn usual Mondays – I should have written to you but my engagements in preaching which is every evening except Saturday somewhere, with a variety of other things have kept me so employ'd. I have had no time for writing except to my dear Elizabeth. I knew she had inform'd you of me – I recd a letter from her Yesterday thro divine goodness she is well her Father recd a letter from her by the same Post. I hope to see you next Monday evening, tho' it is with difficulty I have resisted the united importunity of yr Friends to stay another Sab. with them. I thank you for your affecte wishes for my staying with you a few days & one Sab. but this will not, cannot, be. I shall yn have been from home a month. My design is to stay with you a few hours, perhaps till Wednesday morning & yn go for S / Salisbury / as fast as ye Coachman will drive, tho' not perhaps so fast as I shall wish – I was in hopes our good Father would have staid in Town over this week 'till my return, my duty to him, I shou'd be glad to see him Will you endeavour to inform Mr & Mrs Hilton in a day or two yt Mrs Collier ye old Woman to whom they sent by me when I was last at N– (c) is very ill, had been confined to her bed several weeks, & is I find in necessitous circumstances, I don't know if I do right in soliciting a small portion of their bounty for her, if they think so, I will do whatever they command, if I have the orders this week – My love to them, & beg their pardon for the liberty I have thus taken. I'll do it myself when I see ym – You want to know ye state of Religion in these parts. I have not time to write much, but can say upon ye whole it is pleasing. The Congregatn in College Lane yt I am now supplying is large about 700. & there are a great many godly eminent Xtians among ym & I think more of ye spirit of religion yn is to be found in Churches & Congregats in general. The Villages about N– 1, 2, 3, 4 & 5 miles distant & fm which a good part of their N. comes afford a most pleasing appearance in a religious sense. They are in general large, the people earnest to hear ye gospel with much attentn Farmers living in ym some of whom feel much of ye power of godliness & lay out themselves to encourage & support ye preaching, & you may almost at any / service / have from 1 to 300 people glad to hear you in ym O how different from ye little, wretched, cursed places about us. Tho there are many pleasing situats in this County for Village preaching I suppose Northton has ye preference of ym all. I hope God will give ym a godly, able, willing Minister; who will prove himself a Labourer. Its a pity they should have a lazy drone where there is so much to do – I wish you & I felt what you express a desire for, more love too & zeal for God, let us beg & pray ye Lord for it. I could say much on this head but must forbear – I was at Olney last week had a pleasing & profitable interview with Bror Sutcliff I intend going to Walgrave Wednesday, & Kettering to see Bror Fuller Thursday & back to N– Friday. (d) Pray for & believe me to be with earnest wishes for your best interest & Your Very Affecte Bror

J Saffery

NB. Love to your dear Susan & her Sisters &c

If our dear Father is not under an absolute necessity of returning this week I should like to spend one day in London with him & tell him this with my duty.

NOTES: [a] Saffery/Whitaker Papers, acc. 142, I.A.(20.), Angus Library. Address: Mr Shoveller | 19 Upper Newman Street | Oxford Street | London. Postmark: 25 August 1795.
[b] Apparently Rev. Joseph Horsey of Portsmouth was visiting his daughter and son-in-law in London at this time.
[c] Northampton, where Saffery had been supplying the Baptist congregation in College Lane, a congregation still seeking a replacement for John Ryland, Jr., now the minister at Broadmead in Bristol.
[d] Andrew Fuller (1754-1815) joined the Baptist congregation at Soham in 1769, and would eventually become the congregation's pastor at a young age. His study of scripture and reading of Jonathan Edwards and some other writers led him to espouse an evangelical Calvinist position, with his influential work, The Gospel Worthy of All Acceptation (1785), being the fruition of that study. He subsequently influenced numerous ministers among the Particular Baptists to follow his evangelical preaching with an 'open call' to unbelievers, a movement that became known as 'Fullerism'. He left Soham in 1782 for the Baptist church at Kettering, where he remained the rest of his life.

▲*Letter written by Rev. John Saffery to his brother-in-law Rev. John Shoveller Sr, 23 Aug 1795.*[76]

Joseph Ivimey. John Shoveller was instrumental in founding a new congregation in a neighbouring community at Marie-le-bonne, where he took out a lease of land at Green Row in August 1798.[39] Along with a Mr Knight and Mr James Saffery, brother of Rev. John Saffery, they regularly preached there at the turn of the 19th century.[40] But at the same time John remained a principal in the ropemaking and ships chandlery partnership with John Parmeter at East Street, Portsmouth, having succeeded to his fathers business in 1798.

Between 1803 and 1814, Rev. Shoveller ministered to congregations at Romsey, Hampshire, at Pembroke Street, Plymouth Dock (replacing William Steadman, formerly at Broughton), and at Newport on the Isle of Wight.[41] On 22nd March 1812, the foundation stone of a new Independent Chapel was laid in King-street, Portsea, by the Rev. John Griffin, who by increasing the congregation had occasioned the necessity for the new building.

In addition to these ministries, John kept on with his father's business. Although the enterprise experienced difficult periods when parts of their property had to be leased out to tenants, and administrators stepped in to foreclose on stock in trade with bankruptcy proceedings against the business in 1810, John Shoveller remained involved with 'Shoveller & Parmeter' until at least 1827, when his partner John Parmenter died.

In 1814 Rev. John Shoveller Sr. accepted the call to pastor the Baptist congregation at Poole, where he preached until 1826, returning at that time to 17 Marlborough Row, Portsea, where in March 1829 he took out a lease on Marie-le-Bonne Chapel in Green Row.[42] He would continue to preach in retirement until his 85th year.[43]

John and Susannah Shoveller produced at least three children, who in turn left a prodigious number of descendants (*see 3.1 Descendants of Rev. John Shoveller Sr. & Susannah Horsey*). Their surviving children were Elizabeth Shoveller (1783-1826),[44] Susanna Shoveller (1785-1861),[45] and Rev. John Shoveller Jr. (1796-1832),[46] who were all baptised at the Meeting-House Alley, Baptist Church in Portsea. Susanna married on the 1st November 1803 at St Mary's Church, Portsea to William (1785-1846), the son of William Ellis Sr. and Mary King, producing seven sons and three daughters.[47] Elizabeth married two years later on the 20th November 1805 at St Thomas' Church, Portsmouth to Joseph (1780-1861),

3.1 Descendants of Rev. John Shoveller Sr. & Susannah Horsey

Shoveller | Horsey

Rev. John SHOVELLER (1760-1851), married firstly on the 4th February 1783 at St. Mary's Church, Portsea to Susannah (1759-1816), daughter of Rev. Joseph Horsey & Susannah Todd, with issue:

1. Elizabeth Shoveller (1783–1826), baptised 24th Oct 1783 at Meeting House Alley Baptist Church, Portsmouth. She married on 20th Nov 1805 at Saint Thomas Church, Portsmouth, Hampshire to Joseph PAFFARD (1794-1861)[77] She died and was buried on the 23rd April 1826,[78] aged 43 at Portsea, Hampshire, with issue:

1.1 Elizabeth Carter Paffard (1810-1904), married in 1831 to James THOMPSON (1814-?), with issue:
a. Elizabeth Thompson (1834-?)
b. John THOMPSON (1836-1921)
c. Sarah Thompson (1838-?)
d. Fanny Thompson (1842-?)

1.2 Rebecca Carter Paffard (1812-1851), married on 18 May 1834 at Alverstoke, Hampshire to Richard WILLIAMS, a master tailor, with issue:
a. Rebecca Paffard Williams (1836-?)
b. Sarah Ann Williams (?-?)*

1.3 James Carter PAFFARD (1814-1866), married on 1st Sep 1833 at St Martin in the Fields, London to Mary Ann Jupe (1812-1886), with issue:
a. Mary Anne Paffard (1834-1895)
b. James Joseph Thomas PAFFARD (1836-1914)
c. George Wallis PAFFARD (1839-1903)
d. Maria Louisa Paffard (1840-?)
e. Mary Jane Paffard (1840-?)
f. Matilda Paffard (1840-?)
g. Walter Scott PAFFARD (1841-1866)
h. Charles (PAFFARD 1847-1848)*
i. Elizabeth Paffard (1849-1881)

2. Susanna Shoveller (1785-1861), was born in 1785 and likely baptised at Meeting House Alley Baptist Church, Portsmouth. She married on the 1st Nov 1803 at St Mary's, Portsea to William ELLIS (1785-1846), with issue:

2.1 William ELLIS (1804-1873), married in 1828 to Sarah Bigwood (1804–1855), with issue:
a. William Cuzens ELLIS (1830–1875)
b. Sarah Ellis (1834–1893)
c. Mary Ellis (1840–1864)
d. Emma Ellis (1843–1937)
e. George ELLIS (1845–1909)

2.2 John ELLIS (1807-1894), married firstly tin 1835 to Margaret Rebecca Grant (1815-1907). he married secondly in 1836 to Ann Jane Helier (1818-?), with issue:
a. Robert William ELLIS (1837-1923)
b. Margaret Rebecca Ellis (1846-1952)
c. Sarah Elizabeth Ellis (1847-?)

d. Clara Jane Ellis (1850-?)

2.3 Joseph Horsey ELLIS (1808-1875), married in 1835 to Anne Sophia Gamsby (1812–1906), with issue:
a. Adelaide Wellesley Ellis (1832–1898)

2.4 Robert Bowyer ELLIS (1811-1894), married in 1835 to Margaret Rebecca Grant (1815-1907), with issue:
a. Robert W. ELLIS (1837-1923)
b. Edward William ELLIS (1841-?)
c. Margaret Rebecca Ellis (1846-?)
d. Sarah Elizabeth Ellis (1847-?)
e. Clara Jane Ellis (1850-)

2.5 James ELLIS (1814-?), married in 1842 to Fanny Coxon (1817-1875), with issue:
a. George Coxon (1844-1922)
b. William H. (1845-1931)
c. Albert (1847-?)
d. Mary Ann (1849-1895)
e. Fanny (1852-?)
f. Milly (1857-?)

2.6 Susan Shoveller Ellis (1816-1876), married in 1838 to Richard Elliott VARDY (1814-1883), with issue:
a. Susan Mary Vardy (1839-1880)
b. Annie G. Vardy (1840-1928)
c. Albert Richard VARDY (1841-1900)
d. Frances Sarah Vardy (1843-1906)
e. Emily Vardy (1844-1896)
f. Julia Vardy (1845-1917)
g. Jane Vardy (1847-1908)
h. William Ellis VARDY (1848-?)
i. Amelia Vardy (1851-1869)
j. Joshua Alfred VARDY (1853-1944)
k. Harriet Shoveller Vardy (1861-1952)

2.7 Mary Ellis (1818-?), married in 1849 to Samuel Davies BRIGHT (1822-1906), with issue:
a. Female Bright (1852-1852)*

b. Susan Mary Bright (1854-1936)
c. Hannah Shoveller Bright (1855-1851)
d. Anne T. Bright (1856-1942)
e. Samuel Ellis BRIGHT (1857-1882)
f. Ellen Jane Bright (1859-1860)*
g. Amy Dora Bright (1861-1944)
h. Stillborn Bright (1865-1865)*

2.8 George ELLIS (1820-1873), married firstly in 1835 to Phoebe Pledger (1811-1853), with issue:
a. George ELLIS (1836-1858)*
b. Selina Ellis (1838-1893)
George married secondly in 1840 to Sarah Frith (1822-?), with issue:
c. Henry William ELLIS (1841-1907)
d. John ELLIS (1843-1919)
e. Harriett Ellis (1845-1911)
f. Phoebe Ellis (1847-1850)*
g. Albert ELLIS (1850-1898)

2.9 Samuel ELLIS (1821-1892), married in 1847 to Sarah Foster (1826-1881), with issue:
a. Frederick Foster ELLIS (1849-1928)
b. Emma Sarah Ellis (1850-1927)
c. Charles Samuel ELLIS (1854-1917)
d. Louisa Agnes Ellis (1854-1927)
e. Clara Miriam Ellis (1856-1903)
f. Sydney Herbert ELLIS (1858-1905)
g. Howard James Shoveller ELLIS (1864-1928)

2.10 Ann Ellis (1822-?), married in 1844 to James SMITH (1822-?), with issue:
a. William SMITH (?-?)

3. Rev. John SHOVELLER Jr. (1796-1831), was born then baptised 4th Aug 1796 at Meeting House Alley Baptist Church, Portsmouth, Hampshire. He married on the 13th Apr 1819 to Eliza Guyer Horsey (1797-1826), dau. of the Rev. Richard Horsey of Taunton, at Melksham, Wiltshire, who unfortunately died in May 1826 without issue. John married secondly to Dorothea Toms (1808-1831) in May of 1829, but tragically became a double widower when he lost his second bride Dorothy in childbirth, aged just 23 in January 1831... the infant also dying either at birth or soonafter.
a. Infant Shoveller (1831-1831)
Praying for a change of luck, he left England to minister for the Baptist Church at Kingston, Jamaica, but died there on the 6th December 1831, at just 35 years of age. He left whatever he had to his sister Susannah and her husband, his brother-in-law Mr. William Ellis.

Rev. John SHOVELLER married secondly on the 13th July 1826 at St. Michael's Church, Melksham to Sarah (1777-1870), daughter of Joseph & Mary Hook, without issue.

* Died before adulthood - d.s.p.
(Some names not listed in the index.)

Letter from… Rev. John Shoveller, Portsmouth, to Rev. John Saffery, Bratton

18th August 1799

My dear Brother

I catch a moment or two off this Sacred day to write you a line just as the post is going to say that it was my fixed intention to have been with you on Yesterday in company with Mr Horsey, & to have gone with you on your Brattonian expedition, [a] but Mr H. thought proper to decline, & as I could not get a Companion I concluded it would be best for the present to decline also, & in the course of a few days we mean some of us to pay our respects to your amiable & lovely Bride, Our prayer is that God may earnestly bless her to you & you to her & both to the Church of God where Providence has plac'd you.

My dearest sends her kindest love to your dear Maria & our dear friend Mrs Whitaker & Mr ??? we have never had the pleasure of seeing her since she abandoned the name of Andrews – we shall always be exceedingly happy to see any of you in our quarter –

On Tuesday I find Mr Kemp & Miss Rolfe mean also to join hands – our new married couple are pretty hearty – O if there had but been a spice of grace in that business, the Husband methinks would have been worth accepting, but as Father Medley used to say, we must let that pass." [b]

Wishing you the best presence & of course the best comforts & remaining dear Brother.

Yours very Affectionately
John Shoveller

NOTES: [a] Reference is to Saffery's departure for Bratton to retrieve MGA [Maria Grace Andrews - his future second wife] for their wedding, which occurred two days after the date of this letter.
[b] Reference to Samuel Medley (1738-99), pastor of the Baptist congregation at Byrom Street, Liverpool from 1772-99, and a hymn writer.

▲*Letter written by Rev. John Shoveller Sr. to his brother-in-law Rev. John Saffery, 18 Aug 1799.*[79]

the son of James Paffard and Hannah Garrett, producing two daughters and a son.[48]

After his school years, John Shoveller Jr., studied at the Bristol Baptist Academy and followed in the footsteps of his father as a minister, serving at Baptist congregations in Melksham (Wiltshire), Bridgenorth (Shropshire), Penzance (Cornwall), and Henley-on-Thames (Oxfordshire).[49] Rev. John Shoveller Jr. married on the 13th April 1819 at St Mary Magdalene Church, Taunton in Somerset to Eliza Guyer Horsey (1797-1826),[50] daughter of the Rev. Richard Horsey of Taunton, but she died in 1826 without issue.[51] Rev. John Shoveller Jr. married secondly on the 6th April 1829 at St Sidwell's Church, Exeter in Devon to Dorothea (1808-1831),[52] the daughter of Humphrey and Eleanor Toms, but she died also, in childbirth on the 13th January 1831 along with their stillborn child.[53]

Praying for a change of luck, Rev. John Shoveller Jr. left England in mid 1831 to replace Rev. James Coultart, another missionary friend of the Safferys, as minister of the Baptist Church in Kingston, Jamaica, but he succumbed to sickness and died there in early December of 1831,[54] and was likely buried at the Maypen Cemetery. His will bequethed his few possessions to his nieces and nephews and the repayment of a loan to his brother-in-law, William Ellis.

Following the death of his first wife Susannah (nee Horsey) on the 7th February 1816,[55] Rev. John Shoveller Sr. took some time before marrying secondly on the 13th July 1826 at St Michaels Church, Melksham to Sarah (1777-1870), the daughter of Joseph and Mary Hook of Melksham, Wiltshire, but without further issue.[56]

The Rev. John Shoveller Sr. was a philanthropic and concerned resident of Portsmouth, and he supported and subscribed to many causes including families that suffered catastrophies such as fire (1814), the Baptist Missions of the East and West Indies (1824), the petitioning of parliament to abolish slavery (1830), representative reform (1830), subscriptions for the poor (1830), Miss Durant's Seminary (1830), the Female Penitentiary at Landport (1832), the Baptist Missionary Society (1833), Friends of Portsmouth, Portsea and Gosport Seamen's Chapel and School for the children of seamen (1836), the building of new churches in Portsmouth and Portsea (1837), a Building Fund for the refurbishment of Meeting House Alley Chapel (1844) and the Portsmouth, Portsea and Gosport Hospital (1846) aswell as many other worthy causes.

The Rev. John Shoveller Sr. died in March 1851 at 17 Marlborough Row, Portsea in Hampshire, at 90 years of age, outliving all his siblings and most of their offspring. He bequethed his assets to his second wife Sarah (nee Hook) and his only surviving child Susannah Ellis, and was buried in the Ebenezer Chapel burial ground at Portsea.[57] His

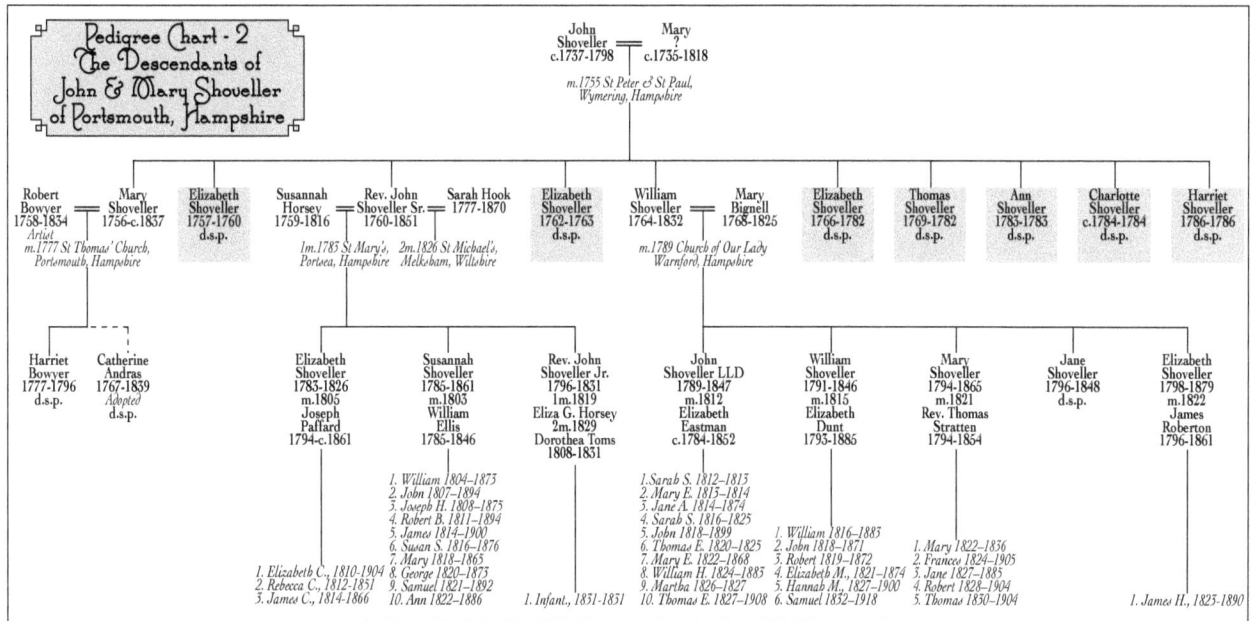

Pedigree Chart - 2
The Descendants of
John & Mary Shoveller
of Portsmouth, Hampshire

John Shoveller c.1737-1798 = Mary ? c.1735-1818
m.1755 St Peter & St Paul, Wymering, Hampshire

- Robert Bowyer 1758-1854 Artist = Mary Shoveller 1756-c.1837 m.1777 St Thomas' Church, Portsmouth, Hampshire
- Elizabeth Shoveller 1757-1760 d.s.p.
- Susannah Horsey 1759-1816 = Rev. John Shoveller Sr. 1760-1851 = Sarah Hook 1777-1870 1m.1785 St Mary's, Portsea, Hampshire; 2m.1826 St Michael's, Melksham, Wiltshire
- Elizabeth Shoveller 1762-1763 d.s.p.
- William Shoveller 1764-1832 = Mary Bignell 1768-1825 m.1789 Church of Our Lady Warnford, Hampshire
- Elizabeth Shoveller 1766-1782 d.s.p.
- Thomas Shoveller 1769-1782 d.s.p.
- Ann Shoveller 1783-1785 d.s.p.
- Charlotte Shoveller c.1784-1784 d.s.p.
- Harriet Shoveller 1786-1786 d.s.p.

Children:
- Harriet Bowyer 1777-1796 d.s.p.
- Catherine Andras 1767-1839 Adopted d.s.p.

- Elizabeth Shoveller 1783-1826 m.1805 Joseph Paffard 1794-c.1861
  1. Elizabeth C., 1810-1904
  2. Rebecca C., 1812-1851
  3. James C., 1814-1866

- Susannah Shoveller 1785-1861 m.1803 William Ellis 1785-1846
  1. William 1804-1873
  2. John 1807-1894
  3. Joseph H. 1808-1875
  4. Robert B. 1811-1894
  5. James 1814-1900
  6. Susan S. 1816-1876
  7. Mary 1818-1865
  8. George 1820-1873
  9. Samuel 1821-1892
  10. Ann 1822-1886

- Rev. John Shoveller Jr. 1796-1831 1m.1819 Eliza G. Horsey 2m.1829 Dorothea Toms 1808-1831
  1. Infant., 1831-1851

- John Shoveller LLD 1789-1847 m.1812 Elizabeth Eastman c.1784-1852
  1. Sarah S. 1812-1813
  2. Mary E. 1813-1814
  3. Jane A. 1814-1874
  4. Sarah S. 1816-1825
  5. John 1818-1899
  6. Thomas E. 1820-1825
  7. Mary E. 1822-1868
  8. William H. 1824-1885
  9. Martha 1826-1827
  10. Thomas E. 1827-1908

- William Shoveller 1791-1846 m.1815 Elizabeth Dunt 1793-1885
  1. William 1816-1885
  2. John 1818-1871
  3. Robert 1819-1872
  4. Elizabeth M., 1821-1874
  5. Hannah M., 1827-1900
  6. Samuel 1852-1918

- Mary Shoveller 1794-1865 m.1821 Rev. Thomas Stratten 1794-1854
  1. Mary 1822-1836
  2. Frances 1824-1905
  3. Jane 1827-1885
  4. Robert 1828-1904
  5. Thomas 1830-1904

- Jane Shoveller 1796-1848 d.s.p.

- Elizabeth Shoveller 1798-1879 m.1822 James Roberton 1796-1861
  1. James H., 1823-1890

▲LEFT: Drawing of 'The Sleeping Congregation,' by William Hogarth (1736). RIGHT: The high infant mortality rate in late 18th century England meant that approximately one in every three children did not make it to their fifth birthday, with John & Mary Shoveller's children being even less.

▲*Although Portsmouth was one of the largest towns on the English south coast, and residents carried on with their normal day to day lives, the presence of the massive military and naval forces and establishments was inescapable. TOP: Print of the Saluting Battery and Barracks, at Point Battery, Portsmouth (c.1830). ABOVE: Waterside Portsmouth street with the fence of the moat and entry to the sallyport to the left.*

second wife Sarah Shoveller lived into her 94th year, and died with probate in 1870.[58]

Sarah Shoveller - Effects under £5000. Late of Portsea in Southampton, widow. Died 20 July 1870 at Marlborough Row, Portsea. By Eliza and Charles Townsend Hook of Portsea & Snodland near Maidstone, Kent, being niece and nephew executors.

Probate for Sarah Shoveller, 1870 [59]

4. Elizabeth Shoveller (1762-1763)

The second child named Elizabeth by John and Mary Shoveller was baptised on the 2nd May 1762 at St. Mary's Church, Portsea, but like the first she died as an infant, and was buried at St Mary's Portsea on the 15th May 1763.[60] Her death was likely caused by disease brought about by the unsanitary conditions of the town at this time, as both Portsea and Portsmouth were overflowing with refuse.

In 1764 a body of men called the Improvement Commissioners was set up in Portsea, who were given the power to pave and clean the streets. They also appointed a man called a 'scavenger' to collect rubbish each week with a cart. In 1768 a similar body was set up in

Old Portsmouth.

5. William Shoveller (1764-1832)

John and Mary Shoveller's second son was William Shoveller, who was baptised on the 22nd April 1764 at St. Mary's Church, Portsea, and resided with his family in Portsmouth.[61] He became a cutler and silversmith and married in 1789 to Mary Bignell. William died in 1832, but he was destined to become the grandfather of Thomas Eastman Shoveller, and his family and descendants are discussed in much greater detail in Chapter 5.

6. Elizabeth Shoveller (1766-1782)

In a third attempt to name a daughter Elizabeth, John and Mary Shoveller's fourth daughter was baptised on the 19th October 1766 at St. Mary's Church, Portsea and initially seemed to have broken the spell.[62] Regrettably we know little of her, except that she likely attended Portsmouth Grammar School along with her siblings. However, the name Elizabeth proved once again to be ominous, as despite reaching the age of 16 she also died, and was buried at Portsea on the 26th March 1782.[63]

7. Thomas Shoveller (1769-1782)

The Shovellers celebrated the arrival of a third son when Thomas Shoveller was born in 1769. Like his siblings, he was baptised on the 23rd April 1769 at St. Mary's, Portsea,[64] and likely also attended Portsmouth Grammar School. By 1776 Portsmouth had introduced street lighting with oil lamps and from 1783 they appointed night watchmen to patrol the streets. The new suburb of Portsea soon outgrew its boundaries, which was initially known as Old Portsmouth. Nevertheless, it was not until the 1770s that the town walls were extended to include the new suburb.

The Shoveller household at this time consisted of five children including Mary (20), John (16), William (12), Elizabeth (10) and young Thomas (7) in addition to their parents. But Portsmouth and Portsea had long been a breeding ground for all manner of diseases, with cramped streets, poor living conditions and nutrition being responsible for high loss of life. There was no refuse collection as such, so rubbish was mostly left lying in the streets. Drainage, if it existed at all, was inadequate. People, and most particularly the poor were surrounded by dirt and filth, and the habit of keeping pigs, which would run loose and

3.2 Descendants of William Shoveller Sr. & Mary Bignell

William SHOVELLER (1764-1832), was a cutler and tanner. He married on the 3rd January 1789 at the Church of Our Lady, Warnford, Hampshire to Mary (1768-1825), daughter of John Bignell of Warnford, with issue:

1. John SHOVELLER, LLD (1789-1847), born 21st Oct 1789 in Poole, Dorset. He married on the 24th March 1812 at St Mary's Church, Portsea to Elizabeth (c.1784-1852), daughter of Thomas Eastman and Sarah Sabine of Portsmouth, with issue:
1.1 Sarah Sabine Shoveller (1812 - 1813)*
1.2 Mary Elizabeth Shoveller (1813 - 1814)*
1.3 Jane Allen Shoveller (1814 - 1874)
1.4 Sarah Sabine Shoveller (1816 - 1825)*
1.5 John SHOVELLER (1818 - 1899)
1.6 Thomas Eastman SHOVELLER (1820 - 1825)*
1.7 Mary Elizabeth Shoveller (1822 - 1868)
1.8 William Henry SHOVELLER (1824 - c.1883)
1.9 Martha Shoveller (1826 - 1827)*
1.10 Thomas Eastman SHOVELLER (1827 - 1908)

2. William SHOVELLER Jr. (1791-1846), born 5th March 1791 in Portsea, Hampshire. He married on the 13th May 1815 at St Martin In The Fields Church, Westminster, London to

Elizabeth(1794-1885), daughter of John Dunt and Hannah Heal of London, with issue:
2.1 William SHOVELLER (1816 - 1883)
2.2 John SHOVELLER (1818 - 1871)
2.3 Robert SHOVELLER (1819 - c.1872)
2.4 Elizabeth Meta Shoveller (1821 - 1874)
2.5 Hannah Mary Shoveller (1827 - 1900)

2.6 Samuel SHOVELLER (1832 - 1918)

3. Mary Shoveller (1794-1865), baptised on the 14th Oct 1794 at home at Queen St, Portsea. She married on the 23rd May 1821 at St Mary's Church, Portsea to Rev. Thomas (1794-1861), son of Thomas Spender Stratten and Frances Dawes of Holt, Wiltshire, with issue:
3.1 Mary Stratten (1822 - 1836)
3.2 Frances Stratten (1824 - 1905)
3.3 Jane Stratten (1826 - 1885)
3.4 Robert STRATTEN (1828 - 1904)
3.5 Thomas STRATTEN (1831 - 1904)

4. Jane Shoveller (1796-1848), baptised 13th April 1796 at home at Queen St, Portsea, and died a spinster in 1848 .

5. Elizabeth Shoveller (1798-1879), born 20th March 1798 at home at Queen St, Portsea. She married on the 26th June 1822 at St Mary's Church, Portsea to James (1796-1861), the son of Richard Roberton VI and Mary Rayner of Portsea, with issue:
5.1 James Henry ROBERTON (1823 – 1890)

* Died before adulthood - d.s.p.
(Some names not listed in the index).

spread further muck, did not help at all, with illnesses such as smallpox and typhoid fever striking down the people.[65]

Many of the doctors at that time were scathing of the conditions that people had to endure. Dr Engledue described the island of Portsea as "one huge cesspool... 160,000 cesspools daily permitting 30,000 gallons of urine to penetrate the soil." Dr Martin described the Portsmouth Point as "deficient in every requisite to health, comfort and cleanliness." It was obvious that these conditions were implicated in various epidemics, even if the doctors could not understand how this was so.[66]

Tragically, young Thomas Shoveller succumbed to an unknown malady, perhaps cholera or smallpox and he died at 13 years of age in 1782. But the Shoveller's were determined folk and didn't abandon the hope of trying again for more children. However, a conundrum arises at this point, if the press reports regarding Mary Shoveller are to be believed. Mary's death notices reported that she attained the very respectable age of 93 by the time of her death in 1818, which meant she was born in 1725. Problematically, this birthdate not only placed Mary, most unusually for the time, as being 12 years senior to her husband, but how could she supposedly deliver another three children between the ages of 58 to 62? Perhaps the news report was incorrect and she died at age 83, in which case her year of birth would have been 1735. This would place her much closer in age to her husband and her final three deliveries would be more credulous. All that appears certain by contemporary reports is that John and Mary Shoveller did indeed witness 'seven of their young ones being delivered into the gloomy tomb.'[67]

Unfortunately, child mortality was a fact of life, even for the royal family during those times, and the only protection against it was to produce a large brood of children. By 1800 approximately one in every three children born in Portsea did not survive to their fifth birthday, but John and Mary Shoveller persisted without pause or delay, and delivered three more girls in Portsea.[68] As a safeguard, very few infants who survived their first few days of life escaped baptism, thus there are records of these Shoveller baptisms, although almost

▲Painting looking south towards 'The Poynt' at Portsmouth, Hampshire (unknown artist, c. 1850).

▲1900 photograph of Marlborough Row, Portsea, home to Rev. John Shoveller Sr., which has now been consumed within HM Dockyard, Portsea.

nothing else of them is known. Tragically, all three of these infants also died, each death being no less meaningful and all being a time of great grief for the Shoveller family.

8. Ann Shoveller (1783-1783)

Ann Shoveller was born, baptised and died all in the same year, and was buried at Portsea on the 19th August 1783.[69]

9. Charlotte Shoveller (c.1784-1784)

Evidence of Charlotte Shoveller's birth or baptism has not been found, but she died and was buried at Portsea on the 2nd March 1784.[70]

10. Harriet Shoveller (1786-1786)

Harriet Shoveller too was born, baptised and died all in the same year, and was likely buried on the 21st August 1786 in Portsea.[71]

While their eldest child Mary had relocated to London following her marriage to Robert Bowyer in 1777, both of the brothers Rev. John Sr. and William essentially remained in Portsmouth, along with their families. Taking into account all ten of John and Mary Shoveller's children, only their eldest son Rev. John Shoveller Sr., was left alive by 1840, residing with his second wife Sarah at 17 Marlborough Row in Portsea.

But what of William, the second son, youngest of the three survivors and the only other son of John and Mary Shoveller to reach adulthood? It is through him and his wife Mary Bignell, that the ancestral path to Thomas Eastman Shoveller lies. This genealogy therefore continues with an examination of the Hampshire family that William Shoveller joined in marital bondage, which can be identified as the Bignells of Warnford. It is their unremarkable, yet engaging story that must next be told.

▲ *A South east view of Portsmouth, published according to an Act of Parliament on the 28th March 1765, by I. After Waters (artist, fl.1765, Royal Collection Trust). Printed for Jn. Ryall at Hogarth's head, Fleet Street, London.*

References

1. Hantsphere - 'Portsmouth and its people 1800-1850' [http://www.hantsphere.org.uk/portsmouth-and-its-people-1800-1850].

2. Baptisms for the infant children of John & Mary Shoveller , St Mary's, Portsea, Hampshire (England, Select Births and Christenings, 1538-1975).

3. Mary Shoveller - Baptism held on the 25th Apr 1756 at Saint Marys, Portsea, Hampshire (England, Select Births and Christenings, 1538-1975).

4. Hantsphere - 'Portsmouth and its people 1800-1850,' op. cit.

5. Mary Shoveller & Robert Bowyer - marriage held on 14 Jul 1777, at Saint Thomas, Portsmouth, Hampshire (England, Select Marriages, 1538-1973).

6. Robert Bowyer - Baptism held on the 18th Jun 1758 at Saint Thomas, Portsea, Hampshire (England, Select Births and Christenings, 1538-1975).

7. Gentleman's Magazine, lix, 1789, p. 281.

8. Manley, K.R., (1969) Robert Bowyer (1758–1834), 'Artist, Publisher and Preacher,' Baptist Quarterly, 23:1, 32-46, [DOI: 10.1080/0005576X.1969.11751273].

9. Manley, K.R., (1969). op. cit., p.33.

10. Hake, M.K., (1925). 'Catalogue of Engraved British Portraits preserved in the Department of Prints and Drawings in the British Museum,' vi, p.461.

11. Graves, A., (1905). 'The Royal Academy of Arts. A Complete Dictionary of Contributors and their work from its foundation in 1769 to 1904,' i, s.v 'Bowyer.'

12. Information kindly supplied by Mr. J.H. Mayne, Deputy Keeper, Department of Paintings, Victoria & Albert Musuem (from Manley, K.R., (1969). op. cit.).

13. Manley, K.R., (1969). op. cit., p.34.

14. Earland, A., (1911). 'John Opie and his Circle,'incorporated family reminiscences 'taken down by Mrs. Asquith, from the reminiscences of Mrs. Stratton, Mrs. Bowyer's niece and adopted daughter, and used by kind permission of Miss Alice M. Westerdale, grand-daughter of Mrs. Stratton' (p.70, note 2).

15. Earland, A., (1911). op. cit.

16. Harriet Bowyer - Burial held on the 6th August 1796 at Portsea, Southampton (England, Select Deaths and Burials, 1538-1991).

17. Baptist Register, iii, 1798-1801, p.100.

18. Manley, K.R., (1969). op. cit., p.38.

19. Naomi Clifford Books & Talks - Catherine Andras, Model-Maker to Royalty (2018). [https://www.naomiclifford.com/catherine-andras-model-maker-to-royalty/?unapproved=98617&moderation-hash=280992f7e4fd1b0912733c431e84fe51#comment-98617].

20. Earland, A., (1911). op. cit., p.69.

21. Naomi Clifford Books & Talks - Catherine Andras, Model-Maker to Royalty (2018). op. cit.

22. Naomi Clifford Books & Talks - Catherine Andras, Model-Maker to Royalty (2018). op. cit.

23. Robert Bowyer - Death notice (The Belfast Newsletter, 17 June 1834, p.3).

24. Robert Bowyer - Death notice (Gentleman's Magazine, n.s, ii, 1834, p.221).

25. Catherine Andras - Will, 1837 (England & Wales, Prerogative Court of Canterbury Wills, 1384-1858 [PROB 11: Will Registers [1839-1841], Piece 1910: Vaughan, Quire No 251-300 (1839)).

▲LEGEND: 1. South Sea Castle; 2. New Hospital for Sick Seamen; 3. Block house fort; 4. Gosport; 5. The Saluting Battery & Magazine; 6. the Spur Battery; 7. The King's Baston; 8. Governor's House; 9. Portsmouth Church; 10. Felton's Gibbett.

26. National Portrait Gallery - Robert Bowyer [https://www.npg.org.uk/collections/search/person/mp08110/robert-bowyer].

27. Manley, K.R., (1969). op. cit., p.43.

28. Elizabeth Shoveller - Baptism held on the 4th December 1757 at Saint Marys, Portsea, Hampshire (England, Select Births and Christenings, 1538-1975).

29. John Shoveller - Baptism held on the 6th Apr 1760 at Saint Marys, Portsea, Hampshire (England, Select Births and Christenings, 1538-1975).

30. John Shoveller - 'Caulker,' apprenticed to John Hatcher of Portsea, 12 Jan. 1780 (UK, Register of Duties Paid for Apprentices' Indentures, 1710-1811).

31. Ivimey, J., (1830). 'A History of the English Baptists', Vol.4, Isaac, Taylor & Hinton, London, p.486.

32. Ivimey, J., (1830). op.cit., p.487.

33. Ivimey, J., (1830). op.cit., p.488.

34. Ivimey, J., (1830). op.cit., pp.491-92.

35. Ivimey, J., (1830). op.cit., p.491.

36. Rev. John Shoveller Sr. & Susannah Horsey - Marriage held on the 4th Feb 1783, at Saint Mary's, Portsea, Hampshire (England, Select Marriages, 1538-1973).

37. Printed and sold in Portsea by James Horsey. Sold also by Seeley, Williams, and Button, London; James, Bristol; Saffery, Salisbury; and Jolliffe, Crewkerne, 1803.

38. Rev. John Shoveller Sr. - Biography from 'Nonconformist and Dissenting Studies, 1650-1850,' Biographical Indexes 'S' [https://sites.google.com/a/georgiasouthern.edu/dissenting-studies-1700-1850/biograph/s]).

39. Rev. John Shoveller Sr. (Dissenting Minister), Lease/Release of land in Green Row, August 1798 (on Card at Portsmouth History Centre).

40. Rev. John Shoveller Sr. - Biography, op. cit.

41. Rev. John Shoveller Sr. - Biography, op. cit.

42. Rev. John Shoveller Sr. (Dissenting Minister), Lease of Marie-le-Bonne Chapel in Green Row, March 1829 (on Card at Portsmouth History Centre).

43. Rev. John Shoveller Sr. - Biography, op. cit.

44. Elizabeth Shoveller - Baptism held on the 24th October 1783 at Meeting House Alley Baptist Church, Portsea, Hampshire (England & Wales, Non-Conformist and Non-Parochial Registers, 1567-1970).

45. Susannah Shoveller - Born approx. 1785 at Portsea, Hampshire (Kingston, District 10, 1861 England Census for Susan Ellis).

46. John Shoveller Jr. - Birth registered on the 4th August 1796 at Meeting House Alley Baptist Church, Portsea, Hampshire (England & Wales, Non-Conformist and Non-Parochial Registers, 1567-1970).

47. Susannah Shoveller & William Ellis - Marriage announcement (Hampshire Telegraph, 7th Nov. 1803).

48. Elizabeth Shoveller & Joseph Paffard - Marriage announcement (Hampshire Telegraph, 25th Nov 1805, p.3).

49. Rev. John Shoveller Jr. - Biography, op. cit.

50. Rev. John Shoveller Jr. & Eliza Guyer Horsey - Marriage announcement (Bristol Mirror, 17 April 1819).

51. Rev. John Shoveller Jr. & Dorothea Toms - Marriage announcement (Royal Cornwall Gazette, 18 April 1829).

52. Eliza Shoveller (nee Horsey) - Death notice (Staffordshire Advertiser, 20 May 1826).

53. Dorothea Shoveller (nee Toms) - Death notice (Oxford Journal, 22 January 1831)

54. Rev. John Shoveller II - Obituary (Hampshire Telegraph, 27th Feb 1832 p.4); & Rev. John Shoveller Jr. - Death notice (Reading Mercury, 5 March 1832).

55. Susannah Shoveller (nee Horsey) - Death notice (Hampshire Chronicle, 12 Feb 1816).

56. John Shoveller & Sarah Hook - Marriage held on the 13 July 1826, in Melksham Church, Wiltshire (England, C of E Marriage and Banns, 1754-1916).

57. Rev. John Shoveller - Death, March 1851, Portsea, Hampshire (England & Wales, Civil Registration Death Index, 1837-1915).

58. Sarah Shoveller (nee Hook) - Death notice (Hampshire Advertiser, 27 July 1870).

59. Sarah Shoveller - Probate notice, 20th July 1870 at Southampton, Winchester (England & Wales, National Probate Calendar (Index of Wills and Administrations), 1858-1966, 1973-1995).

60. Elizabeth Shoveller - Baptism held on the 15th May 1763 at Saint Marys, Portsea, Hampshire (England, Select Births and Christenings, 1538-1975).

61. William Shoveller - Baptism held on the 22nd April 1764 at Saint Marys, Portsea, Hampshire (England, Select Births and Christenings, 1538-1975).

62. Elizabeth Shoveller - Baptism held on the 19th October 1766 at Saint Marys, Portsea, Hampshire (England, Select Births and Christenings, 1538-1975).

63. Elizabeth Shoveller - Burial held on the 26th March 1782 at St. Mary's, Portsea, Hampshire (England, Select Deaths and Burials, 1538-1991).

64. Thomas Shoveller - Baptism held on the 23rd April 1769 at Saint Marys, Portsea, Hampshire (England, Select Births and Christenings, 1538-1975).

65. Hantsphere - 'Portsmouth and its people 1800-1850,' op. cit.

66. Hantsphere - 'Portsmouth and its people 1800-1850,' op. cit.

67. Fuller, A., (1800). 'Memoirs of the late Rev. Samuel Pearce,' Button, Gardiner & Williams, London, p.185.

68. Statista - O'Neill, Aaron (2019). 'Child mortality in the United Kingdom 1800-2020,' Published - 9th Sep 2019 [https://www.statista.com/statistics/1041714/united-kingdom-all-time-child-mortality-rate/].

69. Ann Shoveller - Burial held on the 19th August 1783 at Portsea, Hampshire (England, Select Deaths and Burials, 1538-1991).

70. Charlotte Shoveller - Burial held on the 2nd March 1784 at Portsea, Hampshire (England, Select Deaths and Burials, 1538-1991).

71. Harriet Shoveller - Burial held on the 21st August 1786 (England, Select Deaths and Burials, 1538-1991).

72. Wikipedia - Robert Bowyer [https://en.wikipedia.org/wiki/Robert_Bowyer].

73. Wikipedia - John Newton [https://en.wikipedia.org/wiki/John_Newton].

74. Wikipedia - Amazing Grace [https://en.wikipedia.org/wiki/Amazing_Grace].

75. Rev. John Saffery - Biography (Nonconformist and Dissenting Studies, 1650-1850, Biographical Indexes 'S' [https://sites.google.com/a/georgiasouthern.edu/dissenting-studies-1700-1850/biograph/s]).

76. Saffery/Whitaker Papers, acc. 142, I.A.(20.), Angus Library.

77. Elizabeth Shoveller & Joseph Paffard - Marriage, op. cit.

78. Elizabeth Paffard - Burial held on 23rd April 1826 at Portsea England (Select Deaths and Burials, 1538-1991 [Ref: 919762/34])

79. Saffery/Whitaker Papers, op. cit.

Further Reading

Billingsley, Naomi, (2021). 'The Great Bowyer Bible': Robert Bowyer and the Macklin Bible 1. Journal of Illustration 8:1, pages 51-80.

Boulton, J. & Davenport, R. (2015). Few Deaths before Baptism: Clerical Policy, Private Baptism and the Registration of Births in Georgian Westminster: a Paradox Resolved.' Local Popul Stud., Spring; (94):28-47. PMID: 26536752.

Callender, Sir Geoffrey, (1941). 'The Effigy Of Nelson In Westminster Abbey', The Mariner's Mirror, 27:4, 307-313, DOI: 10.1080/00253359.1941.10658776.

Portsmouth City Libraries, (2011). 'The Portsmouth Encyclopedia: A History of Places and People in Portsmouth, with an Index to Streets' compiled by Alan King (Historical Collections Librarian).

Ridoutt, Frederick (Ed., 1888). 'The Early Baptist History of Portsmouth,' Kessinger Publishing [2010].

Chapter Four

THE BIGNELL ANCESTORS

(Paternal maternal antecedents of Thomas Eastman Shoveller)

William Shoveller Sr. (1764-1832) was the second and youngest son of John and Mary Shoveller and was baptised on the 22nd of April 1764 at St. Mary's Church in Portsea.[1] He grew up with his family in the vicinity of Portsea, and the comfortable existence created by his father's successful ropemaking and merchant marine business likely saw William admitted to Portsmouth Grammar School. Just prior to William's ninth birthday began an event which was to unleash worldwide implications when the American War of Independence commenced on the 19th April 1775, with the Declaration of Independence being signed on the 4th July 1776.

Of course, William was too young at the time, but he made a decision quite early on to equip himself with a trade, a lifeskill that he could rely upon for income, although one not necessarily related to the maritime world. Taking a different stance to his older brother, he avoided involvement in matters of religion, but preferred instead to take up an apprenticeship as a cutler and silversmith.

▲ Duties paid to James Gibbs for WIlliam Shoveller's apprenticeship, 23 January 1779 (Register of Duties Paid for Apprentices Indentures).

55555

555555555555

55

William demonstrated a penchant for fine work early on and by age 14 he was sent to London to be apprenticed as a cutler, one who made and sold cutlery, under James Gibbs. Duties paid for his apprenticehip were registered on the 18th February 1779 and he may very well have moved in with the Gibbs family at St George Hanover Square, in London.[2] James Gibbs, also known as Gibbs & Lewis, was a successful metalworker, silver and goldsmith at that time whose business flourished from around 1775 to at least 1804, and he traded out of No. 137 New Bond Street, London.[3]

The learning of a trade through an apprenticeship, in which a young person was placed with and formally bonded to a master, had its roots back in the 16th century, when it was generally accepted as a means of providing technical training for boys. The Statute of Apprentices of 1563, sometimes called the Statute of Artificers, made apprenticeship compulsory for anyone who wished to enter a trade, and this law remained on the statute

▲TOP: A copy of the billhead later used by Gibbs & Lewis - 'Manufacturing Cutlers' of 137 New Bond St, London. The Bill-head in the Heal Collection (Heal,52.43) states "Bought of James Gibbs, Cutler..." The bill is dated 1791 and also states "Bought of Gibbs & Lewis Manufacturing Cutlers..." Heal's annotations on mount: "Compare trade-card in A.H. collection of Joseph Gibbs, cutler, at the 'Half Moon & Star' in New Bond St. (The British Museum - James Gibbs [https://www.britishmuseum.org/collection/term/BIOG247715]). ABOVE: A print of 'The London Coach', between Portsmouth and London, which travelled the London road and passed directly through the village of Warnford, Hampshire, c.1780.

BIGNALL, James, of H.M.S. Glasgow, gunner, 21, b., & Elizabeth Arminer, of
    Gosport, sp., at G., 24 July, 1776.
BIGNELL, Jonathan, of Itchen-Abbots, 23, b., & Joan Wickham, of New Alresford,
    25, sp., at Weeke, St. Maurice, or St. Thomas, Winchester, 15 June, 1690.
BIGNELL, Stephen, of Dummer. wheelwright, 21, b., & Henrietta Eames, of the s.,
    21, sp., 7 Oct., 1819. William Bignell, of the s., wheelwright, bondsman.
BIGNELL, William, of Herriard, yeoman, & Margaret Matthews, of the s., sp., at
    Winslade, 3 Nov., 1736.
BIGNELL, William, of Warblington, b., & Sarah Till, of the s., a minor, with c. of
    her f., Thomas Till, at W., 23 Jan., 1798.
BIGNELL, William, of Itchen Abbas, 21, b., & Eliza Gillingham, of St. John,
    Winchester, 20, sp., with c. of her f., James Gillingham, at I. A., 19 June,
    1835. Aff.
BIGNELL, Robert, of Bighton, blacksmith, b., & Elizabeth Ewens, of the s., sp.,
    at B., 13 Oct., 1710.

Name:	Francis Bignell
Gender:	Male
Marriage Date:	17 May 1769
Marriage Place:	Bishops Waltham,Hampshire,England
Spouse:	Mary Cook
FHL Film Number:	1042025

▲ TOP (Left): Allegations for Bignell marriage licences in Hampshire. (Right): Francis Bignell Jr. & Mary Cook - Marriage registration for the 17th May 1769 at Bishops Waltham, Hampshire (England, Select Marriages, 1538-1973). ABOVE: Thomas Milne's 1791 map of Warnford, West Meon and the London Road, Hampshire.

books until 1814. In that long period, no man could in theory set up as a workman, or as a master until they had served a seven year apprenticeship, which ensured a minimum standard and a continued supply of labour in particular trades.

By the 17th century the payment of a fee or 'premium' to the master became the usual practice, although this varied greatly from trade to trade. In some specialised trades, particularly in London, very high apprenticeship fees were demanded as masters feared that newcomers could copy the relevant skills and prejudice their own work.[4]

Having committed himself to a seven year apprenticeship in London, it is safe to say that young William travelled regularly between Portsea and the capital. As this well trodden route linked London with the country's main naval base, the appropriately named 'London Road,' was obviously at the centre of national events over the centuries. Back in 1688, the road was the dramatic escape route for the Catholic baby son of King James II, who was smuggled out of the country to escape the forces of Protestant William of Orange, when he landed in the West country.

Amongst other famous journeys on that road was that of Admiral John Byng (1704-1757), the only Royal Navy admiral to be executed. Byng was placed before a firing squad for "failing to do his utmost" in battle, which led to a British defeat and the French capture of Minorca in 1756. He received a hostile reception along the road from Greenwich to Portsmouth where he was executed on the deck of "HMS Monarque" on the 14th March 1757.[5] And of course, Admiral Lord Nelson himself travelled regularly from Portsmouth to the Admiralty in London, along this very route.

Nonetheless, travelling the London Road on horseback or by coach in those days had its risks. Many people actually wrote their will before setting off on their travels, with the everpresent danger of crime and road accidents, "quite apart from the likelihood of catching a severe cold, if you were sitting on the outside of the coach."

Criminals like Dick Turpin in the 1730s, and infamous highwaymen like Jerry Abershaw, attacked travellers on the northern section of the road and in reality were far from their glamorous reputations, being "both ruthless and violent, and they prayed upon all types of travellers, not just the wealthy." There were also 'gibbets' along the length of the road, trees where criminals would be hung to serve as deterrents to a life of crime.

In any event, the 76 mile journey took time and as travelling at night was frought with danger, at least two or three stopovers were required somewhere along the way. The most likely and equidistant towns on the trip were Guildford and West Meon/Warnford, and it was perhaps while stopping over in the latter that William met his future bride... Mary Bignell. It is therefore necessary at this point to delve into the background and ancestors of the Bignell family.

The Bignell Ancestors

The unusual and curious name of Bignell is of Anglo-Saxon origin, and is predominantly a locational surname that derives from a contracted form of either of the places named Bickenhall in Somerset, or Bickenhill in Warwickshire. The place in Somerset is recorded in the Domesday Book of 1086 as 'Bichehalle', and as 'Bikenhal' in the 1243 Assize Court Rolls of the county, and means 'Bica's or Bicca's hall', or 'hill.' It is derived from the Olde

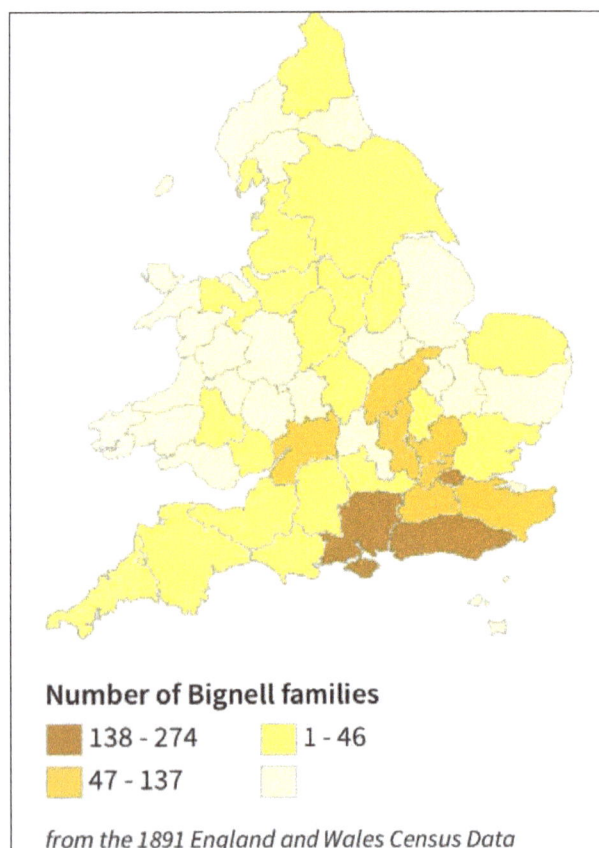

Number of Bignell families

- 138 - 274
- 47 - 137
- 1 - 46

from the 1891 England and Wales Census Data

▲ LEFT: Distribution and density of Bignell families across England and Wales in 1891 (Ancestry). RIGHT (Above): The countryside around Warnford, Hampshire. (Below): The River Meon at Warnford, Hampshire.

John Bignall	
mentioned in the record of John Bignall and Elizabeth Boxall	
Name	**John Bignall**
Spouse's Name	Elizabeth Boxall
Event Date	25 Sep 1765
Event Place	Bramshot,Hampshire,England

Jenny Bignell	
England Births and Christenings	
Name	**Jenny Bignell**
Gender	Female
Christening Date	15 May 1774
Christening Date (Original)	15 MAY 1774
Christening Place	LONG DITTON AND TOLWORTH,SURREY,ENGLAND
Mother's Name	Elizabeth Bignell

John Bignell	
England Deaths and Burials	
Name	**John Bignell**
Gender	Male
Burial Date	28 Jun 1804
Burial Place	Warnford, Hampshire, England

Sir WILLIAM WYNNE.KillD. Dean of the ARCHES, and Judge of the Prerogative Court of Canterbury. There is no Portrait taken of him, he always resisting all application to sit to an Artist. Mr. Bockton his Proctor took His resemblance of Him as he sat giving Judgment. It is as faithfully copied by Mrs. Crosswell. widow of Richard-Henry Crosswell LL.D.inAldown in 1819.

AYLWARD, John, of Warnford, w., & Jenny Biswell, of Portsea, 21, sp., at P., 10 Feb., 1803.

▲LEFT COLUMN: 1-John Bignall & Elizabeth Boxall - Marriage held on the 22nd Sep 1765 at Bramshot, Hampshire, were possible ancestors of John Bignell (England Marriages, 1538-1973). 2-The baptism of a Jenny Bignell was held on the 15th May 1774 at Long Ditton & Tolworth, Surrey (England Births & Christenings, 1538-1975). 3-John Bignall - Burial was held on the 28th June 1804 at Warnford, Hampshire (England Deaths & Burials, 1538-1991). RIGHT: Silhouette of the Right Honourable Sir William Wynne, Judge of the Prerogative Court who granted probate for John Bignell's will in 1804. ABOVE: John Aylward & Jenny Biswell [sic. Bignell] - Marriage held on the 10th Feb 1803 at Portsea, (Hampshire, England, Allegations for Marriage Licences, 1689-1837).

English pre 7th century personal name 'Bic(c)a,' from 'becca,' pickaxe or mattock, with either 'hyll,' hill, or 'heall,' hall.[6]

Locational surnames were developed when former inhabitants of a place moved to another area, usually to seek work, and they were hence best identified by the name of their birthplace. Modern derivatives of this surname can be found recorded as Bicknell, Bignell, Bignall and Bignold. The very first recorded spelling of the family name was found to be that of Thomas de Bikenhulle, which was dated 1214, in the 'Curia Regis Rolls of Warwickshire,' during the reign of King John, from 1199 to 1216.[7] More recent registrations of the name from London Church records include those of the marriage of Thomas Bignell and Marie Hide at St. Gregory by St. Paul, on January 30th 1610, and the christening of Joseph, son of Robert Bignell, on June 5th 1636, at St. Mary Whitechapel, in Stepney.

With the small village of Warnford being the epicentre and hereditary residence of Mary Bignell and her family in Hampshire over a number of generations, an overview of this town is both relevant and appropriate.

The Village of Warnford, Hampshire

There is evidence in the form of barrows or burial mounds of the occupation of Warnford from early times. The barrow and associated Saxon boundary bank at Sheepbridge is registered as a 'Scheduled Monument', and both are referred to in a land charter dating from the time of King Aethelstan in the early 900's. The Domesday Book records Warnford and also Upwarnford, which is believed to have covered the northern part of the parish.[8]

Today, the civil parish of Warnford lies in the City of Winchester district of Hampshire,

▲ The 'Church of Our Lady' and graveyard at Warnford, Hampshire, where Mary Bignell and William Shoveller Sr. celebrated their marriage on the 3rd January 1789, and also the likely burial site of Mary's father John Bignell.

and covers 1283 hectares (3170 acres). It is situated south of Kilmeston and Hinton Ampner, north-east of Exton, west of West Meon and falls naturally into two parts: the comparatively low-lying land bordering the River Meon on the south and east through which runs the main road from West Meon to Droxford; and the down-country on either side, Wheely Down and Beacon Hill reaching the heights of 500 ft. and 659 ft. respectively.[9]

The population in 2019 was estimated at 220, which has not markedly changed since the 18th century.[10] The George and Falcon pub and hotel, which is grade II listed and dates to the 16th century is located near the centre of the village. The ruins of the 13th century St. John's or King John's House behind the church, are also Grade 1 listed. Warnford Park is itself Grade II listed as a park and garden, and was the site of the manor house, renamed 'Belmont' in the 19th century and demolished in the 1950s. Warnford once had two water mills where grain was ground to make flour for the villagers, and the town was surrounded by three huge fields where the villagers worked. The parish contains a considerable number of other listed buildings, including the 'Farmhouse', 'Well House' and 'Granary at Bere Farm', 'Abbey House, ' which was formerly the rectory, 'North Lodge' and the adjacent gateway into Warnford Park, 'Papermill Cottage' and 'Riversdown House'.[11]

The Bignell's Of Warnford

Perhaps the first identifiable, although unverified Bignell ancestor was a John Bignell (c.1670-?), who married in August of 1694 at Warnford, Hampshire to Elizabeth Tyler (c.1675-?).[12] They produced a son in John Bignell (c.1695-c.1760), who married about 1715 in Warnford to Ann Roberts, and from that union came Francis Bignell Sr. (c.1715-c.1793).[13]

Although the records are difficult to authenticate, it seems likely given the uncommon surname and the isolated rural location, that Francis Bignell, who married on the 12th April

1737 at Rowner, near Gosport, Hampshire to Ann Hellyar (c.1718-1779),[14] were the parents of John Bignell Sr. (1743-1804), and the progenitors of Mary Bignell and her offspring to William Shoveller Sr. The evidence reveals that Francis and Ann Bignell produced a large brood who, in contrast to the high infant mortality experienced in the larger towns like Portsmouth, mostly all survived into adulthood. The birth and baptismal registrations for the children of Francis and Ann Bignell of Warnford, were found in the first register book (1541–1771) of the Church of Our Lady at Warnford, although little is known of most of them, except for John Bignell Sr. (*see 4.1 Descendants of Francis Bignell & Ann Hellyer*).[15] Francis Bignell himself was likely buried at Meonstoke on the 16th November 1793.[16]

John Bignell Sr. (1743-1804)

Records held by the Church of Our Lady at Warnford reveal that John Bignell was born on the 10th November and baptised on the 19th November 1743 at Warnford, Hampshire.[17] The Bignell's were at Warnford during the same period as Admiral Lord Nelson of the Royal Navy, and their farmhouse was located just a few miles from 'Fir Hill Manor' at Droxford,

Johns Bignell Sr.'s Will & Copyhold

Copyhold was a form of customary land ownership common from the late Middle Ages into modern times in England. The name for this type of land tenure is derived from the act of giving a copy of the relevant title deed that is recorded in the manorial court roll to the tenant; not the actual land deed itself. The legal owner of the manor land remained the mesne lord, who was legally the copyholder, according to the titles and customs written down in the manorial roll.[33,34] In return for being given land, a copyhold tenant was required to carry out specific manorial duties or services. The specific rights and duties of copyhold tenants varied greatly from one manor to another and many were established by custom. By the 19th century, many customary duties had been replaced by the payment of rent.

Copyhold was directly descended from the feudal system of villeinage which involved giving service and produce to the local lord in return for land. Although feudalism in England had ended by the early 1500s,[35] forms of copyhold tenure continued in England until being completely abolished by the Law of Property Act in 1925.

▲ *The will of John Bignell Sr. of Warnford, revealed that he possessed a number of freehold properties. TOP (Left): River Meon, by the former mill at Corhampton, Hampshire. (Right): The Old Corhampton Mill, of which John Bignell Sr. held a 'copyhold' interest on the River Meon, Hampshire. ABOVE (Left): Bridge and Ford over river Meon from Lippen Lane end, 1910. (Right): Warnford village from the Hill, c.1906.*

Last Will & Testament of John Bignell Sr., of Warnford, Hampshire
Drafted - 21 May 1803 & Proved 29 Dec 1804

Translation

In the name of God Amen, **John Bignell** of Warnford in the County of Southampton being at this time of sound disposing & minds and memory blessed be God, do make, publish and declare this my last will and testament in manner as following. First, I give to my son **John Bignell** and his heirs for ever all that moiety of a freehold estate situate and lying in the parish of Portsea in the County of Southampton in the occupation of ??? ??? and _____ Spurrel?, also I give to my son a house and small plots of ground adjoining and a small meadow railed the ????? situated in the parish of Meonstoke, the house occupied by **Edward Shayer**?, The small piece of ground adjoining in the occupation of **William Bignell** and a small meadow railed the ???? occupied by **Thomas Aylward**, Also I give to **my wife** my aforesaid estate that ??? live in during her life, And after her decease I give it to my daughter **Mary** and her heirs forever and whereas on the thirty first day of July in the year of one thousand seven hundred and eighty, I did surrender unto the hands of the Lord of the house of Meonstoke by the ARREPTAURE? of **Charles Knott** Steward, a messuage with the garden containing an ??? with the appurts and a meadow railed, Barn ??? containing by estimation half a acre on the North part of the Kings Highway and also railed at ???? Wadden containing three acres one close railed & Hawksbury containing five acres one close railed & ???????? containing fourteen acres with the appurts and also two closes of arable land containing by estimation sixteen acres held by three? several copies of Court Roll of the said Manor to and for such uses intents and purposes as I shall in my last will and testament ?????? now I the said **John Bignell** in pursuance of the said surrender do give and devise all those my said copyhold estates to my daughter **Jenny** and her heirs according to custom of the said Manor wherein on the ninth of January in the year one thousand eight hundred and one I did surrender into the hands of the Lord of the Manor of Bishops Waltham by the ARREPTAURE? of **William ?????**, Clerk of the bailiwick of Bishops Waltham a cottage with a messuage of ??? pasture land heretofore of **John Simmington** in the EYTHING? of Waltham held by one other copy of Court Roll and two Crofts of Bond Land with a curtalage adjoining on the North of the same ???? towards East Mills in the ?????? aforesaid held by one other copy and ???? parcel of land of the ???? soil of ??? land lying in ??? lane toward East Mill railed coppin Mill in the ???? aforesaid held by one other copy and one cottage with a curtalage heretofore of **John ??????** situated on the East part of Bazewell? Street in the EYTHING? of Waltham held by one other copy to and for such uses interests and purposes as I shall in my last will and testament ????? now I **John Bignell** in pursuance of the said surrender do give and devise all those this my said copyhold estates to my daughter **Mary** and my daughter **Jenny** equally between them, also I give to my daughters **Mary** and **Jenny** and their heirs equally between them all that my freehold estate situated in the parish of Corhampton containing a messuage and cornmill with all the buildings and lands thereunto belonging, Also I give to **my wife** the sum of sixty pounds a year to be paid to her during her life by my two daughters **Mary** and **Jenny** out of their rents and profits that shall arise from Corhampton Mill and the house at Bishops Waltham in the occupation of _____ ????? Also I give to **my wife** my household goods to make use of as long as she lives and after her decease to be equally divided between my three children **John**, **Mary** and **Jenny**, Also I give to my son **John** and his eldest son **John** that he had by his first wife four hundred pounds that I have in the three percent ??? all the rest that is personal property Bonds Debts Mortgages Notes after my just debts and funeral expenses are paid I give to my son **John**, my daughter **Mary** and my daughter **Jenny** share and share alike, Lastly I constitute and appoint my son **John Bignell, John Aylward** and my son-in-law **William Shoveller** to be joint executors of this my last will and testament put my hand and seal the 21st day of May in the year of our Lord Christ one thousand eight hundred and three... **John Bignell**.

Signed, sealed, published and ????? by the above named testators to be his last will and testament in the prescence of us whose names are under written who at his request have set our hands as witnesses hereunto...
James Martin, John ???? & ???????????

This Will was proved at London the twenty ninth day of December in the year of our Lord one thousand eight hundred and four before the **Right Honourable Sir William Wynne**, Knight, Doctor of Laws, Master, Keeper of Commissary of the Prerogative Court of Canterbury, lawfully constituted by the oaths of **John Aylward** and **William Shoveller**, two of the Executors named in the said will to whom administration was granted of all and singular the goods chattels and credits of the said deceased having been first sworn by commission duly to administer power reserved of making the like grant to **John Bignell** the son and other executor named in the said will.

▲ *The Will of John Bignell Sr., proved on the 29th December 1804 (England & Wales, Prerogative Court of Canterbury Wills, 1384-1858 [PROB 11: Will Registers (1802-1804), Piece 1418: Heseltine, Quire No 801-1804]).*

4.1 Descendants of Francis Bignell Sr. & Ann Hellyer

Francis BIGNELL Sr. (c.1715-c.1793), married on the 12th April 1737 at Rowner, near Gosport to Ann Hellyer (c.1718-1779), with issue:

1. Ann Bignell (1738-1747) was born & baptised 21 Apr 1738, but died and was buried in Warnford on the 7 June 1747.*

2. Mary Bignell (1739-?) was born 25 Nov & baptised 8 Dec 1739.

3. Elizabeth Bignell (1741-?) was born 9 Dec & baptised 26 Dec 1741, although an Elizabeth Bignell was buried in Warnford in July of 1779.

4. John BIGNELL Sr. (1743-1804) was born 10 Nov & baptised 19 Nov 1743. John married (unknown), with issue:
4.1 John BIGNELL Jr. (1767-?) was born & baptised 11 May 1767, and married twice with issue:
  a. John BIGNELL III (1803-?)
4.2 Mary Bignell (1768-1825), was born & baptised 13 Dec 1768. Married on the 3rd Jan 1789 at Warnford to William SHOVELLER (1764-1832), with issue:
  a. John SHOVELLER (1789-1847)
  b. William SHOVELLER (1791-1846)

Bignell | *Hellyer*

  c. Mary Shoveller (1794-1865)
  d. Jane Shoveller (1796-1848), spinster, d.s.p.
  e. Elizabeth Shoveller (1798-1879)
4.3 Jenny Bignell (c.1782<1813), married on 10 Feb 1803 at Warnford to John AYLWARD (1784-1843), no issue.

John Bignell was also a witness - "In the presence of John

Bignell & John Winter, Gharry Hayes & Grace Trodd, both of Warnford, were married by banns, on 30 November 1765; and in the presence of John Bignell & James Thorne & Hester Backman, William Ironmonger & Sarah Hayes, both of Warnford, were married on 17 April 1775."

5. Francis BIGNELL Jr. (1745-?) was born & baptised 26 Dec 1745, married on the 17 May 1769 at Bishops Waltham to Mary Cook (?-?) of the parish, in the church by licence. Groom signed & X bride made her mark in the presence of John Bull & James Cole.

6. Hannah Bignell (1747-?) was born 24 May & baptised 7 June 1747.

7. Sarah Bignell (1752-?) was born 21 Dec & baptised 30 Dec 1752.

8. Jane Bignell (1756-?) was born Dec 1756. Married on the 16 Oct 1778 at Bishops Waltham to Robert WOODMAN (?-?) of the parish of Fareham, in the church by licence. Both signed in the presence of Sarah & Richd Cole.

* Died before adulthood - d.s.p.
(Some names not listed in the index).

▲TOP: The likely descendants of Francis Bignell Sr. & Ann Hellyer of Warnford, Hampshire. ABOVE The ruins of Bishops Waltham Palace, Hampshire, the history of which includes a roll call of Medieval and Tudor kings and queens that visited the town to stay at the palace. The name of the town is Saxon, being derived from the words 'wald' (forest) and 'ham' (settlement). It is a medieval market town situated at the source of the River Hamble with a well-preserved high street and many listed buildings. It has a foot in the South Downs National Park and is located at the midpoint of a long-established route between Winchester and Portsmouth.36

where Nelson occasionally stayed over on his way to London. Residing in this community, John Bignell Sr. is likely to have been a farmer, with little else known of him except through declarations made in his 1803 will. The document disclosed that John Bignell was a freehold owner of a number of properties in Portsea, Meonstoke, Hawksbury, Corhampton Mill and Bishops Waltham, with other additional property holdings including over 60 acres of leased land. John Bignell's will affirmed that his property at Warnford went to his unnamed wife, who was alive in 1804, and that he was the father of John Bignell Jr. (c.1767-?), Mary Bignell (1768-1825) and Jenny Bignell (c.1782<1813), as well as father-in-law to William Shoveller Sr. (1764-1832), and John Aylward (1784-1843).

Unfortunately, research has not confirmed a marriage for John Bignell Sr. or the name of his wife, although the following marriage registrations from 'England Marriages (1538-1973)' are all possibilities:[18]

Pedigree Chart - 3
The Descendants of
John Bignell of
Warnford, Hampshire

John Bignell Sr. c.1743-1803 = Elizabeth Boxall [UV]

m.1765 at Bramshot, Hants

Aylward

1m? ? = John Bignell Jr. c.1767>1804 = 2m? ?

Mary Bignell c.1769-1825 m.1789 at Warnford William Shoveller Sr. 1764-1832

Jenny Bignell c.1774>1803 d.s.p. — John Aylward 1784-1843 = Maria Burcher <1792>1833

m.1805 at Portsea   m.1813 at St Cross

John Bignell III <1803-?

John Shoveller LLD. 1789-1847 m.1812 Elizabeth Eastman c.1784-1852

William Shoveller Jr. 1791-1846 m.1815 Elizabeth Dunt 1793-1885

Mary Shoveller 1794-1865 m.1821 Rev. Thomas Stratten 1794-1854

Jane Shoveller 1796-1848 d.s.p.

Elizabeth Shoveller 1798-1879 m.1822 James Roberton 1796-1861

Nine Aylward Children

1.Sarah S. 1812–1813
2. Mary E. 1813–1814
3. Jane A. 1814–1874
4. Sarah S. 1816–1825
5. John 1818–1899
6. Thomas E. 1820–1825
7. Mary E. 1822–1868
8. William H. 1824–1883
9. Martha 1826–1827
10. Thomas E. 1827–1908

1. William 1816–1885
2. John 1818–1871
3. Robert 1819–1872
4. Elizabeth M., 1821–1874
5. Hannah M., 1827–1900
6. Samuel 1832–1918

1. Mary 1822–1856
2. Frances 1824–1905
3. Jane 1827–1885
4. Robert 1828–1904
5. Thomas 1830–1904

1. James H., 1825-1890

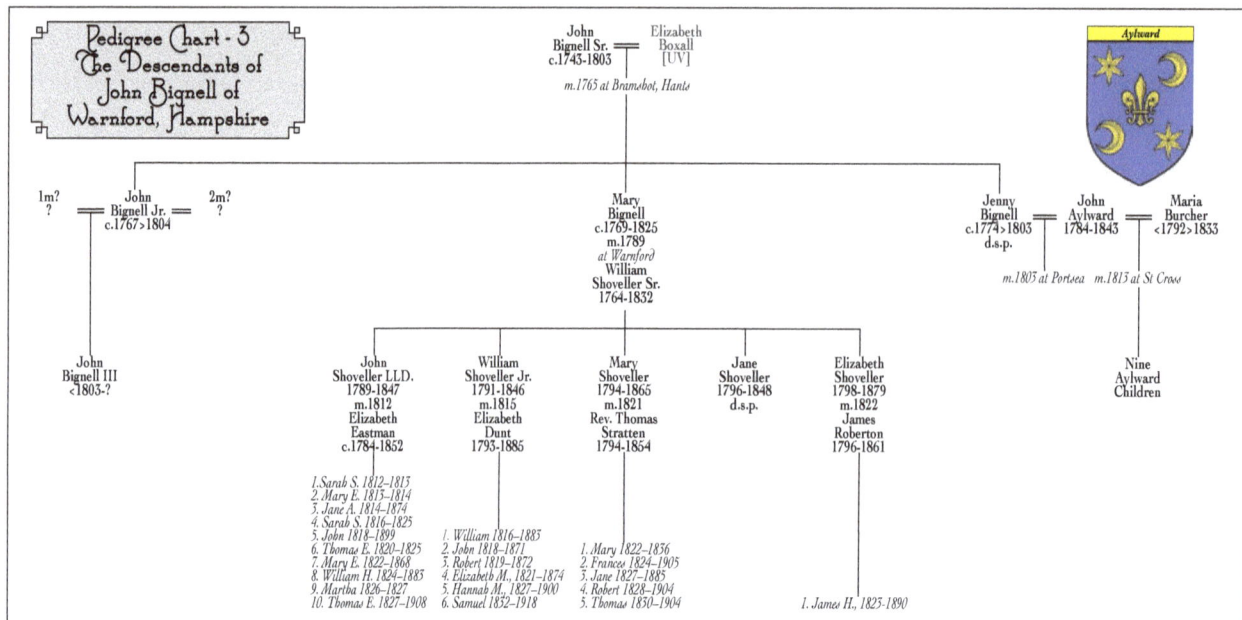

▲ *Pen & ink drawing of the village of West Meon, Hampshire, where John Bignell Sr. possessed a house and other small plots of land.*

- A John Bignall married at Ockley, Surrey on the 4th May 1762 to
Elizabeth Currington (80km E of Warnford).
- A John Bignall married at Bramshot, Hampshire on the 25th Sept 1765 to
Elizabeth Boxall (30km NE of Warnford).
- A John Bignall married at Castlethorpe, Buckinghamshire, on the 21st Oct 1768 to
Mary Seabrook (160km N of Warnford).
- A John Bignall married at Stoke-Damerel, Devonshire, on the 5th Sept 1768 to
Diana Taylor (280km SW of Warnford).
- A John Bignel married at Falmer, Sussex, on the 9th July 1769 to
Ann Web (100km E of Warnford).

While the Bramshot wedding to Elizabeth Boxall looms largest by virtue of its proximity to Warnford, John Bignell Sr's actual wedding could realistically have been any of the above,[19] with other as yet unidentified registrations that cannot be ruled out. What is known, is that the following descendants evolved from the union of John Bignell Sr. and his unnamed wife (*see Pedigree Chart 3*).

1. John Bignell Jr. (1767>1804)

John Bignell Jr. was baptised on the 11 May 1767 at Warnford, Hampshire,[20] and mentioned in the will of his father in May 1803,[21] which also disclosed that he had a son by a first wife, who was also named John Bignell (<1803-?). Unfortunately, neither of the wives are mentioned by name, with no further details having been found of his occupation, any additional children or his death.

2. Mary Bignell (c.1769-1825)

Mary Bignell was born on the 13th December 1768 at Warnford,[22] and was also mentioned along with her husband William Shoveller Sr., in the will of her father in May of 1803.[23] All we know of Mary begins with her marriage on the 3rd January 1789 at the Church of Our Lady at Warnford, to William (1764-1832), the son of John and Mary Shoveller of Portsea.[24] Mary and William were destined to become the grandparents of Thomas Eastman Shoveller, and their family and descendants are discussed in greater detail in the next chapter.

3. Jenny Bignell (c.1782<1813)

Jenny Bignell may have been born in 1774, but was more likely born in 1782, although neither baptism has been confirmed. She was however, mentioned in the will of her father in May 1803,[25] and married on the 10th February 1803 at St Marys Church, Portsea to John Aylward (1784-1843).[26,27,28] Jenny died most likely without children, sometime prior to her husband's second marriage to Maria Burcher in November 1813,[29] with whom he went on to father at least nine children.

John Bignell Sr. was buried in the Warnford Church graveyard on the 28th June 1804,[30] with his will being proved in London on the 29th December 1804, under the auspices of the Right Honourable Sir William Wynne, Judge of the Prerogative Court.[31]

WINCHESTER,

SATURDAY, FEBRUARY 19.

Last week was married, Mr. John Aylward, of Peak Farm, in this county, to Miss Bignell, of Warnford.

▲ Postcard of the George Hotel in the quaint village of Warnford, Hampshire, c.1900 (Emm's Series Postcards). INSET: Announcement of the marriage of Jenny Bignell and John Aylward, which occurred on the 10th February 1803 at Winchester (Hampshire Chronicle, 21 Feb 1803).

Having explored what is known of John Bignell Sr. and his children, the ancestral pathway to Thomas Eastman Shoveller passes through his daughter Mary. The beneficiaries of John Bignell Sr. were his children John Jr., Jenny, and Mary along with his son-in-law William Shoveller Sr., and although his wife was not mentioned by name in his will, we know that she outlived him.[32] While little information has been uncovered about Mary Bignell's life, this genealogy next explores the life and events of Mary Bignell and her husband William Shoveller Sr.

References

1. William Shoveller - Baptism held on the 22nd April 1764 at Saint Marys, Portsea, Hampshire (England, Select Births and Christenings, 1538-1975)

2. William Shoveller - Duties Paid to James Gibbs for Apprenticeship Indenture, 23 January 1779 (Portsea, Universal British Directory, 1791, Pt.2).

3. James Gibbs of Gibbs & Lewis - 'Manufacturing Cutlers' of 137 New Bond St, London (The British Museum - James Gibbs [https://www.britishmuseum.org/collection/term/BIOG247715]).

4. Family Search - Apprenticeship In England [https://www.familysearch.org/en/wiki/Apprenticeship_in_England].

5. Cavendish, Richard, (2007). 'The Execution of Admiral Byng, History Today, Vol.57, No.3, March [https://www.historytoday.com/archive/months-past/execution-admiral-byng].

6. Surname DB - Bignell [https://www.surnamedb.com/Surname/Bignell].

7. Surname DB - Bignell, op.cit.

8. British History Online - William Page, (Ed.,1908). 'A History of the County of Hampshire: Parishes: Warnford,' London, Vol. 3, pp. 268-273. [http://www.british-history.ac.uk/vch/hants/vol3/pp268-273, accessed 5 June 2022].

9. British History Online - William Page, (Ed.,1908)., op.cit.

10. City Population - Warnford, Hampshire, England [citypopulation.de].

11. Local Histories - Tim Lambert, (2021). 'A History of Warnford' [https://localhistories.org/a-history-of-warnford/].

12. Knightroots - John Bignell & Elizabeth Tyler - Marriage held in August 1694 at Warnford, Hampshire [Marriages, p.87 - https://www.knightroots.co.uk/parishes/warnford].

13. Knightroots - 'Bignell/Bignall' in Warnford, Hampshire [https://www.knightroots.co.uk/parishes/warnford].

14. Knightroots - 'Bignell/Bignall' in Warnford, Hampshire, op.cit

15. Francis Bignell - Baptisms held at 'Church of Our Lady,' Warnford, Hampshire (England, Hampshire Parish Registers, 1538-1980).

16. Francis Bignele - Burial held on the 16 Nov 1793 at Meonstoke, Hampshire (England, Select Deaths and Burials, 1538-1991).

17. Knightroots - 'Bignell/Bignall' in Warnford, Hampshire, op.cit

18. 'England Marriages' (1538-1973).

19. John Bignall & Elizabeth Boxall - Marriage held on the 22nd Sep 1765 at Bramshot, Hampshire (England Marriages, 1538-1973).

20. John Bignell Jr. - Baptism held on the 11th May 1767 at Warnford, Hampshire (Births & Baptisms, Church of Our Lady, Warnford, Hampshire [1541-1771])

21. John Bignell - Will, Proved 29th December 1804, op. cit.

22. Mary Bignell - Born on the 13th December 1768 at Warnford, Hampshire (Births & Baptisms, Church of Our Lady, Warnford, Hampshire [1541-1771]).

23. John Bignell - Will, Proved 29th December 1804, op. cit.

24. William Shoveller & Mary Bignell - Marriage held on the 3 Jan 1789, Portsea (Hampshire Allegations for Marriage Licences, 1689-1837, Vol 2).

25. John Bignell - Will, Proved 29th December 1804, op. cit.

26. Jenny Biswell [sic. Bignell] & John Aylward - Marriage held on the 10th Feb 1803 at St Marys, Portsea, (Hampshire, England, Allegations for Marriage Licences, 1689-1837).

27. Miss [Jenny] Bignell & John Aylward - Marriage held on the 10th Feb 1803 at Winchester (Hampshire Chronicle, 21 Feb 1803).

28. Knightroots - John Aylmer - Baptism held on 14 Nov 1784 at Warnford, Hampshire [https://www.knightroots.co.uk/parishes/warnford].

29 John Aylward & Maria Burcher - Marriage held on the 10 Nov 1813 at St Cross, Hampshire,(England, Allegations for Marriage Licences, 1689-1837).

30. John Bignell - Burial held on 28th June 1804 at Warnford, Hampshire (England, Hampshire Bishop's Transcripts 1680-1892).

31. John Bignell - Will, Proved 29th December 1804 (England & Wales, Prerogative Court of Canterbury Wills, 1384-1858 [PROB 11: Will Registers (1802-1804), Piece 1418: Heseltine, Quire No 801-1804]).

32. John Bignell - Will, Proved 29th December 1804, op.cit.

33. Wilkes, J. (1815). "Lord". Encyclopaedia Londinensis. Vol. 13. J. Wilkes, 1815. p. 661. Retrieved 15 January 2019. Lord is also a title.... Lord mesne is he that is owner of a manor, and by virtue thereof hath tenants holding of him in fee, and by copy of court-roll; and yet holds himself of a superior lord called lord paramount.

34. "Reports of cases: House of Lords". The Jurist. n.s. S. Sweet. 10 (1): 893-895. 1865. Retrieved 13 January 2019.

35. "The End of Feudalism" in J.H.M. Salmon, Society in Crisis: France in the Sixteenth Century (1979) pp 19–26.

36. Wikipedia - Bishops Waltham [https://en.wikipedia.org/wiki/Bishop%27s_Waltham].

Further Reading

British Listed Buildings, "Church of Our Lady, Warnford, Hampshire," Grade 1 [www.britishlistedbuildings.co.uk].

"Church Of Our Lady, Warnford - 1296978 | Historic England," [www.historicengland.org.uk].

Hampshire County Council - 'Meon Valley Trail.'

Hampshire County Council - "Warnford," Hampshire Treasures, Vol., 1 pp.305-311.

Knightroots - Warnford for 'Bignell/Bignall' [https://www.knightroots.co.uk/parishes/warnford].

'Parishes: Warnford', in A History of the County of Hampshire: Volume 3, ed. William Page (London, 1908), pp. 268-273. British History Online http://www.british-history.ac.uk/vch/hants/vol3/pp268-273 [accessed 5 June 2022].

Chapter Five

WILLIAM SHOVELLER & MARY BIGNELL

(Paternal grandparents of Thomas Eastman Shoveller)

The folk of Portsmouth were familiar with the sight of departing ships and small conveys, but it never ceased to be a spectacle and a cause for patriotic celebration, such as when the ships departed for North America filled with troops and supplies for various campaigns of the American War of Independence.

However, when 11 ships full to the gunwhales with felons, convicts and three years of supplies set sail from Portsmouth for far away Botany Bay, it was a completely different spectacle and a sight for the townsfolk to behold, as thousands of their kin lined the harbour and commiserated over final farewells.

Captain Arthur Philip had initially scheduled the First Fleet to depart on the 10th May, but the sailors of the "Fishburn" refused to do so until a pay dispute was resolved,[1] after which the fleet was finally able to set sail on the 13th May 1787.[2] Today, a memorial plaque and a statue of anchor chains stands at the Portsmouth waterfront as a monument to commemorate that auspicious day. Seven months later, "HMS Bounty" quietly slipped out of Portsmouth Harbour on the 23rd December 1787, on a voyage to Tahiti, with a mission to propogate 'Artocarpus altilis' otherwise known as the breadfruit trees of Tahiti.[3]

The Marriage of William Shoveller & Mary Bignell

These were insignificant events back then, and something just as inconsequential occurred about this time when William Shoveller, who was working some 55 miles away in Poole, Dorset, proposed to his future wife Mary Bignell. After a respectful courtship interval, their marriage went ahead at the Church of Our Lady in Mary's village of Warnford, Hampshire, on the 3rd January 1789.[4] Mary was just 20 years of age and required the consent of her father. The guests were comprised of Mary's father John Bignell Sr. and mother, her 22 year old brother John Bignell Jr., and younger sister Jenny Bignell. Guests from William's family would have included his parents John and Mary Shoveller, his 33 year-old sister Mary and her husband Robert Bowyer, who just three months later was appointed 'Miniature Painter in Ordinary' to King George III, along with William's older brother Rev. John Shoveller Sr. and his wife Susannah (nee Horsey). William's nieces Harriet Bowyer (12), as well as Elizabeth (6) and Susannah Shoveller (4) would also have been present amongst other uncles, aunties and friends.

Essentially, all that is known and recorded of Mary Bignell is her marriage to William Shoveller Sr. in 1789. Their choice of wedding venue was the ancient 'Church of Our Lady,' which is of Saxon origin begun by St Wilfrid the Saint, who had converted the South Saxons to Christianity about 675-680 AD. However, the church was rebuilt in the Middle Ages and restored again in 1906, but retains to this day relics of its early Saxon legacy.[5,6] The Grade 1 listed structure is located in Warnford Park to the south of the village, and contains registers of baptisms (1541–1771), marriages (1604–1764) and burials (1617–1771) in its first book. The second book contains baptisms (1783–1812), marriages (1735–1800) and burials (1782–1812), the baptisms and burials (1771–1783) having being lost, and the third book contains marriages (1800–1812).[7]

The newlywedded Mr and Mrs William Shoveller, initially returned to Poole, as William was likely finishing off work commitments, and possibly exploring opportunities to establish a cutlery and silversmithing business. However, a few months later Mary's pregnancy adjusted their plans, and on the 21st October, their first child John Shoveller arrived and was baptised two weeks later on the 6th November 1789.[8] The baptism was held at the Skinner St, Independent Church in Poole, and was officiated by the Rev. Edward Ashburner, after which the young family returned to Portsea. While no one at the time could have realised the significance of that day, some 16 years later young John Shoveller would become well aware of the importance of his birthday, as it marked Admiral Nelson's indomitable victory over the combined French and Spanish navies at the Battle of Trafalgar in 1805.

LEFT: A cutlery/silversmith shop where smaller pieces were made was often referred to as a jewelry shop. The workmen here are shown melting the metal, hammering on an anvil, soldering with a mouth blow pipe, and setting the stones. RIGHT: Examples of fine silverware from the 17th and early 18th centuries, by Diderot. [48]

Shoveller John, *Coal-merchant*
Shoveller Wm. *Cutler and Silverſmith*

▲*William Shoveller shaped, repaired and sold knives, cutlery and other items of silver. TOP (Left): Silver flatware typical of the period; (Right) The elegant design of this teapot, by Paul Revere Jr, 1796 was in keeping with the fine taste of the late 18th century. MID (Left): Charles II Antique Silver Porringer, by Samuel Hawkes; (Right): 18th century antique silver cutlery. ABOVE: Apposing directory listings of William Shoveller as a Cutler & Silversmith, with his father John Shoveller listed as a Coal-merchant (Portsea, Universal British Directory, 1791, Pt.2).*

By Christmas of 1790, William and Mary Shoveller had returned from Poole to await the birth of their second child, and at the same time William set about establishing a residence and silversmithing business in Portsea. Young William Shoveller Jr. was born in early March and baptised at the Shoveller home in Queen Street, Portsea on the 26th March 1791, which was officiated by Mr. William Dunn, Protestant Dissenting Minister.[9] Dissenting was a term used for Protestant religious groups and individuals who refused to conform to the Church of England, and with whom they otherwise had very little in common. The term concealed major differences between the different denominations in matters of doctrine, church governance and attitudes to the ministry.

Cutler & Silversmith

By all accounts, William Shoveller was a diligent and talented tradesman, but he was not destined to be one of the great silversmiths, and no examples of his silver work have been found. The wealth accumulated by his father John Shoveller at Portsmouth Point likely helped him to establish his silver business, which he ran out of a shopfront at 117 Queen Street, Portsea. By 1792, William was listed in the Universal British Directory (1792-98) as a qualified 'cutler and silversmith.'[10] Back then, a person who made or sold cutlery was known as a cutler. In the United States, cutlery was more usually known as silverware or flatware where it had the more specific meaning of knives and other cutting instruments. Although the term silverware is used irrespective of the material composition of the utensils, the term tableware has come into use to avoid the implication that they are made of silver. Most silversmiths during the late 18th century were fabricating silver tableware in the form of dishes, bowls, candlesticks and flatware as opposed to jewellery.

A silversmith today crafts objects and turns silver sheet metal into hollow ware in the form of dishes, bowls, porringers, cups, candlesticks, vases, ewers, urns, flatware (silver cutlery) and other articles of household silver, church plate or sculpture, which may also include the making of jewelry. However, the terms 'silversmith' and 'goldsmith' are not synonyms as although the techniques, training, history and guilds were largely the same, the end product varied greatly as did the scale of objects created. Although most goldsmiths usually worked with silver, the reverse was not the case.[11]

Hallmarks reveal whether a piece is 'Britannia gauge' by a stamp indicating the purity of the silver, which is called the assayer's mark. The date mark is a letter indicating the exact year in which the piece was made, and each silver maker has his or her own unique maker's mark. The hallmark is usually indicated by a set of initials inside an escutcheon. While all records prior to 1681 were destroyed in a fire at the Goldsmiths Hall in London,[12] William's work came afterwards. However, while William Shoveller would have been required by law to hallmark his work to record its date and maker, regrettably none of his silver or cutlery work has been identified by the authorities (*see Appendix C*).

Baptisms of William Shoveller Sr. & Mary Bignell's Children

▲LEFT COLUMN: 1-Marriage of William Shoveller & Mary Bignell on the 3rd Jan 1789 at Warnford (Hampshire Allegations for Marriage Licences 1689-1837, Vol.2). 2-John Shoveller - Born 21 Oct 1789 & baptised 6 Nov 1789 at Skinner St, Independent Church, Poole, Dorset (Non-Conformist & Non-Parochial Registers, 1567-1970). 3-William Shoveller Jr., Birth & baptismal registration from the 'Non-Conformist & Non-Parochial Registers, 1567-1936, Independent Church, Portsea, Hampshire (5 March 1791). RIGHT COLUMN: 1-Mary Shoveller, Birth & baptismal registration from the 'Non-Conformist & Non-Parochial Registers, 1567-1936, Independent Church, Portsea, Hampshire (5 Feb 1794); 2-Jane Shoveller (9 Mar 1796); 3-Elizabeth Shoveller (20 March 1798), held at England & Wales, Non-Conformist and Non-Parochial Registers, 1567-1936 (Portsea, Hampshire, King St (formerly Orange St) Independent Church). ABOVE: Land Tax Redemption for William Shoveller Sr, showing his tenants in 1798.[49]

▲A 16th to 19th century communal punishment, the pillory was never meant to be lethal. Transgressors were placed in the stocks for a period of time for minor crimes to shame and embarrass, with community members passing judgement by throwing garbage or sometimes even human excrement at the victims, or flowers if they felt the accused to be wrongly convicted (Artist unknown).

Residing mostly in Portsmouth throughout this period would have been both an anxious and fascinating experience as the bulk of Great Britain's naval and associated merchant shipping was concentrated there. It is therefore probable that William turned a good income through sales of his cutlery and silverware to officers and seaman of the Royal Navy, and travellers as well as the Portsmouth gentry. At the same time, William didn't limit his activities entirely to the fabrication of silver, as there is evidence that he also acquired and leased property.[13]

It is unsurprising, given the squalid living conditions and short lives faced by many of the inhabitants, that crime was a regular part of everyday life in Portsmouth and Portsea. An undermanned and underpaid police force that was regularly assaulted and was susceptible to drunkenness and bribery did not help matters. Drunk sailors, unemployed labourers, loose women and vagrant children all contributed to the impoverished situation in differing ways. Crime was punished harshly, with the pillory and transportation to Australia being two of the most common sentences. Children were often treated in the same way as adults, receiving harsh punishments.

The punishment of crime in the early 19th century was significantly different to the present day, with a much greater emphasis on the protection of property. It was not unusual for those found guilty of stealing to receive sentences of transportation, while offences such as prostitution were far less harshly punished. The Hampshire Telegraph reported that a William Stentford was sentenced to "seven years transportation for stealing ducks," whereas Martha Chamberlain was sentenced to "twelve months and to stand in the pillory" for

▲ *Portsmouth Roadstead around 1792, painted by John Hagan.*

enticing servant girls into prostitution.[14]

Following the dethroning and guillotining of King Louis XVI and his wife Marie Antoinette of France in 1793, the ramifications of the French Revolution (1792–1802) leading into the Napoleonic Wars (1803-1815), dominated the twenty years from 1795, and began to affect everything and everybody. The turmoil was particularly felt in Portsmouth, where the 'wooden wall' of the Royal Navy was the main deterrent to French invasion.

During this period, William and Mary Shoveller were primarily engaged in business and the establishment of their family, with their third child Mary Shoveller, arriving on the 5th February and being baptised on the 14th October 1794.[15] Jane Shoveller arrived next on the 9th March 1796 and was baptised on the 13th of April.[16] This year saw a giant leap forward in medicine when Edward Jenner administered the first smallpox vaccination, which had killed an estimated 400,000 Europeans each year during the 18th century, including five reigning monarchs.[17] The fifth and final child in the Shoveller family was Elizabeth, who was born on 20th March 1798.[18] All the Shoveller children save John, were baptised at their home in Portsea, under the auspices of the Independent Baptist Church, the latter three being christened by the newly installed Baptist minister in Portsmouth, the Rev. John Griffin.[19]

Three months after Elizabeth's final delivery saw the sad death of William's father John Shoveller, who was buried on the 8th June 1798 in Portsea.[20,21] His generous will left William and his two siblings with a more than sufficient inheritance in both cash and property.[22] The year 1798 ended after lurching through yet another anxious period when the French supported 'Irish Rebellion' narrowly failed to overthrow British rule in Ireland.[23]

With the ever-present need for naval manpower throughout this period, it was not uncommon in Portsmouth for 'press gangs' to descend on revellers at the end of an evening, searching for those attempting to avoid their duty to become seamen. Such actions were supposed to only recruit eligible men, but little distinction was made by the gangs. At best this could mean a night aboard ship for release on the grounds of exemption the next morning, or at worst a new career as a sailor. Interestingly, despite being residents in the naval capital of England, none of the Shoveller family seem to have been cacheted into naval service in this way.

Admiral Lord Nelson

During this anxious period, all of Great Britain and its colonies were reliant on the Royal Navy to stave off a possible French invasion, and everyone looked to Admiral Lord Horatio Nelson (29 September 1758 – 21 October 1805), 1st Viscount Nelson, 1st Duke of Bronte, KB, and flag officer of the Royal Navy.[24] His inspirational leadership, uncanny grasp of strategy and unconventional tactics brought about a number of decisive British naval victories throughout the French Revolutionary and Napoleonic Wars. He was then, and still now is widely regarded as one of the greatest naval commanders in history.

Nelson had a close association with Portsmouth, and is renowned for the defeat of Napoleon's navy at the Battle of Trafalgar on the 21st October 1805, as well as for many other great naval triumphs. Nelson's progress before the Battle of Trafalgar was closely followed by the Hampshire Telegraph, with regular naval missives appearing in its pages. The level of local interest was demonstrated in a review of the local Free Mart Fair of 1805,

Admiral Lord Horatio Nelson (1758-1805)[50]

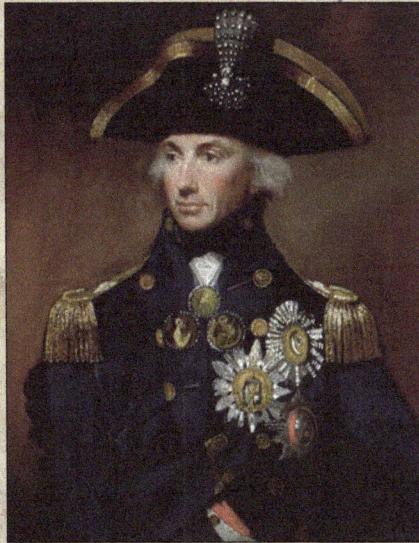

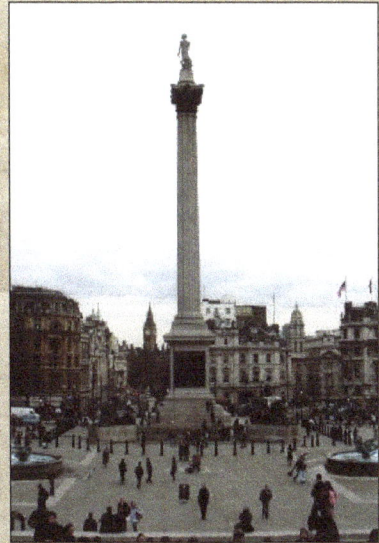

▲ Two images of Vice Admiral & Admiral Horatio Lord Nelson, by Lemuel Francis Abbott (1799). RIGHT: With Nelson's effigy standing atop the column, even 210 years on, Trafalgar Square is still considered as the heart of London.

Nelson's final departure from Portsea Island was probably the most significant, as it marked his final port of call in Britain before departing to fight at the Battle of Trafalgar. Nelson was not necessarily always fond of Portsmouth as a destination and in a letter to Lady Hamilton on the 20th May 1805 he described it as "that horrid place", but his opinion seemed much more positive on his last visit. The Hampshire Telegraph detailed how Lord Nelson arrived at the George Inn on Saturday, 14th September 1805. The report observed that "a number of people followed his Lordship and cheered him when he embarked." Other sources suggest that Nelson tried to leave the George Inn secretly by the back door into Penny Street, but was soon surrounded by a crowd on Southsea Common. Apparently, Nelson's one hand was shaken so much by members of the crowd that he said "I wish I had two hands and then I could accommodate more of you."

News of Nelson's victory and his death on the 21st October reached Portsmouth on the 7th November 1805. Initially there was a period of great celebration, with bells rung and ships firing volleys, but Nelson's sacrifice was also remembered, with bells ringing muffled peals the next day as a tribute. Nelson's body returned to Portsmouth aboard "HMS Victory" on the 2nd December, but was then taken up the Thames to London. The Hampshire Telegraph carried a long and in-depth report of the funeral. Within three years of the 'Battle of Trafalgar,' Nelson's monument on Portsdown Hill, Portsmouth was erected, paid for voluntarily by his officers and men.

William Shoveller Sr. lived in the same period as Nelson and his tanning business located at Westmeon, was only a few miles north of 'Fir Hill Manor' at Droxford, Hampshire, where Lord Nelson often overnighted when he was on shore leave.

Napoleon's Planned

▲Napoleon inspecting his invasion troops at Boulogne on the 15th August 1804. ▼BELOW: The Fort Blockhouse, Portsmouth. BOTTOM: View from the 'Saluting Platform at Portsmouth' by E.W. Cooke. The Square is in the background with the semaphore tower on top.

Fort Blockhouse

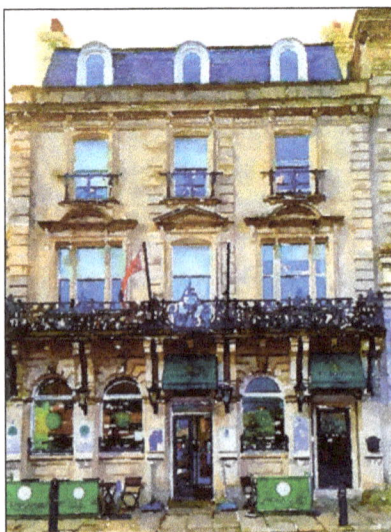

which began by asking "Is there any news from Lord Nelson?" So the fate of the fleet and its admiral was of the utmost importance and interest to the people of Portsmouth, and to the entire country.

The Rise of Napoleon

Britain's nemesis, Napoleon Bonaparte was five years younger than William Shoveller, being born in Ajaccio, Corsica on the 15th August 1769, but following his brilliant tactical command of French forces, he dominated a large slice of history from 1796 when he first took command of the French Army.

But the British fleet under the command of Admiral Nelson sought retribution and destroyed the French navy in the Battle of the Nile in 1798, to isolate Napoleon's supplies and communications in Egypt.[25]

▲Painting of 'The Ship Leopard Hotel,' Portsmouth, by Tracy Rockwell (2016).

The first French Army of England had gathered on the Channel coast in 1798, but an invasion of England was sidelined by Napoleon's concentration on campaigns in Egypt and against Austria, and shelved in 1802 by the Peace of Amiens.

From 1803 to 1805 a new army of 200,000 men, known as the Armée des côtes de l'Océan (Army of the Ocean Coasts) or the Armée d'Angleterre (Army of England), was gathered and trained at camps at Boulogne, Bruges and Montreuil. Napoleon also seriously considered using a fleet of troop-carrying balloons as part of his proposed invasion force and appointed Marie Madeline Sophie Blanchard as an air service chief, though she said the proposed aerial invasion would fail because of the winds. Though an aerial invasion proved a dead-end, the prospect of one captured the minds of the British print media and public.

Britain continued to be on high alert with their defences to the anticipated invasion. With the flotilla and encampment at Boulogne visible from the south coast of England, Martello towers were built along the English coast to counter the invasion threat, and militias were raised. Unfounded rumours of a massive flat French invasion raft powered by windmills and paddle-wheels and a secretly-dug channel tunnel spread via the print media, as did caricatures ridiculing the prospect of invasion. A naval raid on Boulogne was also carried out in October 1804 and British fleets continued to blockade the French and Spanish fleets needed to gain naval superiority long enough for a crossing.

Before any French flotilla could cross however, Napoleon had to gain naval control of the English Channel, and quipped... "Let us be masters of the Channel for six hours and we are

Invasion of England[51]

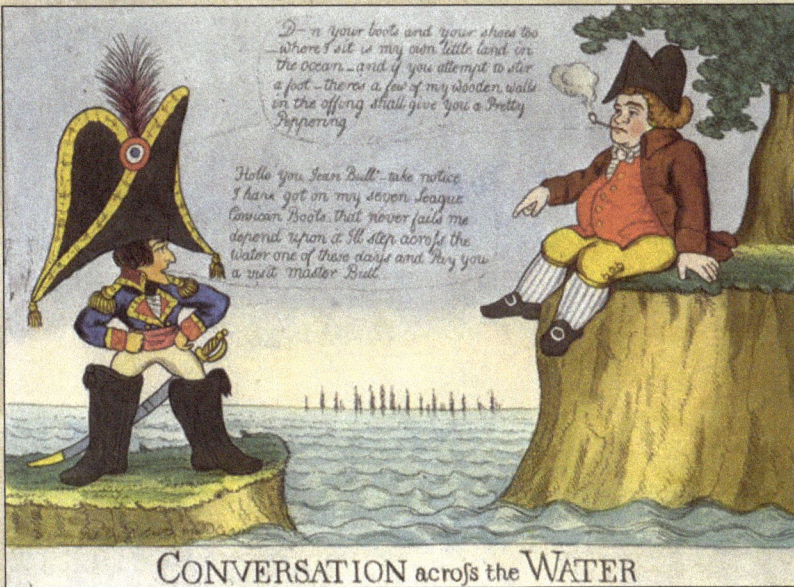

CONVERSATION across the WATER

▲Cartoon of a conversation between 'Bony' and John Bull, with reference to the 'wooden wall' being the Royal Navy. ▼BELOW: Memorial plaque at the Trafalgar Cemetery on Gibraltar. BOTTOM: The 1711 doorway to "HM Dockyard" at Portsea.

TRAFALGAR CEMETERY
HERE LIE THE REMAINS OF SOME WHO DIED OF WOUNDS AT GIBRALTAR AFTER NELSON'S GREAT VICTORY IN OCTOBER, 1805, THOSE KILLED DURING THE BATTLE HAVING BEEN BURIED AT SEA. OTHER GRAVES DATE FROM 1798.

Yet the Napoleonic juggernaut rolled on, and France gradually became the master of all Europe. Despite the ascendancy of Napoleon, the United Kingdom of Great Britain and Ireland came into being on the 1st January 1801, with King George III becoming its first monarch.[26]

On the 18th May 1804, Napoleon was presented with the title of "Emperor of the French" by the Senate. He was solemnly crowned, after receiving the Iron Crown of the Lombard kings, and was consecrated by Pope Pius VII in Notre-Dame de Paris.[27]

About this time, Napoleon's planned invasion of the United Kingdom heavily influenced British naval strategy and the fortification of the coast of southeast England. The British populace were fearful of an assault by the French and were solely dependent on the might of the Royal

masters of the world." He envisaged doing this by having the Brest and Toulon Franco–Spanish fleets break out from the British blockade, and then sail across the Atlantic to threaten the West Indies. This, he hoped, would draw off the Royal Navy force under William Cornwallis defending the Western Approaches. The Toulon and Brest fleets could then rendezvous at Martinique, quickly sail back across the Atlantic to Europe and defeat what parts of the English Fleet had remained in the Channel, take control and defend and transport the invasion force, all before the pursuing fleets could return to stop them.

This plan was typical of Napoleon in its dash and reliance on fast movement and surprise, but such a style was more suited to land than to sea warfare, with the vagaries of tide and wind and the effective British blockade making it ever more impractical and unlikely to succeed as more and more time passed. Only the Toulon force eventually broke out on 29 March 1805 and, though it managed to cross the Atlantic, it did not find the Brest fleet at the rendezvous and so sailed back to Europe alone, where it was met by the force blockading Rochefort and Ferrol, and defeated at the Battle of Cape Finisterre then forced back into port. Therefore, on 27 August 1805 Napoleon used the invasion army as the core of the new Grande Armée and had it break camp and march eastwards to begin the Ulm Campaign. Thus, by the time of the Battle of Trafalgar on 21st October 1805, the invasion had already been called off, which further guaranteed British control of the Channel rather than preventing the invasion. The comment attributed to Admiral John Jervis "I do not say they [the French] cannot come, I only say they cannot come by sea" had been proved right.

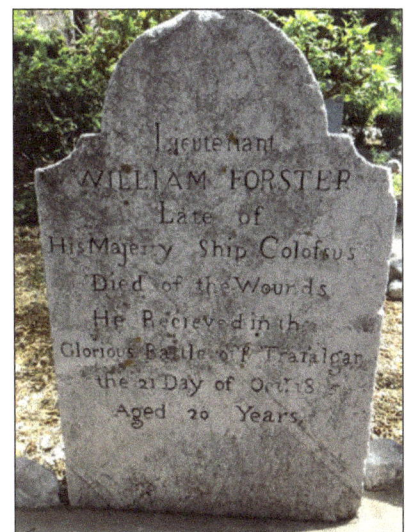

▲Headstone at the cemetery on Gibraltar for Lt William Forster, killed at Trafalgar.

Nelson's flagship "HMS Victory" arrives at Portsmouth after the Battle of Trafalgar with the Admiral's body on board, her flag draped at half mast.

Navy for protection.[28]

The many residents, institutions and businesses of Portsmouth of course, saw much more of the war than the rest of the country. They continually witnessed the half-shattered ships returning for repair, the hundreds of wounded soldiers and sailors being hospitalised, and the intensity of the logistics operations surrounding HM Dockyard at Portsea.

On the other hand, Napoleon realised that unless the Royal Navy could be defeated, his planned invasion of England was futile. Today, the site of the French invasion camp at Boulogne is marked by a 53-metre column, the tallest of such monuments in France, which is topped by a statue of Napoleon.[29]

At sea, the French were no match for the Royal Navy, which was confirmed by Admiral Nelson's victories at the Nile and Trafalgar. But the loss of Nelson at the latter aboard his flagship "HMS Victory," which is now dry docked in Portsmouth as a tourist attraction, was a crushing blow for Britain.[30]

It took a further ten years to defeat and exile Napoleon, which finally occurred after the Duke of Wellington's famous victory at the Battle of Waterloo in 1815. It was

William Shoveller Sr., Gentleman

▲LEFT COLUMN: 1-Advertisement for the sale of William Shoveller Sr.'s Silver Business (Hampshire Telegraph, 9th July 1804, p.3). 2-William Shoveller Sr. - Hiring Tanners (Hampshire Telegraph, 3 Nov. 1806 , p.2). 3-William Shoveller Sr. - Journeyman tanners required (Hampshire Telegraph, 7 Sep 1807). 4-William Shoveller Sr. - Tan-Yard Auction (Hampshire Telegraph, 1st Feb 1808, p.2). 5-Death notice for Mary Shoveller (nee Bignell, in Hampshire Telegraph, 26th Sept 1825, p.4). RIGHT COLUMN: 1-William Shoveller Sr. & John Shoveller (LLD) - Tan-Yard Sale (Hampshire Chronicle, 9 Nov. 1807, p.4). 2-William Shoveller Sr. - Property Sale (Hampshire Chronicle, 5 June 1820, p.4). 3-William Shoveller Sr. - Gentleman of Surrey St, Portsea (now Portsmouth City Centre, from 1830 Pigot's Directory). ABOVE: The elegant townhouses at Landport Terrace, Portsmouth, where William & Mary Shoveller spent their final years.

Tanning & Tannerys[52]

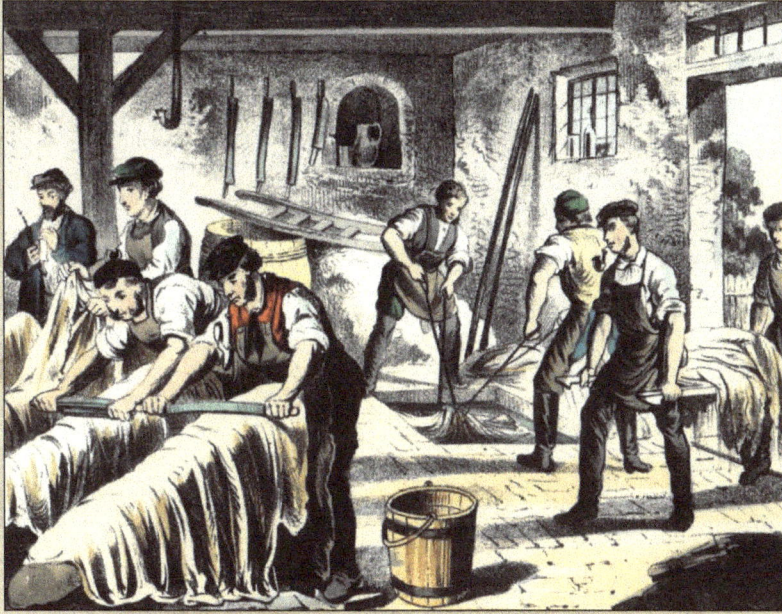

Tanning operations of the early 19th century were lucrative, but it was a messy, smelly business.

Tanning is the process of treating skins and hides of animals to produce leather, and a tannery is the place where the skins are processed. Tanning hide into leather involves a process which permanently alters the protein structure of skin, making it more durable and less susceptible to decomposition, and coloring.

Before tanning, the skins are dehaired, degreased, desalted and soaked in water over a period of six hours to two days. Historically this process was considered a noxious or "odoriferous trade" and relegated to the outskirts of town. Tanning used tannin, an acidic chemical compound from which the tanning process draws its name, derived from the bark of certain trees. An alternative method, developed in the 1800s, was chrome tanning, where chromium salts are used instead of natural tannins.

The English word for tanning is from medieval Latin tannāre, derivative of tannum (oak bark), from French tan (tanbark), from old-Cornish tann (red oak). These terms are related to the hypothetical Proto-Indo-European 'dhonu' meaning 'fir tree'. The same word is source for Old High German tanna meaning 'fir', related to modern Tannenbaum. Despite the linguistic confusion between quite different conifers and oaks, the word tan referring to dyes and types of hide preservation is from the Gaulic use referencing the bark of oaks, the original source of tannin, and not fir trees.

Ancient civilizations used leather for waterskins, bags, harnesses and tack, boats, armour, quivers, scabbards, boots, and sandals. Tanning was being carried out by the inhabitants of Mehrgarh in Pakistan between 7000 and 3300 BCE.[i] Around 2500 BCE, the Sumerians began using leather, affixed by copper studs on chariot wheels. The Hebrews tanned with oak bark, and the Egyptians, with babul pods. The Romans used bark, certain woods, and berries. The Arabs tanned with bark and roots, and in the Middle Ages they reintroduced the art into Europe via Spain. By the 18th century the value of materials such as oak bark, sumac, valonia, and hemlock was well established. The procedure, essentially unchanged in modern times, involves soaking hides in vats of increasingly strong liquors, or liquid extracts of vegetable tannin.

Formerly, tanning was considered a noxious or "odoriferous trade" and relegated to the outskirts of town, among the poor. Indeed, tanning by ancient methods is so foul-smelling that tanneries are still isolated from those towns today where the old methods are used. Skins typically arrived at the tannery dried stiff and dirty with soil and gore. First, the ancient tanners would soak the skins in water to clean and soften them. Then they would pound and scour the skin to remove any remaining flesh and fat. Hair was removed by soaking the skin in urine,[ii] painting it with an alkaline lime mixture, or simply allowing the skin to putrefy for several months then dipping it in a salt solution. After the hair was loosened, the tanners scraped it off with a knife. Once the hair was removed, the tanners would 'bate,' or soften the material by pounding dung into the skin, or soaking the skin in a solution of animal brains. Bating was a fermentative process that relied on enzymes produced by bacteria found in the dung. Among the kinds of dung commonly used were those of dogs or pigeons.[iii]

Traditionally the actual tanning process used vegetable tanning. In some variations of the process, cedar oil, alum or tannin was applied to the skin as a tanning agent. As the skin was stretched, it would lose moisture and absorb the agent. Following the adoption in medicine of soaking gut sutures in a chromium (III) solution after 1840, it was discovered that this method could also be used with leather and thus was adopted by tanners.[iv]

----

i. Possehl, Gregory L. (1996). Mehrgarh in Oxford Companion to Archaeology, edited by Brian Fagan. Oxford University Press.

ii. Kumar, Mohi (August 20, 2013). "From Gunpowder to Teeth Whitener: The Science Behind Historic Uses of Urine". smithsonian.com. Retrieved December 16, 2018.

iii. Johnson, Steven (2006). The Ghost Map. New York: Riverhead Books. pp. 4, 263..

iv. "A history of new ideas in tanning - Leather International". www.leathermag.com. Archived from the original on 2 January 2017. Retrieved 27 April 2018.

only then that the British populace and ordinary citizens like the Shovellers, could settle down to what would became a golden era for the British Empire.

In the midst of the war with France, William Shoveller Sr. sold out of his silversmithing business in July of 1804, to enter into an animal skins and tanning enterprise.[31] William may have been motivated to switch to tanning as the influx of animal pelts arriving from Canada and the United States, were streaming through Portsmouth and likely generating substantial profits.

Mary Shoveller's father John Bignell Sr., passed on in this same year and was buried on the 28th June 1804 in the church cemetery at Warnford.[32] He nominated William Shoveller Sr. as joint executor of his will, and Mary received the family estate at Warnford along with other leasing properties as her inheritance.[33] The name and date of death for John Bignell's wife has not been found.

William purchased his tannery sometime in 1805 and set up operations at Westmeon for his eldest son and heir John Shoveller. But young John had already known to be an excellent classical scholar, and had decided upon a legal career.

This forced William to realise that the tanning industry was both a difficult and oderous occupation and by 1807, he had put the entire inventory, the property at Westmeon and the business, up for sale.[34]

William's son John was later to study at Oxford University, and matriculated at that eminent institution in 1817.[35] From around this time, William Shoveller Sr. was designated as a 'gentleman,' a term which although was losing its original intention, was nevertheless indicative of persons of independent means.

"As William Harrison put it in his 'Description of England' (1577), to "live without manual labour, and thereto is able and will bear the port, charge and countenance of a gentleman," could "for money have a coat and arms bestowed upon him by heralds... and [be] reputed for a gentleman ever after."

Encyclopedia Brittanica [36]

By the early 1800s William and Mary Shoveller's children were coming of age, and one by one they began to marry. The eldest son John Shoveller, was first to the alter when he married on the 24th March 1812 at St. Mary's Church in Portsea, to Elizabeth (c.1784-1852), the daughter of Thomas Eastman and Sarah Sabine of Portsea, a wealthy local cabinetmaker and auctioneer.[37] Next was William Shoveller Jr., who married on the 13th May 1815 at St Martin in the Fields, London to Elizabeth (1794-1885), the daughter of John Dunt and Hannah Heale.[38]

In 1818, William Shoveller's mother Mary, passed away on the 7th January, while staying with her son Rev. John Shoveller Sr. and family at Poole, Dorset, reportedly at 93 years of age, although it seems more likely that she was 83.[39] Next to wed was William's daughter Mary, who married on the 23rd May 1821 at St. Mary's, Portsea to Rev. Thomas Stratten (1794-1854), a congregational minister.[40] The last of William and Mary's children to the alter was Elizabeth, who walked down the aisle on the 26th June 1822 at St. Mary's,

▲*Fashions of the Regency period. LEFT: Early 19th century portrait of a young lady, oil on canvas by an unknown artist (unrelated). RIGHT: Early 19th century gentleman wearing a ruffled shirt with neckcloth, oil portrait by an unknown French artist, c.1810 (unrelated, Philadelphia Museum of Art).*

▲ TOP (Left): The 'Ship Anson Inn', Portsmouth. (Right): Queen Street, Portsea was both the business address and residence for William Shoveller Sr. and family, being on the main shopping precinct for centuries and the first port of call for most visiting sailors to the town. ABOVE: Maritime activity at Portsmouth Point, Hampshire about 1835, showing a paddle steamer at left, which were first introduced around 1821.

Portsea with a draper named James (1796-1861), the son of Richard Roberton VI and Mary Rayner, a family which stretched back some 12 generations.[41]

Apart from these few records, further information about William Shoveller Esq, has not come to light, except that through his business acumen he had evidently become sufficiently wealthy to provide his children with a good education, which included his eldest son John, who received a doctoral degree from Oxford University.

The death of King George III on the 29th January 1820, brought an end to a remarkable reign after having been 60 years on the throne. His son King George IV, George Augustus Frederick (1762-1830), who had already served as the Prince Regent during his father's final mental illness since the 5th February 1811, was crowned King of the United Kingdom

Last Will & Testament of William Shoveller Sr., of Portsea
Drafted - 7th January 1832 & Proved 3rd September 1832

Translation

This is the last will and Testament of one **William Shoveller** of Portsea in the county of Southampton, Gentleman made this seventh day of January in the year of our lord 1832 whilst I am of sound and disposing mind, memory and in understanding whereby I humbly renounce my soul to Almighty God and dispose my worldly estate and effects in manner following, that is to say I give and devise unto my son **John Shoveller** all that messuage, tenement or dwelling house with ??? yard and garden thereto belonging situate lying and being on the North side of Sandwich Street in the town of Portsea containing in width from east to west on the North and South sides of 17 feet of our size and in depth from North to South on the east and west sides there of 50 feet of a size or thereabouts and also all that messuage tenement or dwelling house yard and garden thereto belonging situate lying and being on the north side of Sandwich Street aforesaid in row obtaining in breadth from east to west at the North and South ends thereof 15 feet passage and in depth from North to South at the east and west sides there of 50 feet of passage or thereabouts to hold said ??? messuages tenements or dwelling houses with their rights members and appurtenances unto and to the use of my said son **John Shoveller** his heirs and assigns for ever, I give devise and bequeath all that my ??? messuage tenement or dwelling house with the appurtenances thereunto belonging situate and being in East Street Portsmouth in the said county onto my said son **John Shoveller** his executors admons and assigns for his and their own absolute use and benefit and I hereby give and bequeath unto my said son all such sum and sums of money that may be owe from him to me at the time of my decease and ??? all the rest and residue of my estate and effects both real and personal I give devise and bequeath the same respectively unto my sons in law the **Rev Thomas Stratten** of Sunderland in the county of Durham dissenting Minister and **James Roberton** of Portsmouth aforesaid draper and my daughter **Jane Shoveller** their heirs executors admons and assigns upon trust that they my said trustees and the survivors or survivor of them and the heirs executors and admon's of such survivor do and soon as conveniently can be after my decease absolutely sell and dispose of my said real and personal estate so devised and bequeathed to them as aforesaid either by public sale or private contractas to them him or her shall soon seem meet and make and execute all such conveyances and assurances as shall be necessary or proper for perfecting the sale or transfer thereof and as to the monies to arise by the sale or sales of the said trust estates some thing ??? and other produce thereof in the interim at all other money herein before bequeathed to them upon trust to pay and divide, and I do hereby give and bequeath the same unto and equally between my four children namely my son **William Shoveller** and my daughters **Mary** the wife of the said **Thomas Stratton** the said **Jane Shoveller** and **Eliza** the wife of the said **James Roberton** share and share alike and I nominate and appoint to said **Thomas Stratton, James Roberton** and **Jane Shoveller** executors and executrix is of this my will and I do here by declare order and direct that the ??? receipts in writing of my said trustees or the survivors or survivor of them or the heirs executors or admons of such survivor shall be good and effectual discharges to ??? or purchasors of all any part of my said real and personal estate here subject ??? to be sold and that such purchaser or purchasors shall not be answerable for the inapplication or non-application of the money in such receipt or receipts acknowledged or expressed to be received and it is my will and meaning that my said trustees and executors before named or ??? of them shall not be liable to answer or make good any loss or losses that shall or my happen to my estate and effects unless in same shall appear to happen by or through their or either of their wilful neglect or ??? and that the one of them shall not be answerable for the others or other of them for the acts or deeds of the other of them but each of them for their own separate acts and deeds only and further I do hereby direct that my said trustees and executors ??? and may pay reimburse themselves himself and herself out of the said trust monies and promises all reasonable and necessary costs charges and expenses whatsoever that thay or either of them shall bear pay all be put unto in or about the execution of this is my will and lastly I do here by revoke and make void all former and other wills by me made in witness whereof I have to the bottom of the two first sheets of this my will the whole whereof is contained in three sheets of paper subscribed my name and to this third and last sheet set my hand and seal in the day and year first above written

William Shoveller signed sealed published and declared by the said **William Shoveller** the testator as and for his last will and Testament on the day of the date in the presence of us who have hereto subscribed our names as witnesses in his presence at his request and in the presence of each other

J.H. Paffard - John Heywood Jr - R.J. Warner

Proved at London 3rd Sept 1832 before the judge by the oaths of the **Rev Thomas Stratton, James Roberton** and **Jane Shoveller** spinster the daughter the executors to whom Admon was granted having been first sworn by common duty to administer.

▲ *The Will of William Shoveller, proved 3 Sep 1832 (England & Wales, Prerogative Court of Canterbury Wills, 1384-1858 [Prob 11- Will Registers, 1832-1834, Piece 1806, Tenterden, Quire No.601-650, 1832]).*

of Great Britain and Ireland, and King of Hanover at his coronation at Westminster Abbey, on the 19th July 1821.[42]

A few years later, Mary Shoveller (nee Bignell) died unexpectedly on the 21st September 1825, at her home at Landport Terrace, Portsmouth, aged 57.[43] By then the world was evolving rapidly as just one week later, the world's first public passenger railway opened for business between Stockton and Darlington.[44] At the same time out in Portsmouth Harbour the moored convict hulks, still brimming with languishing prisoners, slowly rotted away, while life for the lower classes remained a harrowing experience.

In Pigot's 1830 Directory William Shoveller Sr., was again listed as a 'gentleman' and was residing at Surrey St, Portsea,[45] but he died two years later in mid 1832, aged 68, well before both of his older siblings.[46] A search of the burial records at St. Mary's Church in Portsea, may at some stage reveal the location of his tomb. His 1832 will made generous provisions for his five children as well as his sons-in-law James Roberton and the Rev. Thomas Stratten.[47]

William and Mary Shoveller produced a family of five children with only one daughter Jane, remaining unmarried. While their eldest son John became a schoolmaster and qualified in legal studies, he nevertheless produced the largest family with ten children. But the other siblings also had good sized families with younger brother William Jr. producing six, and sister Mary bringing forth five children from their respective marriages. Fortunately, both William and Mary Shoveller survived long enough to witness the birth of all of their 22 grandchildren, including Thomas Eastman Shoveller in 1827, and it is their engaging stories that are the subject of the next chapter.

References

1. Clune, D. & Turner, K. (Eds, 2009), 'The Governors of New South Wales, 1788-2010,' The Federation Press, Sydney, p. 34.
2. Hunter, John (1793), An Historical Journal of the Transactions at Port Jackson and Norfolk Island - chapter1, Project Gutenberg Australia, retrieved 16 October 2021.
3. Wikipedia – "HMS Bounty" [https://en.wikipedia.org/wiki/HMS_Bounty].
4. William Shoveller & Mary Bignell - Marriage held on the 3 Jan 1789, at the Church of Our Lady, Warnford (Hampshire Allegations for Marriage Licences, 1689-1837, Vol 2).
5. "Church Of Our Lady, Warnford - 1296978, Historic England." [www.historicengland.org.uk.].
6. Lambert, Tim. 'A History of Warnford' [https://localhistories.org/a-history-of-warnford/].
7. A. 'Parishes: Warnford', in A History of the County of Hampshire: Volume 3, ed. William Page (London, 1908), pp. 268-273. British History Online http://www.british-history.ac.uk/vch/hants/vol3/pp.268-273 [accessed 5 June 2022].
8. John Shoveller - Baptism held on 6 Nov 1789 at Skinner St, Independent Church, Poole, Dorset (England & Wales, Non-Conformist and Non-Parochial Registers, 1567-1970).
9. William Shoveller - Baptism held on 6 Nov 1789 at the family residence at Queen St on Portsmouth Common, Hampshire, Independent (England & Wales, Non-Conformist and Non-Parochial Registers, 1567-1936).
10. William Shoveller - Listed as 'Cutler & Silversmith' (Hampshire - Universal British Directory, 1792-1798).
11. Wikipedia - Silversmith [https://en.wikipedia.org/wiki/Silversmith].
12. Wikipedia - Silver Hallmarks [https://en.wikipedia.org/wiki/Silver_hallmarks].
13. William Shoveller - Property Sale (Hampshire Chronicle, 5 June 1820, p.4).
14. Hantsphere Heritage In Place - Portsmouth and its people 1800-1850 [http://www.hantsphere.org.uk/portsmouth-and-its-people-1800-1850].
15. Mary Shoveller - Baptism held on 14 Oct 1794 at the family residence at Queen St on Portsmouth Common, Hampshire, Independent (England, Select Births and Christenings, 1538-1975).
16. Jane Shoveller - Baptism held on 13 Apr 1796 at the family residence at Queen St on Portsmouth Common, Hampshire, Independent (England, Select Births and Christenings, 1538-1975).
17. Wikipedia - Edward Jenner [https://en.wikipedia.org/wiki/Edward_Jenner].
18. Elizabeth Shoveller - Born on 20 Mar 1798, and baptised at the family residence at Queen St on Portsmouth Common, Hampshire, Independent (England, Select Births and Christenings, 1538-1975).
19. Sense Of Place South East - Rev. John Griffin [http://www.sopse.org.uk/ixbin/hixclient.exe?a=query&p=gateway&f=generic_objectrecord_postsearch.htm&_IXFIRST_=26123&_IXMAXHITS_=1&m=quick_sform&tc1=i&tc2=e&s=14_5T9hgIyY], [accessed 12 June 2022].
20. John Shoveller - Death notice (Hampshire Chronicle, 9 June 1798, p.4).
21. John Shoveller -Burial held on the 8th June 1798 at Portsea, Hampshire (England Deaths & Burials, 1538-1991).
22. John Shoveller - Will, proved on the 14th August 1798 (England & Wales, Prerogative Court of Canterbury Wills, 1384-1858 [Prob 11- Will Registers, 1796-1798, Piece 1311, Walpole, Quire No.527-569, 1798]).
23. Brittanica - Irish Rebellion [https://www.britannica.com/event/Irish-Rebellion-Irish-history-1798].
24. Brittanica - Horatio Nelson [https://www.britannica.com/biography/Horatio-Nelson].
25. Brittanica - Battle of the Nile [https://www.britannica.com/event/Battle-of-the-Nile].
26. Brittanica - Act of Union [https://www.britannica.com/event/Act-of-Union-United-Kingdom-1801].
27. Wikipedia - Emporer of the French [https://en.wikipedia.org/wiki/Emperor_of_the_French].
28. Wikipedia - Napoleon's Planned Invasion of the United Kingdom [https://en.wikipedia.org/wiki/Napoleon%27s_planned_invasion_of_the_United_Kingdom].

29. Wikipedia - Napoleon's Planned Invasion of the United Kingdom, op. cit.

30. Wikipedia - The Death of Nelson, 21 October 1805 [https://en.wikipedia.org/wiki/The_Death_of_Nelson,_21_October_1805].

31. William Shoveller - Silver Business Advertisement (Hampshire Telegraph, 9th July 1804, p.3).

32. John Bignell - Burial held on the 28 June 1804 at Warnford, Hampshire (England, Select Deaths and Burials, 1538-1991).

33. John Bignell - Will, proved on the 29th December 1804 (England & Wales, Prerogative Court of Canterbury Wills, 1384-1858 [PROB 11: Will Registers (1802-1804), Piece 1418: Heseltine, Quire No 801-1804).

34. WIlliam Shoveller - Tan-Yard Auction (Hampshire Telegraph, 1st Feb 1808, p.2).

35. John Shoveller - Oxford University (Extract from Alumni Oxoniensis: 1715 to 1886, The London Public Record Office, Chancery Lane, London England. Located in the Reference Section).

36. Britannica, The Editors of Encyclopaedia. "gentleman". Encyclopedia Britannica, 29 Aug. 2018, https://www.britannica.com/topic/gentleman. Accessed 10 June 2022.

37. John Shoveller & Elizabeth Eastman - Marriage held on the 24 Mar 1812 at St. Mary's, Portsea (Hampshire Allegations for Marriage Licences, 1689-1837, Vol 2).

38. William Shoveller Jr. & Elizabeth Dunt - Marriage held on the 13 May 1815, at St Martin in the Fields, Westminster (London, England, Church of England Marriages and Banns, 1754-1921).

39. Mary Shoveller - Death notices (Oxford Uni & City Herald, 17th Jan.1818; Salisbury and Winchester Journal, 12th Jan. 1818; Hampshire Telegraph, 12th Jan. 1818, p.4).

40. Mary Shoveller & Rev. Thomas Stratten - Marriage held on the 23 May 1821, at St. Mary's, Portsea, Hampshire (England, Select Marriages, 1538–1973).

41. Elizabeth Shoveller & James Roberton - Marriage held on the 26 Jun 1822, at St. Mary's Church, Portsea, Hampshire (England, Select Marriages, 1538–1973).

42. Brittanica - George III [https://www.britannica.com/biography/George-III].

43. Mary Shoveller (nee Bignell) - Death notice (Hampshire Telegraph, 26th Sept 1825, p.4).

44. Brittanica - Stockton & Darlington Railway [https://www.britannica.com/topic/Stockton-and-Darlington-Railway].

45. William Shoveller - Gentleman of Surrey St, Portsea (now Portsmouth City Centre, from 1830 Pigot's Directory).

46. William Shoveller - Burial held on the 10 Jun 1846, All Souls, Kensal Green, Kensington and Chelsea (London, England, Church of England Deaths and Burials, 1813-1980).

47. William Shoveller - Will, proved on the 3 Sep 1832 (England & Wales, Prerogative Court of Canterbury Wills, 1384-1858 [Prob 11- Will Registers, 1832-1834, Piece 1806, Tenterden, Quire No.601-650, 1832]).

48. Ford, Thomas K. (2018). 'The Silversmith In Eighteenth-Century Williamsburg,' [https://www.gutenberg.org/files/58066/58066-h/58066-h.htm].

49. William Shoveller, Land Tax Redemption, Southampton, 1798 (UK, Land Tax Redemption, 1798).

50. Wikipedia - Horatio Nelson, 1st Viscount Nelson [https://en.wikipedia.org/wiki/Horatio_Nelson,_1st_Viscount_Nelson].

51. Wikipedia - Napoleon's Planned Invasion of the United Kingdom, op. cit.

52. Wikipedia - Tanning (leather) [https://en.wikipedia.org/wiki/Tanning_(leather)].

Chapter Six

Shoveller

Bignell

THE DESCENDANTS OF
WILLIAM SHOVELLER & MARY BIGNELL

Eastman

Dunt

Stratten

Roberton

By 1812, Britain was heavily committed to the Peninsula War in Spain and Portugal against Napoleon. To make matters worse, the U.S. President James Madison, enacted a 90 day embargo on trade with the United Kingdom, which sparked off another war between Britain and the Americans known as the War of 1812. Portsmouth once again went onto a war footing, and with Nelson's flagship "HMS Victory" now retired from service, Britain prayed for strength.

At this time the traditional religions were undergoing change and being shaken up by adherents of the non-conformist movement. The Baptists were known to have had a presence in Portsmouth since the early 1640s, with records revealing that the first pastor was a Mr. Wentworth, who was followed by Richard Drinkwater and then Thomas Bowes. Up until the passing of the Toleration Act in 1688, when dissenters were protected from persecution, the Baptists had been forced to meet in secret, but on the enactment of legislation, Thomas Bowes gave a parcel of land in the garden of his property in St. Thomas' Street, Portsmouth for a lease of 99 years.

Around 1700, many of Bowes' congregation left to form their own mainstream Baptist church, meeting initially in a barn on Portsmouth Common. In 1704 Edward Parsons bought some land in West Dock Field and used part of it to erect a Meeting House, which

**Pedigree Chart - 4
The Descendants of
William & Mary Shoveller
of Portsea, Hampshire**

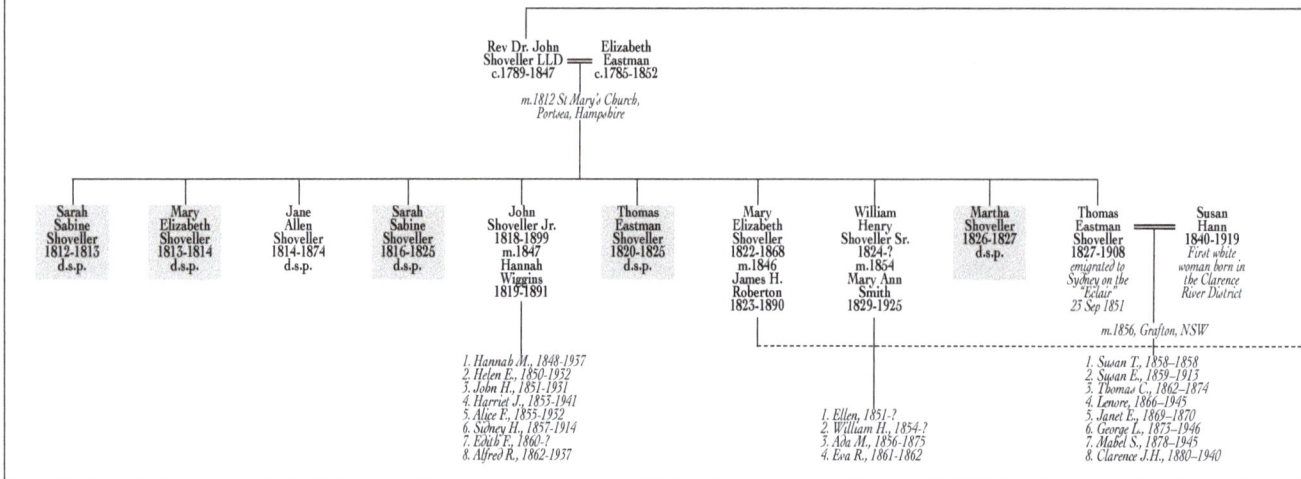

Rev Dr. John Shoveller LLD c.1789-1847 ═══ Elizabeth Eastman c.1785-1852

m.1812 St Mary's Church, Portsea, Hampshire

- Sarah Sabine Shoveller 1812-1813 d.s.p.
- Mary Elizabeth Shoveller 1813-1814 d.s.p.
- Jane Allen Shoveller 1814-1874 d.s.p.
- Sarah Sabine Shoveller 1816-1825 d.s.p.
- John Shoveller Jr. 1818-1899 m.1847 Hannah Wiggins 1819-1891
- Thomas Eastman Shoveller 1820-1825 d.s.p.
- Mary Elizabeth Shoveller 1822-1868 m.1846 James H. Roberton 1823-1890
- William Henry Shoveller Sr. 1824-? m.1854 Mary Ann Smith 1829-1925
- Martha Shoveller 1826-1827 d.s.p.
- Thomas Eastman Shoveller 1827-1908 *emigrated to Sydney on the "Eclair" 25 Sep 1851* ═══ Susan Hann 1840-1919 *First white woman born in the Clarence River District*

m.1856, Grafton, NSW

John Shoveller Jr. issue:
1. Hannah M., 1848-1937
2. Helen E., 1850-1952
3. John H., 1851-1951
4. Harriet J., 1853-1941
5. Alice F., 1855-1932
6. Sidney H., 1857-1914
7. Edith E., 1860-?
8. Alfred R., 1862-1937

William Henry issue:
1. Ellen, 1851-?
2. William H., 1854-?
3. Ada M., 1856-1875
4. Eva R., 1861-1862

Thomas Eastman issue:
1. Susan T., 1858-1858
2. Susan E., 1859-1915
3. Thomas C., 1862-1874
4. Lenore, 1866-1945
5. Janet E., 1869-1870
6. George L., 1873-1946
7. Mabel S., 1878-1945
8. Clarence J.H., 1880-1940

6.1 Descendants of Rev. Dr. John Shoveller LLD & Elizabeth Eastman

Rev. Dr. John SHOVELLER (1789-1847), was a schoolmaster and independent minister. He married in 1812 at St Mary's Church, Portsea to Elizabeth (c.1785-1852), the daughter of Thomas Eastman and Sarah Sabine of Portsmouth, with issue:

1. Sarah Sabine Shoveller (1812 - 1813)* born 1812, died 1813.

2. Mary Elizabeth Shoveller (1813 - 1814)* born 1813, died 1814.

3. Jane Allen Shoveller (1814 - 1874), born 1814, was a spinster and died 1874, no issue.

4. Sarah Sabine Shoveller (1816 - 1825)* born 1816, died aged 9 years in 1825.

5. John SHOVELLER Jr. (1818 - 1899), born 1818, married on the 18th May 1847 at St Ann's Blackfriars, London to Hannah (1819-1891), the daughter of William Wiggins & Rebecca

Shoveller | *Eastman*

Gulley, died in 1899, with issue (see Chap.15).

6. Thomas Eastman SHOVELLER (1820 - 1825)* born 1820, died aged 5 years in 1825.

7. Mary Elizabeth Shoveller (1822 - 1846), born 1822, married on the 29th September 1846 at Banbury, Oxfordshire to her first cousin James Henry (1823-1890), the son of James Roberton Sr. and her aunt Elizabeth Shoveller of Portsea, Hampshire, died aged just 46 in 1868, with issue (see Chap.15).

8. William Henry SHOVELLER (1824 >1883), born 1824, married in 1854 at St Pancras, London to Mary Ann Smith (c.1829-?), with issue (see Chap.15).

9. Martha Shoveller (1826 - 1827)* born 1826, died 1827.

10. Thomas Eastman SHOVELLER (1827 - 1908), born 1827, voyaged throughout the Pacific, married on the 6th March 1856 at Anglican Church, Grafton, N.S.W. to Susan (1840-1918), the daughter of John Hann & Mary Matilda Thompson, died in 1908, with issue (see Chap.15 & 20).

* Died before adulthood - d.s.p.
(Some names not listed in the index).

---

had seating for up to 200 people. It was built of stone obtained from the demolition of Netley Abbey and was initially called Meeting House Alley, but known much later as Kent Street Baptist Chapel. By 1730 the congregation had raised sufficient funds to buy the chapel and in 1750 extended it to include a Baptistery. Prior to that date baptisms were carried out at Milton Farm, in the moat around Portsmouth or in the great morass on Southsea Common. The beginning of the 19th century saw five more chapels spring from the original congregation at Meeting House Alley.[1]

Descendants of William & Mary Shoveller

The Shoveller siblings Mary (1756), John (1760) and William (1764), had all been baptised into the Church of England at St Mary's Church in Portsea. While some of John and Mary Shoveller's ten grandchildren were also baptised into the Church of England, their religious devotion gradually shifted to the Baptists and Independents under the influence of ministers like the Rev. Joseph Horsey and the Rev. John Griffin. Indeed, all of William and Mary Shoveller's children were baptised into the independent faith. This movement was generally known as non-conformist or English Dissenters, which were essentially Protestant Christians who had separated from the Church of England during the 17th and 18th centuries.[2] English Dissenters opposed state interference in religious

William Shoveller Sr. 1764-1832 = Mary Bignell 1768-1825
m.1789 Church of Our Lady, Warnford, Hampshire

- William Shoveller Jr. 1791-1846 = Elizabeth Dunt 1793-1885
  m.1815 St Martin in the Fields, Westminster
- Mary Shoveller 1794-1865 = Rev. Thomas Stratten 1794-1854
  m.1821 St Mary's Church, Portsea, Hampshire
- Jane Shoveller 1796-1848 d.s.p.
- Elizabeth Shoveller 1798-1879 = James Roberton 1796-1861
  m.1822 St Mary's Church, Portsea, Hampshire

Children of William Shoveller Jr. & Elizabeth Dunt:
- William Shoveller 1816-1883 m.1837 Elizabeth Bailey 1814-?
- John Shoveller 1818-1871 m.1854 Mary Ann Rudkin 1830-?
- Robert Shoveller 1819-1872 d.s.p.
- Elizabeth Meta Shoveller 1821-1874 d.s.p.
- Hannah M. Shoveller 1827-1900 m.1873 James H. Roberton 1823-1890 d.s.p.
- Samuel Shoveller 1832-1918 m.1875 Margaret H. Morgan 1847-1901 emigrated to London, Ontario, Canada

Children of Mary Shoveller & Rev. Thomas Stratten:
- Mary Stratten 1822-1856 d.s.p.
- Frances Stratten 1824-1905 m.1849 John Shaw Westerdale 1820-1865
- Jane Stratten 1826-1885 d.s.p.
- Robert Stratten 1828-1904 m.1855 Elizabeth R. Linton 1834-1878
- Thomas Stratten 1830-1904 m.1857 Mary Irving 1835-1891 d.s.p.

Children of Elizabeth Shoveller & James Roberton:
- James H. Roberton 1823-1890 1m.1846 Mary E. Shoveller 1822-1868 2m.1873 Hannah M. Shoveller 1827-1900 d.s.p.

1st Cousins

Under William Shoveller 1816-1883:
- ...e, 1855-?
- ...liam, 1850>1922
1. Alice, ?>1933
2. Mary J., 1857-1933
3. John H., 1860-1943

Under Samuel Shoveller:
1. Hampton W., 1876-1951

Under Frances Stratten / John Shaw Westerdale:
1. Mary F., 1850-1938
2. Charlotte B., 1856-1944
3. Alice M., 1862-1927

Under Robert Stratten:
1. Mary G., 1858-1927
2. Frances E., 1859-1927
3. Edith A., 1862-1928
4. Thomas, 1863-?
5. Lucy A., 1865-1954
6. Robert A., 1872-1872

Under James H. Roberton:
1. Alice M., 1848-1848
2. Alfred J., 1850-1921
3. Henry S., 1852-1916

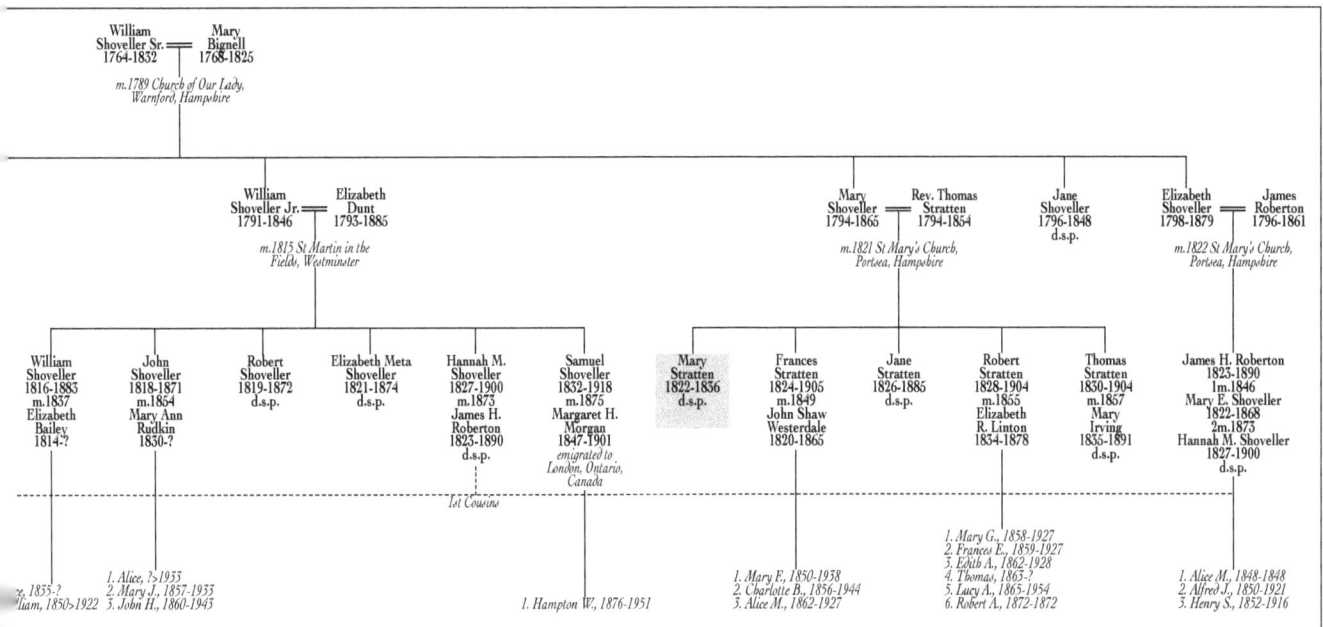

BURIALS in the Year 1846 in ALL SOULS' CEMETERY, established by The General Cemetery Company, under Stat. 2 & 3 WILLIAM IV. c. 110.

Name.	Abode.	When Buried.	Age.	By whom the Ceremony was performed.
William Shoveller No. 10130	21 Lisle Street Leicester Square St Ann Westminster	10 June 1846.	55.	Rev. R.N. Overbury

▲ William Shoveller Jr.- Burial held on the 10 June 1846 at All Souls' Cemetery, Kensal Green, London (England, C of E Deaths & Burials, 1813-2003).

matters, and founded their own churches, educational establishments and communities.[3] Many emigrated to the New World, especially to the 13 Colonies and Canada, where they played a pivotal role in the spiritual development of North America. What is known of William and Mary Shoveller's five children and their descendants to date is illustrated in Pedigree Chart 4.

1. Rev. Dr. John Shoveller (1789-1847)

The eldest son of William Shoveller and Mary Bignell was John Shoveller, who was born on the 21st October 1789, and baptised on the 6th November 1789 at the Skinner St. Independent Church in Poole, Dorset.[4] He was the youngest of his siblings to wed at the age of 23, when he married on the 24th March 1812 at St. Mary's Church in Portsea, to Elizabeth (1785-1852), the daughter of Thomas Eastman and Sarah Sabine of St George's Square, Portsmouth.[5] John soon after established a school he called 'King's House Academy' in Portsmouth, and later enrolled at Oxford University for a law degree. He and Elizabeth produced ten children, although only five survived to adulthood (*see 6.1 Descendants of Rev. Dr. John Shoveller & Elizabeth Eastman*). John Shoveller was destined to be the father of Thomas Eastman Shoveller, and his family and descendants are discussed in much greater detail in chapters 13 and 14.

Documents of William Shoveller Jr. & Elizabeth Dunt

◄1815 Marriage License for William Shoveller Jr. & Elizabeth Dunt (London and Surrey, England, Marriage Bonds and Allegations, 1597-1921). ▲LEFT: Attestation of birth and baptism for Elizabeth Dunt (24 June 1793). RIGHT: An 1880 photograph of Lisle St, entitled "No. 18 to 27 Lisle St, Soho," the home of William Shoveller Jr. & Elizabeth Dunt and family. ▼BELOW: 1885 Elizabeth Shoveller (nee Dunt) - Probate (England & Wales, National Probate Calendar (Index of Wills and Administrations), 1858-1995 [1885, Shackel-Szapira]).BOTTOM: Attestations of births and baptisms for the children of William Shoveller Jr. & Elizabeth (nee Dunt) - William Shoveller (16 May 1816), John Shoveller (19 June 1918), Robert Shoveller (9 Nov 1819), Elizabeth Meta Shoveller (14 Dec 1821), Hannah Mary Shoveller (14 Aug 1827), and Samuel Shoveller (23 March 1832).

SHOVELLER Elizabeth.

Personal Estate £548 1s. 9d.

25 July. Administration of the Personal Estate of Elizabeth Shoveller late of Almonry House Battle in the County of **Sussex** Widow who died 18 June 1885 at Almonry House was granted at the **Principal Registry** to Hannah Mary Roberton (Wife of James Roberton) of Almonry House the Daughter and one of the Next of Kin.

6.2 Descendants of William Shoveller Jr. & Elizabeth Dunt

Shoveller

Dunt

William SHOVELLER (1791-1846), born 1791. After moving to London he became a currier and married on the 13th May 1815 at St. Martin in the Fields, London to Elizabeth (1793-1885), daughter of John & Hannah Dunt, with issue:

1. William SHOVELLER (1816 - 1883), born in 1816, William was baptised on 16th May 1816 at Lisle St, London, Middlesex. He married in July 1837 at the Strand, London to Elizabeth Bailey (1814-?). William was a 'currier' involved in the leather trade and was residing at 33 Carter St, Newington at the time of the 1881 English Census. His death details are unknown, with issue:

1.1 Alice Shoveller (1835 - ?), possibly married in 1869, husband and issue unknown.

1.2 William SHOVELLER (1850>1922), leather merchant, married firstly to Kezia West (?-?), with issue:
  a. Florence H. Shoveller (1875-?)
William married secondly on the 8th Oct 1892 at St Andrews Church, Streatham, London to Georgiana (1867-1922), daughter of Edward Overton and Emily Lowe, with issue:
  b. Marjorie Georgiana Shoveller (1894-1976), no issue.

2. John SHOVELLER (1818 - 1871), born in 1818, John was baptised on 19th June 1818 at 21 Lisle St, London, Middlesex. He married in mid 1854 to Mary Ann Rudkin (1814-?) registered at St. Giles, London, with issue:

2.1 Mary Jane Shoveller (1857-1933), born 29th May 1857 in London, but emigrated to Canada about 1893, where she never married and died at York, Ontario on the 27th Dec 1933. She was buried at Prospect Cemetery on the 2nd Jan 1934. No issue.

2.2 John Henry SHOVELLER (1860-1943), emigrated to Canada, worked as a farmer and married on the 2nd October 1900, at York, Ontario to Mary Ellen Green (1866-?). Mary was also born in England, with issue:
  a. Ruth Shoveller (1902-1933).

2.3 Alice Shoveller (? >1933), emigrated to Canada, and signed the death certificate of her sister Mary Jane, but details of any marriage, issue or death are unknown.

3. Robert SHOVELLER (1819 - c.1872), born in 1819, Robert was baptised on 9th Nov 1819 at 21 Lisle St, London, Middlesex. At the time of the 1841 English Census he was residing with his parents at 21 Lisle St, Westminster, London. He may have married in 1860 to Mary Ann Harden (?-?) at Blean in Kent, and may have died there in 1872? Issue unknown.

4. Elizabeth Meta Shoveller (1821 - 1874), born in Dec 1821, Elizabeth Meta was baptised on 14th Dec 1821 at Gloucester Place, Kentiot Town. At the time of the 1841 English Census she was residing with her parents at 21 Lisle St, Westminster, London. She died a spinster at Thanet, Kent in April 1874. No issue.

5. Hannah Mary Shoveller (1827 - 1900), baptised on 14th August 1827 at 21 Lisle St, London, Middlesex. Hannah Mary lived for most of her life with her family until at the age of 46, she married her widowed first cousin James H. ROBERTON (1823-1890) on the 15th January 1873 at Whitefield's Memorial Church, London. She became mother to James' two adult sons, who would have known her from birth, as their true mother (Mary Elizabeth Shoveller) was also first cousin to both Hannah and James... it was a triangle of first cousins. Hannah died at Tunbrdge, Kent in 1900. No issue.

6. Samuel SHOVELLER (1832 - 1918), born on 23rd March 1832 at 21 Lisle St, London, Middlesex. He emigrated to Canada, arriving sometime before 1871, three of their great grandchildren in Mary Jane, John Henry and Alice Shoveller, as emigrants, as was recorded on the 1871 Canadian Census. He worked as a clerk and married on the 25th September 1875, at London, Middlesex, Ontario, Canada, to Margaret Harriet Morgan (1847-1901), who was born in Canada, according to the rites of the Baptist Church, with issue:

6.1 Hampton Walter Dunt SHOVELLER (1876-1951), married Liza Teresa Barley (1878-1945) on the 25th May 1898 at Lion's Head, Bruce County, Ontario, Canada, with issue:
  a. Morgan Erling SHOVELLER (1899-1945)
  b. Herbert Barley SHOVELLER (1902-1967)
  c. Walter Ross SHOVELLER (1905-?)

* Died before adulthood - d.s.p.
(Some names not listed in the index).

◀Three photographs of Almonry House, Battle in Sussex including the sitting room of the impressive home of Elizabeth Shoveller (nee Dunt).
▼A side view of the lead-light windows and blooming wisteria at the home of Elizabeth Shoveller (nee Dunt), at Almonry House. Almonry House, known earlier as the Almonry, is one of the more striking buildings in Battle, and behind it is a quiet and beautiful garden. A building may well have been there since the 1090s when Battle was first laid out by the monks.

2. William Shoveller Jr. (1791-1846)

The second son of William and Mary Shoveller was William Shoveller Jr., who was born on the 5th March and baptised on the 26th March 1791, which was officiated by Mr. William Dunn, Protestant Dissenting Minister, at their home in Queen St, Portsea.[6] William became a 'currier,' which was a specialist in the leather processing industry. After the tanning process, the currier applied the techniques of dressing, finishing and colouring to a tanned hide to make it strong, flexible and waterproof.[7] The leather is stretched and burnished to produce a uniform thickness and suppleness, and dyeing and other chemical processes give the leather its desired finish. After currying, the leather is then ready to pass to the fashioning trades such as saddlery, bridlery, shoemaking and glovemaking.[8]

William married on the 13th May 1815 at St Martin in the Fields, London to Elizabeth (1794-1885), the daughter of John and Hannah Dunt,[9] and the couple produced six children after moving to London (*see 6.2 Descendants of William Shoveller Jr. & Elizabeth Dunt*). William Shoveller Jr's family resided at 21 Lisle St, Leiscester Square for over 30 years, but he was the first of his five siblings to die in 1846, aged 55, being buried at All Souls

6.3 Descendants of Mary Shoveller & Rev. Thomas Stratten

Mary Shoveller (1794-1865), born in 1794, married on the 23rd May 1821 at St Mary's, Portsea, Hampshire to Rev. Thomas (1794-1854), son of Thomas Spender Stratten and Frances Dawes, with issue:

1. Mary Stratten (1822 – 1836), born 27th April 1822 at Bishop Wearmouth, Durham, England. She died at age 14 and was buried on the 30th Oct 1836, in the General Cemetery, Kingston Upon Hull.

2. Frances Stratten (1824 - 1905), born about 1824 possibly at Bishop Wearmouth, Durham. Frances married in 1st quarter of 1849 at Hull to John Shaw WESTERDALE (1820-1865), with issue:

2.1 Mary Frances Westerdale (1850-1938), married in 1872 at Hull to John William WRIGHT (1838-1883), with issue:
  a. Baby Wright (?-?)*
  b. Freda Wright (?-?)
  c. Hilda Wright (1874–1953), married in 1896 at Keighley, Yorkshire to John Clifton TOWN (1868–1944), JP, with issue.
  d. Winifred Wright (1876–1951), died a spinster, aged 75.
  e. Gertrude Mary Wright (1881-?), unknown.
  f. John Harold WRIGHT (1883-1978), married in 1921 at Keighley, Yorkshire to Sara 'Cis' Stell (1895–1974), with issue.
  g. Wilfred WRIGHT (1884-1961), married in 1915 at Knaresborough, Yorkshire, to Dorothea Elliot (1886–1961), with issue.

2.2 Charlotte Blyth Westerdale (1856-1944), married in 3rd quarter 1891 at Sculcoates, Yorkshire to Rev. James Samuel WOLSTENCROFT (1856-?), with issue:

Stratten *Shoveller*

a. Alfred Stratten WOLSTENCROFT (1894-1964), married in 2nd quarter of 1941 at Warwick, Warwickshire to Louisa Dorothy M. Folkes (1900-1976), no issue.
  b. Emily Agnes Wolstencroft (1896-1992), died a spinster, aged 96.

2.3 Alice Margaret Westerdale (1862-1927), died a spinster, aged 65 on 8th Sep 1927 at Glen-a-lua Hornyold Rd, Malvern, Worcestershire.

3. Jane Stratten (1826 - 1885), born 1826 and baptised 14 Nov 1826 at Bethel Chapel Villiers Street-Independent Church, Bishopwearmouth, Durham, England. She died as a spinster on the 31st March 1885 at Hallgate, Cottingham, Yorkshire.

4. Robert STRATTEN (1828 - 1904), born 27 Oct 1828 at

Bishopwearmouth, Durham, England. Married in 1855 to Elizabeth Robinson Linton (1834-1878). Died 3 April 1904 at Hessle, Yorkshire, England, with issue:

4.1 Mary Gertrude Stratten (1858-1927), married in 1891 at Sculcoates, Yorkshire to Alfred Lomas JOY (widower), no issue.

4.2 Frances Elizabeth Stratten (1859-1827), schoolteacher, died a spinster on 4th Jan 1927, buried at St Peter Cowleigh Bank's Church burial ground, Malvern, Worcestershire, England.

4.3 Edith Annie Stratten (1862-1928), died a spinster, buried at St Peter Cowleigh Bank's Church burial ground, Malvern, Worcestershire, England.

4.4 Thomas STRATTEN (1863-1943), unknown.

4.5 Lucy Agnes Stratten (1865-1954), an artist and sculptor, died a spinster.

4.6 Robert Arnold STRATTEN (1872-1872)*

5. Thomas STRATTEN (1830 - 1904), born 22 July 1830, baptised on 30 Aug 1830 at Bethel Chapel Villiers Street-Independent, Bishopwearmouth, Durham, England. Married on 8 July 1857 at Hull, Yorkshire to Mary Irving (1835-1891). Died 11 September 1904 at Kingston-Upon-Hull, Yorkshire, England, leaving a substantial sum of £23,017 to two apparently unrelated beneficiaries. No issue.

* Died before adulthood - d.s.p.
(Some names not listed in the index).

▲ *Thomas & Mary Stratten (nee Shoveller) resided at the grand Milton House, Anlaby Rd, at Kingston Upon Hull, Yorkshire.*

Documents of Mary Shoveller & Rev. Thomas Stratten

STRATTEN Mary.
Effects under £2,000.

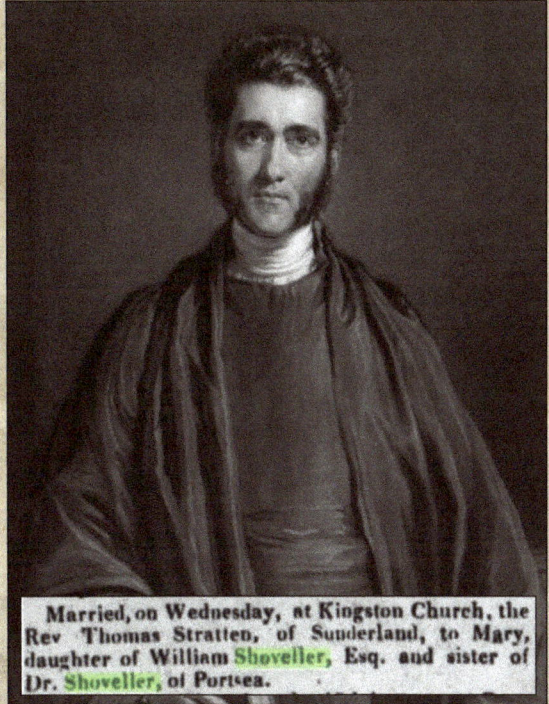

23 December. The Will of Mary Stratten late of the Borough of **Kingston-upon-Hull** Widow deceased who died 11 December 1865 at the Borough aforesaid was proved at **York** by the oath of Thomas Stratten of the Borough aforesaid Merchant the Son the sole Executor

STRATTEN Jane.
Personal Estate £1,457 19s. 11d.

15 May. The Will of Jane Stratten formerly of the Borough of Kingston-upon-Hull but late of Hallgate in Cottingham in the East Riding of the County of York Spinster who died 31 March 1885 at Cottingham was proved at York by Robert Stratten of Tower Hill in Hessle in the said East Riding Bank Manager and Thomas Stratten of Milton-terrace Anlaby-road Kingston-upon-Hull Gentleman the Brothers the Executors.

Married, on Wednesday, at Kingston Church, the Rev. Thomas Stratten, of Sunderland, to Mary, daughter of William Shoveller, Esq. and sister of Dr. Shoveller, of Portsea.

STRATTEN Mary of Milton-house Anlaby-road Kingston-upon-Hull (wife of Thomas Stratten) died 19 December 1891 Probate **London** 28 November to George Foster Holmes farmer Effects £16082 7s. 8d.

STRATTEN Robert of Hessle Yorkshire died 3 April 1904 Probate **London** 14 June to Thomas Stratten esquire Effects £1104 11s. 6d.

STRATTEN Thomas of 252 Anlaby-road Kingston-upon-Hull J.P. died 11 September 1904 Probate **York** 5 October to Michael Campbell gentleman and Alexander Porteous commercial-clerk Effects £23017 11s. 5d.

▲LEFT COLUMN: 1-Rev. Thomas Stratten & Family - Kingston Upon Hull (1841 England & Wales Census, Yorkshire, Myton, 7); 2-1865 Mary Stratten (nee Shoveller) - Probate (England & Wales, National Probate Calendar (Index of Wills and Administrations), 1858-1995 [1865, Saberton-Szabo]); 3-1885 Jane Stratten - Probate (England & Wales, National Probate Calendar (Index of Wills and Administrations), 1858-1995 [1885, Shackel-Szapira]). RIGHT: Rev. Thomas Stratten painted by Thomas Goff Lupton, after John Linnell. INSET: 1821 Mary Shoveller & Rev. Thomas Stratten - Marriage notice (Hampshire Chronicle, 28 May 1821). ABOVE: Probate for Mary Stratten (nee Irving) 1891, and Robert & Thomas Stratten, 1904 (England & Wales, National Probate Calendar (Index of Wills and Administrations), 1858-1995). ▼BELOW: The Fish Street Chapel at Kingston-Upon-Hull, ministry of Rev. Thomas Stratten, was built in 1782, at a cost of £1575, to replace Blanket Row. Enlarged in 1802 for 1,050 sittings, then restored and modernised, internally and externally in 1869. Demolished 1984, now covered by housing to the east of Fish Street.

▲ TOP (Left): Hull was heavily industrialised by the middle of the 19th century. (Right): Memorial for Rev. Thomas Stratten at the General Cemetery in Kingston-Upon-Hull, Yorkshire. ABOVE: Now completely demolished, the 'Thomas Stratten School' was established in 1880 in Londesborough Street, Hull, East Riding of Yorkshire.

Cemetery, London.[10] William's wife Elizabeth later moved to the town of Battle in Sussex, where she took up residence in the ancient, but beautiful 'Almonry House,' a listed building that may well have been there since the 1090s when the town of Battle was first laid out by the monks. Elizabeth outlived William by almost 40 years, before passing away in 1885.[11]

3. Mary Shoveller (1794-1865)

The eldest of William and Mary Shoveller's daughters was Mary Shoveller, who was baptised on the 14th October 1794, by the Rev. John Griffin at their home at 117 Queen St, Portsea.[12] After the death of her cousin Harriet in 1796, this Mary became quite close to her Aunt Mary and Uncle Robert Bowyer, possibly even residing with them for a time and as a result, she was bequethed an inheritance from the will of Bowyer's adopted daughter, Catherine Andras.[13] Mary married on the 23rd May 1821 at St. Mary's, Portsea, in Hampshire, by Rev. R.H. Cumyns to a congregational minister, the Rev. Thomas (1794-1854), son of Thomas Spender Stratten and Frances Dawes,[14] and the couple produced five children (*see 6.3 Descendants of Mary Shoveller & Rev. Thomas Stratten*).

Originally from Sunderland, the Rev. Thomas Stratten trained at Hoxton College and was appointed to the ministry at the Fish Street Congregational Church in Kingston-Upon-Hull in 1831. He was an able and valuable minister and was the author of several well-written tracts and sermons, like his contribution entitled "The Book of the Priesthood,"

Documents of Elizabeth Shoveller & James Roberton

James Roberton, Son of James and Eliza Roberton was born 31st May 1823 — and Baptised 30th Nov. 1823 in the Parish of Portsea. By me John Griffin

157

Married on Wednesday last, by the Rev. R. H. Cumyns, Mr. Roberton, linen-draper, High-street, Portsmouth, to Eliza, youngest daughter of Mr. William Shoveller, of Portsea.

ROBERTON Eliza.
Personal Estate under £2,000.

25 July. The Will of Eliza Roberton late of 33 Burghley - road Kentish Town in the County of **Middlesex** Widow who died 2 July 1879 at 33 Burghley-road was proved at the **Principal Registry** by James Roberton of 33 Burghley-road Gentleman the Son the sole Executor.

ROBERTON James.
Personal Estate £4,931 15s. 8d.

8 January. The Will with a Codicil of James Roberton formerly of 33 Burghley-road Highgate-road in the County of Middlesex afterwards of Battle in the County of Sussex but late of Tunbridge Wells in the County of **Kent** Gentleman who died 7 December 1890 at Tunbridge Wells was proved at the **Principal Registry** by Alfred James Roberton of Jerningham House Tunbridge Wells and Henry Shoveller Roberton of Jerningham House Gentlemen the Sons two of the Executors.

ROBERTON Alfred James of 20 Arundel-road **Tunbridge Wells** died 10 October 1921 Probate **London** 30 November to Frank Robertson bank official. Effects £1769 4s. 8d.

◄LEFT COLUMN: 1-James Roberton - Born 31 May & Baptised 30 Nov 1823 at King St (formerly Orange St) Independent Church), Portsea (England & Wales, Non-Conformist and Non-Parochial Registers, 1567-1936); 2-1822 Eliza Shoveller & Mr. Roberton - Marriage notice (Hampshire Chronicle, 1 July 1822); 3-1879 Eliza Roberton (nee Shoveller) - Probate England & Wales, National Probate Calendar (Index of Wills and Administrations), 1858-1995 [1879, Rabey-Sly]); 4-1890 James Roberton Jr. - Probate (England & Wales, National Probate Calendar (Index of Wills and Administrations), 1858-1995 [1891, Raay-Seys]); 5-1921 Alfred James Roberton - Probate (England & Wales, National Probate Calendar (Index of Wills and Administrations), 1858-1995 [1921, Quackenbush-Syrett]). ▼BELOW: James Henry Roberton & Mary Elizabeth Shoveller - Marriage held on 29th Sept 1846 at Parish Church, Banbury (Oxfordshire, England, Church of England Marriages and Banns, 1754-1930). BOTTOM: Marriage certificate for James [Henry] Roberton, widower & Hannah Mary Shoveller, held on the 15th January 1873 at Whitefields Memorial Church, and registered in the Parish of Pancras, London (England & Wales, Civil Registration Marriage Index, 1837-1915).

18**46**. Marriage solemnized at the Parish Church in the Parish of Banbury in the County of Oxford

No.	When Married.	Name and Surname.	Age.	Condition.	Rank or Profession.	Residence at the Time of Marriage.	Father's Name and Surname.	Rank or Profession of Father.
402	September 29th	James Roberton / Mary Elizabeth Shoveller	full / full	Bachelor / Spinster	Chemist / —	Charlton upon Medlock Lancashire / Horse Fair	James Roberton / John Shoveller	Gentleman / Independent Minister

Married in the Parish Church according to the Rites and Ceremonies of the Established Church by Licence by me, J. Marden

This Marriage was solemnized between us, James Roberton / Mary Elizabeth Shoveller
in the Presence of us, John Shoveller L.L.D. / John Shoveller junior / Jane Alice Shoveller

	MARRIAGE REGISTER.						MARRIAGE REGISTER.	
DATE OF MARRIAGE	NAME AND SURNAME	AGE	CONDITION	RANK OR OCCUPATION	RESIDENCE	FATHER'S NAME AND SURNAME	SIGNATURE OF OFFICIATING MINISTER	
1873 Jan 15 No. 24	James Roberton / ~~James Roberton~~	49	widower	Chemist	4 Maitland Park Road	James Roberton (deceased)	James Charles Lane	
	Hannah Mary Shoveller	45	Spinster	—	1 Dane Row Margate	William Shoveller (deceased)	witness by J. Woodward	

with another volume on the "Tithes." He took part in a vigorous controversy which raged in Hull on the subject of ecclesiastical establishments about the year 1834, and published a "Review of the Hull Ecclesiastical Controversy." A secession from his congregation took place in 1841 when Albion Chapel was erected for their accommodation.[15] The Rev. Thomas Stratten died in 1854 and his memorial stands in the General Cemetery at Kingston-Upon-Hull, Yorkshire.

> "By the early nineteenth century the population in Hull was increasing rapidly and the town was expanding. From well established congregations like that in Fish Street emerged other non-conformist churches, such as Nile Street (1827), Cogan Street (1833) and Albion Street (1842). It has even been said that Fish Street Congregational Church was one of the chief centres of non-conformist life in the whole country. Two noteworthy ministers at Fish Street were George Lambert (1769-1816) and Thomas Stratten (1832-1854). Stratten was particularly noted for opening the doors of membership more widely to the young and for improving the music of the church, the first church organ being built in 1853."

From... Hull History Centre: Fish St Congregational Church [16]

4. Jane Shoveller (1796-1848)

William and Mary Shoveller's second daughter Jane, was baptised on the 13th April 1796 by the Rev. John Griffin, at the Shoveller home at 117 Queen St, Portsea.[17] Unfortunately little is known of her, except that she never married and died in mid 1848, a spinster in Portsea, aged just 52.[18]

5. Elizabeth Shoveller (1798-1879)

Their final child Elizabeth Shoveller, otherwise known as 'Eliza', was born on 20th March 1798 and also baptised by the Rev. John Griffin, at the Shoveller home at 117 Queen St, Portsea.[19] Like her siblings, Elizabeth probably attended school in Portsmouth. She married on the 26th June 1822 at St. Mary's, Portsea to a draper named James Roberton (1796-1861). [20]A draper was originally a term for a retailer or wholesaler of cloth that was mainly for clothing, but they additionally operated as cloth merchants and haberdashers.

The surname of Roberton is of territorial origin from the ancient manor of that name, and was one of the oldest untitled families in the parish of Roberton, Lanarkshire in Scotland.

▲ TOP (Left): The Grade II listed 'Jerningham House', Tunbridge Wells, was the residence of James Henry Roberton. (Right): Memorial for John Henry Shoveller (1860-1943), a great grandson of William & Mary Shoveller, who emigrated to Ontario, Canada and died there in 1943. ABOVE: Photograph of Portsmouth Point, just 300m from John Shoveller's (bc.1737) ropery on East Street, c.1900. By 1848 all of William and Mary Shoveller's children and descendants had left Portsmouth.

▲ The son of Elizabeth & James Roberton, was James Henry Roberton, who worked as a chemist in the township of Tonbridge Wells, Kent. It was he that married his first cousin Mary Elizabeth Shoveller, at Banbury in 1846, the daughter of John Shoveller L.L.D., and sister of Thomas Eastman Shoveller, producing three children. After Mary's death in 1868, James Henry Roberton married another first cousin in Hannah Mary Shoveller, at Camden in 1873, but without issue.

James and Elizabeth Roberton managed to produce one son in James Henry Roberton (1823-1890), who was born on the 31 May 1823, and baptised 30th November 1823 by the Rev. John Griffin at the Orange St. (later King St.) Independent Church, Portsea.[21] After almost 40 years of marriage, James Roberton died in 1861, and Eliza Roberton (nee Shoveller) ended her days on the 2nd July 1879 at Chetwynd End, Shropshire, England.[22]

Their son and heir James Henry Roberton, became a pharmacist and wedded his first cousin, Mary Elizabeth Shoveller (1822-1868), the daughter of John Shoveller L.L.D. on the 29th September 1846 at St Mary's, Banbury, Oxfordshire,[23] from which marriage they produced a daughter and two sons. The daughter was Alice Mary Roberton (1848-1848), who was born at Chorlton, but died aged just six months on the 28th June 1848.[24] Their eldest son was Alfred James Roberton (1851-1921), who married in 1895 at Newton-Abbot, Devon to Mary Phillips (1857-?),[25] but he died without issue on the 10th October 1921.[26] The second son was Henry Shoveller Roberton (1852-1916), who married in October of 1886 at Tonbridge Wells, Kent to Annie Laura Elizabeth Edwards (1849-1939),[27] and died at Tonbridge in June 1916, issue unknown.[28]

Following the death of his first wife Mary Elizabeth in 1868, James Henry Roberton aged 50, married secondly on the 15th January 1873 at Camden, Middlesex to another first cousin in Hannah Mary Shoveller (1827-1900), the daughter of William Shoveller Jr., who was then 46, but without issue.[29]

The union between William and Mary Shoveller delivered five children, all of whom survived to adulthood and were baptised by dissenting ministers into the independent faith. Although William and Mary both remained in Portsmouth until their deaths, all their children and descendants gradually moved away from the port town.

The ancestral path to Thomas Eastman Shoveller descends through John Shoveller LLD, their first child and eldest son. This genealogy therefore continues with an examination of another Hampshire family to join the Shovellers through matrimony, who were the antecedents of John Shoveller's wife Elizabeth Eastman, which for convenience could be classified as the 'Eastman's of Portsmouth,' and it is their industrious story that must next be told.

References

1. History In Portsmouth - 'The Ebenezer Baptist Chapel' [http://historyinportsmouth.co.uk/places/ebenezer.htm].

2. Cross, F. L.; Livingstone, E. A., eds. (13 March 1997). The Oxford Dictionary of the Christian Church (3rd ed.). USA: Oxford University Press. p. 490.

3. Parker, Irene (1914). Dissenting academies in England: their rise and progress, and their place among the educational systems of the country (2009 2nd ed.). Cambridge University Press. ISBN 978-0-521-74864-3.

4. John Shoveller - Born on 21 Oct 1789, and baptism held on 6 Nov 1789 at the Independent Church, Poole, Dorset (England, Select Births and Christenings, 1538-1975).

5. John Shoveller & Elizabeth Eastman - Marriage held on the 24 March 1812, at St Mary's, Portsea (Hampshire Allegations for Marriage Licences, 1689-1837, Vol 2).

6. William Shoveller - Baptism held on 6 Nov 1789 at the family residence at Queen St on Portsmouth Common, Hampshire, Independent (England & Wales, Non-Conformist and Non-Parochial Registers, 1567-1936).

7. The Worshipful Company of Curriers - Historical Background [https://www.curriers.co.uk].

8. Wikipedia - Currier [https://en.wikipedia.org/wiki/Currier].

9. William Shoveller & Elizabeth Dunt - Marriage held on the 13 May 1815, at St Martin in the Fields, Westminster (London, England, Church of England Marriages and Banns, 1754-1921).

10. William Shoveller - Burial held on the 10 June 1846 at All Souls' Cemetery, Kensal Green, London (England, C of E Deaths & Burials, 1813-2003).

11. Elizabeth Shoveller (nee Dunt) - Died 18th June 1885, Probate (England & Wales, National Probate Calendar (Index of Wills and Administrations), 1858-1995 [1885, Shackel-Szapira]).

12. Mary Shoveller - Baptism held on 14 Oct 1794 at the family residence at Queen St on Portsmouth Common, Hampshire, Independent (England, Select Births and Christenings, 1538-1975).

13. Catherine Andras - Will, 1837 (England & Wales, Prerogative Court of Canterbury Wills, 1384-1858 [PROB 11: Will Registers [1839-1841], Piece 1910: Vaughan, Quire No 251-300 (1839)).

14. Mary Shoveller & Rev. Thomas Stratten - Marriage held on the 23 May 1821, at St Mary's, Portsea, Hampshire (England, Select Marriages, 1538–1973).

15. Genuki: HULL: Hull-Fish Street Congregational Church History up to 1868. [https://www.genuki.org.uk/big/eng/YKS/ERY/Hull/Hull-FishStreetCongChurch].

16. Hull History Centre: Fish Street Congregational Church [http://catalogue.hullhistorycentre.org.uk/files/l-dcfs.pdf].

17. Jane Shoveller - Baptism held on the 13 Apr 1796 at the family residence at Queen St on Portsmouth Common, Hampshire, Independent (England, Select Births and Christenings, 1538-1975).

18. Jane Shoveller - Death registration, 3rd quarter of 1848, Portsea Island, Hampshire (England & Wales, Civil Registration Death Index, 1837-1915).

19. Elizabeth Shoveller - Born on 20 Mar 1798, and baptised at the family residence at Queen St on Portsmouth Common, Hampshire, Independent (England, Select Births and Christenings, 1538-1975).

20. Elizabeth Shoveller & James Roberton - Marriage held on the 26 Jun 1822, at St. Mary's Church, Portsea, Hampshire (England, Select Marriages, 1538–1973).

21. James Roberton - Born 31 May & Baptised 30 Nov 1823 at King St (formerly Orange St) Independent Church), Portsea (England & Wales, Non-Conformist and Non-Parochial Registers, 1567-1936).

22. Eliza Roberton (nee Shoveller) - Died 2nd July 1879, Chetwynd End, Shropshire - Probate (England & Wales, National Probate Calendar (Index of Wills and Administrations), 1858-1995 [1879, Rabey-Sly]).

23. James Henry Roberton & Mary Elizabeth Shoveller - Marriage held on the 29th Sept 1846 at Parish Church, Banbury (Oxfordshire, England, Church of England Marriages and Banns, 1754-1930).

24. Alice Mary Roberton - Burial held on the 28th June 1848 at Manchester (UK, Records of the Removal of Graves and Tombstones, 1601-1980).

25. Alfred James Roberton & Mary Phillips - Marriage held 2nd quarter of 1895, registered at Newton Abbot, Devon (England & Wales, Civil Registration Marriage Index, 1837-1915).

26. Alfred James Roberton - Death on 10 Oct 1921 at Tunbridge Wells, Kent, Probate granted 30 Nov 1921(England & Wales, National Probate Calendar [Index of Wills and Administrations], 1858-1966, 1973-1995).

27. Henry Shoveller Roberton & Annie Laura Elizabeth Edwards - Marriageheld in 1887 (

28. Henry Shoveller Roberton - Death registered 2nd quarter 1916 at Tonbridge Wells, Kent (England & Wales, Civil Registration Death Index, 1916-2007).

29. James H. Roberton (widower) & Hannah Mary Shoveller - Marrriage held on the 15th January 1873 at Whitefields Memorial Church, and registered in the Parish of Pancras, London (England & Wales, Civil Registration Marriage Index, 1837-1915).

Chapter Seven

THE EASTMAN ANCESTORS
(Maternal paternal antecedents of Thomas Eastman Shoveller)

While genealogy has been defined as "an account or history of the descent of a person or family from an ancestor; the enumeration of ancestors and their children in natural order of succession," it is sometimes asked "of what use is it?" 'The question might with almost equal propriety be asked concerning the kindred sciences of history and biography, for if there is utility in preserving a record of events, or of the life and character of individuals, then science which embraces, as it is now understood and practiced, in a considerable degree both these features, must also be interesting and profitable.

The founders of Portsmouth and Portsea were a reverent, conscientious and industrious people, and a consideration of their lives, their hardships and their achievements, cannot fail to prove salutary. It is both a natural and honorable ambition on the part of any man to have his genealogy traced, but unfortunately there are some who cannot see the necessity or desirableness of having their pedigrees ascertained, or of preserving any papers or documents bearing upon them, that they may have their descent defined and arranged in authentic genealogical order.

Most people appear content with mere tradition and simple details of their lineage, without being at pains to authenticate them by reference to proper records or regular genealogical authorities. But to their credit, the Eastmans in general, have taken a good deal of interest in the subject. There is a satisfaction to most persons in being able to trace their lineage to remote ancestors, in knowing where they lived, and what scenes and hardships, prosperity and adversity, they passed through, and in recollecting what benefits they conferred on their posterity.

Number of Eastman families

- 88 - 174
- 30 - 87
- 1 - 29

from the 1891 England and Wales Census Data

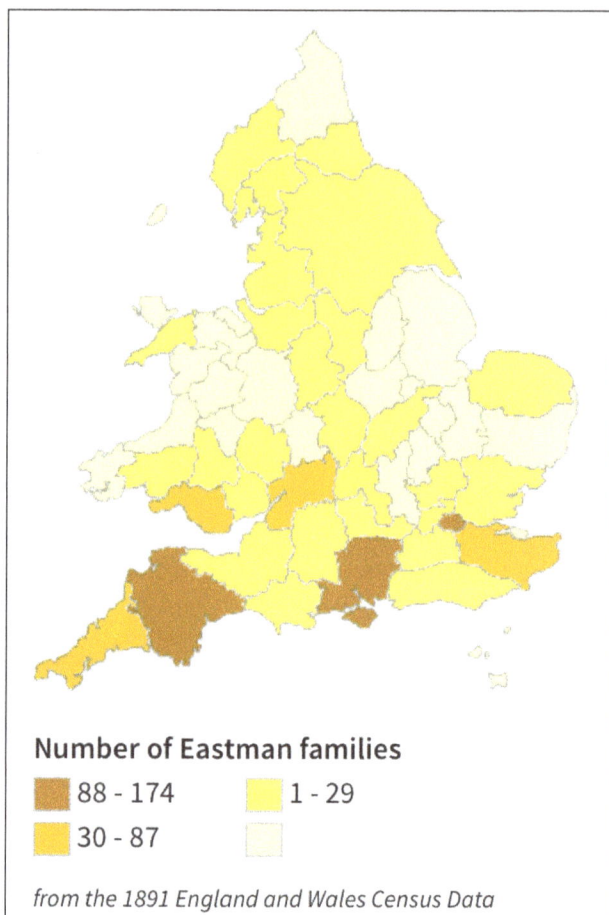

▲ *LEFT: The Portsmouth waterfront was a constant hive of activity. RIGHT: Distribution and density of Eastman families across England and Wales in 1891.*

Although nothing certain is known of Roger Eastman previous to his emigrating to America, his origins in Salisbury serve as a suitable epoch from which to commence an account of his family and descendants. Roger Eastman and the first settlers in Salisbury and adjoining towns were Puritans and as such were under the tyranny of the Tudors and Stuarts, and many left their native country to enjoy civil and religious liberty. They did not strive to accumulate property, to live in ease and splendor, or acquire fame. They had vastly higher and holier views and aims, to obey God and prepare themselves for heaven.

These sons of the forest had sound hearts, were firm in their resolutions and persevering in effort. Their faith in God never failed. They kept constantly in view the grand design of their emigration to America and overcoming the wilderness. It might under other circumstances seem unbecoming in us to speak of the virtues of the descendants of our ancestors, but in a history of the family it would seem strange if we did not find some who rose to eminence. We find more of the Eastman name in America who became college graduates than any other. Many have become ministers, lawyers, members of congress and many have held other public positions. Many have also been mechanics, inventors and farmers.[1]

The Surname of Eastman

The English surname Eastman is patronymic in origin, being derived from the name of the father, in this case, Eastman means "son of Easthund." This surname derives from the Olde English pre 7th century personal name Eastmund, a compound of the element 'east' meaning 'grace,' plus 'mund,' protection. The name is first recorded as Estmunt in the

Domesday Book of 1086 for Suffolk. One Ricardus filius (son of) Estmund appears in the 1195 "Pipe Rolls of Essex." In the Hundred Rolls of Cambridge for the year 1273 there is a record of Geoffrey, Cecil and Hugh Esthund.[2] Over the years the ending of the name was changed to 'man.'

First found in Suffolk, England, where they held a family seat from very ancient times, the surname emerges in the early half of the 13th century, when a John Eastmunde was recorded in the 1277 "Assize Court Rolls of Somerset" and an Alan Esmund in the 1285 "Fine Court Rolls of Essex." In the 'modern' idiom the name has a number of variations including Eastmunt, Esmund, Estman, Yeastman, Eestman, Eastmun, Eastmen, Eastmin, Eastment, Astman, Esmond and Esmonde.

While research into the Eastman family is ongoing, it is obviously an old family and it seems likely that the origins of this branch of the Eastman's were from Portsmouth, in Hampshire. On the 23rd May 1686, Allexander Eastman, an infant was christened in St. Katherines by the Tower, London. An early recorded spelling of the family name is shown to be that of Stephen Estmund, a witness, which was dated 1227, in the "Assize Court Rolls of Buckinghamshire," during the reign of King Henry III, who was known as "The Frenchman." Some of the first settlers of this family were Roger Eastman, who settled in Massachusetts in 1636, Mary Eastman, who immigrated to Maryland in 1671, and James Eastman, who arrived in Barbados in 1679.

The Eastman Blazon

The Eastman blazon is described in latin as 'gules in the dexter chief point an escutcheon

▲ *The Portsmouth Point pubs were a favourite site for Auctioneers like Thomas Eastman, painting by P. Richardson (1904).*

argent charged with a lion rampant sable.' Gules denotes military fortitude and magnanimity. The lion signifies strength, courage and a foe against fear. Sable denotes prudence, mystery and secrecy. In English it is a red shield with a silver gold escutcheon in dexter chief, charged with a black lion.

The crest is a swan collared and lined proper. An advisor with Burke's Peerage in 1991, explained that the collared swan at the top of the crest signifies the Eastman family were connected to royalty by way of servitude in the arts. They were most likely court poets and musicians at the time this crest was designed, as the collar with the chain signifies the lack of personal freedom. The crest also signifies protection, grace and favour, all traits one would need to be affiliated with royalty.

Eastmans of Downton & Nunton, Wiltshire

During the summer of 1910 the Downton parish register was searched for Eastman records by Charles R. Eastman, when some notes on the origin of the Downton Eastmans of Wiltshire were published in the Granite Monthly, a New Hampshire magazine, for December of that year and the following October.[3] Thanks to the generosity at that time of Mr. George Eastman of Rochester, New York, it was possible to engage the services of an expert antiquary, Mr. Charles H. Hoppin, for the purpose of making a complete transcript of the early Eastman family records preserved in the Wiltshire archives. From the large quantity of material collected by this historian a selection was made relating to the direct

'Ships off the Gunwharfe at Portsmouth, 1770', by Dominic Serres (c.1792-93) from the National Maritime Museum, Greenwich.

ancestral line of the pioneer, and previously mentioned American colonist Roger Eastman.

The progenitor of this line of whom authentic records have been preserved was John Eastman of Charleton, who left his original will dated 26th April 1564, which was proved on the 9th May 1565. He noted therein that his father was buried in "the churche of Saynt Lawrence in Downton" and directed that he also be buried there. John had at least two sons including Roger, and made bequests to William, "my sonne" and to William's children in John, William, Walter and Florence. He named his son Roger as his Executor, and granted bequests to him and his sons John and William.[4] The Latin note appended to John Eastmans will may be modernized as follows:

> "The above-written will of John Estmann, late of Downton In our Jurisdiction of the Archdeaconry of Salisbury, deceased, was proved before Master John James, bachelor of law, official of the Lord Archdeacon of Salisbury, on the ninth day of the month of May in the year of our Lord 1565, and by him approved, etc., and [administration] was granted, etc."
>
> *From... "English Origin of the Eastman Family", by Charles R. Eastman* [5]

There is also a John Eastman Sr. of Nunton, an adjoining village, who may have been a cousin of John of Charleton. John of Nunton also left a will that was found in the Archdeaconry Court of Sarum (modern Salisbury), dated 23 December 1557.[6] In it he named various Eastmans, presumably related, including Raffe of Charleton, Alen of Charleton, John of Charleton, Richard of Charleton, John of West Harnham "and Roger Eastman his brother of Downton," Walter (spelled "water") of Charleton, William of Charleton, and Joan, "the daughter of Roger Eastman."[7]

Roger Eastman's father John Eastman, died in February 1604 and was buried on the 17th of that month. His original will is on file in the Consistory Court of Sarum. He had seven or eight children, among whom was Nicholas, born between 1564 and 1570 (probably after the death of his grandfather, John). Roger married Barbara (surname probably Rooke), also of Charleton, but died after 1625. His eldest brother was William, born before 1564, who married an Edith, who died in 1605. William remarried two years later, but the name of his second wife has not survived. He and his eight sons resided in Downton, Wiltshire and included William, John, Nicholas, Edith (d. 1607), Walter, Roger, Mary and Thomas.

Until comparatively recently nothing was known of the origin of the Eastman family of America beyond the fact that the first colonist of that name in New England, Roger Eastman, sailed for Boston in the ship "Confidence" in 1638, and was one of the original settlers at Salisbury in Massachusetts Bay. The new settlement by the name of 'Merrimac' was founded largely by Wiltshire emigrants, and a number of these, including heads of families by the names of Rolfe, Sanders, Whittier and Eastman, came from the parish of Downton, a few miles south of the shire town of Wiltshire.

Another of the earliest Eastmans was John Eastman, of Romsey in county Southampton, who was buried in the Abbey at Romsey. His will dated 24th September 1602, was proved on the 22nd October 1602:

"To son Roger Eastman all lands whatsoever in default to son John, also to Roger, 100 marks at 14, to be paid by my father Roger Eastman, to my son John 50 pounds at 14, to daughter Elizabeth and Margaret when 21 or married 40 pounds each. Ditto to child my wife now goith with, to servant Elizabeth Head 5 pounds. Residuary legate and executrix, wife Anne; overseers, Roger Eastman, Michael Mackeall and Mathew Mundsy. Witnesses: Walter Godfrey, Giles Newe, Thomas Stote."

From..."History & Genealogy of the Eastman Family in America," by G.S. Rix [8]

▲ The Spice Island Inn on Portsmouth Point was conceived in 1991. Originally three old smugglers pubs, the building is Grade II listed and dates back to the 1700's, the name was derived from being the first place spices were landed from Jamaica.

EASTMAN, Edward, of Basingstoke, publican, & Jane Holder, of the s., sp., at B., or Basing, 24 Nov., 1723.

EASTMAN, Lawrence, of Alton, barber, b., & Anne Bayley, of the s., sp., at A., or Holybourne, 4 March, 1708.

EASTMAN, Joseph, of Shirley, gardener, w., & Sarah Jameson, of Millbrook, w., at M., 13 Aug., 1808. John Eastman, of Shirley, bondsman.

EASTMAN, Joseph, of Shirley, publican, w., & Mary Haynes, of All Saints, Southampton, 21, sp., at A. S., 7 Dec., 1813.

EASTMAN, Thomas, of Alton, felmonger, & Ann Taylor, of Stratton, sp., at Brown Candover, or S., 18 Sep., 1736.

▲ TOP: A crowd watches the arrival of Royal Navy ships at Portsmouth Harbour, c.1780, by Thomas Rowlandson (V&A Museum). ABOVE: Records of early Eastman marriage licences in Hampshire (England, Allegations for Marriage Licences, Vol, 1, 1689-1837).

Thomas Eastman & Baptism

Unfortunately, none of these branches have proved a line of descent to our ancestor Thomas Eastman (c.1752-1816) of Portsmouth, and more research is necessary before any possible links can be verified. While the ancestral path to Thomas Eastman Shoveller stems from Thomas Eastman, unfortunately no Eastman ancestors have been identified earlier than the mid-1750s. However, his 1816 headstone stated that he was 64, revealing that Thomas Eastman was likely born around the year 1752,[9,10] most probably in the vicinity of Hampshire, but not being able to substantiate his birth or parentage precludes further research into his Eastman ancestry at this stage.

Despite the following possibilities being recorded across England from 1745 to 1756, research has not been able to verify a birth or baptism for Thomas Eastman in Hampshire or elsewhere:

1745 Thomas Eastman - Baptism held 20 Jan 1745 at Heworth, Durham (Peter Eastman - Father, from England Births & Christenings,1538-1975)

1747 Thomas Eastman - Baptism held 12 Mar 1747 at Gwennap, Cornwall (Henry & Mary Eastman - Parents, from England Births & Christenings,1538-1975)

1750 Thomas Eastman - Baptism held 26 Jan 1750 at Gwennap, Cornwall (William & Jane Eastman - Parents, from England Births & Christenings,1538-1975)

1753 Thomas Eastman - Baptism held 9 Feb 1753 at Bideford, Devon (William & Christian Eastman - Parents, from England Births & Christenings,1538-1975) - Married Grace (Harding) Rodd.

1753 Thomas Eastman - Baptism held 18 Feb 1753 at St Sepulchre Newgate, London (John & Mary Eastman - Parents, from England Births & Christenings,1538-1975)

1754 Thomas Eastman - Baptism held 27 Aug 1754 at Bull Lane Independent, Stepney, London (John & Lydia Eastman - Parents, from England Births & Christenings,1538-1975)

1756 Thomas Eastman - Baptism held 21st November 1756 at Saint George The Martyr, Canterbury, Kent (Edward & Hester Eastman - Parents).

Our Thomas Eastman could be amongst any of the above, or there may even be other as yet unidentified baptisms. Unfortunately, the lack of evidence prevents any speculation into Thomas's background at this stage. All that appears certain and verifiable for the existence of Thomas Eastman begins with his marriage on Christmas Day of 1780 in Portsmouth.

Although evidence shows that Thomas Eastman married Sarah Sabine in 1780, not knowing his parents precludes further speculation into the Eastman ancestry at this stage. However, what of his wife Sarah Sabine? Although the lives and descendants of Thomas and Sarah Eastman are explored in detail in chapters 11 and 12, it is through Sarah Sabine that yet another ancestral branch of Thomas Eastman Shoveller eminates. Therefore, this genealogy continues with an examination of the origins of the Sabine family, and it is their remarkable genealogy that must next unfold.

References

1. Rix, G.S. (1905). 'History And Genealogy Of The Eastman Family In America,' Concord, New Hampshire, pp.5-6.

2. Geni - Eastman Genealogy and Eastman Family History Information [https://www.geni.com/surnames/eastman].

3. Eastman, Charles R., (1917). 'Genealogy of the Harvey Eastman (1777-1829) Branch of the Eastman Family,' Pub. by G. Eastman.

4. Eastman, Charles R., (c.1912). "A Sixteenth Century Eastman Will," The Granite Monthly, pp.372-373.

5. The New York Genealogical and BiOj-Tiraphical Record. See also article on the English Origin of the Eastman Family, by Charles R. Eastman, in the Granite Monthly, December, 1910.

6. John of Nunton will at Archdeaconry Court of Sarum (modern Salisbury), dated 23 December 1557 [Book-4, Folio-117].

7. Eastman, Charles R., (1911). "Wills of Early English Eastmans," The Granite Monthly, Oct, pp. 312-314.

8. Rix, G.S. (1905). op. cit., p.7.

9. Thomas Eastman, Buried on the 21 Nov 1816 at Titchfield, Hampshire (Vital, England, Hampshire Bishop's Transcripts, 1680-1892).

10. Thomas Eastman, Buried on the 21 Nov 1816 at Titchfield, Hampshire (England, Select Deaths & Burials, 1538-1991).

Chapter Eight

THE SABINE ANCESTORS
(Maternal maternal antecedents of Thomas Eastman Shoveller)

The ancient Sabines were an Italic people that lived in the central Apennine Mountains of the Italian Peninsula, also inhabiting Latium north of the Anio well before the founding of Rome. They divided into two populations just after Rome's beginning, which is described by Roman legend although the division, however it came about, is not legendary. The population closer to Rome transplanted itself to the new city and united with the pre-existing citizenry, beginning a new heritage that descended from the Sabines, but was also latinized. The second population remained a mountain tribal state, coming finally to war against Rome for its independence along with all the other Italic tribes. Afterwards, it too became assimilated into the Roman Republic.[1]

The Sabines of Rome

There is little record of the Sabine [*pronounced 'Say-bin'*] language, however there are some glosses by ancient commentators, and one or two inscriptions have been tentatively identified as Sabine. There are also personal names in use on Latin inscriptions from the Sabine country, but these are given in Latin form. Robert Seymour Conway, in his 'Italic Dialects,' gives approximately 100 words, which vary from being well-attested as Sabine to being possibly of Sabine origin. In addition to these he cites place names derived from the

Sabine, sometimes giving attempts at reconstructions of the Sabine form.[2] Based on all the evidence, the Linguist List tentatively classifies Sabine as a member of the Umbrian group of Italic languages of the Indo-European family of latin-speakers called the Sabine's. Their territory originally straddling the modern regions of Lazio, Umbria and Abruzzo Sabinum. To this day, it bears the ancient tribe's name in the Italian form of Sabina. Within the modern region of Lazio (or Latium), Sabina constitutes a sub-region, situated north-east of Rome, around Rieti.

The origins of these Sabines cannot be determined with certainty, but they are believed to have occupied the region of current Lazio since prehistoric times and, once the Roman Republic was established, they assimilated into the culture and became citizens of Rome.[3,4]

Dionysius regarded Lista as the mother-city of the Aborigines.[5] Ancient historians debated the specific origins of the Sabines. Zenodotus of Troezen claimed that the Sabines were originally Umbrians that changed their name after being driven from the Reatine territory by the Pelasgians. However, Porcius Cato argued that the Sabines were a populace named after Sabus, the son of Sancus, a divinity of the area sometimes called Jupiter Fidius.[6] In another account mentioned in Dionysius's work, a group of Lacedaemonians fled Sparta since they regarded the laws of Lycurgus as too severe. In Italy, they founded the Spartan colony of Foronia, near the Pomentine plains, and some from that colony settled among the Sabines. According to this account, the Sabine habits of belligerence, aggressive or warlike behavior

The Rape of the Sabine Women[62]

According to Roman historian Livy, the abduction of the Sabine women occurred in the early history of Rome shortly after its founding in the mid-8th century BC and was perpetrated by Romulus and his predominantly male followers. It is said that after the foundation of the city, the population consisted solely of Latins and other Italic people, in particular male bandits. With Rome growing at such a steady rate in comparison to its neighbours, Romulus became concerned with maintaining the city's strength. His main concern was that with few women inhabitants there would be no chance of sustaining the city's population, without which Rome might not last longer than a generation. On the advice of the Senate, the Romans then set out into the surrounding regions in search of wives to establish families with. The Romans negotiated unsuccessfully with all the peoples that they appealed to, including the Sabines, who populated the neighbouring areas. The Sabines feared the emergence of a rival society and refused to allow their women to marry the Romans. Consequently, the Romans devised a plan to abduct the Sabine women during the festival of Neptune Equester. They planned and announced a program of games to attract people from all the nearby towns. According to Livy, many people from Rome's neighboring towns, including Caeninenses, Crustumini, and Antemnates attended the festival along with the Sabines, eager to see the newly established city for themselves. At the festival, Romulus gave a signal by "rising and folding his cloak and then throwing it round him again," at which the Romans grabbed the Sabine women and fought off the Sabine men. In total, thirty Sabine women were abducted by the Romans at the festival. All of the women abducted were said to have been virgins except for one married woman, Hersilia, who became Romulus' wife and would later be the one to intervene and stop the ensuing war between the Romans and the Sabines. The indignant abductees who were captured and not actually raped, were implored by Romulus to accept the Roman men as their new husbands.

▲LEFT: A Roman Republican denarii, minted by Lucius Titurius Sabinus in 89 BC. The Sabine king Titus Tatius is portrayed on the obverse. The reverse depicts the abduction of the Sabine women by Roman soldiers. RIGHT: The worship of Semo Sancus Sanctus Dius Fidius was imported into Rome at a very early period by the Sabines who first colonized the Quirinal Hill in Rome.

▲ *'The Rape of the Sabine Women' was a popular theme for classical artists, such as in this piece by Peter Paul Rubens (1639-40).*

and prudence in avoiding waste were known to have derived from the Spartans.[7] Plutarch also mentions, in the 'Life of Numa Pompilius' that the, "Sabines, declared themselves to be a colony of the Lacedaemonians." Plutarch also wrote that Pythagoras of Sparta, who was Olympic victor in the foot-race, helped Numa arrange the government of the city and many Spartan customs introduced by him to the Numa and the people.[8]

Tradition suggests that the population of the early Roman kingdom was the result of a union of Sabines and others. Some of the gentes of the Roman republic were proud of their Sabine heritage, such as the Claudia gens, assuming Sabinus as a cognomen or agnomen. Some specifically Sabine deities and cults were known at Rome eg., Semo Sancus and Quirinus, and at least one area of the town, the Quirinale, where the temples to those latter deities were located, had once been a Sabine centre. The extravagant claims of Varro and Cicero that augury, divination by dreams and the worship of Minerva and Mars originated with the Sabines are disputable, as they were general Italic and Latin customs, as well as Etruscan, even though they were espoused by Numa Pompilius, second king of Rome and a Sabine.[9]

It is probably true to say that the surname Sabin(e) is the subject of more curiosity and guesswork than any of those other English surnames which are reminiscent of the classical age of Europe, such as Alexander, Valentine, Phillips, Austin, Hilary, Oliver, Anthony and so on. Of course the connection between the Sabine heritage of Italy and the Sabine surname is purely coincidental, although its influence cannot be completely ruled out. What is apt to come first into the mind of a person who encounters the name Sabin(e) is the romantic

▲ *Early photograph of 'Hammonds Bridge' at Titchfield, Hampshire, by Raphael Tuck & Sons Ltd, London.*

story of the seizure of the ancient Italian Sabines, as French and English history books translate. This mental association is rather different in character from that which occurs in the case of the other classical surnames. Part of the reason for this is that the name Sabin(e) is associated with a tribe, while the other names are associated with individuals, such as Alexander the Great, Macaulay's "stout Austin," and Mark Antony the lover of Cleopatra. The encounterer of a Sabin(e) thinks, with remarkable confidence, that he has before him a descendant of the ancient Sabines or Romans. Yet it is safe to say that this ready assumption is never paralleled by his regarding an Alexander or a Phillips as a representative of the Macedonians or the Greeks.

The Surname of Sabine[10]

Before saying more of the true origin and character of the surname Sabin(e), let it be acknowledged that the classical association that Sabin(e) parents have sometimes been led into bestowing Roman or Italian Christian names on their innocent offspring, is very powerful. This accounts for the first name of Lorenzo Sabine (1803-1877), a distinguished New England writer and legislator, whose ancestors emigrated from England in the early part of the 17th century. He was fortunate as compared with one of his cousins, who faced the world under the given style of Alberto. Less terrifying were the mainly neo-Latin names of the seven children of Thomas Sabine, an attorney of Dorchester, all born between 1808 and 1816, who were: Dorseti John Edmund, Gustavus Adolphus, Lucius Theodore, Georgina Theresa, Harriet Sophia, Julia Frances and Louisa Maria.

In the course of time such baptismal names came to be used as hereditary surnames. The main process of adopting hereditary surnames took place in England approximately between 1250 and 1550, for though the use of surnames had been introduced from France by the Romans at the time of the Conquest, the practice was then only at its beginning even among the French, and was very slow to be adopted in England.[11] The English surname

Sabin(e) was originally a personal or baptismal name, as was cited in the opening paragraph of this discussion, like a vast number of other names like Randolph, John(s), Edward(s), Miles (Milo), Godwin, Pearce, William(s), Geoffrey, Thomas etc.

The surname Sabin(e) has not been entirely the result of the adoption of an exotic name under the influence of Norman culture or of classical learning. It was sometimes a conversion of the Anglo-Saxon names Savin, Sawin, Sewine and Sibwine, all of which forms are found on coins of the period, and in the Domesday Book as Sbern, Sebbi, Sibbi and Saba (a diminutive of Saebeorht or Saberct) were likewise pre-Conquest names, which possessed the potentiality of being Latinized or Gallicized into Sabin(e). Indeed, after the Conquest, when Saxon names were regarded with disfavour, when the Saxon language was confined to the lower orders of society, and when all writing was done in French and Latin, such changes did not even depend on the volition of the name owners. The unlettered, that is the vast majority were at the mercy of the clerks, who recorded people's names in such forms as were suggested by their own taste, knowledge and by how they were pronounced.[12]

It is unquestionable that the story of the seizure of the Sabinae, 'the Sabine women' was the reason why Sabine became an extremely popular baptismal name, which records reveal it to have been during the 13th, 14th and 15th centuries. This popularity may seem a little surprising today, but it must be remembered that in the feudal period people looked for inspiration to other sources than novels and films. The story of the Sabines was then no mere piece of academic knowledge, nor was its telling restricted by the dark repressive spirit that later descended on England. It was popular history, like the history of Alexander the Great, whose name in a variety of spellings, has become one of the commonest surnames in almost every country of Europe.

As a symbol of feminine desirability, Sabin was also considered an appropriate name for a girl, as was Alexander for boys, but as surnames were mainly inherited from the fathers,

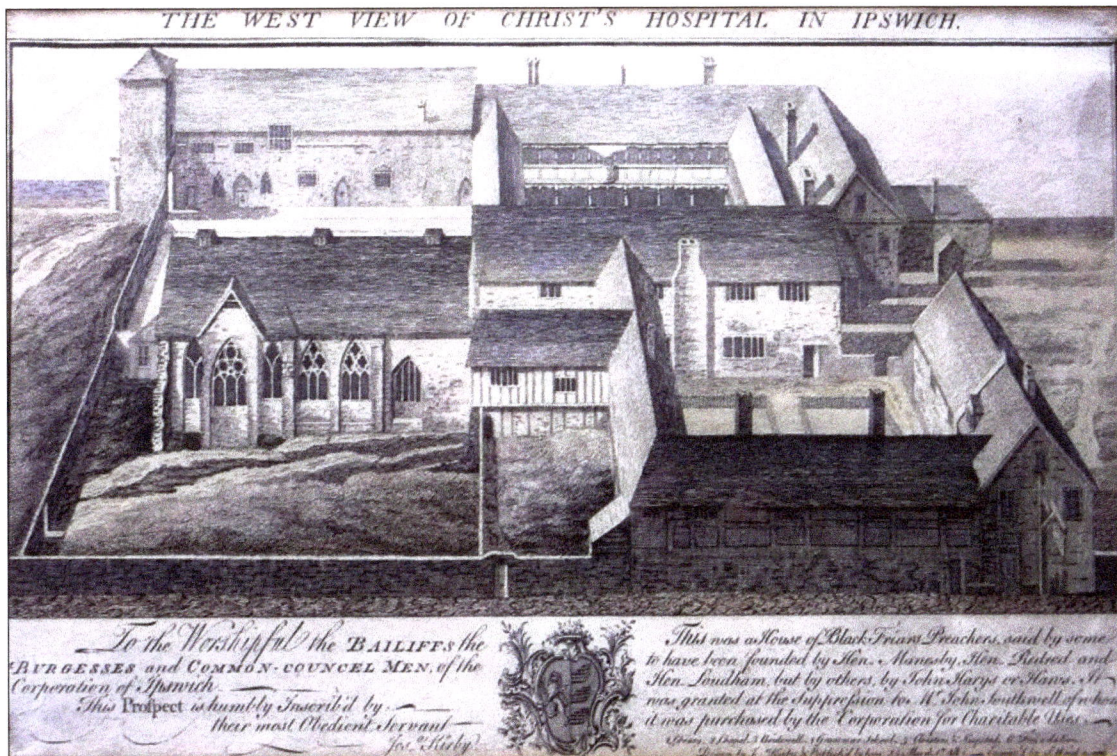

▲ Conventual buildings of Ipswich Blackfriars, which were sold by a William Sabyn in 1541, as they appeared to Joshua Kirby in 1748.

Sabin(e) has not survived as a surname to anything like the same extent as Alexander. It is however, a more frequent name in England than in France, where possibly the Salique law, which denied succession to females, may have tended to lesson its inheritance.[13] Thus, while Sabin(e) is partly a continuation of ancient Germanic name forms, it owes its present form to the fame of the Roman legend among the Norman-English. But the classical spelling did not completely triumph for Sabben, Savin and Sawin may still be encountered. It is the same for Sabb and Sabey, which are diminutives of Sabin(e), and signify "little Sabin(e)" or "the child of Sabin(e)." For example, the name of Alderman Avery Sabine, mayor of Canterbury, was variously spelled Sabine, Savine, Sabyn and Savin, even in the same official document; and Sabin, Sabins, Sab and Sabey were significantly grouped together in the tiny county of Huntingdon, as shown by its early wills.[14]

The Origins of Sabine in England

A paper written by W. H. W. Sabine provides a list of instances of Sabine surnames from 600-1200AD, with 'Savin' occurring frequently in the Domesday Book (*see Appendix D*).[15] In England, the common variants were represented by Sabin, Sabine and Sabyn in Cambridgeshire and Norfolk in the 13th century. The Anglo-Saxon name Sabine comes from Sabinus and Sabine, which are the masculine and feminine forms of the name, respectively. There were three saints named Sabinus and one named Sabine, but "in England, the woman's name was much the more common."

The surname Sabine was first found in Norfolk where a record of that name was discovered in the Latin form Sabina (1186-1210) and then in the Curia Regis Rolls for Kent and Surrey in 1220. Later in Huntingdonshire, Rogerus filius Sabini was registered there in 1252. Richard Sabin was found in the Assize Rolls for Warwickshire in 1221 and a John Sabine was recorded in the Hundredorum Rolls for Cheshire in 1279. The same rolls also included Alexander Sabine in Essex. In Somerset, ancient English rolls listed Sabyna

▲ *A view across the fields to St Peter's Church and the village of Titchfield, Hampshire.*

▲Some members of the Sabine family that developed around Canterbury in Kent, became quite influential. LEFT: General Joseph Sabine (c.1661-1739), soldier & Governor of Gibraltar. RIGHT: General Sir Edward Sabine (1788-1883), KCB, FRS, English astronomer, scientist, ornithologist, explorer and President of the Royal Society.

Vesy and William Sabyn, during the first year of King Edward III's reign. Laurence William Savona (fl. 1485), was a Franciscan of London who graduated D.D. at Cambridge, where in 1478 he wrote his 'Margarita Eloquentiae' in three books.

The relatively recent invention that did much to standardize English spelling was the printing press. Before that, even the most literate people recorded their names according to how it sounded. The spelling variations under which the name Sabine have appeared include Sabine, Sabbe, Sabin, Sabyn, Sabben, Saban, Savin and many more.

Famous & Notable Sabines

Notable persons amongst the Sabine ancestors in England include General Joseph Sabine (c.1661-1739), a British Army officer who came from a family settled at Patricksbourne, Kent. Joseph was appointed captain lieutenant to Sir Henry Ingoldsby's regiment of foot on the 8th March 1689, captain of the grenadier company, major and then general, ahead of his appointments as Governor of Berwick-upon-Tweed and Gibraltar.[16] His grandfather was Avery Sabine (1570-1648), a three time mayor and alderman of the City of Canterbury.

Joseph Sabine (1770-1837), was an English lawyer and naturalist, eldest son of Joseph Sabine of Tewin, Hertfordshire.[17] And General Sir Edward Sabine KCB FRS (1788-1883), was an English astronomer, scientist, ornithologist and explorer, President of the Royal Society, fifth son and ninth child of Joseph Sabine, Esq., of Tewin, Hertfordshire.[18]

William Sabyn of Ipswich

With one or two exceptions, no Sabines appear in Hampshire until the reign of King Henry VII, when the first of the Sabines to figure at all prominently in public records, which have survived, first rose to attention.[19] The following account of William Sabyn of Ipswich, Suffolk comes from an appendage to the election record, in William H. Richardson's 1886 edition of the 'The Annalls of Ipswche.'[20, 21]

▲ *William Sabyn was a ship owner and helped to transport the Royal Army to France before heading north. He was quickly recruited into the army, and his gallant service helped his later career as a naval commander, merchant and official, sitting in the 1539 parliament through his connection with the Howard family.*

William Sabine, also Sabyn or Sabyan (c.1491–11 April 1543), of Ipswich, Suffolk, was an English merchant, ship-owner, naval sea-captain and municipal figure.[22,23,24,25] He later became a Member of Parliament (MP) for Ipswich in 1539, with Edmund Daundy.[26,27]

William was the son of John Sabyn, or Sabyan, Esq., who in 1516 received a life annuity of 12d. a day for being in arms in the king's service.[28] He had an only sister and coheir to his father, named Elizabeth Sabyn.[29] During his father's lifetime William came to hold a position of importance as a captain in the Royal Navy. At the onset of King Henry's war with France in April to July 1512, Sabyn commanded a ship of 120 tonnes bearing his own name "The Sabyne, which carryied 60 soldiers, 34 mariners and four gunners with two servitors."[30]

In April 1513 he was sent with despatches to the King from Admiral Sir Edward Howard[31] and returned to the fleet at Brest just too late to prevent or join the celebrated engagement in which that Admiral was killed.[32] These events he described in a letter to Thomas Wolsey while under sail on 30 April 1513. Sabyn recounted that the attack was not conducted as he would have advised, and that "now we be bodys withowte a hed."[33] With "the king's army royal now on the sea," he was captain, with John Jermy the master of "The Less Bark", of 240 tons, carrying 193 men.[34] In August of 1513 he was again listed as captain on "The Sabyn" with 101 men, among the hired ships.[35] In September 1513 he was present at the Battle of Flodden Field, an English victory against the Scots.

During the winter of 1513-1514 he was appointed to cruise between Dover and Calais,[36] where payments show that he had 40 soldiers, 55 mariners and 5 gunners.[37] In January 1515 he was in command of the King's ships ordered to the Firth,[38] in support of Margaret Tudor, King Henry's sister.[39] He was then described as "Vice-admiral" when a list was drawn up of the men mustered in four of the king's ships under him in Grimsby Roads in 1516.[40] In November 1517, while upon the French coast, he became involved in a dispute with the French commanders on the subject of piracy, but eventually, on the production of the king's warrant, obtained restitution of a royal vessel called "The Black Barke."[41] On the 20th October 1518 he was appointed one of the king's Serjeants-at-arms, with a salary of 12d a day.[42]

By the 10th May 1522 he was again in northern seas, whence writing to Lord Admiral the Earl of Surrey, on coming into Skate Road, he said that he had "fired into Leith and Kinghorn, and after attacking a ship at anchor, which was rescued by the country people, had captured a ship of Copenhagen, laden with rye, which his servant was to repair and bring to Ipswich." He added that if he had had two good ships to land 500 men, he would have burnt half-a-dozen villages.[43] A few days after, on his homeward voyage, he chased a Spaniard, and next two French vessels off Orford Ness, finally putting into Orwell Haven, where he had left his boat.[44] In the succeeding month he accompanied the admiral to Dartmouth, and assisted him in the selection of a harbour in which to lay the great ships for the winter.[45]

Sabyn was admitted a freeman of Ipswich in 1519, and in August 1527 acted swiftly to win the appointment as successor to Sir Edward Echyngham in the controllership of the Ipswich customs.[46] He served as one of the two Bailiffs elected annually to the Assembly of Ipswich in 1536-1537 and in 1539-1540, in conjunction with which he held justiciary powers.[47] In 1537 he was elected an Ipswich Portman, under the proviso that he obtain the king's license to occupy the office, which he held until his death.[48] As a municipal leader in the town he was also its representative in Parliament in 1539, perhaps assisted by his association with Sir Ralph Sadler, whom he named supervisor of his probate.[49]

During this period William Sabyn cooperated with various other merchants,[50] of whom the most prominent was Henry Tooley, founder of the town's almshouses in Foundation Street.[51] Upon the suppression of the Ipswich Blackfriars Monastery in 1538, the site and conventual buildings were at first leased to Sabyn, who had premises adjacent, and were finally sold to him in November 1541, to hold in chief for the twentieth part of a Knight's fee.[52] In his will written in 1542 he refers to them as "my house and mansion place late

▲ 'The Old Mill, Milford on Sea, New Forest,' situated in the rural Hampshire landscape, painted by Georgiana or Helen Kendall.

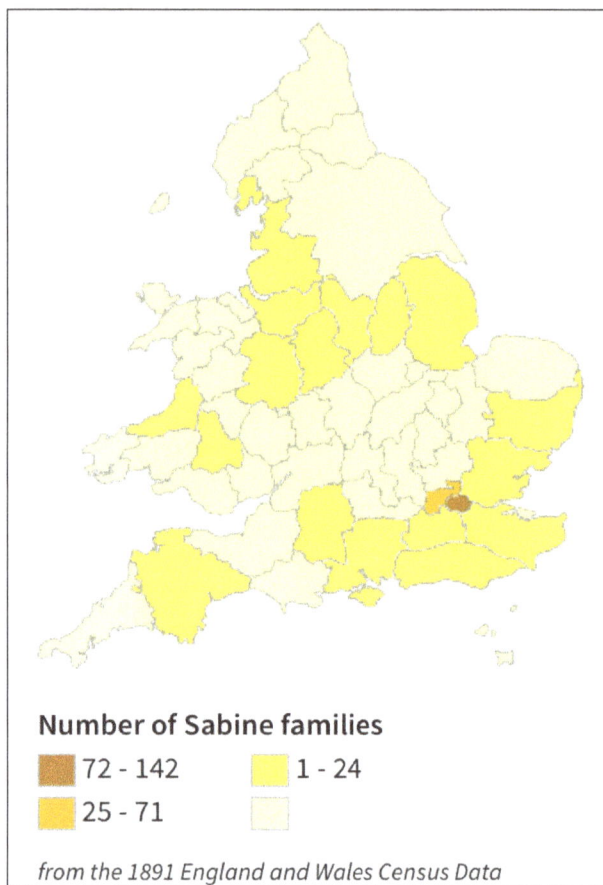

▲ LEFT: Distribution and density of Sabine families across England and Wales in 1891 (Ancestry). RIGHT: The Bell tower of St Peter's Church, Titchfield, Hampshire.

Number of Sabine families
- 72 - 142
- 25 - 71
- 1 - 24

from the 1891 England and Wales Census Data

called the Blakffreres in Ippiswiche." The will also shows that he owned various premises and tenantries in the towns of Mendlesham and Stowmarket, and also two tenements at the University of Cambridge opening against the Cambridge market, one occupied by Master Hacher and one by Mistress Cheeke. His ship "The James of Ipswich," was to be kept working after his death until it was sold.[53] His tenures of various quays in the neighbourhood of St Mary Key are listed in a Rental of 1542.[54]

William Sabyn bore arms... 'Sable three bees [or flies] or, two and one,' which appeared carved in stone and glass, in the church of St Mary Key, or at the Quay, Ipswich.[55] In his will Sabyn requested burial in the chapel of this church where his first wife was buried. St Mary Key stands between the former curtilage of the Blackfriars and the historic quay of Ipswich. Henry Tooley's grave and monument were in the same church.

Sabyn married firstly to Alice ("Alse"), who was living in 1518,[56] and secondly to Margaret, the widow of John Cole, who survived to marry a third time to Thomas Maria Wingfield, son of Sir Richard Wingfield.[57] Sabyn's designated heir was William Attwood of Aspall, Suffolk, son of Reynolde Attwood of London, a son of William Attwood of Staughton (Bedfordshire), and Elizabeth Sabyan (William's sister).[58] Thomas Attwood alias Smythe, the brother of Reynolde, and his son Sabyn Attwood, were also beneficiaries of his will.[59]

The principal executor of the will was William West "otherwise Sabyn", whom William called his godson, probably the same man who became a bailiff of Ipswich in 1550 and 1556.[60] Within weeks of Sabyn's death William Atwood brought a plea against William West claiming that his own grandmother Elizabeth (now Danvers) was in league with his uncle Thomas Smythe to disinherit him.[61]

Although many of these antecedants are notable in terms of their achievements, no direct ancestral links have been established with any known Sabine ancestors at this stage. However, the next chapter focuses on the ancestry of Thomas Eastman's wife Sarah Sabine, which examines the Sabine family of Titchfield, Hampshire.

References

1. Wikipedia - Sabines [https://en.wikipedia.org/wiki/Sabines].

2. Conway, Robert Seymour (1897). The Italic Dialects Edited with a Grammar and Glossary. Cambridge: University Press. pp. 351–369.

3. "I Sabini e l'agricoltura: origine, storia, leggende, pastorizia, coltivazioni". Un Mondo Ecosostenibile (in Italian). 2021-02-20. Retrieved 2021-12-10.

4. Riposati, Benedetto (1985). Convegno di studio: Preistoria, storia e civiltà dei Sabini (in Italian). Centro di studi varroniani.

5. Dionysius of Halicarnassus. "Book I.14". Roman Antiquities. Twenty-four stades from the afore-mentioned city stood Lista, the mother-city of the Aborigines, which at a still earlier time the Sabines had captured by a surprise attack, having set out against it from Amiternum by night.

6. Dionysius of Halicarnassus. "Book II.49". Roman Antiquities. But Zenodotus of Troezen, a...historian, relates that the Umbrians, a native race, first dwelt in the Reatine territory, as it is called, and that, being driven from there by the Pelasgians, they came into the country which they now inhabit and changing their name with their place of habitation, from Umbrians were called Sabines. But Porcius Cato says that the Sabine race received its name from Sabus, the son of Sancus, a divinity of that country, and that this Sancus was by some called Jupiter Fidius.

7. Dionysius of Halicarnassus. "Book II.49". Roman Antiquities. There is also another account given of the Sabines in the native histories, to the effect that a colony of Lacedaemonians settled among them at the time when Lycurgus, being guardian to his nephew Eunomus, gave his laws to Sparta. For the story goes that some of the Spartans, disliking the severity of his laws and separating from the rest, quit the city entirely, and after being borne through a vast stretch of sea, made a vow to the gods to settle in the first land they should reach; for a longing came upon them for any land whatsoever. At last they made that part of Italy which lies near the Pomentine plains and they called the place where they first landed Foronia, in memory of their being borne through the sea, and built a temple to the goddess Foronia, to whom they had addressed their vows; this goddess, by the alteration of one letter, they now call Feronia. And some of them, setting out from thence, settled among the Sabines. It is for this reason, they say, that many of the habits of the Sabines are Spartan, particularly their fondness for war and their frugality and a severity in all the actions of their lives. But this is enough about the Sabine race.

8. Plutarch. "1". Numa. Pythagoras, the Spartan, who was Olympic victor in the foot-race for the sixteenth Olympiad (in the third year of which Numa was made king), and that in his wanderings about Italy he made the acquaintance of Numa, and helped him arrange the government of the city, whence it came about that many Spartan customs were mingled with the Roman, as Pythagoras taught them to Numa. And at all events, Numa was of Sabine descent, and the Sabines will have it that they were colonists from Lacedaemon. Chronology, however, is hard to fix, and especially that which is based upon the names of victors in the Olympic games, the list of which is said to have been published at a late period by Hippias of Elis, who had no fully authoritative basis for his work. I shall therefore begin at a convenient point, and relate the noteworthy facts which I have found in the life of Numa.

9. Bunbury, Edward Herbert (1857). "Sabini". In Smith, William (ed.). Dictionary of Greek and Roman geography. Vol. II Iabadius—Zymethus. Boston: Little, Brown and Company.

10. Sabine, W.H.W., (1953). 'Sabin(e) - The History Of An Ancient English Surname. Illustrated By A Chronological List Of Instances From Saxon Times To The Nineteenth Century; Together With Numerous Pedigrees, Etc.,' Colburn & Tegg, London & New York.

11. Gosta Tengvik, Gosta, (1938). 'Old English Bynames,' p.12.

12. Sir Thomas Duffus Hardy, Rotuli Litterarum Clausarum, 1833, vol.i, pp. iv-vi. The tendency of clerks to air their learning was illustrated at a somewhat later period by their recording Bakehouse as Bacchus, Fishwick as Physick, Pettifer as Potiphar, etc. See under those names in C. Bardsley, (1901). 'A Dictionary of English and Welsh Surnames'.

13. C. Bardsley, (1901).op, cit *, pp, 5-6) shows that a considerable number of English surnames have come from girl-names, citing Margnretts, megson, Ibson (from Isabel), Avice (from Heloise), Tennyson or Dennison (from Dioniso), etc.

14. Robert Ferguson, (1864).'The Teutonic Name-system Applied to the Family Names of France, England', Williams & Norgate, London.

15. Sabine, W.H.W. 'The Surname Sabin(e) - Its Origin and Development from circa 1200,' p.47 (in Roberts, G.B. (1985). 'English Origins of New England Families - From the N.E. Historical and Genealogical Register,' 2nd Series, Vol.3, Genealogical Pub Co, Baltimore).

16. Wikipedia - Gen. Joseph Sabine (British Army Officer) [https://en.wikipedia.org/wiki/Joseph_Sabine_(British_Army_officer)].

17. Wikipedia- Joseph Sabine [https://en.wikipedia.org/wiki/Joseph_Sabine].

18. Wikipedia - Gen. Sir Edward Sabine [https://en.wikipedia.org/wiki/Edward_Sabine].

19. W.H. Richardson (ed.), The Annalls of Ipswche. The Lawes, Customes and Governmt of the Same, by Nathll Bacon 1654 (S.H. Cowell, Ipswich 1884), pp. 212-13 (note b) (Internet archive). (Note: references in this text to the Letters and Papers of Henry VIII are to the Rolls Series, First Edition of 1862, etc.).

20. Wikipedia - William Sabine [https://en.wikipedia.org/wiki/William_Sabine].

21. W.H. Richardson (ed.), The Annalls of Ipswche. The Lawes, Customes and Governmt of the Same, by Nathanial Bacon 1654 (S.H. Cowell, Ipswich 1884), pp. 210-14 (Internet Archive).

22. W.H. Richardson (ed.), The Annalls of Ipswche. The Lawes, Customes and Governmt of the Same, by Nathll Bacon 1654 (S.H. Cowell, Ipswich 1884), pp. 212-13 (note b) (Internet archive). (Note: references in this text to the Letters and Papers of Henry VIII are to the Rolls Series, First Edition of 1862, etc.).

23. He is mis-called William "Aubyn" in W. Page (ed.), A History of the County of Suffolk, Vol. 2 (William Constable, London 1907), p. 123, an error repeated elsewhere.

24. J. G. Webb, 'William Sabyn of Ipswich: an early Tudor Sea-officer and Merchant', The Mariner's Mirror 41 (1955), issue 3, pp. 209-221 (Taylor & Francis online). Subscription required.

25. 'The will of William Sabyn, Sergeant at the Arms of Ipswich, Suffolk', P.C.C. 1543 (Spert quire). Inquisitions post mortem: The National Archives, C 142/68/2; WARD 7/1/63; E 150/643/44.

26. J. Pound, 'Sabine, William (by 1491-1543), of Ipswich, Suff.', in S.T. Bindoff (ed.), The History of Parliament: the House of Commons 1509-1558 (from Boydell & Brewer, 1982), History of Parliament online.

27. W.H.W. Sabine, Sabin(e): The History of an Ancient English Surname (London and New York 1953), pp. 20-21 and pp. 70-74 (Internet Archive). Note: this author's analysis of Sabyn's will and the persons named in it is inexact.

28. '2736. Fees and Annuities', in J.S. Brewer (ed.), Letters and Papers, Foreign and Domestic, Henry VIII, II: 1515-1518 (HMSO, London 1864), at p. 876 (British History Online).

29. 'Atwood of Aspall', in W. Metcalfe (ed.), The Visitations of Suffolk made by Hervey, Clarenceux, 1561, Cooke, Clarenceux, 1577, and Raven, Richmond Herald, 1612 (William Pollard/Editor, Exeter 1882), p. 2 (Internet Archive).

30. A. Spont (ed.), Letters and Papers relating to the War with France, 1512-1513, Naval Records Society, Volume 10 (1897), p. 9 (Internet Archive); Letters and Papers, Henry VIII I: 1509-1514, p. 551 (British History Online).

31. 'Letter of Sir Edward Howard to Henry VIII, 17 April 1513', in Spont, The War with France in 1512-1513, pp. 126-29, at p. 128 and note 1 (Internet Archive); 'The King's Book of Payments, April 1513', Letters and Papers, Henry VIII, II, p. 1460 (British History Online).

32. Spont, The War with France in 1512-1513, pp. xxxvi-viii (Internet Archive).

33. Spont, The War with France in 1512-1513, pp. 141-44 (Internet Archive).

34. '3980. Navy', in J.S. Brewer (ed.), Letters and Papers, Henry VIII, Rolls Series, Vol. I Pt. 1 (Rolls Series) (1862), at p. 552 (Internet Archive).

35. 'Naval payments', Letters and Papers, Henry VIII, Vol. I Pt. 2, pp. 1029-30, no. 2304.3,4 (Hathi Trust).

36. '4474. Navy', in Letters and Papers, Henry VIII, Vol. I Pt 1, p. 677-78 (Internet Archive).

37. '5112. Expences of the war', in Letters and Papers, Henry VIII, Vol. I Pt 1, p. 813 (Internet Archive).

38. '63. Dacre, Magnus and Williamson', in Letters and Papers, Henry VIII, Vol. II Pt 1 (1864), p. 17 (Hathi Trust).

39. A. Hewerdine, The Yeomen of the Guard and the Early Tudors: The Formation of a Royal Bodyguard (I.B. Tauris & Co. Ltd., London and New York 2012), pp. 84-85 (Google).

40. The National Archives (UK), ref. E 101/61/23 (Discovery).

41. Letters and Papers, Henry VIII, Vol. II Pt 2, (1864), p. 1184 no. 3772 and p. 1188 no. 3786 (Hathi Trust).

42. Letters and Papers, Henry VIII, Vol. II Pt 2, (1864), p. 1384, no. 4509 (Hathi Trust).

43. '33. Wm. Sabyn to Surrey', in Letters and Papers, Henry VIII, Vol. III Pt. 2 (1867), Appendix, pp. 1581-82 (Hathi Trust).

44. '2357.ii. Fitzwilliam to [Wolsey]', in Letters and Papers, Henry VIII, Vol. III Pt. 2, p. 999 (Hathi Trust).

41. '2355. Surrey to Henry VIII', in Letters and Papers, Henry VIII, Vol. III Pt. 2, p. 997 (Hathi Trust).

46. S.J. Gunn, Charles Brandon, Duke of Suffolk, c.1484-1545 (Oxford 1988), pp. 98-99.

47. 'William Sabine', 1491-1543 of Ipswich, Suff. in History of Parliament [https://www.historyofparliamentonline.org/volume/1509-1558/member/sabine-william-1491-1543].

48. W.H. Richardson (ed.), The Annalls of Ipswche. The Lawes, Customes and Governmt of the Same, by Nathanial Bacon 1654 (S.H. Cowell, Ipswich 1884), pp. 210-14 (Internet Archive).

49. 'William Sabine', 1491-1543 of Ipswich, Suff. op. cit.

50. The National Archives, Early Chancery Proceedings, Brownrigge v Towley, ref: C 1/1175/52 (Discovery).

51. J.G. Webb, Great Tooley of Ipswich: Portrait of an Early Tudor Merchant, Suffolk Records Society (Boydell Press, 1970), p. 22.

52. '35. The Dominican Friars of Ipswich', in Page, A History of the County of Suffolk, Vol. 2, p. 123 (Internet Archive) - in which he is mis-called "William Aubyn".

53. Will of William Sabyn, Sergeant at the Arms of Ipswich, Suffolk (PCC 1543, Spert quire).

54. A.M. Breen, 'Appendix X. Documentary Research', in K. Heard,(ed. R. Goffin), Western Triangle (former Cranfield's Mill garage), Star Lane/College Street, Ipswich, Archaeological Post-Excavation Assessment, Suffolk County Council Archaeological Service Report no. 2013/141 (March 2014), at pp. 109-11 (Suffolk Archaeology grey literature pdf).

55. Sabine, Sabine: History of an Ancient English Surname, p. 82 (Internet Archive); G.R. Clarke, The History and Description of the Town and Borough of Ipswich (S. Piper, Ipswich/Hurst, Chance & Co., London 1830), p. 270 (Google)

56. The National Archives, Early Chancery Proceedings, ref C 1/499/17 (Discovery), Dameron v. Bailiffs of Ipswich: view original at AALT.

57. 'William Sabine', 1491-1543 of Ipswich, Suff. op. cit.

58. 'Atwood of Aspall', in W. Metcalfe (ed.), The Visitations of Suffolk made by Hervey, Clarenceux, 1561, Cooke, Clarenceux, 1577, and Raven, Richmond Herald, 1612 (William Pollard/Editor, Exeter 1882), p. 2 (Internet Archive).

59. Will of William Sabyn, Sergeant at the Arms of Ipswich, Suffolk (PCC 1543, Spert quire).

60. Richardson (ed.), The Annalls of Ipswche, p. 246, n. (Internet Archive).

61. Sabine, Sabine: History of an Ancient English Surname, p. 73-74; The National Archives, Early Chancery Proceedings ref. C 1/935/33 and 34 (Discovery), At Wudd v Weste.
[https://en.wikipedia.org/wiki/Edward_Sabine].

62. Wikipedia - The Rape of the Sabine Women [https://en.wikipedia.org/wiki/The_Rape_of_the_Sabine_Women].

Chapter Nine

THE SABINES OF TITCHFIELD

Founded by the Meon tribe, the village of Titchfield, Hampshire is located at the bottom of the Meon Valley and dates from the 6th century during Anglo-Saxon times, two centuries before the Vikings invaded Britain. Evidence of Roman occupation abounds in the local area and Titchfield's accessibility from its once natural tidal harbour suggests that it benefited from navigable access at high tide that would have allowed shallow keel vessels to travel up the Meon Valley. Some of Titchfield's oldest jetty styled houses and buildings in South Street date from the 13th century and feature top floors that extend over the pavements. There is some debate about the origin of the name Titchfield, as it was recorded as 'Ticefelle' in the Domesday Book in 1086.[1]

Titchfield thrived on agriculture and sea trade. Geographically, it is an ideal location to live and prosper with rich soils supporting sheep farming and a thriving port that, before it was blocked off in 1611, facilitated trade via Hill Head on the busy Solent. A canal was built to connect Titchfield with the Solent, which runs along the western edge of Titchfield Haven. The town was referred to as a thriving marketplace in medieval times and one has to presume that floating trade elevated its already busy market and local tannery trade. Today, the canal is somewhat overgrown, but it has a footpath which follows the canal on one side and the Titchfield Nature Haven on the other on its route to Meon beach, where Titchfield harbour once existed. The termination of the canal resulted from an act of the 3rd Earl of Southampton, which was by all accounts unpopular with the rationale being undocumented.

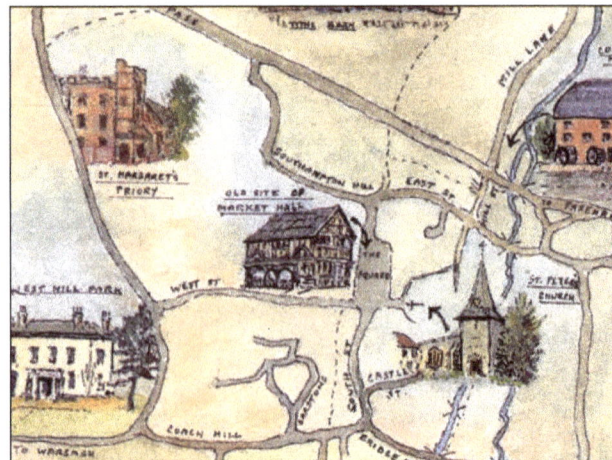

▲ TOP (Left): Old map of the village of Titchfield 'Parryche.' (Right): Street map of Titchfield showing South Street, St Peters Church and The Square. ABOVE: Thomas Milne's 1791 map of Titchfield and Fareham, Hampshire.

The Village of Titchfield [2]

The following description of Titchfield has been borrowed from the Titchfield History Society. "Titchfield's principal historic landmark is the Abbey, founded early in the 13th century by Peter de Roches, the Bishop of Winchester for the Premonstratensian canons, known as the White Canons, a Catholic religious order founded on the continent. The Abbey has been frequented by many Kings and Queens and in 1445 it was the location for the marriage of King Henry VI to Margaret of Anjou. So significant an event was this that a lion was brought in chains to the Abbey for the ceremony, all the way from the Tower of London. The dissolution of the Monasteries, ordered by King Henry VIII and effected by Thomas Cromwell, saw Titchfield Abbey's converted into a fine country residence and the building is today known as Place House. The conversion of the Abbey into Place House was undertaken by Thomas Wriothesley, who was richly rewarded for his royal allegiance by being granted the title 1st Earl of Southampton, and he received the Titchfield and Beaulieu Abbey's estates.

Place House was clearly on the royal circuit as its visitors included Edward VI, Elizabeth I, Charles I and his queen Henrietta Maria. Charles I spent his last night at Place House before fleeing to Carisbrooke Castle on the Isle of Wight, and this refuge became his prison for a year and a half before his execution in 1649. Place House was the home of

Henry Wriothesley, the 3rd Earl of Southampton most famously remembered as William Shakespeare's patron. It is conjectured whether Shakespeare perhaps spent his 'lost years' between 1685 and 1692 as a school teacher in Titchfield, as there is reference to some of his plays being first performed in Place House. The old school house still survives across the road from Place House.

Unfortunately, Place House was left to ruins in 1781. The Delme family who owned it re-purposed some of its stone fabric to build Cams House on Fareham Creek. Abbey stone can also be found in local dwellings and a fireplace has even been salvaged and built into the Georgian village pub, known as the Bugle Inn. The Abbey still stands tall and proud and it is easy to imagine the lives and ways of monks, kings and queens, its banqueting halls and royal weddings and even the premier of a Shakespearean play.

St Peter's was the first church to be built on the south coast in approximately 680 A.D. when Saint Wilfrid travelled from Northumbria and ventured up the Meon Valley building churches on his way. Anglo-Saxon stone in the church has been dated to that period, and Norman and other additions have been built on since then. In St Peters church there is a magnificent marble monument that commemorates Thomas Wriothesley, his wife Lady Jane and their son Henry Wriothesley, the family being interred in the crypt now known as the Southampton Chapel. The Montagu family of Beaulieu descend from the Wriothesley family and Lord Montagu takes a keen and active interest in historic Titchfield.

The Great Barn near the Abbey is a grade 1 listed structure. It dates back to the 15th century and is a fine example of a medieval monastic timber framed aisled barn. It probably stored grain and other essential supplies for the village, but there are stories that it may

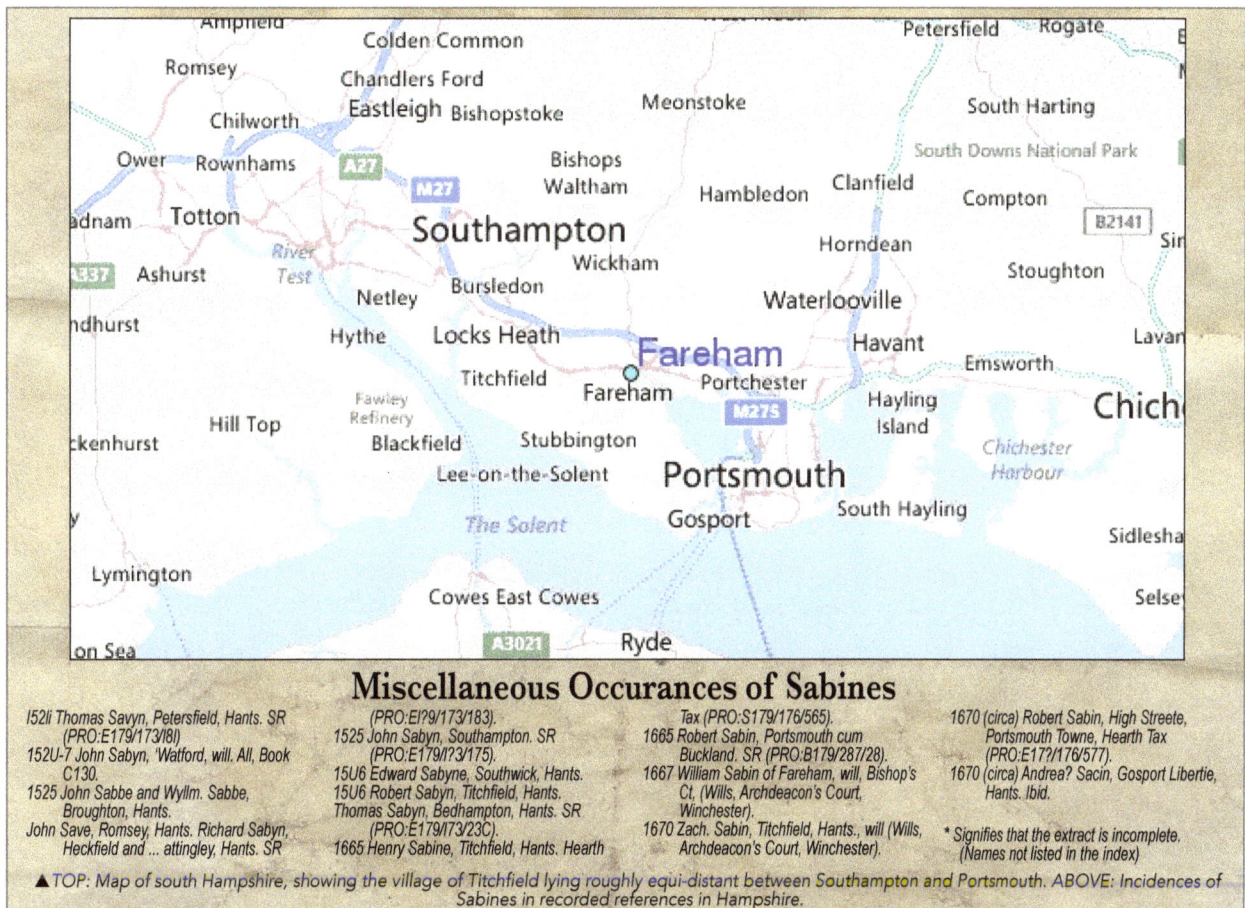

Miscellaneous Occurances of Sabines

152li Thomas Savyn, Petersfield, Hants. SR (PRO:E179/173/181).

152U-7 John Sabyn, 'Watford, will. All, Book C130.

1525 John Sabbe and Wyllm. Sabbe, Broughton, Hants.

John Save, Romsey, Hants. Richard Sabyn, Heckfield and ... attingley, Hants. SR

(PRO:EI79/173/183).

1525 John Sabyn, Southampton. SR (PRO:E179/I73/175).

15U6 Edward Sabyne, Southwick, Hants.

15U6 Robert Sabyn, Titchfield, Hants. Thomas Sabyn, Bedhampton, Hants. SR (PRO:E179/173/23C).

1665 Henry Sabine, Titchfield, Hants. Hearth

Tax (PRO:S179/176/565).

1665 Robert Sabin, Portsmouth cum Buckland. SR (PRO:B179/287/28).

1667 William Sabin of Fareham, will, Bishop's Ct. (Wills, Archdeacon's Court, Winchester).

1670 Zach. Sabin, Titchfield, Hants., will (Wills, Archdeacon's Court, Winchester).

1670 (circa) Robert Sabin, High Streete, Portsmouth Towne, Hearth Tax (PRO:E172/176/577).

1670 (circa) Andrea? Sacin, Gosport Libertie, Hants. Ibid.

* Signifies that the extract is incomplete. (Names not listed in the index)

▲ TOP: Map of south Hampshire, showing the village of Titchfield lying roughly equi-distant between Southampton and Portsmouth. ABOVE: Incidences of Sabines in recorded references in Hampshire.

also have stored supplies for Henry V and that he visited the barn before he sailed to France prior to the great battle at Agincourt in 1415. Some believe he made his famous rallying speech there, but this may be a repeat story as Edward III also sailed to France from the Titchfield coastal area to do battle at Crecy in 1346. It is recorded that Henry V rested in the town before Agincourt and Charles I did the same before his imprisonment at Carisbrooke.

The rebuilt barn has established itself as a much loved local amenity in recent times and Titchfield's local theatre group the 'Titchfield Festival Theatre' regularly hosts Shakespeare's plays in the iconic setting. The barn has also proved itself to be a romantic and very successful wedding venue. Stimulated by the 19th century Enclosure Acts, the

Occurences of Sabines in Hampshire

Richard Sabyn, Heckfield and ... Mattingley, Hants. SR (PRO:E!?9/173/183).

1525 John Sabyn, Southampton. SR (PRO:E179/I?3/175).

15U6 Edward Sabyne, Southwick, Hants.

15U6 Robert Sabyn, Titchfield, Hants.

Thomas Sabyn, Bedhampton, Hants. SR (PRO:E179/173/23C).

1665 Henry Sabine, Titchfield, Hants. Hearth Tax (PRO:S179/176/565).

1665 Robert Sabin, Portsmouth cum Buckland. SR (PRO:B179/287/28).

1667 William Sabin of Fareham, will, Bishop's Ct, (Wills, Archdeacon's Court, Winchester).

1670 Zach. Sabin, Titchfield, Hants., will (Wills, Archdeacon's Court, Winchester).

1670 (circa) Robert Sabin, High Streete, Portsmouth Towne, Hearth Tax (PRO:E17?/176/577).

1670 (circa) Andrea? Sacin, Gosport Libertie, Hants. Ibid.

1693 Robert Sabb in, Portsmouth, will (Wills, Archdeacon's Court, Winchester).

1693 Edward Sabbin, Ripley, Hants., will (Wills, Archdeacon's Court, Winchester).

1693 Edward Saben m. Joan Brexey, at Sopley, Hants., 19 Feb. (HER).

1693 William Saber m. Judeth Downer at Brading, I.O.V, 17 July. (HER).

1693 Mary Saben m. John Brenton at Sopley, Hants., 8 June. (HER).

1693 Edith Sabon, Portsmouth, will. (Wills, Archdeacon's Court, Winchester).

1693 Henry Sabon, Titchfield, Hants, will (Wills, Archdeacon's Court, Winchester).

1693 Edw. Elliott m. Joan Saben at Sopley, Hants., 6 Feb. (HIR).

1693 Joshua Sabin, citizen aid weaver of London, aged U9, son of Robert Sabin of same, applied for confirmation of a Shield of arms. (KC).

1693 Richard Emey m. Jane Saben at Sopley, Hants., 1 July. (HIR).

1718 Licence granted Bushell Ranches of H.E.S. Captain to marry Elizabeth Sabine of Portsmouth (No Ref).

1720 William Sabbin of Titchfield, Hants, will (Wills, Archdeacon's Court, Winchester).

1721 Mary Sabin, widow, m. Isaac Read, artificer, at Titchfield. Lie. 27 July. (HEA).

1723 Sara Sabin of Shirley, Hants, vd.ll. (VAT).

1723 Nicholas Sabins of Preston Candover, Hants., will (Wills, Archdeacon's Court, Winchester).

1737 James Sabben of Titchfield, glazier, and Martha Lamport, at Titchfield, St. Faith's, or Chilcomb, Lie 1 Feb (HLA).

1780 Thomas Eastman of Portsea, cabinet maker, 21, ba., and Sarah Sabine of the sane, 21, sp., at Portsmouth, Lie, 25 Dec. (Wk).

1801 Thomas Charles Flaxman, Esq., of Southampton, & Eliz. Sabben at Portsea. Lie, 30 April (KEA).

* Signifies that the extract is incomplete. (Names not listed in the index)

▲TOP: Early painting of Place House, Titchfield after its conversion from Titchfield Abbey to a manor. ABOVE (Left): Print of Titchfield, 31 Oct 1772 by Godfrey, showing its defensive walls. (Right): Contemporary painting of Place House, Titchfield, now a ruin, by B.P. Hansford.

▲ *Workers upgrading the road on the outskirts of the village of Titchfield, Hampshire, c.1750.*

local strawberry industry has recently experienced remarkable growth in production, and by following the coastal road south of Titchfield in early summer, travellers can encounter some of the best strawberries in Hampshire.

During World War 2, Allied troops were billeted in the surrounding farms to practice the Normandy beach landings. The Meon shore was used to practice beach landings where the training involved live rounds being fired over the soldiers heads towards the cliffs to simulate the action that lay ahead.

For 150 years there has been an annual Titchfield Carnival, which parades through the village. This became a huge event with local floats supported by all sorts of communities and clubs. The history of this event suggests that Titchfield doesn't easily forget, the carnival stemming from the villages want to display its discontent with the 3rd Earl's damming of the harbour. Every year an effigy of the 3rd Earl was publicly burnt and the carnival evolved at the hands of the infamous Titchfield Bonfire Boys. Sadly, the carnival has lately been paused due to burgeoning running costs."

Sabines in Hampshire

While registrations of the surname provide the basic material for a study of the name Sabin(e) throughout England and the southern counties, unfortunately some of the registrations for Hampshire have been corrupted and are difficult to read. The first mention of Sabines in Hampshire were found in 'miscellaneous instances' of that name, which provide some references to dates and locations, although no early verified links have been established to the Titchfield Sabines.

St Peter's Church , Titchfield

Extracts of 'miscellaneous incidences' of the name from the parish registers of St. Peter's Church, Titchfield form the basis of researching the Sabines of Titchfield. According to W. H. W. Sabine, the first mention of a Sabine in the village of Titchfield, Hampshire was John

The Titchfield Emblem[13]

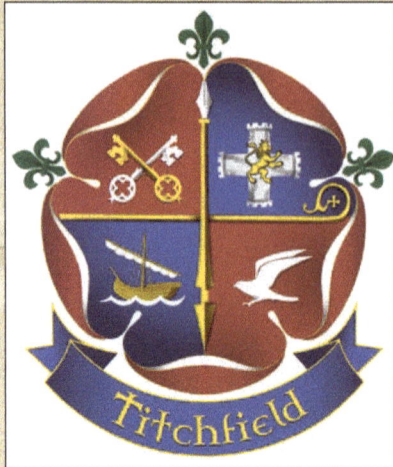

The Titchfield Emblem surround is embraced with red petals to represent the Lancastrian dynasty, and with white tips representing the York dynasty. The white tips also symbolise purity relating to what was once a religious Roman Catholic building – Titchfield Abbey. The two roses are separated out from the well-known Tudor Rose which originated later in history. Three Fleur de Lys have been chosen to substitute the green fronds of the Tudor Rose. The Fleur de Lys indicates Henry V in particular, but also other regal influences. Fleur de Lys can also be found in the Premonstratensian Canons coat of arms who founded the Abbey. Finally the Fleur de Lys can still be seen on the existing floor tiles in the Abbey.

The Four Quadrants:

Top Left - symbolises one of the village's oldest heritages – the very ancient Anglo-Saxon St. Peters Church founded by Saint Wilfred in 680 AD. His Bishops Crozier is also included as the horizontal divide between the top and bottom half of the Emblem. A similar Crozier was used by Premonstratensian Canons in their coat of arms when they inhabited Titchfield commencing in the 13th Century and built Titchfield Abbey in 1232 AD.

Top Right - symbolises the 4 remaining towers of the iconic Titchfield Abbey in the shape of a cross. The towers are slightly white to symbolise the white canons who once occupied the Abbey. A yellow lion in the middle of the towers represents the lion brought into the Abbey for the royal wedding of Henry VI and Margaret of Anjou in 1445 AD. The lion was returned to the Tower of London after the royal ceremony.

Bottom Left - symbolises Titchfield as an ancient port before it was closed-off from the sea at Hill Head. It is represented by an old Anglo-Saxon ship in the Emblem. Ships would have come and gone from Titchfield for War (Battle of Crecy, Edward III 1346 AD, and Battle of Agincourt, Henry V 1415 AD) and trade to and from the tanneries including the wool industry.

Bottom Right - symbolises Titchfield Haven Nature Reserve with a white bird, which could also represent the White Falcon from the Wriothesley coat of arms flying away.

One can also see a yellow spear running vertically down the centre of the Emblem dividing the left and right quadrants. This represents Shakespeare's spear found on the old Shakespeare coat of arms. Shakespeare was friendly with the 3rd Earl of Southampton in 1593/94, which is reflected in the dedication of his only two poems. Shakespeare is also thought to have taught as a teacher in Titchfield in the late 1500s AD.

The scroll at the bottom is quite gothic with a Capital 'T' as a cross, and a small 't' as a sword.

▲ LEFT: An old farm house on the outskirts of Titchfield. RIGHT: The 'Mill' at Titchfield, Hampshire.

Sabbyn, probably a shopkeeper or smallholder in 1525, in a tax entry on a valuation of 20s, written by a clerk in a court hand, which simply read:[3]

"John Sabbyn in goode · xx s · iiij d."

The decline in the number of entries of Sabines after the Restoration is due to the fact that they were Puritan members of the Church of England, and their vicar, the Rev. Urian Oakes, refused to subscribe to the Act of Uniformity, which was enforced in August, 1662. The vicar was thereupon ejected, and with his sympathisers formed a dissenting body, in which infants were baptized without recourse to the parish church. Consequently, records belonging to the period from 1590 to about 1800 were made for Mr. W. H. W. Sabine by the incumbents, but these do not purport to be complete in number or in detail.[4]

The following incomplete copies of headstone inscriptions relate to Sabines on Titchfield tombstones, and were made for W. H. W. Sabine in 1923 by Miss E. Foot, of Titchfield, one of whose ancestors was a Sabine:[5]

"Sacred.... Isaac Sabine Who Died 30th 1786 Aged 48"

· · · · · · ·

"1830 (?) Also of Jane Pink daughter of the above John and Mary Sabine, who died Feb fifth 1887(?) Aged 73 years."*

· · · · · · ·

"James Sabine The Son of above Died 1820 (?). Mary Sabine Daughter of the above who Died July 1823 Aged 62 (?) years."

· · · · · · ·

"Samuel Sabine who departed this life 29th November 1831, Aged 48 years. Also of Mary Wise relict of the above, Who died April 23rd 1814 Aged 79."

· · · · · · ·

"To the Memory of John Sabine who died 20th February 1832 Aged 60 years. Also of Mary Sabine wife of above who died 3rd Sep"

While Sabine families were seemingly well spread across England and Wales, two prominent 16th century branches emerged out of Canterbury in Kent, and Titchfield in Hampshire. And while it seems certain that the Canterbury and Hampshire Sabines had a common progenitor at some time in the past, no clear connection between these groups has been found to date (*see Appendix E*).

It would be superfluous, especially having regard to the limitations of this work, to copy out the complete pedigree published by William Henry Waldo Sabine, but his investigations into the ancestry of the Rev. James Sabine have been reproduced in the next chapter.[6]

The Sabines of Titchfield, Hampshire appear not to have been enobled as there is no known recognised blazon for this branch. Therefore, it seems appropriate to adopt the recently sanctioned 'Titchfield Emblem', as a symbolic badge to represent the rich history of Titchfield village. The emblem was devised by four locals with the first ideas starting in 2017 in the Queen's Head Inn. To date there has been minimal cost involved with the design of the Titchfield Emblem as it has remained within the local community. Many historic events were considered, which have been included in the Titchfield Emblem.

The Sabines of Titchfield

Records for the Sabines of Titchfield are based on parish registers, wills and other family records, and have been placed on a diagram for easier interpretation (*see Pedigree Chart 5*).[7] The first known Sabine ancestor from Titchfield was William Sabine (1567-1606), who married on the 24th September 1592 at Titchfield, to Agnes Woodde (1552-1638), and was buried at Titchfield on the 20th August 1638. Little else is known of William Sabine's

▲ TOP (Left): Colour postcard of St Peter's Church, Titchfield. (Right): Photograph of the interior of St Peter's Church. LEFT: Early drawing of St Peter's Church, surrounded by memorial headstones. ABOVE: Close-up of the alter at St Peter's Church, Titchfield, Hampshire.

Occurences of Sabines from the Records of St Peter's Church, Titchfield

1590 Apr, Bapt. Wyllyn Saben the xxx day.
1590 May, Buried Agnes Saben the vii daye,
(There is also an entry for 7 Feb, 1590 of the burial of Julya, whose surname might conceivably be Saben, but it is very doubtful what it is.)
1592 Sep, Married William Sabin to Agnes Woodde the 24 daye.
1593 Jun, Bapt. Acha (Zachariah) Sabbin the 24 daye.
1595 Feb, Bapt. Rosse (Rose) Sabbine the 22nd daye.
1596 Jul, Married Christopher Sibine and Margaret Fypes (Phipps).
1597 Apr, Bapt. Elisabeth Sabbine the 24 daye.
1600 Feb, Bapt. Margery Sabeye the (? 22nd) daye.
(The Register at this period contains also entries relating to persons named Sabedye).
1600 Aug, Married John Benson and Alice (? Sabine).
1606 Aug, Buried William Sabine was buried the 30th day of this month.
1608 Oct, Married Richard Sabine and Marie Bushe the 29th daye.
1609 Oct, Bapt. William Sabin the xi day. I6IU Nov. Bapt. Thomas Sabbine, 29th day.
1616 Mar, Bapt. Richard Sabbin the xxiii day.
1619 Jul, Bapt. Peter & Frances Sabbine the first day.
1619 Jul, Buried Frances Sabbine the (?

12th) day.
1623 Apr, Buried Peter Sabbine the 27th day.
162ix Jan. Bapt. Henry Sabbine the 6th day.
1626 Apr, Married Thomas Coward and Rose Sabbine the xxth day.
1626 May, Married Zache Sabbinn and Alice Langley/Longline the 7th day.
1627 Jan, Bapt. (? Edward) Sabbinn of (? Richard) Sabbinn the 14th day, (a very faint and faded entry).
1627 Mar, Bapt. George Sabhinne of Zache Sabbin the 18th day.
1629 Mar, Bapt. William Sabbinn of Zache Sabbine the 8th day.
1629 Dec, Bapt, Robert Sabbine and Richard Sabbinn of Richard Sabbine the 16th day.
1631 Feb, Bapt. Thomas Sabbin of Zachi Sabbin the 20th day.
1632 Feb, Bapt. Mary Sabben of Zach Sabben the 9th day.
1632 Mar, Buried Thomas (? Sabin) servant to the right honorable Earle of Southampton the 21st day.
(A section of the Register from... March 1633 to day 1634 is missing).
1635 July, Bapt. Zacher Sabben of Zacher the 25th day.
1636 Oct, Married Ralph Sabben and Anne (7 Gwen or Craven) the 12th day.
1637 Dec, Bapt. Mary Sabben of Ralph Sabben the 3 day.
1638 Apr, Bapt. Henry Sabben of Zache

Sabben the ?th day.
1638 Aug, Buried Widdowe Sabben the mother of Zache Sabben the twentyth day.
1642 Jun, Buried Richard Sabben the first day.
161*3 Nov. Bapt. John Sabben of Ralph Sabben the 29th day.
16BU Apr, Buried Nicholas Sabben the 17 dav.
I6Bli Oct, Buried Mary Sabben widow the IRth day.
1650 Feb, Buried Anthony Sabben the 18th day.
1651 May, Buried (no Christian name) Sabben of Ralph Sabben of Stubbington the 17th day.
1657 Nov, Buried Ralphe Sabbin the son of Ralphe Sabbin the 28th day.
1658 Aug, Buried Simon Sabb the 5th day.
1658 Nov, Buried Anne the wife of Ralph Sabbin the 21 day.
1662 May, Buried Ralfe Sabben of Stroud Green the l?th day.
1663 Sep, Bapt. Henry Sabben of Henry Sabben the 17th day.
I66ii Jun, Buried Henry Sabben of Henry Sabben the 22nd day.
1670 Jul, Buried Zachariah Sabbin the 7 day.
1692 Sept, Married William Laidnan and Sara Saben the 22 day.
1706 Dec, Married Henry Saben & Jane Brice the 24 day.
1712 Mar 30, Married William Sabbin and Hary Kewit, both of the Town.
1719 Aug 15, Buried William Sabbine of the

Town.
1728 Apr 5th, Buried Sarah Savine widow of Titchfield (Dissenter).
1728 Dec, Buried Sarah Sabbin daughter of William Sabbin and Eary of Titchfield, Dec. HLth,
1731 Dec 30, Married William Ardren and Sarah Sabbine of the Town, by Banns.
1739 Buried Jane Sabine.*
17U5 Sep 23, Buried Thos Sabben
1755 Buried Henry Sabbin.*
1756 Apr 10, Buried William Sabine.
1760 Jun 22, Buried Thos Sabine an inf.
1761 Married William Sabine and Anne Rogers.*
1762 Buried Hannah Sabbin.*
176U Buried William Sabbin.*
1765 Baptised Elizabeth Sabbin.*
1765 Buried Aliza Sabbin.*
1779 Sep 3, Buried James Sabine.
1780 Married Daniel Sabine and Ann Prince.*
1782 Buried John Sabine.*
1786 Buried Isaac Sabine.*
1797 Buried Charles Sabine.*
1803 Buried Elisa Sabine.*
180U Buried Charles Sabine.*
1829 Feb 11, Buried Patience Sabine of Titchfield, aged 66.

* Signifies that the extract is incomplete. (Names not listed in the index)

SABBEN, James, of Titchfield, glazier, b., & Martha Lamport, of St. Mary Calendar, Winchester, 28, sp., at T., St. Faith's, or Chilcomb, 1 Feb., 1737.

SABBIN, James, of St. Peter Cheesehill, Winchester, 52, w., & Elizabeth Allee, of St Peter Colebrook, 45, w., at St. P. Cheesehill, 22 Feb., 1805.

SABBIN, John, of St. Peter Cheesehill, Winchester, cabinet maker, 22, b., & Elizabeth Hill, of the s., 22, sp., at St. P. C., 31 Jan., 1806.

SABIN, Edward, of Sopley, farmer, 22, b., & Leah Pope, of the s., 19, sp., with c. of her guardian, Francis Pope, of the s., farmer, 3 July, 1773.

SABINE, Isaac, of Portsmouth, tailor, 21, b., & Elizabeth Fielder, of All Saints, Southampton, 21, sp., at A. S., 3 Feb., 1802. Henry Fielder, of South-ampton, shopkeeper, bondsman.

SABINE, John, of St. James's, Bury St. Edmund's, co. Suffolk, 23, & Adelaide-Isham Epps, of All Saints, Southampton, 23, at A. S., 4 Jan., 1825. Aff.

SABINE, William, of Gosport, grocer, 21, b., & Jane-Perry Young, of Portsmouth, 21, sp., at P., 1 Aug., 1810. James Sabine, of Portsmouth, baker and grocer, bondsman.

▲ TOP: Miscellaneous occurences of Sabines from the records of St Peter's Church, Titchfield, Hampshire. ABOVE: Allegations for Sabine marriage licences in Hampshire (England, 1689-1837, Vol. 2).

life except that he was likely involved in farming, and was buried at Titchfield, on the 30th August 1606, with records revealing that they produced three children in Zachariah Sabbinn [sic. Sabine], who was baptised on the 24th June 1593; Rose Sabine (1594-1640) who was baptised on the 22nd February l595, and subsequently married on the 20th April 1626 to Thomas Coward; and Elizabeth Sabbine (1597-1667), who was baptised on the 24th April 1597, and later married a Mr. Wheatfield.[8]

William Sabine was succeeded by his son and heir Zachariah Sabbinn (1593-1670), who married Alice Langley (or 'Longline', 1600-1638) on the 7th May 1626 at Titchfield. He was buried on the 17th July 1670, but left a family of seven with George Sabbinne being baptised 18th March 1627, who probably died young; William Sabbinn, was baptised 8th March 1629; Thomas Sabbin, was baptised on the 20th February, 1631, but probably died young; Mary Sabben, was baptised on the 9th February 1632, but probably also died young; Zachariah Sabine, was baptised on the 25th July 1635; possibly Anne Sabine, no baptism found; and Henry Sabine, who was baptised on the 7th April 1638.[9]

Zachariah was succeeded by his youngest son Henry Sabine (1638-1687), who married Sarah Elizabeth (surname unknown, c.1640-1728), who herself was buried in Titchfield on the 5th April 1728. Henry's will was proved at Winchester in 1687, which revealed three children in Henry Sabine, baptised 17th September 1663, and buried 22nd June 1668; possibly a Sarah Sabine, who was baptised in 1673 and married William Haidman on the 22nd September 1692; and William Sabine, who was baptised about 1682.[10]

This Henry Sabine was succeeded by his son William Sabine (1682-1719), who married Mary Hewitt (1686-1760), but he died aged just 37 and was buried on the 15th August 1719 at Titchfield. This couple produced three children in James Sabine, who was baptised about 1710; William Sabine, who was likely baptised about 1711; and Sarah Sabine, who died unmarried and was buried at Titchfield on the 11th December 1728. Mary survived William, and married secondly in 1721 at Titchfield to Isaac Read.[11]

The next chapter explores the link between the Sabine ancestors of Titchfield and the son and heir of William Sabine, who was James Sabine (1710-1779). James married twice and in doing so produced some 14 children, although only nine would live to adulthood, and just six of those went on to produce families of their own.[12] An extensive account of the descendants of each of James Sabine's children is reported in the next chapter.

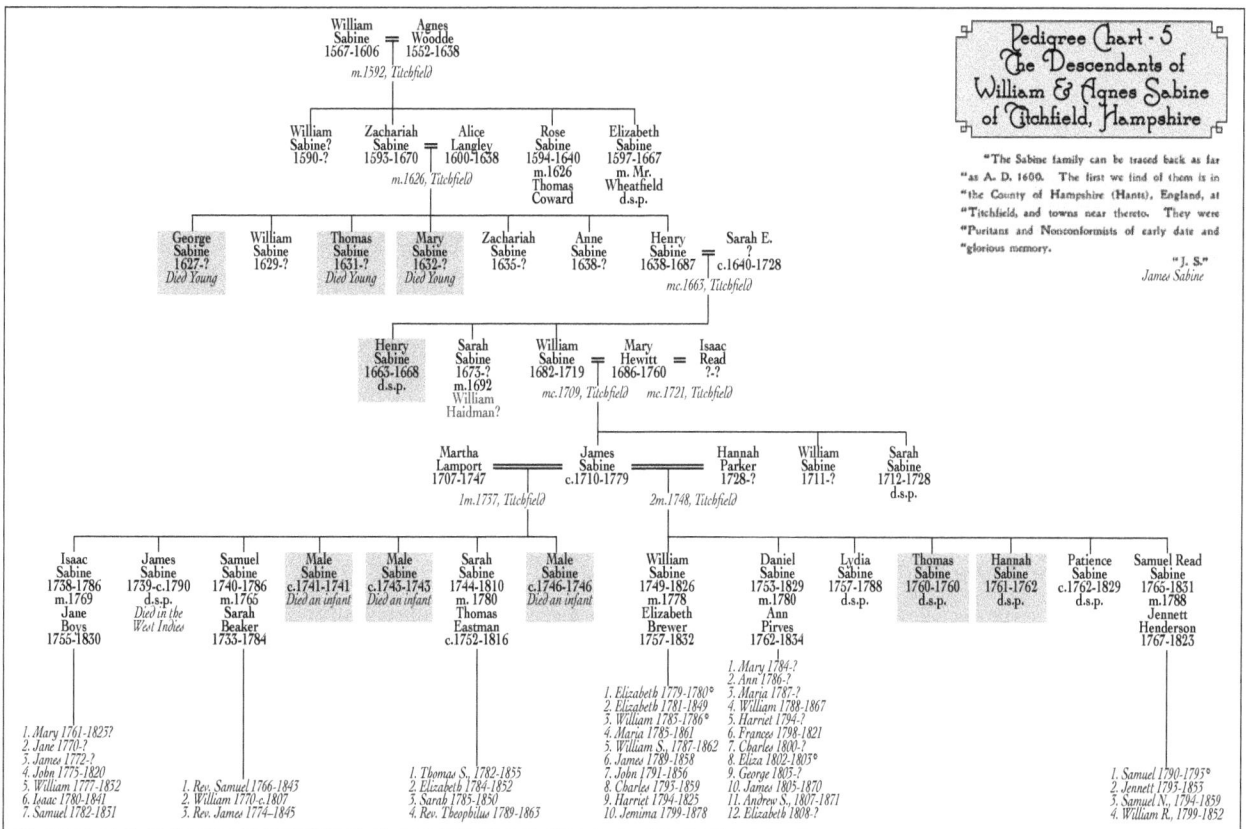

Pedigree Chart - 5
The Descendants of William & Agnes Sabine of Titchfield, Hampshire

"The Sabine family can be traced back as far "as A. D. 1600. The first we find of them is in "the County of Hampshire (Hants), England, at "Titchfield, and towns near thereto. They were "Puritans and Nonconformists of early date and "glorious memory.
"J. S."
James Sabine

▲ Chart 9.0 This chart reveals how the Sabine ancestors of descend from William Sabine (1567-1606) & Agnes Woodde (1552-1638) of Titchfield, Hampshire, (Derived from... 'Ancestry of the Rev. James Sabine' by W.H.W. Sabine, pp.53-56 (in Roberts, G.B., (1985). 'English Origins of New England Families - From the N.E. Historical and Genealogical Register,' 2nd Series, Vol.3, Genealogical Pub Co, Baltimore.).

References

1. Titchfield History Society - Titchfield History In Brief [https://titchfieldhistory.com/about-the-history-society/].

2. Titchfield History Society, op. cit.

3. Sabine, W. H. W. (1953). 'Sabine (e) - The History Of An Ancient English Surname. Illustrated By A Chronological List Of Instances From Saxon Times To The Nineteenth Century; Together With Numerous Pedigrees,' London And New York.

4. Sabine, W. H. W., 'Ancestry of the Rev. James Sabine', p.53 (in Roberts, G.B.,(1985). 'English Origins of New England Families - From the N.E. Historical and Genealogical Register,' 2nd Series, Vol.3, Genealogical Pub Co, Baltimore).

5. Sabine, W. H. W. (1953), op. cit.

6. Sabine, W. H. W. (1953), op. cit.

7. 'Ancestry of the Rev. James Sabine' by W.H.W. Sabine, op.cit., p.54.

8. 'Ancestry of the Rev. James Sabine' by W.H.W. Sabine, op.cit., p.54.

9 . 'Ancestry of the Rev. James Sabine' by W.H.W. Sabine, op.cit., p.54.

10 . 'Ancestry of the Rev. James Sabine' by W.H.W. Sabine, op.cit., p.54.

11. 'Ancestry of the Rev. James Sabine' by W.H.W. Sabine, op.cit., p.54.

12. 'Ancestry of the Rev. James Sabine' by W.H.W. Sabine, op.cit., p.55.

13. Titchfield History Society, op. cit.

Chapter Ten

THE DESCENDANTS OF JAMES SABINE OF TITCHFIELD

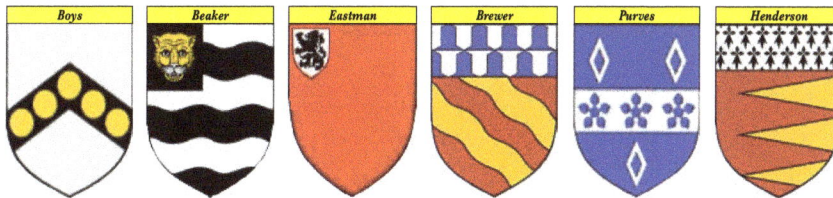

Williiam Sabine (c.1682-1719) of Titchfield, Hampshire, was succeeded by his son and heir James Sabine (1710-1779), who married firstly on the 1st February 1737 at St. Mary's Church, Titchfield to Martha Lamport [sic. Lamborn]. Together they produced a family of seven children, although three of their sons died in infancy.[1] The following information is what is known to date of the four surviving offspring of James and Martha Sabine of Titchfield, Hampshire, and lists their respective known descendants some of whom emigrated to the colonies.

10.1 Descendants of Isaac Sabine & Jane Boys [9]

Isaac SABINE (1738-1786), married on the 20th July 1769 at Titchfield, Hampshire to Jane Boys (1755-1830). He died at Titchfield in 1786, leaving a widow and a large family:

1. **Mary Sabine (1761-1823)**, mother unknown?

2. **Jane Sabine (1770-?)**, was apprenticed to Roger Gough as a 'cordwoman' on the 1st October 1791. Possibly married 23 Feb 1797 St. Mary, Southampton, Hampshire to Robert FIELDER, but issue and death details unknown.

3. **James SABINE (1772-?)**, likely married to Elizabeth, and became proprietors of the 'Crown & Anchor' in King's Head Court, Shoe Lane, issue and death details unknown.

4. **John SABINE (1775-?)**, marriage, issue and death details unknown.

5. **William SABINE (1777-1832)**, marriage, issue and death

details unknown.

6. **Isaac SABINE Jr. (1780-1841)**, a tailor, married on the 4th Feb 1802 at All Saints, Southampton, Hampshire to Elizabeth (1781–1848), daughter of Henry Fielder, shopkeeper of Southampton, with issue:

5.1 Jane Sabine (1805-?)

5.2 Andrew Samuel SABINE (1807-1871), b. 27 May 1807, bp. 29 Apr 1808 at King St. (formerly Orange St.) Independent Church by Rev. John Griffin.

7. **Samuel SABINE (1782-1831)**, married Mary Wise (1735-1814), who died 23rd April 1814. Samuel departed this life 29th November 1831, aged 48 years, issue unknown.

* Died before adulthood - d.s.p.
(Some names not listed in the index).

10.2 Descendants of Samuel Sabine & Sarah Beaker [10]

Samuel SABINE (1740-1786), was listed as a baker in Portsmouth Common, Hampshire in the 1784 Hampshire Directory. He married on the 5th February 1765 at Fareham, Hampshire to Sarah (1733-1784 [b. 16 August 1733 and d. 5 February 1784]), daughter of Henry Beaker and Mary of Fareham, with issue (see also 'Sabine of Boston'):

1. Rev. Samuel SABINE (1766-1843), was married firstly to a woman named Jeanette ??? (?-?), with issue:

1.1 Samuel SABINE (?-?) and two other sons, who were raised and lived in London.

1.2 Jeanette Sabine (?-?), who married Mark REED and lived in London.

1.3 Deborah Sabine (?-?), who married on the 8th July 1832 at St. Botolphs in London to James SEVERS, and removed to Canada.

Samuel married secondly on the 11th Jan 1831 at Dartmouth, MASS to Mary Gifford (?-?), but later died on the 20 October 1843, at Dorchester, MASS., aged 77 years.

2. William SABINE (1770-c.1807), (see 'Sabine of Prince Edward Island - Based on material supplied by Jago Sabine Esq. of West Point.') married on the 20th June 1790 at Old Church, Saint Pancras, London to Ann Willett (1768-?), daughter of Thomas Gardener and Mary Smith. William may have been buried on the 26th April 1807 at St James, Piccadilly, Westminster OR on Prince Edward Island, Canada, with issue:

2.1 Sarah Ann (1791–1881), married George MOORE (1781–1861), with issue:
a. George Benjamin MOORE (1808-1880)
b. William Sabine MOORE (1811-1879)
c. James William MOORE (1813-1875)
d. Charles MOORE (1815-1890)
e. Mary Ann Moore (1818-1889)
f. Samuel MOORE (1820-1909)
g. Henry Baker MOORE (1826-1886)
h. Charlotte Elizabeth Moore (1832-1918)

2.2 Samuel Gardiner SABINE (1799-1873), married firstly sometime before 1824 at Prince Edward Island, Canada to Anne Griffin (1804-?), with issue:
a. Sarah U Sabine (1824-?)
b. William Henry SABINE (1826-?)
c. Charles Thomas SABINE (1831-1909)
d. Eliza Ann Gardiner Sabine (1834-?)
e. Charlotte Willet Adelaide Sabine (1836-1923)
f. Mary Sabine (1839-?)
g. Hannah Sabine (1840-?)

Samuel married secondly on 17 Oct 1851 at Prince Edward Island, Canada to Eliza Jane Bateup (1810-1900), with issue:
h. Isaac SABINE (1852-1912)
i. Ann Elizabeth Sabine (1854-?)
j. William Henry Gardiner SABINE (1856-?)

2.3 Henry Baker SABINE (1802-1863), married on the 30th March 1830 at Charlottetown, Prince Edward Island, Canada to Martha I. Jago (1799-1875), a Bible Christian missionary from Cornwall, England, with issue:
a. William Gardiner SABINE (1831-1916), married Sarah Gardiner Clarke (1836-?), with issue:
a1. Avangeline Elizabeth Sabine (1857-?)
a2. Alice Martha Sabine (1861-1945)
a3. Albert Edward SABINE (1863-?), married Nellie Graves.
a4. Annie Victorino Sabine (1866-?), married John GODKIN.
a5. Caroline Amelia Sabine (1868-1939)
a6. Ida May Sabine (1871-1951)
a7. Ernest E. SABINE (1874-?)
b. Elizabeth Cross Sabine (1832-1858)
c. May Ann Rundell Sabine (1835-1862)
d. Sarah Sabine (1837-1856)
e. Rev. Thomas Jago SABINE (1839-1906), a Methodist minister at various places in Ontario, married Janie Fawkes of Charlottetown, P.E.I, with issue.
f. Caroline Sabine (1841-1917)
g. Ann Willett Sabine (1843-1934)
h. Charles Moor SABINE (1846-1865)
i. Samuel Henry SABINE (1849-1911), married Mary Ferguson at Charlottetown, with issue:
i1. Stella Sabine, married Fred Fraser, Oak Hill, K.B,
i2. Annie Sabine, of Honolulu, Hawaii, unmarried
i3. Ernest Jago SABINE (?-?), b. West Point, P.E.I. 26 Nov, married 9 Feb 1921 at Olenwood, P.E.I., to Lulu Edna Gorrill, with issue:
i. Helen Marie Sabine, b. 3 March 1922, married Wendell PHILLIPS at Springfield 23 Sep 19U2, with issue: Jean Elaine Phillips; Wendell Wayne Phillips; John Ernest Phillips.
ii. John Ernest Sabine, b. 16 Ap. 1892ii, joined the R.C.A.F. in the Great War II, and d. 1915 when the Lancaster bomber in which he was mid-upper gunner was lost with all its

crew during its 32nd flight over enemy territory.
iii. Leslie Theodore Sabine, b. 17 Nov. 1930.
iv. Christopher Irving Ferg. SABINE, b. 26 Sep 1932.
v. Annie Lulu Sabine, b. 2 Jan 1936
vi. Amos Wavell SABINE, b. 7 Apr 19E1, married with issue: Eva Sabine; Albert Theodore SABINE.

2.4 Mary Elizabeth Sabine (1807-?), married on the 3rd February 1831 at Prince Edward Island, Canada to John N. Clark (1804-?), with issue:
a. Frances Ann Clark (1832-?)
b. Eliza Eleanor Clark (1834-1917)
c. Sarah Gardner Clark (1836-?)
d. William Thomas CLARK (1838-?)
e. John Henry CLARK (1841-?)
f. Samuel Sabine CLARK (1843-1912)
g. Martha Matilda Clark (1844-?)
h. Joseph Francis CLARK (1849-?)
j. Mary Jane Clark (1851-?)

3. Rev. James SABINE (1774–1845), (see 'Sabine of Boston'), was born on the 26th May 1774, at Fareham, Hants, England, and married 1stly on the 19th August 1800, to Ann (?-1837) only daughter of Isaac Danford, Esq., attorney at law, County Of Gloucester, England, with issue:

3.1 Ann Sabine (1802-1879), b. 12 Sep 1802, at Uley, England, and married on 4 Mar 1830 in Grace Church, Boston, to Rev. Henry BLACKALLER (1798-1867), who was born 18 May 1798 in England. He died 21 Jun 1867, at Gallipolis, Ohio. She died May 1879, at Pomeroy, Ohio, with issue:
a. Henry Mortimer BLACKALLER (1838-1867), b. 15 July 1838, died 12 July 1867, at San Antonio, Texas, while a 1st lieutenant in the 9th Regiment of Cavalry, U.S. Army.
b. Jeffrey Theodore BLACKALLER (1841-1851)*, born 16 Apr 1841, died 10 May 1851.
c. James Sabine BLACKALLER (1844-?), b. 7 Oct 1844, married 6 Jun 1867 at Gallipolis, Ohio to Lalla James Donnally (?-1882), who died at Pomeroy, Ohio, 3 May 1882, with issue:
c1. Lavinia Sabine Blackaller (1868-?), b. 21 Nov 1868.
c2. Henry Mortimer BLACKALLER (1871-?), b. 22 Sep 1871.
c3. Arthur Morris BLACKALLER (1873-?), b. 24 May 1873.
c4. Danford Sabine BLACKALLER (1879-1879)*, b. 7 Sep 1879, d. 8 Sep 1879.
James married secondly on the 7 Oct 1885, to Georgina Doane Onderdonk, no issue.
d. Lavinia Sabine Blackaller (?-?), married 6 Oct 1892 at Lancaster, Ohio to Clarence Wells GOSS (?-?), with issue:
d1. Donnally Wells Goss (1894-?), b. 12 Feb 1894.
e. Arthur Morris BLACKALLER (?-?), married 28 Feb 1897, to Helen Louise Sullivan., with issue:
e1. Arthur Morris BLACKALLER (1897-?), b. 31 Dec 1897.
e2. Helen Louise Blackaller (1900-?), b. 29 Oct 1900.

3.2 Danford SABINE (1804-1805)*, b. 9 Jul 1804, at Croyden, England, died 3 Jul 1805, d.s.p.

3.3 Caroline Sabine (1806-1850), b. 23 May 1806 at Deptford, England, married 13 Nov 1834 at Bethel, VT to John Spooner SMITH (1790-1872), M. D., of Randolph, VT, and d. 7 Dec 1850, at Randolph. Dr. Smith was b. at Windsor, VT, 25 Aug 1790, and d. at Randolph, 8 Dec 1872, with issue:
a. Ann Caroline Smith (1837-?), b. 30 Apr 1837.
b. John Sabine SMITH (1843-1900), b. 24 Apr 1843; d. 6 Nov 1900.
c. Ann Caroline Smith (?-?), married 1 Aug 1867, to Patrick H. MURPHY (?-?), of Randolph, VT. They resided in New York City where he practiced dentistry for many years.
d. John Sabine SMITH (?-1900) married 15 Nov 1899, to Alice Clara Sawyer (?-?, of Randolph VT, and d. 6 Nov 1900, in New York City, where he had practiced law for many years.

3.4 Mariam Sabine (1808-1890), b. 10 Feb 1808, at Greenwich, England, married 5 Nov 1844, in Boston, MA, to Matthius APPLEBY (1809-?), who was b. 6 Oct 1809. He d. 8 Jul 1883, at Terre Haute, Indiana. She d. 20 Feb 1890 at the same place, no known issue.

3.5 Emma Sabine (1809-1887), b. 13 Dec 1809, at Tunbridge, England and married 26 Sep 1827, at Boston, MA, to Hiram JACOBS (1801-1874), who was b. 12 Mar 1801, at Thompson, CONN. He d. 29 Mar 1874, in Boston. She d. 27 Jan 1887, in Chicago, ILL, with issue:
a. Ignatius Hiram JACOBS (1829-1830)*, b. 20 Jun 1829; d. 2 Feb 1830.
b. William Henry JACOBS (1830-1834)*, b. 6 Dec 1830; d 16 Apr 1834.
c. James Sabine JACOBS (1832-1858), b. 27 Nov 1832; d. 6 Feb 1858.
d. Emma Louisa Jacobs (1835-1851)*, b. 19 Jan 1835; d. 17 Mar 1851.
e. Sarah Adaline Jacobs (1839-?), b. 7 Nov 1839. She married 21 Apr 1864, at Boston, MA, to Joseph Grafton PARKER SR. (?-?). They removed to Chicago in 1880, with issue:
e1. James Jacobs PARKER (1866-?), b. 6 Aug 1866, and married 9 Jun 1891 at Chicago, ILL, to Madaline Kern (?-?), with issue:
i James Irving PARKER (1893-?), b. 26 Jun 1893.
ii Grafton Lenone PARKER (1897-?), b. 29 Aug 1897.
e2. Joseph Grafton PARKER JR. (1868-?), b. 25 May 1868, and married in 1893, at Chicago, ILL, to Bertha Hilgard (?-?), with issue:
i. Robert Roy PARKER (1896-?), b. in 1896.
ii. Joseph Grafton PARKER III (1900-?), b. 1 Apr 1900.
iii. Sarah Marie Parker (1903-?), b. 31 Aug 1903.
e3. Emma Louise Parker (1874-?), b. 20 Jan 1874, and married 28 Jan 1897, in Chicago, ILL, to Arthur Lee HARDIN (?-?), of Kentucky, with issue:
i. Ione Adaline Hardin (1897-?), b. in 1897.
ii. John Grafton HARDIN (1899-?), b. 1 Apr 1899
iii. Arthur Lee HARDIN (1903-?), b. 15 Sep 1903.

3.6 John Theodore SABINE (1811-1851), b. 31 Mar 1811, at Tunbridge Wells, England; graduated from the Boston Latin School in the class which entered in 1821. Graduated in 1830 from Williams College, MASS. Ordained deacon in the Protestant Episcopal Church, 2 Jun 1833, at Bethel, VT, by Bishop Hopkins, and ordained presbyterian Sep 1840, at Woodstock, VT. He married on 8 Sep 1836 at Grace Church, Boston, to Marinette Dickinson (1813-1872), who was b. 7 Oct 1813, at Chatham, CONN and d. 8 May 1872 at Newtonville, MASS. He preached in Clappville (Leicester), MASS., Fairfield, St. Albans, Highgate, Manchester and Bethel, VT. At the formation of the parish of the Church of the Messiah, in Boston, in the fall of the year 1843, he consented to supply the pulpit and preached for seven months, although Rev. George M. Randall, afterwards Bishop of Colorado, was called as the first rector. In 1848 he was one of the editors of a weekly newspaper called the 'American Cabinet and Boston Athenaeum,' devoted to art, science, literature etc. He died at 43 Harvard Street, Boston, on 15 Mar 1851, with issue:
a. James SABINE (1837-1894), born at Highgate, VT, died in Washington, D. C., issue unknown.
b. Marinette Sabine (1840-?), b. 3 Mar 1840, at Manchester, VT, and married 10 Jan 1860, in Grace Church, Boston, to Henry Asa GORE (1834-1864), who was b. 14 Oct 1834, at Preston, CONN., and d. 9 Aug 1864, at Minneapolis, MINN., with issue:
a1. Marinette Dickinson Gore (1860-?), b. 20 Dec 1860, and married 5 Feb 1891, in Brooklyn, NY., to Edward Wolcott CHURCH (1863-?), who was b. 22 May 1863, at Washington CONN, with issue:
i. Marinette Church (1892-?), b. 20 July 1892.
Marinette married secondly on 24 Nov 1869, at Newtonville, MASS. to Carlos GORE (1843-?), brother of preceding, who was b. 24 Feb 1843, at Preston, with issue:
a2. Carlos Sabine GORE (1871-1889)*, b. 20 Jun 1871, d . 17 Aug 1889.
a3. Josephine Cook Gore (1874-1875)*, b. 26 May 1874; d . 5 May 1875.
a4. Calvin Howard GORE (1876-?), b. 14 Apr 1876.
6.3 John Dickinson SABINE (1843-?), b. 9 Oct 1843, in Boston.

3.7 Eusebia Sabine (1813-1873), b. 20 Feb 1813, at Tunbridge, Engand, and married 7 Jan 1840 to Asaph Bemi s CHILD (1813-1875), M.D. who was b. 22 Aug 1813, at Bethel, VT. She d. 15 Sep 1873, at South Boston, MASS., and he d. 17 Aug 1875, at West Fairlee, VT, with issue:
a. John Theodore CHILD (1841-1893), b. 13 Jun 1841, d 30 Mar 1893. He married 4 Jun 1863, at Somerville, MASS., to Sarah Gerry (1844-?), who was b. 14 Jan 1844. He d. 30 Mar 1893, at Malden, MASS., with issue:
a1. Sarah Gertrude Child (1864-?), b. 10 Jun 1864, and married 19 Mar 1900, at Malden, to Charles Wesley WOOD (?-?), of New York City, with issue:
i. Hazel Gertrude Wood (1901-?), b. 29 Sep 1901.
a2. Madeleine Eusebia Child (1866-?), b. 26 Sep 1866, and married 12 May 1897 at Malden, MASS., to William Seldon UDALL (?-?), of Strafford, VT.
a3. Ruth Lavinia Sabine Child (1868-?), b. 7 Dec 1868
a4. Earnest Theodore CHILD (1872-?), b. 1 Feb 1872, and married 8 Jun 1898, at Jamaica Plain, MASS., to Mary Elizabeth Wallace (?-?), with issue:

i. Lachlan Wallace CHILD (1901-?), b. 30 Jun 1901.
b. Henry CHILD (1847-1847), b. 13 Jan 1847; d. 19 Jan 1847.
c. Charles Edward CHILD (1853-?), b. 31 Jul 1853, and
married 14 Jun 1886, at Manchester, N.H., to Rebecca
Emogene Harris (1852-?), b. 14 Dec 1852, at Lowell, MASS.

3.8 Uleyetta Sabine (1814-1839), b. 23 Jul 1814, at Tunbridge,
England. The name Uleyetta is evidently based on Uley,
Glos., where from 1800 to 1808, the Rev, James Sabine held
his first appointment as a minister. She married Nov 1837,
to Rev. Dexter POTTER (1803-1881), a clergyman of the

Protestant Episcopal Church. b. 9 Jan 1803. She d. 25 Jul
1839, at Poquetanock, CONN. He d. 2 Apr 1881, with issue:
8.1 Uleyetta Sabine Potter (1839-1859), b. 25 Jul 1839; d.
15 Dec 1859.

3.9 Lavinia Indiana Sabine (1817-1849), b. 18 Jul 1817, at St.
John's , Newfoundland, and married 22 Sep 1846 in Boston,
to Robert H. RALSTON (1814-1859), who was b. 12 Dec
1814, at Bethel, VT. She d. 9 May 1849, at Lockport, N.Y. He
d. 5 August 1859, at the same place, with issue:
9.1 Mary Ann Ralston (1847-1847)*, b. Jul 1847; d. in infancy.

9.2 LAVINIA SABINE Ralston (1849-1903), b. 3 Mar 1849; d.
30 Jan 1903.

3.10 Ignatius James Jackson SABINE (1819-1822)*, b. 20 Dec
1819, in Boston, MASS. d. 15 Dec 1822.

Rev. James Sabine married 2ndly on 11 Oct 1840 at Trinity
Church, Bridgewater, Mass, to Mrs Dorcas W, Monroe (1787-
1880), but without issue.

* Died before adulthood - d.s.p.
(Some names not listed in the index).

Reverend James Sabine [12]

REV. JAMES SABINE

REV. JOHN THEODORE SABINE

Rev. James Sabine (1774-1845), was born on the 26th May 1774, at Fareham, Hants, England, the 3rd son of Samuel and Sarah Sabine and the grandson of James and Martha Sabine of Titchfield. He married on the 19th August 1800, to Ann (?-1837) the only daughter of Isaac Danford, Esq., attorney at law, County Of Gloucester, England. Sabine entered the Presbyterian ministry in England about 1800, and moved his growing family around the following postings: Uley, Gloucestershire (1800-04); Croyden, Surrey (1804-06); Deptford and Greenwich, London (1806-08); Tunbridge Wells, Kent (1808-15); and Tottenham, near London (1816).

He then left England with his wife and seven children, sailing on the 6th May 1816 from London, and arrived on the 15th of the following month at Saint John's, Newfoundland where he preached until after the two great fires which devastated that city. He then removed to Boston, where he arrived with his family on the 18th July 1818, and soon commenced to preach in Boylston Hall, corner of Washington and Boylston streets. The society thus started became the Essex Street Church, the corner stone of which was laid on the 26th January 1819, and the church was dedicated 15th December 1819. In the course of two years differences arose and by a vote of the 6th March 1822, it was resolved to withdraw to Boylston Hall. This body retained the name of Essex Street Church until the 26th November 1823, when they were received into the Londonderry Presbytery. Thus they became the Second Presbyterian Church of Boston, although they were known as the 'First Prebyterian Church.' He again moved his family through St. John's, Newfoundland (1816-18); Boston, Massachusetts (1818-30); and finally Bethel, Vermont (1830-45).

In 1828 Rev. Sabine withdrew from the Presbyterian Church, took orders in the Protestant Episcopal Church, and was ordained priest by Bishop Griswold. He was received at Grace Church, Temple Street, Boston, as its first rector and was, in 1830 transferred to the diocese of Vermont, becoming the rector of Christ Church, Bethel, where he preached for fifteen years. In addition to having numerous sermons published, Rev. Sabine wrote on "Ecclesiastical History," (Boston, 1820).

His first wife died on the 2nd October 1837, at Bethel, and on 11th October 1840, he married secondly to Mrs Dorcas W. Monroe, widow of Rev. Matt Monroe (d. 8 Apr 1836), at Trinity Church, Bridgewater, Mass, without further issue. He died 2nd October 1845, at the home of his daughter, in Randolph, Orange County, Vermont, aged 71 years and was buried at Old Christ Church Cemetery in Bethel, Vermont. He was survived by Dorcas, who died on the 14th October 1880 at Newport, RI, aged 93, and six of his ten known children.[11]

Martha Lamport (1707-1747)

Martha Lamport's [sic. Lamborn] ancestry may be from noble origins, and she could very well be a descendant of Josiah Lamborn (1659-1749), who was born near Easthampstead, Berkshire.[2] Martha was apparently the sister of a Robert Lamborn who emigrated to Australia, and may even have been the daughter of John Lamborn, who had a daughter baptised at Chiseldon, Wiltshire on the 25th March 1714, not far from Titchfield, but these links are unverified at present. Her children from James Sabine were as follows:

1. Isaac Sabine (1738-1786)

James and Martha's eldest and first son was Isaac Sabine, who was born and baptised at Titchfield in 1738. He married on the 20th July 1769 at Titchfield to Jane Boys (1755-1830), and they produced six children (*see 10.1 Descendants of Isaac Sabine & Jane Boys*). Isaac Sabine died aged 48 at Titchfield in 1786,with his headstone revealing that he also fathered a Mary Sabine (1761-1823) to an unknown mother.

2. James Sabine Jr. (1739-c.1790)

Little is known of James Sabine Jr., who was born and baptised at Titchfield in 1739, but he apparently died unmarried in the West Indies, which was at that time the heart of Britain's sugar and slave trade.

3. Samuel Sabine (1740-1786)

Samuel Sabine was born and baptised at Titchfield in 1740. He married on the 5th February 1765 at Fareham to Sarah Beaker (1733-1784), and they produced at least three sons (*see 10.2 Descendants of Samuel Sabine & Sarah Beaker*).[3]

4. Sarah Sabine (1744-c.1812)

Sarah Sabine was born and baptised at Titchfield in 1744. She married on the 25th December 1780 at St. Mary's, Portsea to Thomas Eastman (c.1752-1816), with her family and descendants discussed in greater detail in Chapter 11 (*see 10.3 Descendants of Sarah Sabine & Thomas Eastman*).[4]

James Sabine's first wife Martha Lamport passed away on the 5th November 1747, and was buried at Titchfield alongside three of her deceased infant sons (#'s 5 to 7), with her headstone memorialising all four deaths:

> "To the Memory of Martha the wife of James Sabine who departed this life November 15th 1747 aged 40 years. Also three of the sons who departed in their infancy."[5]

Hannah Parker (1728-?)

After the death of his first wife, James Sabine married secondly on the 21st November 1748 in the neighbouring town of Fareham, Hampshire to Hannah Parker[6] and they produced a further seven children, although only five of these survived to adulthood. Stemming from James and Hannah Sabine's children were descendants that emigrated to Canada, the United States and to Australia.

10.3 Descendants of Sarah Sabine & Thomas Eastman [13]

Sarah Sabine (1744-1810), married on the 25th December 1780, at St Mary's, Portsea to Thomas EASTMAN (c.1752-1816), cabinetmaker & auctioneer of Portsea, with issue:

1. Thomas Sabine EASTMAN (1782-1855), married in 1805 to Mary Eglon (1780-1866), with issue:
1.1 Miriam Eastman (1806-1886)
1.2 Eliza Eastman (1807-1875)
1.3 Thomas EASTMAN (1809-1860)
1.4 Sarah Eastman (1810-?)
1.5 Jane Eastman (1812-1898)
1.6 George EASTMAN (1813-1869)
1.7 Mary Elizabeth Eastman (1813-1813)*
1.8 Mary Elizabeth Eastman (1815-1848)
1.9 Charlotte Eastman (1817-1819)*
1.10 Theophilus EASTMAN (1819-1819)*
1.11 Ann Eglon Eastman (1821-1841)
1.12 William Henry EASTMAN (1824-1869)

2. Elizabeth Eastman (c.1784-1852), married in 1812 to John SHOVELLER LLD (1789-1847), with issue:
2.1 Sarah Sabine Shoveller (1812-1813)*
2.2 Mary Elizabeth Shoveller (1813-1814)*
2.3 Jane Allen Shoveller (1814-1874)
2.4 Sarah Sabine Shoveller (1816-1825)*
2.5 John SHOVELLER (1818-1899)
2.6 Thomas Eastman SHOVELLER (1820-1825)*
2.7 Mary Elizabeth Shoveller (1822-1868)
2.8 William Henry SHOVELLER (1824-?)
2.9 Martha Shoveller (1826-1826)*
2.10 Thomas Eastman SHOVELLER (1827-1908)

3. Sarah Eastman (c.1785-1850), died unmarried.

4. Theophilus EASTMAN (1789-1863), married 1stly in 1816 to Mary Adlam (1792-1849), with issue:
4.1 Thomas EASTMAN (1819-1820)*
4.2 Mary Adlam Eastman (1822-1822)*
4.3 Samuel EASTMAN (1824-1900)
4.4 Martha Adlam Eastman (1826-1827)*
4.5 Sarah Selenia Eastman (1828-1905)
4.6 Theophilus Adlam EASTMAN (1828-1829)*
4.7 Emma Eastman (1833-1868)
4.8 Jabez Ebenezer EASTMAN (1839-1922)

Theophilus married 2ndly in 1857 to Emma Arter (1834-1860), with issue:
i. Annie Arter (1860-1861)*

* Died before adulthood - d.s.p.

ANCESTRY OF THE REV. JAMES SABINE

Contributed by WILLIAM H. W. SABINE, of Hampstead, London, England

In 1904 John Dickinson Sabine published in Washington "The Family and Descendants of the Rev. James Sabine", a Congregational minister who arrived in Boston in 1818, and whose ten children have today very numerous representatives in the United States, and whose surname was already well-known in America through the family of William Sabin(e) of Rehoboth (in 1643; see THE REGISTER, vol. 101, p. 264).

The author of the above-named genealogy was able to give full details of the descendants of the Rev. James Sabine, and to prefix some particulars of his parents and grandparents, who lived in the small Hampshire town of Titchfield, long a stronghold of Independency or Congregationalism, and associated with an early President of Harvard.

It may therefore be of genealogical interest to record as fully as possible the ancestry of the Rev. James Sabine.

The earliest known references to the Sabin(e) name in Hampshire do not take us so far back as is the case in several other English counties. A deed in the writer's possession, dated 1520, and relating to the town of Stockbridge, is witnessed by "Johe Bendeby the Ballie de Stockbrydge pdnte Johe Sabyn Constabul Gibin etc." The Subsidy Rolls (P.R.O.) name the following Sabin(e)s in Hampshire at the dates given: John Sabyn, Southampton, 1524; John Sabbyn, Titchfield, 1525; Richard Sabyn, Heckfield, 1525; John Sabine, Winchester, 1530; John Sobyn [sic] and Isabel Sabine, West Hursley, 1530; Edward Sabine, Southwick, 1546; Robert Sabyn, Titchfield, 1546.

The small town of Titchfield in or near which lived the immediate ancestors of the Rev. James Sabine, is one of great antiquity. It is named in Domesday Book (1086) as Ticefelle, a mill and a market being mentioned; in later centuries the name appears as Tichefelde. Formerly a small port, with a tidal harbour, the town stands near the mouth of a stream called the River Meon which empties itself into Southampton Water. The harbour ceased to exist in 1611, when the Earl of Southampton closed the mouth of the river to reclaim the land. This must have seemed a tremendous event locally, and the parish register solemnly records "the shutting out of Titchfield haven by one Richard Talbottes industrie under God's permissione".

Today the quiet little town can show the interested visitor the ruins of the Premonstratensian Abbey of St. Mary (founded 1222), and the fascinating parish church of St. Peter, part of which is authoritatively believed to date from the 9th century or even earlier, while the greater part of the existing building belongs to the 12th, 13th, and 14th centuries.

The surviving registers of the church begin in 1589, and one of the first entries reads: Baptized Apryll 1590 Wyllÿm Saben the xxx day.

Thereafter entries of the Sabin(e) name are extremely numerous until the Restoration of Charles II, when the Puritan vicar, the Rev. Urian Oakes, declined to comply with the Act of Uniformity (1662), and was ejected. As soon as the Cavalier persecution died down sufficiently, Oakes assisted in the organization of an Independent (Congregational) Church at Titchfield; he then returned to Cambridge, Mass., to become pastor of the church there, and eventually President of the College. He had originally been taken there by his parents in 1640.

After the ejectment of the vicar whose religious opinions were in accord with their own, the Sabin(e)s and other Independents appear to have ceased almost completely to have their children baptized in the parish church, and to have celebrated their marriages whenever possible in other parishes. Praiseworthy as this faithfulness is from one point of view, it is a little trying for the genealogist to turn page after page of the registers for but scant return. Fortunately wills and other sources do help to fill in gaps in the later period, and the following pedigree of the Rev. James Sabine is based entirely on reliable records:

1. WILLIAM SABINE was buried 30 Aug. 1606. He married in Titchfield, 24 Sept. 1592, AGNES WOODDE, who was buried 20 Aug. 1638.

Children:

2. i. ZACHARIAH SABBINN, bapt. 24 June 1593.
   ii. ELIZABETH SABBINE, bapt. 24 April 1597; m. —— WHEATLAND.

2. ZACHARIAH SABBINN, baptized in Titchfield 24 June 1593, died 7 July 1670. He married, 7 [?] May 1626, ALICE LONGLINE.

Children:

   i. GEORGE SABBINN, bapt. 18 March 1627.
   ii. WILLIAM SABBINN, bapt. 8 March 1629.
   iii. THOMAS SABBIN, bapt. 20 Feb. 1631.
   iv. MARY SABBEN, bapt. 9 Feb. 1632.
   v. ZACHARIAH SABBINN, bapt. 25 July 1635.
   vi. ANNE SABINE.
3. vii. HENRY SABINE, bapt. 7 April 1638.

3. HENRY SABINE, baptized in Titchfield 7 April 1638. He married SARAH ——, who was buried 5 April 1728. His will was proved in Winchester in 1687.

Children:

4. i. WILLIAM SABINE, b. about 1682.
   ii. HENRY SABINE.

4. WILLIAM SABINE, born about 1682, buried in Titchfield 15 Aug. 1719. He married MARY ——, who survived him, and married, in 1721, Isaac Read.

Children:

   i. WILLIAM SABINE.
5. ii. JAMES SABINE, b. about 1710.
   iii. SARAH SABIN, d. unm. Buried in Titchfield 11 Dec. 1728.

5. JAMES SABINE, born in Titchfield about 1710, buried there in 1779. He married first, in 1737, MARTHA LAMPORT, who died 15 Nov. 1747, aged 40 years; and secondly, in 1748 or 1749, HANNAH PARKER.

Children by first wife:

   i. ISAAC SABINE, d. in Titchfield in 1786.
6. ii. SAMUEL SABINE.
   iii. JAMES SABINE, who, it is stated, died or was lost in the West Indies.
   iv. SARAH SABINE, m. in 1780 THOMAS EASTMAN of Portsea.

Children by second wife:

   v. WILLIAM SABINE, b. in Titchfield in 1749; d. at his home in Islington in 1826 and was buried in the churchyard 4 December; m. ELIZABETH BREWER, daughter of the Rev. Samuel Brewer, Congregational minister in Stepney.
   William Sabine went to London as a young apprentice, becoming Fire Surveyor to the London Assurance Company*, and owner of considerable property in the city. About 1799 he built a new chapel in Titchfield, and gave it to the Congregationalists, who still use it. One of his sons, James, emigrated to Canada, whence a number of descendants have moved to the United States.
   vi. DANIEL SABINE.
   vii. PATIENCE SABINE, d. unm. in Titchfield in 1829, aged 66.
   viii. LYDIA SABINE, d. unm. in Guildford, Surrey. Will proved in 1788.

6. SAMUEL SABINE married, about 1765, SARAH BEAKER of Fareham, near Titchfield, born 16 Aug. 1733, died 5 Feb. 1784.

Children:

   i. SAMUEL SABINE, b. in 1766; d. in Dorchester, Mass., 20 Oct. 1843.
   ii. WILLIAM SABINE, who lived in Prince Edward's Island.
7. iii. JAMES SABINE, b. 26 May 1774.

7. JAMES SABINE, born in Fareham, Hampshire, 26 May 1774, died in Bethel, Vt., 2 Oct. 1845. He married ANN DANFORD, born 19 Sept. 1774, daughter of Isaac Danford, attorney-at-law.

He was a student at Hoxton Academy, and entered the Congregational ministry, receiving his first appointment in Uley, Gloucestershire. His next appointment was to the church at George Street, Croydon, one of the oldest Congregational† churches in England. He arrived at St. John's, Newfoundland, in 1816, accompanied by his wife and seven children, thence proceeding in 1818 to Boston, Mass., where he stayed twelve years.

For further details of the Rev. James Sabine and his descendants reference should be made to the genealogy named at the beginning of this article, which was compiled by one of the descendants. The present writer trusts that the earlier matter now offered will prove of interest.

---

*Not to "the city" as stated by John D. Sabine.
†J. D. Sabine mistakenly implied that it was a Presbyterian church.

TITCHFIELD, HAMPSHIRE, ASSOCIATIONS WITH NEW ENGLAND: — When referring to the Earl of Southampton's having closed the port of Titchfield in 1611 (THE REGISTER, vol. 104, p. 259), the writer omitted to point out that this was the Earl (Henry Wriothesley, third Earl of Southampton, born in 1573, died in 1624, the patron of Shakespeare, and believed by some to be the "Mr. H. W." of the "Sonnets") who "helped to equip Weymouth's expedition to Virginia in 1605, and became a member of the Virginia Company's council in 1609.... In April 1610 he helped to despatch Henry Hudson to seek the North-west Passage, and was an incorporator both of the North-west Passage Company in 1612, and of the Somers Island Company in 1615. He was chosen treasurer of the Virginia Company on 28 June 1620, etc." (see "Dictionary of National Biography"). From the rare printed list of "Supplies [sent] to Virginia in Anno 1620" we learn that "the Right Honorable the Earle of Southampton and the Company" sent and provided, among other ships, "The May-Flower of 140 Tuns in August 1620 with 100 persons" aboard.

The Earl's family seat was Place House in Titchfield, which village and manor he owned. Hence, in connection with the suggestion that William Sabin (of Rehoboth in 1643) was a native of Titchfield, it is worth noting that among the entries in the Titchfield parish register is the following: "March 1632. Buried. Thomas Sabin servant to the Right honorable Earl of Southampton the 21st day." This would be the fourth Earl, son of the third Earl.

Hollis, N. Y.   W. H. W. SABINE.

*P. 53, this volume.

▲ 'Ancestry of the Rev. James Sabine' by W.H.W. Sabine, p.53 (in... Roberts, G. B. (1985). 'English Origins of New England Families - From the N.E. Historical and Genealogical Register,' 2nd Series, Vol.3, Genealogical Pub Co, Baltimore).

10.4 Descendants of William Sabine & Elizabeth Brewer [14]

William SABINE (1749-1826), who settled in London, was some years surveyor to the city, married on the 19th May 1778 at St Mary Hill, London to Elizabeth (1757-1832), the daughter of Rev. Samuel Brewer, a Congregational Minister in Stepney, who was born 17th June 1723 at Rendham, Suffolk. William died at Islington, London on the 26th Nov 1826, leaving a numerous family:

1. Elizabeth Sabine (1779-1780), died an infant.

2. Elizabeth Sabine (1781-1849), married 16 Oct 1811 at St Mary, Islington, to William BROOKS (1786-1867), with issue:

2.1 Charles William BROOKS (1815-1874), b. 29 Apr 1815, d. 23 Feb 1874, who was well known under the pen name, "Shirley Brooks." married in 1854 to Emily Marguerite Walkinshaw (1827-1880), with issue:
a. Reginald Shirley Walkinshaw BROOKS (1854–1888)NEW Louise (1847-?)
b. Cecil Cunningham BROOKS (1857-?)
Charles William married 2ndly to Josephine Catharine (Kate) Brooks (1825-?), with issue:
c. Louise Brooks (1847-?)
d. Charles William BROOKS (1849-?)
e. Shirley William Alban Brooks (1850–1851)

2.2 Frances Sabine Brooks (1820-1820)*

2.3 William BROOKS (1821-1882) married 1854 to Caroline Wallach Or Marcus (1825-?), with issue:
a. Charles William BROOKS
b. Amy Mary Brooks (1857-1903)
c. Arthur Sabine BROOKS (1860-1900)
d. Nathalie Henrietta Brooks (1861-1951)

2.4 Sophia Brooks (1822-?), died unmarried.

2.5 David William BROOKS (1828-?), died unmarried.

3. William SABINE (1783-1786), died a child.

4. Maria Sabine (1785-1861), married Basil PIFFARD.

5. William S. SABINE (1787-1862), b. 17 Jan 1787, married on the 16 October 1815 to Elizabeth (1794-1887), daughter of Richard Townend (1756-1837), of Middleton, Leeds. She was born 9 May 1794 and died 5 July 1887 at Bromley, Kent. William died on the 3 Apr 1863 at Bath, Somerset, with issue:

5.1 William Townend SABINE (1817-1852) M.R.C.S., born 17 October 1817 at Camberwell, and married about 18U1 at Brockdish, nr. Karlesden, Norfolk to Anne Churchill. William died on the 26th July 1852 at Cores ^nd, Wooburn, Bucks, with issue:
a. William Churchill SABINE (1852-1940), b. 9th September 1852 at Wcobum, and married on the 22 June 1882 at Holy Trinity Church, Beckenham, Bucks., to Lavinia Ann Fox (1854-1940). William died on 14th October 1940 at Leigh-on-Sea, Essex. She was b. on 1? December 1854 and d. 6 December 1940 at Derby, with issue:
a1. Harold Willian Townend Churchill SABINE (1884-?) was b. 8 November 1884, and married on the 3 September 1910 at St. Gabriel's Church, Cricklewood, Hose Putnam, with issue:
i. Roger Harold Churchill SABINE (19??-?), b. 17 Oct. 19H.
ii. Barbara Sabine (1917-?), b. 25 Feb. 1917.
iii. Brenda Lavinia Sabine (1918-?), b. 2b Bee. 1918.
iv. Pamela Hope Sabine (1921-?), b. 12 April 1921.

6. James SABINE (1789-1858), born London, married on the 13 March 1816 at Saint George The Martyr, Southwark, Surrey, England to Susannah Black (1796-1881), migrated to Canada about 1832, with issue. He d, 2 March 1858 at Brockville, Ontario, (see 'Sabine of Brockville, Ontario' & based on material supplied by Mrs. W. D. Lighthall of Westmount, Quebec, Canada, and on material supplied by Mrs. Elizabeth H. Sloane of Philadelphia):

6.1 James Edward SABINE (1817-1899), married 1849 to Jane Morgan (1823-1853), with issue:
a. Adam Brown SABINE (1857-1934)
b. William Gerald SABINE (1857-1938)
c. Suzie Tassie Sabine (1860-1889)

6.2 Susan Sabine (1818-1903), unmarried, d. Winnipeg, MAN.

6.3 Alexander Frederick SABINE (1819-1901), married 1stly in 1842 to Susan Whitney Lyman (1821-1867) with issue:
a. Theodore Clement SABINE (1843-1906), married 1873 to Frances Ella Drake (Sabine) (1857-1937), with issue:
a1. Frederick Raphael SABINE (1878-1939)
a2. Clarence E. SABINE (1881-1881)
a3. Otto Bauman SABINE (1882-1957)
a4. Shirley Harter SABINE (1887-1935), married 1stly to Anna K. Sabine (1887-?). He married 2ndly to Anna Lee Wilson (Sabine) (1884-1964), d.s.p.
b. Bertha Wenham Sabine (1844-1921)
c. Alice Helen Sabine (1846-1931)
d. Herbertt Willard SABINE (1848-1848)*
e. Edward Ernest Black SABINE (1849-1849)*
f. Frank Gerrard SABINE (1850-?)
g. Alexander Frederick SABINE (1852-1852)*
h. Wilmer Harris SABINE (1854-1855)*
i. Anna Lyman Sabine (1858-1901)
j. Frederika Victoria Sabine (1863-1950), married in1891 at St. Clements Church, Philadelphia to Frank Patterson Hill (1862-1935), with issue:
j1. Winifred Cheston Hill (1891-1961), m, 8 Oct. 1919 at Grace Church, Mount Airy, Phila., to Thomas Francis KOSSITER, d.s.p.
j2. Helen Willard Millicent Hill (1893-1977), married 26 Apr 1920 at Grace Church, Mount Airy, Phila., to Cohn Blair THOMSON (marriage dissolved without issue).
j3. Miriam Pomeroy Lyman Hill (1901-?), married 3 May 1929 at Grace Church, Lount Airy, Phila., to Lt. Lester Joseph TACY U.S.A., a West Point graduate and later a Lt-Colonel, who d. a prisoner of the Japanese in World War II after serving at Bataan and Corregidor, Philipines;
j4. Elizabeth Whitney Hill (1903-1988), married 1st Herbert Edward WHITING of Philadelphia, and 2nd William SLOANE, Jr., of Norfolk. Virginia (both marriages dissolved without issue).
j5. Frank Patterson HILL (1907-1982), m, 27 June 1936 in Philadelphia, to Nettie Louise Brown, dau. of Harry and Anna Barbara Brown of Catasaqua, Pa, with issue:
i Penelope Hill, b. Germantown, PA.
ii Patricia Hill, b. Oreland, PA. 12 May 1982
iii Cynthia Hill, b. Oreland, PA. 8 Feb. 1985
k. Frederick Victoria SABINE (1864-?)
l. Ernest Shirley Brooks Sabine (1866-1866)*
Alexander married 2ndly in 1872 to Jane Boyce Lee (1834-1901)

6.4 Mary Ann Sabine (1824-1902), a deaf mute, d. unmarried.

6.5 Joseph Brooks SABINE (1825-1881), married in 1862 to Harriet H Butterfield (1832–1916), he died London, with issue:
a. Herbert Alvin SABINE (1866-?)

6.6 Herbert Lachlan SABINE (1827-1885), b, Homerton, London, married about 1860 to Margaret May Cameron (1830-1907), with issue:
a. James Ewen SABINE (1861-1929)
b. Susannah Sabine (1865-?)
c. Jeanette Wilks Sabine (1869-?)
d. Hannah Sabine (1873-?)
e. Bertha Sabine (1876-?)
f. John A. SABINE (1879-?)

6.7 Jeanette Sabine (1831-1912), married Quinton McKENDRICK (1828-?), with issue:
a. Chas. G. McKENDRICK (1853–1937)
b. Helen McKendrick (1857-?)
c. Ruth J. McKendrick (1859-?)
d. Clara McKendrick (1866-?)

6.8 Charles SABINE (1834-1834)*, d.s.p.

6.9 Alice Truman Sabine (1836-1902), b. Brockville, married 1862 to John Aston WILKES (1833-1881), with issue:
a. Lucy May Wilkes (1862-1871)*
b. Henry Aston WILKES (1866-1950)
c. Cybella Charlotte Wilkes (1868-1958)
d. Edward Albert Oxnard WILKES (1873-1873)*
e. John Frederick WILKES (1875-1954)
f. Charles Herbert WILKES (1878-1965)

7. John SABINE (1791-1856) (see 'Sabine of Australia' - Based on information supplied by Sir Robert R. Garran (K.C.M.G.). John Sabine was b. in 1791, probably in Islington, Middlesex, married 5 Jan 1525 at All Saints', Southampton, to Adelaide Isham Eppes, who was born 1800, and died 1885 at Glenelg, SA. He died Adelaide, South Australia in 1856. They lived first at Bury St. Edmunds, Suffolk before emigrating to Australia about 1850, with issue:

7.1 John Randolph SABINE (1826-1902). married in 1854 to Katharine Hardcastle (1833–1893), with issue:
a. Isabelle Randolph Sabine (1855–1920), married Mr. RAMSBOTTOM, issue unknown.
b. Catherine Clara Sabine (1857–1863)
c. William Randolf Eppes SABINE (1859–1924)
d. Mary Adelaide Sabine (1861–1957), married WELLS, with issue:
d1. Enid Wells, married with issue.
d2. Haisie Wells, married with issue.
d3. Alice Wells, died unmarried
e. Melina Hardcastle Sabine (1863–1952)
f. John Randolph SABINE (1867–1936)
g. Edith Annie Sabine (1869–1926)
h. Henry Rudolph SABINE (1871–1926)

7.2 Edith Brewer Sabine (c.1830-190), died unmarried.

7.3 Mary Isham Sabine (1830-1923), married 1 Dec 1854 at Adelaide to Andrew GARRAN (b. in England 1825, d. 1901), editor of the Sydney Morning Herald, and a member of the NSW Legislative Council, with issue:
a. Mary Eppes Garran (1856-1930), unmarried.
b. Winifred Isham Garran (1858-1935), unmarried.
c. Helen Sabine Garran.
d. Elsie Clement Garran
e. Lucy Randolph Garran, married Herbert HARPER
f. Sir Robert Randolph GARRAN, (1867-1957, K.C.M.G.), Commonwealth Solicitor-General. He. married on 7 Apr 1902 at Sydney to Hilda Mary Robson (1873-1936), with issue:
f1. Richard Randolph GARRAN (1903–1991)
f2. John Cheyne GARRAN (1905–1976)
f3. Andrew GARRAN (1906–1965)
f4. Sir Isham Peter GARRAN (1910–1991)
g. Adelaide Maud Garran*, died in infancy.
h. Beatrice Briscoe Garran*, died in infancy.

7.4 Clement SABINE (1833-?), married 6 Mar 1862 at Congregational Chapel Freeman St, Adelaide, South Australia, to Ann Glenn Clarke (1843-1921), with issue:
a. Clement Egbert Eppes SABINE (1862-1898), unmarried.
b. Andrew Garran SABINE (1864-1921), d. unmarried.
c. Adelaide Isham Mary Sabine (1866–1866), d. unmarried.
d. Ernest Maurice SABINE (1867-1957), a Police magistrate in S. Australia, married with issue;
e. Edith Ethelwyn Sabine (1870-1934), d. unmarried.
f. Mary Sabine, who married 1stly Hamilton Hope OSBORNE of H.o.W., with issue of two daus. and a son:
f1. Anthony Hope OSBORNE (1908-1943), a Captain in the Royal Greys, married Primrose Phyllis Salt, with issue:
i Duncan Norton Hope OSBORNE
f2. Mary Sabine (1871-1959),
Mary married 2ndly Captain Reginald HORTEN, R.N. of Downs House, Xalding, liaidstene
g. Charles Glenn SABINE (1875-1931), unmarried.
h. Robert Routh SABINE (1876–1941), who went to West Australia, married with issue.
i. Adelaide Isham Elizabeth Sabine (1878-1921)
j. Helen Sabine (1880-1971), married Edward WAKEFIELD, with issue:
j1. Edward WAKEFIELD who d. unmarried.
j2. Winsome Wakefield. married Norman PICKERING, solicitor, Sydney.
j3. Kate 'Kitty' Sabine, married David CROSSLEY, farmer, without issue.
k. Alice Katherine Ann Sabine (1882-1954)
(NB: the foregoing ten children of Clement Sabine are not necessarily in the correct order of birth.)

7.5 Eustace Powhatan Sabine (1838-1902), m, ?, with issue:
a. Eric Sabine, d, 1939, m, Gertrude Scott, with issue:
a1. Kora Sabine, married
a2. Leslie Sabine, married
a3. Sheila Sabine, married
a4. Kathleen Sabine, married
a5. Gordon SABINE, unmarried.
a6. Patience Sabine, married
b. Annie Sabine, married 1st to Sydney Thow, and 2nd Travers Hartley FALKINER, but d.s.p.
b1. Hubert SABINE, d. unmarried Feb, I 69 I 1
b2. Edgar SABINE, married Kate Mary Poole, with issue:
i Marjorie Hope Sabine unmarried.
ii Helen Mary Sabine unmarried.
iii John Rolfe SABINE married Ruth Welch, with dau.
iv Mary Elizabeth Sabine
v. Harry SABINE, married Diemel, and had daus.
vi. Reginald SABINE, d. Oct. 19L6, married, Kate Doliman, with issue:
Ian SABINE, unmarried, and...
Jefferson SABINE, married with one son.

For other Sabines in Australia, see Oswestry pedigree below.

8. Charles Waldo SABINE (1796-1859), (see 'Sabine of Oswestry, Shropshire'). Charles Sabine, attorney, was b. Islington, Middlesex, 25 March 1796, married 6 Oct. 1825 at St, Oswald's, Oswestry, to Margaret (12 May 1800-?), dau. of Alderman Thomas Hughes. Charles d. 3 June 1859 at Oswestry, with issue:

8.1 Charles Edwyn SABINE (1827-1874), b. Oswestry 11 Feb 1827, married 17 July 1860 at St. Oswald's, Oswestry, to Edith Elizabeth (1832-1887), dau. of Thomas and Edith Ann (Smith) Hill. She was b. 1 June 1832, and d. 6 Apr 1887. Charles d. 21 Nov. I874, with issue:
a. Miriam Edith Sabine (1862-1936), b. 2 July 1862, d. 8 May 1936 at Paddington, London, died unmarried
b. Charles Shirley SABINE (1864-1946), b. 21 Dec 1863, d.s.p* Melbourne, Australia, 19H6, m, Lydia Dyer, a widow.
c. Henry Wilmshurst SABINE (1865-1955), b. 9 Jan. 1865, married ? Nov 1899 at St. Michael's, Aberystwith, to Mary Goderich (1875-?), dau. of William and Hannah (Lloyd) Goderich of Sandbach, Cheshire, with issue:
c1. Charles Shirley Wilmshurst SABINE (1900-), b. 11 Sep. 1900.
c2. William Henry 'Waldo SABINE (1903-?), b. 2 Apr 1903, married Ellen, dau. of George W. Borcherding of New York.
c3. Margaret Edith Sabine (1906-?), b. 21 July 1906,

married Charles Shirley 'Wilmhurst SABINE, b. Birkenhead 11 Sep 1900, married 25 April 1924 at Melmerby, near Ripon, Yorkshire to Clara Harbottle, with issue:
 i. Margaret Ann Sabine, b. Harrogate 15 Apr 1926.
 ii. John Charles Henry SABINE, b. 9 June 1929*
 iii. Joseph Anthony Hill SABINE, b. 6 June 1931.
 iv. Cynthia Mary Sabine, b. 5 Aug 1935*
d. Arthur Woolmer SABINE (1866-1919), b. 17 Aug. 1866, d, Shrewsbury, 19 July 1919, ra. Sarah Humphreys (b. 1872), dau. of David Humphreys of Llanfair, Montgomeryshire, with issue:
 d1. Charles Reginald SABINE (1897-?), b. Oswestry, married to Hilda Varney, issue - Margaret Josephine Sabine.
 d2. Margaret Ellaline Sabine (1899-1912)
 d3. David Cyril Woolmer SABINE (1901-?), married Maud Pryce (1900-?), dau. of Edward Pryce of Bicton, Shropshire, with issue:
  i David Shirley SABINE (1923-?), killed during R.A.F. training.
  ii Rosemary Ann Sabine, b. 29 Sept. 19R0
 d4. Phyllis Doreen Sabine (1903-?)
 d5. Edith Olive Sabine (1908-?) married Frank Thompson RICHARDSON.
e. William Herbert SABINE (1868-1909), died unmarried
f. Reginald Waldo SABINE (1869-1870)*, d.s.p.
g. Cyril Edward SABINE (1871-1895), died unmarried

h. Margaret Ellen Sabine (1873-1911), married Henry Minshull SMYTHE.

8.2 Emma Sabine (1827-1916)?

8.3 Miriam Jemima Sabine (1829-1862), married Dr Edward Wilnshurst TAIT, of Highbury, Islington, with issue:
a. Edward Sabine TAIT, M.D, d. about 19hl> m* Frances ?, with issue
 a1. Alice Tait, who married Dr. WHITE
 a2. Charles TAIT
 a3. Henry Brewer TAIT, F.R.C.S,, F.R.C.P, of Kighgate

8.4 Henry Waldo SABINE (1830-1869), b. 20 Dec 1830, d. gold prospecting in Australia, 1869, unmarried.

8.5 Margaret Elizabeth Sabine (1832-1890), b. 22 Dec, 1832, d. Highbury, Islington, 23 Apr I890, unmarried.

8.6 William Hubert SABINE (1835-1870), b. 4 Aug 1834, at Oswestry, Shropshire, emigrated to Australia with his brother Waldo, m, Augusta Maria Elliott (1850-1929), who after his death m, a newspaper proprietor in Deniliquin, N.S.W. He d. 20 Dec 1870, with issue:
a. Charles Waldo SABINE (1869-1950), married Muriel Bowden, with issue:
 a1. Noel SABINE, married with Betty and Evelyn
 a2. Keith SABINE, married "Jo" Tindale with son Nicholas
 a3. Greville SABINE, married Lois Attwood and had sons Phillip and Nigel
 a4. Beryl Sabine, married Kemrais
 a5. Eric SABINE, married Evans
b. Miriam Margaret 'Minnie' Sabine (1871-1953), unmarried,d. in Marrickville, Sydney.

9. Harriet Sabine (1794-1825), buried June 1825 at St. Mary's, Islington.

10. Jemima Sabine (1799-1878), married James Guerard PIFFARD (1801-1852), stockbroker, with issue:

10.1 John Guerard PIFFARD (1832-1842)*

10.2 Bernard PIFFARD(1833-1916), married 1stly on 2 Dec 1858 at St Clement Danes, Westminster to Alice Matilda Watts (1843-1891), with issue:
a. Clara Piffard (1868-?)
b. Edgar James Guerard PIFFARD (1872-1933)
c. Elfrida Beatrice Piffard (1873-1952)
d. Alice Theodora Piffard (1877-1942)
Bernard married 2ndly to Edith Marion Ward (1850-?), no issue.

10.3 Albert PIFFARD (1834–1909), married in 1867 to Henreitta Elizabeth Gimingham (1852-?), with issue:
a. Guerard B. E. PIFFARD (1870-1883)
b. Isabel Sabine Piffard (1870-1927)
c. Josephine Mary Piffard (1872-1885)
d. Cecilia Piffard (1875-1947)
e. Helen Constance Piffard (1877-1955)
f. Hubert Shirley PIFFARD (1879-1908)
g. Basil Eyre PIFFARD (1883-?)

10.4 Reginald PIFFARD (1836-1912), died unmarried

10.5 Waldo PIFFARD (1837-1838)*, d.s.p.

10.6 Basil Antoine PIFFARD (1840–1870), died unmarried

* Died before adulthood - d.s.p.
(Some names not listed in the index).

▲TOP (Left): Portraits of Adelaide Isham Eppes (1800-1885) and her husband John Sabine (1791-1856), who emigrated to Adelaide from Titchfield about 1850.

8. William Sabine (1749-1826)

The first of his seven children to his second wife was William Sabine, who was born and baptised in Titchfield in 1749 and later settled in London. He was for some years a surveyor to the city and married on the 19th May 1778 at St Mary Hill, London to Elizabeth (1757-1832), the daughter of the Rev. Samuel Brewer, a dissenting minister from Stepney, who himself was born 17th June 1723 at Rendham, Suffolk. William died at Islington, London on the 26th November 1826, leaving a numerous family (*see 10.4 Descendants of William Sabine & Elizabeth Brewer*).

▲ *Views of the south coast village of Titchfield, in Hampshire.*

10.5 Descendants of Daniel Sabine & Ann Pirves [16]

Daniel SABINE (1754-1829), with John Sabine (half-nephew) Daniel was listed as a baker in Titchfield, Hampshire in the 1792-98 Universal British Directory, and married on the 7th October 1780 at Titchfield, Hampshire to Ann Pirves (1762-1834), and raised his family at Titchfield.

1. Mary Sabine (1784-?), married 1808 at Titchfield, Hampshire to James GROVE (1776-1849), with issue:

1.1 Maria Grove (1811-1874), died unmarried.

1.2 Elizabeth Grove (1816-1851), died unmarried.

1.3 Ruth Knight Grove (1817-1897), died unmarried.

1.4 Jemima Grove (1821-1878), married 1846 to John FOOT (1821-1869), with issue:
 a. Jemima Grove Foot (1848-1919)
 b. Ann Foot (1852-1936)
 c. John FOOT (1855-?)
 d. Elizabeth Foot (1858-1949)
 e. James William FOOT (1863-1900)

2. Ann Sabine (1786-?), died unmarried.

3. Maria Sabine (1787-1874), died unmarried.

4. William SABINE (1788-1867), married in 1810 to Jane Perry Young (1789-1883). He died in 1867 in Barnet, London, with issue:

4.1 William SABINE (1815-1899), married 1840 to Caroline Cope (1808-1871), with issue:
 a. Caroline Sabine (1844-1901)
 b. Frances Sabine (1848-1861)
 c. William SABINE (1851-1888)

4.2 Ebenezer SABINE (1833-1906), married 1863 to Emily Sarah Goodes (1834-1925), with issue:
 a. Charles Orton SABINE (1860-1942)
 b. Ellen Sabine (1864-1925)
 c. Herbert Frank SABINE (1865-1922)
 d. Emily Sarah Sabine (1867-1908)
 e. Harry Ebenezer SABINE (1869-1936)
 f. Howard William SABINE (1870-1928)
 g. Clarence Edward SABINE (1871-1895)
 h. Harry F. SABINE (1872-?)

5. Harriet Sabine (1794-?), married in 1817 to Henry LUCAS (1794-1870), with issue:

5.1 Susannah Lucas (1819-1841), died unmarried.

6. Frances 'Fanny' Sabine (1798-1821), died unm. and buried on 14 Nov 1821 at Titchfield, Hampshire, aged 23.[18]

7. Charles SABINE (1800-1803)*, died a child.

8. Eliza Sabine (1802-1803)*, died an infant.

Sabine	Purves

9. George SABINE (1803>1839), married in 1839 to Ann Davison (1815-?), with issue:

9.1 John SABINE (1843-?), bank clerk, died unmarried.

9.2 Fanny Sabine (1845-?), died unmarried.

9.3 Jane Sabine (1847-?), died unmarried.

10. James SABINE (1805-1870), married in 1855 to Sarah Neller (1812-1905), with issue:

10.1 Edward SABINE (1836-1918), married 1stly in 1859 to Lucretia Plumstead (1834-1875), with issue:
 a. May Lucretia Sabine (1860-1863)*
 b. Charles Herbert SABINE (1864-1934)
 c. Edward Frederick SABINE (1869-1938)
 d. Harry SABINE (1873-1885)*
 Edward married 2ndly in 1877 to Emily Taylor (1856-1926), with issue:
 e. Fred SABINE (1869-?)
 f. Mabel Sabine (1877-1968)
 g. Blanche Amy Sabine (1882-1975)
 h. Alice Maud Sabine (1883-1924)
 i. Albert Edward SABINE (1885-1972)
 j. Ethel Eveline Sabine (1891-?)

10.2 James William SABINE (1837-?), married 1865 to Julia Tibbs (1842-1878), with issue:
 a. Alna J. Sabine (1866-?)
 b. Rosina A. Sabine (1869-?)
 c. William Joseph SABINE (1870-?)
 d. Lucretia Sabine (1873-?)
 e. Marian Sabine (1875-?)
 f. Grace Maud Sabine (1877-1969)

10.3 Marian Sabine (1837-?), died unmarried.

10.4 Sarah Anne Sabine (1846-1900), married 1868 to Henry TURNER (1844-?), with issue:

a. Emily Sabine (1870-?)
b. Sarah Caroline Sabine (1871-?)
c. John H. SABINE (1873-?)
d. Lilian Sabine (1874-?)
e. Florence Sabine (1879-?)

10.5 Albert Augustus SABINE (1854-1908), married 1900 to Mary Ann Dalgleish (1856-1911), d.s.p.

10.6 Arthur SABINE (1854-?), died unmarried.

11. Andrew Samuel SABINE (1807-1871), married in 1831 to Ann Eliza Simmons (1810-1884), with issue:

11.1 Edward John SABINE (1834-1918), married 1863 to Sarah Maria Wasem (1841-1909), with issue:
 a. Alfred Edward SABINE (1865-?)
 b. Henry G. SABINE (1869-?)

11.2 Walter Theodore SABINE (1838-1918), married 1864 to Harriet Elizabeth Harris (1841-1893), with issue:
 a. Clara Louise Sabine (1867-1868)
 b. Ada Elizabeth Sabine (1868-1939)
 c. Louisa Rose Sabine (1870-1919)
 d. Teressa A. Sabine (1870-?)
 e. Walter George SABINE (1872-1929)
 f. Lillian Amy Sabine (1875-1955)
 g. William Alfred SABINE (1877-1943)
 h. Thomas Henry SABINE (1882-1963)

11.3 Charles Clifford SABINE (1840-1912), married 1868 to Martha Brickwell (1847-1912), with issue:
 a. Alice Martha Sabine (1868-?)
 b. Charles SABINE (1875-?)
 c. Samuel Andrew SABINE (1876-1942)
 d. Edith Sabine (1879-?)
 e. Amy Sabine (1881-1931)
 f. Bertram SABINE (1884-?)

11.4 Francis John SABINE (1845-1911), married 1867 to Harriet Elizabeth Smith (1845-1925), with issue:
 a. Harriet Elizabeth Sabine (1868-?)
 b. John Francis SABINE (1869-1935)
 c. George SABINE (1872-1912)
 d. Florence Caroline Sabine (1876-1958)
 e. John William SABINE (1878-1957)
 f. Lucy Sabine (1880-?)
 g. Ellen Alice Sabine (1885-?)

11.5 Mary Ann Eliza Sabine (1848-1926), died unmarried.

11.6 Julia Maria Sabine (1850-1926), died unmarried.

11.7 Eliza Ann Eleanor Sabine (1851-1914), died unmarried.

12. Elizabeth Sabine (1808-?), info unknown.

* Died before adulthood - d.s.p.
(Some names not listed in the index).

10.6 Descendants of Samuel Read Sabine & Jennett Henderson [17]

Samuel Read SABINE (1765-1831), married on the 24th August 1788 at Alverstoke, Hampshire to Jennett Henderson (1767-1823), with issue:

1. Samuel SABINE Jr. (1790-1793), * died a child.

2. Jennett Sabine (1793-1853), dress maker, married 24 Feb 1814 at Alverstoke to Mark REED (1784-1841), a draper, with issue:

2.1 Jennett Ann Reed (1817-1898), married Richard Thomas ROHERS, issue unknown.

2.2 Samuel Sabine REED (1823-1861), married in 1846 to Sarah Mary Ann Rexford (1822-1861), with issue:
  a. Amelia Jane Reed (1849-1920), married 24 Aug 1868 at Bethnal Green to John Frederick THACKRAY (1848-?), with issue:
    a1. Amelia Nelly Adelaide Thackray (1871-1945)
    a2. Frederick Victor THACKRAY (1872-1875)*
    a3. Harriet Thackray (1874-1875)*
    a4. Agnes Thackray (1875-1895)
    a5. Clarence THACKRAY (1878-1930)
    a6. Arthur Alfred THACKRAY (1881-1882)*
    a7. John Reed THACKRAY (1883-1884)*
    a8. Lilly G. Thackray (1887-1951)
    a9. Edith May Thackray (1889-1944)
    a10. Edgar Norris THACKRAY (1891-1977)
    a11. Hilton N. THACKRAY (1893-1894)*
  b. Elizabeth Reed (1854-1927), married in 1870 at Islington to John FAIRHEAD (1851-1908), with issue:
    b1. Lizzy Amelia Fairhead (1871-?)
    b2. Ada Fairhead (1873-?)
    b3. John James FAIRHEAD (1874-?)
    b4. Ernest FAIRHEAD (1876-?)
    b5. Florence Edith Fairhead (1880-?)
    b6. Arthur FAIRHEAD (1881-?)
    b7. Edgar FAIRHEAD (1887-?)
    b8. Ethel Fairhead (1888-?)

2.3 James Sabine REED (1825-1886), confectioner, married on 29 Aug 1847 at Stepney to Emma Charlotte Dawson (1829-1867), with issue:
  a. Jennette A. Reed (1852-?)
  b. Mark W. REED (1854-?)
  c. Emily Reed (1857-?)
  d. Charlotte E. Reed (1859-?)
  e. Alfred R. REED (1862-?)

2.4 John Sabine REED (1826-1841)*

2.5 Richard Sabine REED (1828-1890), cigar maker, married 28 Sep 1851 at Stepney to Ann Elizabeth Stinner (1828-1910), no issue.

2.6 Henry Sabine REED (1833-1902), confectioner, married on 21 Nov 1852 at Stepney to Ann Eliza Brown (1833-1887), with issue:
  a. Henry Severs REED (1854-1871)
  b. Frederick Joseph REED (1856-1935)
  c. Catherine Ann Reed (1861-1865)
  d. Phillip H. REED (1864-1952)

Sabine   *Henderson*

e. Arthur Louis REED (1867-1942)
f. Jennett Agnes Reed (1871-1946)
g. Helen Eliza Reed (1876-1946)
h. Rachel Reed (1880-1881)

3. Samuel Reed SABINE (1794-1859), married 14 Aug 1825 at Aldgate, London to Mary Crockwell (1794-1873), with issue:

3.1 Samuel SABINE (1828-1873), died unmarried.

3.2 Mary Ellen Sabine (1830-1891), married 19 Oct 1858 at Stepney to John Frederick LAMBERT (1810-1883), with issue:
  a. Mary Ellen Lambert (1859-?)
  b. Elizabeth Lambert (1861-?)
  c. Jeanette Maria Lambert (1863-?)
  d. John Frederick LAMBERT (1865-1928)
  e. Susan Lambert (1867-?)

3.3 Edwin SABINE (1831-?), details unknown

3.4 Jennett Sabine (1833-1903), married 1 Mar 1852 at Bermondsey to William DYER (1812-1887), emigrated to Victoria before 1860, with issue:
  a. Charles Edwin DYER (1860-1931)
  b. Samuel Warren DYER (?)

3.5 Ebenezer SABINE (1837-?), details unknown

3.6 John SABINE (1839-?), details unknown

4. William Read SABINE (1799-1852), married 1stly in 1826 to Matilda Church (1803-1827), no issue. Married 2ndly on 22 Oct 1832 at Finsbury to Sarah Muskett (1802-1863), with issue:

4.1 William James SABINE (1833-1875), details unknown

* Died before adulthood - d.s.p.
(Some names not listed in the index).

▲ Photograph of St Peter's Church, Titchfield, site of generations of Sabine baptisms, marriages and burials.

Sir Robert Randolph Garran (1867-1957)

Through his son John Sabine (1791-1856), who emigrated to Adelaide in 1850, one of William Sabine's descendants was Sir Robert Randolph Garran, who held the highly revered post of secretary of the Australian Attorney-General's Department, and over the course of three decades provided legal advice to no less than ten Australian prime ministers, from Edmund Barton to Joseph Lyons. Sir Robert Garran was considered an expert in Australian constitutional law, and with John Quick published an annotated edition of the Australian constitution that became the standard reference work.

Sir Robert Randolph Garran, GCMG, QC [18]
2 x Great Grandson of James Sabine & Hannah Parker, of Titchfield, Hampshire

▲LEFT (Top): The Garran home in Canberra, 22 Mugga Way, Red Hill. (Above): The Australian delegation to the Paris Peace Conference, 1919. Garran is seated, second from left, with PM Billy Hughes (centre), and Sir Joseph Cook, second from right. RIGHT: Sir Robert Garran was a second great grandson of James Sabine & Hannah Parker of Titchfield, Hampshire, through his grandparents John and Adelaide Sabine, who emigrated to Australia about 1850.

Sir Robert Randolph Garran, GCMG QC (10 February 1867 – 11 January 1957) was an Australian lawyer who became "Australia's first public servant" – the first federal government employee after the federation of the Australian colonies. He served as the departmental secretary of the Attorney-General's Department from 1901 to 1932, and after 1916 also held the position of Solicitor-General of Australia.

Garran was born in Sydney, the son of the journalist and politician Andrew Garran. He studied arts and law at the University of Sydney and was called to the bar in 1891. Garran was a keen supporter of the federation movement, and became acquainted with leading federalists like George Reid and Edmund Barton. At the 1897-98 constitutional convention he served as secretary of the drafting committee. On 1 January 1901, Garran was chosen by Barton's caretaker government as its first employee for a brief period, he was the only member of the Commonwealth Public Service. His first duty was to write the inaugural edition of the Commonwealth Gazette, which contained Queen Victoria's proclamation authorising the creation of a federal government.

Over the following three decades, Garran provided legal advice to ten different prime ministers, from Edmund Barton to Joseph Lyons. He was considered an early expert in Australian constitutional law, and with John Quick published an annotated edition of the constitution that became a standard reference work. Garran developed a close relationship with Billy Hughes during World War I, and accompanied him to the Imperial War Cabinet and the Paris Peace Conference. Hughes, who was simultaneously prime minister and attorney-general, appointed Garran to the new position of solicitor-general and delegated numerous powers and responsibilities to him. He was knighted three times for his service to the Commonwealth, in 1917, 1920 and in 1937.

In addition to his professional work, Garran was also an important figure in the development of the city of Canberra during its early years. He was one of the first public servants to relocate there after it replaced Melbourne as the capital in 1927. He founded several important cultural associations, organised the creation of the Canberra University College, and later contributed to the establishment of the Australian National University. Garran published at least eight books and many journal articles throughout his lifetime, covering such topics as constitutional law, the history of federalism in Australia, and German-language poetry. He was granted a state funeral upon his death in 1957, the first ever federal public servant to receive one.

Garran's "personality, like his prose, was devoid of pedantry and pomposity and, though dignified, was laced with a quizzical turn of humour." His death "marked the end of a generation of public men for whom the cultural and the political were natural extensions of each other and who had the skills and talents to make such connections effortlessly." At his death, Garran was one of the last remaining people involved with the creation of the Constitution of Australia. Former Prime Minister John Howard, in describing Garran, said: "I wonder though if we sometimes underestimate the changes, excitements, disruptions and adjustments previous generations have experienced. Sir Robert Garran knew the promise and reality of federation. He was part of the establishment of a public service which, in many ways, is clearly recognisable today."

Garran's friend Charles Studdy Daley, remarked at a celebratory dinner for Garran in 1954 that: "There has hardly been a cultural movement in this city with which Sir Robert has not been identified in loyal and inspiring support, as his constant aim has been that Canberra should be not only a great political centre, but also a shrine to foster those things that stimulate and enrich our national life... his name will ever be inscribed in the annals, not only of Canberra, but of the Commonwealth as clarum et venerabile nomen gentibus.

However Garran is perhaps best remembered as an expert on constitutional law, more so than for his other contributions to public service. On his experience of Federation and the Constitution, Garran was always enthusiastic: "I'm often asked 'has federation turned out as you expected?' Well yes and no. By and large the sort of thing we expected has happened but with differences. We knew the constitution was not perfect; it had to be a compromise with all the faults of a compromise. But, in spite of the unforeseen strains and stresses, the constitution has worked, on the whole, much as we thought it would. I think it now needs revision, to meet the needs of a changed world. But no-one could wish the work undone, who tries to imagine, what, in these stormy days, would have been the plight of six disunited Australian colonies."

Garran was made a Commander of the Order of St Michael and St George (CMG) on the day that Federation was completed and Australia created, 1 January 1901, "in recognition of services in connection with the Federation of the Australian Colonies and the establishment of the Commonwealth of Australia", Garran was first knighted in 1917, and was appointed as a Knight Commander of the Order of St Michael and St George (KCMG) in 1920. He was knighted a third time in 1937 when he was made a Knight Grand Cross of the Order of St Michael and St George (GCMG). Shortly after the establishment of the ANU in 1946, Garran became its first graduate when he was awarded an honorary doctorate of laws. He had already been awarded such an honorary doctorate from the University of Melbourne in 1937 and later received one from his alma mater, the University of Sydney in 1952.

9. Daniel Sabine (1753-1829)

Next of James and Hannah Sabine's children was Daniel Sabine, who was born and baptised in Titchfield in 1753. He later married on the 7th October 1780 at Titchfield to Ann Pirves (1762-1834), and together they raised a large family of twelve children at Titchfield (*see 10.5 Descendants of Daniel Sabine & Ann Pirves*).[7]

10. Lydia Sabine (1757-1788)

The third child of James and Hannah Sabine was Lydia, who was born and baptised at Tichfield in 1757, but she died unmarried aged just 21, at Guildford, Surrey.

11 & 12. Thomas & Hannah Sabine

Next came Thomas Sabine (1760-1760), who died an infant in the same year of his birth, and Hannah Sabine (1761-1762), who also died an infant, but two years later. Both were buried at St. Peter's Church cemetery in Titchfield.

13. Patience Sabine (c.1762-1829)

James and Hannah Sabine's sixth child was Patience Sabine, who was born and baptised at Titchfield about 1762. She remained a spinster and died without children in 1829, aged 67. She was buried in February of 1829 at the St Peters Church cemetery in Titchfield.

14. Samuel Read Sabine (1765-1831)

The final child of James Sabine and Hannah Parker was Samuel Read Sabine, who was born and baptised at Titchfield in 1765. Samuel was apprenticed as a cabinetmaker

▲ *Various views of the quaint village of Titchfield, Hampshire.*

▲ 'Titchfield Mill On The River Meon,' drawn by artist John Munnings, (1916-1987).

under Thomas Eastman of Portsmouth, the husband of his half-sister Sarah Eastman (nee Sabine).[8] He married on the 24th August 1788 at Alverstoke, Hampshire to Jennett Henderson (1767-1823), and produced at least four children (*see 10.6 Descendants of Samuel Read Sabine & Jennett Henderson*).

The family patriarch James Sabine, died aged 69 years and was buried in the cemetery at Titchfield on the 31st October 1779. Although far from complete, the aforementioned pedigrees that descend from James Sabine relative to Boston, USA; Adelaide, Australia; Prince Edward Island, Canada; Oswestry and Ripley in Dorset, reveal a world-wide dispersal of the Sabines of Titchfield, yet the name ceased entirely to be found in the village of Titchfield itself after 1890.

Returning to the ancestral trail of Thomas Eastman Shoveller, the next logical pathway in this genealogical journey is to examine the lives, events and descendants of James Sabine's daughter Sarah Sabine and her husband Thomas Eastman, a successful cabinetmaker and auctioneer in Portsmouth, who were married at St. Mary's, Portsea on Christmas day in the year 1780.

▲ TOP: A water colour painting of South Street, featuring the timber framed and thatched roofs of village houses in Titchfield, Hampshire, by B.P. Hansford.
ABOVE: A water colour painting of South Street, with a view toward 'The Square' in Titchfield, Hampshire, by B.P. Hansford.

References

1. Sabine, W. H. W., (1953) 'Ancestry of the Rev. James Sabine', p.53 (in Roberts, G.B.,(1985). 'English Origins of New England Families - From the N.E. Historical and Genealogical Register,' 2nd Series, Vol.3, Genealogical Pub Co, Baltimore).

2. Lamborn, Samuel (1894). 'The Genealogy of the Lamborn Family', M.L. Marion Press, Philadelphia.

3. Sabine, J.D. (1904). 'The Family and Descendants of Rev. James Sabine', Printed for Private Collection, Washington, DC.

4. 'Ancestry of the Rev. James Sabine' by W.H.W. Sabine, op.cit., p.55.

5. Sabine, W. H. W. (1953), op. cit.

6. James Sabin & Hannah Parker, married at Fareham, Hampshire on the 21 st November 1848 (English Marriages 1538-1973, from Family Search).

7. The National Archives, Kew - Will of Daniel Sabine, Baker of Titchfield, Hampshire on 17 December 1829 [PROB 11/1764/225].

8. Samuel Read Sabine - Apprenticed to Thomas Eastman with duties paid in 1781 (UK, Register of Duties Paid for Apprentices' Indentures, 1710-1811).

9. Sabine, W. H. W. (1953), op. cit.

10. Sabine, W. H. W. (1953), op. cit.

11. Sabine, J.D. (1904), op.cit.

12. Find-a-Grave - Rev James Sabine [https://www.findagrave.com/memorial/70960725/james-sabine].

13. Sabine, W. H. W. (1953), op. cit.

14. Sabine, W. H. W. (1953), op. cit.

15. Knightroots - Fanny Eastman, buried at Titchfield, Hampshire - 14 Nov 1821, aged 23 (Page 60 No 479 [https://www.knightroots.co.uk/parishes/titchfield]).

16. Sabine, W. H. W. (1953), op. cit.

17. Sabine, W. H. W. (1953), op. cit.

18. Wikipedia - Robert Garran [https://en.wikipedia.org/wiki/Robert_Garran].

Chapter Eleven

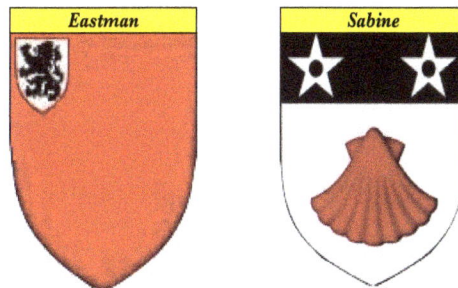

THOMAS EASTMAN & SARAH SABINE

(Maternal grandparents of Thomas Eastman Shoveller)

Despite numerous attempts to research the ancestors of Thomas Eastman, no verified links have been found to date, but he was likely to have been born in the vicinity of Portsea, Hampshire. His memorial headstone erected at Titchfield, Hampshire in 1816 stated that he had reached the age of 64, indicating a birth year of 1752,[1] but not being able to substantiate his actual date of birth, baptism or his parentage precludes any further research into his Eastman ancestors at this stage. He likely came from humble origins to become a successful cabinetmaker, auctioneer and well respected elder amongst his community in Portsea. He took on the role of deacon at the Orange Street (now King Street) Independent Church in Portsea under his close friend Rev. John Griffin, where his children and most of his 32 grandchildren were baptised, and he left a substantial will and legacy for his four offspring.

If Thomas Eastman was indeed born in 1752, it was a memorable year in British history as with George II on the throne, Thomas likely shared his birth year with the celebrated architect John Nash (1752-1835). That year the British Parliament passed a bill to bestow

---

Hampshire, England, Allegations for Marriage Licences, 1689-1837 for Thomas E...

Hampshire Allegations for Marriage Licences Vol 1

EASTMAN, Thomas, of Portsea, cabinet maker, 21, b., & Sarah Sabine, of the s., 21, sp., at P., 25 Dec., 1780.

EASTMAN, Thomas, of Portsea, upholsterer, 23, b., & Mary Eglon, of Holy Rood, Southampton, 23, sp., at H. R., 25 March, 1805.

EASTMAN, Thomas, of Portsea, cabinet maker, w., & Jane Allen, of Havant, w., at P., 22 Apl., 1811.

▲*Allegations of Eastman marriage licences in Hampshire, England, showing Thomas Eastman to his first wife - Sarah Sabine (25th Dec 1780), and Thomas Eastman to his second wife - Jane Allen (22nd Apr 1811), and also for his first born son Thomas Sabine Eastman to his wife - Mary Eglon (25th March 1805).*

▲ *Thomas Eastman was a successful cabinetmaker, upholsterer and auctioneer, and likely produced pieces like this early 19th century upholstered lounge.*

estates forfeited by Jacobites to the Crown, with the revenue being used to develop the Scottish Highlands. And the Murder Act (1751) came into effect, which provided that the bodies of hanged murderers should suffer public dissection or (for men) hanging in the gibbet. And, Robert Clive forced the surrender of French troops in the aftermath of the Siege of Trichinopoly in India.

Growing up in Portsmouth, the hub of the Royal Navy, was no doubt full of adventure for a young boy like Thomas. He lived out his youth during the Seven Years War against France and he would have been witness to the slave trade. However, we know not his parents, his siblings or where he may have been schooled, and although Thomas was obviously apprenticed into the cabinetmaking trade, his master has not been identified.

It seems that Thomas managed to avoid the Royal Navy press gangs in Portsmouth, and resisted calls to enlist in the military for the American Revolution, which ran from 1770 to 1783, but little else is known of him prior to 1780. The first known record of Thomas Eastman was his marriage, which occurred on Christmas day of 1780 to an older, but eligible lady from the small village of Titchfield, Hampshire.

Sarah Sabine (1744-1810)

How Thomas Eastman and Sarah Sabine met is a mystery, but she was the eldest daughter of James Sabine (c.1710-1779) and Martha Lamport (1707-1747), although her mother's surname was more likely to have been a corruption of 'Lamborn.' Sarah was apparently born in the year 1744, but no evidence by way of a baptism exists other than a record listed in the pedigree of her grand nephew Rev. James Sabine (1774-1845).[2] Her parents married on the 1st February 1737 at St. Mary's Church in Titchfield,[3] and produced seven children, although only four survived to become adults that included Isaac (1738-1786), James Jr. (1739-c.1790), Samuel (1740-1786) and Sarah herself.[4]

Tragically, at the age of 40, Martha Sabine unexpectedly died on the 15th November 1747, when Sarah was just three years old. With four children under the age of ten, James required support, and after a respectable mourning period of 12 months he married secondly on the 21st November 1748 in the neighbouring village of Fareham, to Hannah Parker (b.1728). Hannah adopted James' four children, and they had a further seven of their own, although two of these died as infants. From all accounts, James Sabine's nine children from two mothers, grew up harmoniously in Titchfield, and although one son died without trace somewhere in the West Indies, and the two youngest daughters remained spinsters, six went on to marry and produce families of their own.

The Marriage of Thomas Eastman & Sarah Sabine

The marriage of Thomas Eastman and Sarah Sabine occurred on the 25th December 1780 and was registered at St Mary's Church in Portsea, Hampshire.[5] With four of her brothers having already stepped up to the altar, Sarah was 36 by the time of her 1780 wedding to Thomas Eastman, who himself was perhaps only 28. Sadly, Sarah's father James Sabine had died a year before on the 31st October 1779, and was buried in Titchfield. However, her step-mother Hannah, six brothers and their four wives, two sisters and some nine nieces and nephews, were all likely to have attended the celebrations. Thomas' relatives were probably there also, although at this stage, none of these are known.

Just nine months after their wedding a pivotal event occurred with the surrender of Charles Cornwallis, 1st Marquess Cornwallis in the American colonies at Yorktown,

Thomas Eastman & His Apprentices

UK, Register of Duties Paid for Apprentices' Indentures, 1710-1811

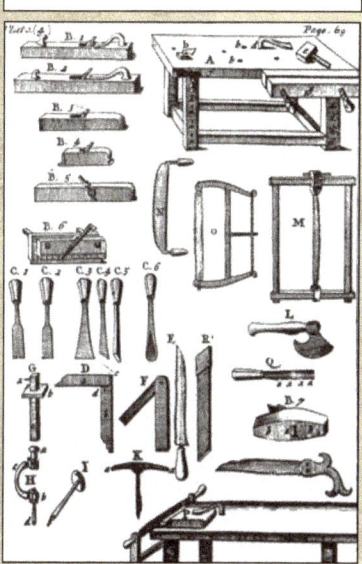

▲ABOVE: Thomas Eastman as a master cabinetmaker took on a number of apprentices including his brother-in-law Samuel Read Sabine (1781); James Coker (1783); Henry Moss (1788); James Blake (1789), and George Blake (1791). RIGHT (Top): The cabinetmakers drill. (Above): Standard tools for cabinetry work in the early 19th century.

Thomas Eastman - Cabinetmaker, Upholsterer & Auctioneer

▲ *Auction notices posted by Thomas Eastman from 1786 to 1807 in 'The Times,' the 'Hampshire Chronicle,' & the 'Hampshire Telegraph,' and in one instance representing his nephew Isaac Sabine Jr. in July 1807.*

Virginia, on the 19th October 1781, which ended the hegemony of British military power in America and encouraged the French to revolt some eight years later. At this same time, Thomas was intent upon building his cabinetmaking business, but was happy to accept his wife's half-brother Samuel Read Sabine, as an apprentice cabinetmaker, at the age of 16 in 1781.[6]

A search of newspaper records for the name Eastman around this period revealed a number of advertisements, showing that by the time of their marriage, Thomas Eastman had become a successful and recognised cabinetmaker in and around the vicinity of Portsea, and within the county of Hampshire. Thomas and Sarah's first child Thomas Sabine Eastman, arrived in 1782, although no record of his baptism has been found.

The Town of Portsea

Portsea uniquely possesses the name of an island, a parish, a manor and a town. The island of Portsea is now occupied by the larger part of the City of Portsmouth and is mainly urban. Portsmouth Harbour is on the western side, Langstone Harbour on the eastern side, while Portsea Island is separated from the mainland to the north by Portscreek, with the Solent lying to the south, before the open sea of the English Channel.

The parish of Portsea, with its church of St. Mary's at Kingston, covered most of Portsea Island. Excluded was the northern strip of Portsea Island including Hilsea, which fell within the parish of Wymering, the crown land of Great Salterns on the eastern side, and the parish of Portsmouth, which was formally separated from the parish of Portsea in 1320.[7]

Even though Portsea was officially created and so-named by an Act of Parliament in 1792, the town had grown up on Portsmouth Common, between the Dockyard and the Mill Pond, from the end of the 17th century onwards. It then consisted of the area north and south of Queen Street, south of the Dockyard and north of the railway, which ran along the former north shore of the Mill Pond.[8]

By 1784, William Pitt the younger, who was almost the same age as Thomas, was appointed Britain's prime minister by King George III. This event coincided with the birth of Thomas and Sarah's first daughter, Elizabeth Eastman who arrived in 1784, which was followed up the next year by the birth of another daughter, Sarah Eastman. Just two years later, Thomas and family would have been eye witnesses to the departure of 'The First Fleet,' consisting of 11 ships carrying over 750 convicts, which departed from Portsmouth for Botany Bay on the 13th May 1787.

By this time, Thomas had become a master cabinetmaker and had established a business

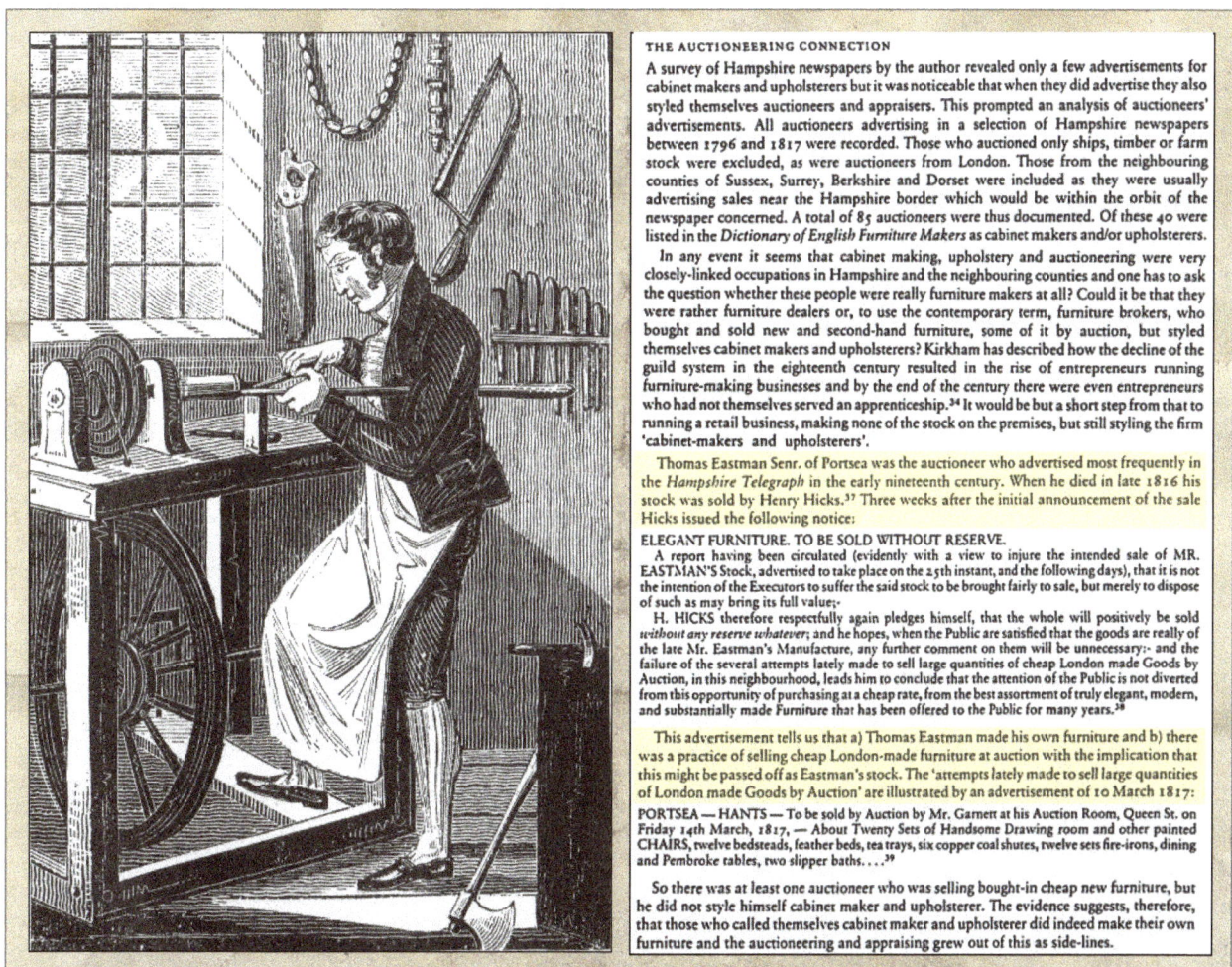

THE AUCTIONEERING CONNECTION

A survey of Hampshire newspapers by the author revealed only a few advertisements for cabinet makers and upholsterers but it was noticeable that when they did advertise they also styled themselves auctioneers and appraisers. This prompted an analysis of auctioneers' advertisements. All auctioneers advertising in a selection of Hampshire newspapers between 1796 and 1817 were recorded. Those who auctioned only ships, timber or farm stock were excluded, as were auctioneers from London. Those from the neighbouring counties of Sussex, Surrey, Berkshire and Dorset were included as they were usually advertising sales near the Hampshire border which would be within the orbit of the newspaper concerned. A total of 85 auctioneers were thus documented. Of these 40 were listed in the *Dictionary of English Furniture Makers* as cabinet makers and/or upholsterers.

In any event it seems that cabinet making, upholstery and auctioneering were very closely-linked occupations in Hampshire and the neighbouring counties and one has to ask the question whether these people were really furniture makers at all? Could it be that they were rather furniture dealers or, to use the contemporary term, furniture brokers, who bought and sold new and second-hand furniture, some of it by auction, but styled themselves cabinet makers and upholsterers? Kirkham has described how the decline of the guild system in the eighteenth century resulted in the rise of entrepreneurs running furniture-making businesses and by the end of the century there were even entrepreneurs who had not themselves served an apprenticeship.[34] It would be but a short step from that to running a retail business, making none of the stock on the premises, but still styling the firm 'cabinet-makers and upholsterers'.

Thomas Eastman Senr. of Portsea was the auctioneer who advertised most frequently in the *Hampshire Telegraph* in the early nineteenth century. When he died in late 1816 his stock was sold by Henry Hicks.[37] Three weeks after the initial announcement of the sale Hicks issued the following notice:

ELEGANT FURNITURE. TO BE SOLD WITHOUT RESERVE.

A report having been circulated (evidently with a view to injure the intended sale of MR. EASTMAN'S Stock, advertised to take place on the 25th instant, and the following days), that it is not the intention of the Executors to suffer the said stock to be brought fairly to sale, but merely to dispose of such as may bring its full value;-

H. HICKS therefore respectfully again pledges himself, that the whole will positively be sold *without any reserve whatever*; and he hopes, when the Public are satisfied that the goods are really of the late Mr. Eastman's Manufacture, any further comment on them will be unnecessary:- and the failure of the several attempts lately made to sell large quantities of cheap London made Goods by Auction, in this neighbourhood, leads him to conclude that the attention of the Public is not diverted from this opportunity of purchasing at a cheap rate, from the best assortment of truly elegant, modern, and substantially made Furniture that has been offered to the Public for many years.[38]

This advertisement tells us that a) Thomas Eastman made his own furniture and b) there was a practice of selling cheap London-made furniture at auction with the implication that this might be passed off as Eastman's stock. The 'attempts lately made to sell large quantities of London made Goods by Auction' are illustrated by an advertisement of 10 March 1817:

PORTSEA — HANTS — To be sold by Auction by Mr. Garnett at his Auction Room, Queen St. on Friday 14th March, 1817, — About Twenty Sets of Handsome Drawing room and other painted CHAIRS, twelve bedsteads, feather beds, tea trays, six copper coal shutes, twelve sets fire-irons, dining and Pembroke tables, two slipper baths....[39]

So there was at least one auctioneer who was selling bought-in cheap new furniture, but he did not style himself cabinet maker and upholsterer. The evidence suggests, therefore, that those who called themselves cabinet maker and upholsterer did indeed make their own furniture and the auctioneering and appraising grew out of this as side-lines.

▲LEFT: An early 19th century cabinetmaker working at his trade. RIGHT: Thomas Eastman was mentioned in the article 'English Newspaper Advertisements As A Source Of Furniture History.' [27]

▲ *Registration of baptism for Theophilus Eastman, youngest son of Thomas and Sarah Eastman, on the 10th January 1790 at Meeting House Alley, Orange St (now King Street), Portsea (Portsea, Hampshire, England & Wales, Non-Conformist and Non-Parochial Registers, 1567-1936).*

called 'Thomas Eastman & Co.' He set up his flourishing enterprise with his partner George Whitbread in St George's Square, opposite the church in Portsmouth, and took out a Sun Insurance policy on the 20th July 1787, on household goods, a house in Butcher St, and £1,100 in stock and utensils.[9] Following soonafter was the birth of their fourth child and second son in Theophilus Eastman, who arrived on the 24th September 1789, and was baptised on the 10th January 1790, at the King St (formerly Orange St.) Church, Portsea, by Mr. William Dunn, Protestant Dissenting Minister.

As a master craftsman, Thomas took on a number of apprentices, many of whom may have stayed on and worked for him including his wife's half brother Samuel Read Sabine (1781); James Coker (1783); Henry Moss (1788); James Blake (1789), and George Blake (1791).[10] Towards the end of the 1780's and with his cabinetmaking business succeeding, Thomas added auctioneering as a side interest to help clear his stock and generate income. Thomas Eastman's auction advertisements revealed that in addition to furniture, he became an auctioneer of many general items including household contents like china, paintings, general goods, carriages and also property. There seemed no limit to the range of items he contracted for sale, and he even auctioned consignments of mahogany logs from Honduras at the docks. Interestingly, about this time, a James Eastman was listed as a cabinetmaker in Portsea, Hampshire in the Universal British Directory of 1792-98, which could very well have been a brother of Thomas?[11]

On the 8th November 1798, Thomas was recorded as an executor on the will of his good friend John Coker of Portsea, a foreman of caulkers at HM Dockyard, Portsmouth. The will included a messuage or tenement in Havant Street, Portsea and the beneficiaries were Thomas Coker (son); Edward Coker (son); Molly Kemp (daughter, wife of James Kemp of Portsea, shipwright); Dinah Doudney (daughter, wife of John Doudney of Portsea, tallow chandler); Mary Gardiner (servant); and poor persons receiving offerings at Orange Street Chapel from Portsea Trustees. The executors were the Rev. John Griffin of Portsea, dissenting minister and Thomas Eastman of Portsea, cabinet maker.[12]

The Reverend John Griffin (c.1769-1834)

Over the years, the Rev. John Griffin became a close family friend of Thomas Eastman and it was he that baptised Thomas and Sarah's children and virtually all their grandchildren. Indeed, John Griffin was the first minister of the spacious King Street Chapel in Portsea, which opened on the 8th September 1813. This splendid Georgian chapel with seating for 2500 and accommodating 3000 when crowded, was a large and lofty structure, with an internal balcony around three sides, but was sadly demolished in 1893. Griffin had earlier been pastor of the Tabernacle in Orange Street, near Southsea Common, which first opened in 1754. He was a progressive and had been active in encouraging vaccination against smallpox, pioneered by Edward Jenner in 1796.[13]

On the 14th July 1789, the Bastille was stormed in Paris by a desperate mob, which heralded the birth of the French Revolution, and the guillotine was first used three years later. By 1793, Britain had joined other European nations in another war against France, mainly through naval engagements in the West Indies and in the Atlantic. However, it wasn't until 1799 that the revolutionaries in France became a mortal threat to England, which was when the British prime minister William Pitt responded by introducing an income tax of 10% to pay for the war.

In preparing for war, Portsmouth once again became a hive of activity and would have

▲ TOP (Left): 'Thomas Eastman & Sons' were notable cabinetmakers in Portsmouth and Hampshire. (Right): The Rev. John Griffin was the first minister of the spacious King Street Chapel in Portsea, opened on 8th September 1813, and the principal trustee of Thomas Eastman's 1816 will. ABOVE (Left): King Street Chapel, Portsea, was opened in 1813 and built to seat 2500 congregants, by I. Stockman (Artist). (Right): Mahogany card table by Henry Hicks of Gosport.

▲TOP: 1906 map of Portsmouth & Portsea, by Wagner & Debe's. ABOVE (Left): Thomas Eastman - 1798, Liberty of Portsmouth (Land Tax Redemption). (Right): Thomas Eastman - 1806 Electoral Register, Portsea.

been an ideal time and place to be profiting from the passing trade. As an auctioneer Thomas Eastman was likely an extroverted character, who became a respected and successful businessman. Over time he developed a formidable reputation and inevitably rose in stature amongst the society in which he lived.

By 1800, Thomas Eastman & Sons were making good headway and he was able to employ servants for his household at 79 St Georges Square in Portsea. At that time male servants were paid from £20 to £60 a year and a female servant from £5 to £15 pounds per year. While these remunerations seem desperately low, room and board were usually also included. Interestingly, coal cost £50 per year, and the rent of a medium sized house in London ranged from £12 to £25 per year. If a family's income was less than £100 for a single person or £200 for a couple, then the head of the house would probably have had to work for a living. London was of course, much more expensive than the countryside.

Thomas continued to grow his business throughout these difficult days, which were to become even more tumultuous in the years ahead. He advertised his goods frequently, and particularly preferred the Hampshire Telegraph as his choice of news outlet.[14] He also became a senior deacon of the church, an office generally associated with lay service, under the patronage of the Rev. John Griffin.

In 1801, the new century heralded the coming Industrial Revolution with William Symington's steam tug, the "Charlotte Dundas", going into service on the Forth and Clyde canal in 1802, while the first census of the United Kingdom revealed the population now numbered approximately nine million people.

▲Description of Portsmouth, Portsea & Gosport in 'Piggotts Directory of Hampshire,' 1828.

A brief lull in the war with France ended in 1803, when hostilities once again broke out and Britain came under the imminent threat of invasion. But this impending peril was terminated on the 21st October 1805, when under Admiral Lord Nelson, the British inflicted a crippling and devastating defeat upon the combined French and Spanish fleet at the Battle of Trafalgar.

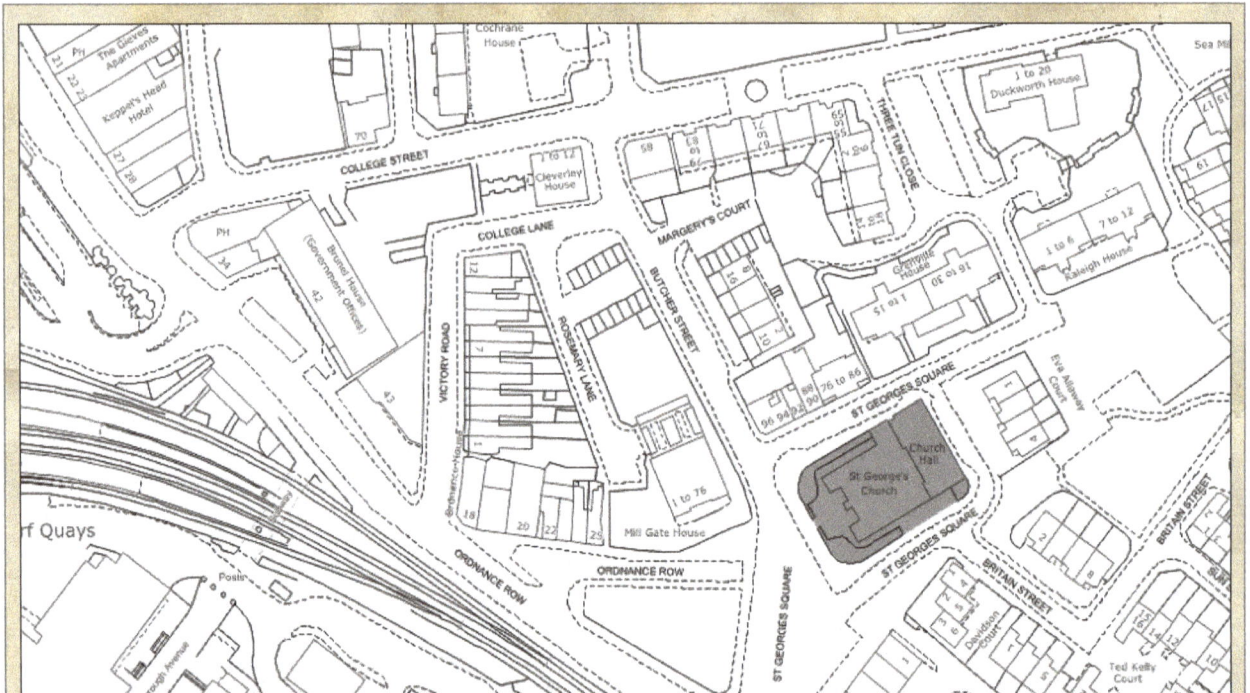

▲TOP: Map of downtown Portsmouth showing the layout of the original streets and St George's Square. ABOVE (Left): An aerial view of St George's Square and the town of Portsea, from the south-west, 1924. (Right): A 1750's drawing of St. Georges Church, in St George's Square, Portsea.

St George's Square [28]

When land was granted for the building of a chapel here in 1752, St. George's Square was waste ground on the southern edge of Portsmouth Common, just north of the Mill Pond. The Square is included in Pigot's Directory of 1830. A triangular space with St. George's Church at the west end, east of Ordnance Row, where (in 1865) it was separated from Britain Street by two blocks of buildings. In 1861 the line of buildings on the south side was continuous westwards across Ordnance Row almost to the Mill Gate, which led to the New Gun Wharf and the Old Portsmouth fortifications. At the east end St. George's Square narrows towards the junction with Kent Street, St. James's Street and Portland Street. On the south side from west to east: Elephant and Castle Inn [no.75], St. George's Foundry with Smith's Shop and Fitting Shop [no.76], [a short section obliterated on library copy of this map], Three Guns pub [no.72] (on 83.7.24 to here), then Britain Street, Little Britain Street, Britain Street, St. George's Brewery (with office and Malt House). On the north side from west to east: Old Gunwharfe, Ordnance Row, Commercial Hotel [Totterdell's], Ordnance Row, Eagle Tavern, St. George's Church (in centre), then Meeting House Alley, leading to Three Tuns Alley (access via covered passage), Unnamed brewery (access via covered passage), Hand in Hand pub, Whitehorse Alley, Wellington Place (access via covered passage), St. George's Passage (access via covered passage), Monday's Court, St. George's Hotel, Plough & Barleycorn pub, Bateman's Alley, Pelican pub. At the west end east of Ordnance Row: St. George's Church with vestry.

▲ TOP (Left): An early 19th century auction being conducted in a library. (Right): Finely worked cabinet bureau featuring numerous draws and pockets.
ABOVE: Cartoon of an 18th century English auction and auctioneer.

Marriages & Grandchildren

The first born son Thomas Sabine Eastman, had married earlier that year on the 25th March 1805 at Holy Rood Church, Southampton to Mary (1782-1866), the daughter of William Eglon and Mary Fry of Newport, Isle of Wight.[15] They began producing children at a prodigious rate with Miriam (b.1806), Eliza (b.1807), Thomas (b.1809), Sarah (b.1810), Jane (b.1812), George (b.1813), Mary Elizabeth (b.1813) and another Mary Elizabeth (b.1815), all arriving prior to 1816.

Thomas and Sarah's daughter Elizabeth Eastman, was next to marry on the 26th March 1812 at St Mary's Church, Portsea to John (1789-1847) LLD, the son of William Shoveller and Mary Bignell of Warnford, Hampshire.[16] They too began producing grandchildren with Sarah Sabine (b.1812), Mary Elizabeth (b.1813), Jane Allen (1814) and another Sarah Sabine (1816) also arriving prior to 1816.

By this time, Thomas Eastman was apparently doing well enough to see him establish an office in London. But sadly by 1810, he had over stepped himself with the expansion of his business, and creditors caught up with him when he was listed in the Bankruptcy Courts.[17] On the 27th July 1811, Thomas Eastman was again listed in the press under 'Dividends from Guildhall, London', as a merchant conducting business in Clements Lane, London.[18]

Unfortunately, likely afflicted by the failure of his London venture, Thomas experienced a further blow with the probable commital of his 66 year old wife Sarah to an asylum, and then her death, which may have occurred when a Sarah Eastman was buried on the 14th June 1812 at Millbrook, Hampshire.[19] With no further evidence of Sarah's death having been found, unless Sarah was committed to an asylum, an 1812 burial for Sarah Eastman creates a conundrum as Thomas had already remarried in April of 1811?

▲ TOP: Painting of an early 19th century family in their drawing room, by James Holland. ABOVE (Left): Thomas Eastman opened an outlet in Clements Lane, London (shown here in 1831, drawn by Thomas H. Shepherd), which proved not to be a success. (Right): Cabinetmakers required a good sized workhouse, storehouse and yard.

Last Will & Testament of Thomas Eastman, of Portsea
Drafted - 30 July 1816 & Proved - 8 January 1817

◀The will of Thomas Eastman of Portsea, Hampshire was written on 30th July 1816, and is a substantial six-page document involving quite some property and thousands of pounds. It references his daughter Sarah Eastman, his sons Thomas Sabine Eastman, and Theophilus Eastman, and his second wife Jane Allen, as well as his eldest daughter Elizabeth, the wife of John Shoveller.

Translation

This is the last Will & Testament of one **Thomas Eastman** of the town of Portsea in the County of Southampton, upholsterer, whereby I humbly recommend my soul to God & dispose of all my worldly Estate, Effects in manner following, that is to say I give & bequeath unto my dear wife **Jane Eastman** an annuity or yearly sum of seventy five pounds for & during the term of her natural life to be paid to her by equal half yearly payments the first payment thereof to be made at the end of the first half year after my decease. I also give and bequeath unto my said wife for and during her natural life all my plate and dinner & also such part of my household furniture and of my books as she shall choose an Inventory being taken of the same & home immediately after ??? ????? I give & dispose of the same as follows. I give to my dau. Sarah Eastman one large Silver Era pot, one ???? pot & one Sugar Boat & the residue of my plate. I give unto my four children **Thomas Sabine Eastman, Elizabeth the wife of John Shoveller, Theophilus Eastman** & the said **Sarah Eastman** to be equally divided between them & I also give unto them in like manner all my linen & books & also the part of my household furniture so bequeathed to & enjoyed by my said wife for her life as aforesaid. I direct that the same shall after her decease be deemed part of the residue of my Estate & Effects. I also give unto my said wife the sum of fifty pounds to be paid to her immediately after my decease all that landhold messuage or dwelling house situate & being No. 79 in St Georges Square in Portsea aforesaid & now in my own occupation together with the warehouse, workshops, yard & appoints thereunto belonging. I give devise and unto my friends the **Rev. John Griffin** of Portsea aforesaid, **Samuel Allnutt** of the same place Druggist, and **Erasmus Jackson**? of Portsmouth in the said county of Southampton ???? their Exors, Admons and Assigns in trust to permit & ???? my said son **Thomas Sabine Eastman** to use and occupy the same house & immediately after the sale of my stock in Trade until such time as my real & personal Estates hereinafter devised & bequeathed respectively In trust to be sold and converted into money shall be sold and converted accordingly by my said son **Thomas Sabine Eastman** paying unto the said **John Griffin, Samuel Allnutt & Erasmus Jackson**? their Exors, Admons or Assigns the yearly rent or sum of one hundred pounds by four equal portions quarterly the first payment thus not to be made at or upon the Expiration of one quarter of a year or three calendar months next after the sale of my stock in Trade & upon this further Trust that they the said **John Griffin, Samuel Allnutt & Erasmus Jackson**? or the survivors or survivor of them or their Exors & Admons of such survivor or the acting Trustees or Trustee for the time being of this my will shall & do when & so soon as my Real & personal Estates hereinafter devised & bequeathed. In Trust to be sold and converted into money shall be sold and converted accordingly & assign & convey the said messuage or dwelling house together with the warehouse, workshop, yard & apperts thereunto belonging unto my said son **Thomas Sabine Eastman**
-four messuages or tenements, stable & yard in Warblington, St, Portsmouth - in the occupation of Mr MisGibbons, Mr. Taplin & Mr. Smut
-messuage or dwelling house, storehouse & timber yard situate in the Old Rope Walk, in the town of Portsea, occupied by myself & others
-messuage or dwelling house situate on the ???? of a new found ???? intended to be called ??? ??? Buildings - in the occupation of Mr Dunn
-all that messuage being at No. 58 St Georges Square, in the town of Portsea - now in the occupation of my said son **Thomas Sabine Eastman**
-also other messuages, lands and tenements of which I may have any disposing power
-I give & devise unto the said **John Griffin, Samuel Allnut & Erasmus Jackson**?, their sons Exors, Admons & Assigns
-I give & bequeath unto my dau. **Sarah Eastman** the sum of five hundred pounds to be paid to her within twelve months after my decease (except the said legacy of fifty pounds to my said wife)
-I give & bequeath unto my said son **Theophilus Eastman**, his Exors, Admons & Assigns the sum of two thousand pounds to be paid to him or them when & as soon as my real & personal Estates hereinbefore and hereinafter devised & bequeathed
-I give and bequeath the sum of two thousand pounds unto the said **John Giffins, Samuel Allnut & Erasmus Jackson**?, their sons Exors, Admons & Assigns upon trust to lay out & invest the said sum in the purchase of Parliamentary St???? or funds of Great Britain
-I devise that my said dau. **Elizabeth Shoveller** receive dividends from the above mentioned two thousand pounds, for her, not for the debts of her husband or future husbands... it is intended for her maintenance and support during her life or in the event of her decease, her children and equally to be divided between them, but if **Elizabeth Shoveller** should depart this life without bearing any children, the invested sum of two thousand pounds is to be distributed in three equal shares to **Thomas Sabine Eastman, Theophilus Eastman and Sarah Eastman**.
-same as page 3 above, for **Sarah Eastman**
-I give and bequeath unto my executor the said **John Griffin** the sum of fifty pounds, and to each of my other Exors the sum of ten pounds as a mark of respect towards them all & singular... belonging to the trade carried on under the firm of **Thomas Eastman & Son**
-there are other bequeathments in this will, but it is both difficult to read and interpret. etc.

▲The will of Thomas Eastman, proved 8 January 1817 (England & Wales, Prerogative Court of Canterbury Wills, 1384-1858. Held at The National Archives; Kew, England; Prerogative Court of Canterbury and Related Probate Jurisdictions: Will Registers; Class: PROB 11; Piece: 1588).

Thomas Eastman, Clement's-lane, London, merchant, Dec. 8, 15, Jan. 5, at ten. Attorney, Mr. Pasmore, Warnford-court, Throgmorton-street.

trement maker —Thomas Eastman, Clements-Lane, London, merchant.—William Crowder, Alderman-

Died, in Belgrave-square, London, Letitia, wife of Vice-Admiral Sir Charles Ogle, Bart.—In King-street, Portsea, aged 85, Mrs. Eastman, sen.—Aged 78, Mrs. Goodacre, of Gosport.—At Bedhampton, Wm. Read,

HAMPSHIRE.

Married.] At Southampton, Lieutenant Shaw, of the 31st foot, to Miss Light.

At Portsmouth, Lieutenant W. S. Key, of his Majesty's ship Leopard, to Miss S. F. Hurst, eldest daughter of the late Captain H. of the Royal navy.—Lieutenant Truss, to Miss Egton, sister to Mrs. Eastman, jun. of Portsea.

▲ABOVE (Left): 1-Thomas Eastman of Clement's Lane, London - Bankruptcy Listing (Kentish Gazette, 27 Nov. 1810, p.3). 2-Thomas Eastman - Bankruptcy Listing (Chester Courant, 27 Nov. 1810, p.2). 3-1832 Death notice for Mrs. Eastman Sr.- aged 85? (ie. Jane Allen, in Salisbury & Winchester Journal, 26 Nov 1832, p.4). (Right): Marriage announcement for Sarah Eglon to Lt. William Truss of "HMS Le Jupiter" (The Monthly Magazine & British Register, Vol 21, 1806, p.585).

Despite his wife's demise, Thomas seems to have recovered relatively quickly from Sarah's death, and married for a second time to Jane Allen (c.1765-1832) of Havant, Hampshire on the 22nd April 1811 at Portsea.[20] However, Thomas wasn't well and he declined in health over the next five years.

During these years the war continued and the French capture of Madrid provoked a British response that resulted in the Peninsular War, which brought Arthur Wellesley back from India. Suffering from porphyria, King George III was deemed unfit to govern and in 1811 his eldest son became Prince Regent, heralding in the 'regency period.'

In 1813, William Hedley's "Puffing Billy," the first steam locomotive to run on smooth rails, began work at Wylam Colliery, west of Newcastle upon Tyne, and in 1814 Britain and the United States signed the Treaty of Ghent, to end the War of 1812. The French threat was finally vanquished on the 18th June 1815, when the Duke of Wellington defeated Napoleon at the Battle of Waterloo. Following the Napoleonic War the Industrial Revolution shifted into high gear, and profound improvements were made in steam power, which saw the "SS Savannah" make the very first paddle steamship transatlantic crossing in 1819.

It was in 1816 that Thomas Eastman's demise occurred, although he was responsible

▲After the war with France ended in 1815, many Royal Navy ships were unseaworthy and not being needed they commonly had their masts reduced or removed to be re-purposed as prison hulks in Portsmouth Harbour, which became a a familiar sight for the local inhabitants. This view to the south shows rows of dismasted hulks with Portsmouth in the middle distance, the hills of the Isle of Wight in the right background, and the town of Gosport to the right.

enough to leave his affairs in good order. The will of Thomas Eastman of Portsea, Hampshire was written on 30th July 1816, and is a substantial six-page document involving quite some property and thousands of pounds. It references his daughter Sarah Eastman, his sons Thomas Sabine Eastman, Rev. Theophilus Eastman and his second wife Jane (nee Allen), as well as his eldest daughter Elizabeth, the wife of John Shoveller.[21]

The year 1816 brought the marriage of Thomas' youngest child Theophilus Eastman, which occurred at St. Denys, Warminster in Wiltshire on the 17th June 1816 to Mary (1791-1849) the daughter of Thomas Adlam and Martha Gattrall of Warminster.[22] Sadly, it was only a few months later that Thomas Eastman passed away and his body was buried on the 21st November 1816 at Titchfield, Hampshire. Although no memorial has been found, the burial site was likely to have been alongside his first wife Sarah, as Titchfield was her hereditary home.[23]

Thomas Eastman was a frequent advertiser in the 'Hampshire Telegraph', and after he died in 1816 much of his stock was sold at auction by his colleague Henry Hicks. In an advertisement dated 24th March 1817, Hicks declared that not only was the stock to be sold without reserve, but that "it was all of the late Mr. Eastman's manufacture, and not cheap London made Goods."[24] So respected was the business of Thomas Eastman & Co., which had flourished under his directorship from 1787 to 1816, that it was listed in 'The Dictionary of English Furniture Makers 1660-1840.'[25]

Unfortunately, we know only fragments about Thomas Eastman and his family at this stage. Apart from her considerable ancestry, research has failed to find virtually any information about Thomas's first wife Sarah (nee Sabine), with whom he produced four children, and even less about his second wife Jane Eastman (nee Allen), except that she passed away and was buried where she was born in Havant, Hampshire, on the 6th November 1832.[26]

Thomas and Sarah Eastman managed to produce a family of four children that were all fortunate enough to survive into adulthood. Three of these married, from which were brought forth no less than 31 grandchildren, although tragically, almost half of these descendants died as infants. The unique life stories of the four children of Thomas and Sarah Eastman and their descendants are the subject of the next chapter.

References

1. Knightroots - Thomas Eastman, burial held at Portsea - 21 November 1816, aged 64 (Page 26, No, 207 [https://www.knightroots.co.uk/parishes/titchfield]).

2. Sabine, John Dickinson, (1904). 'The Family and Descendants of Rev. James Sabine,' Washington, D.C.

3. James Sabine & Martha Lamport - Marriage held on the 1st February 1737 at Titchfield (Hampshire: Marriage License allegations, Bishop of Winchester, 1689-1837).

4. Sabine, John Dickinson, (1904), op.cit.

5. Thomas Eastman & Sarah Sabine - Marriage on the 25th December 1780 at Portsea, Hampshire, England, (from Hampshire Allegations for Marriage Licences 1689-1837, Vol.1).

6. Samuel Read Sabine - Apprenticed to Thomas Eastman with duties paid in 1781 (UK, Register of Duties Paid for Apprentices' Indentures, 1710-1811).

7. Hoad, Margaret (1981). 'The Origins of Portsmouth' Hampshire Studies presented to Dorothy Dymond, pp.13-15.

8. King, Alan, T. (Ed, 2011). 'The Portsmouth Encyclopaedia: A History of Places and People in Portsmouth, with an Index to Streets,' Historical Collections, Librarian Portsmouth City Libraries [https://www.portsmouth.gov.uk/wp-content/uploads/2020/05/lib-portsmouth-encyclopaedia-2011.pdf].

9. Sun Insurance (1787). Policy for Thomas Eastman & Co (GL MS vol. 345, p. 413).

10. Cabinetmakers apprenticed under Thomas Eastman from 1781 to 1791 at Portsea, Hants. (UK Register of Duties Paid for Apprentice's Indentures, 1710-1811).

11. Hampshire Extracts, [http://specialcollections.le.ac.uk/digital/collection/p16445coll4/id/167705].

12. Portsmouth History Centre (1798). 'Will of John Coker of Portsea, foreman of caulkers, HM Dockyard, Portsmouth.' The National Archives - Ref: X/479A/1/34, [https://discovery.nationalarchives.gov.uk/details/r/c17592a1-8d62-46d9-ac5a-16ac80728c62].

13. Sense of Place, South East - Rev. John Griffin [http://www.sopse.org.uk/ixbin/hixclient.exe?a=query&p=gateway&f=generic_objectrecord_postsearch.htm&_IXFIRST_=26123&_IXMAXHITS_=1&m=quick_sform&tc1=i&tc2=e&s=14_5T9hgIyY].

14. Thomas Eastman in Stabler, John (1991). 'English Newspaper Advertisements As A Source Of Furniture History,' Regional Furniture, Vol. 5, pp.93-102. [http://.regionalfurnituresociety.files.wordpress.com/2017/01/english-newspaper-advertisements-as-a-source-of-furniture-history-john-stabler].

15. Thomas Eastman & Mary Eglon - Marriage held on the 25th March 1805 at Holy Rood, Southampton, Hampshire, England, (from Hampshire Allegations for Marriage Licences 1689-1837, Vol.1).

16. Elizabeth Eastman & John Shoveller LLD - Marriage held on the 24th March 1812 at St Mary's Church, Portsea, Hampshire, England, (from Hampshire Allegations for Marriage Licences 1689-1837, Vol.2).

17. Thomas Eastman of Clement's Lane, London - Bankruptcy Listing (Kentish Gazette, 27 Nov. 1810, p.3).

18. Thomas Eastman - Dividends from Guildhall, London (Kentish Gazette, 28th June 1811).

19. Sarah Eastman - Burial held on the 14th June 1812 at Millbrook, Hampshire (England Deaths and Burials, 1538-1991).

20. Thomas Eastman & Jane Allen - Marriage held on the 22nd April 1811 at Portsea, Hampshire, England, (from Hampshire Allegations for Marriage Licences 1689-1837, Vol.1).

21. Thomas Eastman - Will, 30th July 1816 (England & Wales, Prerogative Court of Canterbury Wills, 1384-1858. Held at The National Archives; Kew, England; Prerogative Court of Canterbury and Related Probate Jurisdictions: Will Registers; Class: PROB 11; Piece: 1588).

22. Theophilus Eastman & Mary Adlam - Marriage held on 17th June 1816 at Stalbridge, Dorset (Wiltshire, England, Church of England Marriages and Banns, 1754-1916).

23. Thomas Eastman - Burial held on the 21 Nov 1816 at Titchfield, Hampshire, England, United Kingdom, Lancashire Record Office and Hampshire Record Office, United Kingdom. (England, Hampshire Bishop's Transcripts 1680-1892," database with images, FamilySearch [https://familysearch.org/ark:/61903/1:1:QLYW-R232: 16 March 2018]).

24. Thomas Eastman in Stabler, John (1991). 'English Newspaper Advertisements As A Source Of Furniture History,' p.102 (Hampshire Telegraph, 3rd March 1817).

25. Beard, Geoffrey & Gilbert, Christopher (1986). 'The Dictionary of English Furniture Makers 1660-1840', Leeds, pp. 263-287. British History Online [http://www.british-history.ac.uk/no-series/dict-english-furniture-makers/e [accessed 16 April 2022].

26. Jane Eastman - Burial held on the 6 Nov 1832 at Havant, Hampshire (England, Select Deaths and Burials, 1538-1991).

27. Thomas Eastman in Stabler, John (1991), op. cit.

28. Portsmouth City Libraries - 'The Portsmouth Encyclopedia' [https://www.portsmouth.gov.uk/wp-content/uploads/2020/05/lib-portsmouth-encyclopaedia-2011.pdf].

Chapter Twelve

THE DESCENDANTS OF
THOMAS EASTMAN & SARAH SABINE

Thomas Eastman was likely born around the year 1752, and most probably in the vicinity of Portsea, Hampshire, but not being able to substantiate his birth or parentage precludes further research into his ancestry at this stage. He likely developed from humble origins to become a skilled cabinetmaker and auctioneer amongst his community in Portsea. He left a substantial will and legacy for his four children, and took on the role of deacon at the Orange Street (now King Street) Independent Church in Portsea under his close friend Rev. John Griffin, where all except one of his 32 grandchildren were baptised. The following information is all that is currently known about Thomas and Sarah Eastman's children and their respective descendants (*see Pedigree Chart 6*).

1. Thomas Sabine Eastman (c.1782-1855)

Although no record of birth or baptism has been found for their first child and heir Thomas Sabine Eastman, he was likely born about 1782, at Portsea and followed in his fathers footsteps as a cabinetmaker and upholsterer. His middle name honoured his maternal heritage and he married on the 25th March 1805 at Holyrood Church, Southampton, Hampshire to Mary (1782-1866), the daughter of William Eglon and Mary Fry of Newport, from the Isle of Wight.[1] Built in 1320, Holyrood Church was one of the

PORTSEA, HANTS.

CABINET and UPHOLSTERY FURNITURE, Brussels and other Carpets, painted Floor Cloths, a fine toned Piano Forte, by Broadwood & Co. in an elegant mahogany case, with carved and turned legs, nearly new; sets of Dining Tables, an excellent Secretaire and Bookcase, brilliant Chimney-glasses of large dimensions, a few Paintings, and various other Effects.

TO be SOLD by AUCTION, by Mr. GARNETT, on Thursday the 19th day of October, 1826, and following day, without reserve, at eleven o'clock each day, by order of the Proprietor, Mr. Thomas S. Eastman, Upholsterer, on the Premises, No. 79, St. George's-square, Portsea; comprising excellent goose and swan feather beds, in deep bordered ticks, hair and wool mattrasses; a good mahogany secretaire and book-case, with glazed Gothic doors, two sets of extensible dining tables, card and Pembroke ditto, a circular rosewood Loo table, wardrobes, and chests of drawers, a music Canterbury, ladies' work table, hat stand, &c.; two Spanish mahogany Grecian sofas, an elegant carved sofa frame unstuffed, several sets of mahogany Trafalgar chairs, imitation rose wood, cane seated, and fancy painted ditto; Brussels, Kidderminster, and Venetian carpets, and painted floor cloths; large chimney glasses (very fine plates), in rich burnished gold frames; dressing glasses; a few lots of paper hangings and borders; canvas for papering on, bed ticks, satin hair seating, a small assortment of brass furniture, &c. &c.

₊ Entrance to the Auction-room from Ordnance Row.

Catalogues, in due time, may be had of the Auctioneer, Piazza, Queen-street; and of Mr. Eastman, on the Premises.

ST. GEORGE'S SQUARE, TOWN OF PORTSEA.

TO be LET, with early possession,—All those valuable and extensive PREMISES, situate in St. George's Square and Ordnance Row, Portsea, now in the occupation of Mr. Thomas S. Eastman, the Proprietor; comprising an excellent and roomy family House, consisting of a large front shop and parlour adjoining, drawing and dining rooms, three principal bed rooms and convenient dressing room, and four rooms in the attic, approached by an excellent stair case. The whole finished in an expensive manner, has excellent and convenient closets, and is replete with well adapted fixtures. The offices consist of two kitchens, cellar, and detached larder, and good paved outlet, rain water tank, &c.—Attached are three capacious and strongly built STORES. A stable and coach-house may be made at a small expence; and two smaller Stores with leaded flat leading therefrom.

The above Premises are well adapted for the Wholesale Provision, Corn Importation, or any other business requiring room; or at a small expence may be made an excellent and capacious Hotel. The whole measuring about twenty-five feet front, by one hundred and five feet deep.

For further particulars or viewing the same, application to be made on the premises.

◄Thomas Sabine Eastman occupied the family residence at 79 St George's Square, Portsea, and continued the cabinetmaking business following the death of his father in 1816 (Hampshire Telegraph, 16th Oct 1826, p.1). ▲The letting of 'all those valuable and extensive premises' at St George's Square & Ordnance Row occurred in 1834 (Hampshire Telegraph, c.1834).

original five churches serving the old walled town of Southampton, England, although the church was destroyed by enemy bombing during the World War blitz in November 1940.

Thomas Sabine Eastman was mentioned in the 1816 will of his father, and inherited his fathers substantial cabinetmaking/auctioneering business in the same year.[2] At the age of 41 in 1823, he was recorded as residing in the family home at 79 St George's Square, Portsea.

"Eastman, Thomas Sabine, 79 St George's Sq., Portsea, Portsmouth, Hants., Cabinetmaker, upholsterer and auctioneer."

1823 Piggotts Directory, Hampshire

By 1830, Thomas Sabine Eastman had added 'undertaking' to his business portfolio in Portsea, but he also opened a 'german repository [Berlin work]' at Union St, Ryde, on the Isle of Wight. By 1839, he had moved his family to Southampton and opened a 'fancy repository,' a shop that offered knick-knacks and toys for children at 60 Above Bar St, Southampton, Hampshire, which fed the market for cheap consumerism.[3]

In addition to labour-saving devices, the Industrial Revolution pioneered the development of new high-quality materials for needlework. In Berlin, embroidery patterns printed on a finely ruled grid and then colored by hand appeared for the first time in the early 1800s. Berlin wool work, simply known as 'Berlin work,' where the embroidery was done by following pre-printed patterns on canvas, became one of the most popular needlework pastimes for nearly a century. Thousands of Berlin-work patterns were printed and sold in needlework shops, one of which was a Berlin Warehouse opened by Mary Eastman (nee Eglon) at 60 Above Bar St, in Southampton.[4]

Commencing the year after their marriage in 1805, Thomas Sabine and Mary Eastman began producing a large brood of 12 children, of which nine survived to adulthood (*see 12.1 Descendants of Thomas Sabine Eastman & Mary Eglon*). While most remained in England, their eldest Miriam (1806-1886), and her husband William Francis Weeks Wilson (1801-1872),

▲ TOP (Left): Marriage registration of Thomas [Sabine] Eastman & Mary Eglon on the 25th March 1805 at Southampton, (from Hampshire Allegations for Marriage Licences 1689-1837, Vol.1). RIGHT: Newspaper announcements for the wedding of Thomas [Sabine] Eastman & Mary Eglon. LEFT COLUMN: Registrations of baptism for the children of Thomas Sabine & Mary Eastman from 1806 to 1824 at the Orange Street (now King Street) Independent Church, Portsea (Portsea, Hampshire, England & Wales, Non-Conformist and Non-Parochial Registers, 1567-1936), with Miriam Eastman (1806); Eliza Eastman (1807); Thomas Eastman (1809); Sarah Eastman (1810); Jane Eastman (1812) and George Eastman (1813). RIGHT COLUMN: Mary Elizabeth (1815); Charlotte (1819); Theophilus (1819); Ann Eglon (1821) and William Henry (1824).

Documents of Thomas Sabine Eastman & Family

Thomas Sabine Eastman
England & Wales Census
1841

Place:	All Saints, Hampshire.
Residence:	Above Bar St, Southampton
Head of House:	Thomas Eastman
Estimated Age:	55
Occupation:	Unknown
Registration District:	Southampton
Folio:	H0107/416/26
Residents:	Mary, wife (55-59)
	Eliza, dau (29-33)
	Mary, dau (21-25)
	Thomas, son (31)
	William, son (17-21)
	Sarah Eastman, sister (50-54)
	Ann Bungy, Servant (32-36)
	Mary Perry, Servant (20-24)

1851

Place:	Newchurch, Hampshire
Residence:	Union Street, Ryde
Head of House:	Thomas S. Eastman
Estimated Age:	69
Occupation:	Retired Auctioneer
Registration District:	Isle of Wight
Folio:	H0107/1664/225
Residents:	Mary, wife (69)
	Eliza, dau (43)
	Jane, dau (39)
	Mary Ann Bungy, Servant (46)
	Sarah Hoskin, Servant (30)

1861

Place:	Newchurch, Hampshire
Residence:	2 Pier Terrace, Ryde
Head of House:	Mary Eastman
Estimated Age:	79
Occupation:	Lodging House Keeper
Registration District:	Isle of Wight
Folio:	H047/657/19
Residents:	Mary, wife (79)
	Eliza, dau (53)
	Jane, dau (48)
	Mary Ann Bungy, Servant (57)

EASTMAN—On the 19th instant, at Southampton, after a long and painful illness, Mary Elizabeth, youngest daughter of Mr. Thomas Sabine Eastman, late of St. George's Square, Portsea.

EASTMAN—On the 27th instant, after a long and painful illness, Mr. Thomas Sabine Eastman, formerly of Portsea, aged 73 years.

Thomas Eastman, R.N.
England & Wales Census
1851

Place:	Portsea, Hampshire
Residence:	Norfolk Square
Head of House:	Thomas Eastman
Estimated Age:	42
Occupation:	Naval Instructor RN, Half Pay
Registration District:	Portsea Island
Folio:	17/H0107/1659/99
Residents:	Sarah, wife (26)
	Miriam, dau (1)
	Thomas, son (0)
	Ann Edwards, Nurse (54)
	Jane Boulton, Servant (19)

DIED.
On the 25th ult., at Ventnor, Anne Fetherstonh', the wife of Charles Coles, esq., of 86, Great Tower-street, and Wimbledon-common, Surrey.
On the 27th ult., at Ryde, after a long and painful illness, Mr. Thomas Sabine Eastman, late of St. George's squre, Portsea.

BIRTHS.
EASTMAN—On the 9th instant, at Southsea, the wife of Thomas Eastman, Esq., H.M.S. Excellent, of a daughter.

BIRTHS.
EASTMAN—In St. George's-square, Portsea, on the 27th ult., the wife of Mr. T. Eastman, R.N., of a son.

BIRTHS.
TAYLOR—On the 1st inst., the wife of Francis Taylor, Esq., Romsey, of a son.
EASTMAN—This day, in St. George's Square, Portsea, the wife of Mr. Thomas Eastman, R.N., of a daughter.

BIRTHS.
WARREN—On the 29th ult., at Purbrook, the wife of Captain R. L. Warren, H.M.S. Cressy, of a son.
EASTMAN—On the 3rd inst., at Southsea, the wife of Mr. Thomas Eastman, R.N., of a son.

BIRTHS.
MC FARLANE—On the 29th ult., at Llanreath House, near Pembroke Dock, South Wales, the wife of Donald Mc Farlane, Esq., of a son.
MACKENZIE—On the 1st inst., in the precincts of the Close, Chichester, the wife of the Rev. D. C. Mackenzie, of a son.
EASTMAN—On the 3rd inst., at Eastern-parade, Southsea, the wife of Thomas Eastman, Esq., R.N., of a son.

BIRTHS.
EASTMAN—On the 24th inst., at Eastern-parade, Southsea, the wife of Mr. Thomas Eastman, R.N., of a daughter.
FORD—On the 21st inst., at Grafton-street, Landport, the wife of Mr. S. Ford, of a daughter.

EASTMAN—On Sunday last, suddenly, of disease of the heart, Mr. Thomas Eastman, R.N., proprietor of the Esplanade House Academy, Southsea.

EASTMAN, Thomas. 23 December. of Thomas Eastman formerly of St. George's square Portsea but late of Eastern Parade Southsea both in the County of Southampton Naval Instructor deceased who died 1 July. The Will of Thomas Eastman formerly of St. George's square Portsea but late of Eastern Parade Southsea... Effects under £5,000. 1860 at Eastern Parade aforesaid, was proved at the Principal Registry by the oath of Sarah Eastman of Eastern Parade aforesaid Widow the Relict and the sole Executrix.

SPICKERNELL—EASTMAN—On the 17th instant, at St. Jude's, Southsea, by the Rev. Thomas Brownrigg, incumbent, George Eastcott Spickernell, Esq., Head Master of Eastman's Naval Establishment, to Sarah, widow of the late Thomas Eastman, Esq., R.N.

Pigot & Co.'s
REFERENCE TO PORTSMOUTH, Directory, &c. Hampshire.

1828 Pigot's Directory, Portsea
CABINET MAKERS AND UPHOLSTERERS.
*Eastman Thos. S. 79, St. George's-sq
Eastman T. S. cabinet mkr 13

1830 Pigot's Directory, Portsea
UNDERTAKERS.
Eastman Thomas Sabine, 79 St. George's square

1830 Robson's Directory, Ryde
Eastman Thomas S. Union st·· German Repository

1839 Robson's Directory, Southampton
Fancy Repositories.—Eastman T. 60 Above Bar st
Thurston John, 35 Above Bar st

1844 Pigot's Directory, Southampton
AUCTIONEERS APPRAISERS & HOUSE, &c. AGENTS.
Eastman Thomas S. 61 Above Bar st
BERLIN WAREHOUSES.
Eastman Mary & Co. 60 Above bar

1849 Post Office Directory, Ryde
Eastman Misses, 5 Above Bar st. Sthmptn
Eastman T. S. 5 Union street, Ryde

▲LEFT COLUMN: 1-Thomas Sabine Eastman - Census for England & Wales [1841, 1851 & 1861]; 2-1848 Death notice of Mary Elizabeth, dau, (Hampshire Telegraph, 25 Nov 1848, p.5); 3-1855 Death notice for Thomas Sabine Eastman (Hampshire Telegraph, 29th Dec 1855, p.5). CENTRE COLUMN: 1-Thomas Eastman, R.N. - Census for England & Wales [1851]; 2-Death notice for Thomas Sabine Eastman (Isle of Wight Observer, 5th Jan 1856, p.4); 3-Notices for daughter Miriam (Hampshire Telegraph, 13th Oct 1849, p.5); 4-Birth of George (Hampshire Telegraph, 1st Jan 1853, p.5); 5-Birth of Eliza (Hampshire Telegraph, 5th Aug 1854, p.5); 6-Birth of William (Hampshire Telegraph, 4th Oct 1856, p.5); 7-Birth of Henry (Hampshire Telegraph, 7th Aug 1858, p.5); 8-Birth of Sarah (Hampshire Telegraph, 26th May 1860, p.5). 9-Death notice for Thomas Eastman, R.N. (Hampshire Telegraph, 7 July 1860, p.5). RIGHT COLUMN: 1-1860 Probate notice for Thomas Eastman, R.N. (England & Wales, National Probate Calendar, 1858-1995); 2-Notice of marriage between Sarah Eastman (widow) & George Spickernell (Hampshire Telegraph, 21 Dec 1861, p.5); 3-Thomas Sabine & Mary Eglon business and residential listings in local directories from 1828 to 1849.

emigrated to Canada in 1836 and reared their family in Ontario, Canada.

Thomas Sabine Eastman died on the 27th December 1855, at Ryde, on the Isle of Wight, but was formerly of No. 79 St. George's Square, Portsea, Hampshire.[5]

Thomas Eastman's Royal Naval Academy

The eldest son of Thomas Sabine Eastman and namesake of his grandfather was another Thomas Eastman, who became a Royal Navy instructor at "HMS Excellent" and later established the prestigious 'Eastman's Royal Naval Academy' at Portsmouth, a proud educational institution that was responsible for later producing no less than 20 admirals and commanders for the Royal Navy.[6,7]

12.1 Descendants of Thomas Sabine Eastman & Mary Eglon [33]

Thomas Sabine Eastman married on 25th Mar 1805 at St. Mary's Church, Portsea to Mary Eglon (1782-1866), with issue:

__1. Miriam Eastman (1806 - 1886)__, was born on the 3rd Feb and baptised on the 14 April 1806 at Orange Street (now King Street) Independent Church, Portsea. She married on the 8 Oct 1828 to William Francis Weeks WILSON (1801-1872), and they emigrated to Canada in 1836, with issue:

1.1 William Ashlin Faye Wilson (1829-1895), was born in 1829 in Hampshire, England. He married in 1854 to Eliza A. Pound (1836-1908). He died in 1895 (aged 65-66) at Ionia County, Michigan, USA, and buried at Tuttle Cemetery, Ionia, Ionia County, Michigan (Section - 1), with issue:
a. William Alfred WILSON (1854-)
b. Ada Miriam "Mary" Wilson (1857-1941)
c. Edwin George Wilson (1858-1948)
d. Culmer P. WILSON (1864-1895)
e. Nellie E. Wilson Adgate Wilson (1870-1945)

1.2 William Francis Wilson (1830-1900), details unknown.

1.3 Alfred Dell Wilson (1832-1918), born Feb 26 1832. He married in 1862 to Mary Dwyer (Apr 27 1837 - Apr 16 1916), Alfred died at Rochester Township, Essex County, Ontario, Canada and was buried at Ruscom United Church Cemetery, Rochester Township, Essex County, Ontario, Canada (Row 17), with issue:
a. Francis W. WILSON (Nov 27 1863 to Apr 16 1928), who married Elizabeth M. Leak (Jan 5 1865 to Dec 6 1928).
b. Miriam Wilson (1865-1940)
c. Mary Dell Wilson (1866-1944)
d. Minnie Wilson (1867-)
e. George A. WILSON (1869-1907)
f. Albert Henry WILSON (1871-)

1.4 Thomas Eastman Wilson (1834-1918), born 4 Nov 1834 in Southampton, Southampton Unitary Authority, Hampshire, England. He married firstly to Elizabeth Abbs (1840-1876),), with issue:
a. William Richard WILSON (1873-1876)
b. Harry Edwin WILSON (1875-1876)
Thomas married secondly in 1878 to Elizabeth Dalgarno (1855-1907), with issue:
c. Edith Ann Wilson (1883-1969), married Revenaugh.
d. James Dalgarno Wilson (1890-1975)
Thomas died on 13 Aug 1918 (aged 83) in Detroit, Wayne County, Michigan, USA and buried at Woodmere Cemetery, Detroit, Wayne County, Michigan, USA (Section A Lot 429).

1.5 Hannah Wilson (1835-1853), died unmarried.

1.6 Miriam Emma Wilson (1835-1853), died unmarried.

1.7 Caroline Ada Wilson (1837-1870), married in 1863 to Alexander Munroe SMITH (1836-1924), with issue:
a. Miriam "Minnie" Florence Smith (1864-1947)
b. Harry John SMITH (1866-1952)
c. Jessie Isabella Smith (1868-1913)

1.8 George Edwin WILSON (1840-1923), married in 1870 to Mary Christine Ferguson (1846-1883), with issue:
a. Emma Margaret Wilson (1872-1954)
b. Mary Caroline Wilson (1873-1874)
c. William Edwin WILSON (1875-1876)
d. George Edwin (Eddie) WILSON (1877-1921)
e. Fergus Alfred Arthur WILSON (1878-1955)
f. Albert Dell WILSON (1880-1969)
g. Robert Bruce WILSON (1882-1933)

George married secondly in 1884 to Mary Gordon McColl (1855-1889), no issue.

1.9 Albert James Wilson (1841-1905), married in 1864 to Anne Robertson Cameron (1843-1920), with issue:
a. Alexander Cameron WILSON (1867-1910), details unknown.

1.10 Arthur Porter Wilson (1844-1934), born 21 Jul 1844, Ontario, Canada. He married Maria Honner on 19 March 1879 in the home of Capt. Thomas Honner, Amherstburg, Essex, Ontario, Canada. Witnesses: Annie Sunderland & Percy Hackett. Arthur died 30 Apr 1934 (aged 89) in Ionia County, Michigan, USA. Buried at Lakeside Cemetery, Lake Odessa, Ionia County, Michigan, USA, with issue:
a. Mary Christiana Wilson (1880-1919), married Evans.
b. Annie Augusta (Infant) Wilson (1882-1882)
c. William Victor Honner WILSON (1885-1963).

1.11 Francis "Frank" Henry Wilson (1848-1894), "Frank Wilson died in Orange township on Wednesday last and was buried on Thursday. He was 46 years of age, and had been a great sufferer from rheumatism for the past seven years, he dying from the results of that disease. In his younger days, before he became crippled, he was a great worker and his services were always in demand, He was deserted by his wife some years ago and had been cared for by relatives." (Portland Observer," Portland, Ionia, Michigan, Wednesday 03 Oct 1894, p.1), with issue:

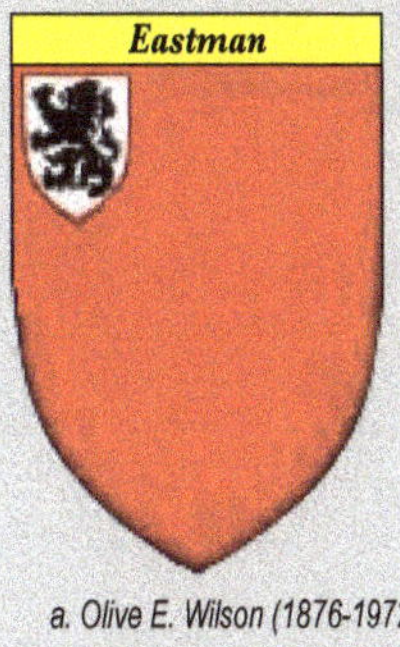

a. Olive E. Wilson (1876-1972), married Rowe.

1.12 Augustus "Gus" Norton Wilson (1853-1913), known as Gus, was born in Ontario, one of many children of William Francis Wilson and Miriam Eastman. He married twice, first in 1904 to Margaret "Maggie" Dalgarno (1875-1958) in Chatham, with two daughters:
a. Clara Ezma Wilson (1889-1965) married McRea
b. ??? Wilson (?-?), details unknown.
Augustus lived in Michigan during both marriages. He had two daughters from his first marriage and two sons from his second marriage. Following his first wife's death in Detroit, Gus married Sarah Ellen Wilson (1853-1899, with issue:
c. William Francis WILSON (1910-1995), Oldest of two sons of Sarah Ellan Willmore and Augustus "Gus" Norton Wilson, his father died in Michigan when he was just a young boy. His mother headed north with her two sons, Bill and Jim, to Eston Saskatchewan where her brother was homesteading. The brother died of typhoid in 1916 and another brother who joined them soon after she arrived drowned in 1920. She continued to farm the land alone until 1932. William had gone on ahead of her to find a place to live near her sisters whereupon the family was reunited in Bellflower California. Their family Kept in touch with the Malcomson's, her sister Alice Malcomson nee Willmore having moved to Califoria before her. They all remained in California until they died. In 1952 William married Margaret Susan Mize.
d. James Augustus WILSON (1913-1972), was born in Detroit Michigan, the youngest son of Augustus Norton Wilson and Sarah Ellen Wilmore. A few months after his father died, the family moved to Eston, Saskatchewan in 1914 to help his uncles farm. A few years after both uncles died the family left Canada in 1932 and settled close to relatives in California. While enlisted as a soldier in WWI James met and married Willa Catherine George 9 April 1943 in Pomona.
Gus's daughters remained in Detroit, but he died when the boys were very young. Sarah and the boys then left Detroit to help her brother work his homestead at Eston, Saskatchewan. After the death of her brothers Sarah remained on the homestead in Eston until 1932, when she moved to California with her two sons to be near family members. Gus died on the 14th Nov 1913 (aged 60) in Detroit, Wayne County, Michigan, USA and was buried at Woodmere Cemetery (Plot, Section A1, Lot 429).

__2. Eliza Eastman (1807 - 1875)__, was born on the 13th July 1807 and baptised on the 7th August 1807 at Orange Street (now King Street) Independent Church, Portsea. She resided with her parents at 79 St George's Square, and at 60 Above Bar St in Southhampton, where she worked in a partnership with her sister Jane as a 'Berlin Wool Trader'. The family later moved to 5 Union St, and then 2 Pier Terrace, at Ryde on the Isle of Wight. She died on the 9th May 1875 at Pier Terrace, leaving a will proved at Winchester, with effects under £20 to her sister Jane, no issue.

__3. Thomas EASTMAN (1809 - 1860)__, was born on the 14 March 1809, and baptised on the 6th May 1809, at the Orange Street (now King Street) Independent Church, Portsea. Thomas Eastman (Royal Navy) worked as a gunnery instructor at "HMS Excellent," a naval shore establishment in Portsmouth Harbour. Thomas married on 26th October 1848 at Milton Lilbourne, Wiltshire to Sarah (1825-1867), the dau. of Joel Jackman (farmer) of Milton. He was promoted to Naval Instructor on the 3rd February 1851 and established Eastman's Royal Naval Academy (The National Archives, Kew ADM 196/74/1036). Thomas Eastman, R.N. died on 1 July 1860 at Eastern Pde, Southsea, Hampshire, aged just 51 years, leaving a will with effects under £5000 to his wife Sarah,with issue:

3.1 Miriam Eastman (1849-1922), born 9th Oct 1849 at Southsea, and baptised 9 May 1852 at Saint Thomas,Portsmouth. Miriam was living at Alton Barnes Rectory, Marlborough, Wiltshire when she died a spinster on the 4 Dec 1922 at Devizes, Wiltshire, leaving a substantial will with effects valued at £5195 15s. 5d. to her brothers William Inglefield Eastman, retired general H.M. Army, and Henry Mervyn Eastman, gentleman, no issue.

3.2 Thomas EASTMAN (1851-1923), a school master, married firstly in 1882 to Eva Francis Leggatt (1863-1887), no issue. He married secondly in 1891 to Rosa Charlotte Yardley (1872-1941). Thomas studied at Cambridge and became a solicitor and died at Applegarth Mark Way, Godalming, Surrey on the 19 Sep 1928, leaving a substantial will valued at £26,034 16s. 1d. proved in London to Harold Wigan insurance broker and Percival Field Walker, solicitor, with issue:
a. Rose Dorothy Violet Eastman (1891-1974), married 1921 to Capt Arnold Henry BLECKLY (1889-1923), with issue:
a1. Lorna Dorothy Bleckly (1922-1996), born iHong Kong, married 1942 at Guildford, Surrey to Capt Thomas Herbert MARTIN (1918-2008, Royal Canadian Artillery), with issue:
b. Lucie Maud Eastman (1893-1983), died unmarried a wealthy spinster with over £40,000 in probate.
c. Brigadier Claude Henry Warrington EASTMAN (1899-1975), MVO, DSO, married 5 Feb 1931 to Lady Mary Agatha (1905-1997), dau. of Hugh Frederick Vaughan [CAMPBELL] (1870-1914), 4th Earl Cawdor of Cawdor Castle, Scotland & Joan Emily Mary Thynne (1872-1945). Their issue:
c1. Sylvia Eastman (1935-2004), married in 1967 to Peter LETH (1920-1987), no issue.
c2. David William EASTMAN (1937-2011), educated at Eton College, Windsor, & married in 1969 to Antonia Catherine Dorman (1947-?), with issue.

3.3 George EASTMAN (1853-?), born late 1853 and baptised 15 Feb 1854 at Portsmouth, Hampshire. He may have married in 1873 at Kingston to either Sarah Blatch or Mary Milton, otherwise information as to his issue or death are unknown.

3.4 Eliza Irvine Eastman (1854-1917), born July 1854 at Portsea, Hampshire, married in 1877 at Lymington, Hampshire to James Newton ROBINSON (1838-1917). She died on 24 Sep 1917, 22 Elphinstone Rd, Southsea, Hampshire leaving a will valued at £143 14s., proved on 23 Nov 1917 in London, bequeathing Arthur Frederick Eastman Robinson, captain H. M. Army, with issue:
a. Blanche Hannington Robinson (1878-?), details unknown.

3.5 General Sir William Inglefield EASTMAN (1856-1941), was an officer in the Royal Marine Artillery. In 1881 he was residing at the "Royal Marine Artillery Brarracks", Eastney, Hampshire. He travelled to Australia, and married on 11 July 1891 at St David's Cathedral, Hobart to Agnes Ida Lewis (1864-1936). He was promoted to Major-General on 7th February, 1912.[1. The Navy List. (March, 1913). p. 24.]. He died on 13 Oct 1941, at Worthing, Sussex, with issue:
a. Lt.-Col. Neil Inglefield EASTMAN (1892-1972), born Exeter, Devon, married in 1922 to Agnese Eudora Wingate, no issue.
b. Thomas Inglefield EASTMAN (1894-1977), born Exeter, Devon, died unmarried.

3.6 Henry Mervyn EASTMAN (1858-1950), born Oct 1858 at Portsea, Hampshire. He married Helen Ashley (1876-1952), dau. of Col Thomas Dyer (Indian Army). Henry died at Rafters Hayling Island on 19th Jan 1950 (aged 76), leaving a will valued at £4,272 17s. 7d., proved on 18 March 1950 in Winchester, bequeathing Helen Ashley Eastman, widow, with issue:
a. Henry Seymour Gordon EASTMAN (1898-1965)

3.7 Sarah Victoria Eastman (1860-1952), born April 1860 at Portsea, Hampshire. Married 20 Jan 1891 at Sculcoates, Yorkshire to Charles Andrew SLADEN (1851-1928). Sarah died on the 16 Dec 1952 (aged 92) at 19 Wayside Rd, Southborne, Bournemouth, Hampshire, leaving a will valued at £4,846 6s. 7d., proved on 28 March 1952 in London, bequeathing her daughter Evelyn Frances Merrett, widow, and nephew Henry Seymour Gordon Eastman (Rubber Planter), with issue:
a. Charles Ethelred SLADEN (1891-1893)
b. Evelyn Frances Sladen (1893>1952), married Merrett.

__4. Sarah G. Eastman (1810 - 1889)__, was born on the 30 Dec. 1810, and baptised on the 10th Feb. 1811, at the Orange Street (now King Street) Independent Church, Portsea. Sarah died April 1889 at Braintree, Essex, England. She married firstly in 1828 to Robert EMMERSON, with issue:

4.1 Frederick EMMERSON (1834-?), details unknown.

4.2 Catherine Emmeline Emmerson (1842-?), details unknown.

Sarah married secondly on the 5th April 1842 at Lymington, Hampshire to Alfred WEEKS (1818-1889), with issue:

4.3 Katherine Emmeline Weeks (1850-1924), married in1873 to Samuel EASTMAN (1824-1900), with issue:
a. Samuel R.A. EASTMAN (1875-1938)
b. Howard Wriothesley R. EASTMAN (1875-1959)
c. Walter Weldon EASTMAN (1877-1968)
d. Harold Alexander Sabine EASTMAN (1878-1970)
e. Katherine Margaret Eastman (1880-1973)
f. Reginald Heber EASTMAN (1883-1966)

__5. Jane Eastman (1812 - 1898)__, was born on the 28 May 1812, and baptised in 1812, at the Orange St. Church, Portsea. She resided with her parents at 79 St George's Square, then 60 Above Bar St in Southhampton, and worked as a 'Berlin Wool Trader' with her sister Eliza. They later moved to 5 Union St, and then 2 Pier Terrace, Ryde on the Isle of Wight. At the 1881 Census she was living with Bernard &

Emily Marvin at Beaconsfield, Ryde, and in 1891 was still with them, living under her own means at 76 Union St, Ryde. She died a spinster at Ryde, Hampshire in April 1898 (aged 85), no issue.

6. George EASTMAN (1813 - 1869), was born on the 6 Dec. 1813, and baptised on the 13th Feb. 1814, at the Orange Street (now King Street) Independent Church, Portsea. He died in January 1869 at South Stoneham, Hampshire, unmarried and without issue.

7. Mary Elizabeth Eastman (1813 - 1813), was born on the 6 Dec. 1813, but died as an infant. No issue.

8. Mary Elizabeth Eastman (1815 - 1848), was born on the 30 Sep. 1815, and baptised on the 23rd Feb. 1816, at the Orange Street (now King Street) Independent Church, Portsea, but died a spinster at Southampton in Oct. 1848 (aged 33), without issue.

9. Charlotte Eastman (1817 - 1819), was born on the 8 July 1817, and baptised on the 19th Sep. 1817, at the Orange Street (now King Street) Independent Church, Portsea. She died an infant and was buried at Portsea, 5 June 1819, aged 22mths.[31] No issue.

10. Theophilus EASTMAN (1819 - 1819), was born and baptised in 1819, at the Orange Street (now King Street) Independent Church, Portsea. He died an infant and was buried at Portsea, 22 April 1819, aged 1.[32] No issue.

11. Ann Eglon Eastman (1821 - 1841), was born on the 13 Sep. 1821, and baptised on the 7th June 1822, at the Orange Street (now King Street) Independent Church, Portsea, but died Portsea, Hampshire and was buried on 1st May 1823 (aged 20) at Titchfield, Hampshire, died unmarried.

12. William Henry EASTMAN (1824 - 1869), as born on the 29 March 1824, and baptised on the 31st Dec. 1824, at the Orange Street (now King Street) Independent Church, Portsea. He travelled to the USA, entering New York on 3rd January 1850, but returned and died on the Isle of Wight in June 1869. Died unmarried and without issue.

* Died before adulthood - d.s.p.
(Some names not listed in the index).

Documents of Miriam Eastman & William Francis Weeks Wilson

Married, on Wednesday the 8th inst. Mr Weeks, of Southampton, to Miriam, eldest daughter of Mr. Eastman, St. George's-square, Portsea.

EASTMAN—On the 11th ult., at the residence of her niece, Above Bar, Southampton, Sarah, daughter of the late Mr. Thomas Eastman, of St. George's Square, Portsea, in the 65th year of her age, beloved by all who knew her.

EASTMAN Eliza.   Effects under £20.

26 June.   The Will of Eliza Eastman late of Ryde in the Isle of Wight in the County of Southampton Spinster who died 9 May 1875 at Ryde was proved at Winchester by Jane Eastman of Ryde Spinster the Sister the sole Executrix.

▲TOP (Left): 1-Miriam Eastman & William Wilson's marriage notice (Hampshire Chronicle, 8 Oct 1828, p.1); 2-1850 Death notice for Sarah Eastman, (Hampshire Telegraph, 2nd Feb 1850, p.5). (Right): 1-Probate notice for Eliza Eastman - 26th June 1875 (England & Wales, National Probate Calendar, 1858-1995). MID (Left): Early photograph of Miriam Weeks-Wilson (nee Eastman). (Right): The eight sons of William F. Sr. & Miriam Wilson (nee Eastman). Standing from left: Thomas Eastman, Augustus Norton, Frank and Albert. Seated: William Francis Jr., Edwin, Fred and Arthur, taken c.1880 at Rochester, Ontario, Canada. The boys were all great grandsons of Thomas and Sarah Eastman. ABOVE: William Francis Weeks Wilson & Miriam Eastman who emigrated to Ontario, Canada in 1836.

The introduction in 1838 of an entrance examination for the Royal Navy, although initially an undemanding test for most, encouraged the development of specialised educational establishments, of which Eastman's Royal Naval Academy was one.[8] Despite its impressive name, the Academy had no formal association with royalty or the navy. It

Eastman's Royal Naval Academy [34,35]

Eastman's Royal Naval Academy, was a preparatory school originally established on the east side of Southern Road (later Burgoyne Road) at Southend, Hampshire. It became one of the best-known private naval academies, and later relocated to Winchester. Between 1855 and 1923 it was known primarily as a school that prepared boys for entry to the Royal Navy. Thereafter, it was renamed Eastman's Preparatory School and continued until the 1940s. According to Jonathan Betts, it was "considered one of the top schools for boys intended for the Navy."

The introduction in 1838 of an entrance examination for the Royal Navy, although initially an undemanding test for most, encouraged the development of specialised educational establishments, of which Eastman's Royal Naval Academy was one. Despite its name, the Academy had no formal association with the Navy. It was founded by Thomas Eastman, a retired naval instructor in 1851, and in 1854 had moved into a purpose-built building on South Parade, Southsea. There it catered primarily for boarders, but did take some day-boys. When Eastman died in 1860 he was succeeded by one of the teaching staff, Dr George E. Spickernell (c. 1833-1901), who was elected a Fellow of the Royal Geographical Society in 1863. He married Eastman's widow Sarah, and a year later he continued on as headmaster until 1885.

The school was four floors high with a huge assembly hall on the ground floor. In the middle was a large pot-bellied stove. There was also a very large kitchen with coal-fired ranges and a conservatory to the rear. A large oak staircase ran from the top to bottom of the building and what looked like bedrooms going off of the floors with cast iron fireplaces in them. The building was largely flat roofed which the last flight of stairs led up to. On the roof were lots of tall yellow chimney pots.

Thomas Eastman's son, Thomas Eastman IV, taught at the school in 1872, around the time that he was attending or due to attend the University of Cambridge, and was again on the staff from 1876. In 1881, he opened his own school at Wallington, Hampshire, also called Eastman's Royal Naval Academy. In 1886, this school moved to Stubbington and in 1894 it moved again to Northwood Park (former home of Philip Vanderbylt), near Winchester, which coincided with a change of name to Northwood Park Naval College, and later became Eastman & Salter Private School.

'IT was a decent place to learn the elements of an English education'. So wrote Robert Scot Skirving who, at the age of twelve, was sent to Eastman's Royal Naval Academy in Southsea in February 1872 as a preliminary to joining the Royal Navy as a cadet. He was at the school for only one year but it was a year which was deeply engraved on his memory, as the account which follows this brief introduction will show.

E.R.N.A., as it was known, was a private school founded in 1851 by a retired naval instructor, Thomas Eastman, primarily to prepare boys for the examination to enter the Royal Navy as cadets. At that time boys went straight to sea provided they passed the exam between the ages of twelve and fourteen and acquired a nomination from a flag officer or a captain.[1] The school's first home was in St George's Square, Portsea, near The Hard, but in September 1854 it moved to a new building at 28 Eastern Parade, Southsea (renamed South Parade twenty years later), on the corner with what is now Burgoyne Street (Fig. 1).[2] The school building later acquired the name Burgoyne House. An advertisement for E.R.N.A., Southsea, in the *Hampshire Telegraph* of 26 April 1856 declared that

Young gentlemen are prepared for entry into Her Majesty's Service, as Naval and Marine Cadets, Masters' Assistants etc, by Mr Thomas Eastman, RN (Five years Naval Instructor of HMS *Excellent*). The situation of the Establishment, commanding as it does an extensive view of the Sea, presents great advantages for exercise with the nautical instruments – affording, by means of the sea horizon, equal facility for making the observations for ascertaining the latitude and longitude, to that on board ship. Terms by the month, quarter or year. Eastern Parade, near the Castle, Southsea.

Eastman died in 1860[3] and was succeeded by George Eastcott Spickernell (c1833–1901) who in 1861 married Eastman's widow Sarah. Eastman's eldest son, also Thomas, was an assistant master at the school in 1872 when aged twenty-one, either taking a year off from Cambridge to help out or perhaps before going up to the university.[4]

The school continued under a succession of headmasters after Spickernell gave it up in 1885, and was closed early in the Second World War. Since 1911 it had been known as Eastman's Preparatory School for Boys. Its building, 28 South Parade, survived the war and was used as the Boarding House of Portsmouth Grammar School from 1946 to 1954. It was pulled down in the 1960s and replaced by Fastnet House, a block of flats.

E.R.N.A., Southsea, never had quite the fame of Dr Burney's Royal Academy which flourished in Gosport from 1791 to 1904,[5] nor of Stubbington House School near Fareham which was run by the Foster family from 1840 to 1962.[6] But certainly E.R.N.A. was considered by distinguished naval officers as a suitable school for their sons, and it had many distinguished alumni, as is well borne out in the account which follows where mention is made of just a few boys who happened to be there in 1872.

From... Owen, Hugh (1991). 'Eastman's Royal Naval Academy, Southsea, In The 1870s,' The Mariner's Mirror, 77:4, pp.379-387.

List Of Royal Navy Officers Educated At Eastman's Royal Naval Academy, Portsmouth [36]

A....
Austin Charles Ackland
Thomas Benjamin Stratton Adair
Bryan John Huthwaite Adamson
Augustine Willington Shelton Agar*
Argentine Hugh Alington
Henry Brooke Anson
Edward Astley Astley-Rushton
B....
Sidney Robert Bailey
Edward Joseph Bain
Casper Boucher Ballard
James Bayley
John Edward Bearcroft
Michael Stephens Beatty
Thomas Parry Bonham
Henry Harvey Boteler
Hector Boyes
Barton Rose Bradford
Joseph Ridgway Bridson
Richard Wyville Bromley
Kennedy Gerard Brooke
Robert Lindsay Burnett*
C....
Cyril St. Clair Cameron

Edward Poore Chapman
Apsley Dunbar Maxwell Cherry
Archibald Cochrane*
William Charles O'Grady Cochrane
James William Combe
William Rooke Creswell*
Cecil James Crocker
Fritz Hauch Eden Crowe
James Cuddy
Robert Stevenson Dalton Cuming
D....
Robert William Dalgety
Leonard Andrew Boyd Donaldson
Henry Percy Douglas*
Martin Eric Dunbar-Nasmith*
Charles Hope Dundas
E....
John Augustine Edgell
George Le Clerc Egerton
Albert Sigismund Elwell-Sutton
F....
Frank Finnis
Charles Morton Forbes*
William Carnegie Codrington Forsyth

George Charles Frederick
G....
Arthur Kimber Gregory
Rupert Thomas Gould*
William Francis Gunn
H....
Thomas Hadley
Charles Harold Evelyn Head
Gilbert Cockshutt Heathcote
George Morris Henderson
Frederick William Fane Hervey*
Fourth Marquess of Bristol
George Hadley Hewett
Heathcote George Hewitt
Edwin Anderson Homan
Peyton Hoskyns
Reginald Becher Caldwell Hutchinson
Richard Hyde
J....
Henry Hastings Jauncey
Percy Johnson
Arthur Townsend Johnstone
Francis Gilbert Jones
Loftus William Jones

K....
Charles William Keighly-Peach
Joseph Montague Kenworthy
Tenth Baron Strabolgi
John Kiddle
Kerrison Kiddle
L....
Geoffrey Layton*
Arthur Macaulay Lecky
Alan Bruce Leslie
George Edgar Lewin
Horace Walker Longden
M....
Kenneth MacLeod
Albert Hastings Markham*
George Lawrence Massey
William McCarthy Maturin
William Henry May*
John Edward Meryon
Archibald Berkeley Milne, 2nd Baronet
William Mitchell Moir
N....
Cecil Rice Nicholl
Edward Hugh Meredith Nicholson
Robert Lascelles Gambier Noel

P....
Alexander Robinson Palmer
Edwin Mansergh Palmer
Philip Colquhoun Pearson
Cyril Peel
John Denton Pinkstone-French*
Richard Anthony Aston Plowden
John Innes Pocock
R....
Stephen Herbert Radcliffe
Harry Holdsworth Rawson*
Frederick Algernon Reyne
Frederick St. George Rich
Charles Hope Robertson
Charles Grey Robinson
Charles William Rawson Royds*
Percy Molyneux Rawson Royds*
Harry Lucius Fanshawe Royle
S....
Edward John Sanderson
Percy Moreton Scott*
Thomas Bodley Scott
Claude Seymour
Edward Hobart Seymour*
Harry Hesketh Smyth

Alexander Eckstein Stewart
Archibald Peile Stoddart
Leslie Creery Stuart
T....
Francis Alban Arthur Giffard Tate
Charles William Thomas
George Stanley Thornley
Philip Francis Tillard
Vernon Archibald Tisdall
Cyril Everard Tower
William Francis Tunnard
W....
Thomas Philip Walker
Herbert Augustus Warren
Philip Hyde Waterer
George Talbot Wingfield
Alfred Leigh Winsloe
Arthur Charles Woods
Maurice Woollcombe
Henry Bruce Wroughton
Y....
George Bennett Weston Young

* Admirals & Commanders listed in the Index.

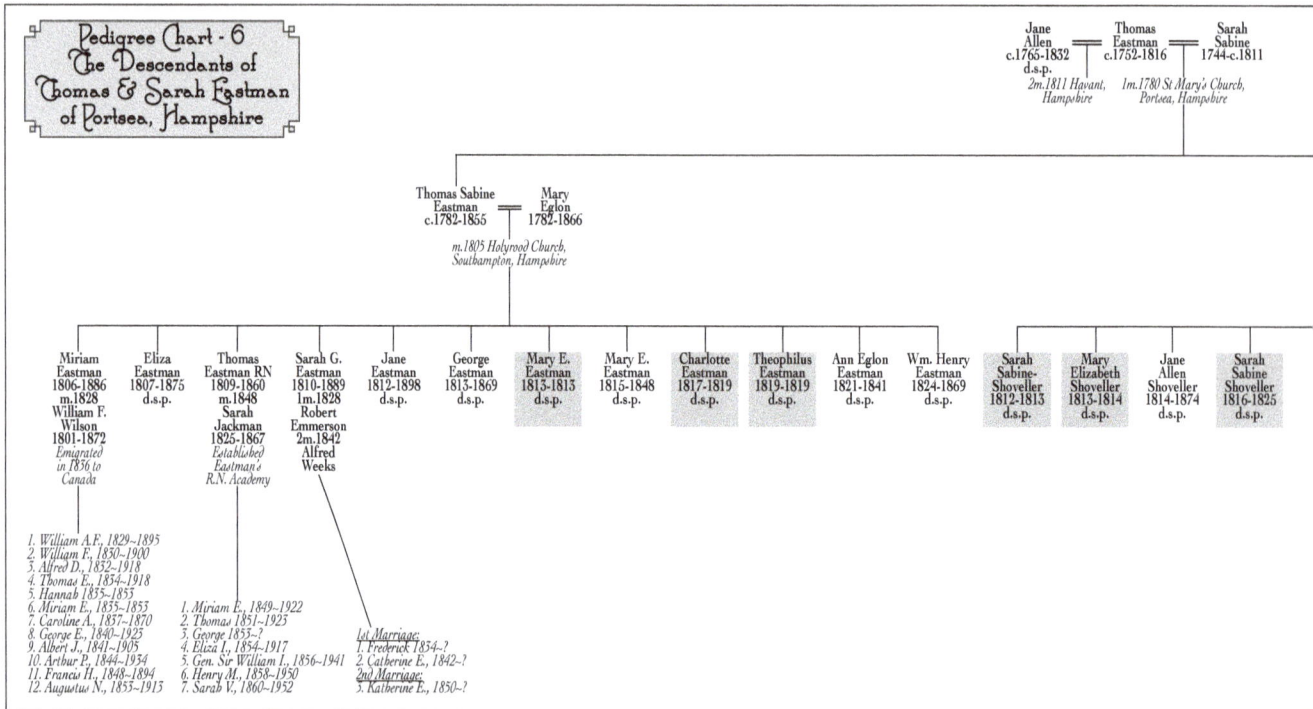

Pedigree Chart - 6
The Descendants of
Thomas & Sarah Eastman
of Portsea, Hampshire

Jane Allen c.1765-1832 d.s.p. === Thomas Eastman c.1752-1816 === Sarah Sabine 1744-c.1811

2m.1811 Havant, Hampshire

1m.1780 St Mary's Church, Portsea, Hampshire

Thomas Sabine Eastman c.1782-1855 === Mary Eglon 1782-1866

m.1805 Holyrood Church, Southampton, Hampshire

| Miriam Eastman 1806-1886 m.1828 William F. Wilson 1801-1872 *Emigrated in 1836 to Canada* | Eliza Eastman 1807-1875 d.s.p. | Thomas Eastman RN 1809-1860 m.1848 Sarah Jackman 1825-1867 *Established Eastman's R.N. Academy* | Sarah G. Eastman 1810-1889 1m.1828 Robert Emmerson 2m.1842 Alfred Weeks | Jane Eastman 1812-1898 d.s.p. | George Eastman 1813-1869 d.s.p. | Mary E. Eastman 1813-1813 d.s.p. | Mary E. Eastman 1815-1848 d.s.p. | Charlotte Eastman 1817-1819 d.s.p. | Theophilus Eastman 1819-1819 d.s.p. | Ann Eglon Eastman 1821-1841 d.s.p. | Wm. Henry Eastman 1824-1869 d.s.p. | Sarah Sabine-Shoveller 1812-1813 d.s.p. | Mary Elizabeth Shoveller 1813-1814 d.s.p. | Jane Allen Shoveller 1814-1874 d.s.p. | Sarah Sabine Shoveller 1816-1825 d.s.p. |

1. William A.F., 1829~1895
2. William F., 1830~1900
3. Alfred D., 1832~1918
4. Thomas E., 1854-1918
5. Hannah 1835~1855
6. Miriam E., 1855~1855
7. Caroline A., 1857~1870
8. George E., 1840~1925
9. Albert J., 1841~1905
10. Arthur P., 1844~1934
11. Francis H., 1848~1894
12. Augustus N., 1853~1913

1. Miriam E., 1849~1922
2. Thomas 1851~1925
3. George 1855~?
4. Eliza I., 1854~1917
5. Gen. Sir William I., 1856~1941
6. Henry M., 1858~1950
7. Sarah V., 1860~1952

1st Marriage:
1. Frederick 1854~?
2. Catherine E., 1842~?
2nd Marriage:
3. Katherine E., 1850~?

Sarah Eastman 16.

This is the last Will and Testament...

▲ TOP (Left): Registration of marriage between Theophilus Eastman and Mary Adlam on 17th June 1816 at Stalbridge, Dorset (Wiltshire, England, Church of England Marriages and Banns, 1754-1916). (Mid): Sample of early 19th century 'Berlin' wool work, which became a a popular pastime when applied to pre-printed patterns, and was a business for Mary and Sarah Eastman. (Right): Portrait of Thomas Eastman, RN, proprietor of Eastman's Royal Naval Academy.
ABOVE: Excerpt of the will of Sarah Eastman - 26th Nov 1841 (England & Wales, Prerogative Court of Canterbury Wills, 1384-1858. PROB 11: Will Registers, 1850-1852, Piece 2125: Vol.1, Quire Numbers 1-50 (1851).Piece: 1588).

was founded in 1851 in the Eastman family home at St. George's Square, Portsmouth by Thomas Eastman, a retired naval instructor who had been five years at the Royal Navy's gunnery training school "HMS Excellent." By 1854 the school had moved into purpose-built premises on South Parade at nearby Southsea. There it catered primarily for boarders

Family Tree

John Shoveller LLD c.1789-1847 == **Elizabeth Eastman** c.1784-1852
m.1812 St Mary's Church, Portsea, Hampshire

Sarah Eastman c1785-1850 d.s.p.

Mary Adlam 1791-1849 == **Rev. Theophilus Eastman** 1789-1863 == **Emma Arther** 1834-1860
1m.1816 St Denys' Church, Warminster, Wiltshire *2m.1857, London*

Children of John Shoveller & Elizabeth Eastman:
- **John Shoveller Jr.** 1818-1899 m.1847 Hannah Wiggins 1819-1891
- **Thomas Eastman Shoveller** 1820-1825 d.s.p.
- **Mary E. Shoveller** 1822-1868 m.1846 James H. Roberton 1823-1890
- **William Henry Shoveller** 1824-c.1883 m.1854 Mary Ann Smith 1847-1925 Emigrated to Sydney on the "Vimeira" 25 Oct 1862, but returned in 1863
- **Martha Shoveller** 1826-1827 d.s.p.
- **Thomas Eastman Shoveller** 1827-1908 Emigrated to Sydney on the "Eclair" 25 Sep 1851 m.1856 Susan Hann 1840-1919

Children of Mary Adlam & Rev. Theophilus Eastman:
- **Thomas Eastman** 1819-1820 d.s.p.
- **Nathaniel A. Eastman** 1821-1821 d.s.p.
- **Mary Adlam Eastman** 1822-1822 d.s.p.
- **Samuel Eastman** 1824-1900 1m.1847 Martha Campkin 2m.1873 Katherine E. Weeks
- **Martha A. Eastman** 1826-1827 d.s.p.
- **Sarah Sabine Eastman** 1828-1905
- **Theophilus A. Eastman** 1829-1829 d.s.p.
- **Emma Eastman** 1833-1868 d.s.p.
- **Jabez E. Eastman** 1839-1922 m.1862 Elizabeth Matthews 1854-1926
- **Anne Ester Eastman** 1860-1861 d.s.p.

Children of John Shoveller Jr. & Hannah Wiggins:
1. Hannah M., 1848~1937
2. Helen E., 1850~1932
3. John H., 1851~1931
4. Harriet J., 1853~1941
5. Alice F., 1855~1952
6. Sidney H., 1857~1914
7. Edith F., 1860~?
8. Alfred R., 1862~1937

Children of Mary E. Shoveller & James H. Roberton:
1. Alice M., 1848~1848°
2. Alfred J., 1850~1921
3. Henry S., 1852~1916

Children of William Henry Shoveller & Mary Ann Smith:
1. Ellen 1851~?
2. William H., 1854~?
3. Ada M., 1856~1875
4. Eva R.J., 1861~1862°

Children of Thomas Eastman Shoveller & Susan Hann:
1. Susan T., 1858~1858°
2. Susan E., 1859~1915
3. Thomas C., 1862~1874°
4. Leonora 1866~1945
5. Janet E.A., 1869~1870°
6. George L., 1873~1946
7. Mabel S., 1878~1945
8. Clarence J.H., 1880~1940

Children of Samuel Eastman:
1st Marriage:
1. Philip M., 1849~?
2. Jessie A., 1851~1919
3. Martha E., 1853~1894
4. Eustace J., 1856~1937
5. Selina M., 1859~1876°
6. Francis 1866~?
2nd Marriage:
7. Samuel R.A., 1875~1938
8. Howard W. R., 1875~1959
9. Walter W., 1877~1968
10. Harold A.S., 1878~1970
11. Katherine M., 1880~1975
12. Reginald H., 1885~1966

Children of Jabez E. Eastman & Elizabeth Matthews:
1. Mary E., 1865~?
2. Frank 1866~1941
3. Edith H., 1867~1961
4. Annie 1868~1957
5. Clara 1871~1952
6. Sydney 1872~1915
7. Phoebe C., 1874~1911
8. Margaret 1876~1945

Page 23.

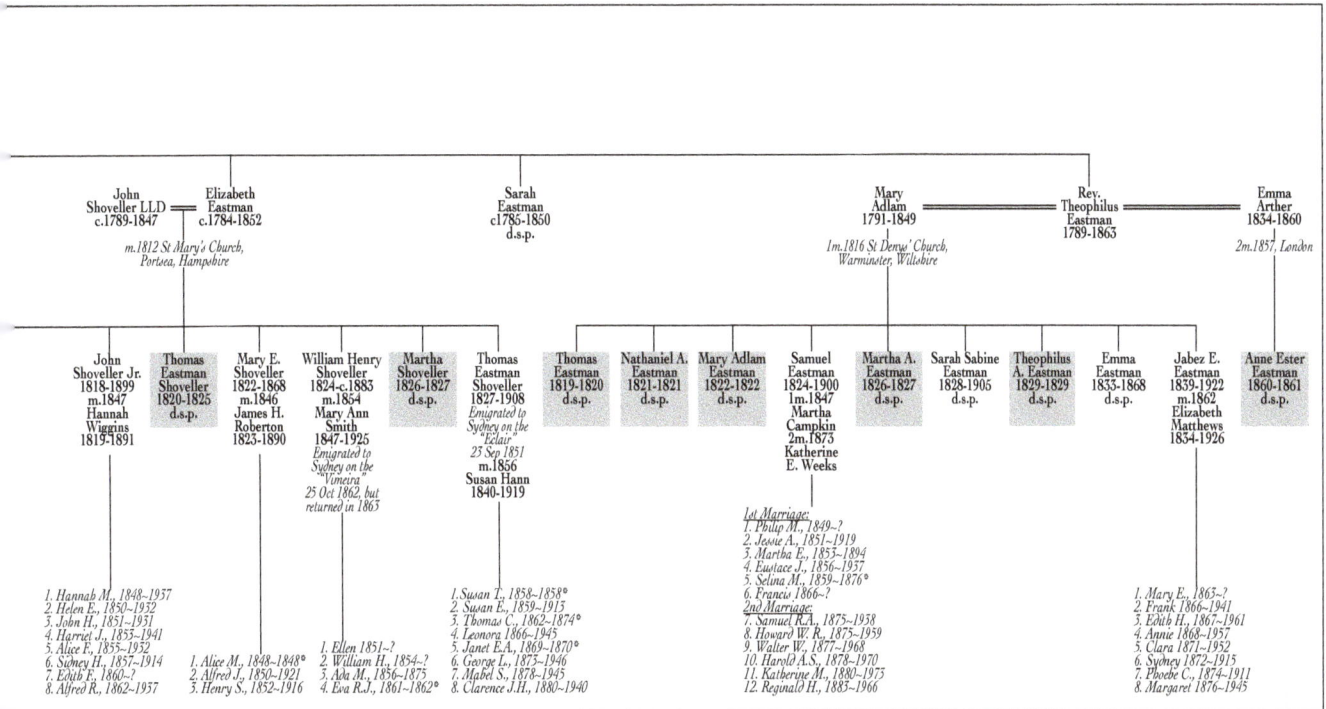

18__. Marriage solemnized in the Parish Church in the Parish of Milton Lilbourne in the County of Wilts.

No.	When Married.	Name and Surname.	Age.	Condition.	Rank or Profession.	Residence at the Time of Marriage.	Father's Name and Surname.	Rank or Profession of Father.
45	Octr 26th	Thomas Eastman / Sarah Jackman	full age	Bachelor / Spinster	Naval Instructr	Portsmouth / Milton	Thomas Sabine Eastman / Joel Jackman	No profession / Farmer

Married in the Parish Church according to the Rites and Ceremonies of the Established Church by me, J. Henry Gale

This Marriage was solemnized between us, Thomas Eastman / Sarah Jackman — in the Presence of us, William Jackman / Louisa Jackman / Anna Church

▲Marriage certificate for naval instructor Thomas Eastman, RN & Sarah Jackman, registered on the 26th October 1848, by Rev. John Henry Gale.

but also took in day-boys.[9] One of his first pupils was Charles Dickens' son, Sydney Smith Haldimand Dickens (1847-72), who enrolled in 1859, and the next year joined the Royal Navy, out of which he made his career.[10] When Thomas Eastman died in 1860 he was succeeded by one of the teaching staff, a Mr. George Spickernell, who married Eastman's widow a year later, and continued on as headmaster until 1885.[11]

The school announced in 'The Lancet' in 1870, that it took boys from the age of nine, offered supervised bathing and boating, and had both a gymnasium and a fives court. It claimed that over 900 pupils had gone on to careers in the armed services.[12] There was a distinct nautical bent to the curriculum, which aside from teaching subjects such as Latin, Greek and English literature, included instruction in the tying of knots, carpentry and the rudiments of navigation. The proximity of the school to the sea was also exploited, especially when naval ships were present.[13]

The Southsea premises on the corner of Burgoyne Road, was four floors high with a huge assembly hall on the ground floor. In the middle was a large pot-bellied stove. There was also a very large kitchen with coal-fired ranges and a conservatory to the rear. A large

12.2 Descendants of Elizabeth Eastman & John Shoveller LLD [33]

Elizabeth Eastman (c.1785-1852), the daughter of Thomas Eastman and Sarah Sabine of Portsmouth, married in 1812 at St Mary's Church, Portsea to John SHOVELLER (1789-1847), a schoolmaster and independent minister, with issue:

1. **Sarah Sabine SHOVELLER (1812 - 1813)*** died an infant.

2. **Mary Elizabeth SHOVELLER (1813 - 1814)*** died an infant.

3. **Jane Allen SHOVELLER (1814 - 1874)**, born 1814, was a spinster and died 1874, no issue.

4. **Sarah Sabine SHOVELLER (1816 - 1825)** born 1816, died aged 9 years in 1825.

5. **John SHOVELLER Jr. (1818 - 1899)**, born 1818, married on the 18th May 1847 at St Ann's Blackfriars, London to Hannah (1819-1891), the daughter of William Wiggins & Rebecca Gulley. John Jr. died in 1899, with issue.

6. **Thomas Eastman SHOVELLER (1820 - 1825)*** born 1820, died aged 5 years in 1825.

7. **Mary Elizabeth Shoveller (1822 - 1868)**, born 1822, married on the 29th September 1846 at Banbury, Oxfordshire to her first cousin James Henry (1823-1890), the son of James Roberton and Mary's aunt Elizabeth Shoveller of Portsea, Hampshire. Mary died aged just 46 in 1868, with issue.

8. **William Henry SHOVELLER (1824 >1883)**, born 1824, married in 1854 at St Pancras, London to Mary Ann Smith (c.1829-?). William died about 1883, with issue.

9. **Martha SHOVELLER (1826 - 1827)*** died an infant.

10. **Thomas Eastman SHOVELLER (1827 - 1908)**, born 1827, voyaged throughout the Pacific, married on the 6th March 1856 at Anglican Church, Grafton, N.S.W. to Susan (1840-1918), the daughter of John Hann & Mary Ann Thompson, died in 1908, with issue.

* Died before adulthood - d.s.p.
(For full details of these ancestors - see Chapter 15.)

oak staircase ran from the top to bottom of the building with dormitories coming off each floor with cast iron fireplaces in them. The building was largely flat roofed which the last flight of stairs led up to. On the roof were many tall yellow chimney pots. The school was subsequently knocked down and today the site is occupied by 'Fastnet House'.[14]

Thomas Eastman's son, Thomas Eastman IV, taught at first at his father's school, but in 1881 opened his own school at Wallington, Hampshire, also called Eastman's Royal Naval Academy. In 1886 he moved his school to Stubbington and in 1894 moved again to Northwood Park, the former home of Philip Vanderbylt, near Winchester. The academy relocated to Winchester in 1898 and was amongst those that were accredited by the Admiralty as examination centres for entrance to the Royal Navy, although the decision to single out a handful of schools in this way led to a successful protest from the Association of Preparatory School Headmasters in 1901. The Association considered the selection of a few was unfair to the remainder.[15] By 1923 the then joint headmasters, Thomas Gilderdale and Donald Mercer, turned the establishment into a general school, which was renamed as Eastman's Preparatory School.[16]

2. Elizabeth Eastman (c.1784-1852)

Although no birth or baptismal record has been found for Elizabeth Eastman, she was born about 1784, and was likely baptised into the Independent Church at her home. She married on the 26th March 1812 at St Mary's Church, Portsea to John Shoveller (1789-1847).[17] Elizabeth was also mentioned in the 1816 will of her father.[18]

As the wife of a schoolmaster, a commissioner inquiring into the state of the registers of births, deaths and marriages across England and Wales, and an independent minister, Elizabeth supported her husband in his important work across various postings. While her husband passed away in 1847, Elizabeth died on the 22nd July 1852, at the residence of her son John Shoveller Jr. at Haverstock Terrace in Hampstead.[19] Elizabeth Eastman and John Shoveller and their descendants are discussed in greater detail in Chapters 13-15 (*see 12.2 Descendants of Elizabeth Eastman & John Shoveller*). It is by their tenth child Thomas Eastman Shoveller (1827-1908), who emigrated to Sydney in 1851, and soon after relocated to Grafton, that this genealogy concludes (*see Chapters 16-20*).

3. Sarah Eastman (c.1785-1850)

Although no birth record has been found for Sarah Eastman, she was likely born and baptised at home about 1785 and never married, remaining a spinster her whole life. She was mentioned in the 1816 will of her father.[20] Sarah resided with her brother Thomas Sabine Eastman and his family following the death of her parents, and in 1830 she was listed as a proprietor in a millinery business partnership with her sister-in-law Mary.[21] She died in her 65th year at the residence of her brother, at Above Bar, Southampton on the 11th January 1850.[22,23]

The will of Sarah Eastman of Portsea, Hampshire was written on the 26th November

Documents of Rev. Theophilus Eastman & Family

Rev. Theophilus Eastman
England & Wales Census

1841

Place:	All Saints, Hampshire.
Place:	Shropshire
Residence:	St Mary's St, Whitchurch
Head of House:	Theophilus Eastman
Estimated Age:	50
Occupation:	Unknown
Registration District:	Wem
Folio:	907/12/14/22
Residents:	Mary, wife (45)
	Samuel, son (15)
	Sarah, dau (13)
	Emma, dau (7)
	Jabez, son (2)

1851

Place:	Newchurch, Hampshire.
Place:	Islington East, Islington, M'sex.
Residence:	94 Rotherfield St, Finsbury
Head of House:	Theophilus Eastman
Where Born:	Portsea, Hampshire
Age:	60, Widower
Occupation:	Ind. Minister
Registration District:	Islington East
Folio:	94/1502/180/26
Residents:	Sarah S., dau.(23)
	Emma, dau (17)

1861

Place:	Newchurch, Hampshire
Place:	Marylebone, London
Residence:	14 Clifton Road, St Johns Wood
Head of House:	Theophilus Eastman
Estimated Age:	71, Widower x 2
Occupation:	Ind. Minister w/ Academy
Registration District:	Marylebone
Folio:	161/90/22/46
Residents:	Sarah S., dau, Governess (23)
	Emma, dau, Governess (27)
	Annie Ester, dau (6 mths)
	John Edward Dyson, boarder/schol (8)
	George Henry Dyson, boarder/schol (7)
	William James Dyson, boarder/schol (6)
	Henry Sparrow, boarder/schol (7)
	Harriet Hopperton, Nurse (57)
	Matilda Burrows, General Servant (22)

FAREHAM GRAMMAR SCHOOL
THE REV. THEOPHILUS EASTMAN, B.A. of Glasgow University, begs respectfully to announce, that the Business of his ESTABLISHMENT, comprehending a Course of Classical, Commercial, and Mathematical Studies, and conducted on principles of the greatest liberality and kindness, to the pupils committed to his care, will be RESUMED on the 28th instant.

Pigot & Co.'s
REFERENCE TO PORTSMOUTH,
Directory, &c. Hampshire.

1830 Pigot's Directory, Fareham
ACADEMIES AND SCHOOLS.
Not otherwise described are Day Schools.
Eastman Rev. Theophilus (gent.'s boarding) West st

1856 Post Office Directory, London
Eastman Jas. Henry, carpenter & builder, ...
Eastman Louisa (Mrs.), butcher, 6 Vittoria pl. Bethnal green
Eastman Rev. Theophilus, B.A. academy, 2 College ter. Steps.gn
Eastman Samuel, agent to Legal & Commercial Life Insu-

1860 Post Office Directory, London
Clifton road, Abbey road (N.W.),
St. John's wood.
1 Carter Mrs. (Clifton lodge)
2 Brown Mrs
3 Knight Charles, esq
4 Robson John, esq
5 Liles Charles, esq
6 Roper Thomas, esq
7 Mudry Rev. John
9 Farquhar John James, esq
11 McBean Miss
14 Eastman Rev. Theophilus, B.A. preparatory school

On Wednesday se'nnight, the Rev. Theophilus Eastman late of Stalbridge, Dorset, and son of the late Mr Thomas Eastman, of Portsea, was publicly set a part to the pastoral office, over the Independent Church at Fareham.

Mr. Samuel Eastman.

On Thursday, October 1st, 1846, Mr. Samuel Eastman, of Highbury College, was publicly ordained to the office of pastor, over the church of Christ assembling at the Independent chapel at Great Eversden, Cambridgeshire.

At ten o'clock a meeting was conducted by the Revds. Messrs. Hebditch, Jones, and Paul, of Highbury College, to implore the Divine blessing on the engagements of the day.

The ordination service was commenced at eleven o'clock, by the Rev. A. C. Wright, of Melbourn, in reading a portion of the Scriptures and prayer. Rev. J. H. Godwin, President of Highbury College, delivered the introductory discourse, from Rom. xiv. 16. Rev. S. S. England, of Royston, proposed the usual questions. Rev. Theophilus Eastman, A.M., (father of the young minister,) offered the dedicatory prayer, with laying on of hands. Rev. Thomas James, of London, delivered the charge to the newly-ordained minister, from 1 Tim. iv. 16. Rev. H. Trigg, of Therfield, closed the solemn and interesting service by prayer. The following ministers were present on the occasion, (most of whom took a part in the devotional services.) Revds. Messrs. Flood, of Melbourn; Gough, of Barrington; Garner, of Harston; Stockbridge, of Guilden Morden;

1862. Marriage solemnized at *the Parish Church* in the *Parish* of *South Hackney* in the County of *Middlesex*

No.	When Married	Name and Surname	Age	Condition	Rank or Profession	Residence at the time of Marriage	Father's Name and Surname	Rank or Profession of Father
1	March 30th 1862	Jabez Ebenezer Eastman	full	Bachelor	Chemist	South Hackney	Theophilus Eastman	Dissenting Minister
		Elizabeth Matthews	full	Spinster	—	South Hackney	Richard Matthews	Grast-Merchant

Married in the *Parish Church* according to the Rites and Ceremonies of the Established Church, by ____ or after *Banns* by me,

This Marriage was solemnized between us, *Jabez Ebenezer Eastman / Eliott ... ..* in the Presence of us, *Alfred Matthews / ... Rose Role*

▲LEFT COLUMN: 1-Rev. Theophilus Eastman - Census for England & Wales [1841, 1851 & 1861]. CENTRE COLUMN: 1-Rev. Theophilus Eastman - meeting attendance at Wakefield (West Yorkshire, Non-Conformist Records, 1646-1985); 2- 1828 Rev. Theophilus Eastman - Notice for Fareham Grammar School (Hampshire Telegraph, 7th July 1828); 3-Theophilus & Mary Eastman business and residential listings in local directories from 1830 to 1860. RIGHT COLUMN: 1-Notice re Rev. Theophilus Eastman, second son of Thomas Eastman of Portsea (Hampshire Telegraph, 11th Oct 1819, p.4); 2-Samuel Eastman (pastor), son of Rev. Theophilus Eastman in Dr. Williams Non-conformist Library, London. Compiled by E. Jane Elliott, 1997. ABOVE: 1862 Marriage registration for Jabez Ebenezer Eastman & Elizabeth Matthews (Wiltshire, England, Church of England Marriages and Banns, 1754-1916).

▲ *TOP (Left): An old photograph of Portsmouth Point at high tide, by A. Fogwill. (Right): Rare colour image of the Theatre Royal at Portsmouth. ABOVE: Abbey Road (formerly Clifton Road) Baptist Church, at St Johns Wood, NW London, the final ministry for Rev. Theophilus Eastman.*

1841, and she bequeathed £300 to her brother Thomas Sabine Eastman. Sarah left her goods, chattels and effects to her unmarried nieces Eliza, Jane and Mary Elizabeth Eastman, and amongst others left her pew at the King St Independant Chapel in Portsea to be shared by her brother Rev. Theophilus Eastman, and sister Elizabeth, the wife of John Shoveller. Sarah's will was proved in London on the 30th January 1851, with Robert Wakeford acting as the Executor.[24]

4. Rev. Theophilus Eastman (1789-1863)

Theophilus Eastman was the fourth and final child of Thomas and Sarah Eastman and was born on the 24th September 1789, and baptised on the 10th January 1790, at the King St (formerly Orange St.) Independent Church, Portsea.[25] He studied first at Gosport and afterwards at Glasgow University, where he graduated with a bachelor's degree in Arts, ahead of becoming a minister in the Independent Church. His first settlement was at Stalbridge, Dorset, after which he removed to Fareham, Hampshire where he established Fareham Grammar School, and became associated with the Rev. Dr. Bogue, as a classical tutor in the Missionary Seminary. He was mentioned in the 1816 will of his father.[26] He married firstly at St. Denys, Warminster in Wiltshire on the 17th June 1816 to Mary (1791-1849) the daughter of Thomas Adlam and Martha Gattrall of Warminster.[27] Their marriage produced nine children *(see 12.3 Descendants of Rev. Theophilus Eastman & Mary Adlam).*

12.3 Descendants of Rev. Theophilus Eastman & Mary Adlam [33]

Thomas Eastman son of Theophilus and Mary. Eastman was born 1819 and baptized 1819 in the Parish of Portsea. By me John Griffin

Martha Adlam Eastman, Daughter of the Revd. Theophilus and Mary Eastman was born 30th April 1826 and Baptized 14th Septr. 1826 at the Chapel of Mr Eastman at Fareham in the County of Hants. By me John Griffin

Mary Adlam Eastman, Daughter of Theophilus and Mary Eastman, was born 22d April 1822 and Baptized 7th June 1822. in the Parish of Portsea. By me John Griffin

Theophilus Adlam Eastman, Son of Theophilus and Mary Eastman, was born 6th Octr. 1828 and Baptized 22 June 1829 at Fareham in the County of Hants. by me John Griffin

Samuel Eastman, Son of Theophilus and Mary Eastman, was born 15th October 1824, and Baptized 31 Dect 1824. at the house of John Shoveller L.P.D. in the Parish of Portsea. By me John Griffin

EASTMAN Jabez Ebenezer of 84 Dalston-lane Hackney **Middlesex** died 14 January 1922 Probate **London** 5 September to Edith Eastman and Annie Eastman spinsters. Effects £268 6s. 6d.

Eastman | **Adlam**

Theophilus Eastman married firstly at St. Denys, Warminster in Wiltshire on the 17th June 1816 to Mary (1791-1849) the daughter of Thomas Adlam and Martha Gattrall of Warminster, with issue:

1. Thomas EASTMAN (1819-1821)*, was born and baptised in 1819, at the Orange Street (now King Street) Independent Church, Portsea. He died as an infant and buried on 15 Sep 1821 at Fareham, Hampshire, aged 2.[37]

2. Nathanial Adlam EASTMAN (1821-1821)*, was born and baptised in 1819, at the Orange Street (now King Street) Independent Church, Portsea. He died as an infant and buried on 11 Sep 1821 at Fareham, Hampshire, aged 8 mths.[38]

3. Mary Adlam Eastman (1822-1822)*, was born on 22 April 1822, and baptised on the 7 June 1822 at the Orange Street (now King Street) Independent Church, Portsea. She died as an infant in Nov 1822 in Portsea, and was buried on 23 Nov 1822 at Titchfield, Hampshire, England.

4. Samuel EASTMAN (1824-1900), was born on 13 Oct 1824, and baptised on the 31 Dec. 1824 at the Orange Street (now King Street) Independent Church, Portsea. He was a wood turner and chair maker and advertised as such in the 1844 Piggotts Directory for Fordingbridge, Hampshire. He was also ordained as a pastor into the Independent Church. Samuel died on the 12 Jan 1900 at Mounstead Burley, Yorkshire. He married firstly in 1847 to Martha (1823-1872), the dau. of Joseph Campkin of Melbourne, Cambridgeshire, with issue:

4.1 Philip Melancthon EASTMAN (1849-), married in 1877 to Emily Mary Ann Hetherington (1848-), with issue:
a. Arthur Hetherington EASTMAN (1879-1977)
b. George Herbert EASTMAN (1881-1974)
c. Philip S EASTMAN (1888-?)
d. Duncan S EASTMAN (1890-?)

4.2 Jessie Anne Eastman (1851-1919), died a spinster. No issue.

4.3 Martha Elizabeth Eastman (1853-1894), died a spinster. No issue.

4.4 Eustace John EASTMAN (1856-1937), married in 1885 to Alice Gertrude Howard (1865-?). He died in Jan 1937 Andover, Hampshire. No issue.

4.5 Selina Mary Eastman (1859-1876), born April 1859 at Mile End, London. Died September 1876 Devonshire, England. No issue.

4.6 Francis EASTMAN (1866-?)

Samuel married secondly in 1873 to to his 2nd cousin Katherine Emmeline (1850-1924), dau. of Alfred Weeks of Lymington, Hampshire, with issue:

4.7 Samuel R.A. EASTMAN (1875-1938), married in 1895 to Susan Emma Roffe (1869-1949), with issue:
a. Doris Fay Eastman (1897-1976).

4.8 Howard W. R. EASTMAN (1875-1959), born 1875 at Derbyshire. He married firstly in 1894 to Annie Elizabeth Dawes (1871-?), with issue:
a. Samuel EASTMAN (1895-?)
b. Katherine Eastman (1900-?)
c. Walter EASTMAN (1902-?)
d. John EASTMAN (1905-?)
Howard married secondly in Oct 1940 in Monmouthshire to Mary A Philpott. No issue.

4.9 Walter Weldon EASTMAN (1877-1968), married firstly in 1899 to Sarah Maude Culverwell (1876-1927), with issue:

a. Winifred Maude Eastman (1901-1975)
b. Dorothy Katherine Eastman (1904-?)
c. Walter Stanley EASTMAN (1906-1981)
d. Harold Victor EASTMAN (1907-1970)
e. Constance Margaret Eastman (1909-?)
Walter married secondly in 1928 to Mary Elizabeth 'Molly' Mallon (1901-?), with issue:
f. Walter Francis 'Frank' EASTMAN (1930-2007)

4.10 Harold Alexander Sabine EASTMAN (1878-1970), married 1901 to Mabel Ingham (1879-?), with issue:
a. Marjorie Eastman (1904-?)

4.11 Katherine Margaret Eastman (1880-1973), married in 1955 to Roy E. HANCOCK (1923-2001), no issue.

4.12 Reginald Heber EASTMAN (1883-1966), married in 1903 to Letitia Lucy Quinn (1884-1949), visited Brisbane on the 23 Jun 1938 aboard the "Strathallan," issue unknown.

5. Martha Adlam Eastman (1826-1827)*, was born on 30 April 1826 at Fareham, Hampshire, England, and baptised on the 14 Sep 1826 at the Orange Street (now King Street) Independent Church, Portsea. She died as an infant in April 1827 and was buried on 17 Apr 1827 at Titchfield, Hampshire, England.

6. Sarah Sabine Eastman (1828-1905), was born in 1828 at Fareham, Hampshire. She was a governess for her fathers Academy School, but had a problem with her spine and spent many years in hospitals for 'incurables' as an invalid. She died a spinster aged 77, and was buried on 12 Oct 1905 at Putney Vale Cemetery, Wandsworth, Surrey. No issue.

7. Theophilus Adlam EASTMAN (1829-1829)*, was born June, and baptised on the 11 Jun 1834 at Argyle Independent Church, at Bath, Somerset. He died as an infant later the same year and was buried on 20 Dec 1829 at Titchfield, Hampshire, England.

8. Emma Eastman (1833-1868), was born on 25 Nov 1833 at Bath, and baptised on the 22 June 1829 at the Orange Street (now King Street) Independent Church, Portsea. She was a governess for her fathers Academy School. She died a spinster in October 1868 (aged 35), at Hampstead, London. No issue.

9. Jabez Ebenezer EASTMAN (1839-1922), was born in Jan 1839 at Liverpool, Lancashire, and became a chemist. Jabez married on 30 Mar 1862 at Hackney, London to Elizabeth (1834-1926), dau. of Richard Matthews of South Hackney, London, a yeast merchant. They resided at High Rd, Tottenham, and 52 Forestdale, Southgate. Jabez died on the 14th Jan 1922 at 84 Dalston Lane, Hackney, and was buried

at Abney Park Trust, (Grave 042636, Loc:B06), leaving a will proved on 5 Sep 1922 in London, valued at £268.6s.6d, which was bequeathed to his spinster daughters Edith and Annie Eastman. They had the following issue:

9.1 Mary Elizabeth Eastman (1863-?), married on the 4 Apr 1890, at St Botolph, Aldersgate, London to Frederick James MACKIE (1865-?). Death & issue unknown.

9.2 Frank EASTMAN (1866-), born 1866 at Tottenham, London. A master butcher, married 13 Feb 1893 at All Hallows, Tottenham, M'sex, to Alice Louise Kate Hibbert (1866-1944), with issue:
a. May Eastman (1897-1992), married in 1924 to Frank Ernest ALDRED (1886-1964), a clerk, no issue.
b. Frank Hibbert EASTMAN (1898-1967), engineer & later hairdresser, married in 1923 to Doris Maud Logsdon (1897-1975), they emigrated to New Zealand, issue unknown.

9.3 Edith Henderson Eastman (1867-1961), born in 1867 at Tottenham, London. Edith dworked as a post office clerk. She died a spinster on 13th May 1961 at Highlands Hospital, London (aged 94), leaving a will valued at £17,448 18s. 11d., proved on 27 July 1961 in London, and bequeathed Peter Ernest Sandford Fawcett and John Barry William Holderness solicitors. No issue.

9.4 Annie Eastman (1868-1957), born in 1868 at Tottenham, London. She died a spinster in Apr 1957 at Southend on Sea, Essex, aged 88. No issue.

9.5 Clara Eastman (1871-1952), born in 1871 at Tottenham, London. Clara married ion 24 Sep1894 at West Ham, Essex to Thomas George MARDELL(1860-1946). She died 23 September 1952 at Oxted & Limpsfield Cottage Hospital, Oxted, Surrey (aged 81), leaving a will valued at £370.14s.18d, proved on 10 Nov 1952 in London, and bequeathed her son Harry George Mardell (Company Secretary), with issue:
a. Harry George MARDELL (1897-)

9.6 Sydney EASTMAN (1872-1915), born 29 Jun 1872 at Tottenham, Middlesex. He was in Cheyenne City, working as a railroad Ttamster in June 1900, before marrying on 25th Dec 1900 to Ethel Sophia Pibel (1878-1957). Sydney died on the 27 Sep 1915 at Belgrade, Nance, Nebraska, USA, with issue:
a. Bessie Cedonia Eastman (1903-1984)
b. Sidney Keith EASTMAN (1905-1951)
c. Frank Creighton EASTMAN (1909-1949)
d. Stanley Pibel EASTMAN (1912-1979)

9.7 Phoebe Charlotte Eastman (1874-1936), born at Tottenham, Middlesex. Charlotte married on the 16th May 1919 at Holy Trinity Church, Dalston in Hackney to Charles WRIGHT (?-?). Details unknown.

9.8 Margaret Eastman (1875-), born 6 Feb 1875 at Tottenham, Middlesex. Margaret died a spinster in Jan 1945 at Brentford, Middlesex. Issue unknown.

Rev. Theophilus Eastman married secondly at Marylebone, London, in April 1857 when he was 67 years old to Emma Arther (1834-1860), who died in childbirth, with issue:

10. Annie Esther Eastman (1860-1861)*, was born in Oct 1860 at Marylebone and despite the death of her mother in child-birth, she survived, but died as an infant in 3rd Quarter of 1861 in Marylebone, London.

* Died before adulthood - d.s.p.
(Some names not listed in the index).

▲ Baptisms for five of the nine children of Theophilus & Mary Eastman, all officiated by Rev. John Griffin from 1819 to 1829 of the Orange Street (now King Street) Independent Church, Portsea (Portsea, Hampshire, England & Wales, Non-Conformist and Non-Parochial Registers, 1567-1936). LEFT COLUMN: 1-Thomas (1819); 2-Mary Adlam (1822); 3-Samuel(1824). RIGHT COLUMN: 1-Martha (1826); Theophilus Adlam (1828); 3-1922 Probate notice for Jabez Ebenezer Eastman (England & Wales, National Probate Calendar, 1858-1995).

Theophilus Eastman's devotion for Christ can be traced to the prayers of his mother Sarah (nee Sabine), and through his father's example as a deacon in the ministry of the Rev. John Griffin at Portsea. After leaving Hampshire, Theophilus administered a boarding-school at Bath, in connection with the ministry of Widcombe Chapel.

"Theophilus Eastman - Sion Place, Parish of Bathwick." [28]

Following his work at Bath, he settled at Ruthin, North Wales, but circumstances over which he had no control obliged him to leave, amidst the tears and prayers of his beloved flock. His next settlement was at Whitchurch, Shropshire, where he remained nearly five years. His final pastorate just four years previous to his decease, was at St Johns Wood, where he resided at 14 Clifton Road, which was later changed to the famous Abbey Road in London.

While at St Johns Wood, Marylebone, Theophilus married secondly at the age of 67

1830 Print of the Saluting Battery and Barracks, at Point Battery, Portsmouth (artist unknown).

years in April 1857 to Emma Arther (1832-1860) and fathered his tenth child.[29] His second wife safely delivered a daughter they named Annie Esther Eastman (1860-1861), but Emma died in childbirth, with the infant passing away at the age of one. On the 22nd of April 1863, the Rev. Theophilus Eastman himself was seized with slight paralysis, from which he never recovered.[30] Although he fathered ten children, although only four of these reached adulthood.

This genealogy continues by exploring the life and descendants of Thomas Eastman's eldest daughter Elizabeth Eastman, who through her marriage to John Shoveller LLD, helped bring together the Shoveller, Bignell, Eastman and Sabine branches of this fervently religious yet distinguished family.

Brigadier Claude Henry Warrington Eastman (1899-1975), MVO, DSO, a great grandson of Thomas Sabine Eastman, married Lady Mary Agatha Campbell (1905-1997), the daughter of Hugh Frederick Vaughan 'Campbell' (1870-1914), 4th Earl of Cawdor Castle, Scotland, on the 5th Feb 1931.

References

1. William Robson & Co. (1839). 'Robson's 1839 Hampshire Directory.

2. Thomas Eastman - Will, 30th July 1816 (England & Wales, Prerogative Court of Canterbury Wills, 1384-1858. Held at The National Archives; Kew, England; Prerogative Court of Canterbury and Related Probate Jurisdictions: Will Registers; Class: PROB 11; Piece: 1588).

3. William Robson & Co. (1839). 'Robson's 1839 Hampshire Directory.

4. Stepanova, Irina (2011). 'Berlin Work: An Exuberance of Color,' PieceWork, March/April.

5. England & Wales Death Indexes 1837-2007. (1855). Death of Thomas Sabine Eastman, at Ryde, Isle of Wight, #40,2B, p.327 (Q3, 1855).

6. Owen, Hugh (1991). 'Eastman's Royal Naval Academy, Southsea, In The 1870s,' The Mariner's Mirror, 77:4, 379-387 [DOI: 10.1080/00253359.1991.10656370].

7. Wikipedia & Portsmouth City Libraries - 'The Portsmouth Encyclopedia' [https://www.portsmouth.gov.uk/wp-content/uploads/2020/05/lib-portsmouth-encyclopaedia-2011.pdf].

8. Leinster-Mackay, Donald P. (1988). "The nineteenth-century English preparatory school: cradle and crèche of Empire?". In Mangan, J. A. (ed.). 'Benefits Bestowed'?: Education and British Imperialism. Manchester University Press. pp. 65–66. ISBN 9780719025174. Retrieved 4 December 2012.

9. Betts, Jonathan (2006). Time Restored: The Harrison timekeepers and R.T. Gould, the man who knew (almost) everything. Oxford University Press. pp. 19–23. ISBN 978-0191620843. Retrieved 4 December 2012.

10. University of Portsmouth. 'Dickens & The Victorian City' [https://dickens.port.ac.uk/background/].

11. "List of Fellows". Journal of the Royal Geographical Society of London. 37: lxvii. 1867. JSTOR 1798511.

12. Owen, Hugh (1991), op.cit.

13. Betts, Jonathan (2006), op. cit.

14. Fandom - Eastman's Royal Naval Academy [https://military-history.fandom.com/wiki/Eastman%27s_Royal_Naval_Academy].

15. "Education for Sons of Gentlemen." The Lancet. 16 July 1870. Retrieved 4 December 2012.

16. "List of Fellows". Journal of the Royal Geographical Society of London, op. cit.

17. Marriage of Elizabeth Eastman & John Shoveller LLD on the 24th March 1812 at St Mary's Church, Portsea, Hampshire, England, (from Hampshire Allegations for Marriage Licences 1689-1837, Vol.2).

18. Thomas Eastman - Will, 30th July 1816, op. cit.

19. England & Wales Death Indexes 1837-2007. (1852). Death of Elizabeth Shoveller (Q3, 1852, Brentford).

20. Thomas Eastman - Will, 30th July 1816, op. cit.

21. Sarah & Mary Eastman - Fordingbridge (1830). 'Piggott's 1830 Hampshire Directory.

22. England & Wales Death Indexes 1837-2007. (1850). Death of Sarah Eastman (Q1, 1850, Southampton).

23. Sarah Eastman - Death notice (Hampshire Telegraph, 2nd Feb 1850, p.5).

24. Will for Sarah Eastman - 26th Nov 1841 (England & Wales, Prerogative Court of Canterbury Wills, 1384-1858. PROB 11: Will Registers, 1850-1852, Piece 2125: Vol.1, Quire Numbers 1-50 (1851).Piece: 1588).

25. Theophilus Eastman - Baptism held on the 10th January 1790 at Meeting House, Orange St, Portsmouth (Portsea, Hampshire, England & Wales, Non-Conformist and Non-Parochial Registers, 1567-1936).

26. Thomas Eastman - Will, 30th July 1816, op. cit.

27. Theophilus Eastman & Mary Adlam - Marriage held on the 17th June 1816 at Stalbridge, Dorset (Wiltshire, England, Church of England Marriages and Banns, 1754-1916).

28. From Dr. Williams Non-conformist Library, London. Compiled by E. Jane Elliott, 1997 (UK, Poll Books and Electoral Registers, 1538-1893).

29. England & Wales, Civil Registration Marriage Index, 1837-1915. (1857). Marriage registration for Thomas Eastman & Emma Arther at Marylebone, London (Q2, 1857 [1a, 898, p.4]).

30. England & Wales Death Indexes 1837-2007. (1863). Death registration for Theophilus Eastman (Q3, 1863, Marylebone).

31. Knightroots - Charlotte Eastman, buried at Portsea, Hampshire - 5 June 1819, aged 22 months (Page 46, No. 361 [https://www.knightroots.co.uk/parishes/titchfield]).

32. Knightroots - Theophilus Eastman, buried at Starbridge, Dorsetshire - 22 April 1819, aged 1 (Page 45, No. 354 [https://www.knightroots.co.uk/parishes/titchfield]).

33. Ancestry, (2022). Descendant data from Ancestry.com.au.

34. Owen, Hugh (1991), op.cit.

35. Wikipedia - Eastman's Royal Naval Academy [https://en.wikipedia.org/wiki/Eastman%27s_Royal_Naval_Academy].

36. Royal Navy Officers Educated At Eastman's Royal Naval Academy [http://www.dreadnoughtproject.org/tfs/index.php/Category:Royal_Navy_Officers_Educated_at_Eastman%27s_Royal_Naval_Academy].

37. Knightroots - Thomas Eastman, buried at Fareham, Hampshire - 15 Sept 1821, aged 2 (Page 59, No. 470 [https://www.knightroots.co.uk/parishes/titchfield]).

38. Knightroots - Nathaniel Adlam Eastman, buried at Fareham, Hampshire - 11 Sept 1821, aged 8 mths (Page 59, No. 469 [https://www.knightroots.co.uk/parishes/titchfield]).

Chapter Thirteen

Shoveller

Eastman

JOHN SHOVELLER & ELIZABETH EASTMAN
(Parents of Thomas Eastman Shoveller)

ohn Shoveller (1789-1847) was the son and eldest child of William Shoveller Sr. and Mary Bignell, and was born on the 21st of October 1789 and baptised soon after on the 6th of November 1789 at the Skinner Street Independent Church in Poole, Dorset, which was officiated by the Rev. Edward Ashburner, Protestant Dissenting Minister.[1]

Throughout his formative years John would have been acutely aware of and accustomed to his nation being continually at war. Indeed, his 16th birthday was a significant one as it marked a day of national celebration, which even today is commemorated annually right across Great Britain and the Empire. On the 21st October 1805, Admiral Lord Nelson soundly defeated the combined French and Spanish fleets at the Battle of Trafalgar, virtually removing in one dominant blow, any threat of invasion by Napoleon Bonaparte and the French Army, with whom England was at war.

Unfortunately Nelson lost his life in the battle and was brought back to London in a cask of rum. His monument to the British nation stands proud today at Nelson's Column in Trafalgar Square, London. But although Admiral Lord Nelson and the Royal Navy had halted the prospect of French invasion after Trafalgar, the French remained dominant on land, and so the war continued.

On his 16th birthday in Portsmouth, John Shoveller's younger siblings consisted of William (14), Mary (11), Jane (9) and Elizabeth (7). Despite living conditions at the time being difficult and with infectious disease a constant threat to young lives, all of these five children lived to adulthood. Few other details have emerged about John's earlier years, except that being a natural scholar, and likely through the patronage of his father, one thing is certain... he received the benefit of and capitalised on an impeccable education, and was likely schooled at Portsmouth Grammar School.

John Shoveller Son of William Shoveller and Mary his Wife, of the Parish of Poole in the County of Dorset (born on the Twenty First Day of October 1789) was baptized on the Sixth Day of November 1789

By me Edward Ashburner { Proteſtant Diſſenting Miniſter.

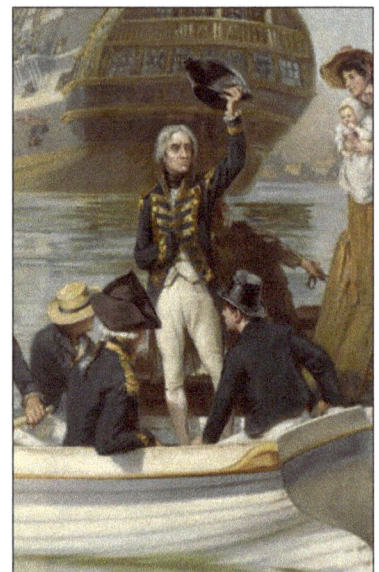

▲ TOP (Left): Portrait of the Rev. Edward Ashburner of Poole, Dorset. (Right): 1789 Birth and baptismal registration of John Shoveller at the Skinner St. Independent Church, Poole, Dorset. ABOVE (Left): The Skinner Street Independent Church at Poole, Dorset, the site of John Shoveller's baptism in November of 1789. (Right): Admiral Horatio Nelson departed from Portsmouth in September 1805 just weeks before his victory and heroic death at the Battle of Trafalgar.

The War Years

By John's 21st birthday in 1810, Napoleon Bonaparte and his Grand Armee were once again rampaging across Europe, with little opposition. By 1812, Napoleon had expanded his force to more than 450,000 men, but ignored repeated advice against an invasion of the Russian heartland, which commenced forthwith on the 24th June 1812.

The Russians avoided Napoleon's objective of a decisive engagement and instead retreated deeper into their country, practicing a scorched earth policy to limit available supplies. They eventually offered resistance outside Moscow on the 7th September, at the Battle of Borodino. The action resulted in approximately 44,000 Russian and 35,000 French dead, wounded or captured, which was likely the bloodiest single day of battle in history, up to that point. Although the French won the day, Napoleon's own account was:

"The most terrible of all my battles was the one before Moscow. The French showed themselves to be worthy of victory, but the Russians showed themselves worthy of being invincible."

Napoleon Bonaparte [2]

After the subsequent Battle of Berezina on the return leg, Napoleon retreated but had to abandon much of his remaining artillery and baggage train. On the 5th December 1812, shortly before arriving in Vilnius, Napoleon left the army in a sledge.

While the war raged on across Europe until 1815, John Shoveller and his fellow Britons were protected from the rapacious French by the absolute supremacy of the Royal Navy, so their lives were fortunately insulated from the tremendous upheavals going on in Europe. The next verifiable record of John Shoveller was his marriage, which occurred in March of 1812 to an eligible young lady from Portsea.

Elizabeth Eastman (c.1784-1852)

Residing in Portsmouth, John and his family were aligned with the non-parochial churchand were members of the Orange St (later King St) Independent Church, with his fervour for God most likely being influenced by the Rev. Joseph Horsey (1737-1802), who ministered there from 1782 until 1802. John's uncle, the Rev. John Shoveller, was also closely involved with the Independent Church in Portsea, and was indeed married to Rev. Horsey's daughter. Following his death in 1802, Rev. Horsey was replaced by the Rev. John Griffen, who soonafter appointed Thomas Eastman as deacon, and it is likely through this connection that Eastman's daughter Elizabeth was introduced to John Shoveller.

Regrettably, research has been unable to find an exact birth or baptismal date for Elizabeth. However, the International Genealogical Index (IGI) contains a marriage for Thomas Eastman and Sarah Sabine, registered at Portsea on the 25th of December 1780,[3] and as Elizabeth's age, upon her death in 1852, was recorded as being 68, it is therefore consistent with her parents marriage date that 1784 was her likely year of birth.[4] In addition to Elizabeth, the IGI reveals three other siblings, the first being Thomas Sabine Eastman who was born about 1782, followed by Sarah in 1785, and the family culminated a few years later with Theophilus, who was baptised on the 10th of January 1790 at Orange St. (now King St.) Independent Church at Portsea.[5] These four children were all mentioned in Thomas Eastman's will, along with John Shoveller as an executor himself.[6]

▲LEFT: 'A Church Of England Congregation Stand' & RIGHT: 'A Victorian family at Church', both drawings from the 'Mary Evans Picture Library', typify the devotion to God and the Church during 18th and 19th century England.

Nelson, Napoleon & Wellesley [39]

▲ TOP: The Battle of Trafalgar, 1805, painted by William Clarkson Stanfield. ABOVE (Left):Napoleon's retreat from Moscow, 1812. (Right-Top): Admiral Horatio Lord Nelson, painted by Lemuel Francis Abbott (1799). (Right-Above): Napoleon Bonaparte, painted by Jacques-Louis David (1812).

Napoleon seized power in 1799, creating a military dictatorship.[26] There are a number of opinions on the date marking the formal beginning of the Napoleonic Wars; 18 May 1803 is often used, when Britain and France ended the only short period of peace between 1792 and 1815.[27] The Napoleonic Wars began with the War of the Third Coalition, which was the first of the Coalition Wars against the First French Republic after Napoleon's accession as leader of France.

Britain ended the Treaty of Amiens and declared war on France in May 1803. Among the reasons were Napoleon's changes to the international system in Western Europe, especially in Switzerland, Germany, Italy and the Netherlands. Historian Frederick Kagan argues that Britain was irritated in particular by Napoleon's assertion of control over Switzerland. Furthermore, Britons felt insulted when Napoleon stated that their country deserved no voice in European affairs, even though King George III was an elector of the Holy Roman Empire. For its part, Russia decided that the intervention in Switzerland indicated that Napoleon was not looking toward a peaceful resolution of his differences with the other European powers.[28]

The British hastily enforced a naval blockade of France to starve it of resources. Napoleon responded with economic embargoes against Britain, and sought to eliminate Britain's Continental allies to break the coalitions arrayed against him. The so-called Continental System formed a league of armed neutrality to disrupt the blockade and enforce free trade with France. The British responded by capturing the Danish fleet, breaking up the league, and later secured dominance over the seas, allowing it to freely continue its strategy. But Napoleon won the War of the Third Coalition at Austerlitz, forcing the Austrian Empire out of the war and formally dissolving the Holy Roman Empire. Within months, Prussia declared war, triggering a War of the Fourth Coalition. This war ended disastrously for Prussia, defeated and occupied within 19 days of the beginning of the campaign. Napoleon subsequently defeated Russia at Friedland, creating powerful client states in Eastern Europe and ending the fourth coalition.

Concurrently, the refusal of Portugal to commit to the Continental System, and Spain's failure to maintain it led to the Peninsular War and the outbreak of the War of the Fifth Coalition. The French occupied Spain and formed a Spanish client kingdom, ending the alliance between the two. Heavy British involvement in the Iberian Peninsula soon followed while a British effort to capture Antwerp failed. Napoleon oversaw the situation in Iberia, defeating the Spanish, and expelling the British from the Peninsula. Austria, keen to recover territory lost during the War of the Third Coalition, invaded France's client states in Eastern Europe. Napoleon defeated the fifth coalition at Wagram.

Trafalgar, Russia & Waterloo

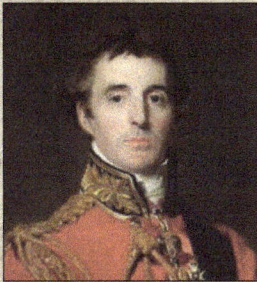

▲ TOP: The Battle of Waterloo, 1815, painted by William Sadler. ABOVE (Left-Top): Lord Arthur Wellesley, the Duke of Wellington, painted by Thomas Lawrence (1814). (Left-Above): Alexander I of Russia, painted by G. Dawe (1826). (Right): The Battle of Waterloo, 1815, painted by Jan Willem Pieneman (1824).

Anger at British naval actions helped push the United States to declare war on Britain in the War of 1812, but it did not become an ally of France. Grievances over control of Poland, and Russia's withdrawal from the Continental System, led to Napoleon invading Russia in June 1812. The invasion was an unmitigated disaster for Napoleon. Scorched earth tactics, desertion, French strategic failures and the onset of the Russian winter compelled Napoleon to retreat with massive losses. Napoleon suffered further setbacks, while French power in the Iberian Peninsula was broken at the Battle of Vitoria the following summer, and a new coalition began the War of the Sixth Coalition.

The coalition defeated Napoleon at Leipzig, precipitating his fall from power and eventual abdication on 6 April 1814. The victors exiled Napoleon to Elba and restored the Bourbon monarchy. But Napoleon escaped from Elba in 1815, gathering enough support to overthrow the monarchy of Louis XVIII, triggering a seventh, and final coalition against him. Napoleon was then decisively defeated at the Battle of Waterloo, and he abdicated again on 22 June. On 15 July, he surrendered to the British at Rochefort, and was permanently exiled to the remote Atlantic island of Saint Helena. The Treaty of Paris was signed on the 20th November 1815, which formally ended the war.

The Bourbon monarchy was restored once more, and the victors began the Congress of Vienna to restore peace to the continent. As a direct result of the war, the Kingdom of Prussia rose to become a great power on the continent,[29] while Great Britain, with its unequalled Royal Navy and growing Empire, became the world's dominant superpower, beginning the Pax Britannica.[30] The Holy Roman Empire was dissolved, and the philosophy of nationalism that emerged early in the war contributed greatly to the later unification of the German states, and those of the Italian peninsula. The war in Iberia greatly weakened Spanish power, and the Spanish Empire began to unravel. Spain would lose nearly all of its American possessions by 1833. The Portuguese Empire shrank, with Brazil declaring independence in 1822.[31]

The wars revolutionised European warfare. The application of mass conscription and total war led to campaigns of unprecedented scale, as whole nations committed all their economic and industrial resources to a collective war effort.[32] Tactically, the French Army redefined the role of artillery, while Napoleon emphasised mobility to offset numerical disadvantages,[33] and aerial surveillance was used for the first time in warfare.[34] The highly successful Spanish guerrillas demonstrated the capability of a people driven by fervent nationalism against an occupying force.[35] Due to the longevity of the wars, the extent of Napoleon's conquests, and the popularity of the ideals of the French Revolution, the principles had a deep impact on European social culture. Many subsequent revolutions, such as that of Russia, looked to the French as their source of inspiration,[36,37] while its core founding tenets greatly expanded the arena of human rights and shaped modern political philosophies, still in use today.[38]

John Shoveller L.L.D., most likely met his future wife Elizabeth Eastman as a fellow parishioner at the Independent Church in Portsea.
▲ *TOP: 'The Village Choir', by Thomas Webster. ABOVE: The Schoolmaster supervising his pupils & early 18th century pupils at play.*

The Schoolmaster

In the year 1811, John Shoveller gave a widely applauded address on the "Excellence of the Hebrew Language," which was perhaps the impetus he needed to launch himself into a new enterprise.[7] On the 22nd July of that year, and at the age of just 22, John Shoveller embarked upon a venture to establish a boarding school he called the 'King's House Academy.' The school was situated on Southsea Common, near Portsmouth and he doubted not "that the attention paid to the health, morals and improvement of the youth… intrusted to his care, will ensure him the honour of future patronage."[8] Despite some issues with the location, with contemporary accounts of the time describing the Common as "a swampy wasteland filled with rubbish and known locally as the Great Morass,"[9] the enterprise proved to be a success.

Mr. Shoveller proclaimed that the school was founded on extensive experience and that he "receives the whole of the scholastic exercises, in every branch under his immediate inspection, which are conducted with especial reference to the disposition, abilities and

King's House Academy

PORTSMOUTH,
SATURDAY, JULY 6, 1811.

KING'S HOUSE ACADEMY,
Southsea-Common, near Portsmouth.

J. SHOVELLER takes this early opportunity of returning thanks to the Parents and Guardians of his Pupils, and begs leave to say, that as he is generally informed that his course of Tuition has given perfect satisfaction, he shall persevere in the same mode, while he doubts not, that the attention paid to the health, morals, and improvement of the Youth, which may be intrusted to his care, will ensure him the honour of future patronage.

J. S. takes the same opportunity to say, that he has just finished his commodious School-Room, in which he flatters himself to receive his Pupils after the present recess.

TERMS.—Board, with the usual branches of Education, including the Hebrew, Greek, and Latin languages; Geometry, Trigonometry, Astronomy, Geography, and Use of the Globes; with Navigation, Merchants' Accounts, and Short-Hand—Forty Guineas per annum.

French and Drawing (which are the only extra charges) at the usual terms. £. s.

Day Boarders taken, and they will enjoy } 5 5 ⅞ qr. all the advantages of the Academy, at.... }

Day Scholars, with equal opportunities.... 2 2

☞ School opens July 22nd.

KING's HOUSE ACADEMY,
SOUTHSEA COMMON, NEAR PORTSMOUTH.

MR. SHOVELLER conceives it is unnecessary to enumerate the advantages of education, at a period of time, when science is so generally cultivated; but he is desirous of directing the public attention to his system of tuition, as, being founded on extensive experience, it cannot fail to give a satisfactory view of the beneficial effects which it is likely to produce. Fully sensible of the time and talents necessary to be employed, in a just and conscientious discharge of the important duties of education, Mr. S. receives the whole of the scholastic exercises, in every branch, under his immediate inspection; by which he is authorized to say, that they will be conducted with especial reference to the disposition, abilities, and prospects of the pupil.

Mr. SHOVELLER having been requested to publish the outline of the system of tuition which he has so successfully followed, he takes this opportunity to say, that he has committed it to the press, and hopes shortly to lay before the public, *A General Introduction to Universal Science.*

TERMS.

Board, with the usual branches of education (including the Hebrew, Greek, and Latin languages, geometry, trigonometry, astronomy, geography and use of the globes, with navigation, merchant's accounts, and short hand) forty guineas per annum.

French and drawing (which are the only extra charges) at the usual terms.

No entrance money required.

Day Boarders taken, and they will enjoy all the advantages of the Academy, at 5l. 5s. per quarter.

Day Scholars, with equal opportunities, 2l. 2s. per quarter.

School opens Jan. 22d.

PORTSMOUTH,
SATURDAY, DECEMBER 26, 1812.

KING's HOUSE ACADEMY, SOUTHSEA.

MR. SHOVELLER desires to inform his Friends, that the SCHOOL will OPEN again for the reception of his Pupils, January 25th.

N. B. There are very few vacancies.

ACADEMY, LANDPORT TERRACE.

J. SHOVELLER begs to acquaint his friends and the public, that he has removed to very commodious premises, in LANDPORT TERRACE (near his late residence), and that he therefore intends to take a few YOUNG GENTLEMEN, as Boarders, in addition to his former limited number.

The School, which is conveniently situated, adjoining the house, opens into an inclosed and spacious play ground.

School opens July 28th.

For an outline of the course of studies recommended to employ the time and engage the attention of his pupils, see Mr. Shoveller's *Essay on Scholastic Education*, sold by Horsey and Whitewood, Portsea, and Longman and Co. London; where may be had also, his *Address on the Study of the Hebrew Language.*

TO SCHOOL ASSISTANTS.

WANTED.—A JUNIOR ASSISTANT. —He should be competent to hear the lower Latin and Greek Classes occasionally, and be willing to make himself generally useful.—Character must be unexceptionable.—Apply to Dr. Shoveller, Grammar School, near Portsmouth; if by letter, post-paid.

DR. SHOVELLER begs to announce his intention of *Retiring from his Establishment* at Midsummer next, for the purpose of devoting himself entirely to the Education of his own Sons, together with EIGHT or TEN YOUNG GENTLEMEN only, on advanced terms. He pledges himself to dispose of his House and Interest to such a person only, as shall combine unexceptionable stability of character, with eminent scholastic attainments; and, that on this point, his relinquishment shall entirely depend.

GRAMMAR SCHOOL, NEAR PORTSMOUTH, } 20th March, 1824. }

DR. SHOVELLER educates a limited number of YOUNG GENTLEMEN, Warnford, Hants, (58 miles from London, and 18 from Gosport.)—His system comprehends in addition to the ordinary branches of education, a complete course of the Greek and Latin Classics, Hebrew (without points) French and the modern Languages, English and Classical Composition, Geography, Astronomy, and use of the Globes, History and Chronology, Natural and Moral Philosophy, the higher branches of the Mathematics, and the principles of the Mechanical Sciences.

☞ Terms, 36 guineas per annum; a few branches only are extra charges.

. The number of Pupils being strictly limited three months notice is necessary previous to a removal.

On Wednesday last, the first stone of a new Independent Chapel was laid, at Warnford, in this county, by John Shoveller, LL.D. who delivered a suitable address on the spot, to a large assemblage from Warnford and the surrounding villages. The stone bore an appropriate Latin inscription by the young gentlemen of the School.

Warnford, near Alton, Hants.

DR. SHOVELLER begs to announce that in his limited number of 12 Young Gentlemen, there will be, after the present holidays, two or three Vacancies, occasioned by the removal of so many of the senior pupils, who have completed their education.

Terms, for Board and Education generally, 36 guineas per annum. A few branches only are extra charges. [6670

John Shoveller established King's House Academy in 1811. ▲LEFT COLUMN: 1-J. Shoveller - Opening of King's House Academy (Hampshire Chronicle, 8 July 1811); 2-Mr Shoveller - King's House Academy Advertisement (Hampshire Chronicle, 30 Dec 1811, p.1). 3- Mr. Shoveller - School Advertisement (Hampshire Telegraph, 28 Dec 1812). RIGHT COLUMN: 1-J. Shoveller - King's House Academy (Hampshire Chronicle, 14 July 1817); 2-Dr. Shoveller - Junior School Assistant Wanted (Hampshire Telegraph, 23 June 1823); 3-Dr. Shoveller - Retiring (Hampshire Telegraph, 22 March 1824); 4-Dr. Shoveller - Educating Young Gentleman at Warnford (Hampshire Telegraph, 10 July 1826); 5-John Shoveller LLD - Stone for New Independent Chapel at Warnford (Hampshire Telegraph, 14 May 1827); 6-Dr. Shoveller - Warnford School (Hampshire Chronicle, 9 July 1827).

John Shoveller established the King's House Academy Boarding School in Portsmouth in 1811. ▲ABOVE: 'At the School Exam' (1862), by Albert Anker (1831–1910), oil on canvas. (Kunstmuseum Bern, Bern, Switzerland. Wikimedia Commons).

prospects of the pupil."[10] The curriculum included hebrew, greek and latin languages, geometry, trigonometry, astronomy, geography, the use of globes with navigation, merchant's accounts and short-hand. French and drawing were the only extra-curricular subjects, which were billed separately. He set his terms (viz. fees) with board for the all-boys school at 40 guineas per annum, which with an enrollment of 20 pupils in todays money, would have rewarded his efforts with a considerable sum upwards of £115,000 per annum. He also accepted day boys at £5.5s, and day scholars were £2.2s per quarter respectively, with no entrance (viz. reservation) money required.[11]

The Marriage of John Shoveller & Elizabeth Eastman

Soon after the commencement of his school, and in the midst of some of the most tumultuous events of the early 19th century, Hampshire Allegations for marriage licences recorded the wedding of John Shoveller and Elizabeth Eastman on the 24th March 1812, at St. Mary's Church in Portsea.[12] Elizabeth was 28, and although her mother Sarah (nee Sabine) had only just recently passed on, her guests most likely included her father Thomas Eastman, and his second wife Jane Allen, who had only themselves wedded in April of 1811. Also attending would have been Elizabeth's 30 year-old brother Thomas Sabine Eastman, and his heavily pregnant wife of seven years Mary (nee Eglon) with their first four children - Miriam (6), Eliza (5), Thomas (3) and Sarah (2). Elizabeth's 27 year-old sister Sarah and 23 year-old brother Theophilus were there, both of whom were unmarried, while it is entirely possible that other Eastman and Sabine relatives including William, Daniel, Patience and Samuel Read Sabine were also present with their families.

Although John Shoveller was just 23, his guests would have included his parents William and Mary Shoveller, and his four as yet unmarried siblings in William Jr. (21), Mary (18), Jane (16) and Elizabeth (14). It is also probable that the Shoveller and Bignell relatives attended, and most likely amongst these was his aunt Mary and uncle Robert Bowyer with their adopted daughter Catherine Andras. His uncle John and aunt Susannah Shoveller, with their children Elizabeth and husband Joseph Paffard, Susannah and her husband William Ellis, and their son John Shoveller Jr. (16), were also likely amongst the guests.

Residing coincidentally at this time at 1 Mile End Terrace, Landport on Portsea Island, was a John and Elizabeth Dickens (nee Barrow), whom being of a similar age, it is not unreasonable to assume, may have been amongst the acquaintences of John and Elizabeth Shoveller. John Dickens (1785-1851) was a clerk in the pay office of the Royal Navy attached to the Portsmouth dockyard, and they delivered a son, the second of eight children on the 7th February 1812, who was baptised at St. Mary's Church, Portsea on the 4th March 1812. His name was Charles John Huffam Dickens (1812-1870),[13] who was to become the greatest novelist of the Victorian era, and although three years later, they moved to London, Portsmouth forever held a special place in young Dicken's heart. It was providential that just three weeks later John Shoveller and Elizabeth Eastman were married by the very same minister, in that very same church.

Over the next 15 years John and Elizabeth Shoveller produced a family of their own, with their first born being a daughter in Sarah Sabine Shoveller. Sarah was born in Portsea on the 21st of December 1812 and was given the namesake of her maternal Sabine ancestors. She followed the Shoveller and Eastman tradition of being baptised into the Independent Church, which occurred on the 30th January 1813, but she sadly died at just eight weeks of age on the 21st of February 1813, and was presumably buried in Portsea.[14]

St Mary's Church, Portsea [40]

SHOVELLER, John, of Portsea, gent., 21, b., & Elizabeth Eastman, of the s., 21, sp., at P., 24 March, 1812.   William Shoveller, of the s., gent., bondsman.

▲ TOP: The first St. Mary's Parish Church, Portsea, built 1170, demolished 1843. ABOVE: John Shoveller & Elizabeth Eastman - Marriage held on the 24 Mar 1812 at St. Mary's, Portsea (Hampshire Allegations for Marriage Licences, 1689-1837, Vol 2)

Though Portsmouth was generally seen to be founded in 1181 by Jean of Gisors in 1164, the Norman lord of the manor, Baldwin de Portsea, informed Henry de Blois, the Bishop of Winchester, that he was giving the church of St. Mary, together with some land, cattle, sheep and hogs to the prior and canons of Southwick Priory.

The old St. Mary's church was built in the 12th century, and served the parish until 1843. The building was a low, short structure with a red tiled roof set with dormer windows. At the west end was a square tower and inside was a gallery and uncomfortable high box pews, with flaps for the poor on their doors. While many family baptisms, marriages and funeral ceremonies were conducted in this church, the Independent Non-Parochial Church in Portsea, under Rev. John Griffin played a larger role in the lives of these families, and this was particularly the case for the Shoveller and Eastman families.

While the use of the Bignell surname was overlooked, Elizabeth was keen to perpetuate her ancestry and she used both Eastman and Sabine as middle names for four of her children, although disturbingly, three of these died young. Indeed John and Elizabeth had great difficulties with their children as only five of their ten offspring survived to

Sarah Sabine Shoveller Daughter of John and Elizabeth Shoveller was born Decr. 21st 1812 and baptised Janry 20th 1813 in the Parish of Patea — By me *John Griffin*

Mary Elizabeth Shoveller Daughter of John and Elizabeth Shoveller was Born Decr 7th 1813 and baptised Febry 13th 1814 in the Parish of Portsea — By me *John Griffin*

Jane Allen Shoveller Daughter of John and Elizabeth Shoveller was born Octr. 22d. 1814 and baptised Decr 27th 1814 in the Parish of Portsea. — By me *John Griffin*

Thomas Eastman Shoveller Son of John and Elizabeth Shoveller, was born 11th April 1820 and Baptised 5 Sept. 1820 in the Parish of Portsea By me *John Griffin*

On Tuesday afternoon, the Sunday School Teachers belonging to the Independent Chapel in King-street, Portsea, held their Annual Meeting in the School Rooms, Orange street, the Rev. John Bristow, of Wilton, in the Chair; when upwards of 600 persons assembled. An interesting Report of the state of the school (since its first formation in 1802) was read by the Secretary, Mr. John Cooke, and many excellent speeches, on the importance of Sunday-school instruction, were delivered by Mr. Shoveller, of King's-terrace, Southsea; the Rev. J. Smedley, of Chichester; and other gentlemen.— Prior to the business of the evening, refreshment was provided and served by the Teachers, highly creditable to the zeal of the Committee.

▲ TOP: The birthplace of Charles Dickens at 1 Mile End Terrace, Landport, Portsea. ABOVE: Mr Shoveller - 'Address on the Importance of Sunday School Teachers' (Hampshire Chronicle, 14 Apr 1817, p.4). ▶Births, baptisms and deaths for eight of the ten children of John Shoveller & Elizabeth Eastman from 1812 to 1827, from the register of the Independent Chapel, King Street (formerly Orange Street), Portsea (Portsea, Hampshire, England & Wales, Non-Conformist and Non-Parochial Registers, 1567-1936). BELOW: John Shoveller's certified statement regarding the birth, baptisms and deaths of his children, signed 4th August 1837. This cherished original document has been passed down through seven generations, and even survived the Grafton floods.

The above are the children of John Shoveller L.L.D., late of Portsea in the County of Southampton and now of Stockwell Green, Surrey, and Elizabeth his wife whose former name was Eastman. All ought to have been registered in their proper places in this book, but some have been inadvertently omitted.

Children	Born	Bapt	Died
Sarah Sabine	21st Dec 1812	30th Jan 1813	21st Feb 1813
Mary Elizabeth	7th Dec 1813	13th Feb 1814	6th May 1814
Jane Allen	22nd Oct 1814	27th Dec 1814	[18th Mar 1874]
Sarah Sabine	19th Jul 1816	17th Sep 1816	6th Jan 1825
John Jr.	10th Jun 1818	14th Jul 1818	[19th Dec 1899]

Mary Elizabeth Shoveller, Daughter of John and Elizabeth Shoveller, born 14th March 1822 and Baptized 7th June 1822. in the Parish of Portsea.
By me John Griffin

William Henry Shoveller, Son of John and Elizabeth Shoveller, was born 30 April 1824, and Baptized 31st Dec. 1824 at their house in the Parish of Portsea.
By me John Griffin

Martha Shoveller, Daughter of John and Elizabeth Shoveller, was born 26th April 1826 and Baptized 9 June 1826. at their house in the Parish of Portsea
By me John Griffin

Thomas Eastman Shoveller, Son of John and Elizabeth Shoveller, was born 25 May 1827 and Baptized 11 July 1827 at their house in the Parish of Portsea
By me John Griffin

adulthood. Their second child was Mary Elizabeth Shoveller, who was delivered on 7th December 1813, and baptised on 14th February 1814, but she also died as an infant on the 6th May 1814. Jane Allen Shoveller arrived next on the 22nd October 1814 and was baptised on the 27th December of that year, and named after Elizabeth's step mother.

SOUTH HANTS
EYE AND EAR DISPENSARY.
AT a large and respectable Meeting of the Subscribers to this Institution, held at the Guild hall, Portsmouth, December 20, 1821,—
The Rev. J. INMAN, D.D. in the Chair,
Committee—D. Howard, Esq. J. Shoveller, LL.D. H. M. Plaistow, Esq. G. Godden, Esq. Capt. Searle, C.B. R.N. and Capt. Travers.
Treasurer—Geo. Grant, Esq.

DIED.—At Upper Clapton, at a very advanced age, the widow of the late H. Pearson, Esq., formerly of Lymington.—At Highway House, Froyle, the wife of T. Pearse, Esq.—At Stoke, aged 49, George Willis, Esq., Captain in the South Hants Militia, and great grandson of the Right Rev. Dr. Richard Willis, formerly Bishop of Winchester.—At Gosport, after a lingering illness, Mrs. Mitchell, relict of the late Mr. John Mitchell, of Portsmouth. Sarah Sabine, second daughter of John Shoveller, LL. D., Landport Terrace, Portsmouth.

▲TOP: John & Elizabeth Shoveller witnessed the burials of five of their ten children. MID: Dr. Shoveller LLD - On the Committee for the Eye & Ear Dispensary (Hampshire Telegraph, 14 Jan 1822). ABOVE: Death notice for nine year old Sarah Sabine Shoveller (Dorset County Chronicle, 13th Jan 1825).

Children	Born	Bapt	Died
Thomas Eastman	11th Apr 1820	8th Sep 1820	18th Jun 1825
Mary Elizabeth	14th Mar 1822	7th Jun 1822	[17th Nov 1868]
William Henry	30th Apr 1824	31st Dec 1824	[Abt.1883]
Martha	26th Apr 1826	9th Jun 1826	1st Apr 1827
Thomas Eastman	25th May 1827	11th Jul 1827	[22nd May 1908]

Witness my hand this fourth day of August, One Thousand Eight Hundred and Thirty Seven.

(Signed) John Shoveller L.L.D, Their Father [Witness Jno. S .Burn]

All the while John Shoveller was advancing his career and about this time he published another essay in Portsea on "The most effectual Methods of advancing Youth in Scholastic Education."[15]

Jane Allen Shoveller was followed by a second Sarah Sabine Shoveller who arrived on the 19th of July 1816 and was baptised on the 17th of September.[16] Toward the end of 1816 Elizabeth sadly lost her father Thomas Eastman, but came into a worthy inheritance with other bequeathments.[17]

By July of 1817, John Shoveller had moved his school from Southsea to 'a very commodious premises' at Landport Terrace, and to promote his establishment and the curriculum he advertised his own publications on education in the form of Mr. Shoveller's 'Essay On Scholastic Education,' so as to "employ the time and engage the attention of his pupils," which was made available from Horsey & Whitewood at Portsea."[18] It was at this time that John Shoveller enrolled in a doctoral degree in law at Oxford University, the purpose of which was likely to strengthen his scholastic qualifications.[19]

In August of 1820, "on account of the property being so far from the proprietor's residence," John Shoveller placed his mother's ancestral property at Warnford, up for auction. It was a substantial home, situated 18 miles from Gosport on the London road, and consisted of "two good parlours in front, a kitchen, a cellar, a sitting room, four good bedrooms with roomy closets, a chaise house, a three stalled stable with loft over, and a garden,"[20] but whether it actually sold is doubtful, as he moved his family there in 1826.

John Shoveller wasn't a litigious man, but neither was he someone that would back away from a fight. The next piece of evidence concerning Dr. Shoveller was as a plaintiff in January of 1825 before D. Howard, Esq, a justice of the Borough, against Henry Levett, a driver and part-proprietor of the London coach "Rocket", for enacting more money than he was entitled to receive, and also for abusive and insulting language. The defendant was

▲ Regency era wedding ceremonies were simple and entirely determined by the prescribed service in the Book of Common Prayer. The only requirements were the clergyman, the parish clerk to ensure formal logging in the register, and two witnesses. All weddings, except those by special license, took place between 8am and noon.

▲In January of 1825, Dr. Shoveller was as a plaintiff before D. Howard, Esq, a justice of the Borough, against Henry Levett, a driver and part-proprietor of the "Rocket", London Coach, "for enacting more money than he was entitled to receive, and for abusive and insulting language."

convicted and fined a penalty of 40s and costs.[21]

The Grammar School, as it was later termed, was still operating through June of 1823, when they advertised for a 'Junior Assistant.'[22] However, by March of 1824, Dr. Shoveller announced his "intention of retiring... for the purpose of devoting himself to the education of his own sons, together with eight or ten young gentlemen only, on advanced terms." He pledged himself "to dispose of his house and interest to such a person only, as shall combine unexceptionable stability of character, with eminent scholastic attainments." But evidently, no one with such esteemed qualifications could be found as in May of 1824, it was announced in the Hampshire Telegraph that Mr. R. Salmon had entered into an agreement to purchase and convert Dr. Shoveller's house in Landport Terrace, into a hotel.[23] After the property transaction was concluded, Dr. Shoveller engaged his brother-in-law Thomas Sabine Eastman to hold an auction of his household furniture, which was advertised in the Hampshire Telegraph together with a full list of its contents. The auction was conducted at the house at 11am on the summer solstice, Wednesday, 21st June 1826.

John Shoveller had obviously inherited the Warnford property from his late mother Mary, who had died unexpectedly on the 21st September 1825, at her home at Landport Terrace, Portsmouth, aged 57.[24] This was confirmed when John moved his family to Warnford in July of 1826. He brought the small school with him, as in July 1827, its vacancies were advertised in the Hampshire Chronicle, "for a limited number of 12 young gentleman, at the reduced rate of 36 guineas per annum for board and education."[25]

Where To From Here?

In the midst of the Industrial Revolution, technological advancements were occurring at breakneck speed and the Menai Suspension Bridge, built by engineer Thomas Telford, opened on the 30th January 1826 between the island of Anglesey and the mainland of Wales. The same year heralded in the formation of the Zoological Society of London, the University of London and the first Cowes Regatta, which was held off the Isle of Wight.

John Shoveller too was changing, as he now began to make other significant decisions, and soon headed off in a new direction that would impact both himself and his family.

References

1. John Shoveller - Born on 21 Oct 1789, and baptism held on 6 Nov 1789 at the Independent Church, Poole, Dorset (England, Select Births and Christenings, 1538-1975).

2. Wikipedia - French Invasion of Russia [https://en.wikipedia.org/wiki/French_invasion_of_Russia].

3. Thomas Eastman & Sarah Sabine - Marriage held on the 25th December 1780 at St. Mary's Portsea, Hampshire, England, (Hampshire Allegations for Marriage Licences 1689-1837, Vol.1).

4. Elizabeth Shoveller (nee Eastman) - Death notices, (Hampshire Telegraph, 24th July 1852, p.5 & London Standard, 24th July 1852).

5. Theophilus Eastman - Baptism held on the 10th January 1790 at Meeting House, Orange St, Portsmouth (Portsea, Hampshire, England & Wales, Non-Conformist and Non-Parochial Registers, 1567-1936).

6. Thomas Eastman - Will, 30th July 1816 (England & Wales, Prerogative Court of Canterbury Wills, 1384-1858. Held at The National Archives; Kew, England; Prerogative Court of Canterbury and Related Probate Jurisdictions: Will Registers; Class: PROB 11; Piece: 1588).

7. John Shoveller - Address on 'The Excellence of the Hebrew Language' (Bibliotecha Brittanica, 1811, p.854).

8. J. Shoveller - Opening of King's House Academy (Hampshire Chronicle, 8 July 1811).

9. Shoveller's School Advertisement (Hampshire Telegraph, 27 June 1825).

10. Mr Shoveller's - King's House Academy Advertisement (Hampshire Chronicle, 30 Dec 1811, p.1).

11. Mr Shoveller's - King's House Academy, ibid.

12. John Shoveller & Elizabeth Eastman - Marriage held on the 24 Mar 1812 at St. Mary's, Portsea (Hampshire Allegations for Marriage Licences, 1689-1837, Vol 2).

13. University of Portsmouth. 'Dickens & The Victorian City' [https://dickens.port.ac.uk/background/].

14. Knightroots - Sarah Sabine Shoveller, buried at Portsea, Hampshire - 26 Feb 1813, aged 2 mths (Page 2, No. 15, but may have been re-buried on the 10th May 1814 at Portsea - Page 9, No. 70) [https://www.knightroots.co.uk/parishes/titchfield]).

15. John Shoveller - Essay on 'The most effectual Methods of advancing Youth in Scholastic Education,' (Bibliotecha Brittanica, 1815, p.854).

16. John Shoveller LLD (father) - 4th Aug 1837, Register of baptisms of all his children from the Independent Chapel, King Street (formerly Orange Street), Portsea (Portsea, Hampshire, England & Wales, Non-Conformist and Non-Parochial Registers, 1567-1936).

17. Thomas Eastman - Will, 30th July 1816, op.cit.

18. J. Shoveller - King's House Academy (Hampshire Chronicle, 14 July 1817).

19. John Shoveller - Oxford University (Extract from Alumni Oxoniensis: 1715 to 1886, The London Public Record Office, Chancery Lane, London England. Located in the Reference Section).

20. Mr. Shoveller - Auction of freehold dwelling at Warnford (Hampshire Chronicle, 7 Aug 1820).

21. Dr Shoveller v. Henry Levett (Hampshire Telegraph, 10 Jan 1825).

22. Dr. Shoveller - Junior School Assistant Wanted (Hampshire Telegraph, 23 June 1823).

23. Dr. Shoveller - Sold House to R. Salmon for a Hotel (Hampshire Telegraph, 8 May 1826).

24. Mary Shoveller (nee Bignell) - Death notice (Hampshire Telegraph, 26th Sept 1825, p.4).

25. Dr. Shoveller - Warnford School (Hampshire Chronicle, 9 July 1827).

26. Jones, Colin (1994). 'The Cambridge Illustrated History of France.' Cambridge University Press. [ISBN 978-0-521-66992-4.1994], pp. 193–194.

27. Kagan, Frederick (2007). 'The End of the Old Order: Napoleon and Europe', 1801–1805. Hachette Books. [ISBN 978-0-306-81645-1], pp. 42–43.

28. Kagan, Frederick (2007), ibid.

29. Dwyer, Philip G. (2014). 'The Rise of Prussia 1700–1830.' [ISBN 9781317887034]. Archived from the original on 7 February 2021. Retrieved 2 October 2020.

30. Ferguson, Niall (2004). 'Empire, The rise and demise of the British world order and the lessons for global power.' Basic Books. [ISBN 0-465-02328-2].

31. Keen, Benjamin & Haynes, Keith (2012). 'A History of Latin America.' Cengage Learning. [ISBN 978-1-133-70932-9]., chpt. 8.

32. Bell, David Avrom (2007). 'The First Total War: Napoleon's Europe and the Birth of Warfare as We Know it.' Houghton Mifflin Harcourt. [ISBN 978-0-618-34965-4]., p. 51.

33. Geoffrey Wawro (2002). 'Warfare and Society in Europe, 1792–1914.' Routledge. p. 9. [ISBN 9780203007358]. Archived from the original on 30 September 2015. Retrieved 18 June 2015.

34. Palmer, Robert Roswell (1941). 'Twelve who Ruled: The Committee of Public Safety, During the Terror.' Princeton University Press, pp. 81–83.

35. Tone, John Lawrence (1996). "Napoleon's uncongenial sea: Guerrilla warfare in Navarre during the Peninsular War, 1808–14". European History Quarterly. 26 (3): 355–382.

36. Shlapentokh, Dmitry (1997). 'The French Revolution and the Russian Anti-Democratic Tradition: A Case of False Consciousness.' Transaction Publishers. [ISBN 978-1-4128-2397-5]., pp. 220–228.

37. Palmer, R. R.; Colton, Joel; Kramer, Lloyd (2013). 'A History of the Modern World: '11th Edition. McGraw-Hill Higher Education. ISBN 978-0-07-759962-1., pp. 81–83.

38. Desan, Suzanne; Hunt, Lynn; Nelson, William Max (2013). 'The French Revolution in Global Perspective. Cornell University Press. [ISBN 978-0-8014-6747-9]., pp. 3, 8, 10.

39. Wikipedia - Napoleonic Wars [https://en.wikipedia.org/wiki/Napoleonic_Wars].

40. Scott, Ken - St. Mary's Church, Portsea [http://www.kenscott.com/portsea/stmarys.htm].

Chapter Fourteen

DR. JOHN SHOVELLER
MINISTER & COMMISSIONER
(Father of Thomas Eastman Shoveller)

Stepping back a decade, the year 1817 marked the deaths of such notable people as novelist Jane Austen (b.1775), and William Bligh (b.1754), and although George III was still the monarch, authority had passed to the Prince Regent, George Augustus Frederick (1762-1830), later George IV in 1811. On the streets, the 'Luddites' were waning, although a last major attack occurred in February, against lace-making machines in Loughborough, when 'habeas corpus' was suspended amidst fears of insurrection. The term "Luddite" was used to describe people who had a dislike for new technologies, but its origin dates back to an early 19th century labor movement that railed against how mechanized manufacturers and their unskilled laborers undermined the skilled craftsmen of the day.

That year also saw the opening of the Waterloo Bridge in London, gas lighting was introduced on stage in London's West End theatres, and Thomas Moore published his 'Lalla Rookh,' an oriental romance.[1] After the victory at Waterloo, Napoleon surrendered to Captain Frederick Maitland of "HMS Bellerophon" on the 15th July 1815, and was exiled to the Isle of St Helena. Fortunately, and most likely due to his standing as a schoolmaster, John Shoveller was able to avoid service in the British forces throughout the entire war, but with the war now resigned to history, people turned to improving their lives.

Doctoral Degree at Oxford University

John's father William Shoveller Sr., who could see the value of a good education, had the foresight to gain a position for his son at Oxford University, to study in the much esteemed field of law. John 'matriculated', which marked the commencement of his studies on the 16th of December 1817 at the age of 28 and he resided at St. Alban's Hall, as was recorded by the following entry in a list of Oxford University Old Boys:

List Of Oxford University Old Boys

"Shoveller, John, s. William, of Poole, Dorset, gent. ST. ALBAN HALL, matriculated 16th December 1817, aged 28. Rev. J. S. formerly of Finsbury Square, L.L.D., died at Banbury, 9th January 1847, aged 57."

Alumni Oxoniensis, 1715 to 1886 [2]

The title L.L.D. refers to a Legum Doctor (Doctor of Laws in English) and was a doctorate-level academic degree in law, or it could also have been an honorary doctorate, depending on the jurisdiction. The double L in the abbreviation indicating the plural, referred to the early practice to teach both Canon Law and Civil Law, and conferred a Doctorate of both laws, although Oxford Archives holds no further records of John Shoveller (*see Appendix F*).

Some 25 years previously in 1792, a University College Club was established in London to commemorate this brilliant period in the history of St. Alban's Hall at Oxford. Of its 33 members, all of whom were at the college between 1764 and 1772, 11 were members of parliament, four of them ministers, 13 were judges, two Lord Lieutenants and the Commander-in-Chief of Scotland. During Wetherell's later years the college failed to maintain its intellectual pre-eminence, although socially it continued to rank high.[3] Under

▲TOP (Left): St Alban's quadrangle at Oxford University. (Right): The coat of arms for Oxford University, and St. Alban's College ABOVE (Left): Engraving of St Albans Hall, Oxford, by David Loggan, c.1600. (Right): Drawing of St Alban's Hall at Oxford University, c.1837.

Documents of Dr John Shoveller L.L.D.

John Shoveller LLD

WARNFORD, HANTS.

TO be SOLD by AUCTION, by WM. WESTON, on Thursday, August 10, 1820, at three o'clock in the afternoon, at the George Inn, Warnford,—All that comfortable, convenient, and respectable FREEHOLD DWELLING-HOUSE with immediate possession, containing two good parlours in front, kitchen, cellar, sitting room, four good bed rooms with roomy closets, a chaise house, three stalled stable with loft over, and garden; pleasantly situated at Warnford, 14 miles from Gosport, on the London road.

On account of the Property being so far from the Proprietor's residence, a Purchaser will have an opportunity of buying a most capital bargain.

, For further particulars, apply to Mr. Shoveller, the Proprietor, on the Premises, or to the Auctioneer, Bishop's Waltham, (if by letter, post-paid).

N. B. The greater part of the purchase money may remain on mortgage, if required.

Upon the hearing of an information on Tuesday last, before D. Howard, Esq. a Justice of the Borough, exhibited by Dr. Shoveller, of Landport Terrace, against Henry Levett, driver and part proprietor of the Rocket, London Coach, under the 50th Geo. 3. for enacting from him more money than he was entitled to receive, and also for using abusive and insulting language; the defendant was convicted in the penalty of 40s. and costs.

R SALMON begs respectfully to acquaint the inhabitants of Portsmouth, Portsea, and Southsea, that he has entered into an agreement with Dr. Shoveller, of Landport Terrace, to take his House for an HOTEL; he is in expectation that the Lease will be executed very soon; and upon obtaining possession at Midsummer next, he will fit up and conduct his Establishment in such a manner as will insure the public patronage.

FULHAM, MIDDLESEX, 6th May, 1826.

LANDPORT TERRACE, SOUTHSEA.

VALUABLE HOUSEHOLD FURNITURE, brilliant Chimney Glass, in burnished gold frame, a fine Piano Forte, by Broadwood and Co. in handsome mahogany case, turned and reeded legs, with brass mouldings and ornaments, a Piano Forte, by Longman and Co. a music stool, ditto Canterbury, large Library Bookcase, School Desks, School Bell, &c.

TO be SOLD by AUCTION, by Mr. T. S. EASTMAN, on Wednesday, 21st June, 1826.—Being part of the HOUSEHOLD FURNITURE, of Dr. Shoveller, quitting his residence at Landport Terrace;—comprising, a mahogany four-post bedstead with handsome japanned cornice, chintz furniture lined throughout with yellow calico, full head cloth drapery, &c. handsomely fringed and trimmed; elliptic and half tester bedsteads, with dimity furnitures, very choice seasoned goose feather beds, a mill puff bed, hair and wool mattresses, blankets and counterpanes; a secretaire and bookcase with glazed gothic doors, a portable secretaire, neat mahogany sideboard, with cellaret drawer, several chests of drawers, a set of extensible dining tables, sets of handsome mahogany trafalgar chairs, rosewood cane seated ditto, two mahogany hall chairs, hat stand, drugget, stair, and other carpets, &c.

May be viewed the morning of sale, which will commence precisely at eleven o'clock.

On Wednesday last, the first stone of a new Independent Chapel was laid, at Warnford, in this county, by John Shoveller, LL.D. who delivered a suitable address on the spot, to a large assemblage from Warnford and the surrounding villages. The stone bore an appropriate Latin inscription by the young gentlemen of the School.

WARNFORD, HANTS.

Brilliant Toned Six-octave Cabinet Piano-Forte, in superb Spanish Mahogany and barrel front; capital Pony, five years old, Chaise and Harness, 15-inch Globes, Compound Microscope, large Magic Lanthorn with slides, &c.

TO be SOLD by AUCTION, by Mr. EASTMAN, on Tuesday, 28th June, 1831,—Part of the HOUSEHOLD FURNITURE, and Effects, of the Rev. J. Shoveller, L.L.D. quitting his residence, as above. The sale to commence at twelve o'clock.

Also, will be SOLD by AUCTION, at the same time and place, the FREEHOLD MESSUAGE, pleasantly situate, and very convenient for a family; containing two parlours, five good bed rooms, with servants' rooms, kitchen, wash-house, pantry, laundry, stable, chaise-house, with all other convenient appurtenances.

Shoveller Dr. (gents. boarding) Landport-terrace, Southsea

A district in the centre of the county of Hants, containing upwards of 300 square miles, was without a dissenting chapel, till, about eight years ago, a member of the Church at Portsea used his exertions to erect one at Westmeon, and subsequently another at Warnford. These two places form part of a cluster of villages, in which there is reckoned a population of 5,000 souls, within three or four miles of the chapels. Having been supplied by the students of the Missionary seminary, on their removal from Gosport, the people were on the point of being left destitute, when John Shoveller, LL.D. from Portsea, fixed his residence among them, and as soon as the church was formed, received a unanimous call to become its pastor; which invitation, after having candidly stated his reasons for supposing that his residence in the neighbourhood might be only temporary, he consented to accept, and on Tuesday, Oct. 6th, he was ordained over the people forming the united Independent church of Westmeon and Warnford. After reading and prayer by the Rev. T. S. Guyer, of Ryde, Isle of Wight, the introductory discourse was delivered by the Rev. Joseph Johnson, of Farnham, and the ordination prayer was offered by the Rev. J. Reynolds, of Romsey; the Rev. John Griffin, of Portsea, then gave a charge to the minister, replete with the most weighty admonition, couched in the most affectionate terms; and the Rev. T. Adkins, of Southampton, addressed a very judicious and impressive sermon to the congregation. It was truly a day to be remembered both by the minister and the people.

▲LEFT COLUMN: 1-The signature of John Shoveller L.L.D., August 1837; 2- 1820 Mr. Shoveller - Auction of freehold dwelling at Warnford (Hampshire Chronicle, 7 Aug 1820); 3- 1825 Dr Shoveller v. Henry Levett (Hampshire Telegraph, 10 Jan 1825); 4- 1826 Dr. Shoveller - Sold House to R. Salmon for a Hotel (Hampshire Telegraph, 8 May 1826). CENTRE COLUMN: 1- 1826 Dr Shoveller - Furniture auction held by his brother-in-law Thomas Sabine Eastman (Hampshire Telegraph, 19 June 1826); 2- 1827 Recognition of a speech given by John Shoveller LL.D., at laying the first stone of the Independent Chapel at Warnford (Hampshire Telegraph, 14th May 1827, p.4); 3- 1830 Rev. J Shoveller LLD - Auction in Quitting his residence (Hampshire Telegraph, 20 June 1831). RIGHT COLUMN: 1-Dr. John Shoveller - Gents Boarding House Advertisement, Southsea (1828 Pigot's Directory, Hampshire); 2-Appointment of John Shoveller LLD in 1829, as the minister of Warnford (The Evangelical Magazine and Missionary Chronicle, Vol VII, London, 1829).

James Griffith (1808–21) the only event of note was the expulsion of Hogg and Shelley "for contumaciously refusing to answer questions proposed to them and for also repeatedly declining to disavow a publication entitled 'The Necessity of Atheism'." Shelley's rooms were on the first floor in the corner of the quadrangle next to the hall.[4]

The Bible Society

Earlier in the summer of 1817, and just a couple of months before his enrollment at Oxford, John Shoveller was swept up in the enthusiasm of a new religious enterprise known as the Bible Society. Perhaps guided by his friend and colleague the Rev. John Griffin of Portsea, John attended and spoke at a number of meetings of the 'Hampshire Auxiliary British and Foreign Bible Society,' with one of his addresses being printed in its entirety by the Hampshire Telegraph:

"On Friday the 10th of October, a very numerous and respectable Meeting was held at the Beneficial Society's Hall, Portsea, for the purpose of forming a Branch Bible Society for the towns of Portsmouth, Portsea, Gosport, Fareham, Wickham & Titchfield, &c.," at which Mr Shoveller began by reflecting... "on the number, variety, and interesting nature of those means, by which mankind progressively attains a state of civilization and refinement, and observed that the British and Foreign Bible Society was an institution, which not only tended to civilize, refine, and adorn this life, but which had a special reference to another, and a better life to come..."

John Shoveller's Address at the Bible Society Meeting, Portsea, 10 Oct 1817 [5]

The British & Foreign Bible Society

AT the THIRD ANNUAL MEETING of the MEMBERS & FRIENDS of the HAMPSHIRE AUXILIARY BRITISH and FOREIGN BIBLE SOCIETY, holden at the Beneficial Society's Hall, Portsea, on Wednesday the 13th of August, 1817,

Sir THOMAS BARING, Bart. V. P. in the Chair—

The Report having been read by the Secretary, it was moved by the Rev. W. S. DUSAUTOY, and seconded by the Rev. JOHN GRIFFIN,

1.—*Resolved unanimously*—That the Report now read, be received and adopted, and that it be Printed under the direction of the Committee.

On a motion of EDWARD CARTER, Esq. and seconded by the Rev. Mr. HAWKINS, it was

2.—*Resolved unanimously*—That the cordial Thanks of this Meeting be given to the Most Noble the Patron, and the Right Honourable the Vice Patrons, for their Patronage.

On a motion of Mr. SHOVELLER, seconded by Mr. HOBBS, it was

Mr. SHOVELLER, after a few reflections on the number, variety, and interesting nature of those means, by which mankind progressively attain a state of civilization and refinement, observed, that the British and Foreign Bible Society was an Institution, which not only tended to civilize, refine, and adorn this life; but which had a special reference to another, and a better life to come. The benefit resulting from such an institution, was, he thought, unquestionably great: that benefit, however, could not be rapid in its progress, and visible at every step; it would be gradual in its advances, and perceptible only, when considerable efforts had been produced; for though the hand of industry might in a few years change the aspect of a country, it often required as many generations to make an alteration in the habits, sentiments, or morals of man. He was sorry, that a neighbourhood so populous and opulent, had not been more prominent in the promulgation of the Sacred Scriptures; and though he lamented, that the inhabitants of these towns had not, any ago, offered their most strenuous co-operation with the friends of this noble Institution, he could not refrain from speaking a few words, if not in defence, at least in extenuation, of the charges which had been brought against them; for he believed, that their activity and zeal could not have been surpassed, when loyalty, liberty, and benevolence had been the order of the day. If,

---

PORTSMOUTH, PORTSEA, GOSPORT, TITCHFIELD, FAREHAM, WICKHAM, &c.

BRANCH BIBLE SOCIETY.

On Friday the 10th of October, a very numerous and respectable Meeting was held at the Beneficial Society's Hall, Portsea, for the purpose of forming a BRANCH BIBLE SOCIETY for the Towns of PORTSMOUTH, PORTSEA, GOSPORT, FAREHAM, WICKHAM, TITCHFIELD, &c.

Mr. SHOVELLER, after a few reflections on the number, variety, and interesting nature of those means, by which mankind progressively attain a state of civilization and refinement, observed, that the British and Foreign Bible Society was an Institution, which not only tended to civilize, refine, and adorn this life; but which had a special reference to another, and a better life to come. The benefit resulting from such an institution, was, he thought, unquestionably great: that benefit, however, could not be rapid in its progress, and visible at every step; it would be gradual in its advances, and perceptible only, when considerable effects had been produced; for though the hand of industry might in a few years change the aspect of a country, it often required as many generations to make an alteration in the habits, sentiments, or morals of man. He was sorry, that a neighbourhood so populous and opulent, had not been more prominent in the promulgation of the Sacred Scriptures; and though he lamented, that the inhabitants of these towns had not, long ago, offered their most strenuous co-operation with the friends of this noble Institution, he could not refrain from speaking a few words, if not in defence, at least in extenuation, of the charges which had been brought against them; for he believed, that their activity and zeal could not have been surpassed, when loyalty, liberty, and benevolence had been the order of the day. If, however, they had been dilatory in their support of the Bible Society, the day was now arrived in which, he trusted, they would show that they had slumbered only, that the zeal of their hearts towards that cause might burst forth at once into a more vigorous and unquenchable flame. He argued that if the Bible was true, its truths were of the highest importance; and if truths so important concerned one individual more than another, they ought to be universally known. He would affirm that they who had it in their power to obtain the Word of God, could not conscientiously withhold it; nor could they who had the means of be-

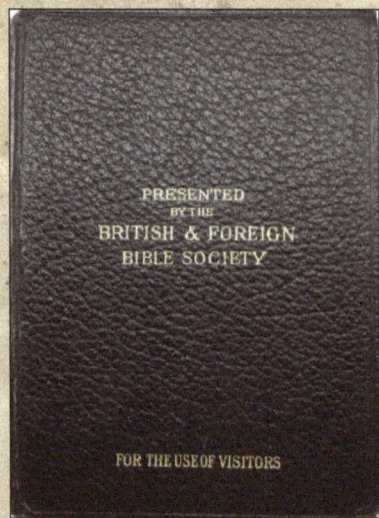

The British and Foreign Bible Society, often known in England and Wales as simply the Bible Society, is a non-denominational Christian Bible society with charity status, whose purpose is to make the Bible available throughout the world.[31]

The Society was formed on 7th March 1804 by a group of people including William Wilberforce and Thomas Charles to encourage the "wider circulation and use" of the Scriptures.[32]

Hearing of plans to provide Bibles at reduced prices for Welsh speakers, at a Religious Tract Society meeting, the Rev. Joseph Hughes asked, 'If for Wales, why not for the kingdom, and if for the kingdom, why not for the world?'

In this meeting, held on the 7th December 1802 in London, lay the foundation for the formation of the British and Foreign Bible Society the following year. The Society was launched on the 7th March 1804, in the London Tavern, Bishopsgate, in the presence of around 300 people.

The British and Foreign Bible Society dates back to when a group of Christians, associated with the Religious Tract Society, sought to address the problem of a lack of affordable Bibles in Welsh for Welsh-speaking Christians. Many young girls had walked long distances to Thomas Charles to get copies of the Bible. Later the story was told of one of them – a young girl called Mary Jones who walked over 20 miles to get a Bible in Bala, Gwynedd.

The British & Foreign Bible Society was not the first Bible Society in the world, the honour going to 'The Bible Society' proper, which was founded in 1779. This organisation still exists and is now called the Naval & Military Bible Society.

Today, the Society's mission is global and its work is organised into two categories: domestic and international.

The Society is part of an international fellowship of over 140 Bible Societies around the world, known as the United Bible Societies. Its entire international programme is delivered on the ground through the close relationship they have with each of their fellow Bible Societies.

---

stowing the precious gift, conscientiously withhold it. He believed no Christian could selfishly monopolise the source of all the happiness which he himself enjoyed; for in the same proportion that he valued the Word of God himself, would be his desire that others should value it also; for, said he, " inseparably connected with the benefit which we derive from the Bible, is the desire to communicate that benefit to all within the sphere of our influence." The capital which had been disbursed by the British and Foreign Bible Society seemed, therefore, to him, to be put out at compound interest.— To show how the Bible could prove injurious to any class of society, was, he acknowledged, a problem too profound for his shallow head to solve, and it was one, he believed, which would not be readily comprehended by a much deeper head than his; he was sorry, therefore, that it should be asserted with so much pertinacity, and maintained with as much obstinacy, as mathematicians would use in defence of their celebrated axioms— one of which declares, that things equal to the same thing are equal also to each other; and a second, as gravely affirms, that the whole of any thing is greater than its part! Many sad forebodings of the serious consequences, which would result from the untainted diffusion of the sacred Scriptures, had reached his ears; but the manner and matter of them all, were to him as ambiguous as the technical phraseology of a recruiting serjeant, who, when he speaks of a *good* man, means one who can handle his musket well. It is pleasing, continued Mr. Shoveller, to take a perspective view of that happy period, when Christianity will influence the conduct of nations as well as individuals; then, and not till then, will its triumph be complete.— That happy period, must come, and the anticipation of it must rejoice our hearts, when they shall no more teach every man his neighbour, and every man his brother, saying, " Know the Lord, for all shall know him, from the least unto the greatest." Much, he thought, had been done by the British and Foreign Bible Society, to accelerate that happy period, and nothing was too much to expect, from an Institution, which but a few years since, was in its secum state, though now like a magnificent oak, it was shooting its fair branches on every side—an institution (in the language of the Latin poet.)—

The Friends of the British and Foreign Bible Society will rejoice to hear that yesterday a Meeting was held at the Beneficial Society's Hall, Portsea, for the purpose of establishing a Branch Bible Society in this populous neighbourhood. It is impossible for us to describe the interest that was produced by the speeches of the several Reverend and other gentlemen who took part in the proceedings of the day. Precisely at twelve o'clock, the Hon. Sir GEORGE GREY, Bart. was called to the Chair, and the business of the day was opened by the Rev. Mr. WEST, one of the Secretaries of the Hampshire Auxiliary Society, who gave a very lucid and able account of the proceedings of the Parent Institution, both at home and abroad, from the period of its commencement, and concluded by moving a string of resolutions, relative to the organization of the Branch Society (which we are under the necessity of deferring till our next publication). This motion was seconded by T. A. MINCHIN, Esq. who forcibly recommended the great objects of the Meeting.—Major-General WILLIAMS then proposed that the Thanks of the Meeting should be given to Lord Howard, of Effingham, for the very kind and handsome manner in which he had consented to become Patron of the Institution, which was seconded by Mr. SHOVELLER.—Mr. THOMAS HOSKINS proposed that the . . . . . should be rendered to Sir . . . . . . Navies of the world. This then, surely, is the spot which should also render itself interesting by the establishment of a Bible Society.

The Meeting was also addressed by the Rev. Messrs. ADKINS, NEALE, and HAWKINS, and by Edw. CARTER, Esq. Mayor of Portsmouth, and Messrs. HOWARD, SHOVELLER, BUCKLAND, &c.

PRESENTED BY THE BRITISH & FOREIGN BIBLE SOCIETY

FOR THE USE OF VISITORS

From 1817 John Shoveller LLD assisted the British & Foreign Bible Society.▲ LEFT COLUMN: 1-Bible Society Meeting (Hampshire Telegraph, 18 Aug 1817); 2-Shoveller - Bible Society (Hampshire Telegraph, 20 Oct 1817, p.3); 3-Mr. Shoveller - Speech at Bible Society Meeting (Hampshire Telegraph, 20 Oct 1817). RIGHT COLUMN: 1-Mr. Shoveller - British & Foreign Bible Society (Hampshire Chronicle, 13 Oct 1817); 2- Shoveller - Hants Aux. Bible Society (Hampshire Chronicle, Aug 1817); 3-Shoveller - Hants Auxiliary Bible Society (Hampshire Chronicle, 18 Aug 1817); 4-Dr. Shoveller - Bible Society (Hampshire Chronicle, 16 Aug 1819)

Throughout and beyond his studies at Oxford, John Shoveller became closely involved with the Bible Society, for which he became for the rest of his life a passionate advocate. He was often reported in the print news as giving addresses and being present at various meetings, including one occasion at a 'Meeting Of The South-East Hants British and Foreign Bible Society,' on the 28th of November 1831. Although the details are unclear, John Shoveller - Schoolmaster, next registered a deed in Portsmouth in 1818.[6] That same year brought the arrival of their first son in John Shoveller Jr., who was born on the 10th of June 1818 and baptised on the 14th of July 1818 by the Rev. John Griffin of the Independent Chapel at King St (formerly Orange St.) Portsea.

When George III died on the 29th January 1820, the 57 year old Prince Regent ascended the throne as George IV, with no real change in his powers,[7] but by the time of his accession, he was obese and possibly addicted to laudanum.[8] Three months later, the first Thomas Eastman Shoveller arrived to John and Elizabeth on the 11th of April, and he was baptised on the 8th of September. The seventh child of John and Elizabeth Shoveller was Mary Elizabeth Shoveller, who was born on the 14th of March 1822 and baptised on the 7th of June.[9] Two years later, another son joined the family in William Henry Shoveller, who arrived on the 30th of April 1824 and was baptised on 31st of December 1824.[10]

Unfortunately, 1825 was not a good year for the Shoveller family as they lost two children in the second Sarah Sabine, aged nine on the 6th of January, and then the first Thomas Eastman, who had turned five on the 18th of June. John Shoveller also lost his mother Mary Shoveller (nee Bignell) that year, when she unexpectedly died aged 57, on the 21st September 1825, at her home at Landport Terrace, Portsmouth.[11]

The Shoveller's perservered with their family nonetheless, and soon after another girl was born in Martha Shoveller on the 26th of April 1826, who was baptised on the 9th of June, although she too died on the 1st of April 1827. Their last child was a second Thomas Eastman, who arrived on the 27th of May 1827, after they had made the move to Warnford. This Thomas was baptised soon after his birth on the 11th of July 1827, which was also conducted at the Independent Chapel at King St (formerly Orange St) in Portsea.[12] Notably, and like the Eastmans, every one of the Shoveller children had been baptised at home by the Rev. John Griffin of the King St (formerly Orange St) Independent Church in Portsea.

Family sources have anecdotally claimed over the years that although John Shoveller had gained a doctorate of law's, he unfortunately couldn't commence a legal practice due to a speech stammer, which apparently affected his speaking ability, although one might be somewhat dismissive of such an allegation given his work and obvious achievements as a schoolmaster and a speaker.

At this time non-conformists in the 18th and 19th century claimed a devotion to hard work, temperance, frugality and upward mobility, with which historians today largely agree. A major Unitarian magazine, the Christian Monthly Repository asserted in 1827:

> "Throughout England a great part of the more active members of society, who have the most intercourse with the people have the most influence over them, are Protestant Dissenters. These are manufacturers, merchants and substantial tradesman, or persons who are in the enjoyment of a competency realized by trade, commerce and manufacturers, gentlemen of the professions of law and physic, and agriculturalists, of that class particularly who live upon their own freehold. The virtues of temperance, frugality, prudence and integrity promoted by religious non-conformity... assist the temporal prosperity of these descriptions of persons, as they tend also to lift others to the same rank in society"

From... "The Politics of the Confessional State, 1760–1832," by Richard W. Davis [13]

The ideas of social equality that gradually came about with the advent of individual

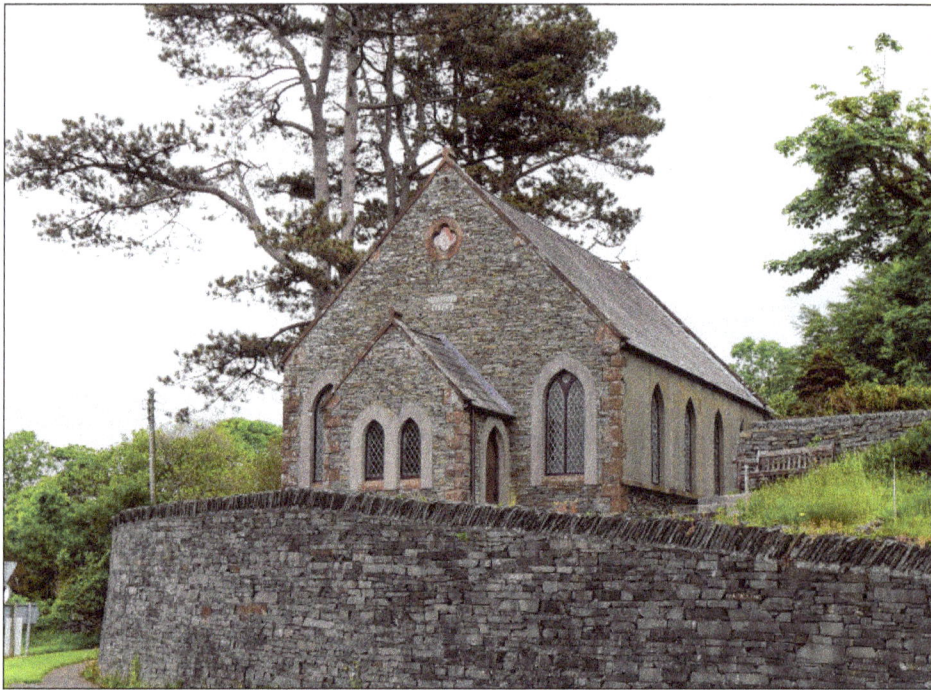

▲ *The Chapel at Warnford, Hampshire, which came about when John Shoveller galvanised the community to erect chapels in Westmeon and Warnford.*

freedoms trickled down to religion, and the movement later known as the 'Second Great Awakening' began about 1790. Specifically, Methodists and Baptists began an effort to democratize religion. Unlike the Episcopalian religion, many ministers in these sects were typically uncultivated, but unlike the Calvinists, they believed and preached salvation for all. By 1830, the Shoveller family could boast at least nine close relatives who spread the word of god as ministers of the independent faith. These included Robert Bowyer (1758-1834), Rev. John Shoveller Sr. (1760-1851), Rev. John Shoveller Jr. (1796-1831), Rev. Thomas Stratten (1794-1861), Rev. Theophilus Eastman (1789-1863) and John Shoveller L.L.D, himself (1789-1847), with the Rev. Samuel Sabine (1766-1843), Rev. James Sabine (1774-1845) and his son Rev. John Theodore Sabine (1811-1851) having emigrated to North America.

Independent Minister

Throughout his life, John Shoveller contributed where he could to various causes, and having moved to a rural village without an Independent Church, he soon galvanised the community to erect two small chapels in Westmeon and Warnford. On the 14th May 1827, just two weeks prior to the birth of his tenth child, he gave a speech at the laying of the first stone for the new Independent Chapel at Warnford.[14] The stone bore an appropriate latin inscription from the young gentlemen of his school, and John Shoveller was thus recognised:

> "A district in the centre of the county of Hants, containing upwards of 300 square miles, was without a dissenting chapel, till, about eight years ago, a member of the Church at Portsea used his exertions to erect one at Westmeon, and subsequently another at Warnford. These two places form part of a cluster of villages, in which there is reckoned a population of 5,000 souls, within three or four miles of the chapels. Having been supplied by the students of the Missionary seminary, on their removal from Gosport, the people were on the point of being left destitute, when John Shoveller L.L.D. from Portsea, fixed his residence among them, and as soon as the church was formed, received a unanimous call to become its pastor; which invitation, after having candidly stated his reasons for supposing that his residence in the neighbourhood might be only temporary, he consented to accept, and on Tuesday, October 6th, he was ordained over the people forming the united Independent Church of Westmeon and Warnford."

The Evangelical Magazine and Missionary Chronicle, Vol VII, London, 1829 [15]

Stockwell Green, Surrey

▲TOP (Left): Kennington Common & Church, c.1830. (Right): Stockwell Green United Reformed Church. MID (Left): The Congregational Chapel at 35 Stockwell Green, where Dr. John Shoveller possibly ministered during the 1830s. First built in 1798 as Stockwell New Chapel for 'a new class of dissenters denominated as Independents' - it also had a small graveyard. The building was considerably extended and given this facade in 1850 by the architect James Wilson. William Booth the founder of the Salvation Army was married here on 17th June 1855. The congregation moved to a smaller premises in 1989 and the building became a mosque. Photograph by M.D. Trace, dated June 1968. (Right): View across Stockwell Green c.1870, showing the Green House, later known as the Haunted House. The Green itself remained open until 1876 when Mr Honey the freeholder, settled a dispute to claim the rights to use the land for building purposes. ABOVE: 1871 Map of Stockwell Green, Surrey showing the location of the Congregational Chapel just below the Green itself.

The Shovellers resided in elegant properties and John Shoveller possibly ministered at the Independent Church at Stockwell Green, Surrey during the mid to late 1830s. ▲ TOP (Left): By 1845, the Shoveller 's were residing at 50 Finsbury Square, London as per this print, 'Temple of the Muses, Finsbury Square, London' drawn about 1831 by Thos. H. Shepherd. Engraved by R. Acon. Jones & Co. (Centre): Business and residential listings for Dr. John Shoveller, in local directories from 1828 to 1845. (Right): Portrait of the 18 year old Queen Victoria for her coronation in London, in 1838. ABOVE: 1817 Antique engraved print of Finsbury Square, London, by J. Greig.

By 1829 John Shoveller had accepted the position as pastor of the newly erected Independent Chapels at Westmeon and Warnford, which after having been a schoolmaster, no doubt altered both his occupation and his direction in life. However, Warnford was always just a temporary move and by June 1831 he had relocated the family back to Portsmouth. In 1832 John Shoveller lost his father William Shoveller Sr., who had reached the age of 68, which was well before either of his older siblings Mary Bowyer and Rev. John Shoveller Sr.[16] It's likely that sometime after this, John Shoveller moved his family once again, this time to London where they resided south of the river at Stockwell Green in Surrey, only 4.5km from Westminster Abbey.

It was while at Stockwell Green that John's esteemed uncle and artist, Robert Bowyer died on the 4th June 1834 at Golden Square, near Piccadilly in London.[17] John and Elizabeth would no doubt have been mourners at his funeral, along with John's aunt Mary Bowyer, and Catherine Andras, their adopted daughter. Considering the vast sum of £300,000 Robert Bowyer claimed to have expended in the cause of British art, he died a comparatively poor

WHITEHALL, *Sept.* 13. | The King has been pleased o direct letters patent to be passed under the Great Seal, nominating Joseph Phillimore, D.C.L.; Henry William Tancred, Esq.; Edgar Taylor, Esq.; the Rev. Dr. Rees, LL.D.; John Bowring, Esq.; John Nicholl, D.C.L.; Robert Winter, Esq.; Saml. Gale, Esq.; John Parker, Esq.; Samuel March Phillipps, Esq.; Thomas Henry Lister, Esq.; and John Shoveller, LL.D. to be his Commissioners for inquiring into the state of the registers of births, deaths, and marriages, not being parochial registers, in England and Wales.

WHITEHALL, SEPT. 13.—The King has been pleased to direct letters patent to be passed under the Great Seal, nominating and appointing Joseph Phillimore, D.C.L.; Henry William Tancred, Esq.; Edgar Taylor, Esq.; the Rev. Dr. Rees, LL.D.; John Bowring, Esq.; John Nicholl, D.C.L.; Robert Winter, Esq.; Samuel Gale, Esq.; John Parker, Esq.; Samuel March Phillips, Esq.; Thomas Henry Lister, Esq.; and John Shoveller, LL.D. to be his Commissioners for inquiring into the state of the registers of births, deaths, and marriages, not being parochial registers, in England and Wales. *Gazette.*

LONDON, &c.

Tuesday's *Gazette* contains the appointment of the following. Gentlemen Commissioners for inquiring into the state of registers of births, deaths and marriages, not being parochial registers, in England and Wales:—J. Phillimore, D.C.L.; H. W. Tancred, Esq.—E. Taylor, Esq.—the Rev. Dr. Rees, L.L.D.—J. Bowring, Esq.—J. Nicholl, D.C.L.—R. Winter, Esq.—S. Gale, Esq.—J. Parker, Esq.—S. M. Philipps, Esq.—T. H. Lister, Esq.—and John Shoveller, L.L.D.

REGISTERS OF DISSENTERS' BIRTHS AND BAPTISMS.—We are happy to inform our readers that there is reason to hope that the existing registers of births and baptisms which have been kept by Dissenting ministers, may yet be received as legal evidence. A few months ago, they are aware, his Majesty was pleased to direct letters patent to be passed under the Great Seal, nominating, constituting, and appointing Joseph Phillimore, D.C.L., Henry William Tancred, Esq., Edgar Taylor, Esq., the Rev. Thomas Rees, LL.D., John Bowring, Esq., John Nicholl, D.C.L., Robert Winter, Esq., Samuel Gale, Esq., John Parker, Esq., Samuel March Phillips, Esq., Thomas Henry Lister, Esq., and John Shoveller, LL.D., to be his Commissioners for inquiring into the state of registers of births, deaths, and marriages, not being parochial registers in England and Wales. We have the pleasure to know that these Commissioners are at work, and that speedily circulars will be addressed by them to Dissenting ministers throughout the Kingdom, with a view to ascertain the state, custody, and authenticity of the documents in question; also, what measures can be taken to collect, arrange, deposit, and preserve them, and also how full force and effect may be given to them as evidence, and to facilitate their reception as such in Courts of Justice. We owe this enlightened and soothing measure to the equitable councils of his Majesty's present ministers, to whom, on many grounds, Protestant Dissenters are greatly indebted.—*Congregational Magazine.*

◄ *TOP: John Shoveller L.L.D., Kings Nomination (Hampshire Telegraph, 19th Sept, 1836, p2). MID: John Shoveller L.L.D., Appointment under Letters Patent (Hereford Journal, 21 Sept 1836). BELOW: Appointment of John Shoveller L.L.D., as Commissioner inquiring into the state of non-parochial births, deaths and marriages (Taunton Courier & Western Advertiser, 28 Sept 1836). ▲John Shoveller L.L.D., Commissioner into registers kept by Dissenting Ministers (Staffordshire Advertiser, 17 Dec 1836).*

The General Register Office of England & Wales [33]

The General Register Office for England and Wales (GRO) was founded in 1836 by the Births and Deaths Registration Act 1836, and civil registration commenced in 1837. Its head is the Registrar General. Prior to the creation of the GRO in 1837, there was no national system of civil registration in England and Wales. Baptisms, marriages and burials were recorded in parish registers maintained by Church of England (Anglican) clergy. However, with the great increase in nonconformity and the gradual relaxation of the laws against Catholics and other dissenters from the late 17th century, more and more baptisms, marriages and burials were going unrecorded in the registers of the Anglican Church.

The increasingly poor state of English parish registration led to numerous attempts to shore up the system in the eighteenth and early nineteenth centuries. The Marriage Act of 1753 attempted to prevent 'clandestine' marriages by imposing a standard form of entry for marriages, which had to be signed by both parties to the marriage and by witnesses. Additionally, except in the case of Jews and Quakers, legal marriages had to be carried out according to the rites of the Church of England. Sir George Rose's Parochial Registers Act of 1812 laid down that all events had to be entered on standard entries in bound volumes. It also declared that the church registers of nonconformists were not admissible in court as evidence of births, marriages and deaths. Only those maintained by the clergy of the Church of England could be presented in court as legal documents. This caused considerable hardship for nonconformists. A number of proposals were presented to parliament to set up centralised registries for recording vital events in the 1820s, but none came to fruition.

Eventually, increasing concern that the poor registration of baptisms, marriages and burials undermined property rights, by making it difficult to establish lines of descent, coupled with the complaints of nonconformists, led to the establishment in 1833 of a parliamentary Select Committee on Parochial Registration. This took evidence on the state of the parochial system of registration, and made proposals that were eventually incorporated into the 1836 Registration and Marriage Acts. In addition, the government wanted to survey things like infant mortality, fertility and literacy to bring about improvements in health and social welfare. The medical establishment advocated this because a rapidly growing population in the northern industrial towns, caused by the Industrial Revolution, had created severe overcrowding, and the links between poor living conditions and short life expectancy were now known.

The answer was the establishment of a civil registration system. It was hoped that improved registration of vital events would protect property rights through the more accurate recording of lines of descent. Civil registration was also to remove the need for nonconformists to rely upon the Church of England for registration, and provide medical data for research. As a result, in 1836, legislation was passed that ordered the civil registration of births, marriages and deaths in England and Wales. This took effect from 1 July 1837. A General Register Office was set up in London and the office of the Registrar General was established.

England and Wales were divided into 619 registration districts (623 from 1851), each under the supervision of a Superintendent Registrar. The districts were based on the recently introduced poor law unions. The registration districts were further divided into sub-districts (there could be two or more), each under the charge of Registrars who were appointed locally.

Although the GRO was not specifically established to undertake statistical research, the early Registrar Generals, Thomas Henry Lister (1836–42) and George Graham (1842–79), built up a Statistical Department to compile medical, public health and hand written actuarial statistics. Much of this work was undertaken in the early to mid-Victorian period by William Farr, the GRO's Superintendent of Statistics. Under these men the Annual reports of the Registrar General became a vehicle for administrative and social reform. In 1840 the GRO also took over responsibility for the decennial census of England and Wales.

In 1871, the GRO came under the supervision of the Local Government Board. During the First World War the GRO was responsible for co-ordinating National Registration, which underpinned recruitment to the armed forces, the movement of workers into the munitions industries, and rationing. However, National Registration was not continued after the war, and the GRO was absorbed into the Ministry of Health in 1919.

man at the age of 76.[18] Mary Bowyer passed away a few years later sometime prior to the preparation of Catherine Andras' will in November 1837, who died herself in early 1839. Catherine bequeathed the Bowyer household treasures to Mary Stratten, Mary Bowyer's niece, the wife of the Rev. Thomas Stratten and the younger sister of John Shoveller L.L.D.[19]

His Majesty's Commissioner

John Shoveller was likely involved with the Independent Church while residing in Stockwell Green when on the 13th September 1836, he received the most welcome news from Whitehall, that along with 11 others, he had been appointed to an important position:

> "The King (ie.William IV) has been pleased to direct letters patent to be passed under the Great Seal, nominating and appointing... his Commissioners for inquiring into the state of the registers of births, deaths, and marriages, not being parochial registers, in England and Wales."

John Shoveller L.L.D., Appointed Commissioner. [20]

John's appointment may well have been due to influential colleagues from St Albans College at Oxford, or through his network of friends in the non-conformist movement, but as a direct result of the work of these 12 Commissioners, the compulsory registration of births, deaths and marriages became law in 1837, across England and Wales,[21] and their report was published in 1838.[22] One of the first things John and Elizabeth Shoveller did at this time was to make certain that important dates regarding their own family were recorded for posterity, and they officially registered full details of the births, baptisms and deaths of all their children.[23] As well as being so closely involved in the process, what compelled him to make this declaration was that the laws regarding the registration of births, deaths and marriages had recently changed, and although registrations were not retrospective, John Shoveller went ahead and submitted the relevant details for his family.[24]

The very next year, at the tender age of just 18 the coronation of Queen Victoria took place on the 28th June 1838, just over a year after she had succeeded to the throne. The procession to and from the ceremony at Westminster Abbey was witnessed by unprecedented crowds as the new railways made it easier for an estimated 400,000 to travel into London from around the country. The Shovellers were residing at 50 Finsbury Square, a fashionable London address at the time, but their home was completely gutted by fire on the 2nd February 1841, luckily they were insured. By June of that year, the first Census of England and Wales was conducted and John Shoveller and his family of seven were recorded as residing at 'North End' in St Johns Wood, Hampstead, with Hannah Gallifant a servant.

DESTRUCTIVE FIRE IN LONDON.—On Tuesday morning, at ten o'clock, a fire originated on the premises of Messrs. Painter and Co., the extensive cabinet-manufacturers, Finsbury-pavement, Moor-fields, which has involved the total destruction of that spacious building. The area occupied by it was almost an acre in extent, and the top of it was surmounted by a dome. The fire, it is supposed, arose from the boiling over of some varnish in one of the warehouses, which was situated under the roof. The loss of property is said to exceed £25,000. No portion of Messrs Painter and Co.'s premises and manufactory are remaining; the whole are burnt to the ground. The firm are insured in the Phœnix Fire Office, but, Mr. Painter states, far below the extent of property consumed. The premises of Dr. Shoveller, No. 50, adjoining, and at the corner of Finsbury-square, are completely gutted. He is insured in the Protestants' and Dissenters' Fire Office. No. 49, Finsbury-square, belonging to Mr. Gregorie, professor, seriously damaged by water;

▲LEFT: 1841 Dr Shoveller - Premises Gutted By Fire (Northern Star, 6th February 1841, p.5). RIGHT: John Shoveller L.L.D. and family moved to 'North End' in St Johns Wood, Hampstead, Middlesex at the time of the first Census (1841 Census for England & Wales, District 7, Edmonton [Folio:28/H0107/674-16]).

Last Will & Testament of the Rev. John Shoveller, LLD
Drafted - 6th December 1846 & Proved - 20 February 1847 [34]

Translation

This is the last will and testament of one **John Shoveller** of Banbury, Oxon, looking for the mercy of God into eternal life through Jesus Christ our Lord. I give, devise and bequeath all and every my household furniture, linen, books, pictures, plate china and glass to my dear wife for and during the term of her natural life and afterwards I direct the same to be divided unto among my surviving children both sons and daughters except that in before such division I give to my daughter **Jane Allen** to the value of fifty pounds of the same as the equivalent to her sisters piano, for to and whereas I have assured my life for one thousand pounds at the Victoria Assurance and also for one thousand pounds at the ????????? and General Assurance. I direct that as soon as these sums may be realized all the monies which have been borrowed by me on mortgage or otherwise to put my sons in business or to reinstate the house in Finsbury Square. After this be forthwithe paid I give and bequeath out of the same to my son **William Henry** three hundred pounds and to my daughters **Jane Allen** and **Mary Elizabeth wife of James [Henry] Roberton** each two hundred and fifty pounds and as to all the rest, residue and remainder of my estate and effects whatsoever and wheresoever both real and personal whether in possession or reversion, remainder or expectancy, I give devise and bequeath the same to my executors hereinafter amentioned upon trust to pay the proceeds of the same unto my dear wife during the term of her natural life and from and after her decease I wish to give, devise and bequeath my entire estate and effects both real and personal unto and among and to be equally divided between all and every of my children both sons and daughters who shall be living at the time of the decease of my said wife and the issue of such of them as shall be dead such issue nevertheless taking only the share which their deceased parent would have been entitled to. In the event of such parent surviving my said wife I give to my sons their respective shares absolutely but as to my daughters it is my will that their shares respectively shall be vested by my executors in some real securities that my said daughters may enjoy the proceeds of the same during their natural lives. And from and after their decease I give and bequeath their shares severally to their children in such shares and at such a time and manner as my said daughters by their last will and testament shall direct. And in case my daughters or either of them should die without lawful issue I direct that their or her shares or share may be divided equally among my other children or the survivors of them and the issue of such as shall be dead, such issue taking only the share which their deceased parent would have been entitled, to share and share alike. And it is my will that if not before then after the decease of my dear wife my executors hereinafter mentioned, their heirs and assigns or the survivor of them shall sell and dispose of all my messuages, land, tenements and hereditaments when and as soon as may appear to them or him convenient, for the most equity that can be obtained for the same and that they or he make and execute all such deeds and conveyances in the law as shall be necessary and proper for the sale and transfer thereof, and I do hereby declare that the receipts of my executors their heirs and assigns or the survivor of them shall be good and sufficient discharge to the purchasers of the said messuages, land, tenements and hereditaments so directed to be sold. And as soon as the said messuages, land, tenements and hereditaments or any part thereof shall be turned into money, that money shall be deemed part of my general estate and be appropriated as by this my last will and testament is directed and until such sales be affected I direct that the proceeds, rents and dividends accruing from my entire estate and effects be after the decease of my said wife received respectively by my children half yearly and in equal shares and proportions and it is my will that in case either of my sons should at any time cast himself upon his mother for maintenance without paying to her forty pounds a year for his board, lodging and washing - my executors hereinafter named shall deduct the sum of forty pounds from the income of my said wife and divide the same from year to year among my other children excluding that one who shall be so maintained by his mother and no longer. And it is my will that my son **William Henry** shall not receive the legacy bequeathed to him in this my will until he shall have been a twelvemonth in some employ equal to his maintenance subsequent to my decease nor the interest of the same but I direct that the interest shall accumulate for his benefit until he becomes entitled to the principle under the above condition and I make this provision because I do not consider him acquainted with any particular business or with business in general without further experience. I appoint my friend **Dr. Charles Waller** of Finsbury Square, London and my son **John Shoveller [Jr.]** my executors with my dear wife as Executrix of this my last will and testament, and I give to my friend **Dr. Waller** of London, a handsome mourning ring.

Lastly, I do hereby revoke and make void all former and other wills made by me at anytime heretofore made by me and declare this day only to be my last will and testament. In witness whereof I the said **John Shoveller** the testator have to this my last will and testament set my hand this twenty sixth day of December in the year of our Lord, One Thousand Eight Hundred and Forty Six.

John Shoveller (L.L.D.)

Signed by the said Testator John Shoveller and acknowledged by him to be his last will and testament in the prescence of us present at the same time and subscribed by us in the prescence of the said testator and of each other.
Thomas Furneaux Jordan, (Baptist Minister) & **Richard Grimbly Jr.**, (Surgeon, Banbury Oxon.)

Proved at London 20th February 1847, before the worshipful **Robert Joseph Phillimore**, Doctor of Laws and surrogate by **Charles Waller**, Doctor of Medicine, **John Shoveller** the son and **Elizabeth Shoveller** widow the relict executors to whom admon was granted the said **Charles Waller** having first made a solemn and sincere declaration or affirmation according to Act of Parliament and the said **John Shoveller** and **Elizabeth Shoveller** having been first sworn duly to administer.

▲ The will of John Shoveller, LLD - proved on the 20th February 1847 (England & Wales, Prerogative Court of Canterbury Wills, 1384-1858. PROB: 11, Will Registers; 1845-1847; Piece: 2051: Vol.4, Quire No. 151-200, 1847).

The Shovellers moved according to John's various postings with the Independent Church, and documents including his will reveal that their residential history began at Landport Terrace, Portsmouth; then Warnford, Hampshire; returning to Portsmouth;

Stockwell Green, Surrey; at No. 50 Finsbury Square in London; North End, St Johns Wood at Hampstead; and toward the end of his life at Horsefair, Banbury in Oxfordshire, where there evolved no less than four 19th-century dissenting churches: the Independent (or Congregationalist) congregation which met in Church Passage and later in South Bar, the Bridge Street Particular Baptists, and the Calvinistic Baptists of West Bar (and later of the Ebenezer Chapel) and South Bar.[25]

Unfortunately, John Shoveller contracted influenza that soon deteriorated into bronchitis, which he reportedly suffered from for several weeks. Sadly, on the 9th of January 1847 his

▲ TOP: Horse Fair Square at Banbury, Oxfordshire about 1890, the town where John Shoveller passed away on the 9th January 1847. ABOVE: Death certificate for John Shoveller - 9th Jan 1847 issued by the ministry he helped to establish (General Registrar Office, Banbury, County of Oxford & Northampton).

CLERICAL OBITUARY.

Jan. 11, at his residence, Colliton House, near Dorchester, the Rev. W. R. Churchill, in the 73d year of his age.

Jan. 8, aged 78, the Rev. Peregrine Curtois, of Longhills, near Lincoln, Rector of Branston, and a Magistrate for the Kesteven division of Lincolnshire.

Jan. 3, at St. George's Place, Canterbury, the Rev. William Sherlock Carey, Rector of Lezant, Cornwall, aged 47.

Jan. 9, at Banbury, the Rev. John Shoveller, LL.D., formerly of Finsbury Square, aged 57.

SHOVELLER.—Jan. 9, at Banbury, the Rev. J. Shoveller, LL.D., ... of Finsbury-square, aged 57.

Shoveller, John, s. William, of Poole, Dorset, gent. ST. ALBAN HALL, matric. 16 Dec., 1817, aged 28. (Rev. J. S., formerly of Finsbury Square, LL.D., died at Banbury, 9 Jan., 1847, aged 57.

DIED.

COLE—On the 21st inst., the Rev. William Hodgson Cole, A.M., Vicar of Wonersh, Surrey, and domestic Chaplain to H.R.H. the late Duke of Gloucester, in the 82nd year of his age.

SHOVELLER—On the 22nd instant, at Ealing, Elizabeth, widow of the Rev. John Shoveller, LL.D., aged 68.

Parish or Township of	Ecclesiastical District of	City or Borough of	Town of	Village of	
St. John Hampstead					

	Name of Street, Place, or Road, and Name or No. of House	Name and Surname of each Person who abode in the house, on the Night of the 30th March, 1851	Relation to Head of Family	Condition	Age of Males	Age of Females	Rank, Profession, or Occupation	Where Born	Whether Blind, or Deaf-and-Dumb
	No 3 Haverstock	Nancy Philpott	Servant	U		23	Housemaid	Middlesex Middlesex Road	
	Terrace Continued	Harriet Williams	Visitor	U		25	Do	Do St Marylebone	
	One House uninhabited								
60	Haverstock	John Shoveller	Head	Mar	32		Civil Service Registrar Generals Office	Hants Portsmouth	1
	Terrace No 5	Hannah Do	Wife	U		32		City of London	
		Hannah M Do	Daur			2		Middlesex St Lukes	
		Helen R Do	Do			1		Do Hampstead	
		Elizabeth Do	Visitor	Wid		67	Proprietor of Houses	Hants Portsmouth	1
		Mary Sherwood	Servant	U		32	House Servant	Herts Pelham	

▲ TOP (Left Column): 1-Death notice for John Shoveller, L.L.D., (Brighton Gazetteer, 21 January 1847); 2-Rev. J. Shoveller L.L.D. - Death notice (London Daily News, 14th January 1847, p.6). (Right Column): 1-John Shoveller, L.L.D., Alumni Entry (Oxford University Alumni, 1715-1886, Vol.IV, p.1292); 2-Death notice for Elizabeth Shoveller (nee Eastman, Hampshire Telegraph, 24th July 1852, p.5 & in the London Standard, 24th July 1852. ABOVE: At 67 years of age, Elizabeth Shoveller (nee Eastman), who was described as a 'Proprietor of Houses,' visited the family of her son John Shoveller Jr. at 5 Haverstock Terrace, Hampstead (1851 England & Wales Census).

body returned from earth to heaven at his home at Horse Fair, Banbury in Oxfordshire.[26] He was just 57 years of age. John Shoveller was obviously a well educated and respected man and further research into his different vocations may in time reveal greater detail of his life and work. The informant on the death certificate was his wife Elizabeth, who was present when he fell asleep. The death was registered on the 11th of January 1847 by William Galsworthy, Registrar.

John made preparations for his family and had the foresight to make provision for his wife and children in a will he made on the 6th December 1846.[27] Nonetheless, his 19 year old son Thomas was omitted due to him not being 'of the age of majority', which at that time was 21 for males and 16 for females if single, or 14 if married.[28] The attainment of such an age was usually referred to as being 'of full age', which was when progeny could claim an inheritance.

Where Rev. John Shoveller L.L.D. was buried is unknown, although a search of the burial grounds around the vicinity of Banbury, Oxfordshire may at some stage reveal his memorial. He was a schoolmaster, an independent minister and religious advocate, a King's commissioner and a classical 'scholar.' Following the death of her husband, Elizabeth Shoveller survived another five years residing both with her spinster daughter Jane Allen and also with her eldest son John Shoveller Jr.[29] But with the passing of time Elizabeth Shoveller (nee Eastman) died on the 22nd July 1852 at Ealing at the age of 68, although her place of burial is also unknown.[30]

John and Elizabeth Shoveller produced a family of ten children, although only five survived to adulthood and just four married. However, some 23 grandchildren were produced from those unions, with one branch being raised in an ancient land on the opposite side of the world. Moving into the 20th century, the next chapter reveals all that is known of John and Elizabeth Shoveller's surviving children, along with individual stories and details for a number of their descendants, one of whom rose to be an Olympic champion.

References

1. Cox, Michael, ed. (2004). 'The Concise Oxford Chronology of English Literature'. Oxford University Press. [ISBN 0-19-860634-6].

2. John Shoveller - Oxford University, op.cit.

3. Ref: 'University College', in A History of the County of Oxford: Volume 3, the University of Oxford, ed. H. E. Salter and Mary D. Lobel (London, 1954), pp. 61-81. British History Online http://www.british-history.ac.uk/vch/oxon/vol3/pp61-81 [accessed 10 June 2022].

4. University of Oxford, College Register, 25 March 1811.

5. John Shoveller's Address at the Bible Society Meeting (Hampshire Telegraph, 20 Oct 1817).

6. Deed registered in 1818 by John Shoveller - Schoolmaster of King's House Academy, Portsmouth (Card #2005P/14 - Portsmouth History Centre).

7. Innes, Arthur Donald (1915). A History of England and the British Empire. Vol. 4. The MacMillan Company.

8. Hibbert, Christopher (2008) [2004]. "George IV (1762–1830)". Oxford Dictionary of National Biography (online ed.). Oxford University Press. [doi:10.1093/ref:odnb/10541].

9. John Shoveller LLD (father) - 4th Aug 1837, op. cit.

10. John Shoveller LLD (father) - 4th Aug 1837, op. cit.

11. Mary Shoveller (nee Bignell) - Death notice (Hampshire Telegraph, 26th Sept 1825, p.4).

12. John Shoveller LLD (father) - 4th Aug 1837, op. cit.

13. Richard W. Davis, "The Politics of the Confessional State, 1760–1832". Parliamentary History 9.1 (1990): 38–49, doi:10.1111/j.1750-0206.1990.tb00552.x, quote p. 41

14. John Shoveller L.L.D., Speech at laying of the first stone for the Independent Chapel at Warnford in May 1827 (Hampshire Telegraph, 14th May 1827, p.4).

15. The Evangelical Magazine and Missionary Chronicle (1829), Vol VII, London.

16. William Shoveller - Burial, 10 Jun 1846, All Souls, Kensal Green, Kensington and Chelsea (London, England, Church of England Deaths and Burials, 1813-1980).

17. Robert Bowyer - Death notice (The Belfast Newsletter, 17 June 1834, p.3).

18. Robert Bowyer - Death notice (Gentleman's Magazine, n.s, ii, 1834, p.221).

19. Catherine Andras - Will, 1837 (England & Wales, Prerogative Court of Canterbury Wills, 1384-1858 [PROB 11: Will Registers [1839-1841], Piece 1910: Vaughan, Quire No 251-300 (1839)).

20. John Shoveller L.L.D., Appointed under Letters Patent (Hereford Journal, 21 Sept 1836).

21. John Shoveller, LLD - Appointment as Commissioner to the General Registrar Office (Staffordshire Advertiser, 17 Dec 1836).

22. Great Britain, by Commissioners Appointed, (1838). "Report of the Commissioners Appointed to inquire into the state, custody and authenticity of certain non-parochial register or records of births or baptisms, deaths or burials, and marriages in England and Wales." George Edward Eyre & William Spottiswoode, London.

23. John Shoveller LLD (father) - 4th Aug 1837, op. cit.

24. John Shoveller, LLD - Appointment as Commissioner to the General Registrar Office (Hereford Journal, 21 Sept 1836).

25. Christina Colvin, Janet Cooper, N H Cooper, P D A Harvey, Marjory Hollings, Judith Hook, Mary Jessup, Mary D Lobel, J F A Mason, B S Trinder and Hilary Turner, 'Banbury: Churches', in A History of the County of Oxford: Volume 10, Banbury Hundred, ed. Alan Crossley (London, 1972), pp. 95-120. British History Online http://www.british-history.ac.uk/vch/oxon/vol10/pp95-120 [accessed 4 December 2022].

26. General Registry Office - John Shoveller Sr. - Death Certificate, 9th Jan 1847 issued by the ministry he helped to establish (GRO, Banbury, County of Oxford & Northampton).

27. John Shoveller - Will, 6 Dec 1846 (England & Wales, Prerogative Court of Canterbury Wills, 1384-1858. PROB: 11, Will Registers; 1845-1847; Piece: 2051: Vol.4, Quire No. 151-200, 1847).

28. Sue Sheridan Walker, 'Proof of Age in Feudal Heirs in Medieval England' (published in Mediaeval Studies, Vol.34, 1973, p.307).

29. 1851 England & Wales Census - John Shoveller Jr. & family (1851 England Census - Class: HO107; Piece: 1510; Folio: 347; Page: 29; GSU Roll: 87844).

30. Elizabeth Shoveller (nee Eastman) - Death notices (Hampshire Telegraph, 24th July 1852, p.5 & London Standard, 24th July 1852).

31. "About us". www.biblesociety.org.uk. Archived from the original on 5 July 2012. Retrieved 30 March 2017. [https://web.archive.org/web/20120705142911/http://www.biblesociety.org.uk/about-bible-society/why-we-exist/].

32. "Our timeline". Bible Society. Archived from the original on 6 April 2016. Retrieved 26 November 2010.

33. Wikipedia - General Register Office for England and Wales [https://en.wikipedia.org/wiki/General_Register_Office_for_England_and_Wales].

34. John Shoveller - Will, 6 Dec 1846, op. cit.

Chapter Fifteen

THE DESCENDANTS OF
JOHN SHOVELLER & ELIZABETH EASTMAN

At the time of John and Elizabeth Shoveller's 1812 marriage, the threat of Britain's invasion by Napoleon's armies had subsided, but the war against France was still rampant and carried on until the 18th June 1815, when the Duke of Wellington delivered victory for Britain and the allies at the Battle of Waterloo. Coincidentally, it was during this beleagured time that the Shoveller's began producing their family. Notably, all of the Shoveller children were baptised by the Rev. John Griffin of the Independent Church at King Street (formerly Orange St.) in Portsea. The following information is what is known to date about each of John and Elizabeth Shoveller's ten children and their descendants (*see Pedigree Chart 7*).

1. Sarah Sabine Shoveller (1812-1813)

Sarah Sabine Shoveller was the first of the family and was born on the 21st December 1812. The infant daughter was baptised on the 30th January 1813 at homr home under authority of the Independent Chapel, King Street (formerly Orange St.), Portsea, and given the maternal family name of Sabine, but she unfortunately died just three weeks later on the 21st February 1813, and was buried at Portsea.[1,2]

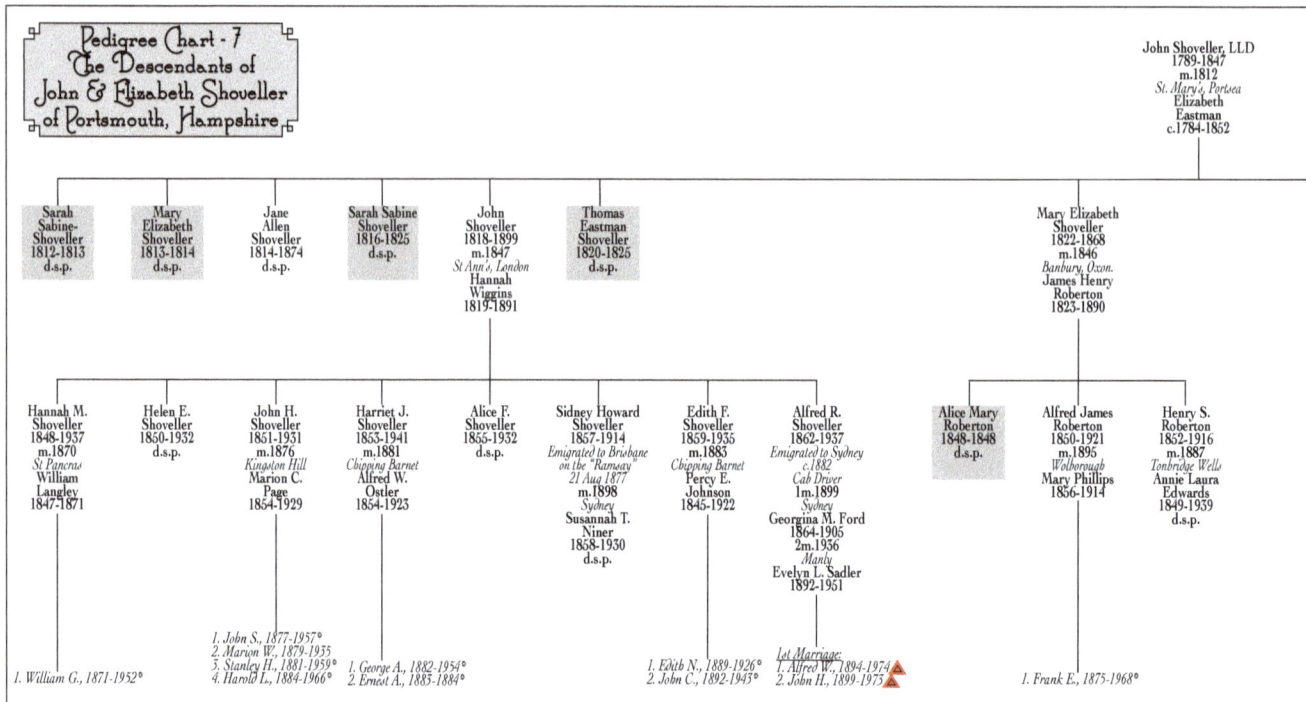

Pedigree Chart - 7
The Descendants of
John & Elizabeth Shoveller
of Portsmouth, Hampshire

John Shoveller, LLD
1789-1847
m.1812
St. Mary's, Portsea
Elizabeth
Eastman
c.1784-1852

Sarah Sabine-Shoveller 1812-1813 d.s.p.	Mary Elizabeth Shoveller 1813-1814 d.s.p.	Jane Allen Shoveller 1814-1874 d.s.p.	Sarah Sabine Shoveller 1816-1825 d.s.p.	John Shoveller 1818-1899 m.1847 *St Ann's, London* Hannah Wiggins 1819-1891	Thomas Eastman Shoveller 1820-1825 d.s.p.			Mary Elizabeth Shoveller 1822-1868 m.1846 *Banbury, Oxon.* James Henry Roberton 1823-1890		

| Hannah M. Shoveller 1848-1937 m.1870 *St Pancras* William Langley 1847-1871 | Helen E. Shoveller 1850-1932 d.s.p. | John H. Shoveller 1851-1931 m.1876 *Kingston Hill* Marion C. Page 1854-1929 | Harriet J. Shoveller 1853-1941 m.1881 *Chipping Barnet* Alfred W. Ostler 1854-1923 | Alice F. Shoveller 1855-1932 d.s.p. | Sidney Howard Shoveller 1857-1914 *Emigrated to Brisbane on the "Ramsay" 21 Aug 1877* m.1898 *Sydney* Susannah T. Niner 1858-1930 d.s.p. | Edith F. Shoveller 1859-1935 m.1883 *Chipping Barnet* Percy E. Johnson 1845-1922 | Alfred R. Shoveller 1862-1937 *Emigrated to Sydney c.1882 Cab Driver* 1m.1899 *Sydney* Georgina M. Ford 1864-1905 2m.1956 *Manly* Evelyn L. Sadler 1892-1951 | Alice Mary Roberton 1848-1848 d.s.p. | Alfred James Roberton 1850-1921 m.1895 *Wolborough* Mary Phillips 1856-1914 | Henry S. Roberton 1852-1916 m.1887 *Tonbridge Wells* Annie Laura Edwards 1849-1939 d.s.p. |

1. *John S., 1877-1957°*
2. *Marion W., 1879-1935*
3. *Stanley H., 1881-1959°*
4. *Harold L., 1884-1966°*

1. *William G., 1871-1952°*

1. *George A., 1882-1954°*
2. *Ernest A., 1885-1884°*

1. *Edith N., 1889-1926°*
2. *John C., 1892-1943°*

1st Marriage:
1. *Alfred W., 1894-1974*
2. *John H., 1899-1975*

1. *Frank E., 1875-1968°*

SHOVELLER Jane Allen.

Effects under £300.

30 March. The Will of Jane Allen Shoveller formerly of Pulbeck Cottage Hampstead but late of Parsons-street Hendon both in the County of **Middlesex** Spinster who died 18 March 1874 at Parsons-street was proved at the **Principal Registry** by John Shoveller the Brother and John Hampden Shoveller the Nephew both of 1 Stanley-gardens Hampstead Esquires the Executors.

HAMPSTEAD POLLING DISTRICT—CONTINUED.

PARISH OF SAINT JOHN, HAMPSTEAD—continued.

6882 Shoveller, John	. . No. 5, Haverstock-terrace, House as occupier . . 5, Haverstock-terrace, Hampstead

TOP: Probate notice for Jane Allen Shoveller - 18th March 1874 (England & Wales, National Probate Calendar, 1858-1995). ABOVE: John Shoveller Jr. - Hampstead Electorate, 1863 Parish of St John, Hampstead (London, Overseer Returns, 1863-1894).

2. Mary Elizabeth Shoveller (1813-1814)

Mary Elizabeth Shoveller was born on the 7th December 1813, and baptised on the 13th February 1814 at home by Rev. John Griffin of the Independent Chapel, King Street (formerly Orange St.), Portsea, but she died three months later on the 6th May 1814.[3]

3. Jane Allen Shoveller (1814-1874)

Jane Allen Shoveller arrived on the 22nd October 1814 and was baptised on the 27th December of that year. and was named in honour of her step-grandmother Jane Shoveller (nee Allen, 1765-1827).[4] Following the death of her father John Shoveller LLD in 1847, Jane lived with her mother and remained a spinster all her life. After her mother's passing in 1852, Jane may have lived independently for a time, but by 1871 she was likely moving between her sister Mary Elizabeth, and her brothers John Shoveller Jr. in Hampstead, and William Henry Shoveller at his Paddington residence in London. Jane Allen Shoveller passed away on the 18th of March 1874, aged 60 years, leaving a will with effects under £300. The above extract provides details of her probate.

William Henry Shoveller Sr.
1824-1883
m.1854
St Pancras
Mary Ann Smith
1829-?
Emigrated to Sydney on the "Vimeira" 25 Oct 1862, but returned in 1863.

Martha Shoveller
1826-1827
d.s.p.

Thomas Eastman Shoveller
1827-1908
Emigrated to Sydney on the "Eclair" 25 Sep 1851
m.1856
Grafton, NSW
Susan Hann
1840-1919

Ellen Shoveller 1851-? m1877? *Kensington* John A. Anderson 1850-?

William Henry Shoveller Jr. 1854-1922 m.1881 *Faversham, Kent* Fanny Wise 1863-1910 *Changed surname to Walker!*

Ada Mary Shoveller 1856-1875 d.s.p.

Eva Rose J. Shoveller 1861-1862 d.s.p.

Susan Theresa Shoveller 1858-1858 d.s.p.

Susan Eva Shoveller 1859-1913 m.1879 Edward R. Meally 1861-1936

Thomas Charles Shoveller 1862-1874 d.s.p.

Leonora Shoveller 1866-1945 1m.1890 John Henry Mackie 1868-1894 2m.1900 Humphrey J. O'Sullivan 1871-1905

Janet E. A. Shoveller 1869-1870 d.s.p.

George Lorraine Shoveller 1873-1946 m.1918 *Rockdale* Mary Luney 1873-1952 d.s.p.

Mabel Susan Shoveller 1878-1945 1m.1902 William Albert Hayes 1875-1902 2m. 1903 Samuel West 1876-1928

Clarence John Hann Shoveller 1880-1940 m.1904 *Sydney* Mary E. White 1883-1952

Children of William Henry Shoveller Jr.:
1. Bessie L., 1882-1958
2. William H., 1884-1951
3. Harriet 1887-?
4. Roseanna 1888-1956
5. Frederick 1890-1956°
6. John 1894-?°
7. Arthur 1896-1961°
8. Albert E., 1901-1961°
9. Horace 1903-1951°

Children of Susan Eva Shoveller:
1. Edward C., 1879-1954°
2. Latona S., 1882-1900°
3. Eva N., 1885-1969

Children of Leonora Shoveller:
1st Marriage:
1. Valtie C., 1891-1974
2nd Marriage:
2. Melecca 1901-1901°
3. Octavia C., 1902-1976
4. Sylvia V., 1903-1914°
5. Goldie A., 1905-1982

Children of Mabel Susan Shoveller:
1. Reginald S., 1904-1951
2. Sibyl S., 1905-1987
3. Sadie M., 1906-1987

Children of Clarence John Hann Shoveller:
1. Thomas E., 1905-1961
2. Susan H., 1907-1978
3. John W., 1909-1978
4. Russell L., 1916-1995 ▲°

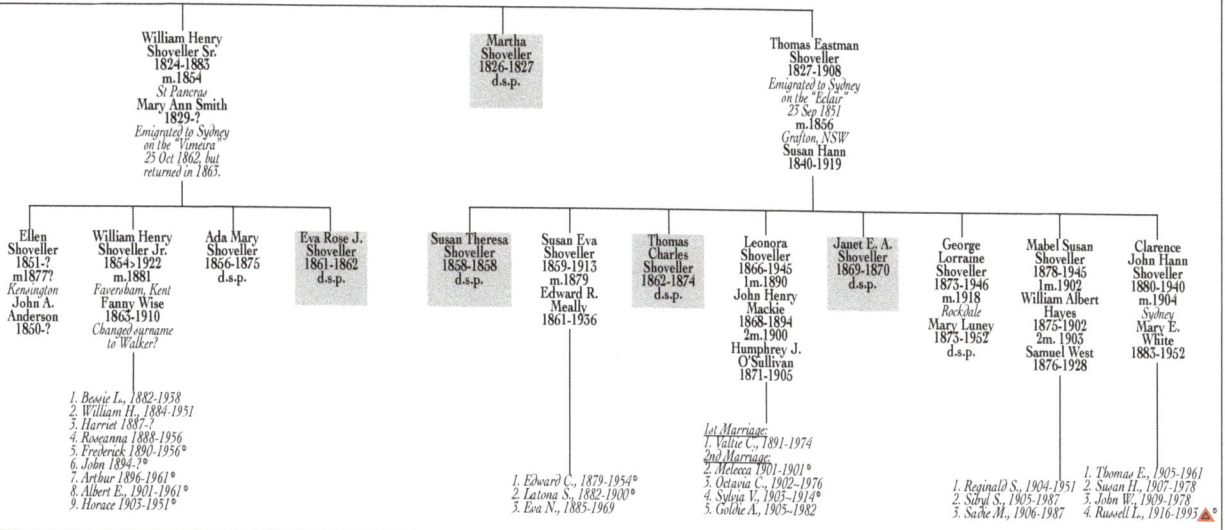

ABOVE: An etching of Hampstead Common, London about 1840, home to John Shoveller Jr. and family..

4. Sarah Sabine Shoveller (1816-1825)

With the war against France having ended in 1815, the second Sarah Sabine Shoveller was born into a relieved nation on the 19th July 1816, and she was again given the maternal family name of Sabine. Sarah was baptised at home by Rev. John Griffin of the Independent Chapel, King Street (formerly Orange St.), Portsea, on the 17th September 1816, but she sadly died at the age of 8 years and 6 months on the 6th January 1825.[5,6] Her death would no doubt have been a dreadful loss to the family, and this event may have been a reason for the Shoveller's relocation to Warnford the next year.

John Shoveller Jr. & Family

184_. Marriage solemnized _at the Church_ in the _Register of _____ in the County of London_

No.	When Married.	Name and Surname.	Age.	Condition.	Rank or Profession.	Residence at the Time of Marriage.	Father's Name and Surname.	Rank or Profession of Father.
334	_May 18th_	_John Shoveller_	_full_	_Bachelor_	_Government Service_	_Finsbury Place_	_Revd. Thos. Shoveller_	
		Hannah Wiggins	_full_	_Spinster_			_William Wiggins_	

Married in the _Parish Church_ according to the Rites and Ceremonies of the _Church of England by Licence_ by me,

This Marriage was solemnized between us, _John Shoveller / Hannah Wiggins_ in the Presence of us,

John Shoveller Jr.
England & Wales Census [48]

1851
Place: St John, Hampstead, ENG.
Residence: Haverstock Terrace
Head of House: John Shoveller
Estimated Age: 32
Occupation: Proprietor of Houses
Reg. District: Hampstead
Folio: 20/HO107/1492-40
Residents: Hannah, wife (32)
Hannah M., dau. (2)
Helen E., dau. (1)
Elizabeth Shoveller, Mother, Visitor (67)
Mary Thorogood, Servant (32)

1861
Place: St John, Hampstead, ENG.
Residence: Haverstock Terrace
Head of House: John Shoveller
Estimated Age: 42
Occupation: Scholar
Reg. District: Hampstead
Folio: 18/RG09/93-81
Residents: Hannah, wife (42)
Hannah M., dau. (12)

Helen E., dau. (11)
John H., son (9)
Harriet J., dau. (7)
Alice F., dau. (5)
Sidney H., son (3)
Edith F., dau. (1)
Mary Ann Charlotte, Servant (26)
Pricilla Stratford, Servant (23)

1871
Place: St. John, Hampstead, ENG.
Head of House: John Shoveller
Estimated Age: 52
Occupation: Reg. Gen. Dept. Agent
Enumeration District: 15
Entry: 18
Residents: Hannah, wife (52)
Helen E., dau. (21)
John H., son (19)
Harriet J., dau. (17)
Alice F., dau. (15)
Sidney H., son (13)
Edith F., dau. (11)
Alfred R., son (9)
Jane Baker, Servant (28)
Susanna Raven, Servant (22)

1881
Place: Chipping Barnet, Herts., ENG.
Residence: Station Road
Head of House: John Shoveller
Estimated Age: 62
Occupation: H.M. Civil Serv, Reg. Gen. Dept.
Registration District: Barnet
Folio: 84/RG11/1369-77
Residents: Hannah, wife (62)
Hannah M. Langley, dau. (32)
Helen E., dau. (31)
Harriet J., dau. (27)
Alice F., dau. (25)
Florence E., dau. (21)
William Langley Jr., g'son (10)
Florence Donisthorpe, Visitor (22)
Amy Lipscombe, Servant (28)
Esther Boulton, Servant (18)

1891
Place: Holdenhurst, Hampshire. ENG.
Ecclesiastical Parish: St Peters
Residence: Alumhurst Road
Occupation: Ret. Super'dent, Reg. Gen. Dept.
Head of House: John Shoveller
Estimated Age: 72
Registration District: Christchurch
Folio: 39/RG12/901-33
Residents: Hannah, wife (72)

Post Office London Directory > 1845

Shoveller John, Gen. Register Off

May 18, Mr. John Shoveller, of Finsbury Place and Banbury, wine Merchant, to Hannah, second daughter of the late Wm. Wiggins, Esq., of High-wood House Hendon.

On the 3d inst., at Haverstock-terrace, Hampstead, Mrs. Shoveller, of a daughter.

LANGLEY—SHOVELLER.—On the 12th inst., at Haverstock Chapel, Maitland Park, (by the Rev. John Nunn, assisted by the Rev. F S. Attenborough, of Leamington,) William Langley, Esq., of Leicester, to Hannah Mary, eldest daughter of John Shoveller, Esq., of Hampstead.

SHOVELLER—PAGE—At Christ Church, New Malden, Mr. John H. Shoveller, of Park-road-villas, Norbiton, to Marion C., daughter of Mr. James Page, of Coombe, Surrey, June 29.

OSTLER—SHOVELLER.—11th inst., at the Baptist Chapel, New Barnet, by the Rev. John Nunn, Minister of Haverstock-hill Chapel, Alfred William Ostler, of Cheltenham-villas, Bournemouth, to Harriet Jessie, third daughter of John Shoveller, of Westmeon, New Barnet.

JOHNSON—SHOVELLER.—On the 6th inst., at the Congregational Church, New Barnet, by the Rev. John Nunn, minister of Haverstock-hill Chapel, Percy E. Johnson, of 179, Dalston-lane, Clapton, to Edith Florence, youngest daughter of John Shoveller, Westmeon, New Barnet.

The Registrar General

General Register Office, June 23rd, 1869.
SIR,—I am directed by the Registrar General to acknowledge the receipt of your letter of the 21st inst., enclosing a return showing your qualification for the Superintendent Register, and in reply to that part which refers to the Register Office, to state that if the convenience for registration purposes will be best secured by the establishment of the office in an easily accessible position within the limits of the district, he will not object to it. The 12th section of the amendment act, 1 Vic. cap. 22, provides for cases such as appear to exist in Lunesdale. The Registrar-General will be glad to receive a ground plan sketch of the proposed office, with an assurance that it is free from damp and capable of being securely closed.
When he has approved of the office he will give the necessary directions for the transfer of such records as should be deposited under your care.
Enclosed herewith are forms to enable you to appoint a deputy.—I am, sir, your obedient servant.
JOHN SHOVELLER,
Pro. Secretary.

TOP: Marriage certificate for John Shoveller Jr. & Hannah Wiggins on the 18th May 1847 at St Andrew By The Wardrobe Church, London (from London C of E Marriages and Banns 1754-1937). MID: John Shoveller Jr., Census Returns' for England & Wales (1851, 1861, 1871, 1881, 1891). ABOVE (Left Column): 1-John Shoveller Jr. with the Civil Service - Gen. Registrar Office (1845 Post Office Directory, London); 2-John Shoveller Jr. & Hannah Wiggins - Marriage announcement (Oxford Chronicle & Reading Gazette, 22 May 1847); 3-Helen Elizabeth Shoveller - Birth (Morning Chronicle, 7 Jan 1850, p.8); 4-Hannah Mary Shoveller & William Langley Sr. - Marriage announcement (Leamington Spa Courier, 21 May 1870, p.5); 5-John Hampden Shoveller & Marion Charlotte Page - Marriage announcement (Pall Mall Gazette, 30 June 1876, p.3); 6-Harriett Jessie Shoveller & Alfred William Ostler - Marriage announcement (Hertford Mercury & Reformer, 14 May 1881. (Right Column): 1-Edith Florence Shoveller & Percy E. Johnson - Marriage announcement (Morning Post, 10 Sept 1883); 2-John Shoveller Jr. as Pro Secretary of the Office of General Registrars - 23 June 1869 (Lancaster Gazette, 3 July 1869).

5. John Shoveller Jr. (1818-1899)

Next to arrive on the 10th June 1818, was their first son John Shoveller Jr., who was baptised at home by the Rev. John Griffin of the Independent Chapel, King Street (formerly Orange St.), at Portsea, on the 14th July 1818.[7] Further mentions of John Shoveller Jr. are recorded in both the will of his father, and in the probate notice of his sister Jane Allen Shoveller.[8,9] Following the Napoleonic Wars the Industrial Revolution shifted into high gear, and incredible technological leaps were made in steam power. Indeed, the year after the birth of John Jr saw the "SS Savannah" make the first paddle steamship crossing of the Atlantic.

While John Shoveller Jr. received an excellent education under the tutelage of his father, little information of his youth has been found, except records reveal that he married just four months after the death of his father, on the 18th May 1847 at St. Ann's Blackfriars, London to Hannah (1819-1891), the daughter of William Wiggins and Rebecca Gulley of Buckland, Berkshire.[10] Following the death of her father in February 1846, Hannah was bequeathed a £50 annual inheritance from a trust established by her father.[11]

While he worked as a wine merchant for some years, John Shoveller Jr. followed in his

SHOEVELLER John of Alumhurst-road Bournemouth died 19 December 1899 Probate London 3 February to Percy Emanuel Johnson gentleman Helen Elizabeth Shoeveller spinster and William Langley architect Effects £6697 2s. 1d.

▲TOP: Probate notice for John Shoveller Jr. - 19th Dec 1899 (England & Wales, National Probate Calendar, 1858-1995). MID: Marriage certificate for John Hampden Shoveller [grandson of John & Elizabeth Shoveller] & Marian Charlotte Page on the 29th June 1876 at Christ Church, New Malden & Coombe, Surrey (from Surrey C of E Marriage and Banns 1754-1937). ABOVE: Haverstock Terrace, Hampstead, residence of John Shoveller Jr. and his sizeable family.

▲ *Somerset House, London, the home of the General Registrar's Office from 1837, for almost 150 years, and workplace of John Shoveller Jr.*

fathers footsteps when he took up a career with the General Registrars Office. In 1844, under George Graham Esq. (Registrar General) John Shoveller Jr. was working as a Clerk, 2nd Class, at 7 and 8 Somerset Place, and also as a Clerk with the Non-Parochial Register Office at Rolls Yard, Chancery Lane, London.[12] By 1870 he had progressed in His Majesty's Civil Service to the post of Pro-Secretary in the General Registrars Office, responsible for birth, marriage and death registrations across all of England and Wales.[13]

John Shoveller Jr. and his family resided at Haverstock Terrace in fashionable Hampstead during the 1850's and 60's, which were terraces in the Grecian-style, built in 1825-26. Almost all the 38 houses on the estate had been completed by 1830, and were occupied by 'persons of quality' with stabling. John and Hannah Shoveller produced eight children, of which six married, and all survived to adulthood *(see 15.1 Descendants of John Shoveller Jr. & Hannah Wiggins)*. Hannah died in late 1891,[14] and John Shoveller Jr. died aged 81 on the 19th December 1899, having moved to Alumhurst Road, Bournemouth.[15]

6. Thomas Eastman Shoveller (1820-1825)

The sixth child of John and Elizabeth Shoveller, was Thomas Eastman Shoveller, who was born on the 11th April 1820. He was baptised by Rev. John Griffin of the Independent Chapel, King Street (formerly Orange St.), Portsea, on the 8th September 1820 and given his mother's paternal family name of Eastman, but he sadly died aged 5, on the 18th June 1825, and was probably buried at Portsea, the second child of John and Elizabeth Shoveller's children to die that year.[16]

7. Mary Elizabeth Shoveller (1822-1868)

Mary Elizabeth Shoveller was born on the 14th March 1822, and baptised by Rev. John Griffin of the Independent Chapel, King Street (formerly Orange St.), Portsea, on the 7th June 1822.[17] Mary survived infancy and was married just four months prior to her father's death, on the 29th September 1846 by the Rev. Thomas Mardon at Banbury, Oxfordshire to her first cousin James Henry (1823-1890), the son of James Roberton and her aunt Elizabeth Shoveller of Portsea, Hampshire.[18]

Stanley Howard Shoveller (1881-1959) [52]

Stanley Howard Shoveller was educated at Kingston Grammar School and was one of the pioneers of hockey at the school in 1897-98. He joined Hampstead Hockey Club aged 18 and was selected for Surrey a year later. Shoveller won the first of his 29 England caps in 1902 and captained the side for more than 10 years until his retirement in 1921 at the age of 40. He scored 76 career goals for England.

Shoveller played for his school 1st XI, which is now Kingston Grammar School, from the age of 14 and was a prolific goal scorer. He was playing for Hampstead Hockey Club before he left school and for Middlesex the year after leaving school. He first played for England three years later (1902) at the age of 21, which was very young in those days. In the following 19 years he played 35 times for England. He also fought in WW1, rising to the rank of captain and was decorated.

His international hockey career spanned two Olympics, London (1908) and Antwerp (1920), winning gold medals in both. That in itself is an achievement unlikely to be equalled again by a British player. His official England record shows that he scored 79 goals in 35 appearances, including 17 hat-tricks. That is an average of more than 2 goals per match. It is possible that this tally could be posthumously increased as 'Shove,' as he was affectionately known, captained the England team that played in an international tournament in Hamburg in 1912 as a substitute for there being no hockey at the Stockholm Olympics. At this event he scored four times against Germany and three against Austria, but at present these two matches do not appear in the England records.

To make Shoveller's record even more remarkable, he did not play in 23 England matches because his work as a stockbroker did not give him the freedom to do so. What an amazing record it might have been had he played in all the 60 matches of his era. No wonder he was called the 'W. G. Grace' of his time, which would qualify him to be the greatest English hockey player ever!

Stanley Howard Shoveller became a successful stockbroker on the London Stock Exchange. He served as a captain with the Rifle Brigade 33rd London Regiment during WWI and in 1915 was awarded the Military Cross. [49,50,51]

A BRITISH HOCKEY HERO

MR. S. H. SHOVELLER, ENGLAND'S HOCKEY CENTRE FORWARD

Although barely twenty-three years of age, Mr. Stanley Howard Shoveller is undoubtedly the most brilliant centre forward at hockey in the country. He is a native of Kingston, but plays for the Hampstead Hockey Club. He learnt the game at Queen Elizabeth's School, Kingston, represented Middlesex in 1899 and 1900, and since then has appeared for Surrey. Mr. Shoveller was first selected for the South in 1901, and has played centre forward for England since 1902.

Copyright, "C. B. Fry's Magazine."

▲TOP: Profile of Stanley Howard Shoveller (C.B. Fry's Magazine, undated). ABOVE: The England Olympic gold medal winning hockey team of 1908, with Stan Shoveller (circled).

▲LEFT: Harold Langley Shoveller & Stanley Howard Shoveller, both great grandsons of John & Elizabeth Shoveller. RIGHT: The Hampstead Hockey Team, c.1912 (Standing): C.H. Eiloart, H. R. Hebert, Back): R. A. Hill, F.W. Orr, E.L. Marsden, J.H. Gunner. (Sitting): R.E. Eiloart, G. Logan, S. H. Shoveller, R.H. Preeston, M. Sherwell.

15.1 Descendants of John Shoveller Jr. & Hannah Wiggins [53]

John SHOVELLER Jr. (1818-1899), married on the 18th May 1847 at St Ann's Blackfriars, London to Hannah (1819-1891), the daughter of William Wiggins & Rebecca Gulley, with issue:

1. Hannah Mary Shoveller (1848 - 1937), was born and baptised in 1848, in the St Lukes District, London. Hannah married on the 12th May 1870 to William LANGLEY Sr. (1847-1871), an architect at Maitland Park, with issue.

1. William LANGLEY Jr. (1871 - ?), died unmarried.

2. Helen Elizabeth Shoveller (1850 - 1932), was born at Haverstock Terrace, Hampstead, and baptised in 1850, but apparently remained a spinster with her family. She lived and died at Bournemouth with her sister Alice.

3. John Hampden Shoveller (1851 - 1931), was born at Haverstock Terrace, Hampstead, and baptised in 1851. He apparently also worked with the Registrar Generals Office (1888). He was married on the 29th June 1876 to Marion Charlotte Page (1854-1929) at Christchurch, New Malden, Kingston, Surrey, with issue:

3.1 John Sydney SHOVELLER (1879 - 1957). Dentist. He married in 1915 to either Mary I. Scully or Mabel Taplin. Issue unknown.

3.2 Marian Winifred Shoveller (1879 - 1935). She was born at Kingston Hill, Surrey in 1879, and married in 1903 to Bertram Waller ATTLEE (1870-1950) at St Lukes Church, Kingston-on-Thames, who was a cousin of Clement Attlee (1883-1967), Prime Minister of Great Britain from 1945 to 1951, with issue:
a. John Bartram Shoveller ATTLEE (1904 - ?). He married in 1932 to either Violet E. Cross or Mabel Smith.
b. Unknown (? - ?)

3.3 Stanley Howard SHOVELLER (1881 - 1959). Stockbroker. English hockey player. He is the only Englishman to win two Olympic gold medals for hockey in 1908 and 1920. He married in 1938 to Vera Mary (1888-1972), only daughter of Sir Henry Smith, no issue.

3.4 Harold Langley SHOVELLER (1884 - 1966). Accountant. He married in 1933 to Lily E. Rose (1910-1975). Issue unknown.

4. Harriet Jessie Shoveller (1853 - 1941), was born at Haverstock Terrace, Hampstead, and baptised in 1853. She may have died in Bath, in 1941. She was married on the 11th

May 1881 to Alfred William OSTLER (1854-1923) at New Barnet, with issue:

4.1 George Arthur OSTLER (1882-1954), married in 1914 Elsie "Bess" Frances Usher (1882-1969, no issue.

4.2 Ernest Alfred OSTLER (1883-1884),* died an infant.

5. Alice Frances Shoveller (1855 - 1932), was born at Haverstock Terrace, Hampstead, and baptised in 1855, but apparently remained a spinster with her family. She lived and died at Bournemouth with her sister Harriet.

6. Sidney Howard Shoveller (1857 - 1914), was born at Haverstock Terrace, Hampstead, and baptised in 1857. In the 1891 Census he was single, a manager at Tallow Melter & Wax Chandlers, living in Whitechapel Rd, London with a 43 year old servant by the name of Ann Poore. He emigrated to Brisbane aboard the "Ramsay" on the 21 Aug 1877, before before his marriage aged 41, to Susannah T. Niner, in Sydney in 1898 (#2262), and died in Waverley in 1914. Issue unknown.

7. Edith Florence Shoveller (1860 - ?), was born at Haverstock Terrace, Hampstead, and baptised in 1860. She was married 6th Sept. 1883 to Percy E. JOHNSON at the Congregational Church, New Barnet. Issue unknown.

8. Alfred Russell Shoveller (1862 - 1937), was born at Haverstock Terrace, Hampstead, and baptised in 1862. He emigrated to Australia sometime before 1892. He married

1stly in Sydney in 1899 (#2237, aged 37), to Georgina Maria Ford (1864 - 1905), with issue:

8.1 Alfred William SHOVELLER (1894-1974). ▲ Born in England in the Reg. District of Milton. Enlisted in the AIF for WWI. Married firstly in 1917 at Mosman (#12326) to Ruby Edwards (1895-1956). He died in 1974 (#53594), with issue:
a. Alfred John Russell SHOVELLER (1918-1975). ▲ Enlisted in the AIF for WWII. Service Number - [NX92938], Place of birth - Redfern, NSW: Place of enlistment - Paddington, NSW : Next of Kin - Ruby Shoveller.
b. Mina Olive C. Shoveller (1921-1967), unmarried, d.s.p.
c. Hazel Shoveller (?-?), issue unknown.
d. Thelma J. Shoveller (1927-?), issue unknown.

8.2 John Harold SHOVELLER (1899-1973). ▲ Born at Manly on the 16th Dec, 1899. Enlisted in the AIF for WWI. He married first in 1922 at Sydney (#4505) to Linda May Dickinson (nee Morrison, 1902-1931). He died at Tumut in 1973, and was buried at Batlow Cemetery with issue:
a. Olive Mina E. Shoveller (1923-2014), married in 1942 at Canterbury to Gordon Clarence DELANY (1918-1997), with issue.
b. John (Jack) Harold SHOVELLER (1919-?). ▲ Born 9 June 1919, Sydney. Married in 1940 to Mavis K. Nursey (1921 - 2006) (#3970) in Mosman. Enlisted in the AIF for WWII - [NX68566]. Issue unknown?
c. Roy Drew SHOVELLER (1920-1956). ▲ Born 23rd Sept 1920, Sydney. Enlisted in the AIF for WWII - [NX69452]. Married in 1948 (#14998) to Dorothy May Nye (1926-1956) at Manly. Committed suicide in 1956, 3 months after the suicide death of his wife in (# 10494). d.s.p.
d. John Alfred SHOVELLER (?-?), ▲, married in 1950 to Betty McConnell (1931-1976) issue unknown. Possibly married secondly before 1980 to Gwendoline Lorraine ?
e. Florence Shoveller (? -?), married in 1950 Manly to Alan Hugh McMurrick (# 12215), issue unknown?
Alfred Russell Shoveller married secondly (aged 74) at Manly in 1936 to Evelyn Laura Alberta Sadler, but died and was buried at Manly on the 5th Feb 1937 (Manly Cemetery - Mix S, 7), no issue:

* Died before adulthood - d.s.p.
(Some names not listed in the index).

The Robertons moved to Oxford St, Manchester, and later to 271 Cecil St, Manchester where James Henry worked as an apothecary or chemist, and they produced a family of three children. First to arrive was Alice Mary Roberton (1848-1848), at Chorlton, Lancashire in 1848,[19] but she died as an infant in the same year.[20] Alfred James Roberton (1850-1921), was born next at Chorlton, Lancashire in 1850,[21] and married in May 1895 at St Paul's, Wolborough in Devon to Mary Phillipps (1856-1914).[22] They in turn produced the only grandchild, Frank Edgar Roberton (1875-1968),[23] who married in July 1930 at Wandsworth to Grace M. Wood,[24] without issue.

#? Alfred William Shoveller (1894-1974)

Albert William Shoveller; Service Number - ??????; Date Of Birth - 1894; Place Of Birth - Manly, NSW; Place Of Enlistment - ??????; Next Of Kin - Shoveller, Alfred Russell (father); Unit - ??????. He was a great grandson of John Shoveller LLD and Elizabeth Eastman.

World War One Service

PRIVATE
ALFRED WILLIAM SHOVELLER
?

SERVICE	AUSTRALIAN ARMY
DATE OF BIRTH	1894
PLACE OF BIRTH	MANLY, NSW
DATE OF ENLISTMENT	?
LOCALITY OF ENLISTMENT	?
PLACE OF ENLISTMENT	?
NEXT OF KIN	SHOVELLER, ALFRED. R.
DATE OF DISCHARGE	?
POSTING AT DISCHARGE	?

#96101 John Harold Shoveller (1899-1973)

▼ AIF Recruits in company drill. John Harold Shoveller enrolled too late and never left Australia or saw action.

COMPANY DRILL 8TH OF THE 31ST 1918

SHOVELLER John Harold; Service Number - 96101; Year of Birth: 1899; Place of Birth - Manly NSW; Place of Enlistment - Manly NSW on 30 Sep 1918; Next of Kin - (Father) SHOVELLER Alfred Russell. He was a great grandson of John Shoveller LLD and Elizabeth Eastman.

World War One Service

PRIVATE
JOHN HAROLD SHOVELLER
96101

SERVICE	AUSTRALIAN ARMY
DATE OF BIRTH	1899
PLACE OF BIRTH	MANLY, NSW
DATE OF ENLISTMENT	30 SEPT 1918
LOCALITY OF ENLISTMENT	MANLY, NSW
PLACE OF ENLISTMENT	MANLY, NSW
NEXT OF KIN	SHOVELLER, ALFRED. R.
DATE OF DISCHARGE	31 DEC 1918
POSTING AT DISCHARGE	TRAINING BARRACKS

#NX92938 Alfred John Russell Shoveller (1918-1975)

▼ Alfred J. R. Shoveller was accepted into the Army, but prevented from active service due to poor sight.

Alfred John R. Shoveller; Service Number - NX92938; Date Of Birth - 20 May 1918; Place Of Birth - Redfern, NSW; Place Of Enlistment - Paddington, NSW; Next Of Kin - Shoveller, Ruby (mother); Unit - HQ Info Pool. He was a great great grandson of John Shoveller LLD and Elizabeth Eastman.

World War Two Service

PRIVATE
ALFRED JOHN RUSSELL SHOVELLER
NX92938

SERVICE	AUSTRALIAN ARMY
DATE OF BIRTH	20 MAY 1918
PLACE OF BIRTH	REDFERN, NSW
DATE OF ENLISTMENT	18 MARCH 1942
LOCALITY ON ENLISTMENT	BANKSTOWN EAST
PLACE OF ENLISTMENT	PADDINGTON, NSW
NEXT OF KIN	SHOVELLER, RUBY
DATE OF DISCHARGE	10 DECEMBER 1943
POSTING AT DISCHARGE	INF POOL

Australian Government
Department of Veterans' Affairs

#NX68566 John Harold Shoveller Jr. (1919-?)

▼ *Australian 2/4th Infantry Battalion carriers at Baalbek in Syria, 1941. (AWM photo #021259).*

John Harold Shoveller; Service Number - NX68566; Date Of Birth - 9 June 1919; Place Of Birth - Sydney, NSW; Place Of Enlistment - Manly, NSW; Next Of Kin - Shoveller, John (father). He was a great great grandson of John Shoveller LLD and Elizabeth Eastman.

World War Two Service

PRIVATE
JOHN HAROLD SHOVELLER
NX68566

SERVICE	AUSTRALIAN ARMY
DATE OF BIRTH	9 JUNE 1919
PLACE OF BIRTH	SYDNEY, NSW
DATE OF ENLISTMENT	10 MARCH 1941
LOCALITY ON ENLISTMENT	MANLY, NSW
PLACE OF ENLISTMENT	PADDINGTON, NSW
NEXT OF KIN	SHOVELLER, JOHN
DATE OF DISCHARGE	20 FEBRUARY 1946
POSTING AT DISCHARGE	2/4 AUSTRALIAN INFANTRY BATTALION

Australian Government
Department of Veterans' Affairs

#NX69452 Roy Drew Shoveller (1920-1956)

▼ *Troops from the 2/4th Battalion attack around Wewak, PNG with tank support, 10th May 1945.*

Roy Drew Shoveller; Service Number - NX69452; Date Of Birth - 23 Sep 1920; Place Of Birth - Sydney, NSW; Place Of Enlistment - Manly, NSW; Next Of Kin - Shoveller, John (father). He was a great great grandson of John Shoveller LLD and Elizabeth Eastman.

World War Two Service

PRIVATE
ROY DREW SHOVELLER
NX69452

SERVICE	AUSTRALIAN ARMY
DATE OF BIRTH	23 SEPTEMBER 1920
PLACE OF BIRTH	SYDNEY, NSW
DATE OF ENLISTMENT	10 MARCH 1941
LOCALITY ON ENLISTMENT	MANLY, NSW
PLACE OF ENLISTMENT	PADDINGTON, NSW
NEXT OF KIN	SHOVELLER, JOHN
DATE OF DISCHARGE	13 FEBRUARY 1946
POSTING AT DISCHARGE	2/4 AUSTRALIAN INFANTRY BATTALION

Australian Government
Department of Veterans' Affairs

#? John Alfred Shoveller (c.1925-1997)

John Alfred Shoveller; Service Number - ??????; Date Of Birth - c.1925; Place Of Birth - Manly, NSW; Place Of Enlistment - ??????; Next Of Kin - Shoveller, John Harold (father); Unit - ??????. He was a great great grandson of John Shoveller LLD and Elizabeth Eastman.

World War Two Service

PRIVATE
JOHN ALFRED SHOVELLER
?

SERVICE	AUSTRALIAN ARMY
DATE OF BIRTH	1925
PLACE OF BIRTH	MANLY, NSW
DATE OF ENLISTMENT	?
LOCALITY OF ENLISTMENT	?
PLACE OF ENLISTMENT	?
NEXT OF KIN	SHOVELLER, JOHN
DATE OF DISCHARGE	?
POSTING AT DISCHARGE	?

Henry Shoveller Roberton (1852-1916), was the third and final child of James Henry and Mary Elizabeth Roberton, born at Chorlton, Lancashire in 1852,[25] and he married in 1887 at Tonbridge Wells, Kent to Annie Laura Edwards (1849-1939),[26] but they were also without issue. Mary Elizabeth Roberton (nee Shoveller) died aged just 46 on 17th November 1868, and was buried in Manchester.[27,28] Her husband James Henry Roberton then moved with his two sons to St Pancras in London, before marrying secondly on the 15th January 1873 at Camden, Middlesex to another Shoveller first cousin in Hannah Mary (1827-1900), daughter of his uncle and aunt William Shoveller Sr. and Elizabeth Dunt, but without further issue.[29] James Henry Roberton died aged 67 in 1890,[30] with his second wife Hannah Mary passing away in 1900.[31]

8. William Henry Shoveller Sr. (1824-c.1883)

A third Shoveller son, William Henry Shoveller was born on the 30th April 1824, and baptised at home on the 31st December 1824 by the Rev. John Griffin of the Independent Chapel, King Street (formerly Orange St.), Portsea.[32] He moved with his parents from Portsea, then to Kilburn in London, and later married in 1854 at St. Pancras to Mary Ann

Documents of Mary Elizabeth Shoveller & Family

1846. Marriage solemnized at the Parish Church in the Parish of Banbury in the County of Oxford

No.	When Married.	Name and Surname.	Age.	Condition.	Rank or Profession.	Residence at the Time of Marriage.	Father's Name and Surname.	Rank or Profession of Father.
402	September 29"	James Roberton / Mary Elizabeth Shoveller	full / full	Bachelor / Spinster	Chemist	Charlton upon Medlock Lancashire / Horse Fair	James Roberton / John Shoveller	Gentleman / Independent Minister

Married in the Parish Church according to the Rites and Ceremonies of the Established Church by Licence by me, T. Mardon

This Marriage was solemnized between us, James Roberton / Mary Elizabeth Shoveller — in the Presence of us, John Shoveller L.L.D. / John Shoveller Junr. / Jane Allen Shoveller

On the 29th of September, at Banbury, by the Rev. Thomas Mardon, Mary Elizabeth, youngest daughter of the Rev. John Shoveller, LL.D., to Mr. John Roberton, of Manchester.

ROBERTON—EDWARDS.—Dec. 29, at Christ Church, Tunbridge Wells, Henry Shoveller Roberton, B.A., B.Sc., younger son of James Roberton, of Forest View, Battle, to Annie Laura, youngest daughter of the late Thomas Edwards, of Watford, Herts.

James Henry Roberton
England & Wales Census [54]

1851
Place:	Manchester, Lancashire
Residence:	Oxford St
Head of House:	James H. Roberton
Estimated Age:	27 (b. Portsmouth)
Occupation:	Chemist
Registration District:	Chorlton
Folio:	HO107/2220
Residents:	Mary Elizabeth, wife (27)
	Alfred J., son (0)
	Henry Jones, Assistant (18)
	Jane A. Shoveller, sister (18)
	Sarah N Des?, Servant (24)

1861
Place:	Manchester, Lancashire
Residence:	271 Cecil St
Head of House:	James H. Roberton
Estimated Age:	38 (b. Southsea)
Occupation:	Chemist (Lodger)
Registration District:	Chorlton
Folio:	70/2884/43
Residents:	Mary Elizabeth, wife (39)
	Alfred J., son (10)

Henry S., son (8)
Fanny Meyer, Lady's Maid (23)
Charles Rosenberg [Lodger] (29)

1871
Place:	St Pancras, London
Residence:	Maitland Park Rd
Head of House:	James H. Roberton
Estimated Age:	47 (b. Portsmouth)
Occupation:	Chemist (Head)
Registration District:	Pancras
Folio:	194/236/91
Residents:	Eliza Roberton, mother (69)
	Alfred J., son (20)
	Maria Shaw, Gen. Servant (24)

1881
Place:	St Pancras, London
Residence:	33 Burghley Rd
Head of House:	James H. Roberton
Estimated Age:	57 (b. Portsmouth)
Occupation:	Ret. Chemist (Head)
Registration District:	Pancras
Folio:	220/70/17
Residents:	Hannah Mary, 2nd wife (53)
	Ann Thackham, Gen. Servant (19)

▲ TOP: Marriage certificate for Mary Elizabeth Shoveller & James Henry Roberton on the 29th Sept 1846 at St Mary's Church, Banbury (from Oxfordshire, C of E Marriages and Banns 1754-1930). MID (Left): Mary Elizabeth Shoveller & John (sic.) Roberton - Marriage notice (Northampton Mercury, 3 Oct 1846, p.3). (Right): Henry Shoveller Roberton & Annie Laura Edwards - Marriage announcement (Northampton Mercury, 8th Jan 1887, p.8). ABOVE: Mary Elizabeth Roberton (nee Shoveller) Memorial headstone - 17 Nov 1868 (Greater Manchester General Cemetery, Manchester, Plot No 3, Church). ◄ James Henry Roberton, Census Returns for England & Wales (1851, 1861, 1871, 1881).

Documents of William Henry Shoveller & Family

SUBURBAN DIRECTORY.

1860 Post Office Directory, London

Shoveller William Henry, Kilburn nw

1870 Post Office Directory, London

Cumberland ter. *Bayswtr.*
(W.) *Artesian road.*

1 Hughes Thos. Essington, booksellr
2 Davidson William, artist
3 Shoveller William Henry

1875 Post Office Directory, London

Sutherland pl. *Bayswater*
(W.), *Artesian road.*
38 Shoveller William Henry

Shoveller William Henry, auctioneer, see Hooper & Shoveller

DEATH.

SHOVELLER.—On the 25th instant, Eva Rosa Jane, the infant daughter of Mr. William Shoveller, of North Grafton, aged 12 months.

FINE LIGHT COUNTER SUGAR, in sound bags of about 56 lbs. each, at 2¼d a lb. by the bag, CASH ; 3d. by the single pound. This surpasses any sugar at the price ever offered in Grafton, and is fully equal to sugar recently sold at 4d.

THOS. & WILLIAM SHOVELLER.

SPIRIT MERCHANTS. — The undermentioned gentlemen have been *Gazetted* as spirit merchants for this district :— Grafton — Messrs. Thomas Shoveller, William Henry Shoveller, Thomas Fisher, and W. B. Campbell. Casino — Messrs. John Grime, and James Stocks.

HEALTH OFFICER.

TO THE EDITOR OF THE EXAMINER.

SIR,—Will you kindly grant me space in your next impression to state that I am desirous of hearing from any gentlemen willing to co-operate with me in memorialising the Council of this Town, upon the necessity of appointing a Health Officer for the Municipality, whose duty should be the general supervision of all food offered for sale in the town. I believe such an officer much needed, and that his attentions would improve the public health.

I am, Sir, Yours, &c.,

WILLIAM H. SHOVELLER.

Economic Stores, Grafton, February 6th.

ALL ACCOUNTS DUE to WILLIAM H. SHOVELLER, are requested to be PAID to the UNDERSIGNED, at an early date.

THOMAS SHOVELLER.

In Grafton itself the parties injured are principally the main storekeepers in Prince street, although there are few streets in which some loss has not been sustained. Probably the largest amount of direct loss is Mr. W. B. Campbell, of the Clarence River Stores and Hall of Commerce, situate at the corner of Prince and Bacon streets. Messrs. Lewenthal and W. H. Shoveller, are also sufferers to a great extent, and Mr. Lawrence of the Criterion Hotel. These three gentlemen, and perhaps we may add Mr. White, are doubtless the heaviest losers. Some of the lower lands were altogether covered, such as in Duke street where the mere tops of cottages peeped above the water. Heavy loss has, we fear, been sustained at Kirchenstadt, and much timber carried away, but we do not know the amount. The bridge over Alumny Creek, known as Pound street bridge, has fallen into the gully ; and this is the only damage of a public nature known to us.

MR. WILLIAM SHOVELLER, lately from GRAFTON. You can hear from your servant that was, by writing to Mrs. SALMONDS, at Mr Holder's, Royal Oak Hotel, Braidwood.

MRS. SALMON would be glad to learn the address of Mr WM. SHOVELLER. Please address to her at Mr McGRATH'S, at 91, Gloucester-street, Sydney.

NOTICE is hereby given, that the Partnership heretofore subsisting between us, the undersigned, William Swift Hooper and William Henry Shoveller, of 10, Albion-place, Hyde Park, Middlesex, as Auctioneers, Valuers, and House Agents, was this day dissolved by mutual consent. All debts due to and owing by the said late firm will be received and paid by the said William Swift Hooper, by whom the business will be carried on.—Dated this 24th day of June, 1875.

William Swift Hooper.
William Henry Shoveller.

Business and residential listings for William Henry Shoveller Sr. from 1860-1875, ▲LEFT COLUMN: 1-William Henry Shoveller at Kilburn (1860 London Post Office Directory); 2-Death notice for William Henry Shoveller's daughter, Eva Rose Jane Shoveller, which occurred in Grafton, NSW (Clarence & Richmond Examiner, 30th Dec 1862); 3-Thos. & William Henry Shoveller - Advertisement for 'Sugar' (Clarence & Richmond Examiner, 24 March 1863, p.1). CENTRE COLUMN: 1-Thomas & William Henry Shoveller - Spirit Merchants (Clarence & Richmond Examiner, 10 Feb 1863, p.2); 2-William H. Shoveller - Health Officer (Clarence & Richmond Examiner, 10 Feb 1863, p.3); 3-William H. Shoveller - Delegating Thomas (Clarence & Richmond Examiner, 14 April 1863, p.1). RIGHT COLUMN: 1-W. H. Shoveller - Flood Victim (SMH, 5 March 1863, p.5); 2-A number of creditors left notices for William Henry Shoveller, but he had already departed for England by then; 3-Notices in search of Mr. Wm. Shoveller (SMH, 30 June 1863, p.1 & SMH, 14 July 1863, p.8); 4-William Henry Shoveller dissolves his Auctioneering partnership in London, 1875 (The London Gazette, 29 June 1875, p.3343). ABOVE: William Henry Shoveller, elder brother of Thomas, arrived in Sydney with wife and family aboard the "Vimeira" on the 25th October 1862. At the time of her launch on June 16, 1851, it was said, the "Vimeira" presented one of the most magnificent and exquisitely finished specimens of naval architecture ever produced by the shipwrights of the Wear. A 'model' of the ship was on show at the Crystal Palace during the 1851 Great Exhibition.

William Henry Shoveller Sr.
England & Wales Census [55]

1861

Place:	Willesden, M'Sex, ENG.
Residence:	Edgeware Rd, Kilburn
Head of House:	William H. Shoveller
Estimated Age:	36
Occupation:	Auctioneers Clerk
Registration District:	Hendon
Folio:	12/RG09/785-71
Residents:	Mary A., wife (32)
Ellen (10), William H. Jr. (7) & Ada (5)	

1871

Place:	Paddington, M'Sex, ENG.
Head of House:	William H. Shoveller
Estimated Age:	44
Occupation:	Auctioneer
Enumeration District:	11
Folio:	12
Residents:	Mary A., wife (42)
	Ellen, dau, (20)
William H. Jr., son, (16)	
Ada M. dau, (15)	
Jane Allen, sister (56)	
Louisa Lee, Servant (20)	

1881

Place:	Kensington, London
Residence:	Acklam Rd
Head of House:	William H. Shoveller
Place:	Kensington, M'Sex, ENG.
Residence:	Acklam Rd, Notting Hill
Head of House:	William H. Shoveller
Estimated Age:	52
Occupation:	Auctioneer
Registration District:	Kensington
Folio:	4/RG11/38-106
Residents:	Mary A., wife (56)
William H. Jr., son, (26)	

▲TOP: 1870 Photograph of the Portsmouth Point. MID 1: William Henry Shoveller Sr.- Census Returns (1861, 1871 & 1881 - Census Returns for England & Wales).MID 2: William Henry Shoveller - Charged with Arson at the Central Criminal Court, the Old Bailey, 9th January 1882 (England & Wales, Criminal Registers, 1791-1892, Middlesex). ABOVE: William Henry Shoveller - Charged with Arson, 28th Dec 1881? (UK, Calendar of Prisoners, 1868-1929, Anglesey-Yorkshire).

Smith (c.1829-?).[33] William Henry Shoveller and his wife produced four children who were all born in London. The children were Ellen (1851), William Henry (1854), Ada Mary (1856), and Eva Rose Jane Shoveller, who arrived in late 1861, just prior to the family's departure for Australia.

William Henry worked as an auctioneers clerk, but at the age of 38, he and his wife decided to emigrate to Australia to join in business with his younger brother Thomas Eastman Shoveller at Grafton, in far off New South Wales. Along with their children Ellen

▲ 'Scene in the Great Clarence Flood of 1863', painted by Conrad Wagner (c.1818-1910). The artist was born in Offenbach, Germany about 1818. He and his wife Katherine arrived in Australia on the "Caesar Goddefroy" on 31st March 1856. He set up a studio in Prince Street, Grafton and worked as a photographer and artist. His studio was later taken up by his son-in-law John W. Lindt (1845-1926). Wagner was secretary of the German Club in Grafton for quite a number of years. This painting was the subject of an original poem by Henry Kendall (1839-1882), who also spent some time in the area as clerk to a solicitor. Both the painting and the original manuscript of the poem hang in Schaeffer House, home of the Clarence River Historical Society in Grafton. Wagner died on the 1st August 1910, said to be aged 92, and was interred in the Church of England Cemetery at Waverley, Sydney. Described as a genial artist, 'the quintessence of politeness [who] wears the orthodox cap, and smokes the equally orthodox long-stem pipe', his son remarked that he was the epitome of Kendall's painter-poet, and an impractical businessman.

(11), William Henry Jr. (8), Ada (6) and Eva (1) they sailed from England aboard the "Vimeira," of 1037 tons, under Captain Swanson, which departed from the Downs, off Deal, Kent, on the 4th July and arrived in Sydney on the 25th October 1862, after 114 long days at sea.[34]

Transferring his family onto a coaster for the much shorter journey north to Grafton, William Henry immediately launched himself into business with his brother Thomas in Grafton, virtually from the day of his arrival in late October 1862, and quickly advertised himself as a storekeeper, and was also gazetted as being a spirit merchant in the district.[35,36] Sadly, after surviving the long and arduous journey to Australia, their infant daughter Eva tragically died in Grafton on Christmas Day of 1862.[37]

Right on its heels of little Eva's death, another disaster occurred for William Henry and family with the devasting Grafton floods of February 1863, where William Henry Shoveller's new trading enterprise was completely and utterly ruined.[38] Having saved themselves, but losing everything else, William Henry and his wife realised just how dangerous rural New South Wales could be. While the 'Second Battle of Fredericksburg' took place on the 3rd May 1863, in Virginia, during the American Civil War, another more personal battle loomed between William Henry and his wife Mary Ann, in Grafton. William Henry Shoveller was now intent on evading financial ruin caused by the recent floods, and likely driven by his distraught spouse, they made the difficult decision to return via the most grueling voyage to England, rather than remain in such a hostile environment.

William probably had to borrow the return passage fare to England for himself and his family from his brother Thomas, who himself had no alternative but to remain and struggle on. In what was an unusually long delay from their dates of birth, both young William Henry Jr. and Ada Mary Shoveller were baptised on the 3rd of May 1863 in Grafton, aged nine and seven years respectively,[39] likely as an 'insurance measure' prior to the exhausting and dangerous voyage that lay ahead. The very next day, William Henry Shoveller and family were listed as passengers departing from Grafton aboard the paddlesteamer "Agnes Irving" on the 4th May 1863, which arrived in Sydney two days later. From there, the Shovellers departed for England, although details of their homeward passage have not been found, the anonimity perhaps being due to William Henry Shoveller's intentions to evade his creditors.

Back in London, and eight years on, William Henry Shoveller and family were next recorded in the England and Wales Census' of 1871 and again in 1881, where William had established a partnership with William Swift Hooper as an auctioneer, valuer and house agent.[40] Then, seemingly in a moment of depression, William Henry Shoveller was charged with 'feloniously and maliciously setting fire to certain things in a building,' on the 28th December 1881, although no conviction or sentence seems to have been recorded.[41] While no information about the place or date of his death has been found, he may have been committed to an asylum, possibly in 1883?

William Henry and Mary Ann Shoveller produced four children, of which only two survived to adulthood. The eldest, Ellen Shoveller married in 1877 at Kensington to John Alexander Anderson (1850-?), although no issue came from the union. The other surviving child, William Henry Shoveller Jr., became a blacksmith and married in 1881 at Faversham, Kent, to Fanny (1862-1910), the daughter of John Wise and Elizabeth Goldsmith, and they more than made up for the lack of grandchildren by producing nine offspring, although for some unknown reason about 1883/84, they changed their name to Walker *(see 15.2 Descendants of William Henry Shoveller Sr. & Mary Ann Smith).*

15.2 Descendants of William Henry Shoveller Sr. & Mary Ann Smith [53]

William Henry SHOVELLER (1824-c.1883), married in 1854 at St Pancras, London to Mary Ann Smith (c.1829-?), with issue:

1. Ellen Shoveller (1851 - ?), was born in 1851. She married in 1877 at Kensington, to John Alexander ANDERSON, issue unknown.

2. William Henry SHOVELLER Jr. (1854 > 1922), was born on the 23rd Sep 1854 at St. Pancras, London, and became a blacksmith. He married on the 15 Apr 1881 at Faversham, Kent, to Fanny (1862-1910), the daughter of John Wise and Elizabeth Goldsmith. She was buried at Cheriton Road Cemetery, Folkestone, Kent. (N.B: This family was listed as 'WALKER' on their 1881 England & Wales Census return, with different siblings using different surnames), with issue:

2.1 Bessie Louisa Shoveller (1882-1938), married firstly c.1905 to Frederick William BLUNDEN (1885-1965), with issue:
a. Frank William BLUNDEN (1906-1971), married in 1936 to Nellie Mary Palmer (1914-2003), with issue:
  a1. Brian William BLUNDEN (1943-2016)
  a2. Colin Robert BLUNDEN (1947-1993)
b. Harriet Frances Blunden (1909-?), died unmarried.
Bessie married secondly on the 7th Jan 1911 at Folkestone, Kent, to Thomas ELLIOTT (1889-1969), with issue:
c. Dorothy L 'Doris' Elliott (1912-1998), married in 1932 to Walter Samuel Tickner (1908–1973), with issue:
  c1. Gordon ELLIOTT (1933-1998)
d. Thomas George ELLIOTT (1913-1990), married in 1939 to Joan Bishop (1918-2000), with issue:
e. Emily May Elliott (1914-?), married in 1935 to Frederick Prior HAYTER (1915-1993), with issue:

2.2 William Henry Walker [SHOVELLER] III (1884-1951), was a labourer prior to his marriage, and convicted on multiple occasions of petty thievery. He married on the 8th Feb 1904 at the Church of Annunciation, Brighton, Sussex to Francis

Caroline (1883-1966) the daughter of Cornelius Swaysland, bricklayer, with Herbert & Ellen Weedon as witnesses. He retrieved himself by joining the Royal Sussex Regiment and was promoted to Lance Corporal and awarded the War Badge & Certificate, with issue:
a. Doris Ida Gertrude Shoveller (1905-1972), married on the 8th Feb 1925 to Sidney Charles BURT (1898-1960), with issue:
  a1. Stanley Gordon BURT (1927-1992), married firstly in 1949 at Brighton, Susses to Doris F. J. Dunmore, with issue. May have married twice more with issue from each marriage.
  a2. Ronald Charles BURT (1929-2014), married 1957 at Brighton, Sussex to Daphne Aspinall, with issue.

2.3 Harriet Francis Walker [Shoveller] (1887-?), married on the 2 Nov 1911 at Montreal, Québec, Canada to Alexander Thomas BATCHELOR (1885-1947), with issue:
a. Gordon BATCHELOR (1912-1980), married in ???? to Gladys Gilmour (1913-1988), with issue:
  a1. Allan Gilmour BATCHELOR (1947-1996)

b. Elise Batchelor (1915-?), issue unknown.
c. Walter Stewart BATCHELOR (1918-1986), married in 1945 at Chelsea, London to Rose Maud Birch (1920-2005), with issue:
  c1. J. Carroll Dailey Batchelor

2.4 Roseanna Walker [Shoveller] (1888-1956), married in 1909 at Elham, Kent to Thomas James TUNBRIDGE (1888-1971), with issue:
a. Nellie Thomasina Tunbridge (1910-1995), married in Oct 1933 at Elham, Kent to Leslie D. HAYMAN (1906-1978), with issue
  a1. Ronald J. D. HAYMAN (1936-2007)
b. Violet Esther Tunbridge (1912-2007), married firstly in 1936 to Jonathan William BISCOE (1915-?), with issue:
Violet married secondly in 1957 to Peter W. SOLE (?-?), no issue.
c. Leonard Thomas TUNBRIDGE (1915-1977), no issue.

2.5 Frederick WALKER [SHOVELLER] (1890-1956), d.s.p.

2.6 John WALKER [SHOVELLER] (1894-?), d.s.p.

2.7 Arthur WALKER [SHOVELLER] (1896-1961), d.s.p.

2.8 Albert Edward WALKER [SHOVELLER] (1901-1956), d.s.p.

2.9 Horace WALKER [SHOVELLER] (1903-1951), married in 1926 to Eliza Beatrice Lilian Barnes (1906-1992), d.s.p.

3. Ada Mary Shoveller (1856 - 1875), was born on the 24th Dec 1856 at St. Pancras, London. She died in 1875 at Kensington, aged 19, no issue.

4. Eva Rose Jane Shoveller (1861 - 1862)*, was born in late 1861 at Hendon, London, but died as an infant on the 25th Dec 1862, at Grafton, NSW, d.s.p.

* Died before adulthood - d.s.p.
(Some names not listed in the index).

WILLIAM HENRY SHOVLER ...
Bound over—Hove—2nd February, 1899—
Stealing leather (as Wm. Hy. Walker).
Fined—Hove—22nd June, 1900—Stealing
ginger beer (as Wm. Hy. Walker).
Bound over—Brighton—30th Oct., 1901—
Attempted robbery from a till (as Wm.
Hy. Walker).
1 month's H.L.—Brighton—6th Aug., 1902
—On enclosed premises (as Wm. Hy.
Walker).
6 months' H.L.—Chichester County Sessions
—8th Jan., 1903—Stealing money (as
Wm. Hy. Walker).
Once fined for assault in 1902.

FOLKESTONE.

ALLEGED THEFT OF RINGS. — At the
Borough Police Court on Friday William Henry
Shoveller was charged with stealing three gold
rings from the jeweler's shop of Mr. Metherell,
Guildhall Street. Prisoner was arrested at Canterbury on Thursday morning, and when told
by P.C. Johnson what the charge was he said
he wished to plead guilty on condition that the
magistrates would settle the case as he had just
done two months. The evidence showed that
the prisoner was seen behaving suspiciously in
the prosecutor's shop in July, and when asked
what he was doing said he had come to buy
a watch key, but had dropped a shilling behind the counter. He left the shop without
purchasing anything, and subsequently three
rings were missing from a ledge at the top of
the till. On July 25th P.S. Sharpe had occasion to go to the prisoner's house, and on the
mantelpiece he found the three rings, which
had been reported to the police as having been
stolen. Prisoner asked the magistrates to deal
with the case, but they decided to send him for
trial at the quarter sessions.

▲LEFT: 'Queen Street, Portsea', c.1900, painted by an unknown artist. RIGHT: William Henry Shoveller III (1884-1951), a great grandson of John & Elizabeth Shoveller, became a petty criminal. (Above): William Henry Shoveller III (1884-1951) - List of offences from 1903 (UK, Calendar of Prisoners, 1868-1929). (Below): William Henry Shoveller III - Report of Theft (Whitstable Times & Herne Bay Herald, 24 Sept 1910, p.7).

9. Martha Shoveller (1826-1827)

Martha Shoveller was born on the 26th April 1826, and baptised just prior to moving to Warnford on the 9th June 1826 by Rev. John Griffin of the Independent Chapel, King Street (formerly Orange St.), Portsea, but she unfortunately died 11 months later on the 1st April 1827.[42]

10. Thomas Eastman Shoveller (1827-1908)

A second Thomas Eastman Shoveller was the last of John and Elizabeth Shoveller's ten children. He arrived on the 27th May 1827 at Warnford, Hampshire, and was baptised on the 11th July 1827 at his home by Rev. John Griffin of the Independent Chapel, King Street (formerly Orange St.), Portsea.[43] Thomas travelled with his family to his father's various postings, but was not mentioned individually in the will of his father, who died unexpectedly on the 9th January 1847, because he hadn't yet reached 21, the 'age of majority'.[44]

By late 1848, and at just 22 years of age, he embarked on a 'world adventure,' and eventually arrived in Sydney aboard the "Eclair" in 1851,[45] before moving north to become a pioneer of the fast developing Clarence River district of northern New South Wales. He married on the 6th March 1856 at the Anglican Church, Grafton, to Susan Hann (1840-1919),[46] the first white child born in the Clarence District, and then opened the Clarence

---

15.3 Descendants of Thomas Eastman Shoveller & Susan Hann [53]

Thomas Eastman SHOVELLER (1827-1908), was born on the 27th May 1827 at Warnford, Hampshire. He emigrated to Australia in 1851, and married in 1856 at Christ Church, Grafton to Susan Hann (1840-1919), the first white child born in the Clarence River District, with issue:

1. **Susan Theresa Shoveller (1858 - 1858)***, died an infant.

2. **Susan Eva Shoveller (1859 - 1913)**, born 1859, married in 1879 at Christ Church, Grafton to Edward R. MEALLY (1861-1936), with issue (see Chapter 20).

3. **Thomas Charles SHOVELLER (1862 - 1874)***, drowned in the Clarence River, aged 11, no issue (see Chapter 20).

4. **Lenore Shoveller (1866 - 1945)**, born 1866, married firstly in 1890 at Christ Church, Grafton to John Henry MACKIE (1868-1894), with issue (see Chap.15 & 20).
Lenore married secondly in 1900 at St Mary's Cathedral,

Shoveller | Hann

Sydney to Humphrey Joseph O'Sullivan (1871-1905), with issue (see Chapter 20).

5. **Janet E. A. Shoveller (1869 - 1870)***, died an infant.

6. **George Lorraine SHOVELLER (1873 - 1946)**, born 1873, married in 1918 at Rockdale, Sydney to Mary Luney (1873-1952), no issue (see Chapter 20).

7. **Mabel Susan Shoveller (1878 - 1945)**, born 1878, married firstly in 1902 in Sydney to William Albert HAYES (1875-?), no issue.
Following her divorce, Mabel married secondly in 1903 at Sydney, NSW to Samuel WEST (1876-1928), with issue (see Chapter 20).

8. **Clarence John Hann SHOVELLER (1880 - 1940)**, born 1880, married in 1904 at Sydney to Mary Elizabeth White (1883-1952), with issue (see Chapter 20).

* Died before adulthood - d.s.p.

▲LEFT: The 'Shoveller's Arms', East Street, Old Portsmouth, started life as the 'Three Tuns', and stood close to the Camber Dock. Owned by the Pike Brewery in the 19th century and latterly Brickwoods, the name change came about in 1905. In 1928 the pub closed and the licence was transferred to the 'Jolly Taxpayer' in Copnor (no known relationship to Shoveller's). RIGHT: Old photograph of cottages on Marlborough Row, Portsea.

River Stores with the help of his mother-in-law. Thomas and Susan produced a family of eight children, although only five reached adulthood and produced families of their own (*see Chapter 20*). After a fascinating life, and almost a century after the marriage of his parents in Portsea in 1812, the last of the Shoveller family, Thomas Eastman Shoveller died in Grafton, northern New South Wales on the 22nd May 1908.[47]

In following the descent of John Shoveller's youngest and fourth son, this genealogy next examines the fascinating life, events and descendants of Thomas Eastman Shoveller, and briefly explores the ancestry of his wife Susan Hann, in the remaining chapters of this book (*see Chapters 16-20*).

References

1. John Shoveller LLD (father) - 4th Aug 1837, Register of baptisms from the Independent Chapel, King Street (formerly Orange Street), Portsea (Portsea, Hampshire, England & Wales, Non-Conformist and Non-Parochial Registers, 1567-1936).
2. Knightroots - Sarah Sabine Shoveller, buried at Portsea, Hampshire - 26 Feb 1813, aged 2 mths (Page 2, No. 15, but may have been re-buried on the 10th May 1814 at Portsea - Page 9, No. 70) [https://www.knightroots.co.uk/parishes/titchfield]).
3. John Shoveller LLD (father) - 4th Aug 1837, op. cit.
4. John Shoveller LLD (father) - 4th Aug 1837, op. cit.
5. John Shoveller LLD (father) - 4th Aug 1837, op. cit.
6. Sarah Sabine Shoveller - Death notice (Dorset County Chronicle, 13th Jan 1825).
7. John Shoveller LLD (father) - 4th Aug 1837, op. cit.
8. John Shoveller - Will, 6 Dec 1846 (England & Wales, Prerogative Court of Canterbury Wills, 1384-1858. PROB: 11, Will Registers; 1845-1847; Piece: 2051: Vol.4, Quire No. 151-200, 1847).
9. Jane Allen Shoveller - Probate notice, 18 March 1874 (England & Wales, National Probate Calendar, 1858-1995).
10. Marriage certificate for John Shoveller Jr. & Hannah Wiggins on the 18th May 1847 at St Andrew By The Wardrobe, London (from London C of E Marriages and Banns 1754-1937).
11. William Wiggins - Probate, 5 Feb 1846, Hendon, Middlesex (England & Wales, Prerogative Court of Canterbury Wills, 1384-1858).
12. John Shoveller - (The British Imperial Calendar, on General Register of the United Kingdom, 1844, p.185).
13. John Shoveller Jr. as Pro Secretary of the Office of General Registrars - 23 June 1869 (Lancaster Gazette, 3 July 1869).
14. Hannah Shoveller (nee Wiggins) - Death registration, Dec 1891 (England & Wales, Civil Registration Death Index, 1837-1915).
15. John Shoveller Jr. - Probate notice, 19 Dec 1899 (England & Wales, National Probate Calendar, 1858-1995).
16. John Shoveller LLD (father) - 4th Aug 1837, op. cit.
17. John Shoveller LLD (father) - 4th Aug 1837, op. cit.
18. Mary Elizabeth Shoveller & James Henry Roberton - Marriage held on the 29 Sep 1846, at St Mary's Church, Banbury (from Oxfordshire, C of E Marriages and Banns 1754-1930).
19. Alice Mary Roberton - Birth registration in Mar Qtr, 1848 at Chorlton, Lancashire (England & Wales, Civil Registration Birth Index, 1837-1915 [Vol 20, p.200]).
20 Alice Mary Roberton - Death registration in Sep Qtr, 1848 at Chorlton, Lancashire (England & Wales, Civil Registration Death Index, 1837-1915 [Vol 20, p.99]
21. Alfred James Roberton - Birth registration in Dec Qtr, 1850 at Chorlton, Lancashire (England & Wales, Civil Registration Birth Index, 1837-1915 [Vol 20, p.184])

22. Alfred James Roberton & Mary Phillips - Marriage held in May 1895 at St Paul's Church, Wolborough (Devon, England, Church of England Marriages and Banns, 1754-1920 [Vol 5b, p.290]).

23. Frank Edgar Roberton - Birth registration in Dec Qtr, 1875 at Portsea Island, Hampshire (England & Wales, Civil Registration Birth Index, 1837-1915 [Vol 2b, p.449])

24. Frank Edgar Roberton & Grace M. Wood - Marriage held in July 1930 at Wandsworth, London (England & Wales, Civil Registration Marriage Index, 1916-2005 [Vol 1d, p.1721]).

25. Henry Shoveller Roberton - Birth registration in Jun Qtr, 1852 at Chorlton, Lancashire (England & Wales, Civil Registration Birth Index, 1837-1915 [Vol 8c, p.320]).

26. Henry Shoveller Roberton & Annie Laura Edwards - Marriage held in Dec Qtr 1887 at Tonbridge Wells, Kent (England & Wales, Civil Registration Marriage Index, 1837-1915 [Vol 2a, p.1093]).

27. Mary Elizabeth Roberton - Burial, 17 Nov 1868, Manchester General Cemetery, Manchester, England (UK and Ireland, Find a Grave Index, 1300s-Current).

28. Mary Elizabeth Roberton (nee Shoveller) Monument - 17 Nov 1868 (Greater Manchester General Cemetery, Manchester, Plot No 3, Church).

29. James Roberton & Hannah Mary Shoveller - Marriage, 15 Jan 1873, Whitefield's Memorial Church, Camden, Middlesex (London, England, Non-conformist Registers, 1694-1931).

30. James Roberton - Probate notice, 7 Dec 1890, Kent, England (England & Wales, National Probate Calendar, 1858-1995).

31. Hannah Mary Roberton - Death registration, June 1900, Tonbridge, Kent, England (England & Wales, Civil Registration Death Index, 1837-1915).

32. John Shoveller LLD - 4th Aug 1837, op. cit.

33. William Henry Shoveller & Mary Ann Smith - Marriage registration, Sep 1854, St Pancras, London (England & Wales, Civil Registration Marriage Index, 1837-1915).

34. Mr. & Mrs. Shoveller & 4 children - Passengers on "Vimeira" - Arrived Sydney (Sydney Mail, 25 Oct 1862, p.5).

35. Thos. & William Shoveller - Advertisement (Clarence & Richmond Examiner, 24 March 1863, p.1).

36. Thomas & William Henry Shoveller - Spirit Merchants (Clarence & Richmond Examiner, 10 Feb 1863, p.2).

37. Eva Rose Jane Shoveller - Death notice (Clarence & Richmond Examiner, 30th Dec 1862).

38. 1863 (03) William H Shoveller - Flood Victim (Empire, 5 March, p.5).

39. William Henry Shoveller Jr. (No. 21/3/32) & Ada Mary Shoveller (No .21/3/33). Baptisms held on the 3rd May 1863 at Grafton (Church of England Archives, Grafton, NSW).

40. William Henry Shoveller dissolves his Auctioneering partnership in London, 1875 (The London Gazette, 29 June 1875, p.3343).

41. William Henry Shoveller - 1882 Jan-1882 Mar, Anglesey-Yorkshire (UK, Calendar of Prisoners, 1868-1929).

42. John Shoveller LLD - 4th Aug 1837, op. cit.

43. John Shoveller LLD - 4th Aug 1837, op. cit.

44. John Shoveller LLD - Will, 6 Dec 1846, op. cit.

45. Thomas Shoveller arrived on the "Eclair" - Shipping Intelligence (Maitland Mercury & Hunter River General Advertiser, 27th Sept 1851, p.3).

46. Thomas Eastman Shoveller & Susan Hann - Marriage held on the 6 March 1856, at C of E Church, Grafton, NSW (NSW BDM #1125/43b).

47. Thomas Eastman Shoveller - Death certificate, 22 May 1908, Grafton, NSW (NSW BDM #433/1908).

48. John Shoveller Jr. - England & Wales Census for 1851, 1861, 1871, 1881 & 1891.

49. Wikipedia - Stanley Howard Shoveller [https://en.wikipedia.org/wiki/Stanley_Shoveller].

50. Olympics.com - Stanley Howard Shoveller, Biography [https://olympics.com/en/athletes/stanley-howard-shoveller].

51. The Hockey Museum - Stanley Howard Shoveller [http://www.hockeymuseum.net/index.php/news/114-hockive-facts/268-hockive-fact-16-the-greatest-ever-english-hockey-player].

52. Kingston Grammar School - Stanley Howard Shoveller [http://archive.kgs.org.uk/authenticated/Browse.aspx?BrowseID=6332&tableName=ta_featureddocuments].

53. Ancestry, (2022). Descendant data from Ancestry.com.au

54. James Roberton Jr. - England & Wales Census for 1851, 1861, 1871 & 1881.

55. William Henry Shoveller. - England & Wales Census for 1861, 1871 & 1881.

Chapter Sixteen

THOMAS EASTMAN SHOVELLER & THE GREAT ADVENTURE

John Shoveller was born in Poole, Dorset and although he had become a schoolmaster and qualified as a lawyer, by 1827 he had accepted a post as an Independent minister in the little village of Warnford, in Hampshire. His wife Elizabeth was born in Portsmouth, the daughter of Thomas Eastman, a successful cabinetmaker and auctioneer, and a devout deacon of the non-parochial Independent Church. It was in Warnford, that Elizabeth delivered their tenth child, an infant son.

On the other side of the world, the whole of Australia was claimed as British territory, when Major Edmund Lockyer formally annexed the western portion of the country in a ceremony at King George Sound on the 21st January 1827. This event was perhaps a omen of destiny as just four months later, Thomas Eastman Shoveller arrived to John Shoveller (L.L.D.) and Elizabeth Eastman, on the 27th May 1827 at Warnford, with fate having already mapped out a future for their young son in the great southern continent.[1]

Thomas was baptised soon after his birth on the 11th of July 1827 at his home by Rev. John Griffin of the Independent Chapel at King St (formerly Orange St) in Portsea.[2] Many cousins and virtually all of Thomas' siblings had been baptised at this very same church under patronage of the Rev. John Griffin.

▲ *Birth and baptism for Thomas Eastman Shoveller, son of John Shoveller & Elizabeth Eastman from the register of the Independent Chapel, King Street (formerly Orange Street), Portsea (Hampshire, England & Wales, Non-Conformist and Non-Parochial Registers, 1567-1936).*

▲TOP: *Thomas Eastman Shoveller was born on the 25th May 1827 in the sleepy Hampshire village of Warnford. ABOVE: The last home of Thomas Eastman Shoveller in England was at Banbury in Oxfordshire, which was famous for its 'Horsefair.'.*

By the time young Thomas turned three years of age on the 27th May 1830, only four of the nine siblings that preceded him had survived, with Jane Allen (15), John Jr. (11), Mary Elizabeth (8) and William Henry (6) making up his elder siblings. The causes of death for those that passed away are unknown, but living conditions in the crowded and unsanitary streets and towns of Portsmouth at the time were not ideal.

Sometime after Thomas' birth in Warnford, the Shoveller family moved back to Portsmouth. Around the time that Thomas turned ten years of age his father moved again, this time from Portsmouth to Stockwell Green in Surrey, and from there to 50 Finsbury Square in London, where he took up a position assisting with the introduction of the new Registrar Generals Department in London.[3] It was while at Finsbury Square that the family home was gutted and they had to make another move to 'North End' at St Johns Wood.[4] With his father engaged as an Independent Minister, the family were naturally immersed in religious matters and events, but in accepting another posting, John Shoveller and his family finally settled at Horsefair, Banbury in Oxfordshire.

Despite their disruptive relocations, one fact is certain, the Shoveller children were all impeccably schooled and undertook their studies under the tuition of their schoolmaster father, "who devoted himself to the education of his own children."[5]

Along with his parents and siblings, Thomas would have no doubt attended the wedding of his sister Mary Elizabeth to James Roberton on the 29th September 1846 at Banbury, in Oxfordshire. But the very next year, brought the tragic death of Thomas' father, John Shoveller L.L.D., who sadly passed away on the 9th of January 1847 at Horse Fair, Banbury, aged just 57.[6] Thomas was only 19 at the time and was not individually named in his father's will as he had not yet attained his majority, which was set at 21, when male progeny could legally claim an inheritance.

Later that same year, and just four months after the death of his father, Thomas' eldest brother John Shoveller Jr. married on the 18th May 1847 at St. Ann's Blackfriars, London to Hannah (1819-1891), the daughter of William Wiggins and Rebecca Gulley of Buckland, Berkshire.[7] Possibly not wanting to fall into matrimony too early himself, it was about this time that young Thomas thought to broaden his life experiences, and he began planning a journey to see much more of the world than just England.

▲ TOP (Left): Travelling by coach was popular across Britain until the onset of the railways during the 1840s. (Centre): A steam engine of the 'London & North Western Company Line' in 1848. (Right): The stateroom on the "Brittania" in which Charles Dickens crossed the Atlantic, in January 1842 would have been similar to Thomas Shoveller's cabin. ABOVE: Painting of the activity at London Docks around the time of Thomas Shoveller's departure from England, in November 1848.

Journey to the South Pacific

It was the legacy that had been bequeathed him through the death of his father that enabled Thomas to embark upon the adventure of his short life to date. While his elder siblings put their father's inheritance to good use in property and toward their future, Thomas was fixed on another course. Despite the well trodden path for young British gentlemen at that time being to take the 'tour of Europe,' Thomas looked much further afield to Australia, New Zealand and the Pacific Islands, which had become a more enterprising and exciting destination. Other than adventure, what motivated Thomas Eastman Shoveller, at just 21 years of age to travel to the other side of the world remains a mystery.

However, over the history of the world, every so often a happening occurs which is immediately recognized as being important by almost everyone. Such events are history's waterfalls, which suddenly channel the flow of human affairs in new directions, and one such pivotal moment was the California gold rush.

BOAT CATASTROPHE, AND THE "LALLA ROOKH" IN DISTRESS, OFF WORTHING.

▲ TOP: The "Lalla Rookh" arrived Auckland on the 18th April 1849, but was wrecked just a year later in a gale off Worthing, England. ABOVE (Left): Drawing of a moari hut, c.1850. (Right): The wide open streets of Auckland as they would have looked to Thomas Eastman Shoveller, on his arrival there in April of 1849.

▲ "The Port of Lambton Harbour, Port Nicholson, New Zealand, comprehending about one third of the water frontage of the town of Wellington." Drawn by Chas Heaphy, engraved by J. C. Armytage, c.1842.

California Gold

The first published announcement of the discovery of gold in California was made on 15th March 1848, in the San Francisco weekly newspaper 'The Californian', which quickly attracted thousands of adventurers from the eastern states of America and across the world. Could the gold rush have been the reason that Thomas Shoveller left his home and family? But why travel to San Francisco via the Pacific... why not take the shorter route across the Atlantic Ocean? His descendants are left only to second guess his motivations and intentions. Fortunately Thomas left an evidence trail that has allowed researchers to piece together his travels over 170 years later.

With the richness of the California diggings being confirmed by December 1848, young men throughout the settled parts of the United States and elsewhere began making plans to set out for the fabulous foothills of the Sierra Nevada. But at that time there were only two realistic routes to California from the eastern United States or Europe, and both were by sea. Although trails across the continent from the Missouri River to California, would eventually carry the greatest number of emigrants, they were closed by snow when news of the gold discovery reached the eastern United States, and it was not feasible to start out by land before late April and May of 1849.

Voyaging by sea was necessary, but there were arguments for and against each of the two principal sea routes. The first route was around Cape Horn to San Francisco Bay. The Cape Horn journey took more time, but it was less complicated in that passengers remained in the same ship all the way. Although part of the course lay through notoriously rough seas, events proved that travellers that chose this route were more certain of reaching California alive and in good health.

The other sea route was via some port on the coast of Mexico or Central America, trekking overland to the Pacific, and then by sea once more to California. There were

Charles Philippe Hippolyte de Thierry [25]

Charles Philippe Hippolyte de Thierry (April 1793 – 8 July 1864) was a nineteenth-century adventurer who attempted to establish his own sovereign state in New Zealand in the years before British annexation.

De Thierry was from a French family that had fled to England following the revolution. He claimed to have been born in 1793 while his parents were fleeing, probably in Grave in the Netherlands. Upon reaching England, his father Charles Antoine de Thierry, claimed the title of Baron Nasher.

De Thierry was enrolled at Magdalen College, Oxford, and claimed to have transferred to a college of the University of Cambridge. There, he met Hongi Hika, the Ngāpuhi Moari chief who was visiting England, and the missionary Thomas Kendall. De Thierry subsequently arranged a purchase of 40,000 acres (16,000 ha) at Hokianga, in Northland, NZ, through Kendall while at Cambridge. The land was bought for the price of about 500 muskets plus powder and ball which de Thierry sent to Sydney, Australia. Hongi Hika uplifted the weapons on his return to Sydney. It was this act that ignited the inter-iwi and inter-hapu Musket Wars in New Zealand, which continued until about 1842.

After travels in North America and the Caribbean, de Thierry came to the Pacific in 1835. In the Marquesas Islands, he announced himself King of Nuku Hiva. By 1837, de Thierry had reached Sydney, where he recruited some colonists to join him in his New Zealand possessions. Arriving at Hokianga, the local Maori rangatira (chiefs) Tāmati Wāka Nene and Eruera Maihi Patuone, rejected his claims, but he was allowed to settle. His settlement was a failure. De Thierry continued to agitate for a French colony led by himself, but this activity was curtailed by the signing of the Treaty of Waitangi in 1840.

During the war of 1845–46 in the north of New Zealand de Thierry moved to Auckland, where he lived in poor circumstances until 1850. In February 1850 he sailed for California, two of his sons having preceded him to the goldfields, but on the way was marooned for a month on Pitcairn Island. After six months at San Francisco, he called at Honolulu in December 1851 and was appointed to the staff of the French consulate, where he served for nearly two years.

In May 1853 de Thierry left Honolulu and returned to Auckland to pursue his land claims and eke out a living teaching music and tuning pianos. His wife died in Auckland in 1856. He became a friend of Bishop J. B. F. Pompallier and Governor Sir George Grey, and between 1854 and 1857, at Grey's urging and with his financial support, began an autobiography in which he presented himself as the principal pioneer colonist of New Zealand, idealistic and misunderstood. In business he experimented in flax processing, and manufactured millboard. By 1860 he had achieved some degree of financial success. He died suddenly in Auckland on the 8th July 1864.

▲ *Baron Charles Philippe Hippolyte de Thierry, with whom Thomas Eastman Shoveller shared a four month voyage throughout the islands of the Pacific in 1850.*

several isthmian crossings that were theoretically feasible: Panama, Nicaragua, Guatemala, Tehuantepec, and Central Mexico. Of these however, only the Panama crossing received extensive use during the gold rush. Although it required longer sea voyages than the other isthmian crossings, traversing Panama offered the shortest land journey, and arrangements to facilitate the journey from sea to sea were more complete. However, the principal drawbacks of this route lay in the climate and hardships of travel on the isthmus, and the insufficiency of ships in the Pacific to carry passengers from Panama to San Francisco.

Of the passengers arriving at San Francisco in 1849 almost 16,000 had sailed around Cape Horn, as compared with 6,500 by way of Panama.[8] But for Europeans, was there another route? Was it possible to round the bottom of Africa, travel via Australia or New Zealand and onward past the Pacific Islands to San Francisco? Not really... so it is likely that Thomas' initial intention was not to fossick for gold, but perhaps he hoped to combine prospecting with a journey of adventure.

As time went it is clear that he significantly altered his plans. What is certain is that Thomas was tearfully farewelled by his mother, brothers and sisters in late 1848, when he embarked aboard the 375 ton barque "Lalla Rookh" heading for New Zealand. Under Captain Harris, the ship sailed from London for Auckland, New Zealand on the 5th November 1848,[9] a destination so far from England that you couldn't go any further without commencing the journey home.

> "The name Lalla Rookh or Lala-Rukh is a term of endearment frequently used in Persian poetry, meaning 'tulip cheeked.' Engaged to the young king of Bukhara, Lalla Rookh goes forth to meet him, but falls in love with Feramorz, a poet from her entourage. The bulk of the work consists of four interpolated tales sung by the poet: "The Veiled Prophet of Khorassan" (loosely based upon the story of Al-Muqanna), "Paradise and the Peri", "The Fire-Worshippers", and "The Light of the Harem". When Lalla Rookh enters the palace of her bridegroom she swoons away, but revives at the sound of a familiar voice. She awakes with rapture to find that the poet she loves is none other than the king to whom she is engaged."
>
> *Encyclopedia Brittanica*[10]

It is uncertain whether the "Lalla Rookh" made any replenishment stopovers on the outward voyage, but it seems likely as the journey took an unusually long 164 days, calling at Port Nicholson at Wellington before finally arriving in Auckland on the 18th April 1849.[11]

Auckland in 1849

Upon his arrival in Auckland, Thomas would have been updated on the gold rush occurring in California, which had by then been underway for 15 months, after the precious metal was first discovered by James W. Marshall at Sutter's Mill in Coloma, California. But the news had slowly leaked out, and it took until early 1849 before the Californian discovery began to draw wealth-seekers from almost every nation on earth.

Rumours of glittering goldfields for the taking spread from California around the globe, with tens of thousands of people leaving their homes and families to chase the dream of quick riches. By mid 1849, 42,000 Americans had headed west overland, but for many others the ocean routes were the quickest and easiest way to reach California, with another 25,000 arriving by ship.

The news of California along with the excitement involved was sufficient motivation for most adventurers. But if Thomas' initial plans were to reach the California goldfields, he certainly wasn't in a rush to do so. In fact, it wasn't until February of 1850, some ten months after arriving in Auckland, that he finally booked passage and headed for San Francisco. So was his outward plan simply to visit New Zealand? Unfortunately, despite a possible but unknown link with New Zealand, there is little evidence to explain how or where he spent his time in Auckland. The estimated population of that settlement in 1849 was only around 7,500 people, while New Zealand as a whole consisted of just 19,543 Europeans, facing a native population of some 67,000 Maoris.

San Francisco

Nevertheless, California was calling to all those that would listen. Thomas eventually booked pasage aboard the 250 ton barque "Noble", under Captain Parker, which departed from Auckland on the 9th February 1850. The ship loaded all the goods it could carry to be sold in the rapidly developing city of San Francisco. Joining the ship were a few paying passengers that included Thomas and another five travellers, which included a well known frenchman by the name of Baron de Thierry.[1213]

However, their hopes of a speedy passage was slowed when the "Noble" made a stopover to take on fresh water at Pitcairn Island, which placed them in direct contact with the descendants of the "Bounty" mutineers, as the Pitcairn population wasn't moved on to Norfolk Island until 1856. Even worse, while the passengers of the "Noble" were ashore, the tides either turned or the winds picked up, and the captain decided it was better to depart than endanger the ship, with the passengers were stranded on Pitcairn Island for a month. But the "Noble" later returned and retrieved the marooned travellers, who eventually arrived in San Francisco on the 24th June 1850.[14]

VIEW OF SAN FRANCISCO, FORMERLY YERBA BUENA, IN 1846-7
BEFORE THE DISCOVERY OF GOLD

▲A view of San Francisco and the hinterland in 1846-47, just prior to the frenzy of the gold rush.

It is more than reasonable to assume that having spent four months in each other's company from Auckland to San Francisco, that friendships evolved between Thomas and his gold seeking companions. But ultimately his efforts on the diggings were in vain as he spent just ten months at the goldfields. However, California was more than likely the place where Thomas realised it was not just the diggers that prospered, and his observations may have fostered an inkling to commence his Clarence River Stores five years later at Grafton.

Having realised that slogging it out on the gold fields wasn't really for him, along with the rough and lawless lifestyle that went with it, Thomas searched for a ship that was heading back to either New Zealand or Australia. But this was no easy task as the promise of fabulous riches was so strong that crews on arriving vessels just deserted their ships and rushed off to the gold fields. Estimates state that approximately 500 ships were completely abandoned, which left deserted ships, rotting hulks and a forest of masts in San Francisco harbour.

Thomas did eventually manage to extricate himself from San Francisco, but it is uncertain exactly when that occurred. A small ship called the "Eclair" was also in San Francisco at this same time, and perhaps Thomas met Captain Peppercorn and joined the vessel directly from San Francisco. Evidence definitely reveals that Thomas acquired passage aboard the "Eclair", which called in to Tahiti, as it was from there that Thomas was registered as a passenger on the small 50 ton schooner, for its voyage to Sydney.In any event, whatever ship Thomas boarded would no doubt have stopped in Hawaii first, then later at Tahiti, from where we know Thomas boarded, or remained aboard the "Eclair", when it sailed for

SEPTEMBER 20 1849

GOLD! GOLD! GOLD!

GOLDEN NEWS FROM THE DIGGINGS.

PHILADELPHIA, Nov. 14.—We have at length quite a budget of California news, in consequence of the arrival of the steamer Empire City, with two weeks' later intelligence from San Francisco. The Empire City is from Chagres, at which port she received the mails from Panama and San Francisco; and the general advices from the gold regions are to October 2. She brings gold dust (duly entered) to the tune of 477,207 dollars; and the passengers have amongst them nearly 500,000 more.

San Francisco, 1849 [26]

The Yelamu group of the Ohlone people resided in a few small villages when an overland Spanish exploration party, led by Don Gaspar de Portolà, arrived on November 2, 1769, the first documented European visit to San Francisco Bay. Seven years later, on March 28, 1776, the Spanish established the Presidio of San Francisco, followed by a mission, the Mission San Francisco de Asis (Mission Dolores), established by the Spanish explorer Juan Bautista de Anza.

Upon gaining independence from Spain in 1821, the area became part of Mexico. Under Mexican rule, the mission system gradually ended, and its lands became privatized. By 1835, Englishman William Richardson erected the first independent homestead, near a boat anchorage around what is today Portsmouth Square. Together with Alcalde Francisco de Haro, he laid out a street plan for the expanded settlement, and the town named 'Yerba Buena', began to attract American settlers.

Commodore John D. Sloat claimed California for the United States on July 7, 1846, during the Mexican–American War, and Captain John B. Montgomery arrived to claim Yerba Buena two days later. Yerba Buena was renamed San Francisco on January 30 of 1847, and Mexico officially ceded the territory to the United States at the end of the war in 1848. Despite its attractive location as a port and naval base, San Francisco was still a very small settlement with inhospitable geography.

However, the California Gold Rush brought a flood of treasure seekers known as "forty-niners" in 1949. With their sourdough bread in tow, prospectors accumulated in San Francisco over rival Benicia, raising the population from 1,000 in 1848 to 25,000 by December 1849. The promise of fabulous riches was so strong that crews on arriving vessels deserted and rushed off to the gold fields, leaving behind a forest of masts in San Francisco harbour. Some of these approximately 500 abandoned ships were used at times as storeships, saloons and hotels, but many were left to rot and some were sunk to establish title to the underwater lot. By 1851 the harbor was extended out into the bay by wharves while buildings were erected on piles among the ships. By 1870 Yerba Buena Cove had been filled to create new land. Buried ships have occasionally been exposed when foundations are dug for new buildings.

▲TOP (Left): The 1849 California gold rush drew thousands of thrill seekers to San Francisco. (Right): Headlines and news from the diggings attracted thousands of prospectors. ABOVE (Left Column): Golden News (Lloyd's Weekly Newspaper, 2nd Dec 1849, p.1). (Right Column): 1-San Francisco and the forest of ships masts in its harbour in 1851. 2-A rare photo of a San Francisco street corner in 1849.

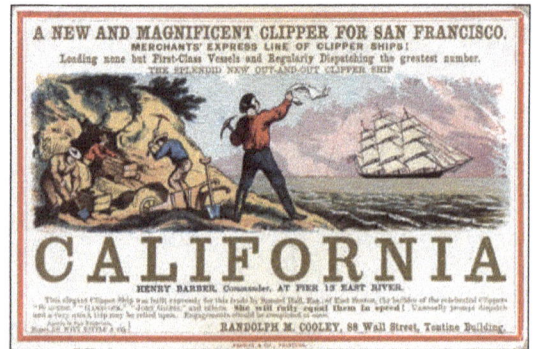

▲ TOP (Left): A sketch of Honolulu Harbour in 1854. (Right): Advertisement for passage to the California goldfields in 1849. ABOVE: A ship departs from San Francisco Bay, leaving the madness of the goldfields behind.

other islands.[15] At the Isle of Pines, the ship loaded up with sandalwood before departing on the 10th September 1851, and arrived after another two weeks in Sydney on the 25th July 1851.[16]

Arrival in Sydney

On the 1st May 1851 the Great Exhibition opened in London. But on the opposite side of the world another gold rush had started when the precious metal was found at Summerhill Creek and Ballarat, and by the 1st July that year, the colony of Victoria formally separated from New South Wales.

Just prior to Thomas' arrival in Australia, a tremendous opportunity opened up when William Tom Jr., John Lister and Edward Hargraves discovered gold on the 5th of February 1851 in the districts surrounding Bathurst in New South Wales. The discovery brought an army of prospectors from the capital cities and across the globe as the population of Sydney and Melbourne swelled with gold seekers. Indeed, the population of Victoria mutiplied from 75,000 in 1851, to over 500,000 just ten years later. It is possible that news of the discovery at Bathurst could have reached San Francisco before Thomas sailed, and this may even have been the reason his turnaround in San Francisco was so swift. Of course, this is mere speculation and we may never know his real aspirations.

During his travels, Thomas Eastman Shoveller was sufficiently independent to pay for his own unassisted passage, while most settlers were arriving as assisted immigrants. Thomas arrived in a burgeoning Sydney via the Isle of Pines (New Caledonia) and Tahiti on the 23rd of September 1851, alone and at the young age of just 24. As a result of their travels together Thomas had befriended the captain of the "Eclair," Mr. F. J. Peppercorn, and they obviously remained in contact as some 12 years later, they were again travelling companions on the paddlesteamer "Agnes Irving" that departed from the Clarence River, and arrived in Sydney on the 12th February 1863.[17] Unfortunately the "Eclair" was not in

Tahiti

The Tahitian rebellion against annexation ended in December 1846 in favour of the French. The Queen returned from exile in 1847 and agreed to sign a new covenant, considerably reducing her powers, while increasing those of the commissaire. The French nevertheless still reigned over the Kingdom of Tahiti as masters. In 1863, they put an end to any British influence and replaced the British protestant missions with the Société des missions évangéliques de Paris (Society of Evangelical Missions of Paris).

Isle of Pines

Melanesian people lived on the island for over 2000 years before the island was first visited by Europeans. Captain James Cook saw the island in 1774 and renamed it on his second voyage to New Zealand. Cook gave the island its name after seeing the tall native pine (Araucaria columnaris). He never disembarked onto the island, but as he saw signs of inhabitance (smoke) assumed it was inhabited. In the 1840s Protestant and Catholic missionaries arrived, along with merchants seeking sandalwood.

The French took possession of the island in 1853 at which time the native Kunies opted for the Catholic religion. In 1872 the island became a French penal colony, home to 3,000 political deportees from the Paris Commune.

▲TOP: Painting of the spectacular welcome of the Tahitians when European ships arrived, during the 18th & 19th centuries. ABOVE: A modern photo of the Isle of Pines (New Caledonia), showing the stands of columnar pine and the pristine reef and waters.

very good shape after her Pacific voyage as it was listed for 'private sale' just two weeks after arriving in Sydney.[18]

Now on the other side of the world, it took months for Thomas to receive news from home. But it was about this time that he was heartbroken at receiving news of the death of his dear mother Elizabeth, who had passed away on the 22nd July 1852, aged 68.[19] Thomas would no doubt have felt helpless as without his parents, it now made little sense to hurry home to England.

By mid 1852, communication between England and Australia was dramatically improved with the arrival of the first steam mail-ship, which sailed from England via Singapore to Sydney in just over two months.

Discovery of Gold in New South Wales [27]

After the California gold rush began in 1848, which caused many people to leave Australia to look for gold, the New South Wales government rethought its position, and sought approval from the Colonial Office in England to allow the exploitation of the colony's mineral resources and also offer rewards for the finding of payable gold.

The first gold rush in Australia began in May 1851 after prospector Edward Hargraves claimed to have discovered payable gold near Orange, at a site he called Ophir. With William Tom Jr. and John Lister, Edward Hargraves found payable gold in February 1851 at the Ophir gold diggings, located at the confluence of Summer Hill Creek and Lewis Ponds Creek. Hargraves was awarded £10,500 (worth $1,125,434 in 2004 values) by the NSW Government. Hargraves had been to the Californian goldfields and had learned new gold prospecting techniques such as panning and cradling. Before the end of the year, the gold rush had spread to many other parts of the state where gold had been found.

Edward Hargraves, accompanied by John Lister, found five specks of alluvial gold at Summerhill near Bathurst in February 1851. Then, in April, John Lister and William Tom Jr, trained by Edward Hargraves, found 120 grams of gold. This discovery, instigated by Hargraves, led directly to the beginning of the gold rush in New South Wales. Gold was also found at the Turon Goldfields at Sofala in June 1851, and also at the Victorian goldfields. The Australian gold rushes changed the convict colonies into more progressive cities with the influx of free emigrants. These hopefuls, termed diggers, brought new skills and professions, contributing to a burgeoning economy.

▲ TOP (Left & Right): In 1851 gold fever struck the Australian colonies with the discovery of payable gold at Ophir, near Bathurst, NSW, and later Ballarat in Victoria. ABOVE: Just like in California, prospectors came from all over the world to find their fortune at the Ophir diggings.

▲TOP (Left): The 'Corrobary', or peculiar dance of the natives of NSW (From William R. Govett's - Notes & Sketches, 1832). (Right): The arrival in Sydney of the "Eclair" 23rd September 1851, showing Thomas Shoveller as a passenger (NSW Archives, Unassisted Immigrant Index 1842-1855, Reel No. 1278), & (Inset): Announcement of the arrival of the "Eclair" showing Thomas Shoveller as a passenger (Shipping Intelligence - Maitland Mercury & Hunter River General Advertiser, 27th Sept 1851, p.3). ABOVE: Sydney town as Thomas Shoveller would have viewed it on his arrival. in 1851.

Steam Communication With England At Last

"The arrival in the Australian ports of the first steam mail-ship from England, is an event of so much importance that we scarely know in what terms we may best congratulate our fellow colonists upon its actual accomplishment. The "Chusan" has made the passage from Southampton to Sydney, calling at St. Vincent, the Cape of Good Hope (at each of which places she was detained five days), and Port Phillip (where she stopped two days), in seventy-nine days, or in sixty-seven days actual running, thus realising our most sanguine hopes. Henceforward, then, we are to have regular steam-communication with our fatherland once a month, by the Cape and Singapore routes alternately."

The Sydney Morning Herald, 5th July 1852 [20]

The Crimean War commenced on the 16th October 1853 between Russia and a British alliance, who feared Russian expansion in the Balkans. While a declaration of war on Russia was pronounced, no immediate attack on Sydney eventuated, but additional battery sites were ordered for Middle and South Heads as defence against anticipated raids by the Russian Navy.[21] But there were other external threats in the Pacific, with France having established a colony at New Caledonia in 1853. The conflict in Crimea stretched out until

▲ The "SS Chusan" was the first steamship to operate a regular mail service between the United Kingdom and Australia, and it arrived in Sydney on the 3rd August 1852 following its first voyage south.

the 30th March 1856, but eventually resulted in an allied victory. Closer to Australia, the Eureka Rebellion materialised, which involved gold miners that revolted against the British colonial administration during the Victorian gold rush.[22] It culminated in the Battle of the Eureka Stockade, which took place on the 3rd December 1854 at Ballarat, between the rebels and the colonial forces of Victoria.

It was during these years that Thomas Shoveller left no trace of his whereabouts. Was he anywhere near Ballarat at this time? Probably not, as evidence reveals that on the 2nd March 1855, a Mr. Shoveller pledged £1 to the 'Patriotic Fund' on behalf of the widows and orphans of those who fell in the Crimean War, when he was likely working with the firm Jones, Smithe & Curtiss in New England. A short time later at Glen Innes, T. E. Shoveller pledged a further 10 shillings toward the same cause on the 14th March 1855.[23]

At this stage, no further evidence has been uncovered as to what Thomas Shoveller may have done or where he ventured following his arrival in Sydney in September 1851, although he had unclaimed mail waiting for him at the Sydney GPO in October 1853.[24] He could have travelled to the new goldfields at Ophir or Sofala near Bathurst, to Bendigo or Ballarat in Victoria, spent his time in Sydney, or perhaps he briefly returned to England? The next confirmed evidence of Thomas Eastman Shoveller was recorded in March of 1856 in the northern NSW township of Grafton.

With Thomas working at Glen Innes in 1855, he had to have travelled down to the Clarence River via the Grafton-Glen Innes Road at some stage, as this was then the only

The Journey of Thomas Eastman Shoveller (1848-1851)

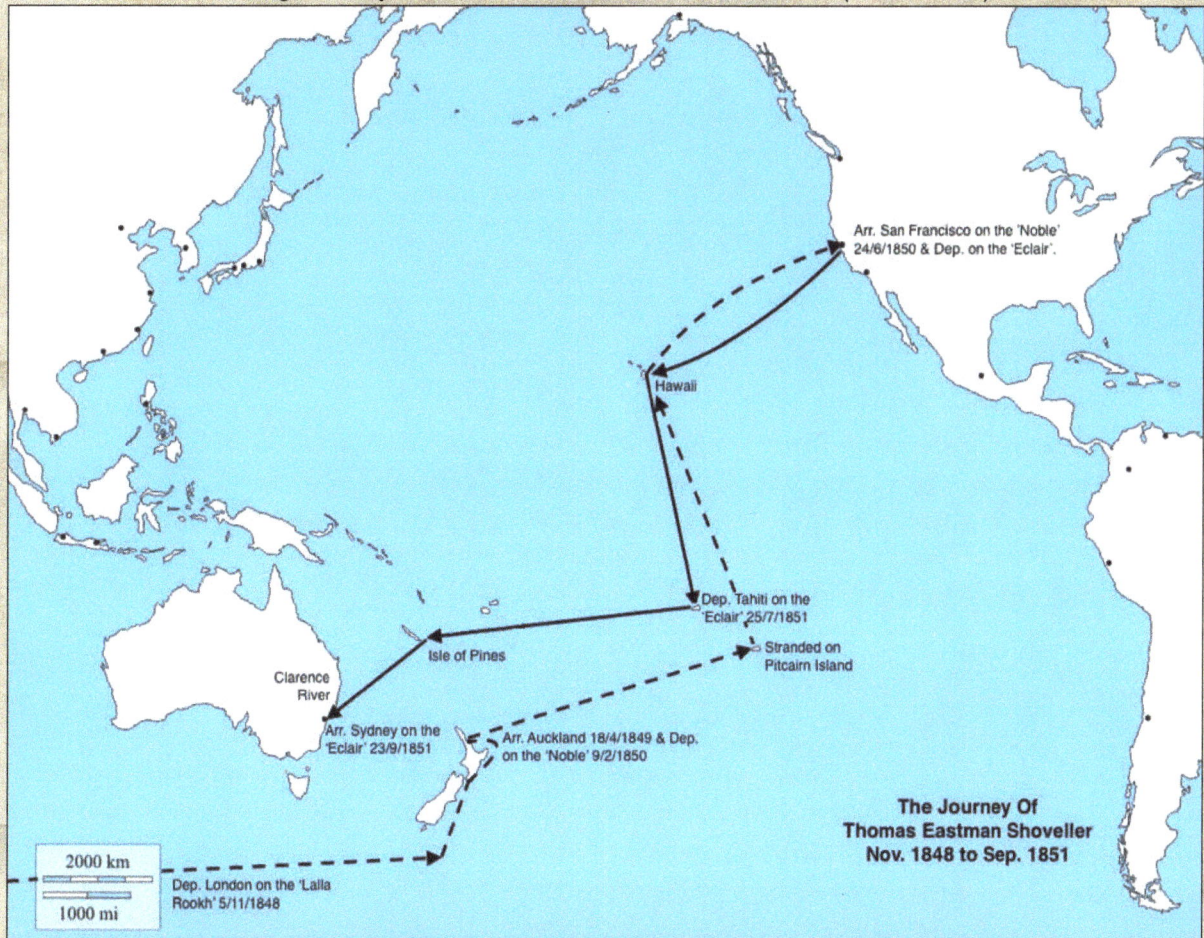

Arr. San Francisco on the 'Noble' 24/6/1850 & Dep. on the 'Eclair'.

Hawaii

Dep. Tahiti on the 'Eclair' 25/7/1851

Stranded on Pitcairn Island

Isle of Pines

Clarence River

Arr. Sydney on the 'Eclair' 23/9/1851

Arr. Auckland 18/4/1849 & Dep. on the 'Noble' 9/2/1850

The Journey Of Thomas Eastman Shoveller Nov. 1848 to Sep. 1851

2000 km
1000 mi

Dep. London on the 'Lalla Rookh' 5/11/1848

The Itinerary

- Departure from London -

"The **Lalla Rookh**", Capt. Harris, was reported as having sailed for New Zealand, 5th November."

Evening Mail, 6 November 1848

- Arrival at Auckland -

"April 18. "**Lalla Rookh**" barque, 373 tons,, Capt. W.H.O. Hains, from London via Wellington, with sundries. Passengers - Captain Parker, Messrs. Gilfillan, Bain, **Shoveller**, Stephen, Fraser, Hansard, and 1 child in Steerage. Brown & Campbell, agents. NB. The 'Lalla Rookh' was wrecked off Worthing, England in a storm in 1850."

Daily Southern Cross, 21 April 1849

- Departure from Auckland -

"Feb. 9. "**Noble**", 251 tons, Capt. Parker, for San Francisco. Exports: 17 hhds brls. ale, 60 tons coal, 25,000 shingles, 3 wheelbarrows, 203 bundles containing 7 houses, 10 bolts canvas, 9 doors, 6 shutters, 67 doors, 21,000 shingles, 2,500 bricks, 51 cases onions, 21 boxes carrots, 3 bales slop...

Passengers -	
Brodie	Mr Walter
Carleton	Mr Hough Esq.
de Thierry	Baron
Shoveller	**Mr T.E.**
Taylor	Mr Allan
Vaile	Mr Samuel"

The Southern Cross, 12 February 1850

- Arrival at San Francisco -

"Arrivals at San Francisco from the colonies since last advices: 24th June "**Noble**", barque, 130 days from Auckland. In a list of vessels lying in San Francisco Bay, published in the Alta California of the 1st July: the "Clyde" of Auckland; the "Eliza" of New Zealand; the "Elizabeth" of New Zealand; the "**Noble**" of Auckland; the "Thomas Lord" of Auckland; and the "William & James" of Auckland."

Sydney Shipping Gazette, Vol 7, 336, 24 Aug, 1850

- Vessels for California -

"The new schooner "**Eclair**", 49 tons built by Mr Peppercorn, at Coromandel (NZ), is also to proceed to Tahiti and San Francisco on her return from a trip to the Great Barrier."

The Southern Cross, 19 February, 1850 p.2

- Arrival at Sydney -

Vessels Name:	"**Eclair**" (Schooner)
Registered:	Honolula
Tonnage:	50
Masters Name:	F. J. Peppercorn
Lading:	Sundries
Sailed:	25th July 1851
Destination:	Sydney
From:	Tahiti via The Isle Of Pines (dep. 10th Sep 1851)
Arrived:	23rd September 1851
Passengers:	Two from Tahiti plus another two from the Isle of Pines.
Passengers:	James Wilson, Edward Rodd **Thomas Shoveller**, William Lee
Nature of Cargo:	Sundries of 4 pax/3 crew
Health Problems:	No deaths / No disease

Maitland Mercury & Hunter River General Advertiser, 27th Sep 1851, p.3

▲At a time when voyaging to Australia and the Pacific was like travelling to the moon, Thomas Eastman Shoveller went much further, visiting Auckland, Pitcairn, Tahiti, California, Hawaii and the Isle of Pines, all before his arrival in Sydney in September of 1851.

route. Plying that road at that very same time as a 'carrier' and bullock driver, just happened to be an ex-convict by the name of John Hann. It is not implausible to contend that they met somewhere and shared camp, which might explain how Thomas Eastman Shoveller was introduced to the Hann family and his future bride, Susan Hann.

No one leaves their home without good reason and Thomas Eastman Shoveller, now 28 years old, probably always intended to return to Britain at some stage, but whether he ever did remains uncertain. With hindsight, what is known is that subsequent decisions and events would have handicapped his attempts to return to England, as he next proposed to the 15 year old daughter of John and Mary Ann Hann in Grafton. Despite the advances in the speed and safety of sea travel, a family was begun soonafter the wedding, which prevented any further attempts to return home in the forseeable future. The next chapter explores the marriage, community activities and business ventures of Thomas Eastman Shoveller, which helped to forge his reputation as a pioneer of the expanding township of Grafton.

The wild beauty of the Clarence River and district lured squatters and settlers alike, with Thomas Eastman Shoveller arriving at Grafton in the early 1850s.

References

1. Birth of Thomas Eastman Shoveller, from the register of the Independent Chapel, King Street (formerly Orange Street), Portsea (Hampshire, England & Wales, Non-Conformist and Non-Parochial Registers, 1567-1936).

2. Baptism of Thomas Eastman Shoveller, from the register of the Independent Chapel, King Street (formerly Orange Street), Portsea (Hampshire, England & Wales, Non-Conformist and Non-Parochial Registers, 1567-1936).

3. Appointment of John Shoveller, LLD as Commissioner for the General Registrar Office (Hereford Journal, 21 Sept 1836 & Staffordshire Advertiser, 17 Dec 1836).

4. Dr Shoveller - Premises Gutted By Fire (Northern Star, 6th February 1841, p.5).

5. Dr. Shoveller - Retiring (Hampshire Telegraph, 22 March 1824).

6. Death notice for John Shoveller, LLD (Brighton Gazetteer, 21 January 1847).

7. John Shoveller Jr. & Hannah Wiggins - Marriage held on the 18th May 1847 at St Andrew By The Wardrobe, London (from London C of E Marriages and Banns 1754-1937).

8. Kemble, John Haskell (1949). 'The Gold Rush by Panama, 1848-1851.' Vol. 18, No. 1, Rushing for Gold (Feb., 1949), pp. 45-56, University of California Press. [https://www.jstor.org/stable/3634427].

9. "Lalla Rookh" - Departure from London (Evening Mail, 6 November 1848).

10. Wikipedia - Lalla Rookh [https://en.wikipedia.org/wiki/Lalla_Rookh].

11. Thomas Shoveller - Passenger on "Lalla Rookh" - Arrival in Auckland (Daily Southern Cross, 21 April 1849).

12. Thomas Shoveller - Passenger on the "Noble" - Departure from Auckland (The Southern Cross, 12 February 1850).

13. Raeside, J.D. (1977). "Sovereign Chief: A Biography of Baron De Thierry," The Caxton Press, Christchurch.

14. Thomas Shoveller - Passenger on "Noble" - Arrival in San Francisco [Sydney Shipping Gazette, Vol 7, 336, 24 Aug, 1850].

15. Thomas Shoveller - Passenger arriving Sydney on the "Eclair" 23rd September 1851 (NSW Archives, Unassisted Immigrant Index 1842-1855, Reel No. 1278).

16. Thomas Shoveller - passenger on the 'Eclair' (Shipping Intelligence - Maitland Mercury & Hunter River General Advertiser, 27th Sept 1851, p.3).

17. Thomas Shoveller & Peppercorn - Passengers on "Agnes Irving" (SMH, 13 Feb 1863, p.4).

18. Schooner "Eclair" - Private Sale (SMH, 8th October 1851, p.1).

▲ "The new schooner "Eclair" 49 tons built by Captain F. J. Peppercorn, at Coromandel, is also to proceed to Tahiti and San Francisco on her return from a trip to the Great Barrier." ('Vessels for California ' in The Southern Cross, Tuesday, 19th February 1850 p.2). Thomas Eastman Shoveller journeyed from San Francisco aboard the "Eclair", a vessel that would have resembled this small 50 ton schooner, eventually arriving in Sydney on the 23rd September 1851.

19. Elizabeth Shoveller (nee Eastman) - Death notices (Hampshire Telegraph, 24th July 1852, p.5 & London Standard, 24th July 1852).

20. Steam Communication With England At Last (The Sydney Morning Herald, 5th July 1852).

21. Wilson, G.C. (1985) 'Sydney Harbour Fortifications Archival Study', part 1, unpublished report to NSW National Parks and Wildlife Service, p.14.

22. Corfield, Justin; Wickham, Dorothy; Gervasoni, Clare (2004). The Eureka Encyclopedia. Ballarat: Ballarat Heritage Services. [ISBN 978-1-87-647861-2].

23. Mr. T. E. Shoveller - 10s donation to the Patriotic Fund (Maitland Mercury & H.R. Gen. Advertiser, 14th March 1855, p.1).

24. Thomas E. Shoveller - Unclaimed Letters at General Post Office, Sydney (NSW Govt Gazette, 14 Oct 1853, p.1798).

25. Wikipedia - Charles de Thierry [https://en.wikipedia.org/wiki/Charles_de_Thierry].

26. Wikipedia - San Francisco History [https://en.wikipedia.org/wiki/San_Francisco#History].

27. Wikipedia - Discovery of Gold in NSW [https://en.wikipedia.org/wiki/New_South_Wales_gold_rush].

Chapter Seventeen

Shoveller

Hann

THOMAS EASTMAN SHOVELLER & SUSAN HANN

On the world stage, the year 1856 brought the Treaty of Paris, which was signed on the 31st March to end the Crimean War, Queen Victoria instituted the Victoria Cross as a British military decoration, and a fire destroyed Covent Garden Theatre in London. Closer to Australia, Van Diemen's Land was renamed Tasmania, and the United Kingdom gave Norfolk Island to the population of the colony at Pitcairn Island, most being direct descendants of the "Bounty" mutineers. It was also the year Thomas Eastman Shoveller married a young 15 year old lass, who was already notable as being the first white child born in the entire Clarence River District.

Susan Hann's parents were Australian royalty... ex government servants and both transported for seven years. Her father John Hann Sr. (1800-1857) was from Dorset and had been convicted of stealing, for which he was transported aboard the "Guildford" that arrived in Sydney on the 5th March 1824. He was also a recalcitrant and his lack of discipline later landed him at the penal settlement for second offenders at Port Maquarie. Susan's mother was Mary Ann Thompson (1816-1882), a Londoner who had been transported for 'pledging a shawl' and she arrived in Sydney on the 2nd February 1833, on board the "Fanny." They were introduced to one another at the Parramatta Female Factory and soonafter married at St John's Church, Parramatta on the 18th February 1835.

Due to John Hann's skill with timber and having had some experience as a boat builder, they were selected by Thomas Small for an expedition to the Clarence River on board the 14.5m schooner "Susan" in 1840, and they brought their three young children with them. The first settlement on the Clarence River was at Ilarwill on Woodford Island,[1] and in the process these intrepid travellers became pioneers of the far north coast region of NSW. The discovery and settlement of the Clarence River and the fascinating story of the Hanns and

tion 60874/92/CS

NEW SOUTH WALES

Registration of Births, Deaths and Marriages Act, 1973

BAPTISMS

Number	3106/Vol 30A
CHILD	
Christian name	Susan
When born	29th December, 1840
Date of ceremony	8th August, 1845
Where ceremony performed	The Clarence River
Where registered	-
PARENTS	
Father	John HAND
Mother	Mary THOMSON
Abode	Clarence River
Quality or profession	Shepherd
Sponsors	-
By whom the ceremony was performed	John McConnell

I, Robert Noel Miller
hereby certify that the above is a true copy of particulars recorded in a register of
Church of England Baptisms kept by me

Issued at Sydney,
on 8th January, 1992

Deputy   Principal Registrar

▲ *The 1845 baptismal certificate of Susan Hann, showing her birth on the 29th December of 1840, with her abode listed simply as the 'Clarence River' as there were no settlements between Port Macquarie and Moreton Bay at that time.*

their ancestors is available in the volume 7 entitled of the Rockwell Genealogies entitled "To The Big River," (*see also Appendix G - Clarence River & Grafton Timeline*).

Susan Hann (1840-1919)

Susan Hann was the fourth child of John Hann Sr. and Mary Thomson and was born on the 29th of December 1840, at Ilarwill on Woodford Island in the Clarence River.[2] Her 40 year old father was originally born in West Stour, Dorset, and was listed as a shepherd on her birth certificate. Her 25 year old mother was born in Clerkenwell, London, but was not listed as having a separate occupation. No one knew it then, but Susan was the first white female child born on the north coast of NSW. It was not until five years later, on the 8th of August 1845 however, that she was able to be baptised when the Rev. John McConnell, who rode around the unsettled districts, administered the rites of the Church of England.

Susan was preceded by three elder siblings, who were all born in Sydney. The first of which Jane Hann, was born at Dural, Sydney on the 1st of January 1835, and baptised at St. John's Church, Parramatta on the 14th August 1836.[3] Joseph Hann, was born on the 11th of July 1836 also at Dural and was baptised on the same day as his older sister.[4] Then John Hann Jr. arrived next on the 3rd March 1838 at Castle Hill and was baptised on the 15th April of that year.[5]

It was likely around 1839 while employed at Small's Kissing Point property, that Susan's parents were asked to join John Small's journey to what was then known simply as the Big River and in doing so, became some of the earliest pioneers of the region. The obituary of Susan's mother, Mary Ann Hann, which was written in June 1882, reported that after residing for some years in Parramatta she accompanied her husband, a ship-wright and boat-builder, to the Clarence "about 42 years ago." The obituary stated that they first resided on Woodford Island (likely at 'Ilarwill' near Maclean), where her husband worked at his trade as a boat builder.[6] The obituary of Susan's sister Jane Olive (nee Hann), added that she arrived as a six year-old child with her parents aboard the schooner "Susan" and lived on Woodford Island with the Small family.[7]

The Hanns spent time on Edward Ogilvie's 'Yugilbar' and at 'Copmanhurst' over the next few years where Susan's father found work as a boat builder, shepherd and carrier before the family eventually moved into the developing township of Grafton.

"Copmanhurst was taken up by Joseph Hickey Grose in 1839. This was the first station upon which stock were placed in the district. The Superintendent, when I arrived in 1840, was a Mr Houston. He was shortly afterwards succeeded by Mr Lardner. About this time there was at Copmanhurst, in Grose's employ, Mr and Mrs Hann, the parents of the numerous family of that name in this and adjoining districts. There is another old man still living I believe, although I have not seen him for some time past, who came to Copmanhurst at the same time. His name was James Halcup, but he was commonly known as 'Jim the Splitter'."

Thomas Bawden [8]

▲TOP: Susan Hann was the first white child born on the beautiful Clarence River, shown here at sunset. ABOVE (Left): Picnicking by the banks of the Clarence River, c.1875. (Right): An early photograph of Glen Innes Court House, c.1865.

Susan was followed by Sarah Hann, who was born on the 2nd June 1842 at Copmanhurst Station, and the two sisters were baptised at the same time on the 8th August 1845.[9] The next to arrive was Mary Ann Hann on the 15th July 1843 in the growing settlement of Grafton, and baptised on the 14th July 1844.[10] Then Lucy Hann, the seventh child in the Hann family, was born on the 15th November 1845 registered as the Clarence River, and she was baptised on the 30th July 1847.[11] Two years later George Hann was born at 'Yugilbar Station' on the 16th December 1847, but he was baptised at Grafton on the 21st December 1849.[12] Emily Hann was born on the 7th October 1851 again registered only as the Clarence River and baptised a month later on the 9th of November.[13]

An interesting statistic by the time Emily Hann was born in the year 1851, was that the entire population of the Clarence, Richmond and Tweed River Districts totalled not more than 1700 persons. This figure is notable as by this time the Hann family had resided in and around the developing township of Grafton for at least eleven years and were eye-witnesses to the influx of settlers. The last child born into the now large Hann family was William Hann, who arrived on the 10th April 1854 and was baptised on the 2nd of July at Grafton.[14]

Being of Anglican faith, the Hann family would have attended church when possible, however the pioneering members of the clergy in the early days had enormous distances

▲ TOP: An early photo of Thomas Shoveller's 'Clarence River Stores', on the corner of Prince and Bacon Streets, Grafton. ABOVE (Left): The trucks of the future, a bullock dray typically used by carriers of the 1850's, one of whom was Susan Hann's father, John Hann. (Right): A typical bark slab hut erected by pioneers.

▲TOP (Left): A 19th century painting of a gum flower bouquet. (Right): Thomas Fisher's 'Grafton Stores' followed on from Thomas Shoveller's 'Clarence River Stores'. ABOVE: A description of the Clarence District in 1854, written by William Gardner.

to travel in order to reach their parishioners. Although he had a roving brief, more regular services were only established after Rev. John McConnell was appointed clergyman for the region.

There was obviously a large span in terms of years between the Hann children, so much so, that Susan's mother was seven months pregnant with her last child at the same time her first child, Jane Hann aged 19, was married to William Olive on the 23rd January 1854 at Grafton.[15] Susan Hann was the witness for her sister's wedding ceremony although she was aged only 13 at the time.

Up until the arrival of the railway in 1903, most goods arriving in the region came by ship and supplies were landed at Lawrence and then transported by horse and bullock teams to the outlying settlements and up to Glen Innes. It is probable that the younger Hann children attended a 'bush school' at Grafton. By 1851, Governor FitzRoy had officially named the flourishing town as 'Grafton', after his grandfather, Augustus Henry FitzRoy, 3rd Duke of Grafton, who was a former Prime Minister of the United Kingdom.

While little is known of Susan's childhood or teen years, she and her siblings would have roamed as free spirits, with the Australian bush as their playground. While the daily chores were endless, there were fortunately plenty of helping hands in this family, with virtually everything becoming a lesson in life. Susan therefore was a genuine country girl and grew up as what became known at that time as a 'currency lass'. In 1849, J. P. Townsend wrote that "whites born in the colony... are called 'the currency', meaning they were different to English born children who had emigrated." The next we hear of Susan is when at just 15 years of age, she met and was betrothed to her future husband.

The Marriage of Thomas Eastman Shoveller & Susan Hann

How, when and where Thomas Shoveller and Susan Hann met is unknown, but it seems hard to envisage a young 15 year old girl falling in love with a 28 year old Englishman.

Shoveller notices posted from 1857 to 1859. ▲LEFT COLUMN: 1-Thomas Shoveller - Letters Awaiting (SMH, 7 Feb 1857, p.1); 2-Thomas Shoveller - Agent (Moreton Bay Courier, 30th May 1857, p.10); 3-Thomas Shoveller - Elected Councillor of Second Ward & Snakes (Moreton Bay Courier, 21 Sep 1859). CENTRE COLUMN: 1-Thomas Shoveller - Agent for 50 Acre Farm (Maitland Mercury, 10th April 1858, p.1); 2-Thomas Shoveller - Notice of Spirit Merchants (NSW Govt Gazette, 20 February 1857 [Issue No. 25], p.351); 3-Thomas Shoveller - Spirit Merchant (NSW Govt Gazette, 1 January 1858 [Issue No. 1], p.5); 4-Thomas Shoveller - Spirit Merchant (The Maitland Mercury & Hunter River Gen. Advertiser, 20 July 1858, p.3). RIGHT COLUMN: 1-Thomas Shoveller - Spirit Merchant (SMH, 19th July 1958, p.5); 2-Thomas Shoveller - Notice of the birth of daughter Susan Theresa (The Armidale Express & NE Gen. Advertiser, 29 May 1858, p.2); 3-Thomas Shoveller - Notice of the death of daughter Susan Theresa (The Armidale Express & NE Gen. Advertiser, 11 Sep 1858, p.2).

First clergyman appointed to Grafton was the Rev. John O'Connell (Church of England) in 1842 with responsibility for the Clarence and Richmond Rivers.

A church was built at the corner of Duke and Victoria Streets in 1854. The Diocese of Grafton and Armidale was created in 1867 with the first bishop, the Rt. Rev. William Collinson Sawyer, drowned in the Clarence on the night of March 15, 1868. On July 25, 1884, the John Horbury Hunt designed Christ Church Cathedral was opened and dedicated. In the words of Professor J. M. Freeland, the cathedral is unique in the world. The Diocese of Grafton was established in 1914 with the Rt. Rev. Cecil Henry Druitt first bishop.

South Grafton was the cradle of the Catholic Church on the North Coast, with the first St. Patrick's Church (and school) opening on September 15, 1857.

Priests from Armidale visited the Clarence regularly from 1846, with the first resident priest, Father Murphy, appointed in January 1862. The foundations of the first St. Mary's Church were laid on September 8, 1866. In 1887, the Diocese of Grafton was formed with Dr Doyle the first bishop. The name was later changed to Diocese of Lismore with the bishop living in Lismore. The Diocese of Armidale was created in 1869.

Application   54329/81 MN

NEW SOUTH WALES

Registration of Births, Deaths and Marriages Act, 1973

MARRIAGES

Marriages solemnized in the District of Clarence River, in the County of - New South Wales.

Number   1125 Vol: 43B

Thomas Eastman Shoveller   of   the   ~~Parish~~ District of   and Clarence, Bachelor

Susan Hann   of   the   ~~Parish~~ District of Clarence, Spinster

were married in this   Church, Grafton   by   License

with consent of   Parents   this   6th

day of   March   in the year   1856

By me   Arthur E. Selwyn, Minister of the District of Clarence River.

This marriage was solemnized between us   { Thomas Eastman Shoveller
Susan Hann

In the presence of   { James Johnson   of Grafton   Norman Cowan
Ellen Ford   of Grafton   John Hann

I,   John Brettell Holliday,
hereby certify that the above is a true copy of particulars recorded in a Register of Church of England   Marriages kept by me

Issued at Sydney,
on   14th May, 1981.   Principal Registrar

▲ TOP (Left Above): The 1856 signed wedding papers for Thomas Eastman Shoveller and Susan Hann in the Grafton Church register. (Left Below): The original Anglican Church on the corner of Victoria and Duke Streets, Grafton, venue for the marriage of Thomas Eastman Shoveller & Susan Hann in March 1856. This pencil drawing is attributed to Mrs. Selwyn, the ministers wife, c.1860. (Right): Father Arthur E. Selwyn, minister of Grafton and the District of Clarence River from 1854 to 1867. ABOVE (Left-Up): Early Churches & Churchmen (from John Moorhead, John (1984). 'Grafton: The First 125 Civic Years, Grafton Municipal Council). (Left-Down): Thomas Shoveller's advertisement for Sharp's Wharf was aimed at the New England Wool Trade (Armidale Express & NE Gen. Advertiser, 23 Aug 1856, p.1). (Right): The marriage certificate of Thomas Eastman Shoveller and Susan Hann, 6th March 1856 (NSW BDM #1125/43B).

SHIPPING RECORD

ARRIVAL—OCTOBER 2.
GRAFTON, steamer, 210 tons, Wiseman, from Clarence River
September 30. Passengers—Miss Hand, Messrs. Shoveller,
Small, Gregory, Robertson, Day, and 16 in the steerage. Agents,
Kirchner and Co.

AGENTS FOR THE "ARMIDALE EXPRESS."
Bathurst—Mr. William Craigie, Orange
Bendemeer—Mr. Henry Perry
Bundarrah—Mr. J. Mulligan
Byron—Mr. Colin Ross
Drayton—Mr. Edward Lord, postmaster
Dundee—Mr. G. Cobley
Glen Innes—Mr. James Martin
Grafton, South—Mr. Norman Cowan
      North—Mr. Thomas Shoveller, postmaster
Gulligal—Mr. Abraham Johnson

Grafton Store.
THOMAS SHOVELLER begs to announce to his friends that he has just
received a Large and Varied Assortment,
among which will be found none but
FIRST-CLASS GOODS.

All that can be said within the compass
of an advertisement will fail in giving to
the public anything but a most inadequate
conception of the many novelties which will
be found in this, the largest assortment
upon the Clarence.

T. SHOVELLER is now prepared to exe-
cute wholesale orders at a figure which he
conscientiously believes will deter many
wholesale buyers from purchasing in Syd-
ney. On Sale—
W. I. RUM, 30 o.p.
Sperm Candles
Axle Blocks
Bar and Rod Iron
Drapery
Boots and Shoes
Furnishing Ironmongery
Tools
Oilman's Stores
Byass's Ale and Porter
Port and Sherry
Every requisite for a station.   40

THOMAS SHOVELLER, Store-
keeper, Prince's Street, North Grafton,
begs to inform his friends, that he has received
and has now on hand, all descriptions of GE-
NERAL STORES, which he is retailing at
the lowest remunerative prices.
            THOMAS SHOVELLER.
North Grafton, June 28.   12

THOMAS SHOVELLER, Store-
keeper, North Grafton, begs to inform
the public of Grafton and its neighbourhood,
that he has been appointed AGENT for the
SYDNEY FIRE INSURANCE COMPANY,
and will now insure Houses and Property under
the regulations and conditions of the above
Company.
North Grafton, June, 1859.   13

THOMAS SHOVELLER,
STOREKEEPER,
Prince Street, North Grafton,
BEGS to inform his friends, and the public of
Grafton and its vicinity, that he has re-
ceived, and has now on hand, all descrip-
tions of
GENERAL STORES,
which he is retailing at the lowest remunerative
prices.
            THOMAS SHOVELLER.
North Grafton, June 28.   12

Surveyor General's Office,
Sydney, 21st October, 1857.
TITLE DEEDS READY FOR DELIVERY.
THE Deeds specified in this List being
ready for delivery, on payment of the
authorised fee, (to the Grantees or their Agents
duly empowered,) it is requested that early ap-
plication may be made for them at this Office.
Authorities must bear the signature of the
Grantees, attested by a Magistrate.

A sale of Crown Lands, situated near North
Grafton, took place at the Court-house on the
19th, with the following results:—

Lot.	A.	R.	P.	Purchaser.	£.	s.	d.
1.	28	0	0	R. Johnson	28	0	0
2.	31	0	0	A. Maclennan	31	0	0
3.	38	0	0	John Stuart	38	0	0
4.	35	0	0	R. Macaulay	35	0	0
5.	63	0	0	Elliott & Porter	63	0	0
6.	30	0	0	C. J. Walker	30	0	0
7.	22	0	0	Ditto	22	0	0
8.	25	0	0	J. Handcock	25	0	0
9.	27	0	0	C. J. Walker	27	0	0
10.	40	0	0	Ditto	40	0	0
11.	52	0	0	Ditto	65	0	0
12.	12	2	0	Elliott & Porter	25	0	0
13.	8	2	0	T. Shoveller	17	0	0
14.	12	1	0	J. Sharpe	184	7	3
15.	15	0	0	S. Avery	30	0	0
16.	15	0	0	S. Adrian	30	0	0
17.	15	0	0	S. Avery	32	0	0
18.	11	1	0	J. Sharpe	143	0	3
19.	14	2	20	Ditto	162	12	1½
20.	20	0	0	No offer.			
21.	20	0	0	under water.			
22.	20	0	0				
23.	16	2	0	J. Sharpe	231	17	6
24.	18	0	5	C. J. Walker	58	12	0
25.	10	0	0	J. Collins	28	0	0
26.	10	0	0	A. Livingstone	30	0	0
27.	15	0	0	J. Collins	35	5	0
28.	15	0	0	J. Lilbach	59	0	0
29.	3	1	0	Ann Barrett	10	11	3
30.	9	0	0	W. Collie	28	7	0
31.	20	0	0	Ditto	75	0	0
32.	7	0	0	J. Lambert	18	18	0
33.	20	0	0	J. Jackschon	41	0	0
34.	8	0	0	A. Lambert	17	12	0
35.	24	0	0	J. Baker	72	0	0
Sold.	670	3	5		£1725	3	4½
				Deed Fees	32	10	0
				Total	£1757	13	4½

Particulars of Land Sale, held at the
Police Office North Grafton, on the
31st December, 1857. Upset price
£8 per acre.

Town of South Grafton.

Lot.	r.	p.	Purchaser.	£	s.	d
1	2	0	T. Ryan	4	5	0

Town of North Grafton.

2	2	0	P. Greaves	4	4	0
3	2	0	Ditto	4	5	0
4	2	0	J. Wonderlick	4	2	0
5	2	0	J. Siebert	4	0	0
6	2	0	J. Stocken	4	0	0
7	2	0	J. Klobe	4	0	0
8	2	0	Ditto	4	1	0
9	2	0	W. Crouch	5	2	0
10	2	0	Ditto	6	6	0
11	2	0	Ditto	5	6	0
12	2	0	Ditto	4	2	0
13	2	16	W. Lambert	7	0	0
14	2	0	Ditto	7	2	0
15	2	0	W. A. Greaves	8	5	0
16	2	0	John Baker	6	10	0
17	2	0	Ditto	8	5	0
18	2	0	Ditto	9	7	0
19	2	8	W. Collie	6	6	0
20	2	0	T. Shoveller	4	1	0
21	2	0	W. Collie	5	10	0
22	2	0	Ditto	6	6	0
23	2	0	Ditto	6	10	0
24	2	0	H. Robinson	6	13	0
25	2	0	Ditto	7	1	0
26	2	0	J. Baker	8	10	0
27	2	0	Ditto	11	3	0
28	2	0	Ditto	8	10	0
29	2	0	Ditto	8	3	0
30	2	0	Ditto	7	1	0
31	2	0	Mildred	6	6	0
32	2	0	Ditto	6	6	0
33	2	0	W. H. Becke	6	0	0
34	2	0	F. Robinson	6	6	0
35	2	0	J. Baker	9	0	0
			Deed fees	35	0	0
				£257	14	0

The fees are according to the Scale at the end
of the List.
Parties applying for Deeds are particularly
requested to state the numbers placed against
those they may require.
         GEO. BARNEY,
           Surveyor General.

1480 Shoveller Thomas, ditto, 2 roods, allotment
No. 2 of section 93.
1481 Ditto, ditto, 2 roods, allotment No. 3 of
section 93.

A sale of Crown lands took place at
Grafton on the 13th. The land brought
forward consisted of 47 farms, varying
from 40 to 66 acres each. Twenty-six
were sold; the remainder, being principally poor stony ridges, unsuited for agricultural purposes, were passed by, and
are now open for selection at the upset
price of £1 per acre.

The following is the result of the sale.

Lot.	A.	R.	P.	Purchaser.	£	s.	d.
1.	43	0	0	Donald Cameron	44	0	0
3.	43	0	0	Thomas Ryan	252	11	0
4.	45	0	0	John Beel	46	0	0
6.	51	0	0	Do	57	7	0
10.	55	0	0	D. R. Gale	56	0	0
21.	51	0	0	Angus Cameron	52	5	0
22.	52	0	0	Do	58	9	0
23.	50	0	0	Donald Cameron	58	5	0
24.	49	0	0	Do	62	0	0
25.	49	0	0	Hugh Cameron	50	0	0
26.	47	0	0	Thomas Shoveller	48	0	0
27.	46	0	0	J. E. Chapman	47	0	0
28.	50	0	0	Richard Bligh	56	0	0
29.	46	0	0	Do	49	0	0
30.	42	0	0	Do	49	0	0
31.	45	0	0	Wm. Cowan	46	0	0
32.	53	0	0	Do	54	5	0
34.	50	0	0	Henry Wright	51	0	0
36.	55	0	0	Angus Cameron	56	5	0
37.	61	0	0	Do	62	5	0
38.	49	0	0	John Cameron	50	0	0
39.	52	0	0	Do	53	5	0
40.	56	0	0	Do	57	5	0
41.	46	0	0	Christina Cameron	47	0	0
42.	44	0	0	Donald Cameron	45	0	0
43.	47	0	0	Do	48	0	0
26.	1235	0	0	acres realised	£1556	19	0

Grafton, May 13th, 1858.

Result of land sale at Grafton, 31st
May, 1858:—

Lot.		r.	p.	Purchaser.	£	s.	d.
1.	2	2	0	W. A. B. Greaves	18	12	6
2.	2	2	0	do	25	2	6
3.	2	2	0	do	19	5	0
4.	2	2	0	do	30	2	6
5.	0	2	8	Joseph Pahm	5	1	0
6.	0	2	8	John Kratz	8	5	0
7.	0	2	8	do	8	0	0
8.	0	2	8	Edward Inergens	7	0	0
9.	0	2	8	William Amos	9	0	0
10.	0	2	8	John Baker	12	15	0
11.	0	2	8	do	13	0	0
12.	0	2	8	Henry Maurice	8	17	0
13.	0	2	8	William Amos	10	5	0
14.	0	2	8	do	7	10	0
15.	0	2	8	do	9	5	0
16.	0	2	8	do	8	5	0
17.	0	2	8	do	9	5	0
18.	0	2	8	Dugald Cameron	7	0	0
19.	0	2	8	George Grobs	7	0	0
20.	0	2	0	Thomas Shoveller	14	0	0
21.	0	2	0	do	11	0	0
22.	0	2	0	do	9	5	0
23.	0	2	8	Richard Ball	9	1	0
24.	0	2	8	John Baker	9	0	0
25.	0	2	8	do	8	11	0
26.	0	2	8	do	8	11	0
27.	0	2	8	John Wonderlich	9	1	0
28.	0	2	8	Henry Miller	10	0	0
29.	0	2	8	William Galleford	10	0	0
30.	0	2	8	Richard Ball	10	2	0
31.	0	2	8	William Lambert	11	5	0
32.	0	2	8	George Fisher	10	1	0
33.	0	2	8	Alfred Lardner	10	15	0
34.	0	2	8	George Walker	12	18	0
35.	0	2	8	do	12	2	0
36.	0	2	8	John Baker	12	0	0
37.	0	2	8	do	13	0	0
38.	0	2	8	Henry Baker	12	0	0
39.	0	2	8	Adam Maclean	10	15	0
40.	0	2	8	do	10	5	0
				Deed fees	40	0	0
	34	0	24	Total	486	3	6

Shoveller notices posted from 1857 to 1858. ▲LEFT COLUMN: 1-Shoveller - Passage aboard the "SS Grafton" from Clarence River to Sydney (Empire, 3 Oct 1857, p.5); 2-Thomas Shoveller - Postmaster (The Armidale Express & NE Gen. Advertiser, 21 Nov 1857, p.6); 3-Thomas Shoveller - Grafton Store (The Armidale Express & NE Gen. Advertiser, 28 Nov 1857, p.6); 4-Thomas Shoveller - Storekeeper advertisement, placed in the 1st edition of the Grafton Newspaper (Clarence & Richmond Examiner, 26th July 1859, p.1); 5-Thomas Shoveller - General Stores Advertisement (C&RE, 22 Nov 1859, p.1). CENTRE COLUMN: 1-Thomas Shoveller - Title Deeds (NSW Govt Gazette, 3 November 1857, p.2093); 2-Thomas Shoveller - Crown Lands (The Moreton Bay Courier, 5 December 1857, p.2); 3-Thomas Shoveller - Grafton, Land Sale (The Moreton Bay Courier, 20 January 1858, p.2). RIGHT COLUMN: 1-Thomas Shoveller - Crown Lands (The Moreton Bay Courier, 26 May 1858, p.2). 2-Thomas Shoveller - Land Sale (The Moreton Bay Courier, 30 June 1858, p.3).

GRAFTON

School of Arts

CLARENCE RIVER.

FROM OUR OWN CORRESPONDENT.

SCHOOL OF ARTS.—The members of the School of Arts held a soiree in the National School-room, on the evening of the 27th July, which was well attended, 125 persons having sat down to the table. The room was profusely decorated with flags, evergreens, mottoes, transparencies, &c. The table was most liberally supplied by the ladies, and the affair went off with satisfaction to all parties. After the removal of the cloth the Rev. A. Selwyn took the chair, and the business of the half-yearly meeting was proceeded with by the Secretary, Mr. Becke, reading the report, from which it appeared that the institution has advanced in usefulness, and number of members far beyond the most sanguine expectations of its promoters, the number of members who have joined it during the first six months being 51. The library consists of 216 volumes of books principally of an instructive character; the number of books circulated was stated to be 270, with an increasing taste for reading among the members. Five addresses had been delivered during the half-year, viz.:—

1. Opening Lecture.—Industrial Investments; by Mr. James Page.
2. Geology in connection with Scripture—Rev. A. Selwyn.
3. Plants suitable for cultivation on the Clarence—Mr. Lardner.
4. A Visit to St. Petersburg—Mr. A. Page.
5. Reading from Shakespere (Merchant of Venice)—Mr. H. Maurice.

A debating class is in active operation, and several essays have been read and discussed. The singing class has made considerable progress under the able direction of Mr. James Page, and arrangements have also been made for commencing the following classes:—

Drawing, and instruction in the German language—Mr. C. Wagner.
Arithmetic and Mathematics—Mr. J. Page.
Writing and Reading—Mr. A. Page.

The Treasurer (Mr. Lardner) announced that the receipts from members amounted to £73 5s. 6d., and the expenditure to £44 18s. 6d. The balance, £28 7s. carried to the Building Fund.

The voting papers having been handed in, the scrutineers reported that the whole of the former officers and committee were re-elected, viz.:—

R. Bligh, Esq., President. The Rev. A. Selwyn, the Rev. J. Collins, C. J. Walker, E. M. Ryan, C. G. Tindal, and Bruce M'Dougal, Esqs., Vice-Presidents. Mr. A. Lardner, Treasurer. Mr. W. H. H. Becke, Secretary. Mr. James Page, Librarian. Messrs. W. Greaves, W. Collie, T. Shoveller, H. Maurice, A. Hyde, S. Avery, J. Penzer, T. Horton, W. Cowan, junr., D. Kirk, A. Page, and W. Lambert, Committee for the ensuing year.

Considerable inconvenience being felt for want of a suitable building for the purposes of the institution, a resolution was then passed, empowering the committee to raise subscriptions, and make arrangements for the erection of the necessary buildings as soon as possible, it was also announced that the Government had promised a very suitable allotment of land as a site, and that £100 would be placed upon the estimates towards a building fund, on condition of a similar sum being raised by private contributions.

Votes of thanks having been given to the lecturers, teachers of classes, officers and committee, for their zealous and gratuitous exertions in advancing the interests of the institution, to the donors of books, and to the ladies for doing the honors of the table, the company broke up, highly pleased with the evening's proceedings—which, with the exception of some slight disagreement as to the site of the proposed building, passed off in the most satisfactory manner.

The singing class performed several pieces during the evening, which materially assisted in giving success to this first attempt at a public soiree in Grafton.

CLARENCE RIVER.

GRAFTON SCHOOL OF ARTS.

(FROM OUR OWN CORRESPONDENT.)

At a meeting of the Committee of the Institution, held at the National School-house, North Grafton, on Thursday, December 10, Mr. William Collie in the chair. Members of the Committee present—Messrs. Alfred Lardner, David Kirke, J. Penzer, James Page, Alfred Page, George Robinson, and W. H. H. Becke, Secretary.

It was proposed by Mr. J. Page, and seconded by Mr. Podmore, " That efforts be made to get in the amount of subscriptions promised, by the last Thursday in January, 1858."—Carried.

A letter was read by the secretary from Mr. James Page, offering to give the opening lecture of the institution on the second Wednesday in January; subject, " Industrial Investments."

Mr. Kirke proposed, and Mr. Lardner seconded, " that Mr. Page's offer be accepted, and that the secretary be instructed to give public notice of the same in Grafton."—Carried.

Ordered by the Committee that the lecture be free of charge to the public, and that the subject be open to discussion after the lecture.

Proposed by Mr. Alfred Page, and seconded by Mr. Kirke, " that the secretary be instructed to ascertain the cost of printing the Rules of the Institution, and to report the same to the Committee at their next meeting."—Carried.

A letter was read by the secretary from seven members of the institution, addressed to the Committee, requesting that a Debating Class may be appointed.

Proposed by Mr. Becke, and seconded by Mr. Lardner, " that a Debating Class be appointed accordingly, and that this class meet the first and third Wednesday in each month, at 7 p.m., and subject to the general rules of the institution."

Mr. Becke handed in to the chairman a list of the subscribers, amounting to £50.

The meeting adjourned.

List of Subscribers to the Grafton School of Arts:—

	£ s. d.		£ s. d.
R. Bligh, Esq., P.M.	3 3 0	D. R. Gale	1 0 0
Rev. A. F. Selwyn	3 0 0	W. Robertson	1 0 0
Wm. Collie	1 0 0	E. M. Ryan	3 3 0
C. J. Walker	3 0 0	W. Robertson	1 0 0
Rich. Payne	1 0 0	E. M. Ryan	3 3 0
A. Page	1 0 0	C. G. Tindal	3 3 0
J. Penzer	1 0 0	G. Podmore	1 0 0
W. H. Hughes Becke	1 0 0	D. Kirke	1 10 0
Alfred Lardner	1 0 0	P. Shea	1 0 0
James Page	1 0 0	J. P. Jones	1 0 0
J L. Travers	2 2 0	J. Gilmore	1 0 0
T. Shoveller	1 0 0	W. Archer	1 0 0
A. Hyde	1 0 0	Jno. Edgar	1 0 0
J. E. Chapman	1 0 0	Messrs. Robertson, Brothers	5 0 0
J. R. Elliott	1 0 0	J. R. Pate	1 0 0
H. H. Elliott	1 0 0	J. Havinden	1 0 0
Rev. J. Collins	1 0 0	C. E. Porter	2 2 0
Jas. Gregory	1 0 0		
			£59 3 0

In accordance with the terms of a circular, issued on the 31st of October, a meeting of parties favourable to the establishment of a School of Arts for the Clarence district, assembled at the Grafton National School-house, on the 11th ultimo. Amongst those present were the Rev. Mr. Selwyn, Rev. Mr. Collins, Messrs. Bligh, Walker, &c.

The chair was occupied by Mr. Bligh, who briefly addressed the meeting, explaining its object, which was the establishment of an institution for the Clarence River, and which it was proposed to call " The Grafton School of Arts." He believed Mr. Becke would be able to give them some very valuable information before they dispersed.

The Rev. A. Selwyn then moved, " That it is expedient to establish a literary institution in Grafton, to be called 'The Grafton School of Arts;' that its object shall be the moral and mental improvement of its members by means of the establishment of a literary and reading room, the delivery of lectures, and formation of classes, a museum, &c."

Mr. Lardner proposed the next resolution, " That the officers of the institution be ex officio members of committee; that the following gentlemen be requested to act as members of committee, viz.:—Mr. W. B. Greaves, Mr. William Collie, Mr. Penzer, Mr. James Page, Mr. David Kirke, Mr. W. Robertson, Mr. Alfred Page, and Mr. T. Shoveller; that the committee have power to receive subscriptions and donations for the institution, and that this committee endeavour to commence operations the first week in January, of which due notice shall be given by the secretary."

▲TOP (Left): Thomas Shoveller - Committeeman, School of Arts (Moreton Bay Courier, 18 August 1858, p.4). (Right): Thomas Shoveller - Subscriber to the Grafton, School of Arts (Moreton Bay Courier, 6 January 1858, p.3). ABOVE: Thomas Shoveller - Committee member of the School of Arts (SMH, 14 December 1857, p.5).

▲TOP: The commodius layout of the first Grafton Public School. ABOVE: The Grafton Hospital first began operating in July 1863, with Thomas Eastman Shoveller being elected as one of its first trustees.

Thomas had obviously journeyed to the Clarence River around mid 1855, and while there are many possibilities as to what actually eventuated between them, it is probable that Thomas was introduced to Susan by her father John Hann Sr.

Regardless of how they met, documents reveal that Thomas Eastman Shoveller and Susan Hann were married at the Anglican Church in Grafton on the 6th of March 1856. In fact, theirs was the first marriage to be celebrated in the original Anglican church, which stood on the corner of Duke and Victoria Streets.[16] Thomas was 13½ years older than Susan and was listed as a bachelor with no occupation recorded, and Susan was obviously a spinster, both residing in the District of Clarence. The ceremony was witnessed by James Johnson and Norman Cowan for Thomas, and Ellen Ford for Susan with her father John Hann, signing his permission, as she was obviously under age.[17] The ceremony was conducted by the Rev. Arthur E. Selwyn, Minister of the District of Clarence River from 1854 to 1867.[18]

Other than the odd friend, Thomas would have had few guests, but the deficit was more than made up by Susan's family, which included her parents John and Mary Ann Hann, and her 21 year old sister Jane, with her new husband William Olive (1822-1894) and infant

Grafton Improvement Association

CLARENCE RIVER.

(From the Correspondent of the Moreton Bay Courier, August 15.)

The Grafton Association held their half-yearly general meeting on the 3rd August, when the following report was read to the members by the Secretary :—

"GENTLEMEN—So short a time has elapsed since the annual meeting of the association took place, that we have but very little to report. The principal subjects which have engaged the attention of your committee since the last meeting took place, are—1st. The state of the roads (more particularly with reference to the proposed new route to Tenterfield). 2nd. The utterly neglected condition of the streets of the town ; and 3rd. The conduct of our representative during the past session of Parliament.

Moved by Mr. COWAN, seconded by Mr. ARCHER— "That the report of the road committee now read be received, and that the committee be empowered to collect subscriptions for carrying out the same. That Messrs. Avery, Shoveller, and Hyde, be added to the road committee, and that a Memorial be prepared to the House of Assembly, praying for a grant of money to open the road."

GRAFTON.

[FROM OUR CORRESPONDENT]

NOVEMBER 6.—A project for opening a new road to New England, which has been agitated by the Grafton Improvement Association several times during the past two years, has been again revived, and is exciting a lively interest in this town. The rapid development of the Timbarra gold fields has awakened our storekeepers and tradesmen from their usual apathy, and they have at last discovered that good roads to the interior are absolutely necessary to develope the resources of the district, and to promote the interests of the inhabitants.

With the view of again bringing this subject under the consideration of the Government, a public meeting was held in the National School-house, North Grafton, on Tuesday last. Mr. W. A. B. Greaves in the chair.

Mr. Lardner having been called upon to state what steps had been taken in the matter, read extracts from the correspondence, and the proceedings of the association, from which it appeared that upwards of two years ago the Government were requested by a public meeting to cause the line to be surveyed, and to make a grant of money to open the same, and representing that upwards of 30 miles in a distance of 90 could be saved by its adoption, with a much sounder tract of country to be traversed, than the old road could ever become, and that no serious obstacles existed to prevent the adoption of this route. A

Moved by Mr. A. HYDE, seconded by Mr A. PAGE, and carried, "That the following gentlemen be requested to form a committee to carry out the objects of this meeting, viz : Messrs. A. Lardner, W. Cowan, C. Chauvel, S. Avery, T. Horton, W. Oville, S. Cohen, J. T. Jones, G. R. Elliott, J. Penzer, J. Page, T. Bowden, Mr. Chapman, treasurer, and Mr. T. Shoveller, secretary."

GRAFTON.

(From the Armidale Express, Jan. 23.)

CAPTURE OF A DESPERADO.—On the 9th instant, Constables Kelly and Bossman, of the Grafton police, were at the Travellers' Rest Inn, thirty-two miles from Grafton, on duty. Shortly after arriving there, they saw a man coming down the range in front of the place ; at first he made as if he were intending to call, but suddenly turned off, and went along the road. Kelly, thinking to obtain some information from him connected with the duty he was on, hailed him, but the man still continued going on. Kelly then followed him, whereupon he took to his heels, and Kelly called on Bossman to bring one of the horses out of the stable. On taking to his heels the fellow dropped a bundle, which was afterwards found to contain a pair of percussion pistols, nearly new, Blakemore and Sons makers, with swivel ramrods. Bossman succeeded in running the fellow down, about a mile from the house, in the bush ; upon getting up to him, he said, "What do you want ?" Bossman said, "I want to speak to you ;" whereupon he turned round, and struck the constable on the head with a stick, followed by a second blow on the horse's head, causing the horse to swerve away, when the fellow immediately ran off in another direction. Bossman jumped off, collared him, and threw him twice ; the second time he received a deep stab near the right nipple, penetrating the lungs. He then made a second attempt to stabb Bossman, but the latter, being a powerful man, succeeded in raising his head, and held him until Kelly, who was by this time close at hand, came up. Kelly had to use some very persuasive means before the fellow would relinquish the knife. Kelly then, brought him to the house. Bossman, being in a very bad state from loss of blood, and the breath escaping from the wound, a messenger was despatched to Grafton, where he arrived about 11 p.m. As a doctor could not be got to go, Mr. Bligh, P.M., started immediately, Mr. Shoveller having supplied him with a horse, and there being but one constable in the town, viz.—the chief, Mr. Pate, innkeeper, of North Grafton, with great and commendable spirit volunteered his services to accompany Mr. Bligh. They started with the prisoner from the Travellers' Rest on the day after arriving there, and yesterday lodged him in the lock-up ; Kelly having been left to assist Bossman down. We are happy to say he is under the skilful care of Dr. Little, and he is a good way of recovery. Upon the prisoner at the time of his capture were notes, &c., to the amount of £50. An inquiry was held yesterday, before R. Bligh, Esq., P.M., when the prisoner was committed to take his trial for stabbing Constable Bossman. The trial was hardly over when the Tenterfield mail arrived, bringing information from the chief constable at Tenterfield that a man named John Lock had been shot and robbed of £54 by a fellow named John Williams, near Tenterfield, and that the police were on his track. The prisoner now in the lock-up answers the description given by Mr. Gordon, and there can be but little doubt that he is the man. He was no doubt making his way to Sydney. Great praise is due to the Constables Bossman and Kelly for their conduct in this affair, as also Mr. Pate, who acted in such a spirited and patriotic manner in the emergency.

SAILING MATCH AT THE CLARENCE.—A match came off at Grafton, on the 23rd instant, for £20 a-side, between Mr. Bligh's Betsy, and Mr. Bawden's Eclipse (open boats), under canvass. The usual Grafton regatta course twice over. The gun fired for the start precisely at ten minutes after one p.m., the Eclipse going away from her moorings with a good lead ; the Betsy, getting into difficulties, jibed once or twice ; she, however, managed, in consequence of the lightness of the wind, to overhaul the Eclipse, and at the rounding of the upper buoy was at a very short distance in the rear. From this, however, the Eclipse gradually kept gaining ground, rounding the lower and upper buoy second time, and was off Shoveller's when the Betsy rounded the lower buoy ; it was now quite palpable that the latter stood no chance, unless some accident occurred to the blue boat. The suspense was soon at an end by the Eclipse coming in a winner in capital style, in one hour and 30 minutes, the Betsy bringing up at her original mooring at the Ferry Wharf, not attempting to go round the lower buoy the second time. Great praise is due to Mr. Duncan Campbell, who fitted out the Eclipse, for the capital manner in which he rigged and sailed her. This boat sailed as the Kate in the late regatta, coming in third.—*Cor. of Era.*

▲LEFT (Top): Thomas Shoveller - on The Grafton Association Committee (Empire, 26 August 1857, p.5). (Above): Thomas Shoveller - Committee secretary for a new road to New England (SMH, 9 November 1858, p.8). RIGHT (Top): Thomas Shoveller - Capture Of A Desperado (The Maitland Mercury & Hunter River Gen. Advertiser, 28 January 1858, p.5). (Above): Thomas Shoveller - Sailing Match (The Maitland Mercury & Hunter River Gen. Advertiser, 14 March 1858, p.3).

children Sarah (1) and Edwin (0). The rest of Susan's siblings were all as yet unmarried and included Joseph (20), John Jr. (18), Sarah (16), Mary Ann (13), Lucy (11), George (9), Emily (5) and William (2). Just nine days after their wedding, the "Caesar Godeffroy" arrived in Grafton with 182 German immigrants to the Clarence River, of which many descendants are residents today.

Unfortunately the year after brought the demise of Susan's father, John Hann Sr. who died on the 2nd of March 1857 in a freak and tragic accident, leaving his wife Mary Ann Hann alone with eight children.[19] While on the road and in heavy rain, John Hann apparently turned his bullocks loose and camped for the night under a tree... the ground being very squashy, when a large tree fell across the wagon during the night, forcing the dray into the soft ground and slowly crushing Hann who was sleeping beneath it. He was brought back and buried on the Hann property on the corner of Prince and Bacon Streets in Grafton.[20] Although Joseph (20) and John Jr. (19) were old enough to fend for themselves, their father's death left Sarah (14), Mary Ann (13), Lucy (11), George (7), Emily (5) and William (2½) in the care of their mother, although she was obviously assisted by her two married daughters in Jane Olive (22) and Susan Shoveller (16).

Wharfinger, Spirit Merchant & Storekeeper

At some stage in the mid to late 1850s, Thomas Shoveller accepted the responsibility of being a 'wharfinger' at Grafton, an archaic term for a person who was the keeper or owner of a wharf. The wharfinger took custody of and administered goods delivered to the wharf. They typically had an office on the wharf or dock, and were responsible for the day-to-day activities including slipways, keeping tide tables and resolving disputes. Thomas set himself

▲ABOVE (Left): View of South Grafton from Wilsons Hill in 1873. (Right): 'Clarence River Blacks', photographed by J.W. Lindt, c.1880
ABOVE: The Grafton Post and Telegraph Office opened in 1863.

▲ TOP: The eastern side of Prince Street, Grafton looking south-east from Pound St, with Pott's Beehive Store in the foreground, and the School of Arts in the background, about 1872. ABOVE: The paddlesteamer "Agnes Irving" loading up at the Grafton Wharf, c.1870.

up as an agent of sorts, and a point of contact for people trying to find each other through newspaper notices. One of his first advertisements in Grafton was for 'wharf services' in August of 1856.[21]

Thomas also saw potential in the liquor trade, and on the 20th February 1857, the 1st January 1858 and the 20th July 1958, the authorities listed Mr Thomas Shoveller as a registered wholesale spirit merchant for the District of Grafton. Following experience gained at the gold diggings in California or perhaps at gold fields in NSW, and other visits to Sydney aboard vessels like the paddlesteamer "Grafton," Thomas realised a need for a storekeeping business in Grafton. With support from Susan's mother, they decided that a store should be built on the Hann land in Grafton. It is believed that Mary Ann Hann had the store built for Thomas in 1858, and that he cut down the scrub on the land himself. He placed weekly advertisements in the local papers for his general store, and also took on the duties of postmaster.

At the same time he turned to the accumulation of property, mostly through buying up at Crown Land sales. A sale of Crown Lands situated near North Grafton took place at the Court House on the 19th November 1857, and on 17th April 1858 for Special Country Lots, with Thomas purchasing Lot 13 (8/2/0) for £17, and Lot 9 (4/2/0) for £22.[22]

From 1857 onwards, the township of Grafton progressed at a rate of knots and Thomas Shoveller, along with a number of other community minded citizens, were at the forefront of organising a number of improvements. By August of 1857 Thomas was appointed to the Grafton Road Committee.

But "the School of Arts was undoubtedly the principal cultural institution in town, which was an asset that had no competitor for a large radius around the town."[23] Thomas both subscribed to and was most passionate about this community facility and served in various capacities over a number of years. The Institution for the Grafton School of Arts, was formed on the 3rd July 1858, and on the 2nd September 1859, Thomas was appointed as an officer of the Organising Committee.[24]

By then Thomas and Susan had welcomed their first child, Susan Theresa Shoveller into the world on the 15th May 1858.[25] She was baptised on the 5th of August, but sadly died soon after. As a local businessman, Thomas was now on the way to becoming a prominent member of the local community when he gave an address on behalf of the residents of Grafton District supporting Mr. C. J. Walker, and expressing confidence in his integrity.[26]

On the 26th July 1859, an advertisement for 'Thomas Shoveller, Storekeeper' was placed in the very first edition of the Clarence and Richmond Examiner.

THOMAS SHOVELLER
Storekeeper
Prince Street, North Grafton,
Begs to inform his friends and residents of Grafton
And its vicinity that he has received and now has on hand
All descriptions of general stores,
Which he is retailing at the lowest renumerative prices.

Clarence & Richmond Examiner, 26th July 1859, p.1. [27]

Just four weeks later, Susan Shoveller delivered Susan Eva Shoveller, who was born on 24th August 1859 at North Grafton, although her baptismal date hasn't yet been found.[28] Thomas stated in the birth certificate that he was 30 years old (actually 32), originally born in Warnford, Hampshire, England and gave his occupation as a storekeeper. Susan Shoveller was listed as being the 19 year old mother, who was born at Woodford Island on the Clarence River.

Alderman of Grafton Municipal Council

Around this time, things really began happening in Grafton especially in regard to the formation of a municipality. On Friday the 16th of September, and just three weeks after the birth of his daughter, Thomas Shoveller was elected as an alderman (Second Ward) in the inaugural Municipal Council of Grafton. It is obvious from the transcript of the first meeting that these gentlemen were forward thinkers as some very important initiatives were taken in that inaugural Council meeting for Grafton. Thomas Shoveller and John Edward Chapman both declared their intention to stand for the position of Mayor. Mr. T. Bawden then suggested that a ballot take place when Mr. Shoveller was called to the chair pro-tem, and Messrs Bawden and Kennedy were requested to act as scrutineers.

In the ballot, seven declared for Chapman, who obviously voted for himself, leaving Thomas and Mr. Jones as the only two votes for Shoveller. Therefore, the bootmaker won over the storekeeper and became the first Lord Mayor of Grafton. The meeting is notable however, in that Thomas Shoveller was actually the very first Chairman of the Municipal Council of Grafton, even if it was just for a temporary period to conduct the election.[29]

Duke of Clarence

Duke of Grafton

Minutes and Proceedings of the Municipal Council of Grafton

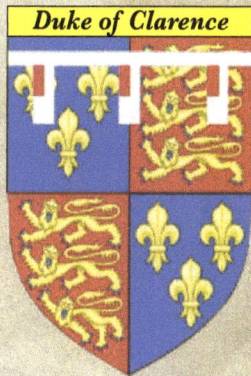

John E. Chapman

Thomas Bawden

Minutes and Proceedings of the 1st Municipal Council Meeting, Grafton Court House, 16 September 1859

Meeting called for the purpose of electing a chairman. Present:

Mr. Thos. Bawden	*Auctioneer*
Mr. William Cowan	*Hotelkeeper*
Mr. Patrick Kennedy	*Storekeeper*
Mr. J.T. Jones	*Hotelkeeper*
Mr. John Edward Chapman	*Bootmaker*
Mr. Thos. Shoveller	**Storekeeper**
Mr. Samuel Avery	*Farmer*
Mr. Richard Payne	*Farmer*
Mr. William Lambert	*Farmer*

Some introductory remarks being made by Mr. Chapman.

Prop. by Mr. Chapman, Sec. by Mr. Jones:

"That **Mr. Thomas Shoveller** be elected chairman."

Prop. by Mr. Avery, Sec. by Mr. Cowan:

"That Mr. Edward Chapman be elected chairman."

Mr. Bawden suggested that a Ballot should take place when **Mr. Shoveller** was called to the chair pro tem: and Messrs Bawden and Kennedy were requested to act as Scrutineers. The result of the Ballot was for:

Mr. Chapman = 7; **Mr. Shoveller = 2**

Majority for Mr. Chapman = 5

Mr. John Edward Chapman having signed the Declaration was at once conducted into the Chair.

The Chairman having returned thanks for the kind wishes expressed towards him and acknowledged the great honour conferred upon him. The following resolutions were admitted to the Council:

Moved by Mr. Bawden, Sec. by Mr. Lambert:

"That the title of the Members of the corporation should be Chairman and Councillors" After some discussion an Amendment was...

Moved by Mr. Avery, Sec. by Mr. Cowan:

"That the Members of this Corporation shall be known and recognised by the names of Mayor and Alderman subject to the approval of His Excellency the Governor General and the Executive Council of New South Wales" Carried.

Moved by Alderman Bawden, Sec. by Alderman Payne:

"That a Committee be appointed for the purpose of framing By Laws and Standing Orders for the government of the Municipality, such Committee to consist of the Mayor, Alderman Cowan, **Shoveller** and Lambert" Amendment was...

Moved by **Alderman Shoveller**, Sec. by Alderman Kennedy:

"That a Committee be appointed for the purpose of framing Standing Orders for regulating the proceedings of this Municipality, the Committee to consist of the Mayor, Alderman Cowan, **Shoveller** and Lambert" Carried.

Notice of Motion by Alderman Bawden:

1st "That application be made to the government for such lands as they may be pleased to Grant or place under the Control of this Council for the following purposes, viz":

Town Commonages each side of River	*do*
Cemeteries	*do*
Market places and Wharves	*do*
Rec. Grounds, Botanical Gardens	*do*
Race Course and Bathing places	*do*
Council Chamber or Town Hall	*do*

Hospital and other Benevolent purposes intended by Act of Incorporation to be in charge by this Council.

Notice of Motion by Alderman Bawden:

2nd "That the Government be requested to furnish the Council with a Map of the Towns of North and South Grafton and a book of reference."

Notice of Motion by Alderman Bawden:

3rd "That in the opinion of this Council the assessment of the Municipality should be commenced at once, and with that view this Council do now take best mode of carrying it out."

Notice of Motion by Alderman Bawden:

4th "That this Council meet on Thursday Evening at 7 o'clock for the despatch of business" J. E. Chapman - Mayor adjourned meeting.

▲TOP (Left): The arms of the Duke of Clarence, who later became King William IV, for which the Clarence River was named. (Mid): Minutes of the 1st Grafton Council meeting, showing Thomas Shoveller's bid for Mayor of Grafton. (Right): The arms of the Duke of Grafton, a former Prime Minister of the United Kingdom, and namesake for the settlement. ABOVE (Left): Photographic portrait of Mr. John Edward Chapman (1819-1908), the man who defeated Thomas Shoveller's bid to become Grafton's First Mayor. (Right): Photographic portrait of Mr. Thomas Bawden (1833-1897).

It is also interesting that within four years of selling the very first lots of land in the new town of Grafton, the people had asked for and obtained permission to govern themselves as a municipality. Early on, the streets were wide and mostly covered with brush, but by October of 1859, new councillors of the municipality called for the clearing of the streets for the better convenience of trade and traffic.

> "The very next year, Mr. Alfred Lardner was elected Mayor. At about the same time Mr. James Page was appointed first Council Clerk, which position he held until his death in May 1877. Thomas Shoveller was elected Treasurer and Messrs. W.A.B. Greaves and Arthur Hyde were elected Auditors.

Grafton and District: Fifty Years of Progress [30]

The 1860's

Mr and Mrs Thomas Shoveller returned to Grafton after buying goods in Sydney, and were listed as passengers aboard the steamer "Grafton," on the 20th November 1860.[31] But the next year, Thomas sold his business to William Campbell when it became officially known as the Clarence River Stores. Although, it is likely that Susan's mother Mary Ann Hann, still retained ownership of the premises.

▲ TOP: Photo of the Dobie St Bridge over Alumny Creek, looking west from the corner of Dobie & Queen Streets, Grafton, which was largely funded by Thomas Shoveller. ABOVE: Thomas' wife Susan Shoveller, who herself was named after Thomas Small's ship, the "Susan", was asked to christen the bridge over Dobie Street and "broke upon it a bottle of wine," naming it after her little girl, Susan Eva Shoveller, so it became known as 'Susan's Bridge.'

▲*Looking west to Susan Island on the Clarence River, painted by A.H. Fullwood, c.1894.*

Thomas didn't last long on the Grafton Council and had resigned his position by 1860, but he remained an active member of his community. In September of that year, he signed his name to a petition for the rather hopeful 'Separation of the Clarence District from NSW', which obviously never succeeded.[32]

By 1861, events in North America were becoming increasingly ominous and by April the situation had descended into Civil War between the north and the south, although these events had little bearing on the faraway colony of New South Wales.

Thomas was also a trustee for the Grafton Hospital, along with Clark Irving, C.J. Walker, W.A.B. Greaves, James Page, Alfred Lardner, Samuel Avery, Rev. A. E. Selwyn, William Kirchner and Rev. William Fidler. The foundation stone was laid on the 16th December 1862, and the Hospital was completed in July of 1863.[33,34]

By May of 1862, Thomas was amongst others listed as creditors in Thomas Bawden's insolvency proceedings, and this may have caused some animosity between them. Thomas Shoveller was listed as being owed the considerable amount of £142.9s.11d, with no notice of these monies ever being realised.[35]

Susan's Bridge

There are conflicting reports as to who the bridge over Dobie Street was named, and even Joan Allerton of the Clarence River Historical Society at Grafton was not able to find a correct answer. However, in March of 1862 a new bridge crossing over Alumny Creek at Dobie Street, was completed and officially opened... largely funded by Thomas Shoveller. Susan Shoveller was asked to christen the structure and "broke upon it a bottle of wine", naming it after her little girl, Susan Eva Shoveller, so it became known as 'Susan's Bridge'. Unfortunately, the bridge was swept away 14 years later by the 1876 flood!

"Mr. Thos. Shoveller also offered £70 towards the construction of a bridge over Alumny Creek in Dobie St. This offer was accepted and a bridge erected at a cost of £185. Mr. John Strauss Jr. being the contractor."

Grafton and District: Fifty Years of Progress [36]

GRAFTON ECONOMIC STORES,
PRINCE-STREET,
NORTH GRAFTON,
NEAR THE BANK.

W. H. SHOVELLER having purchased the business lately carried on by Mr. John M'Fadden, begs respectfully to inform the inhabitants of Grafton and the Clarence District, that he has added to the stock a large and varied assortment of

NEW GOODS,

Of the best quality, in each department, which he is prepared to sell at the VERY LOWEST PRICES FOR CASH.

AMONG THEM ARE :—

Elegant novelties in ladies' dresses, mantles, shawls, &c.,
Pretty summer bonnets
Straw ditto of the same shapes
A large quantity of ladies' and children's hats
Trimmed ditto
Children's summer suits, in Knickerbocker's and Hungarian braiding
An extensive choice of ladies' and gentlemen's BOOTS, of the fashionable makes
Gentlemen's summer suits, and hats.

THE PROVISION DEPARTMENT

will be found supplied with all the usual stores of the best quality, with the addition of Christmas Niceties.

Pudding currants, 5½d., and 6d., per lb.
Ditto raisins, 8d., per lb.
Finest table muscatels, 1s., per lb.
Best tea, 2s. 3d. per lb.
Choice ground coffee, 1s. 4d., per lb.
Ditto in tins, 3½, 7, and 14 lbs.
Sugar, from 3½d.
Finest chrystal ditto, 6d.
Loaf ditto, 8d.
Delicate ground spices.
Ditto essence flavourings.
Nice bottled fruits, and jams.
Dried apples.
Fresh pickles
Preserved oysters, lobsters, salmon, sardines.
Selected sauces.
Confectionary.

A QUANTITY OF USEFUL AND ORNAMENTAL BASKETS

IRONMONGERY,
&c., &c.

PRETTY BONNETS.

Admirers of those becoming articles of dress, are respectfully informed that a number of exceedingly ladylike style are now on view at

THE SHOW ROOMS
OF THE
ECONOMIC STORES,
PRINCE-STREET,
NEAR THE BANK.
Prices from 9s. 9d. to 17s. 6d.

LOCAL INTELLIGENCE.

NOMINATION OF AN ALDERMAN FOR EAST WARD.

The nomination of an Alderman for the above Ward, caused by the retirement of Mr. Shoveller, took place on Tuesday last, at the Court House, North Grafton.

SHIPPING.

ARRIVALS—September 5.
Grafton (s.), 200 tons, Captain Creer, from Clarence River 7th instant. Passengers—Mrs. Lewthall, Miss Lyons, Messrs. M'Evilly, Shoveller, West, and twenty-seven in the steerage. C. and R. N. Company, agents.

SHIPPING.

ARRIVALS—November 21.
R. H. Talbot, American ship, 591 tons, Captain Noyes, from Manila 6th August. Passengers—Mr. Andrews and servant. Captain, agent.
Grafton (s.), 200 tons, Captain Creer, from the Clarence River 20th instant. Passengers—Mr. and Mrs. Shoveller, Miss M'Kenzie, and 17 in the steerage. C. and R. N. Co., agents.
November 22.
City of Sydney (s), 700 tons, Captain Moodie, from Melbourne 19th instant. Passengers—Mrs. Huntley, Miss Wright, Mrs. and Miss Chisholm, Mr. and Mrs. Moore, Mr. and Mrs. Moore, Mr. and Mrs. Holmes, Mrs. Gantor, Captain Edwards, Messrs. Whittingham, Peak, Holmes, Bryan, Kelly, and 26 in the steerage. A. S. N. Co., agents.

WEDNESDAY.
SHOVELLER V. HANN.

This was an action to recover the sum of £31 2s. 9s. being the balance of an account. Defendant did not appear. Verdict for the full amount. Mr. Michael for plaintiff.

SHOVELLER V. YATES.

This was an action for goods sold and delivered. Defendant did not appear. Verdict for plaintiff, £6 9s. 8d.

SHOVELLER V. HENRY.

This was an application for a writ of CA SA, to enforce the payment of £9 14s. 6d., being the balance of an account. It appeared from the argument of Mr. Michael, who appeared for plaintiff, that a verdict had been obtained for the amount in the Small Debts Court, an execution issued, and the defendant sold off, the proceeds of which sale realised only 9s., although he had been informed that the defendant at the time resided in two comfortably furnished rooms, the furniture of which was not owned by him, in addition to which he was in constant employ and well able to pay the amount now in question.

GRAFTON CHRISTMAS RACES,
TO COME OFF ON
BOXING DAY,
THE 26TH OF DECEMBER, 1862.
STEWARDS:

THOMAS SHOVELLER | JOHN HANCOCK
THOMAS BAWDEN | ARTHUR HYDE
J. E. CHAPMAN |

Clerk of the Course — SAMUEL AVERY.

SHIPPING.

ARRIVAL—February 12.
Agnes Irving (s), 500 tons, Captain Creer, from Clarence River 11th instant. Passengers—Miss Ward, Messrs. Jacobs, Peppercorn, Shoveller, and 17 in the steerage. C. and R. N. Co., agents.
Gertrude, American barque, 558 tons, Captain Bartlett, from San Francisco December 8. Passengers—Mr. and Mrs. Ohio and son, Mr. Goldsmith, and 3 in the steerage. G. A. Lloyd and Co., agents.

ABSTRACT OF SALES BY AUCTION DURING THE WEEK.

MR. HENRY MAURICE.—At Mr. Shoveller's Store, Queen-street, Grafton, This Day, and three following days, commencing each day at 11 o'clock prompt, the whole of the Stock-in-Trade, consisting of Drapery, Haberdashery, Hosiery, Millinery, Groceries, Oilmen's Store, Perfumery, Fancy Goods, Ironmongery, Tin Ware, Hollowware, Crockery, Glassware, Plated Ware, Saddlery, Wines, Spirits, Beer, &c., &c., also, Weighing Machine, Scales, Dray and Harness, Horse, Milch Cows, House-Furniture, Culinary Utensils and a lot of sundries.

WHEN YOU MARRY, BUY FURNITURE AND BEDDING FROM T. & W. SHOVELLER, WHO HAVE ALWAYS ON HAND A CHOICE SELECTION OF GENERAL HOUSEHOLD FURNITURE, at prices hitherto unheard of. The QUEENSWARE is made up exclusively of first class workmen. The MATTRESSES and PALLIASSES are made properly, by a regular Sydney mattress maker.
CHAIRS are in great variety; Single and double IRON BEDSTEADS, handsome, strong, and CHEAP.
Elegant PIER GLASSES, 21s., worth 3 s., and all the necessaries for furnishing a house at the same CHEAP RATE.
THOS. & WILLIAM SHOVELLER.

FINE LIGHT COUNTER SUGAR, in sound bags of about 56 lbs. each, at 2¾ a lb. by the bag, CASH ; 3d. by the single pound. This surpasses any sugar at the price ever offered in Grafton, and is fully equal to sugar recently sold at 4d.
THOS. & WILLIAM SHOVELLER.

AN ADDITION OF
£3000 WORTH OF FRESH GOODS,
Carefully selected by THOMAS SHOVELLER personally, and bought at the lowest price at which CASH could procure them.
THOS. & WILLIAM SHOVELLER.

A FEW LARGE SIZED BUSH SADDLES,
All complete, with crupper, only £3 19s. each ; worth at least £5 10s. only a few of them are still remaining.
THOS. & WILLIAM SHOVELLER.

CHOICE STYLES IN CHALLIES, 9¾d a yard
Fancy lined silk parasols, 2s. 11d.
Checked angola cloth, 2 yards wide, 3s. 11d.
A large variety of plaids, all wool, from 1s. 0½.
Russell cord, in all colours, 1s. 3d.
Fancy quilting (beautiful for ladies' jackets)
Ladies' fine white cotton stockings, 5½ a pair
A variety of belts and braces.
A large and miscellaneous assortment of ladies' underclothing
Hearth rugs, genteel patterns, 3s. 9d.
Hollands, linens, hosiery, blankets, flannels, shirts, &c., &c., at a wonderful reduction in price
Prints, wide width, warranted fast colours, 6½d a yard
Plain colours and checked flannels, all wool, 2s. 6d. a yard
Short blinds, window curtains, window Holland, &c., &c.
Stout millers' moleskin, 1s. 5d. a yard
Chenelle hair nets, 11d.
Black coburg, 8½d a yard
Boys' knickerbocker suits in every material, remarkably low.
Men's stout tweed trousers, 9s. 9d.
All wool crimean shirts (gentlemen's patterns), at 6s. 9d.
Full sized gents' white shirts, 3s. 8d.
An immense stock of ladies' and gentlemen's BOOTS and SHOES, from 2s. 3d. a pair (worth 4s. 6d.), having been BOUGHT FOR CASH BY THOMAS SHOVELLER, during his late VISIT TO SYDNEY, at which time he embraced every opportunity of buying up all CHEAP GOODS procurable for ready money.
THOS. & WILLIAM SHOVELLER.

Shoveller notices posted from 1860 to 1863. ▲LEFT COLUMN: Advertisement for William Shoveller's Economic Stores (The Clarence & Richmond Examiner, 23rd December, 1862, p.3). CENTRE COLUMN: 1-'Thomas Shoveller - Resigns from Council (C&RE, 13 March 1860, p.2); 2-Shoveller - Shipping on the "Grafton" (SMH, 10th Sept 1860, p.4); 3-Shoveller - Shipping on the "Grafton" (SMH, 22 Nov 1860, p.4); 4-Thomas Shoveller - vs 3 x Defendants (C&RE, 4 Nov 1860, p.2); 5-Thomas Shoveller - Race Steward (C&RE, 23 Dec 1860, p.4); 6-Shoveller & Peppercorn - Shipping on "PS Agnes Irving" (SMH, 13th Feb 1863, p.4); 7-Mr. Shoveller's Store - Auction (C&RE, 31 May 1864, p.2). RIGHT COLUMN: Thomas & William Shoveller's - Store Advertisements (C&RE, 24 March 1863, p.1).

It may be that Thomas Eastman Shoveller also purchased an inn at the 'Cross Roads' between Grafton and Lawrence in 1862. Then towards the end of that year, their first son, Thomas Charles Shoveller was born on the 6th October 1862.[37] The Clarence and Richmond Examiner stated that he was born at the Shoveller residence in Queen Street, and they received congratulations from many in the Grafton community.

Despite the good news, Thomas Shoveller still had a number of customers who were indebted to him. On the 4th of November 1862, the local newspaper reported that a number of cases had been brought before the Grafton Court. Thomas had taken action to recover debts from three people, which included £9.14s.6d. from Mr Henry, £6.9s.8d. from Mr Yates, and £31.2s.9d. from Hann, one of his wife's own family, although we aren't sure whether this was his mother-in-law, or one of Susan's brothers.[38]

Family Reunion

Not long after the birth of Thomas and Susan's son, another Mr and Mrs Shoveller arrived in Australia. At this time regular coastal shipping services between Grafton and Sydney were well established, and on the 5th of November 1862, Thomas departed Grafton on the "Urara" for the purpose of effecting a family reunion in Sydney. Thomas' older brother, William Henry Shoveller, had emigrated from England aboard the "Vimeira" with his wife Mary Ann, and their four children Ellen (11), William Henry Jr. (8), Ada (6) and their new baby Eva Rose (1). Under Captain Swanson, the "Vimeira" at 1037 tons was a large and comfortable vessel, and she had been once hailed as the most beautiful ship afloat, but on this journey had departed from the Downs, off Deal, Kent, on the 4th July, arriving in Sydney on the 25th October 1862.[39]

After 15 years, and having lost their dear mother in the years between, the reunion of the brothers would have made for an emotional rendezvous. After taking in the sights of Sydney, the reconciled brothers returned to the Clarence aboard the "SS Grafton", and were warmly greeted at the wharf by Susan Shoveller and a multitide of Hann relatives.

With much support from Thomas, William immediately proceeded to use his hard earned English pounds to establish a merchant business on Prince St, near the Bank, which between them they called the 'Grafton Economic Stores,' and advertisements were placed in the local newspaper to promote the enterprise.[40,41,42]

In what was a joyous moment on the 21st December 1862, both Shoveller families and many Hann relatives gathered to celebrate the baptism of Thomas and Susan's new son Thomas Charles, at the Anglican Church in Grafton. Then, hoping for a bright future ahead, William Henry Shoveller placed a long advertisement in the local newspaper just two days before Christmas 1862, which featured a fascinating inventory of the kinds of products that settlers of that period required and utilised.[43]

In keeping with his community mindedness, Thomas was scheduled to act as a steward at the Grafton Christmas Races to come off on Boxing Day 1862, but their optimism was replaced by a tragedy that befell both Shoveller families, and Thomas surely didn't proceed with his commitment.[44] Unfortunately, the calamity that struck on Christmas Day was only the first blow in a series of events that would severely test the resolve and determination of both Thomas and William Shoveller and their families.

References

1. Lee, Stuart (2003). 'Riverboats of the Clarence", Port of Yamba Historical Society, Yamba, p.7.

2. NSW Dept of BDM. (1840). Birth & Baptism Certificate for Susan Hann, 8th August 1845 (#3106/Vol. 30A).

3. NSW Dept of BDM. (1835). Birth & Baptism Certificate for Jane Hann, 1st January 1835 (#609/1835 V1835609 20).

4. NSW Dept of BDM. (1836). Birth & Baptism Certificate for Joseph Hann, 11th July 1836 (#610/1836 V1836610 20).

5. NSW Dept of BDM. (1838). Birth & Baptism Certificate for John Hann, 3rd March 1838 (#597/22).

6. Mary Matilda Hann (nee Thompson) - Death notice (The Sydney Mail & NSW Advertiser, 8 July 1882, p.74).

7. Jane Olive (nee Hann) - Obituary (Clarence & Richmond Examiner, 5th Oct, 1889.)

8. Bawden, Thomas (1886). John Hann - Report of the death (The Bawden Lectures; The First Fifty years of Settlement on the Clarence, Clarence River Historical Society, p.120).

9. NSW Dept of BDM. (1842). Birth & Baptism Certificate for Sarah Hann, 2nd June 1842 (#3105/30).

10. NSW Dept of BDM. (1843). Birth & Baptism Certificate for Mary Ann Hann, 15th July 1843 (#2870/28).

11. NSW Dept of BDM. (1845). Birth & Baptism Certificate for Lucy Hann, 15th Nov 1845 (#2724/32).

12. NSW Dept of BDM. (1847). Birth & Baptism Certificate for George Hann, 16th Dec 1847 (#3153/1849 V18493153 34A).

13. NSW Dept of BDM. (1851). Birth & Baptism Certificate for Emily Hann, 7th Oct 1851 (#3444/37).

14. NSW Dept of BDM. (1854). Birth & Baptism Certificate for William Hann, 10th April 1854 (#4346/40).

15. NSW Dept of BDM. (1854). Marriage Certificate for Jane Hann & William Olive at Grafton, 23rd January 1854 (#1148/41).

16. Wedding Announcement for Eva Meally & Frederick Della Ca (Grafton Argus, 16th Oct 1912).

17. NSW Dept of BDM. (1856). Marriage Certificate for Thomas Eastman Shoveller & Susan Hann at the Church, Grafton, 6th March 1856 (#1125/43B).

18. Australian Dictionary of Biography - Arthur Edward Selwyn (1823–1899), by Rex Davis [https://adb.anu.edu.au/biography/selwyn-arthur-edward-4557].

19. NSW Dept of BDM. (1857). Death certificate for John Hann Sr., 2nd March, 1857 (#2879/1857).

20. Bawden, Thomas (1886). John Hann Sr. - Report of the death (The Bawden Lectures; The First Fifty years of Settlement on the Clarence, Clarence River Historical Society, p.120).

21. Thomas Shoveller's advertisement for Sharp's Wharf (Armidale Express & NE Gen. Advertiser, 23 Aug 1856, p.1).

22. Thomas Shoveller - Crown Lands (The Moreton Bay Courier, 17 April 1858, p.2).

23. Kass, Terry (2009). Grafton: Jacaranda City on the Clarence-A History, Clarence Valley Council, p.91.

24. Grafton School of Arts (1859). Committee among Officers of the Institution for the Grafton School of Arts, 2nd Sept 1859.

25. NSW Dept of BDM. (1858). Birth & Baptism Certificate for Susan Theresa Shoveller, 15th May 1858 (#7416/1858).

26. Thomas Shoveller - Address to G.J. Walker on the 25th August 1858 (Selwyn Papers, Mitchell Library, NSW, A 737, p.311).

27. Thomas Shoveller - Storekeeper (Clarence & Richmond Examiner, 26th July 1859, p.1).

28. NSW Dept of BDM. (1859). Birth & Baptism Certificate for Susan Eva Shoveller, 24th August 1859 (#258/7801).

29. Grafton Municipal Council (1859). Minutes and Proceedings of the Municipal Council of Grafton Court House, 16 September 1859.

30. Grafton Municipal Council, (1910). 'Grafton and District: Fifty Years of Progress 1859-1909', Grafton, p.35.

31. Mr & Mrs Shoveller - Passengers on "SS Grafton" - Arrived Grafton (SMH, 22 Nov 1860, p.4).

32. The Clarence River Separation Question (Empire, 29 Oct 1861, p.8); Thomas Shoveller - Separation from NSW (Clarence & Rich. Ex, 27th Sep 1902, p.2).

33. Davies, R. E. (1957). 'History of the Clarence River,' in the Daily Examiner, 20 February 1957.

34. Paine, K. (2005). 'History of Grafton Hospital,' Clarence River Historical Society, p.8.

35. Thomas Shoveller - Insolvency Court (Clarence & Rich. Ex, 27th May 1862, p.2).

36. Grafton Municipal Council, (1910). op.cit, p.41.

37. NSW Dept of BDM. (1862). Birth & Baptism Certificate for Thomas Charles Shoveller, 6th October 1862 (#8141/1862).

38. Thomas Shoveller - vs 3 x Defendants (C&RE, 4 Nov 1860, p.2).

39. Mr. & Mrs. Shoveller & Four children [William Henry Shoveller] - Passengers on "Vimeira" - Arrived Sydney (Sydney Mail, 25 Oct 1862, p.5).

40. Thomas & William Shoveller - Store Advertisement (C&RE, 24 March 1863, p.1).

41. Thos. & William Shoveller - Advertisement (Clarence & Richmond Examiner, 24 March 1863, p.1).

42. Thomas & William Henry Shoveller - Spirit Merchants (Clarence & Richmond Examiner, 10 Feb 1863, p.2).

43. Advertisement for William Shoveller's Economic Stores (The Clarence & Richmond Examiner, 23rd December, 1862, p.3).

44. Thomas Shoveller - Race Steward for Christmas Races (Nth Australian & Qld Gen. Ad, 13th Nov 1862, p.3).

Chapter Eighteen

Shoveller

Hann

THE SHOVELLER FAMILY & THEIR TROUBLES

Internationally, the election of Abraham Lincoln as U.S. President in 1860 lead the southern states to form the Confederate States of America in February of 1861, which launched the United States into the American Civil War, and the Emancipation Proclamation to free slaves in rebel areas came into law on the 1st January 1863. Later that year, the Union victory at the Battle of Gettysburg in July, was the turning point of the war in favour of the Union. In London the tube opened on the 10th January 1863, becoming the oldest underground railway network in the world, and Louis Pasteur's experiments in the early 1860s proved the germ theory of disease.

However, life remained difficult in Australia, with the ill-fated explorers Burke and Wills, dying at Cooper's Creek in June 1861, after trekking from Melbourne to the Gulf of Carpentaria. This disaster was followed up by scotsman John McDouall Stuart (1815-1866), one of the most accomplished of all Australia's inland explorers, who reached Port Darwin from Adelaide on the 24th July 1862. By early 1863, South Australia had taken control of the Northern Territory, which was previously part of the colony of New South Wales.

In the northern rivers district of New South Wales, rain had been falling intermittantly throughout the spring of 1862 and the ground was already saturated by mid-December. It was at this joyous time of year, with a future full of promise, that calamity struck when William and Mary Ann Shoveller's one year old daughter Eva, died on Christmas Day. It was a shattering loss at what should have been the happiest time of year.[1,2] Little Eva's body was buried in a sombre ceremony at the Grafton cemetery, and the distraught couple would have questioned why they had come all the way from England, simply to bury their children.

As THE UNDERSIGNED intends VISITING SYDNEY shortly, to make EXTENSIVE CASH PURCHASES, he will feel obliged by all parties indebted to him settling their last year's accounts, at an early date.
THOMAS SHOVELLER.

▲ *Recent map of Grafton, showing the location of Susan Island, the main town, South Grafton and the cemeteries. INSET: 1863 Thomas Shoveller - Notice to debtors just prior to the big flood (C&RE & NE Advertiser, 27 Jan 1863, p.3).*

▲ TOP: Illustration of the 1863 Clarence River Floods. ABOVE (Left & Mid): Two illustrations of the devastating 1863 floods at Grafton. (Right): Scene during the Great Clarence Flood of 1863, painted by Conrad Wagner.

Of Drought and Flooding Rains

By February 1863, settlements along the Clarence River were reporting record-breaking rains with minor floodwaters inundating the entire district, claiming the lives of people and causing extensive damage to riverside towns and farms. The flood followed two months of wet weather that had brought an end to a severe drought. The relief felt after the drought had broken was short lived in the Grafton region as concerns grew over the saturation of the countryside throughout January and early February.

Observers noticed a rapid rise in the Clarence River on February 14th and warned others that the flood risk was increasing. Later that night Grafton received the heaviest rainfall of the season and the flood conditions worsened. At its peak, the floodwaters rose more than seven metres above the high water mark.[3]

Homes, crops and livestock were lost all along the river while the small town of Tabulum suffered severely as four men leading drays were washed away. The rise of water was so rapid that it left a number of people trapped on roofs and in trees. The local newspaper described the rescue efforts of three local men.

"They swam to several persons who had been twenty-four hours clinging to trees and by means of ropes brought them to places of safety. Several lives were saved in this manner,"

Sydney Morning Herald, 5 March 1863[4]

Brothers Thomas and William Henry Shoveller had invested everything into their new venture and had even taken on a licence to sell spirits. But the flood was indiscriminate and devastated everything in its path. William and his wife were exasperated by the catastrophic turn of events. Fortunately all the family had survived, but William Henry Shoveller and family, packed up whatever they had left and by early May had made the momentous decision to sail home to England. William Henry left in such a hurry that a number of creditors he had accounts with, searched for and even advertised for his whereabouts.

Thomas's family and his in-laws the Hann's, had no other option than to clean up, repair the damage and carry on. Thomas was appointed as a trustee of the No. 2 Building Society in April 1863,[5] and by January 1864 he was listed as the Grafton agent for the Sydney Insurance Company, obviously trying to capitalise on the recent flood devastation.[6] Thomas continued operating his ruined store, but it wasn't enough to prevent him from falling into insolvency.

The Queen vs Thomas Shoveller

On the 22nd of August 1863, Susan Shoveller departed Grafton on the paddlesteamer

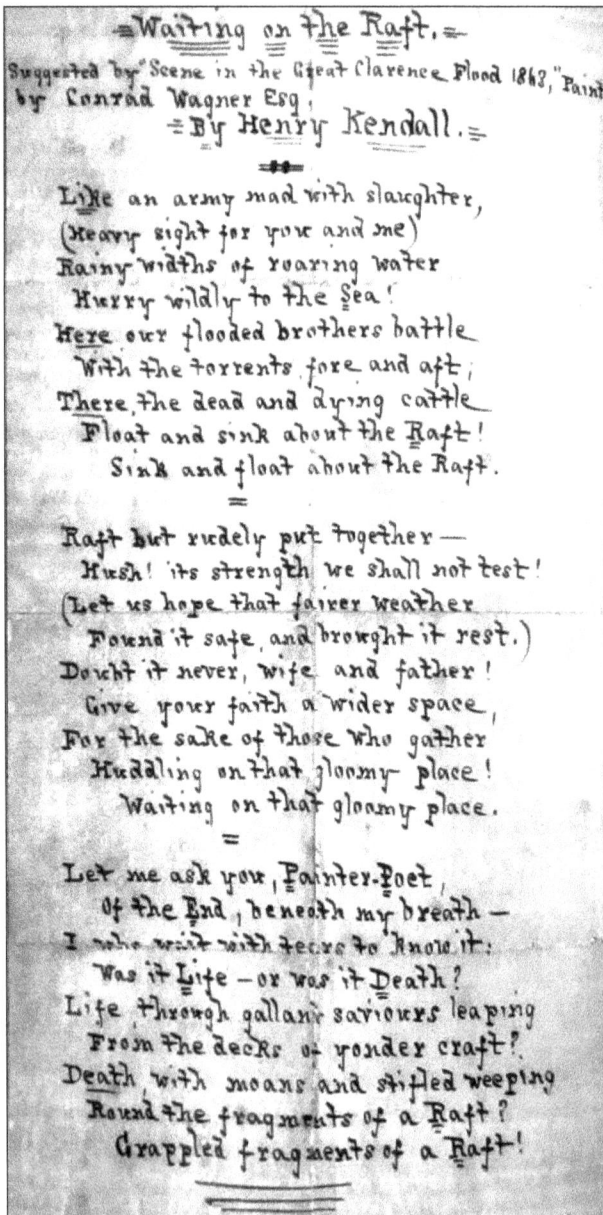

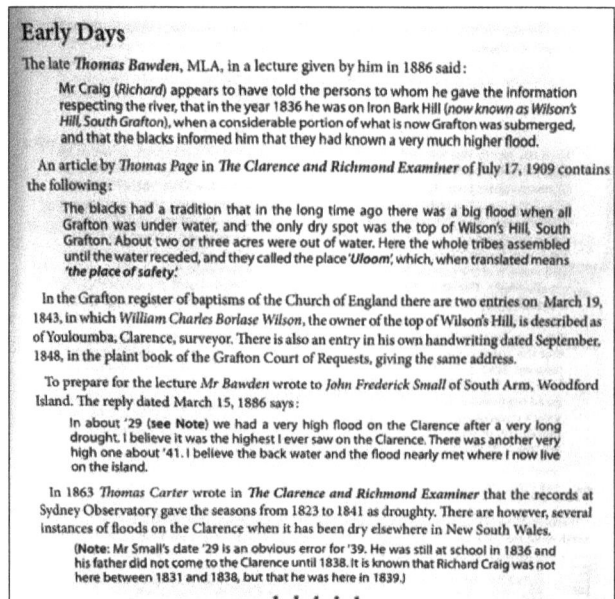

THE GREAT FLOOD IN CLARENCE RIVER.
LOSS OF NINE LIVES.
(From the Clarence and Richmond Examiner, February 24.)

WITHIN the period of the occupation by white men of the district of the Clarence, no calamity has befallen it so great as that which it is this week our painful duty to record. Not more than three or four months have elapsed since the water was salt or brackish nearly up to the First Falls; but since Christmas the weather has been often showery: this has gone on increasing until, about the end of January, "a fresh" warned us that the country above was reaching the point of saturation, and many foresaw that a continuance of rain must result in a more destructive one. The rain did continue, and must have been general over the whole of this site of the country, as we find that Morpeth was flooded on the south, and it is plain that the same weather stretched northward. The consequence is that we are this week called on to chronicle the highest and by far the most destructive flood recorded on the river; resulting in some loss of life (probably more than is yet accurately discovered), and a general devastation of property which we fear will be severely felt for a long time.

Early Days

The late *Thomas Bawden*, MLA, in a lecture given by him in 1886 said:

Mr Craig (*Richard*) appears to have told the persons to whom he gave the information respecting the river, that in the year 1836 he was on Iron Bark Hill (*now known as Wilson's Hill, South Grafton*), when a considerable portion of what is now Grafton was submerged, and that the blacks informed him that they had known a very much higher flood.

An article by *Thomas Page* in *The Clarence and Richmond Examiner* of July 17, 1909 contains the following:

The blacks had a tradition that in the long time ago there was a big flood when all Grafton was under water, and the only dry spot was the top of Wilson's Hill, South Grafton. About two or three acres were out of water. Here the whole tribes assembled until the water receded, and they called the place '*Uloom*', which, when translated means '*the place of safety*'.

In the Grafton register of baptisms of the Church of England there are two entries on March 19, 1843, in which *William Charles Borlase Wilson*, the owner of the top of Wilson's Hill, is described as of Youloumba, Clarence, surveyor. There is also an entry in his own handwriting dated September, 1848, in the plaint book of the Grafton Court of Requests, giving the same address.

To prepare for the lecture Mr Bawden wrote to *John Frederick Small* of South Arm, Woodford Island. The reply dated March 15, 1886 says:

In about '29 (see Note) we had a very high flood on the Clarence after a very long drought. I believe it was the highest I ever saw on the Clarence. There was another very high one about '41. I believe the back water and the flood nearly met where I now live on the island.

In 1863 *Thomas Carter* wrote in *The Clarence and Richmond Examiner* that the records at Sydney Observatory gave the seasons from 1823 to 1841 as droughty. There are however, several instances of floods on the Clarence when it has been dry elsewhere in New South Wales.

(Note: Mr Small's date '29 is an obvious error for '39. He was still at school in 1836 and his father did not come to the Clarence until 1838. It is known that Richard Craig was not here between 1831 and 1838, but that he was here in 1839.)

▲*LEFT: 'Waiting On The Raft,' poem by Henry Kendall. RIGHT (Top): 'The Great Flood In Clarence River - Loss of Nine Lives' (SMH, 5 March 1863, p.5). (Above): Clarence River Floods - The Early Days (from Ford, p.15).*

The Queen vs. Thomas Shoveller

CENTRAL POLICE COURT, SYDNEY.

FRIDAY, FEBRUARY 19TH.

[FROM OUR SPECIAL REPORTER.]

Before Mr. Ross, J.P.

THE QUEEN v. THOMAS SHOVELLER AND WILLIAM LEVY LAWRENCE.—CONSPIRACY.

Thomas Shoveller and William Levy Lawrence, were charged with conspiring to defeat the object of the Acts of Council, relating to Insolvency, and to cheat and defraud the creditors of Thomas Shoveller; that in pursuance of such conspiracy, Thomas Shoveller, and William Levi Lawrence did remove and conceal, and assist in removing and concealing, part of the personal estate of the said Thomas Shoveller, to the value of £300—that is to say, a large quantity of three-bushel bags, files, oval boilers, soap, candles, pickles, oils, pearl barley, pepper, American axes, &c., &c.

The defendants pleaded " Not Guilty "

CENTRAL CRIMINAL COURT—THURSDAY.

Before Mr. Justice Milford.

CONSPIRACY.

Thomas Shoveller and William Levy Lawrence were indicted for having, at Grafton, on the 24th October, 1863, conspired together to defraud the creditors of the said Thomas Shoveller, by the secretion of certain goods which Shoveller ought to have included among the assets conveyed on that day to trustees for the benefit of his creditors.

The defendants pleaded not guilty.

The case for the Crown was conducted by the Attorney-General and Mr. Dalley, the latter gentleman appearing on behalf of Shoveller's creditors. Mr. Darvall, Q.C., appeared for the defendants.

This case was precisely similar to that of the Queen v. Shoveller and Tupper, tried on Tuesday last. The only difference between the two cases was that of the change in defendants, Lawrence taking the place of Tupper, both of whom were charged with assisting Shoveller to remove goods from the premises of the latter, for the purpose of defrauding the creditors.

The trial occupied the whole of the day.

The jury, after deliberation, found both prisoners guilty.

Sentence—Two years' imprisonment in Darlinghurst gaol.

Upon the announcement of the verdict, the prisoner Lawrence fainted, but speedily recovered.

The Court adjourned at nine o'clock until the 17th May next.

NEW TRIAL MOTIONS.

THE QUEEN V. SHOVELLER AND LAWRENCE.

This was a motion for a new trial of a case of misdemeanour tried at the last sittings of the Central Criminal Court, before Mr. Justice Milford.

The prisoners Shoveller and Lawrence had been both tried and convicted of conspiracy to defraud the creditors of the former, by the concealment of certain goods which ought to have formed part of Shoveller's estate then under assignment to trustees.

A new trial was moved for upon the ground—first, evidence had been excluded of a conversation after a witness had spoken as to part of it. Secondly, that there was no such evidence of action in concert as was necessary to constitute, in law, a conspiracy. Thirdly, that the verdict was repugnant, inasmuch as it was a general verdict upon all the counts, whereas it ought to have been a verdict on one count only. Fourthly, that there was no evidence to sustain the verdict upon any of the counts.

Mr. Darvall, Q.C., and Mr. Isaacs, appeared in support of the motion; and the Attorney-General and Mr. Dalley in support of the conviction.

The argument was not concluded.

LEGISLATIVE ASSEMBLY.

WEDNESDAY.

SENTENCES ON LAWRENCE AND SHOVELLER.

Mr. FORSTER asked the Attorney-General—1 With reference to the recent mitigation of sentence granted or promised by the Executive Government to Lawrence Levy, or Levy Lawrence, and Thomas Shoveller, both formerly of Grafton, sentenced to two years' imprisonment for being concerned in fraudulent insolvency—To what extent, under what circumstances, and on what recommendation was such mitigation granted or promised? 2. Was the mitigation granted in either case without or against the recommendation of the judge who tried the case; and, if so, under what circumstances?

Mr. COWPER said the mitigation in the case of Lawrence was to this extent:—He was sentenced to two years' imprisonment, in April, 1864, and in April, 1865, he was released. A petition in his favour, signed by a large number of highly respectable persons, was presented to his Excellency the Governor. This petition was sent to the judge who tried the prisoner, and who was not unfavourable to the mitigation, but was quite willing that such remission should be granted. It was much the same in regard to Shoveller. Shoveller was retained in prison till her Majesty's birthday. In both cases the judge was applied to, and made no objection to leave it entirely with the Executive, as they thought it not unreasonable for the mitigation to be granted.

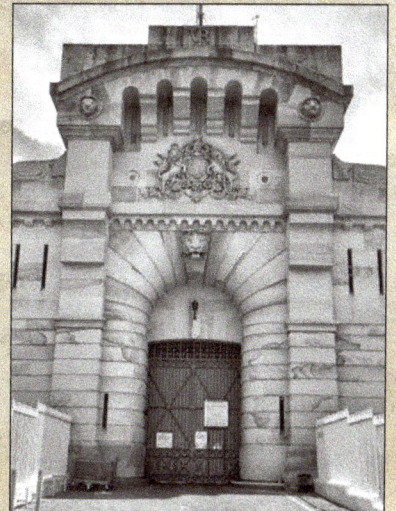

▲LEFT COLUMN: 1-*The Queen v Shoveller* (*Clarence & Rich. Ex*, 1 March 1864, p.2); 2-Criminal Court - *The Queen v Shoveller* (Empire, 8 April 1864, p.2); 3-Thomas Shoveller - New Trial (SMH, 14 June 1864, p.4); 4-Thomas Shoveller - Mitigation of Sentence (Clarence & Rich. Ex. 20th June 1865, p.3). RIGHT (Top): Entrance to Darlinghurst Gaol, 1865. (Mid): Darlinghurst Gaol from Burton St, 1870. (Above-Left): The hand written petition for William Levy Lawrence, February 1865. (Above-Right): The imposing entrance to Bathurst Gaol, to which Thomas Shoveller was transferred in May 1864.

SUPREME COURT RETURN OF CONVICTIONS.

A RETURN of all Prisoners convicted at the Gaol Delivery holden at Sydney, in the Month of March and April 1864.

Name of Prisoner.	Offence.	Date of Conviction.	Judge.	Sentence.	Recommendation, or Remarks.	Disposal.
Thomas Shoveller and	Conspiracy to defraud creditors	April 7th	Milford	Imprisonment in Darlinghurst gaol for two years		
William Levy Lawrence	Conspiracy to defraud creditors	do	do	Imprisonment in Darlinghurst gaol for two years.	then tried to be moved from this case.	

1864

No.	NAME.	CON.	SHIP.	WHERE BORN.	RELIGION.	TRADE.	AGE.	HEIGHT. Feet. In.	MAKE.	COMPLEXION.	COLOR of HAIR. EYES.	EDUCATION.	REMARKS.
939	Thos. Shoveller		Lala Rookh	44	England	Prot	Storekeeper	37				R & w	
940	Wm Levy Lawrence		D. Wellington	52	do	Prot	do	34				R & w	

1864

DATE.	NO.	NAME.	COMMITTED. By whom.	Where.	When.	OFFENCE.	SENTENCE.	DISPOSED OF. How.	When.
April 7	939	Hos. Shovener	S.C. Court	7 April	Sydney	Conspiring to defraud Creditors	Confine 2 Years	To Bathurst Gaol	23 June 1864
	940	Wm Levi Lawrence				do	do 2 Years		13 April 1865

No 2

Particulars of the Conviction of twenty five prisoners whom it is proposed to transfer from Darlinghurst Gaol to Bathurst Gaol in consequence of the overcrowded state of the former establishment.

No	Name	Age	Where and when Convicted			Offence	Sentence	Remarks
17	Thomas Shoveller	37	Sup C Court	7 April	1864	Conspire to defraud	2 Years Impt	Convicted with Lawrence who is to be sent to Bmt gaol
18	Charles Smith	33	Sess 2S	16 Oct	1863	Felony	3 Yrs Labor	
19	William Taylor	15	Sydney Sess	16 Feby	1863	Larceny	2 Years Labor	
20	Wm White or Yellow Billy	22	Maitland CC	4 Oct	1863	Horse stealing	2 Years Labor	
21	Chas Marshall or Herbert	38	Dorolignan CS	4 April	1864	Uttering Forgery	2 Years Labor	
22	George Crosby	50	Sup C Court	2 April	1864	do	3 Years Labor	
23	Ah Kee al Ah Sins	30	Bathurst CC	8 Sept	1863	Larceny	3 Years Labor	
24	Richard Jenkins		Yass Sess	16 Feby	1864	do	2 Years Labor	
25	Charles Willis	23	Braidwood 2S	16 Nov	1863	do	10 Months Labor	

For the Sheriff

Darlinghurst Gaol 6 May 1864

Deputer

June 1864

No.	Name					Trade or Calling		Admitted When	Where	Purpose	Disposed of How	When	Offence
161	John Gough				Catholic	Castle	Birckbryan	28 June	Darlinghurst Gaol	3 Years Labor	Discharged from Labor	July 28 1864	Horse Stealing
	Thomas Shoveller	Lala Rookh				Prot	Storekeeper	28 June	Darlinghurst Gaol	2 Years Impt	by remission of the sealing of the Croaking the Governor	May 24 1865	Convicted with Lawrence

▲ TOP: The Court Conviction of Thomas Shoveller; 2-Darlinghurst Gaol 'Entrance Book' entry for Thomas Shoveller; 3-Darlinghurst Gaol 'Description Book' entry for Thomas Shoveller; 4-Transfer paper between Darlinghurst and Bathurst Gaols, 6th May 1864; 5-Darlinghurst Gaol 'Entrance Book' entry for Thomas Shoveller.

1865.

LEGISLATIVE ASSEMBLY.

NEW SOUTH WALES.

PRISONERS LEVEY AND SHOVELLER.

(ADMINISTRATION OF JUSTICE.)

Ordered by the Legislative Assembly to be Printed, 14 November, 1865.

RETURN to an *Address* of the Honorable the Legislative Assembly of New South Wales, dated 7 November, 1865, praying that His Excellency the Governor would be pleased to cause to be laid upon the Table of this House,—

"(1.) Copies of all Letters and Communications to the "Executive Government, in reference to the liberation of "the prisoners Levey and Shoveller, and all Answers to said "Communications.

"(2.) All Minutes of the Executive bearing on this subject.

"(3.) Copies of the Opinions of the Judge or Judges who "were consulted as to the release of these prisoners, and "every Communication from the Judge or Judges to the "Executive on the subject."

(Mr. Buchanan.)

SCHEDULE.

NO.		PAGE.
1.	David L. Levy to the Colonial Secretary, forwarding Petitions on behalf of William Levy Lawrence. 8 February, 1865	
2.	Under Secretary to Mr. Justice Milford, requesting His Honor's report on the Petitions. 13 February, 1865	6
3.	Mr. Justice Milford to the Colonial Secretary, in reply. 16 February, 1865	6
4.	Under Secretary to Mr. D. L. Levy, in reply to No. 1. 28 February, 1865	6
5.	Do. to the Sheriff, 28 February, 1865	6
6.	Renewal of Petitions forwarded in No. 1. 14 April, 1865	6
7.	Under Secretary to Sheriff, directing the liberation of Lawrence, 13 April, 1865	6
8.	Do. to Mrs. Lawrence, 13 April, 1865	7
9.	Do. to Inspector General of Police, 13 April, 1865	7
10.	Petition of Susan Shoveller, praying the remission of the sentence passed upon Thomas Shoveller	7
11.	Under Secretary to Mr. Justice Milford, requesting His Honor's report upon the Petition. 30 March, 1865	8
12.	Mr. Justice Milford to the Under Secretary, in reply. 4 April, 1865	8
13.	Under Secretary to Visiting Justice of the Bathurst Gaol, authorizing the liberation of Shoveller. 25 April, 1865	9
14.	Do. to Inspector General of Police, 25 April, 1865	9
15.	Do. to Mr. Justice Milford. 25 April, 1865	9

No. 3.

MR. JUSTICE MILFORD *to* COLONIAL SECRETARY.

Supreme Court,
16 February, 1865.

SIR,

I have the honor to report upon the petition of William Levy Lawrence convicted, together with Thomas Shoveller, on the 7th April, 1864, of conspiracy to defraud the creditors of Thomas Shoveller, at Grafton, on the 19th October, 1863. The evidence established, to the satisfaction of the Jury, that Thomas Shoveller, who was a shopkeeper at Grafton, being in difficulties, came to Sydney in October, 1863, for the purpose of arranging with his creditors, and got them to accept an assignment of the estate upon certain trusts. During his absence, Lawrence, to whom he was indebted, with the consent of Mrs. Shoveller, took away goods to satisfy his debts, and other goods apparently for the benefit of Shoveller. The latter purchased the estate, and afterwards returned to Grafton, when many of the goods taken away were returned to Shoveller. The proof, in a great measure, depended upon the evidence of one Mackay—the manager of Shoveller, and a party to the transaction—with whom Shoveller had quarrelled; but I had no reason to think the verdict was wrong. The two prisoners, Shoveller and Lawrence, were found guilty of a conspiracy to defraud their creditors—a misdemeanor of such frequent occurrence as to call for a severe sentence in order to check its perpetration. Whether, the sentence having been passed, and the prisoners having suffered a part of the punishment directed, it may be thought right to remit any part of the unexpired term of imprisonment, is rather a matter for the Executive Government than for the Judge. Probably, however, the sentence itself may have had nearly as great an effect on the public as the continuance of the punishment to the end of the term of imprisonment would have, and if so, perhaps some remission might be granted.

I have, &c.,
SAML. FREDK. MILFORD.

PRISONERS LEVEY AND SHOVELLER. 7

No. 10.

PETITION OF MRS. SHOVELLER.

To His Excellency the Right Honorable SIR JOHN YOUNG, Baronet, &c., &c., &c.

The humble Petition of Susan Shoveller, of Grafton, wife of Thomas Shoveller, a prisoner in Her Majesty's Gaol, Bathurst,—

RESPECTFULLY SHEWETH :

That your Petitioner's husband was tried, in conjunction with one William Levi Lawrence, at the Central Criminal Court, on the 6th April, 1864, and convicted, before His Honor Judge Milford, of conspiracy to defraud, and sentenced to two years' imprisonment.

Your Petitioner would respectfully point out that her husband was convicted wholly upon the unsupported testimony of a discharged servant, who, in his evidence, was compelled to admit having himself been the first mover (during the absence in Sydney of your Petitioner's husband) in forming a conspiracy with Lawrence; and your Petitioner's husband, upon reaching home, was placed in the awkward position of either taking M'Kay (the discharged servant) to the Police Office or keep silence, which silence was construed into a ratification of their actions.

Your Petitioner would also, with all due deference, respectfully draw your attention to the letter from Lawrence to M'Kay, brought in by the Crown on behalf of the prosecution, in which M'Kay is enjoined twice in a short letter not to make any of the movements known to your Petitioner, alleging she had been already repeatedly asked and refused to allow any goods to leave the premises, on the ground of not having received any instruction from her husband for their removal.

Your Petitioner would further state, that her husband has resided in Grafton almost from boyhood, and, until this unfortunate circumstance, was respected by the inhabitants of the entire district, having held the office of Honorary Treasurer to several of the leading local institutions.

Your Petitioner would further add, that she with two children are left entirely unprovided for, owing to the incarceration of her husband, and humbly trusts, therefore, that your Excellency will be graciously pleased, in this instance, to exercise the prerogative of mercy, by granting a remission of sentence.

And your Petitioner, &c.

SUSAN SHOVELLER.

WE,

---

8 PRISONERS LEVEY AND SHOVELLER.

WE, the undersigned, have pleasure in bearing testimony to the general character of Mr. Thomas Shoveller, at present a prisoner in Her Majesty's Gaol, Bathurst. He has resided in Grafton during the past fourteen years, and was, up to the period of his incarceration, respected in the district as an upright, respectable business man, enjoying the confidence of all those with whom he was brought in contact, and has faithfully discharged the duties of Honorary Treasurer to several of our leading local institutions.

It will afford us much pleasure to hear of his release from Gaol.

C. G. Tindal, Ramorine	Henry Cuthbert, Grafton
Ed. Potts, draper, Grafton	T. S. Loewenthal, Grafton
T. Bawden, J.P., Mayor of Grafton	John Edwd. Chapman, Regent Park,
Alfred Lardner, J.P., Grafton	Clarence River
R. Pirey	Wm. Stueley, builder, Grafton
Arthur Hyde, Grafton	Ald. Wm. S. White, Grafton
W. J. Starling, Grafton	P. C. Greaves, Grafton
C. M. A. Shannon	Alderman J. P. Jordan
James L. Michael	Christian Kraus
Henry Maurice, Grafton	W. Attwater, Grafton
G. Keegan, Grafton	E. B. Maides
James T. Jones	James Gregory, Grafton
James Laird, Grafton	George Robinson, Grimsby House,
Richard Bell, Grafton	Grafton
William Layton	Richard Payne, Grafton
Edwd. C. Lisman, Grafton	William James, Grafton
Lewis Jacobs, Grafton	W. H. Schröder
Thomas Gogean	John Holmstien, Grafton
Ald. Charles Avery, Grafton	John James, Grafton
Wm. Cowan, South Grafton	John Gilmore, Grafton
Chas. J. Grant, North Grafton	Thomas Wray, Grafton
Richard Stevenson, Grafton	S. J. Lyons, Grafton
John Davies	William S. Mayne, Wesleyan
Daniel Moyes, Grafton	Minister
C. Wagner, Grafton	John M'Fadden, Grafton
James Page, Grafton	Walter Hindmarsh
Robert Matheson, Grafton	Edward Greenwood, Grafton
Alexander Fairweather	James S. Drew, Grafton.

Parsonage, Grafton,
15 March, 1865.

HAVING been applied to, to give my testimony to the character of Thomas Shoveller, late storekeeper in this place, with a view to obtaining a mitigation of the sentence which he is now fulfilling, I can certify that, up to the time of his conviction, he enjoyed the respect and confidence of many, as evidenced by the various offices of public trust to which he was appointed.

ARTHUR E. SELWYN,
Minister of Church of England, Grafton.

No. 11.

PRINCIPAL UNDER SECRETARY *to* MR. JUSTICE MILFORD.

Colonial Secretary's Office,
Sydney, 30 March, 1865.

SIR,

I am directed to request the favour of your Honor's report upon the accompanying petition for mitigation of the sentence of two years' imprisonment, passed by you upon the prisoner named in the margin.

I have, &c.,
W. VALLACK.

No. 12.

MR. JUSTICE MILFORD *to* COLONIAL SECRETARY.

Supreme Court,
4 April, 1865.

SIR,

In answer to your letter of the 30th ultimo, relating to the case of Thomas Shoveller, convicted with W. Levy Lawrence of conspiracy, I have the honor to refer you to my report of the 17th February last, on the case of Lawrence: the observations there made by me apply as well to the one case as the other.

I have, &c.,
SAML. FREDK. MILFORD.

No. 13.

PRISONERS LEVEY AND SHOVELLER. 9

No. 13.

PRINCIPAL UNDER SECRETARY *to* VISITING JUSTICE, BATHURST GAOL.

Colonial Secretary's Office,
Sydney, 25 April, 1865.

SIR,

Referring to the petition in favour of the prisoner named in the margin, praying for a mitigation of his sentence of two years' imprisonment in Bathurst Gaol, I am desired by the Colonial Secretary to inform you, that His Excellency the Governor has been pleased to authorize the remission of Shoveller's sentence on Her Majesty's next Birthday, the 24th proximo.

2. You will, therefore, cause the prisoner to be liberated accordingly, provided no other cause exist for his detention.

I have, &c.,
W. VALLACK.

No. 14.

PRINCIPAL UNDER SECRETARY *to* INSPECTOR GENERAL OF POLICE.

Colonial Secretary's Office,
Sydney, 25 April, 1865.

SIR,

I am desired by the Colonial Secretary to inform you, that His Excellency the Governor has been pleased to authorize the remission, on the 24th proximo, Her Majesty's Birthday, of the sentence of two years' imprisonment in Bathurst Gaol, passed upon Thomas Shoveller, for conspiracy, and that the necessary instructions have been given for carrying this decision into effect.

I have, &c.,
W. VALLACK.

No. 15.

PRINCIPAL UNDER SECRETARY *to* MR. JUSTICE MILFORD.

Colonial Secretary's Office,
Sydney, 25 April, 1865.

SIR,

In acknowledging the receipt of your Honor's report of the 4th instant, I am desired by the Colonial Secretary to inform you, that the Governor has been pleased to authorize the remission, on Her Majesty's next Birthday, the 24th proximo, of the remainder of the sentence of two years' imprisonment in Bathurst Gaol, passed upon Thomas Shoveller, for conspiracy, and that the necessary instructions have been given for carrying this decision into effect.

I have, &c.,
W. VALLACK.

▲*Documents (items 3 & 10-15) printed by the NSW Legislative Assembly (lower house) concerning the prisoners Levey and Shoveller, whose sentence had essentially provided a lesson to all those colonists who were defrauding creditors and escaping their bankruptsy obligations, 1865.*

"Agnes Irving" and while no children were travelling with her, no one could have foreseen the troubles that lay ahead. Unfortunately, the storekeeping business in Queen Street wasn't going well for Thomas and by late 1863, with his debtors unable to pay their bills, he had great difficulty paying his own, and by the 24th October, he had thoroughly exhausted the patience of his creditors. However, rather than make him an outright bankrupt they agreed to an assignment of his assets, stock in trade, real property and book debts to allow him time to trade out of his troubles.

His main creditor was his brother-in-law, William Olive (carrier), whom Thomas owed £113.4s.4d. The other 61 creditors combined were owed approximately £335, an average of just £5.10s. per person. The deed of assignment provided a detailed listing of Thomas Shoveller's assets, inventory, creditors and debts at that time. Then on the 19th October 1863, while trying to trade out of his insolvency predicament, Thomas hid some of his assets, but fell foul of the law when he was charged with 'cheating and defrauding his creditors by removing and concealing part of his personal estate, to the value of £300.'[7]

The trial was held at the Central Criminal Court in Sydney before Mr. Justice Milford. The devastating and unprecedented outcome was that Thomas Shoveller along with his two accomplices Mr Tupper and Mr Lawrence, were found guilty by the jury, with

Thomas Eastman Shoveller - Deed of Assignment

J. O. 23/6/4

Sir,

I am directed to inform you that your letter of the 20th instant requesting that Thomas Shoveller may remain in Darlinghurst Gaol for a period of three months has been laid before His Honor the Chief Justice who considers that the reasons advanced therein would not justify the prisoner's detention in Sydney inasmuch as his removal has been ordered by the Government

Landed Property:

Powell & Queen Streets... (allotment, 0.5 acre-unimproved)	£50
Racecourse... (2 x allotments, 0.5 acre-unimproved)	£50
Dobie & Queen Streets... Dobie (allotment) & Queen St. (2 x allotments, on part is a good dwelling house, Store and wood outbuildings)	£600
South Grafton... bought from Bawden (2.5 acres-unimproved)	£50
Lawrence... (2 x allotments-unimproved)	£10
Lawrence... (allotment from Crown-unimproved)	£5
Prince Street... (allotment, with a Store or Shop)	£350
Powell Street... cnr block (4-5 allotments,slab house & kitchen)	£180
	£1,295

Stock In Trade & Other Personal Estate & Effects:

Drapery, Ironmongery, Grocery and other goods now in shop in Queen Street occupied by Thomas Shoveller...
- Spirits, Wines, Heavy Ironmongery, Grocery and other goods in Store adjoining that Shop.
- Chairs, Corn shellers, Barrow, Wheels, Zinc, Pump, Treacle and other goods in the Stable.
- Salt, Zinc, Bath Bricks and other goods in Hut.
- Boots, Shoes and other goods in store room at house of Thomas Shoveller.
- Crockery, Glassware, Lamps, and other goods in 'Room known as the Crockery or Earthenware Room' in the house of the said Thomas Shoveller.
- Millinary, Drapery and other goods in shop in Prince Street.
- Four shares in the Grafton Building Society.
- Tooloom Gold in possession of Edward Chapman.
- Sundries - 4 horses, 2 cows and calves, 1 spring cart and harness, 1 dray and harness, 1 saddle.
- Household Furniture [omitted here].
- Office furniture - 1 pigeon holes, 1 deal table, 1 letter spring.
- Cash in hand - about £25.

▲LEFT: Sketch of a courtroom scene from the 1860's, showing the wigged barristers with the accused in the dock. RIGHT (Top): Thomas Shoveller - in Sheriffs Letters, c.1863 (NSW, Sheriff's Papers 1829-1879). (Above): The full list of landed property, stock in trade and other personal estate and effects of Thomas Eastman Shoveller as valued and listed by the Bailiff in 1863, for the purpose of repaying creditors.

▲TOP: Drawn view of Prince St, Grafton about 1874, showing the offices of the Clarence & Richmond Examiner. ABOVE: Shoveller notices posted from 1866 to 1869. (Above Left): 1-Thomas Shoveller - passenger on the "PS Grafton"(Clarence & Rich. Ex, 23 Jan 1866, p.2); 2-Thomas Shoveller - Defendant 'Servants Claim' (Clarence & Rich. Ex, 18th June 1867, p.2). (Above Mid): Thomas Shoveller - Plaintiff 'Detaining cedar' (Clarence & Rich. Ex, 8th Oct 1867, p.2). (Above Right): 1-Shoveller - passenger arriving Sydney on the "PS Agnes Irving"(Empire, 16th March 1869, p.2); 2-Thomas Shoveller - Plaintiff in Forgery (NSW Police Gazette, 6 March 1867, p.88); 3-Notice of the birth of Janet E. A. Shoveller (C&RE, 7th Dec 1869).

each sentenced to two years imprisonment in Darlinghurst Gaol![8] On the 6th May 1864 Thomas was transferred to Bathurst Gaol "in consequence of the overcrowded state of the Darlinghurst establishment." From this point on, Thomas's hard fought reputation, which had been carefully cultivated over the years, now counted for nothing. By May of 1864, in absentia, Thomas was forced to sell his entire stock-in-trade to pay off his creditors and help fund his legal costs, while at the same time a motion to begin a new trial was filed.[9]

By February 1865, 'a petition in his favour, signed by a large number of highly respected townsfolk of Grafton, headed by the Rev. Arthur E. Selwyn,' was presented to his Excellency the Governor, the Right Hon. Sir John Young.[10] This caused the presiding judge, Justice Samuel Frederick Milford to refer the case to no less than the NSW Legislative Assembly at Parliament House on Macquarie St., reasoning that:

"The two prisoners, Shoveller and Lawrence, were found guilty of a conspiracy to defraud their creditors - a misdemeanor of such frequent occurrence as to call for a severe sentence in order to check its perpetration. Probably, however, the sentence itself may have had nearly as great an effect on the public as the continuance of the punishment to the end of the term of imprisonment would have, and if so, perhaps some remission might be granted."
Justice Samuel Frederick Milford [11]

The sentences for both Thomas Shoveller and William Lawrence were subsequently mitigated and they were consequently both released in April of 1865.[12] The case later became the subject of an enquiry by the Attorney General (prosecutor) in June 1865, but they took no further action. The full proceedings of this case were most unusually documented and printed by the NSW Legislative Assembly.

The whole affair had been a 'show trial' to curb the increasing fraudulent behaviour of bankrupts trying to evade their creditors. Until then, such a crime was only punishable as a misdemenour, with an accompanying fine. The fact that people could now be handed a gaol conviction for such trivial fraud, sent shock waves through the colony, and Thomas Eastman Shoveller became a scapegoat through which the message was conveyed to the population.

Grafton Develops

The mid 1860's marked a rather difficult economic time in the Clarence region, as rust had destroyed the wheat crops. Cotton and wool were no longer viable industries after the American Civil War had come to an end, and many of the farmers lived on credit from the local stores. The Ramornie Meat Works liberated the district from falling into complete decline when it opened in 1866 and saved the cattle men from ruin.

Meanwhile, the adoption in 1864 of the Newton Boyd route for the main road between the Clarence River and New England was strongly opposed by Grafton residents, partly because considerable business would be redirected through South Grafton where the road terminated. The blow was softened however, by the establishment of a steam punt, to operate daily, from sunrise to sunset, across the river between the two towns. The punt, which was 62 feet long and 24 feet wide, was driven by a six horsepower steam engine, and was launched in August 1868, coming into full service shortly after.

While residing at the 'Cross Roads', Thomas and Susan had delivered another daughter

▲ Two of the first brick homes in Grafton were erected on Duke Street, next to the Anglican Church, photo by T. Rockwell.

Thomas Shoveller's 'Flying Horse Inn'

Name.	Situation.	Sign of House.
	GRAFTON.	
Berry Theresa	Prince-street	Royal Hotel
Black Walter	Wolli	Wolli Hotel
Cohen Samuel	Ulmarra	Ulmarra Hotel
Cowan William	Grafton	Grafton Hotel
Curry Patrick	Grafton	Commercial Hotel
Cowan Norman	Grafton	Maclean Hotel
Creer Edward	Grafton	Commercial Hotel
Davison Arch. W.	Laurence Town	Laurence Hotel
Foran Jno. Francis	South Grafton	Harp of Erin
Gray Frederick	Grafton	Tattersall's Hotel
Holmston John	Grafton	Criterion Hotel
Jacobs Lewis	Grafton	Queen's Hotel
Jones James T. (now Tankard John).	Brushgrove, Woodford Island.	Royal Hotel
Laird James	Grafton	Freemason's Hotel
Laird David	Richmond Road	Junction Inn
M'Lennan Donald	South Grafton	Australian Hotel
M'Fadden John	Grafton	Victoria Hotel
M'Lachlan Jno.	Rocky Mouth	Argyle Hotel
M'Fadden Jno. junr.	Grafton	Court House Hotel
Matheson William	Ulmarra	Caledonian Hotel
Miller John	Grafton	Star Hotel
Ross John	Palmer's Island	Taloumbi Hotel
Shoveller Thomas	Laurence Road, Grafton.	Flying Horse
Silva Margery	Near Maclean	Commercial Hotel
Small James	Little River	Pick and Shovel
Strauss John	North Grafton	European
Warrell James	Woodford Island	Brushgrove Hotel

Land Selections - Leonora Shoveller
- selected 18 April 1867.
Leonora Shovellar, Grafton, 40 acres, Co. of Clarence, parish of Lawrence, at the junction of the Lawrence and Richmond Road, bounded on the west by the Lawrence Road and on the north by the Richmond Road, adjoining W. Olives selection of 40 acres, two miles south of the Traveller's Rest Inn, selected by Samuel Davidson, on the 25 March 1862, and forfeited. [Ref CRE 23 April 1867]

Thomas Shoveller
- selected 26 November 1868
Lawrence, 60 acres, County of Clarence, Parish of Banyabba, bounded on the east by the Lawrence Road; on the west by the Grafton Road; and on the north by W . Olive's 40 acres, now held by T. Shoveller in fee simple. [Ref CRE 8 December 1868]

FINDING INNKEEPING REPUGNANT TO MY TASTES AND HABITS, and having inducements held out for returning home, I have determined upon DISPOSING OF MY HOUSE, I shall therefore be happy to treat with any respectable party, who may wish to either RENT or PURCHASE THE INN, known by the sign of the

"FLYING HORSE,"

situated at the junction of the Grafton, Lawrence, New England and Richmond River Roads. The house is in full trade, and from the fact of its being the only public-house between the Clarence and Richmond Rivers, a distance of 75 miles, it is obvious that its business position is unparalleled. There is little doubt but that the weekly receipts exceed that of many of the town houses, while the attendant expenses are trifling as compared with them.

THOMAS SHOVELLER.

Grafton, Lawrence, New England and Richmond River Roads.

HAVING PURCHASED THE PREMISES at the junction of the Grafton and Lawrence Roads, known as the CARRIERS' HOME, I intend OPENING the same upon the 1st July, upon an improved scale. The house will henceforth be known by the sign of the

FLYING HORSE.

A MORE COMMODIOUS HOTEL WILL BE ERECTED FORTHWITH to enable me the more fully to carry out the desired object.

THE ACCOMMODATION AFFORDED TO TRAVELLERS AND THEIR HORSES, will be of a character unequalled at roadside inns generally, my aim being to ensure a repetition of a visit once made.

THE CHARGES in all cases will be strictly moderate. The SPIRITS will be of the best brands obtainable, and the culinary arrangements will be liberal. The PADDOCKS and YARDS will be much improved, and GREEN FOOD will be grown for Travellers' horses, in addition to HAY and CORN being constantly kept.

I shall attach to this Hotel a

GENERAL STORE
AND
BUTCHERS' SHOP,

to meet more fully the requirements of all passers by.

THOMAS SHOVELLER, Proprietor.

Thomas Shoveller's 'Flying Horse Inn' was situated at 4983 Pringles Way, Banyabba [Lot 210, DP 1051740]. ▲LEFT COLUMN: 1-Thomas Shoveller - Licensee of the Flying Horse Inn, 1868 (Certificates for Publican's Licences, NSW, 1830-1849 & 1853-1899). 2-Thomas Shoveller - The Flying Horse Inn (C&RE and NE Advertiser, 9 July 1867, p.1). ▶TOP (Mid): Land Selections for Leonora Shoveller (C&RE, 23rd April 1867), & for Thomas Shoveller (C&RE, 8th Dec 1868). (Right): Thomas Shoveller - Finding Innkeeping Repugnant (C&RE and NE Advertiser, 28 Jan 1868, p.1). MID: Getting around pre-1900 meant travelling by horse and wagon or gig. BOTTOM: Travelling anywhere by road was a rough and ready experience, which normally took longer and was more comfortable than the steamships.

on the 13th of November 1866, who they named Leonora.[13] Thomas Shoveller was quick to select land in Leonora's name on the 18th of April 1867. Forty acres were taken up at the junction of the Lawrence Road and the Richmond Road in the county of Lawrence. The property adjoined William Olive's 40 acres, Susan Shoveller's brother-in-law, which was two miles south of the Travellers Rest Inn. However, the Shovellers didn't fulfill the required conditions of the selection, and the property was forfeited to the Crown on the 22nd of September that year.[14]

By June of 1867, Thomas Shoveller was back before the courts for alleged non-payment

1.

2.

3.

Coastal Ships of

The Clarence & Richmond River Steam Navigation Company began as the Grafton Steamship Navigation Company, formed on January 24th 1857, consisting of a group of gentlemen with vested interests in the Clarence River area. Directors were Francis Mitchell, Clark Irving and Robert Waterson. The first Auditors were David Jones, who went on to found the famous Sydney retail firm that still bears his name, and a Mr Grant Tindall of the Ramornie Station and Meatworks on the Clarence River. In 1860 the company name changed to the Clarence & Richmond River Steam Navigation Company, then they renamed the concern to the Clarence & Richmond & MacLeay River Steam Navigation Company Ltd in December 1888. In 1890 they merged with John See and Company to form the North Coast Steam Navigation Company, and continued servicing all the minor ports along the New South Wales coastline until aggressive competition from the railways and the changing trends of transportation led to the company going into voluntary liquidation on the 18th February 1954.

1. "PS WILLIAM THE FOURTH" (1831-1868), 54 tons. Lbd: 74' x 15'6" x 7'. Wooden paddle steamer, 2 masts built by Marshall & Lowe on the Williams River at Clarencetown New South Wales. Engine manufactured by Fawcett of Liverpool England. Owned by James Hickey Grose of Sydney, she was the first ocean going steamship built in Australia in 1831. Ownership changed to the Brisbane Water Steam Packet Co. in September 1839 and then the General Steam Navigation Co. in 1842. In 1853 she was lengthened to be 77 tons and Lbd: 86' x 14'8" x 8'2". By June 1858 she was supposedly owned outright by W. M. & Edye Manning of the Grafton Steam Navigation Co. February 1860 by the Illawarra Steam Navigation Co. In 1863 she was sent abroad to China where she was purchased in 1864, and operated by A. Ellissen & Co., on the Shanghai - Ningpo route. She was laid up towards the end of December 1868 and despatched to Japan, where records end (Image - PYHS).

2. "PS GRAFTON" (1854-1898), 316 gross tons, 212 net. Lbd: 140'9" x 22'3" x 10'6". Iron paddle steamer of two masts brig rigged and built by J Laird, Birkenhead for R. S. Ross & Partners in 1854. Sold to David Jones & Partners in December 1858. Sold to Clark Irving & Partners (Grafton S. N. Co) June 1860. March 1866 of Clarence & Richmond River Steam Navigation Co. August 1874 owned by J. E. Manning. During 1877 she underwent conversion to be twin screw, as well as dimension increases of 397 gross tons and 270 net with Lbd: 145'5" x 27'6" x 13'6". A deckhouse was added in 1878 and she was lengthened to be 173' x 27'3" x 13'6" and 424 gross tons in 1879. Tonnage became 548 gross after more alterations in 1886. On 12th June 1898 she struck the 'bar' at Strahan inward bound, but returned to open sea only to discover the loss of some of her propellor blades and had been holed under the boiler. She was taken in tow by the steamer "Mahinapua" and attempted the entry into Strahan only to strike the bar again. The tow line parted and she drifted fatally to the shore, becoming a total loss (Image -PYHS).

3. "PS URARA" (1859-1866), 382 tons. Lbd: 180'5" x 24'2" x 11'4". Iron paddle steamer of two cylinders making 120 horsepower, two masts, schooner rigged. Built bt Laird & Sons, Birkenhead as a two funnelled

4.

The coastal steamers of the late 1800's were sleek and beautiful ships. Thomas Eastman Shoveller and family, aswell as many other residents of Grafton and the Clarence River District relied entirely upon the coastal ships of the Grafton Steamship Navigation Company, between Sydney and the Clarence. The operating company morphed through four or five different changes of name prior to their dissolution in 1954. BOTTOM (Right): Passengers relaxing on the deck of a NSW coaster, c.1880. Not pictured here is the "PS BALLINA" (1865-79), of 299 gross tons, 190 net. Her gross tonnage was later reduced to 253 tons. Lbd: 179'4" x 24' x 9'6". She was an iron paddle steamer with two masts as brig-rigged and built at Low Walker-on-Tyne by perhaps C. Mitchell & Co. Owner - J. Alexander. Acquired by the Clarence & Richmond River Steam Navigation Company in February of 1866. The "Ballina" worked the passenger trade between Sydney and the northern New South Wales ports, until she was driven ashore and wrecked on 13th February 1879 at Port Macquarie, New South Wales.

Northern NSW [44]

passenger vessel, capacity of 105 in total of two classes, for this concern. Chartered by the Australasian S N Co for their Sydney - Maryborough service and used on their Melbourne trades during 1862- 63. Wrecked at the Clarence River Heads, New South Wales on 1st May 1866.

4. "PS AGNES IRVING" (1862-79), 439 gross tons, 333 net. Lbd: 203'5" x 24'6" x 11'7". Iron paddle steamer with passenger capacity built by Charles Lungley, Deptford Green, London. Two cylinders of 140 horsepower each. Often described as the favourite paddlesteamer, the "Agnes Irving" plied the Sydney-Grafton route for 17 years, before being wrecked upon the South Spit of the Macleay River, New South Wales, whilst attempting to enter on low tide, 26 December 1879. She was immediately hit by a large swell which drove her onto the spit and the engines became useless (Image - PYHS).

5. "SS NEW ENGLAND" (1869-82), 359 gross tons, 223 net. Lbd: 176'4" x 22'1" x 10'7". Iron steamship, two masts schooner rigged and two cylinders making 270 horsepower. Passenger capacity of 62. Built by T. Wingate & Co., Glasgow for the Clarence and New England S. N. Co, registered Sydney. Wrecked upon the Clarence River bar with a loss of eleven souls on the 27th December 1882 (Image - CRHS).

6. "PS CITY OF GRAFTON" (1876-1920), 825 gross tons, 555 net. Lbd: 207'4" x 26'9" x 11'9". Iron paddlesteamer, two masted schooner rigged. Built by A. Stephen & Sons in Glasgow for this concern. Flush decked passenger vessel, with two cylinders of 33 & 56 inches diameter respectively, making 150 horsepower. Of the North Coast S. N. Co. in a merger of 1890. Laid up 1913 and hulked 1920, then crapped completely.

7. "SS HELEN NICOLL" (1882-1932), 384 gross tons, 246 net. Lbd: 157' x 22' x 10'3". Iron steamship built by Gourlay Bros, Dundee for G. W. Nicoll, Brisbane. Worked on the North Coast of New South Wales in passenger-cargo capacity and remained on that run when sold to John See, Sydney in July 1882. In December 1886, under Captain Frazer, involved in collision with "SS Kielawarra", which sank, off North Solitary Island, NSW, with the loss of 48 lives. Six of these were from the "SS Helen Nicoll" who had jumped across 'for safety'. Of North Coast S. N. Co. upon formation in December 1891. Sold 1896 to A. L. Harrold and sold yet again in 1897 to J. Darling Jr, who kept her on the South Australia - West Australia trade route. Later sold to Jones Bros, Coal Co Ltd, seeing her as a collier only. Demolished with register closed 1932.

8. "SS KALLATINA" (1890-1930), 646 gross tons, 380 net. Lbd: 179'1" x 28'2" x 11'4". Steel steamship built by D. J. Dunlop & Co., Port Glasgow, 1890. Built as a passenger vessel for the Clarence, Richmond & MacLeay River S. N. Co registered Sydney. The only new addition to the Company under this title. September 1891 of this concern working the north coast run. Sold to John Burke Ltd., Brisbane in June of 1921 and altered to measure 628 gross tons and 306 net. J. Burke employed her on the Queensland coastal run, taking in the Gulf of Carpentaria ports until sold circa 1930 and hulked in 1931. Now lying as a breakwater on Moreton Island, off Tangalooma.

▲BOTTOM (Left): A three masted steamship moored on the Clarence River at Grafton, NSW, c.1880. Not pictured here is the "SS HELEN McGREGOR" (1866-75), 168 gross tons, 115 net. Lbd: 123'7" x 20' x 9'3". An iron steamship rigged as a two masted schooner with passenger capacity for 28. She was capable of 40 horsepower. Built by T. Wingate & Co., Whiteinch Glasgow for C. V. Robinson, registered Melbourne, designed for the Launceston to Melbourne trade across Bass Strait. She was acquired in May 1867 by the Clarence & New England Steam Navigation Co., and lengthened in September 1867 to be 152'6" x 20'6" x 9'1" rising to 251 gross tons. Thomas Fisher listed as owner from October 1867 until Clarence & New England S. N. Co took ownership again in September 1873. She struck rocks and sank quickly on a reef at south head when attempting to cross the Clarence River bar with the loss of eight souls on the 12th March 1875. One of her lifeboats had cleared the wreck when it was overturned by a heavy sea, drowning six of the occupants.[98]

of wages to a hired servant, William Wyatt, for which the court ruled in Wyatts favour. Thomas was required to pay 15s. and court costs immediately 'or, in default, the usual alternative' was gaol.[15]

Not long after Lenore's birth, Thomas decided to expand his business portfolio. An advertisement appeared in the Clarence and Richmond Examiner on the 9th of July 1867 informing the public that he had opened the 'Flying Horse Inn' on the 1st July, at Banyabba days ride north of Grafton, which had been previously known as the Carriers Home. He added that he was intending to open a store and a butcher's shop adjacent to the hotel.[16] While working on the property he had a dispute with a cedar supplier, which Thomas took to court and lost, the case being dismissed.[17]

However, making a living as an Innkeeper obviously didn't agree with Thomas as on 28th January 1868, he declared in print that he "found Inn-keeping repugnant to his tastes" and that he was selling the business.[18] Despite this, he was still listed as the licensee of the Flying Horse Hotel, Lawrence Rd. Grafton in the 1869 Return of Publican's Licences.[19]

Thomas no doubt corresponded with his siblings in London, but later that year, sad news arrived concerning the death of his older sister Mary Elizabeth Roberton, who died at the age of just 46 on the 17th November 1868.[20,21]

That same year, the Clarence and Richmond Examiner published a list of free selectors who had obtained land between October 1868 and March 1869, which included an allotment for Thomas' three year old daughter Leonora.[22] It was situated nearest to the town of Lawrence, and was bounded on the east by the Lawrence road, on the west by the Grafton Road and on the north by William Olive's 40 acres, his brother-in-law. Thomas soonafter selected another 60 acres of land nearby the Flying Horse in the parish of Banyabba, County of Clarence.[23]

▲ Thomas Shoveller likely arrived in London in 1869 and would have noticed the frenetic pace of life in London in stark contrast to the relative tranquility of Grafton, NSW in 1869.

Voyage on the "SS Ruahine"

STEAMSHIP RUAHINE for SOUTHAMPTON and WELLINGTON.—Gold, Specie, and general Cargo will be received up to NOON, THIS DAY.
Passengers' baggage also received at the wharf, THIS FORENOON.
Panama Co.'s Offices, Grafton Wharf.

NOTICE TO PASSENGERS per RUAHINE.—This Vessel will be detained until 5 p.m. on MONDAY, in order to receive the English Mail.
Passengers can embark from Moore's Wharf, off which the ship lies.
Panama Co.'s Offices, Grafton Wharf.

STEAMSHIP RUAHINE FOR SOUTHAMPTON and WELLINGTON.—This ship will sail at 5 p.m. THIS DAY. Passengers can embark from Moore's Wharf, off which the vessel lies.
All Accounts against the ship to be rendered THIS MORNING.
Panama Company's Offices, Grafton Wharf.

CLEARANCES —March 22.
Ruahine, steamer, 910 tons Darke, for Southampton. Passengers—Messrs. H. B. Rust, T. Shoveller, R. Richard, Mrs. Richard. R. H. Southwick, J. Kelso.

The Japanese troupe, known as Messrs. Lenton and Smith's, after a successful tour in the colonies, left for China per ship Huntley Castle; and Signor Bertolini and Madame Vitali, late of the Italian Opera troupe, sailed for London, per Ruahine, on Monday.

The Ruahine (s.s.) sailed from Wellington for London, on the 28th ultimo, with 100 first-class and 40 second-class passengers.

The Ruahine's (s.s.) passage from Sydney to Southampton is thus described by Mr. Shield, the purser :—The P. N. Z. and A. R. M. Co.'s s.s. Ruahine, Captain J. W. B. Darke, left Sydney for Southampton on 22nd March ; arrived in Wellington on the 27th, and sailed again with 145 passengers on the 30th; had fair winds from thence to the Horn, the ship at times averaging 9 knots under sail alone. When within about 100 miles of the Straits of Magellan, the weather being thick, with heavy sea and rain, and no signs of improvement, bore up for Cape Horn, instead of going through the Straits, as was originally intended. Rounded the Horn, distant two miles, at 6 a.m. on the morning of 21st April, weather mild and calm, thermometer 47 ; had fair winds from thence till within a few days

of Rio, when it shifted ahead ; arrived at Rio on the 1st of May ; were detained here eight days repairing machinery, having broken one of the piston rods a few days after rounding the Horn. Took in 2000 bags of coffee and 600 tons of coal, and sailed again on the 8th. Light and variable trades from thence to the Line, which was crossed on 15th May. Light N.E. trades prevailed from 17th till arrival at St. Vincent, where we anchored 20th May, at 7 p.m. Took in 350 tons coal, and sailed again on 22nd, at 3 p.m. Had head winds from thence till entrance of Bay of Biscay, after which fine weather and smooth sea. Anchored in the Solent the night of the 2nd June, and entered Southampton Docks next morning. The only casualty on the voyage was the death of an infant of Mrs. Toush-Hooker (second-class passenger) on the 28th April.

The steamer Lady Young, for Melbourne, cleared the Heads yesterday afternoon.

▲TOP (Left): Notices to passengers on the "SS Ruahine" (SMH, 20 March 1869, p.1). (Mid): Notice to passengers on the "SS Ruahine" (Empire, 22 March 1869, p.1). (Right-Up): T. Shoveller - Passenger on the "SS Ruahine" (Empire, 23 March 1869, p.2). (Right-Down): Other passengers on the "SS Ruahine" (SMH, 25 March 1869, p.7). MID: Description of the voyage of the "SS uahine" (from Description of the Voyage from Sydney to Southampton via Cape Horn in SMH, 7 August 1869, p.6) ABOVE: Watercolour of the "SS Ruahine" (1865-1889), by Bowen Watson Nazer, c.1867, which was built at Millwall Shipping Yards in 1865, of 1503 tons, 350hp and twin screw. It primarily ran between Sydney, Wellington, Panama and San Francisco between 1866 and 1889 with some occasional voyages to Britain. It was sold to the West India Royal Mail Line, which changed its name to the "Liffey." (NB. Information came from the back of the above print).

Return To The Motherland

By 1869 Thomas had been away from England for 20 long years, and although his parents were both deceased, his older siblings Jane, John Jr. and William Henry Sr. were all residing in London, so it is possible that he now seized an opportunity to make the long sea voyage home. On 13th March 1869, Thomas Shoveller sailed to Sydney aboard the paddlesteamer "Agnes Irving", one week ahead of commencing his international journey.[24] Thomas had booked onward passage on the The Panama, New Zealand & Australian Royal Mail Co's "SS Ruahine," under captain J.W.B. Darke, which departed from Sydney at 5pm on the 22nd March, bound for Southampton, England via Wellington and Rio de Janeiro.[25,26]

Southampton, Thursday. The screw steamship "Ruahine", Captain J.W.B. Darke, one of the fleet of steamers lately employed in the mail service between Panama and New Zealand, has arrived in this port. She brings home a total of 2139 passengers from Australian and New Zealand ports; 13 boxes of gold weighing 12,946oz, from New Zealand, 800L in specie, 20 packages sundries and also 2,040 bags of coffee from Rio Janeiro. Captain H. B. Benson, late general manager, and Mr A.A. Browne, late superintendent purser, of the Panama, New Zealand and Australian Royal Mail Company, have returned to England by the Ruahine. Colonel, Mrs, and Miss Kitchener, from Otago, and Captain Sellars, from Wellington, are also among the passengers. The Ruahine sailed from Sydney on the 22nd of March, arrived Wellington on the 28th and left on the 30th, arrived at Rio Janeiro on the 1st May, left on the 8th, arrived at St Vincent (Cape Verds) on the 20th and left on the 22nd. She rounded Cape Horn on the 21st April and could not make the Straits of Magellan in consequence of thick and bad weather. The ship was detained at Rio Janeiro effecting some slight repairs to the engines.

The Times [London], 4th June 1869 [27]

▲TOP: The "Sophia Jane" (1826-1845), of 256 tons, was the first paddle steamer to operate in the coastal waters of New South Wales, and was about one third smaller than the "Duke of Edinburgh." She was launched on the Thames in 1826 and after being bought by James Hickey Grose, arrived Sydney in May of 1831.
ABOVE: Thomas and his daughter Eva Shoveller were passengers on the paddlesteamer "Duke of Edinburgh," which arrived Sydney from Levuka, Fiji, on the 16th Nov 1871 (NSW Archives, Australia, Inward, Outward & Coastal Passenger Lists 1826-1972). The "Duke of Edinburgh' was 368 gross tons, with dimensions of 166'3" x 25' x 10'3". She was a wooden auxilliary steamship originally built as a two masted schooner by George Dent at Jervis Bay, Sydney, and was advertised as a passenger carrying mail steamer to Fiji. The year 1876 saw her operating on the Sydney - Townsville - Cooktown service, at times taking in other Queensland ports en route. By April 1879, she was sold to C.G. Lessing, then to Dutch subjects, with her fate unknown.

SALE OF THE GRAFTON FERRY.

The sale of dues to be collected on the Grafton Ferry, took place on Tuesday last, according to announcement. There was only one offer, that of Mr. Charles Mathews, viz. 10s. per annum, at which price it was knocked down, the lessee undertaking to place a good and sufficient steam boat on the ferry within a period of six months from the 1st May next; and in the event of Mr. Mathews failing to do so, the lease only to extend to a period of one year. The lessee entering into a bond to keep the punt and boat in good order and repair. The following is a list of the future scale of charges adopted by the Bench:—

	s.	d.
Foot passengers each	0	3
Horse, drawing or not drawing	1	0
Gig or cart with two wheels	1	6
Waggon, with four wheels &c.	2	0
Cattle exceeding 10 in number	0	6
Ditto not exceeding 10	0	9
Sheep, Pig, or goat	0	2
If more than 10	0	1

The above fees are doubled on Sundays.

In the Supreme Court of New South Wales. (11,784)
IN INSOLVENCY.

In the Insolvent Estate of Thomas Shoveller, of Grafton, in the Colony of New South Wales, accountant.

FIRST AND ONLY MEETING.

WHEREAS the estate of the abovenamed insolvent was, on the 20th day of December, 1873, placed under sequestration, by order under my hand : I hereby appoint a First Meeting of the creditors of the said insolvent, to be holden before the District Commissioner of Insolvent Estates, at the Court House, Grafton, on Thursday, the 29th day of January, A.D. 1874, to commence at 11 o'clock in the forenoon or as soon afterwards as the course of business will permit, for the proof of debts against the said estate, and for the collection, administration, and distribution of the same; that the insolvent may account for his insolvency; for directing the Official Assignee whether the insolvent will be allowed to retain for his own use his household furniture, wearing apparel, beds, bedding, and tools of trade, or any part thereof respectively : And as it now appears that the goods and effects of the insolvent, available for the payment of his debts, are less in value than £100, notice is hereby given, that unless it be shown at said First Meeting that these goods and effects exceed the value of £100, the said Commissioner will summarily proceed to rank the debts which shall then be proved, and will direct the proceeds of the estate to be forthwith distributed by the Official Assignee accordingly.—Dated at Sydney, the 22nd day of December, A.D. 1873.

GEORGE HIBBERT DEFFELL,
Chief Commissioner of Insolvent Estates.

ARTHUR HENRY,
Registrar in Insolvency.

Official Assignee—THOMAS HAMILTON SEMPILL.
6750   8s. 6d.

Grafton.

[FROM OUR CORRESPONDENT.]

4th December.

FATAL ACCIDENTS. — Four fatal accidents have occurred on the Clarence this week. On Monday a steamboat excursion of the Presbyterian Sunday-school children took place, and on the steamer's arrival at the pleasure-grounds, several lads went in the river to bathe. One of them, a son of Mr. T. Shoveller, of Grafton, who could not swim, suddenly got out of his depth into deep water, and was drowned. T. G. Hewitt, Esq., J. Brownhill, Esq., and the Rev. C. R. Curry repeatedly dived, but could not succeed in saving him or finding the body. The body was re covered next day by constables Davies and Travers, and brought into Grafton, where an inquest was held, and a verdict found of accidentally drowned while bathing.

▲TOP: A panorama of the gold mining town of Solferino in 1873, by J.W. Lindt. MID (Left): The new steam punt, which connected the townships of north and south Grafton, c.1872. (Right): Grafton Ferry Sale (Clarence & Richmond Examiner, 28th April 1863, p.2). LEFT: Thomas Shoveller - Insolvency (NSW Govt Gazette, 24 Dec 1873, p.3630). ABOVE: Thomas Charles Shoveller - Drowning (Aust Town & Country Journal, 12th Dec 1874, p.21). RIGHT: Memorial headstone for Thomas Charles Shoveller at Grafton Cemetery.

After a relatively fast voyage of 74 days the "SS Ruahine" arrived in Southampton on the 4th June 1869,[28] but the question is whether Thomas Shoveller actually remained aboard all the way to England. Was his purpose to effect a reunion with his family in England, or was he on a business venture to Wellington? The span of time for which he was absent would definitely favour the former. On the 6th December 1869 another daughter was born in Grafton to Thomas and Susan in Janet Eva Shoveller, and while this occurred in Thomas' absence, she unfortunately died as an infant the following year.[29,30,31]

▲ 'The Bush Post Office', c.1900, postcard painted by A. H. Fullwood. (1905-06 Collection of 24 Postcards of Australia and New Zealand, A.H. Fullwood).

Four months later, Thomas Shoveller returned to Grafton from Sydney aboard the paddlesteamer "Ballina",[32] arriving on the 26th April 1870, which meant that the window of 13½ months to make the return journey and still spend six months in England was entirely possible. Unfortunately, no evidence of a return journey or his arrival back into Sydney has been found.

In 1871, Mrs [Susan] Shoveller made a voyage of her own "with family of three" (Eva, 12; Thomas 9; & Lenore 5), aboard the "Ballina", which sailed from Sydney on the 22nd January, and stopped over at Newcastle on the 24th, and Nelson's Bay on the 29th, before arriving in Grafton.[33] Towards the end of this year Thomas embarked upon another journey, this time to the Pacific Islands in company with his 12 year year old daughter Eva. Although the purpose of the trip is unknown, he and Eva were registered upon arrival into Sydney after having left the Port of Levuka, Fiji on the 16th November 1871, travelling in steerage aboard the 358 ton barque "Duke of Edinburgh", under master John D. Harley.[34]

The frequent coastal journeys continued in 1872 with Mr Shoveller departing from Sydney on the 23rd October, via Newcastle on the 24th to arrive at Grafton aboard the paddlesteamer "New England."[35] On the 17th December Mr Shoveller arrived Grafton after having departed from Sydney on the 9th via Newcastle on the 10th, again aboard the "New England."[36] And having spent Christmas in Sydney, a Miss Shoveller arrived Grafton on New Years Eve having departed from Sydney on the 27th via Newcastle on the 28th, aboard the "SS Helen MacGregor."[37]

By 1873, gold fever had arrived in the Clarence River District with discoveries at Solferino and Dalmorton. Thomas and Susan Shoveller had reason to celebrate themselves with the arrival of their second son George,[38] who was given the unusual middle name of Lorraine, but ominously their lives were about to change once more for the worse.

Bad Luck Comes in Threes

In 1874 a series of sad and tragic events transpired to impact upon the Shoveller family, the first of which was that Thomas had once again fallen into insolvency. The circumstances were that some ten years previously, Thomas had apparently signed a bill/guarantee

▲ Early photograph of 'Ilarwill' on Woodford Island, site of John Small's settlement and the likely birthplace of Susan Shoveller (nee Hann) in 1840.

assuming a debt on behalf of his brother William Henry Shoveller Sr., for quite a large sum of money, which William failed to repay. Thomas was unable to honour the debt, and was dragged into the creditors net. The Clarence and Richmond Examiner reported the proceedings of his insolvency meeting on the 6th January 1874:

> "In the estate of Thomas Shoveller, a single meeting will be held before Captain Sinclair at the Court House, Grafton, on Thursday 29th January, at eleven o'clock, for proof of debts and that the insolvent may account for his insolvency."
>
> *Clarence & Richmond Examiner, 6th January 1874* [39]

With the completion of the Australian Overland Telegraph Line in 1872, Thomas would have received news of the passing of his only surviving sister Jane Allen Shoveller, a spinster aged 60, on the 18th March 1874 at Ealing near London, England.[40] Though this was sorrowful news, another much more tragic event occurred later that year. While on a Sunday School picnic, Thomas and Susan's 11 year old son Thomas Charles Shoveller drowned in the Clarence River on the 30th of November 1874. The parents and the wider community were horrified, with the Examiner reporting the accident:

Fatal and Melancholy Accident.

> "We regret to be called upon to announce the sudden and unexpected death of Thomas Charles Shoveller of Grafton, who with his parents, accompanied the Presbyterian Sunday School excursionists to the Upper Clarence yesterday morning, when immediately after landing, the lad, who was 13 years of age, with a number of others, went for a bathe, when getting beyond his depth was drowned. On his father hearing of the mishap to his son, he hastened to the spot and rushed in, and not being a good swimmer, had a very narrow escape also, being only brought ashore by the exertion of Messrs T. G. Hewitt, Manning and others. Every search was made for the body, and on the sad intelligence reaching town, Senior Constable McCormack drove out, taking grapnels, but up to a late hour last evening, the body had not been recovered. This sad affair cast a gloom over what otherwise would have been a most agreeable excursion. His remains were interred in the Grafton Cemetery on Wednesday last, the Public School children following in the procession, and the greatest sympathy was shown to the parents under the sudden and unexpected heavy domestic bereavement which had befallen them.
>
> *Clarence & Richmond Examiner, 1st December, 1874* [41]

The inquest into the death revealed that young Thomas was a smart, well-behaved, intelligent lad and was indeed a special favourite, so at such a tender age... "it was as if christ and his saints were asleep."[42] An edited version of the inquest was published in the same newspaper in 1891 as part of a selective chronicle of sad and fatal accidents that had occurred in the region over the years.[43]

The tragic death of their eldest and favoured son Thomas Charles Shoveller, would no doubt have severely affected both the Shoveller and Hann families and anyone could appreciate that just three weeks later, the Christmas of 1874 would not have been a happy one in the Shoveller household. But as we all know, life continues and each must weather their own storms, and this was true for Thomas and Susan Shoveller as they approached their twilight years in Grafton.

References

1. Death notice for William Henry Shoveller's daughter, Eva (Clarence & Richmond Examiner, 30th Dec 1862).

2. Eva Rose Jane Shoveller - Buried 26th December 1862 (CRHS (2005). 'Burials in the Grafton District 1850-1896', p.19).

3. Kass, Terry (2009). Grafton: Jacaranda City on the Clarence-A History, Clarence Valley Council, p.292.

4. The Great Flood In Clarence River: Loss of Nine Lives (SMH, 5 March 1863, p.5).

5. Thomas Shoveller - Director of Building Society (Clarence & Richmond Examiner, 5th April, 1904, p.2).

6. Thomas Shoveller - Insurance Agent (Maitland Mercury, 2 Jan 1864, p.6).

7. The Queen v Thomas Shoveller (Clarence & Richmond Examiner, 1 March 1864, p.2).

8. Thomas Shoveller in Criminal Court - The Queen v Shoveller (Empire, 8 April 1864, p.2).

9. Mr. Shoveller's Store - Auction (Clarence & Richmond Examiner, 31 May 1864, p.2).

10. Petition for Mitigation of Sentence (Levey & Shoveller), Submitted to the Legislative Assembly, NSW, February 1865.

11. Justice Milford - Request to Remit Sentences for Thomas Shoveller & Levy Lawrence, 18th February 1865 (NSW Archives).

12. Thomas Shoveller - Mitigation of Sentence (Clarence & Richmond Examiner, 20th June 1865, p.3).

13. NSW Dept of BDM. (1866). Birth Certificate for Leonora Shweller [sic. Shoveller], 13 Nov 1866 (#9029/1866).

14. Lenore Shoveller - Forfeited Conditional Purchases (Clarence & Richmond Examiner, 22 Sept 1867, p.2).

15. Thomas Shoveller - Defendant 'Servants Claim' (Clarence & Richmond Examiner, 18th June 1867, p.2).

16. Thomas Shoveller - The Flying Horse Inn (Clarence & Richmond Examiner and New England Advertiser, 9 July 1867, p.1).

17. Thomas Shoveller - Plaintiff 'Detaining cedar' (Clarence & Richmond Examiner, 8th Oct 1867, p.2).

18. Thomas Shoveller - Finding Innkeeping Repugnant (Clarence & Richmond Examiner and New England Advertiser, 28 Jan 1868, p.1).

19. Thomas Shoveller - Licensee of the Flying Horse Inn, 1868 (Certificates for Publican's Licences, NSW, 1830-1849 & 1853-1899).

20. Mary Elizabeth Roberton - Burial, 17 Nov 1868, Manchester General Cemetery, Manchester, England (UK and Ireland, Find a Grave Index, 1300s-Current).

21. Mary Elizabeth Roberton (nee Shoveller) Monument - 17 Nov 1868 (Greater Manchester General Cemetery, Manchester, Plot No 3, Church).

22. Leonora Shoveller - Selection at Lawrence (Clarence & Richmond Examiner, 23rd April 1867).

23. Thomas Shoveller - Selection at Banyabba (Clarence & Richmond Examiner, 8th Dec 1868).

24. Shoveller - Passenger arriving Sydney "PS Agnes Irving'"(Empire, 16th March 1869, p.2).

25. Notice to Passengers on the "Ruahine" (Empire, 22 March 1869, p.1).

26. T. Shoveller - Passenger on the "Ruahine" (SMH, 25 March 1869, p.7).

27. Arrival of the "Ruahine" in London (The Times [London], 4th June 1869, p.6.).

28. Arrival of the "SS Ruahine" at Southampton (The Times [London], Friday, 4th June 1869, p.6).

29. Janet E. A. Shoveller - Birth announcement (Clarence & Richmond Examiner, 7th Dec 1869).

30. NSW Dept of BDM. (1869). Birth Certificate for Janet E. A. Shoveller, 6th December 1869 (#10165/1869).

31. NSW Dept of BDM. (1870). Death Certificate for Janet E. A. Shoveller, 1870 (#1446/1870).

32. Shoveller - Passengers arriving Grafton on "Ballina" (Clarence & Richmond Examiner and New England Advertiser, 26 April 1870, p.2).

33. Shoveller - Passengers arriving Grafton on "Ballina" (Clarence & Richmond Examiner and New England Advertiser, 3 January 1871, p.2).

34. Thomas & Eva Shoveller - Passengers on "Duke of Edinburgh" Arrived from Levuka, Fiji, 16th Nov 1871 (NSW Archives, Australia, Inward, Outward & Coastal Passenger Lists 1826-1972).

35. Messrs Shoveller - Passengers arriving Grafton on "New England" (Clarence & Richmond Examiner and New England Advertiser, 29 October 1872, p.2).

36. Shoveller - Passengers arriving Grafton on "New England" (Clarence & Richmond Examiner and New England Advertiser, 17 December 1872, p.4).

37. Miss Shoveller - Passengers arriving Grafton on "Helen McGregor" (Clarence & Richmond Examiner and New England Advertiser, 31 December 1872, p.2).

38. NSW Dept of BDM. (1873). Birth Certificate for George Lorraine Shoveller, 1873 (#11288/1873).

39. Thomas Shoveller - Insolvency (Clarence & Richmond Examiner, 6th January 1874).

40. Jane Allen Shoveller - Probate notice, 18 March 1874 (England & Wales, National Probate Calendar, 1858-1995).

41. Fatal and Melancholy Accident (Clarence & Richmond Examiner, 1st December, 1874).

42. The Anglo Saxon Chronicle.

43. Inquest into death of Thomas Charles Shoveller - 30 Nov 1874 (reprinted in Clarence & Richmond Examiner, Undated, 1891).

44. Flotilla Australia: Australian Shipping Lines - Images, Postcards, Photographs & Ephemera of Minor shipping lines and Ship owners registered in NSW. [http://www.flotilla-australia.com/crrsnco.htm#crrsnco-crmrsnco].

Chapter Nineteen

THOMAS & SUSAN SHOVELLER PIONEERS OF GRAFTON

By the time Benjamin Disraeli became British Prime Minister for the second time on the 20th February 1874, the world was marvelling at a number of technological achievements and advancements, especially in the field of communications.

In the United States, Samuel Morse had developed an electromagnetic telegraph in 1837 with the Western Union Telegraph Company being formed after merging with several other companies in 1856. In England, it took 30 years of development and refinement before a branch of the Post Office was organised to run the new telegraph network, but it eventually became their policy to provide telegraph facilities at every post office where money orders could be sent. The network rapidly developed with telegraph offices in London increasing from 95 in 1869 to over 5,000 offices by 1872, when traffic had increased to some 12 million messages per year. By 1875, the Telegraph Street central office in London was the largest telegraph centre in the world, with 450 instruments on three floors working connections both in the UK and worldwide on the Imperial Telegraph Network.[1]

This development greatly narrowed the 'tyranny of distance' experienced in far away lands like Australia, where news could take upwards of three months to reach the colony. But that all changed on the 22nd August 1872 when the Overland Telegraph Line linked Darwin with Adelaide, as after it was connected to the Java-to-Darwin submarine telegraph cable several months later, the communication time with Europe dropped from months to just hours, and Australia was no longer so isolated from the rest of the world. The overland line was one of the great engineering feats of 19th century Australia and probably the most significant milestone in the history of telegraphy in Australia.

Around the same time, the invention of a practical telephone was achieved in March 1876 by the American Alexander Graham Bell, who exhibited his invention at the Philadelphia

International Exposition of 1876. Then Thomas A. Edison, touted as the 'King of Inventors', commercialised his research on the incandescent electric light bulb, before also introducing the phonograph in 1878. The phonograph was the centrepiece exhibit at the fourth Paris International Exposition of 1889.

This was a period when all manner of new inventions were changing the known world, and one that made a huge change in people's lives, and finally brought the world out of darkness was the introduction of electric street lighting. Prior to electricity, people used candles, gas lights, oil lamps and fires to illuminate the dark of night, and despite English chemist Humphry Davy developing the first incandescent light in 1802, it took until the 1870s, before Davy's arc lamp had been successfully commercialized, and was used to light up public spaces. Efforts by Sir Joseph Swan and Thomas Edison led to commercial incandescent light bulbs becoming widely available in the 1880s, and by the early 20th century these had completely replaced arc lamps.

The Electric Light

"Yesterday evening one of the most interesting, and perhaps, most popular sources of attraction... was the electric light exhibited from the roof of the Post Office [in Sydney]. The light was exceedingly brilliant, its power occasionally being sufficient to dazzle the eye with the intensity of sunlight."

The Sydney Morning Herald, 10th November, 1876 [2]

During expeditions made possible by the construction of the Australian Overland Telegraph Line, Europeans arrived in the Australian Western Desert in 1873 when Ayers Rock was first sighted and named, although it was renamed Uluru in 2002. However, on the open oceans the ever-present perils of sea travel continued to claim lives, with over 100 souls being lost when the "SS Gothenburg" struck Old Reef and sank off Bowen, North Queensland on the 24th February 1875.

In the township of Grafton, Thomas Shoveller and family struggled to overcome the shock of their son's tragic death. The terrible loss added to the financial hardship caused by

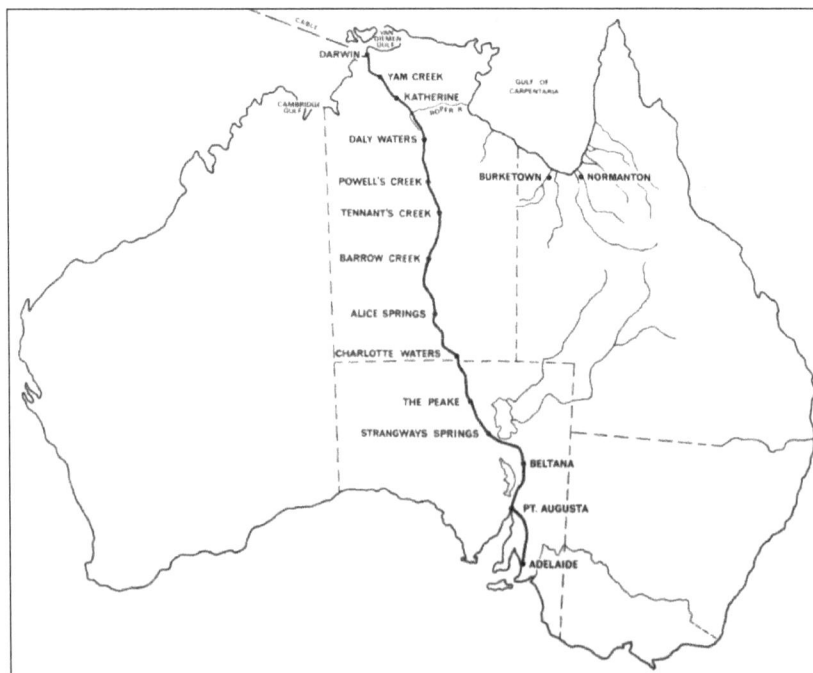

▲LEFT: Map of the Australian Overland Telegraph Line, which was completed in August 1872. Water sources known to Aboriginal people largely determined the route of the Overland Telegraph Line through the dry interior of Australia and, two decades later, guided the route of the Central Australia Railway. RIGHT: Planting the first pole on the Overland Telegraph line to Carpentaria.

Advancements in Communications & Lighting

▲TOP (Left): The telegraph repeater station at Alice Springs, c. 1880. (Right): Various street lights from Morris Tasker & Co. in their 1871 Illustrated Catalogue. ABOVE (Left): Acoustic telephone advertisement by the Consolidated Telephone Co., Jersey City, New Jersey, 1886. (Right): Wood engraving, depicting a public demonstration of new technology at the Royal Society of Victoria in Melbourne (The Illustrated Australian News, 8 August 1878).

Thomas' bankruptcy the year before. These setbacks forced the Shovellers to move across the river where the electoral roll for 1875 revealed they were residing at South Grafton, which involved travelling on the steam punt to reach Grafton on the north side.

On the 27th May 1877, Thomas Shoveller celebrated his 50th birthday. As he faced old age, he could feel proud of his achievements, and if he was riding toward the twilight of his years, the life expectancy of a Shoveller male was somewhere around 70. By 1876-77 the NSW Electoral Roll for the 'Division of The Clarence' revealed that Thomas Shoveller, qualified as a 'household' resident in Grafton.[3]

In June 1877 and again in August 1880 Thomas Shoveller was charged with 'breaching the Attorney Act, when drawing up a certain real estate agreement for payment, he not being a Barrister, Attorney or otherwise legally authorised officer.'[4,5] This was an action brought by the town solicitors to minimise their competition, but it had the desired effect and limited Thomas to acting as an accounting and mercantile agent only.

On the 21st August 1877, a nephew Sidney Howard Shoveller (1857-1914), the son of Thomas' older brother John Shoveller Jr., emigrated to Brisbane aboard the "Ramsay",[6] while his younger brother Alfred Russell Shoveller (1862-1937) also emigrated and settled in the suburb of Manly in Sydney sometime prior to 1892. The two brothers married Australian wives, and their descendants grew up in Sydney, but it is not known to what extent Thomas Shoveller and his family were connected, or remained in touch with these cousins.

About this same time, the last of the old bushranging gangs was the Kelly's in Victoria, led by Australia's most infamous bushranger Ned Kelly. After murdering three policemen in a shootout in 1878, the gang was outlawed and following the raiding of towns and the

▲TOP: Fully clothed Clarence River aboriginals on the main street of Grafton, by J.W. Lindt, c.1895. ABOVE: Shoveller notices posted from 1871 to 1879. LEFT COLUMN: 1-Shoveller - passenger on the "SS Helen MacGregor"(SMH, 25th Dec 1872, p.4); 2-Thomas Shoveller - Auctioneer, Valuer & Accountant (C&RE, 7 Apr 1874, p.8). CENTRE COLUMN: Thomas Shoveller - Treasurer for Queens Birthday Regatta (Clarence & Rich. Ex. 25th May 1875, p.4). RIGHT COLUMN: 1-Thomas Shoveller - Victim of False Pretences, 9 June 1875 (NSW, Govt Gazettes 1854-1930, p.172). 2-Thomas Shoveller - Wine Licence (Clarence & Rich. Ex. 9th Sep 1876, p.2); 3-Thomas Shoveller - Conviction Set Aside (Evening News, 12th June 1877, p.2).

LEFT COLUMN

GRAFTON POLICE COURT.
TUESDAY, AUGUST 3.
BEFORE the Police Magistrate and Mr S. Cohen, J.P.

Thomas Shoveller was charged with drawing a certain agreement connected with real estate for payment, he not being a barrister, attorney, or otherwise legally authorised officer of the Supreme Court.

Defendant pleaded not guilty.

Mr Foott said he appeared in conjunction with Mr Norrie for the prosecution; and said, although Mr C. Dickey's name appeared on the information, the whole of the attorneys were agreed in instituting these proceedings. The charge was for preparing a lease for certain real estate, between Philip Donohue and John Stack, and the document on the face of it showed the necessity of proceedings being taken in the interest of the public. Although it was a lease there was no proviso for re-entry by the landlord, and it was highly necessary all such deeds should be properly prepared. Attorneys had to pass a severe examination, which was a guarantee on their side, and was in the interests, and for the protection, of the public.

John Stack, examined by Mr Norrie, deposed he was a farmer residing at the Coldstream, in the parish of Tyndale; knows Philip Donohue, who resides on Glenugie Creek, and owns freehold land at the Coldstream—9, 10, and 11 of Johnson's estate subdivision; knows defendant Shoveller, and remembers going to him with Donohue on July 20; Shoveller gave the document produced to sign; the signature to it is mine, and Donohue attached his mark; Shoveller signed as attesting witness to both signatures; paid Shoveller 5s for the preparation of the document; Donohue also got a duplicate copy; Donohue took a document to him when he went there, and Shoveller said he would have nothing to do with altering it; they had better have a proper one drawn, and he would do it for 5s; we both agreed to that; we went away, and returned in about half-an-hour; he then had two copies prepared. (Produced his copy). Defendant told Donohue if he wanted a counterpart it would be another 5s; have no doubt that the writing of the document and the signature—Thomas Shoveller—are the same.

By defendant: I had no document when I went into your office; an agreement was laid on your table, and we asked you to add something to the effect that I was to have leave to remove the crop; I asked you to add the first rent was to be paid in 8 months instead of 6; you altered the document, and you then said it would be a hashed up affair, and you would not have it go before any Court; considered if the alteration was made in the original document it would have been sufficient; swear you used the word lease in speaking of what you prepared; will not swear you wrote it; I offered you 2s 6d for altering the document brought, and you wanted 10s.

By Mr. Norrie: The document taken to Mr. Shoveller was not signed by either of us.

By defendant: The agreement was for 1 year.

CENTRE COLUMN

GRAFTON POLICE COURT.
TUESDAY, AUGUST 3.
BEFORE the Police Magistrate and Mr S. Cohen, J.P.

Thomas Shoveller was charged with drawing a certain agreement connected with real estate for payment, he not being a barrister, attorney, or otherwise legally authorised officer of the Supreme Court.

Defendant pleaded not guilty.

RAILWAY MEETING AT GRAFTON.

[BY TELEGRAPH.]
(FROM OUR OWN CORRESPONDENT.)

GRAFTON, WEDNESDAY.

A public meeting was held this evening, at the Theatre Royal, convened by Mr. Marcolino, to advocate a line of railway from North Grafton to Tenterfield. About 300 people were present. Mr. W. Kinnear occupied the chair. A resolution was moved by Mr. J. Geary, and seconded by Mr. Marcolino,—"That in the opinion of this meeting the line of railway proposed from North Grafton to Tenterfield would be the most advantageous to the interests of the Clarence districts, and of the colony generally." An amendment was moved by Mr. W. M. Wilkinson, and seconded by Alderman Murray,—"That this meeting is opposed to any section of the community advocating any definite line to Government, but only advocates a line from Grafton table-land to New England." The amendment was put and lost, the original motion being carried by a large majority. Mr. T. Shoveller was then appointed secretary for the Grafton branch of the North Grafton and Tenterfield Railway League, and a petition to the Minister for Works was adopted, the same to be signed by the chairman and secretary on behalf of the meeting. The business was rather noisy at times when opinions at variance with the objects of the meeting found utterance. The speakers to the resolutions which were carried expressed opinions favourable to the route being left to the Government, but said that as a line was advocated from South Grafton to Glen Innes by others, they felt bound to oppose it. Several speakers spoke strongly against South Grafton being the terminus.

Grafton Police Court.

FRIDAY, AUGUST 31.
(Before the Police Magistrate, and T. Page, J.P.)
S. Shoveller v. T. Shoveller.—An application to have defendant bound over to keep the peace. Defendant was bound over to keep the peace towards complainant in the sum of £40, for a period of three months, and to pay 21s professional costs, and 11s 6d costs of court. Mr. Foott appeared for complainant.

N O T I C E.

Owing to the tardy manner in which accounts due to me come in, I have placed my BOOKS in the hands of Mr. THOMAS SHOVELLER, who is authorised to receive all monies due to me. Mr. Shoveller is also instructed to use for any long standing accounts, which he thinks call for such unpleasant measures being resorted to.

JAMES M'KINNON,
General Blacksmith and Farrier.
Grafton, April 16th, 1886.

RIGHT COLUMN

Grafton - Clarence River
Direct for Sydney

The Favourite steamship -
HELEN NICOLL
will leave the Market Wharf, Market St.
TO-MORROW (SATURDAY) NIGHT, at 9, leaving Grafton for Sydney Wednesday morning.

S.S. AUSTRALIAN
TUESDAY NIGHT, at 9,
To passengers – The accommodation of these steamers is excellent and amidships. Being victualled by the owners, passengers will find every comfort. Return tickets available by either steamer. Horse boxes provided if required.
NIPPER and SEE
129, Sussex Street.

General Notices

THOMAS SHOVELLER
(ACCOUNTANT AND MERCANTILE AGENT)
Offices : Opposite Court-house, Grafton.

Go to SHOVELLER for Bills of Sale.
Go to SHOVELLER for Stock Mortgages.
Go to SHOVELLER for Crop Liens.
Go to SHOVELLER for Leases.
Go to SHOVELLER for Bankruptcy business.
Go to SHOVELLER for Conditional Purchase Transfers.
Go to SHOVELLER for adjusting entangled accounts
Go to SHOVELLER for Wives Judicial Protection Orders.
Go to SHOVELLER for District Court business.
Go to SHOVELLER for Official Correspondence.
Go to SHOVELLER for Petitions.
Go to SHOVELLER for Recovery of Legacies from any part of the world.
Go to SHOVELLER upon all business which you are not able to do for yourself
MODERATE SCALE OF CHARGES throughout.

MR. SHOVELLER'S long and intimate acquaintance with business such as is constantly arising in this district, forms a solid guarantee to constituents that all matters entrusted to him will be efficiently and punctually carried out.

Offices : Opposite the Court-house, Grafton.

Shoveller notices posted from 1880 to 1886. ▲LEFT COLUMN: Thomas Shoveller - Charged with breaching the Attorney Act (Clarence & Richmond Examiner, 7th Aug 1880, p.4). CENTRE COLUMN: 1-Thomas Shoveller - Charged with breaching the Attorney Act cont. 2-Thomas Shoveller - Sec. for Railway Committee (SMH, 20th Apr 1882, p.6); 3-Susan Shoveller - Application For Keeping The Peace (Clarence & Richmond Examiner, 1 Sep 1883, p.4); 4-Thomas Shoveller - Debt Collector Notice (C&RE & NE Advertiser, 27th April 1886, p.3). RIGHT COLUMN: 1-Shipping notices for Grafton & the Clarence River (Sydney Morning Herald, 30th May 1884); 2-Thomas Shoveller - Accountant & Mercantile Agent (C&RE, 3 March 1891, p.3).

robbing of banks in 1879, they earned the distinction of having the largest ever reward placed on their heads. Failing to derail and ambush a police train in 1880, the gang, clad in bulletproof armour that they had devised themselves, engaged in a shootout with the police. Ned Kelly was the only gang member to survive and was later hanged at the Melbourne Gaol in November of 1880.[7]

The Shovellers finally fell in with some good fortune when two more children were born into the family, first with Mabel Susan Shoveller arriving on the 3rd June 1878,[8] and their last child Clarence John Hann Shoveller, being born on the 19th August 1880.[9] Bisecting these two births was the wedding of their eldest daughter Susan Eva Shoveller aged 20, who married Edward R. Meally (1861-1936) at Grafton in 1879,[10] and the young couple produced a grandson for Thomas and Susan in Edward Charles Meally later that year.[11] The Meally's followed up three years later with a daughter they named Latona S. Meally, who arrived in 1882.[12]

However, there were signs that all was not well in the Shoveller household when in August 1883 Susan Shoveller applied to the local court for an injunction to 'keep the peace',

▲ *The rough, but well travelled route to Glen Innes was via the Grafton-Dalmorton Road.*

the equivalent of todays 'apprehended violence order,' although little else is known of this family rift.[13]

Late December of 1881 brought news of the arrest of Thomas' older brother William Henry Shoveller Sr. in London, for 'feloniously and maliciously setting fire to certain things in a building,' and although no conviction or sentence seems to have been recorded, he likely descended into madness and probably died in an asylum in 1883.[14] Six months later, Susan Shoveller lost her mother Mary Ann Hann aged 63, on the 25th June 1882, when a great horde of the family assembled at Grafton to mourn and pay their respects, for the life of their matriarch.[15,16] By November of 1883, it seems Thomas and Susan Shoveller may have been running a lodging house as this was stated in testimony during a perjury case in Grafton.[17]

By this time, travel to and from Sydney had changed considerably with the introduction of the fast and more comfortable coastal steamers that visited Grafton and the Clarence at least twice a week. Advertisements placed by booking agents in the Sydney Morning Herald reveal just how passengers would have organised their travel at the time, embarking from the Market St. Wharf at Darling Harbour in Sydney.[18]

As the years wore on Thomas had evolved into an accountant, mercantile agent and psuedo-solicitor and, setting up an office opposite the Grafton Court House, he was often mentioned in court and in the local newspaper.[19] In February of 1887 he was up against Mr. E. Luttrell, which was 'continued for service', but he also appeared for the plaintiff, a Mr J.R. Love against W. Noud over 'goods sold.' In February 1889, Thomas was in the Small Debts Court for a claim against Thomas Hutchings for cash lent and other items, which went in his favour for the amount of £4.9d and 5s costs. Thomas also made application for a 'Conditional Purchase' of land at Lanitza, South Grafton on the 29th August 1889.[20]

Thomas and Susan's daughter Leonora [Lenore] married John Henry Mackie (1868-1894) on the 3rd March 1890 in Grafton,[21] producing a grandaughter for Thomas and

Susan in Valteveredo Calceolaria Mackie on the 25th March 1891.[22] In November of 1890, Thomas Shoveller was forced to file for bankruptcy for a third time with official notices being posted in the local newspaper.[23,24] By this time the Shovellers had moved back to Grafton proper and were residing in Victoria Street.[25] However, after fathering just one child, his new son-in-law John Mackie proved to be a terrible husband and by all accounts Lenore was lucky to be widowed when he prematurely died aged 26, in 1894.[26]

On the 31st July 1896, after years of public service, negotiation and arbitration through his work as a legal advocate and accountant, Thomas broke down and was admitted to a hospital for the Infirm and Destitute at the Grafton Benevolent Asylum.[27,28] By 1899, word was received from England that his last surviving brother John Shoveller Jr. had died aged 81,[29] which left Thomas as the longest living member of his family.

Shoveller notices posted from 1887 to 1900. ▲LEFT COLUMN: 1-Thomas Shoveller - Plaintiff Clarence & Rich. Ex, 7th May 1889, p2); 2-Thomas Shoveller - Free Selections at South Grafton (C&RE, 31 Aug 1889, p.4); 3-Thomas Shoveller - Bankrupt, Fact & Rumour (Clarence & Rich. Ex, 22 Nov 1890, p.4); 4-Thomas Shoveller - Bankruptcy notice (Clarence & Rich. Ex. 22nd Nov 1890, p.8). CENTRE COLUMN: 1-Thomas Shoveller - Bankruptcy notice (NSW Govt Gazette, 21 Nov 1890, p.8949); 2-Thomas Shoveller - Bankruptcy notice (NSW, Govt Gazettes 1853-1899, No. 8960); 3- Mrs Shoveller - passenger on the "SS Kallatina" (SMH, 21st June 1895, p.4). RIGHT COLUMN: 1-Shoveller - passenger on the "PS City of Grafton" (C&RE, 5th Aug 1899, p.4); 2-Susan Shoveller - Resumption of Land (Govt Gazette of NSW, 7th March 1952, p.721). ABOVE: Thomas Shoveller a resident of Victoria St, in the East Ward of Grafton (Clarence County, 1891 NSW Census).

**N.S.W. Electoral Roll for the Division of Grafton
1898-1899**

No.	Surname	First Name	Residence	Occupation
473	Dalby	Hamlet	Grafton	Bricklayer
889	Hann	George	Grafton	Drover
890	Hann	Hamlet H. H.	Grafton	Carpenter
891	Hann	John Jr.	Coaldale	Farmer
892	Hann	Joseph	Sth Grafton	Labourer
836	Greaves	Charles E.	Grafton	Hotelkeeper
1883	Shoveller	George L.	Pound St, Grafton	Grazier
1884	Shoveller	Thomas	South Grafton	Accountant

▲ TOP (Left): The Grafton and Clarence Basin experienced many floods, but the devastation of the 1890 flood broke all records, reaching a maximum height of 8.13m, or 26' 8" across the entire region. (Right): N.S.W. Electoral Roll for the Division of Grafton, 1898-1899. ABOVE: The 1890 Grafton flood, with the paddlesteamer "City of Grafton" trying to ride out the surges and debris.

Having likely recovered from his hospitalisation, Thomas was listed on the NSW Electoral Roll for 1898-99 in South Grafton, for the Division of Grafton. This Electoral Roll included a large number of close and extended Shoveller and Hann family, which at the same time revealed their various occupations.

Having been widowed in 1894, Lenore married for a second time in 1900, which was held on the 11th July 1900 at St Mary's Cathedral in Sydney to Humphrey Joseph Vincent O'Sullivan (1871-1905).[30] The very next year Thomas was listed as residing at Queen Street, in the North Ward of Grafton, with two other males and one female, likely to have been his children George (28), Mabel (23) and Clarence (21), and it may have been the case that his wife Susan was residing elsewhere with one of her sisters.[31]

An inspection of land records revealed that in 1902, Thomas Shoveller was recorded as owning 40 acres at 'Deep Creek' (*71; C3; 150sq.*), and 37 acres at 'Koolkhan Creek' (*80; C3*) in the Parish of Great Marlow, County of Clarence, Land District of Grafton. Thomas also owned land on the corner of Mary and Dobie Streets in Grafton (*93/Lots 1 to 5 & 6*), for which he had apparently paid just two shillings.

Their daughter Mabel Shoveller was next to marry in secret to William Hayes in Sydney in 1902,[32] but there was no love between them. Mabel soon developed a relationship with a half-caste aboriginal, and a divorce was granted with Hayes, which enabled Mabel to marry for a second time that year to Samuel West, which occurred in Sydney in 1903.[33,34]

In the very next year, Clarence John Hann Shoveller married Mary White, which also occurred in Sydney.[35] Thomas, Susan and family would have undoubtedly been present at most of their children's wedding celebrations if it were possible. But George Shoveller was a late starter and waited until he was 45 before marrying Mary Luney at Sydney in 1918.[36]

TOP: Thomas Shoveller - Lanitza Conditional Purchase, South Grafton (NSW, Govt Gazettes 1853-1899, [May/June 1890] p.3633). MID (Left): Thomas Shoveller - Asylum Admission on the 31 July 1896 (Govt Asylums for the Infirm & Destitute; Register of Inmates Oct 1895-Nov 1896) (Right): Thomas Shoveller - Bronchitis patient 1902 (Hospital & Asylum Records). ABOVE (Left): Notice for Grafton Benevolent Asylum. (Right): Thomas Shoveller - Queen St, North Ward, Grafton (Clarence County, 1901 NSW Census). BOTTOM: Thomas & George Shoveller - Electoral Roll 1903-04 (NSW, The Clarence, Grafton).

▲ The Murwillumbah – Byron Bay – Lismore railway opened in 1894, and was extended to Grafton in 1905, with the North Coast Line reaching South Grafton from Sydney in 1915. Of course Thomas Shoveller would have seen railways, even before he first departed from England back in 1848, but he was nearing his end when the first NSW Government locomotives rolled into Grafton Station. ABOVE: NSW Government Railways E.17 Class Locomotive, No.46. In the first 36 years of its existence the NSW Railways introduced 42 separate classes of locomotives.[53]

On the 1903/04 Australian Electoral Roll, Thomas was listed as an accountant, and his son George as a grazier,[37] while his wife Susan (domestic duties) was listed as residing separately, in Clarence Street, Grafton, all within the electorate of 'The Clarence.'[38] In that year, Thomas was included in a list of persons eligible to be granted an old age pension, which appeared in the newspaper in July of 1904, his annual entitlement being for £26.[39]

As the 20th century dawned the North Coast Railway opened up between Murwillumbah, Byron Bay and Lismore in 1894, which was extended to Casino in 1903 and then to Grafton, which opened the Old Station on the 6th November 1905 as the southern terminus of the original railway line. The development of the line was hampered by the many large rivers that flow out to sea along the North Coast. From the Sydney end, the line ran through Maitland to Paterson and Dungog in 1911, was extended to Gloucester and Taree in 1913 then to Wauchope, Kempsey, Coffs Harbour and the section to South Grafton (now Grafton station) from Glenreagh was completed in 1915. The gap between Coffs Harbour and Glenreagh, which contains five tunnels, was completed in 1922.[40]

Due to its immense span, the Clarence River was the most difficult river to cross and a bridge was not completed until 1932.[41,42] In the meantime, rail services were connected by an innovative rail ferry that could carry an entire train across the river. The opening of the Grafton Road/Rail Bridge in 1932 finally completed the Sydney to Brisbane rail line. It became the first standard gauge inter-capital link, but an unintended consequence of a fast rail service was that it ended the elegant days of travelling by coastal steamship.

The Deaths of Thomas and Susan Shoveller

A new century had turned over and the world was moving on, with a huge leap for mankind occurring on the 17th December 1903, when Orville Wright (1871-1948) and his brother Wilbur Wright (1867-1912), American aviation pioneers, together known as the Wright brothers, were generally credited with inventing, building and successfully flying the world's first motor-operated airplane.[43,44,45] They made the first controlled, sustained flight of a powered, heavier-than-air aircraft with the 'Wright Flyer' four miles south of Kitty Hawk, North Carolina, at what is now known as Kill Devil Hills. The brothers were also the first to invent aircraft controls that made fixed-wing powered flight possible.

DEATH REGISTERED IN NEW SOUTH WALES, AUSTRALIA

Surname of deceased	SHOVELLER
Other names	Thomas Eastman
Occupation	Accountant Old age pensioner
Sex and Age	Male 81 years
Marital status	Married
Date of death	22nd May 1908
Place of death	Milton Street Grafton
Usual residence	-
Place of birth	London England 54 years in N.S.Wales
Father - Surname	SHOVELLER
Other names	John
Mother - Maiden surname	EASTMAN
Other names	Elizabeth
Place of marriage	Grafton N.S.wales
Age at marriage	29 years
To whom married	Susan Hann
Children of marriage	living Eva L. 47 George L. 35 Mabel 30 Clarence J.H. 27 one male and two females deceased
Informant	George Lorraine Shoveller Son Grafton
Cause of death	Valvular disease of heart. Syncope years
By whom certified	T.J. Henry (Registered)
Particulars of burial or cremation	22nd May 1908 Church of England Cemetery Grafton
Particulars of registration	H.F.W. Fletcher District Registrar / Date 22nd May 1908 / Number 433/1908

Death of an Old Resident.

On Thursday death claimed an old resident of Grafton in the person of Mr. Thomas Shoveller, who passed away at the age of 81. He was supposed to be the oldest resident of the district with the exception of one, who is now living on the Orara. Mr. Shoveller was a native of London, but came to this State at an early age, and was identified with the Clarence from considerably beyond half a century ago. He was the first postmaster of the town, was one of the first aldermen when Grafton became incorporated about half a century ago, and his marriage 52 years ago was the first that was celebrated in Christ Church, when it stood on the corner of Duke and Victoria streets, opposite the present Cathedral. The guests at the wedding included the late Mr. Clark Irving, then member for the Clarence, and only one or two who witnessed the nuptials are living at the present time. Susan bridge, that crosses Alumny Creek in Dobie-street, was named after Mrs. Shoveller. In early years Mr. Shoveller took an interest in public matters, and was one of the committee of the School of Arts in 1859. He was engaged in commercial pursuits in the early days of Grafton, and conducted a general store where the Clarence River Stores now stand. Of late, by reason of the infirmities of age, his health began to fail, and it became evident that his end was not far off. He leaves a widow and family of five, of whom two sons and one daughter (Mrs. E. Meally, of Queen-street) reside in Grafton. The funeral took place yesterday, Rev. Mr. King officiating.

Grafton Death

We record with regret the death of an old and respected resident of Grafton, in the person of Mr Thomas E. Shoveller, the same taking place at his residence in Milton Street, late last Thursday evening. Deceased who was 81 years of age and a native of London, came to Grafton 54 years ago, and commenced his career here as a storekeeper and Wharfinger at the old company's wharf, then known as Sharpe's Wharf. He later opened a store in Queen Street and whilst there he and his wife largely subsidised the building of the old bridge over Alumny Creek, connecting the two portions of Dobie-street, and known then (and sometimes now) as Susan's Bridge. His wife (who survives him) he married shortly after his arrival here in the old Anglican Church, which stood in Victoria-street, on the opposite side of the road to the present Cathedral. This lady whose maiden name was Susan Hann, is a native of Grafton and from her it was that the bridge took its name. The deceased was at one time an alderman on the Borough, and was largely responsible for the formation of the Grafton Hospital, and those who knew him best speak of him as a good citizen, who always had the interests of the city at heart. The interment took place at the Grafton Cemetery on Friday. The widow and a family of five, three daughters (one of whom is Mrs E. Meally of Queen Street), and two sons are left to mourn their loss.

The Argus Newspaper, 22nd May 1908

SHOVELLER.—May 21, at Grafton, Thomas Eastmann Shoveller, only surviving son of the late Dr. John Shoveller, LL.D., of London, and dearly beloved father of Mrs. Samuel West, late of Neutral Bay, and Mrs. Lenore O'Sullivan, Miller's Point, in his 81st year. R.I.P. London and New Zealand papers please copy.

▲ TOP (Left): The death certificate of Thomas Eastman Shoveller, 22 May 1908 (NSW BDM #433/1908). (Right): Thomas Shoveller - Death notice and obituary (Sydney Morning Herald, 23 May 1908, p.12). MID: Thomas Shoveller - Obituary (The Argus [Grafton], 22 May 1908). ABOVE: Thomas Shoveller - Obituary (Clarence & Richmond Examiner, 23rd May 1908).

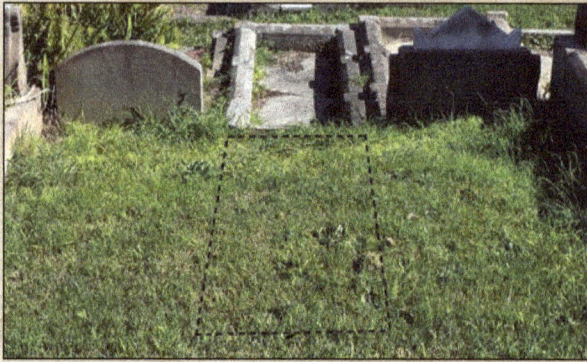

SUSAN SHOVELLER
FIRST WHITE CHILD BORN IN
CLARENCE DISTRICT
1840 - 1919

AN AUSTRALIAN PIONEER

ERECTED BY DR TRACY ROCKWELL (GG GRANDSON) 2016

DEATH TRANSCRIPTION from
NSW Registry of Births, Deaths and Marriages

Transcription requested by	TRACY	ROCKWELL	18-Oct-01
Registration Number	01344		
Date of Death	23 FEB 1919		
Place of Death	123 MITCHELL STREET, GLEBE		
Name	SUSAN SHOVELLER		
Occupation	-		
Sex	FEMALE		
Age	79		
Cause of Death	CARDIAC SYNCOPE, CARDIAC DISEASE, VALVULAR (COMPLICATED WITH SENILITY)		
Duration	SEVERAL YEARS		
Medical Attendant	J. CALDWELL, 22 FEB		
Father	JOHN HANN		
Father's Occupation	BOAT BUILDER		
Mother - Maiden Name	MARY MATILDA THOMPSON		
Informant	GEORGE L. SHOVELLER, SON, 40 CITY RD, SYDNEY		
When Buried	24 FEB 1919		
Where	CHURCH OF ENGLAND CEMETERY, WAVERLEY		
Undertaker	F. DANGAR		
Minister	R. MCKEOWN		
Religion	CHURCH OF ENGLAND		
Witnesses	C. DANGAR, H. WHITBREAD		
Where born	WOODFORD ISLAND, CLARENCE RIVER, NSW		
Time in Colony/State	-		
Place Married	GRAFTON, NSW		
Age at Marriage	ABOUT 16		
Spouse	THOMAS EASTMAN SHOVELLER		
Children of Marriage	LENORE 52, GEORGE L 45, MABEL 40, CLARENCE J H 38, LIVING 2 MALES 1 FEMALE DECEASED		

OLD CLARENCE NATIVE.

There passed away on Sunday last at the residence of her son (Mr. J. Shoveller) at the Glebe, Sydney, the first white female infant born on the Clarence River, in the person of Mrs. Susan Shoveller, aged 80. Her husband predeceased her some years ago. Deceased was born at Woodford Island, Clarence River. The blacks were wild and troublesome at that time, and the old lady could relate many exciting incidents in connection with them. Numbers of them met their death by poisoned flour. She practically resided all her life on the Clarence, and was well known to the old residents. Two sons and two daughters survive, residing in Sydney. She leaves 11 grandchildren and five great-grandchildren. The remains were interred in the Church of England portion of the Waverley cemetery. With her was buried a small testament given her by her late husband 63 years ago. She leaves a number of brothers and sisters, and numerous relatives.

The death of Mrs. H. Shoveller is announced in one of your recent issues. Deceased was one of the Hann family, very old residents of Grafton and the Clarence. Mr. Shoveller conducted a store business here some 60 years ago and resided near Dobie-street bridge, over Alumny Creek, which was called Susan bridge after Mrs. Shoveller.

SHOVELLER.—At her son's (John) residence, 123 Mitchell-street, Glebe, Susan Hann Shoveller, late of Grafton, in her 80th year. Grafton papers please copy.

▲TOP (Left): The unmarked grave of Susan Shoveller at Waverley Cemetery, Sydney. (Right): A suitable proposed memorial for Susan Shoveller's unmarked grave at Waverley Cemetery. MID (Left): Transcript of the death certificate of Susan Shoveller, 23 Feb 1919 (NSW BDM #01344/1919). (Right, Above): Obituary for Mrs Susan Shoveller (The Voice Of The North, 7 March 1919, p.5). (Right, Below): Mrs Shoveller - Death notice and obituary (Northern Star, 7 March 1919, p.7). ABOVE: Susan (Hann) Shoveller - Death notice (Sydney Morning Herald, 24 Feb 1919, p.6).

Sadly on the 22nd of May 1908, after a long and fulfilled life of adventure with numerous ups and downs, Thomas Eastman Shoveller died of valvular disease of the heart, which he had apparently suffered from for a number of years.[46,47] He died at his home at Milton Street in Grafton, and was just five days short of his 82nd birthday. The informant on the death certificate was his son George Lorraine Shoveller, who listed his occupation as an accountant and old age pensioner. George incorrectly recorded that Thomas was born in London (sic. Warnford), England and had been in the colony for 54 years (sic. 57

years). Thomas Shoveller's parents were nevertheless correctly listed as John Shoveller and Elizabeth Eastman.

In regard to Thomas' offspring, George listed his siblings as Eva L. (47), Mabel (30), and Clarence (27), but completely omitted his 42 year old sister Lenore! The certificate also correctly stated that one male (Thomas Charles) and two females (Susan Theresa and Janet) were deceased. Thomas Eastman Shoveller was buried at the Church of England Cemetery in Grafton, apparently on the same day, although the location of his grave or memorial headstone has not been found. The Argus newspaper and the Clarence and Richmond Examiner both published detailed obituaries.[48]

A year after his death in 1909, Thomas was recorded as still owning land, this time in the Parish of Southampton, County of Clarence, Land District of Grafton, with holdings of 66 acres (*15; C.14.R*), and 47 acres (*30; C.14.R*) respectively.

Shortly after Thomas' death, Susan Shoveller moved to Glebe in Sydney to reside between her two sons George and Clarence (John), where she remained in good health for a further

In default of prior payment to the Council of the rates due and in arrear the said land will be offered for sale by public auction by W. M. Dougherty & Co. at Grafton Street, Copmanhurst, adjacent Rest Point Hotel on 13th August, 1965, at 10 a.m.

Owners or Persons having an Interest in the Land	Description of Land (Lot, Section and Dep. Plan Nos. Street, etc.)	Amount of Overdue Rates £ s. d.
MITCHELL, James	Lot 10, Section 1, Lawrence Street, Village of Southgate	28 5 2
PHILIP, Hugh McDonald	Lot 8, Section 9, Clarence Street, Village of Southgate	13 4 1
McDONELL, Charles Joseph; MOFFITT, Robert Delmege	Part portion 88, Great Marlow, D.P. 1,882, Heathcote Street. Lots 2, 3, Section 1.	16 15 2
KIMPTON, Estate Frederick Thomas	Part portion 88, Great Marlow, D.P. 1,882, River Street, Lots 7, 8, Section 2.	38 15 0
SHOVELLER, Susan	Part portion 88, Great Marlow, D.P. 1,882, River Street, Lots 11, 12, Section 2.	33 11 0
LAMAN, Edward John; CLARKE, William	Part portion 88, Great Marlow, D.P. 1,882, River Street, Lots 16 to 18, Section 2.	29 10 11
GRAHAM, Estate William John	Part portion 88, Great Marlow, D.P. 1,882, River Street, Lots 19, 20, Section 2.	29 15 4
CATT, Henry Charles	Part portion 88, Great Marlow, D.P. 1,882, Corner River and Heathcote Streets, Lots 21, 22, Section 2.	29 10 7

In default of prior payment to the Council of the rates due and in arrear the said land will be offered for sale by public auction by W. M. Dougherty & Co., at Shire Council Chambers, on 13th August, 1965, at 2 p.m.

P.O. Box 34,
Grafton.
28th April, 1965.

H. G. GREENAWAY,
Shire Clerk.

1489—£15

▲ TOP: Susan Shoveller received a Rate Defaulters notice from the Grafton Council some 46 years after her death (Govt Gazette of NSW, 7th May 1965, p.67).
ABOVE: A coastal steamer pulling into Grafton wharf, with the township of South Grafton in the background, c.1900.

11 years. It was there that she died of the same disease as her husband, on the 23rd of February 1919,[49,50] with the Clarence and Richmond Examiner in Grafton printing a detailed obituary.[51] Susan was listed on the Probate Index of the Supreme Court of NSW, on the 1st of September 1920.[52] Regrettably, Susan Shoveller was buried by her children in an unmarked grave in the C of E section at Waverley Cemetery (*W14; CE; SL7446*).

The union between Thomas and Susan Shoveller delivered eight children, although only five survived to adulthood. Those that endured produced a further 14 grandchildren, and numerous great grandchildren have since flourished. The final chapter of this book reveals all that is known of Thomas and Susan Shoveller's children and their descendants.

▲ *TOP: The Red Rocks postcard at Copmanhurst, Clarence River, N.S.W, c.1900s. ABOVE: The Foresters Friendly Society was formed in 1834 as the 'Ancient Order of Foresters' (AOF) in Britain, when over 300 branches of the Royal Foresters Society formed the new 'Ancient Order of Foresters'. In 1861, a branch of the AOF was established in Grafton. Is 63 year old Thomas Eastman Shoveller in this unnamed 1890 photograph [either seated center or right rear]?*

Images & Photographs of Grafton Wharf

▲ TOP: Clarence River traffic, with a steamer pulling away from the Grafton Wharf, by Julian Ashton (1851-1942). MID 1 (Left): Steamer loading up at Grafton Wharf. (Right): The town was a hive of activity whenever paddlesteamers, steamships or sailing vessels were at the wharf, c.1900. MID 2 (Left): The approach to the Grafton punt, with the Convent at right. (Right): A driver with his horse and wagon, waiting at the wharf, c.1890. ABOVE: This image of the new Grafton Road/Rail Bridge was taken in 1932, and shows South Grafton (centre), Grafton at the right, and Thomas Eastman Shoveller's long sold property 'Lanitza', at bottom right.

References

1. Wikipedia - Electrical telegraphy in the United Kingdom [https://en.wikipedia.org/wiki/Electrical_telegraphy_in_the_United_Kingdom].

2. The Electric Light (Sydney Morning Herald, 10th November, 1876).

3. Thomas Shoveller - 'Household resident #3952' (Grafton, 'Division of The Clarence,' 1876-77, NSW Electoral Roll).

4. Thomas Shoveller - Conviction Set Aside (Evening News, 12th June 1877, p.2).

5. Thomas Shoveller - Charged with breaching the Attorney Act (Clarence & Richmond Examiner, 7th Aug 1880, p.4).

6. Sydney Shoveller - Arrived Brisbane aboard the "Ramsay" from London, 21 Aug 1877. (Queensland, Australia, Passenger Lists, 1848-1912).

7. Wikipedia - Ned Kelly [https://en.wikipedia.org/wiki/Ned_Kelly].

8. NSW Dept of BDM. (1878). Birth Certificate for Mabel Susan Shoveller - 3 June 1878 (#13336/1878).

9. NSW Dept of BDM. (1880). Birth Certificate for Clarence John Hann Shoveller - 19 Aug 1880 (#15169/1880).

10. NSW Dept of BDM. (1879). Marriage Certificate for Susan Eva Shoveller & Edward R. Meally at Grafton, 1879 (#3246/1879).

11. NSW Dept of BDM. (1879). Birth Certificate for Charles Edward Meally, 1879 (#14355/1879).

12. NSW Dept of BDM. (1882). Birth Certificate for Latona S. Meally, 1882 (#16837/1882).

13. Susan Shoveller - Application to Keeping The Peace (Clarence & Richmond Examiner, 1 Sep 1883, p.4).

14. William Henry Shoveller - 1882 Jan-1882 Mar, Anglesey-Yorkshire (UK, Calendar of Prisoners, 1868-1929).

15. Mrs Hann -Obituary (Clarence & Richmond Examiner and New England Advertiser, 27 June 1882, p.2).

16. Mary Matilda Hann - Obituary (Clarence & Richmond Examiner, 15th July 1882, p.5).

17. Mr & Mrs Shoveller - Lodging House (Clarence & Richmond Examiner and New England Advertiser, 3 Nov 1883, p.3).

18. Shipping notices for Grafton & the Clarence River (Sydney Morning Herald, 30th May 1884).

19. Thomas Shoveller - Accountant & Mercantile Agent (C&RE, 3 March 1891, p.3)

20. Thomas Shoveller - Lanitza, Sth Grafton (NSW, Govt Gazettes 1853-1899, [May/June 1890] p.3633).

21. NSW Dept of BDM. (1890). Marriage Certificate for John Henry Mackie & Lenore Shoveller, 3 March 1890 (#3797/1890).

22. NSW Dept of BDM. (1891). Birth Certificate for Valteveredo Calceolaria Mackie, 25 March 1891 (#14676/1891).

23. Thomas Shoveller - Bankruptcy notice (NSW Govt Gazette, 21 Nov 1890, p.8949).

24. Thomas Shoveller - Bankruptcy notice (NSW, Govt Gazettes 1853-1899, No. 8960).

25. Thomas Shoveller - Victoria St, East Ward, Grafton (Clarence County, 1891 NSW Census).

26. NSW Dept of BDM. (1894). Death Certificate for John Henry Mackie, 1894 (#3418/1894).

27. Thomas Eastman Shoveller - Asylum Admittance, 31 July 1896.

28. Thomas Shoveller - Admission, 31 July 1896 (Govt Asylums for the Infirm & Destitute; Register of Inmates Oct 1895-Nov 1896).

29 John Shoveller Jr. - Probate notice, 19 Dec 1899 (England & Wales, National Probate Calendar, 1858-1995).

30. NSW Dept of BDM. (1900). Marriage Certificate for Lenore Mackie (nee Shoveller) & Humphrey Joseph O'Sullivan, 11th July 1900 (#5186/1900).

31. Thomas Shoveller - Queen St, Grafton (1901 NSW Census).

32. NSW Dept of BDM. (1902). Marriage Certificate for Mabel Shoveller & William Hayes, 1902 (#8434/1902).

33. Mabel Hayes (Shoveller) - Divorced William Hayes (Australian Star, 17 March 1984, p.7).

34. NSW Dept of BDM. (1903). Marriage Certificate for Mabel Hayes (nee Shoveller) & Samuel West, 1903 (#7665/1903).

35. NSW Dept of BDM. (1904). Marriage Certificate for Clarence John Hann Shoveller & Mary Elizabeth White, 1904 (#34/1904).

36. NSW Dept of BDM. (1918). Marriage Certificate for George Lorraine Shoveller & Mary Luney, 1918 (#8020/1918).

37. Thomas & George Lorraine Shoveller, Clarence (Grafton Division, Australia Electoral Rolls 1903-04).

38. Susan Shoveller, Clarence (Grafton Division, Australia Electoral Rolls 1903-04).

39. Thomas Shoveller - Old Age Pension, Grafton (Clarence & Richmond Examiner, 2 July 1904, p.2).

40. NSWrail.net (2021). "North Coast Line." [https://www.nswrail.net/lines/show.php?name=NSW:north_coast]. Retrieved 3 June 2021.

41. NSWrail.net (2021), op.cit.

42. "Crossing the Clarence" Roundhouse, July 1982 pp.4-23.

43. "The Wright Brothers and the invention of the aerial age". National Air & Space Museum. Smithsonian Institution. Archived from the original on August 13, 2015. Retrieved September 21, 2010.

44. Johnson, Mary Ann (September 28, 2001). "Program 3". Following the footsteps of the Wright Brothers: Their sites and stories symposium papers.' Retrieved August 16, 2015.

45. "Flying through the ages". BBC News. March 19, 1999. Archived from the original on October 21, 2014. Retrieved July 17, 2009.

46. NSW Dept of BDM. (1908). Death Certificate for Thomas Eastman Shoveller, 22nd May 1908 (#433/1908).

47. Thomas Shoveller - Death notice (Sydney Morning Herald, 23 May 1908, p.12).

48. Thomas Shoveller - Obituary (Clarence & Richmond Examiner, 23rd May 1908).

49. NSW Dept of BDM. (1919). Death Certificate for Susan Shoveller (nee Hann), 23rd February 1919 (#1344/1919).

50. Mrs Shoveller - Death notice (Northern Star, 7 March 1919, p.7).

51. Mrs Susan Shoveller - Obituary (The Voice Of The North, 7 March 1919, p.5).

52. Susan Shoveller - 1st of September 1920, Probate Index of the Supreme Court of NSW (Deceased Estate Files [1880-1923], No.134/101344).

53. Oberg, Leon (1984). 'Locomotives of Australia 1850's -1980's.' Frenchs Forest: Reed Books. pp.168–170 [ISBN 0 730100 05 7].

Chapter Twenty

THE DESCENDANTS OF
THOMAS & SUSAN SHOVELLER

Thomas Eastman Shoveller likely first arrived in Grafton sometime in the early 1850s, and he remained a resident there for well over 50 years. His wife Susan was the first white child born in the Clarence River District and she resided in the northern capital for almost 70 years, from her birth in 1840 until 1908, before moving south to join her children in Sydney.

Three weeks after Thomas and Susan Shoveller's 1856 marriage, the Treaty of Paris was signed, ending the Crimean War and the threat of Russian invasion of the Australian colonies. It was from this point on that the Shoveller's began producing their family. Although eight known children were born to Thomas and Susan, only five reached adulthood. The following information is what is known to date about each of Thomas and Susan Shoveller's children and their descendants (*see Pedigree Chart 8*).

1. Susan Theresa Shoveller (1858-1858)

After a promising start for the newlyweds, the first child of Thomas and Susan Shoveller was Susan Theresa Shoveller, who was born on 15th May 1858,[1] but she sadly died in the same year.[2]

Early Grafton Schools

The first school was established by James Pillar near the town boundary and close to the racecourse in the 1840s. He was not a qualified teacher and did not pursue a teaching career for long. The next school was set up in 1851 by the first Presbyterian minister, the Rev. John Gibson, near Christopher Creek at South Grafton.

After the first Government sponsored school opened and closed three times from 1852 to 1854, Graftonians applied to the Government for a national school, or what they termed "a proper school."

This school opened late in 1859. School and residence were bounded by Prince, Victoria and Fitzroy Streets. One of the seven teachers who came to Australia from England was James Page, the headmaster and grandfather of Sir Earle Page.

A cyclone practically demolished the school within a few months of its opening. Temporary accommodation was found in Prince Street and an infants' department added in 1865. It was obvious, though, that a fresh start would have to be made.

As local residents paid one-third the cost of erecting school buildings at this time, it was decided to sell the site of the ill-fated school and use the money to finance a school on cheaper land beside Alumy Creek in Queen Street. The Bank of New South Wales bought the former school land and subdivided it.

▲ *TOP: Aquatic activity on the South Grafton riverbank about 1900. ABOVE: Information on early Grafton Schools (from John Moorhead, John (1984). 'Grafton: The First 125 Civic Years', Grafton Municipal Council).*

2. Susan Eva Shoveller (1859-1913)

Susan Eva Shoveller was the second daughter of Thomas and Susan Shoveller, and was born on the 24th August 1859 in Grafton.[3] She grew up in the developing township and attended the local school. At the age of 20, she married Edward (1861-1936), the son of Edward Sr. and Bridget Meally in 1879 in Grafton.[4] Very soon after their wedding, the young couple had a son in Edward Charles Meally who was also born in 1879.[5] A daughter was next to arrive in Latona S. Meally who was born in 1882,[6] but she unfortunately passed away in 1900 at just 18 years of age.[7] The third child to join the family was Eva Nathalia Meally who was born in 1885.[8]

By 1910, Susan's son Edward Charles Meally had married Nellie M. Ford, which took place at the Christ Church Cathedral in Grafton.[9] Two years later in 1912, the Argus newspaper published an article on another wedding, held at the Christ Church Cathedral in Grafton on the 15th of October between Miss Eva [Nathalia] Meally, the only daughter of Susan and Edward Meally of Bacon Street Grafton, and Frederick Charles Della Ca (1893-1959) of Sydney.[10]

Susan Eva Meally sadly passed away prior to her mother in 1913, aged just 55.[11] Few details have arisen about the life of Susan, her family members and descendents, or her husband Edward Meally who lived until 1936.[12] Susan and Edward Meally produced three children, who in turn left a small number of descendents, which continue today (*see 20.1 Descendants of Susan Eva Shoveller & Edward R. Meally*).

Documents of Susan Eva Shoveller & Family

PERSONAL.

The Local Lands Office was the scene of a pleasant function on Friday afternoon, when Mr. District Surveyor Thomas, in his characteristic happy way, presented Mr. F. C. Della Ca with several handsome table requisites to mark the good feeling and esteem in which he is held by his fellow-officers and in anticipation of his entering the married state at an early date. Mr. Della Ca, in a neat and feeling manner responded, thanking the donors. (Mr. Della Ca was married yesterday morning to Miss Meally).

* * * *

At yesterday's wedding of Miss Meally to Mr. Della Ca, as mentioned elsewhere in this issue, one of the most interested spectators was the grandmother of the bride, Mrs Susan Shoveller, who, as Miss Susan Hann, was the first person to be married in the old Church of England (now the Vicarage) by the Rev. A. E. Selwin. She was also (as mentioned in a July issue of the "Argus"), the first white child born on the Clarence River.

* * * *

Della Ca—Meally Wedding.

A quiet wedding was solemnised at Christ Church Cathedral, Grafton, at 8 a.m. yesterday morning, when Miss Eva Meally, only daughter of Mr. and Mrs. E. Meally, of Bacon-street, Grafton, was married to Mr. Frederick Charles Della Ca, of Sydney. Canon Seymour officiated. The bride (who was given away by her father) was tastefully attired in fancy grey material with allover lace yoke, trimmed with silk medallions and apricot silk. The skirt was further enhanced with rows of ruched silk to match. With this costume was worn a black crinoline hat, ornamented with shaded leaves to tone. Miss Mabel Prideaux, as bridesmaid, was also daintly attired in grey, with a large white hat wreathed with berries and foliage. Mr. Horace Kittlety supported the groomsman as best man. Immediately after the ceremony Mr. and Mrs. Della Ca drove to the railway station, where they boarded the train bound for Byron Bay, where the honeymoon is to be spent.—"IRIS."

Lloyd Meally CARR

Lloyd Carr graduated from Sydney in 1944 and gained his MDS in 1953. In the United Kingdom he obtained a Diploma in Public Health Dentistry in 1959. He was an inaugural Fellow of the RACDS and in 1973 was elected a Fellow of the International College of Dentists.

In 1950 he joined the recently forme ACT School Dental Service and became its Director. His appointment to the Dental Health Committee of the NH&MRC from 1973 introduced him to the mainstream of national scientific policy making bodies. In 1973 he was seconded to the Commonwealth Department of Health as Assistant Director-General of Health (Dental Services).

He later became a consultant to the Department as well as many overseas bodies such as WHO and FDI.

He made a very substantial contribution to the advocacy of fluoridation of public water supplies.

His collation and publication of the information recording the outstanding success of his Australian Preventive Dentistry programs is his legacy to his country.

Regrettably, the awarding of the ADA's highest honour was presented posthumously due to his untimely death at sea.

We regret to record the death of Mrs. Meally, wife of Mr. E. Meally, of the "Examiner," which took place on Thursday at her residence Bacon-street. Deceased had been in delicate health for some months past. She was a native of Grafton, and was the eldest daughter of the late Mr. T. Shoveller, one of the oldest residents of the Clarence. Mrs. Meally, who was 51 years of age, leaves a son, Mr. C. Meally, and a daughter, Mrs. Della Ca, both of Grafton. Her mother is still living. The funeral took place yesterday afternoon, Canon Seymour conducting the burial service at the graveside; Rev. W. Higlett and Adjutant Munro holding a short service at the residence. Members of the "Examiner" staff attended by special conveyance, and several acted as pall bearers. A wreath was sent by the proprietor and staff of the journal named, and we extend our sympathy to the bereaved.

MEALLY, Edward Charles.—June 12, 1954, at his residence, 39 Grosvenor Street, Woollahra, dearly loved husband of Frances Meally, loved brother of Eva (Mrs. Carr). At rest.

ELWOOD ELDEST SON OF FRED AND EVA DELLA CA WHO DIED AT DUBBO 9TH NOVR 1926 AGED 13½ YEARS —Also— CHARLES EDWARD MEALLY WHO DIED 12TH JUNE 1954.

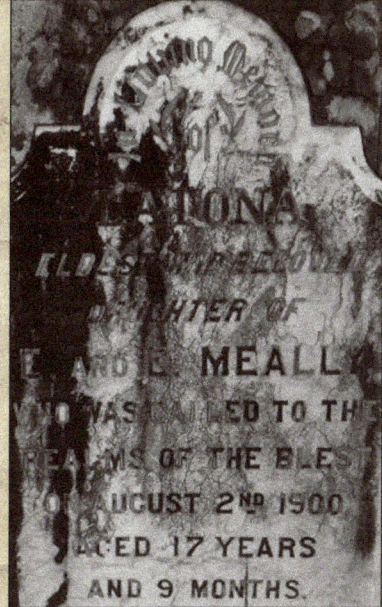

CARR—HAYLLAR. — Dr. and Mrs. Ken Carr, of Moorabbin, have pleasure in announcing the engagement of their only daughter, Margaret Ruth, to Anthony Charles, third son of Mr. and Mrs. H. C. Hayllar, of Moorabbin.

▲LEFT COLUMN: Wedding Announcement for Eva Nathalia Meally & Frederick Della Ca (Grafton Argus, 16th Oct 1912). TOP: Capt. Lloyd Meally Carr - Obituary, 1992. CENTRE COLUMN: 1-Death notice for Mrs Susan Eva Meally (C&RE, 30th Aug 1913); 2-Death notice for Edward Charles Meally, grandson of Thomas Shoveller (SMH, 14th June 1954, p.14); 3-Memorial headstone for Elwood Lorraine Della Ca & Charles Edward Meally (Rookwood C of E Cemetery, Sydney). RIGHT COLUMN: 1-Memorial headstone for Latona S. Meally, daughter of Susan Eva & Edward R. Meally (Grafton Cemetery); 2-Margaret Ruth Carr & Anthony Charles Hayllar - Engagement notice (The Age, 27 January 1970, p.16).

20.1 Descendants of Susan Eva Shoveller & Edward R. Meally [56]

Susan Eva SHOVELLER (1859-1913), married in 1879 at Grafton, NSW to Edward R. MEALLY (1861-1936), with issue:

1. Edward Charles Meally (1879–1954), married firstly in 1910 at Grafton (#12137) to Nellie M. Ford (1888-1959), and resided at 13 Denham St in 'St Albans', Bondi, but Nellie re-married Kingsley Moles in 1926, no issue. Edward married secondly in 1927 at Waverley (#11381) to Frances Carroll (1897-?). Charles died in Sydney in 1854 (#7784), without issue.

2. Latona S. Meally (1882–1900),* died age 17, d.s.p.

3. Eva Nathalia Meally (1885–1969), married in 1912 at Grafton, NSW to Frederick C DELLACA (1893–1959), who later changed their surname to CARR, with issue:

3.1 Elwood Laurraine DELLACA (1913–1926),* died age 13, d.s.p.

3.2 Frederick Edward DELLACA (1917–1970), married in 1940 at Waverley, NSW to Kathleen Norean Dale (1920-?), issue unknown.

3.3 Lloyd Meally CARR (1922–1992) ▲ joined the AIF

with the rank of captain in '60 Dental Unit', during WW2 [#NX204180], married c.1960 at Randwick, NSW to Marion Fawcett (1935–?). Dr Lloyd Meally Carr died as the result of a yachting accident in Twofold Bay on the New South Wales south coast. He was an experienced yachtsman and a former champion at the sport, and sailing was one of the great pleasures of his life. Our deepest sympathy is extended to his wife Marion and his sons Gregory and Philip. Dr Lloyd Carr's greatest professional achievement and his legacy to Australia and Australian Dentistry is the systematic collation and publication of information recording the outstanding success of the Australian preventive dentistry programme that he helped develop and by which he will be remembered and through which he will continue to serve Australia and his profession. His integrity and tenacious pursuit of principle were a monument to a quiet gentleman, leaving issue:
a. Philip CARR (c.1960-?)
b. Gregory CARR (c.1962-?)

3.4 Kenneth Allan CARR (1925–1981), married 1951 at Sydney, NSW to Valma Elizabeth Couper (1927–2010), with issue:
a. Margaret Ruth Carr (1951–?), married in 1970 to Anthony Charles HAYLLAR, with issue:
  a1. Briony Hayllar (?)
  a2. Gavan HAYLLAR (?)

3.5 Male CARR (?-?), issue unknown.

* Died before adulthood - d.s.p.
(Some names not listed in the index.)

Meally / **Shoveller**

Bignell · Clarke · Eastman · Gawpin · Grey · Hann · Hazard · Hewitt · Lamborn

Pedigree Chart - 8
The Ancestors & Descendants of Thomas & Susan Shoveller of Grafton, NSW
▲ = Served in Australian Military Forces

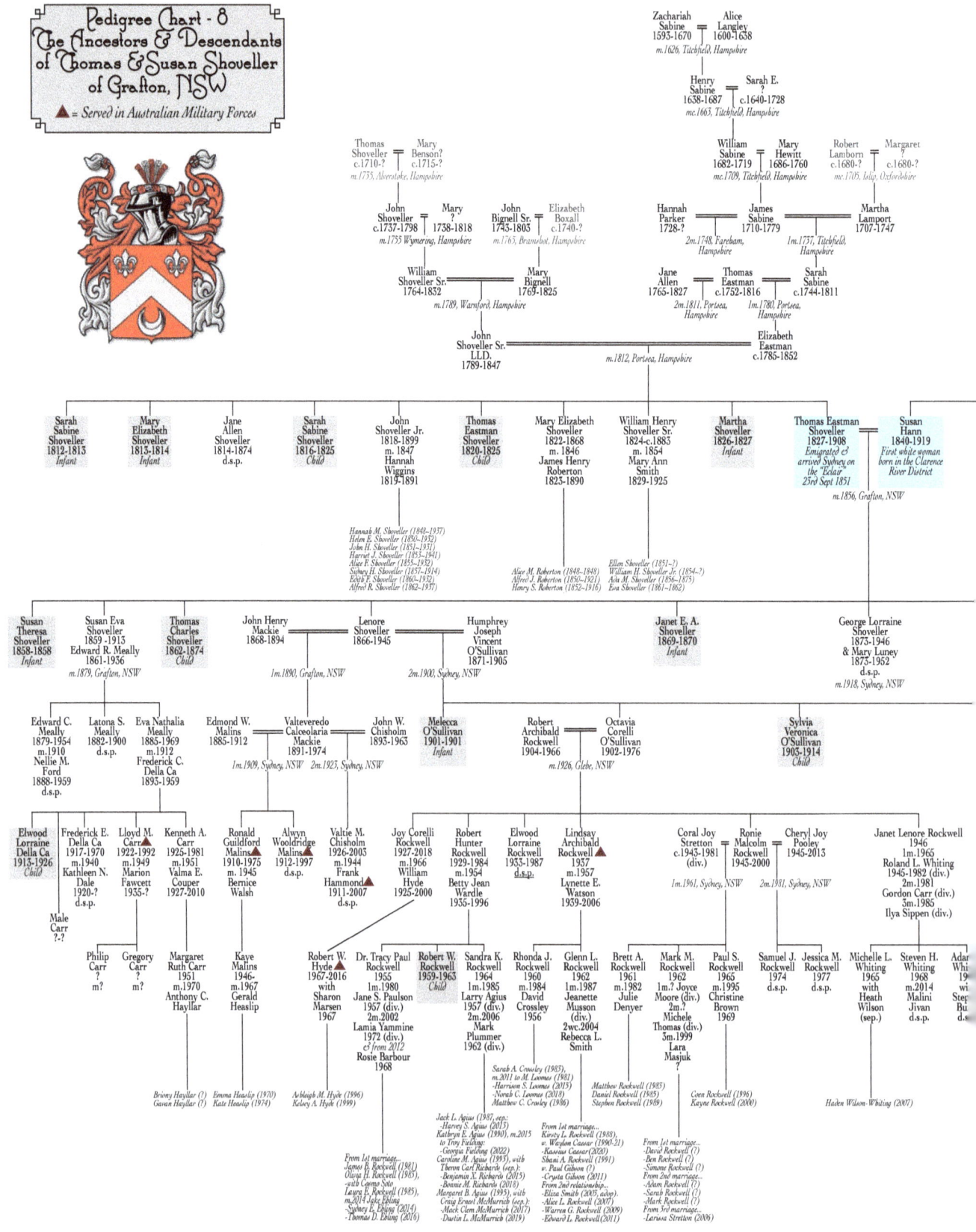

Zachariah Sabine 1593-1670 = Alice Langley 1600-1638
m.1626, Titchfield, Hampshire

Henry Sabine 1638-1687 = Sarah E. ? c.1640-1728
mc.1663, Titchfield, Hampshire

Thomas Shoveller c.1710-? = Mary Benson? c.1715-?
m.1735, Alverstoke, Hampshire

William Sabine 1682-1719 = Mary Hewitt 1686-1760
mc.1709, Titchfield, Hampshire

Robert Lamborn c.1680-? = Margaret ? c.1680-?
mc.1705, Islip, Oxfordshire

John Shoveller c.1737-1798 = Mary ? 1738-1818
m.1755, Wymering, Hampshire

John Bignell Sr. 1743-1805 = Elizabeth Boxall c.1740-?
m.1763, Bramshot, Hampshire

Hannah Parker 1728-? — James Sabine 1710-1779 — Martha Lamport 1707-1747
2m.1748, Fareham, Hampshire; 1m.1737, Titchfield, Hampshire

William Shoveller Sr. 1764-1852 = Mary Bignell 1769-1825
m.1789, Warnford, Hampshire

Jane Allen 1765-1827 — Thomas Eastman c.1752-1816 — Sarah Sabine c.1744-1811
2m.1811, Portsea, Hampshire; 1m.1780, Portsea, Hampshire

John Shoveller Sr. LLD. 1789-1847 = Elizabeth Eastman c.1785-1852
m.1812, Portsea, Hampshire

Sarah Sabine Shoveller 1812-1813 *Infant*
Mary Elizabeth Shoveller 1813-1814 *Infant*
Jane Allen Shoveller 1814-1874 *d.s.p.*
Sarah Sabine Shoveller 1816-1825 *Child*
John Shoveller Jr. 1818-1899 m.1847 Hannah Wiggins 1819-1891
Thomas Eastman Shoveller 1820-1825 *Child*
Mary Elizabeth Shoveller 1822-1868 m.1846 James Henry Roberton 1823-1890
William Henry Shoveller Sr. 1824-c.1883 m.1854 Mary Ann Smith 1829-1925
Martha Shoveller 1826-1827 *Infant*
Thomas Eastman Shoveller 1827-1908 *Emigrated & arrived Sydney on the "Eclair" 23rd Sept 1851* = Susan Hann 1840-1919 *First white woman born in the Clarence River District*
m.1856, Grafton, NSW

Hannah M. Shoveller (1848-1937)
Helen E. Shoveller (1850-1932)
John H. Shoveller (1851-1931)
Harriet J. Shoveller (1853-1941)
Alice F. Shoveller (1855-1932)
Sydney H. Shoveller (1857-1914)
Edith F. Shoveller (1860-1932)
Alfred R. Shoveller (1862-1937)

Alice M. Roberton (1848-1848)
Alfred J. Roberton (1850-1921)
Henry S. Roberton (1852-1916)

Ellen Shoveller (1851-?)
William H. Shoveller Jr. (1854-?)
Ada M. Shoveller (1856-1875)
Eva Shoveller (1861-1862)

Susan Theresa Shoveller 1858-1858 *Infant*
Susan Eva Shoveller 1859-1913 — Edward R. Meally 1861-1936 *m.1879, Grafton, NSW*
Thomas Charles Shoveller 1862-1874 *Child*
John Henry Mackie 1868-1894 — Lenore Shoveller 1866-1945 — Humphrey Joseph Vincent O'Sullivan 1871-1905 *1m.1890, Grafton, NSW 2m.1900, Sydney, NSW*
Janet E. A. Shoveller 1869-1870 *Infant*
George Lorraine Shoveller 1873-1896 & Mary Luney 1873-1952 *d.s.p. m.1918, Sydney, NSW*

Edward C. Meally 1879-1954 m.1910 Nellie M. Ford 1888-1959 *d.s.p.*
Latona S. Meally 1882-1900 *d.s.p.*
Eva Nathalia Meally 1885-1969 m.1912 Frederick C. Della Ca 1893-1959
Edmond W. Malins 1885-1912 — Valteveredo Calceolaria Mackie 1891-1974 — John W. Chisholm 1893-1963 *1m.1909, Sydney, NSW 2m.1923, Sydney, NSW*
Melecca O'Sullivan 1901-1901 *Infant*
Robert Archibald Rockwell 1904-1966 = Octavia Corelli O'Sullivan 1902-1976 *m.1926, Glebe, NSW*
Sylvia Veronica O'Sullivan 1903-1914 *Child*

Elwood Lorraine Della Ca 1913-1926 *Child*
Frederick E. Della Ca 1917-1970 ▲ m.1940 Kathleen N. Dale 1920-? *d.s.p.*
Lloyd M. Carr 1922-1992 ▲ m.1949 Marion Fawcett 1935-?
Kenneth A. Carr 1925-1981 m.1951 Valma E. Couper 1927-2010
Ronald Guildford Malins ▲ 1910-1975 m.1945 Bernice Walsh
Alwyn Wooldridge Malins ▲ 1912-1997 *d.s.p.*
Valtie M. Chisholm 1926-2003 m.1944 Frank Hammond ▲ 1911-2007 *d.s.p.*
Joy Corelli Rockwell 1927-2018 m.1966
Robert Hunter Rockwell 1929-1984 m.1954 Betty Jean Wardle 1935-1996
Elwood Lorraine Rockwell 1933-1987 *d.s.p.*
Lindsay Archibald Rockwell 1937 ▲ m.1957 Lynette E. Watson 1939-2006
Coral Joy Stretton c.1943-1981 (div.) = Ronie Malcolm Rockwell 1943-2000 = Cheryl Joy Pooley 1945-2013 *1m.1961, Sydney, NSW 2m.1981, Sydney, NSW*
Janet Lenore Rockwell 1946 1m.1965 Roland L. Whiting 1945-1982 (div.) 2m.1981 Gordon Carr (div.) 3m.1985 Ilya Sippen (div.)

Male Carr ?-?

Philip Carr ? m?
Gregory Carr ? m?
Margaret Ruth Carr 1951 m.1970 Anthony C. Hayllar 1967
Kaye Malins 1946- m.1967 Gerald Heaslip
Robert W. Hyde ▲ 1967-2016 with Sharon Marsen 1967
Dr. Tracy Paul Rockwell 1955 1m.1980 Jane S. Paulson 1957 (div.) 2m.2002 Lamia Yammine 1972 (div.) & from 2012 Rosie Barbour 1968
Robert W. Rockwell 1959-1963 *Child*
Sandra K. Rockwell 1964 1m.1985 Larry Agius 1957 (div.) 2m.2006 Mark Plummer 1962 (div.)
Rhonda J. Rockwell 1960 m.1984 David Crossley 1956
Glenn L. Rockwell 1962 1m.1987 Jeanette Musson (div.) 2wc.2004 Rebecca L. Smith
Brett A. Rockwell 1961 m.1982 Julie Denyer
Mark M. Rockwell 1962 1m.? Joyce Moore (div.) 2m.? Michele Thomas (div.) 3m.1999 Lara Masjuk ?
Paul S. Rockwell 1965 m.1995 Christine Brown 1969
Samuel J. Rockwell 1974 *d.s.p.*
Jessica M. Rockwell 1977 *d.s.p.*
Michelle L. Whiting 1965 with Heath Wilson (sep.)
Steven H. Whiting 1968 m.2014 Malini Jivan *d.s.p.*
Adam Whi... 19.. wi... Step... Bu... d.s...

Briony Hayllar (?)
Gavan Hayllar (?)

Emma Heaslip (1970)
Kate Heaslip (1974)

Ashleigh M. Hyde (1996)
Kelsey A. Hyde (1999)

From 1st marriage...
James B. Rockwell (1981)
Olivia R. Rockwell (1983), with Cosma Sato
Laura E. Rockwell (1985), m.2014 Jake Ebling
-Sydney L. Ebling (2014)
-Thomas D. Ebling (2016)

Jack L. Agius (1987, sep.)
-Harvey S. Agius (2015)
Kathryn E. Agius (1990), m.2015 to Tiny Fielding:
-Georgia Fielding (2022)
Caroline M. Agius (1993), with Theron Carl Richards (sep.):
-Benjamin X. Richards (2015)
-Bonnie M. Richards (2018)
Margaret B. Agius (1995), with Craig Ernest McMurrich (sep.):
-Mack Clem McMurrich (2017)
-Dustin L. McMurrich (2019)

Sarah A. Crowley (1983), m.2011 to M. Loomas (1981)
-Harrison S. Loomas (2015)
-Norah C. Loomas (2018)
Matthew C. Crowley (1986)

Matthew Rockwell (1983)
Daniel Rockwell (1985)
Stephen Rockwell (1989)

From 1st marriage...
Kirsty L. Rockwell (1988), w. Waylon Caesar (1990-21)
-Rassius Caesar (2020)
Shani A. Rockwell (1991)
w. Paul Gibson (?)
-Cryta Gibson (2011)
From 2nd relationship...
-Elissa Smith (2005, adop.)

From 1st marriage...
-David Rockwell (?)
-Ben Rockwell (?)
-Simone Rockwell (?)
From 2nd marriage...
-Adam Rockwell (?)
-Sarah Rockwell (?)
From 3rd marriage...
-Larissa Stretton (2006)

Coen Rockwell (1996)
Kayne Rockwell (2000)

Haden Wilson-Whiting (2007)

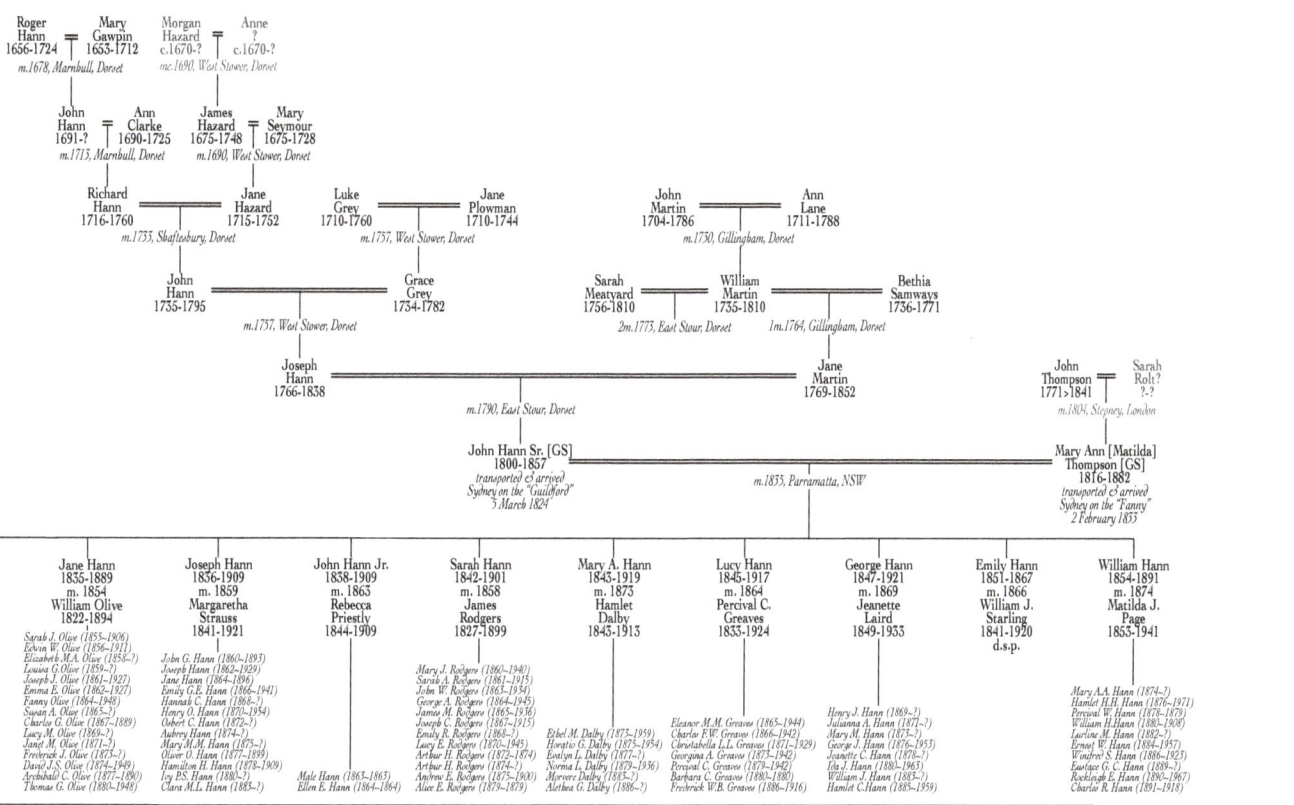

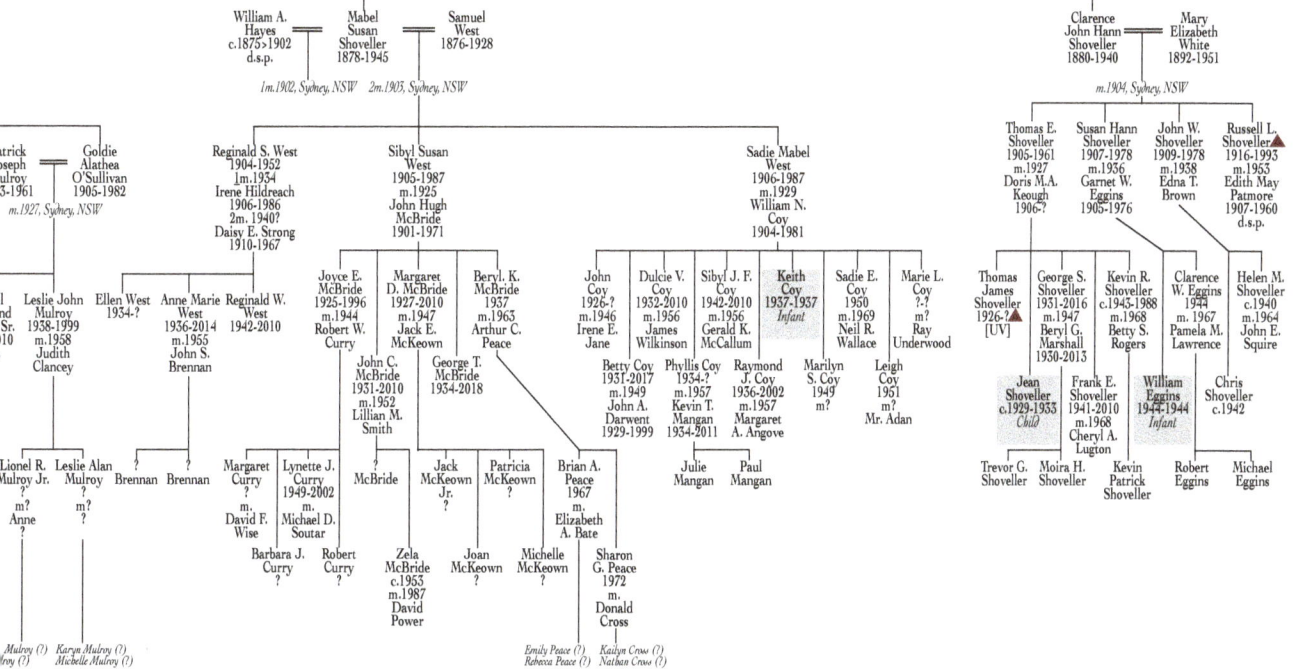

Coats of arms: Lane | Langley | Martin | Plowman | Sabine | Samways | Seymour | Shoveller | Thompson

Roger Hann 1656-1724 = Mary Gawpin 1653-1712
m.1678, Marnhull, Dorset

Morgan Hazard c.1670-? = Anne ? c.1670-?
mc.1690, West Stower, Dorset

John Hann 1691-? = Ann Clarke 1690-1725
m.1713, Marnhull, Dorset

James Hazard 1675-1748 = Mary Seymour 1675-1728
m.1690, West Stower, Dorset

Richard Hann 1716-1760 = Jane Hazard 1715-1752
m.1733, Shaftesbury, Dorset

Luke Grey 1710-1760 = Jane Plowman 1710-1744
m.1757, West Stower, Dorset

John Martin 1704-1786 = Ann Lane 1711-1788
m.1730, Gillingham, Dorset

John Hann 1735-1795 = Grace Grey 1734-1782
m.1757, West Stower, Dorset

Sarah Meatyard 1756-1810 = William Martin 1735-1810 = Bethia Samways 1736-1771
2m.1773, East Stour, Dorset / 1m.1764, Gillingham, Dorset

Joseph Hann 1766-1838 = Jane Martin 1769-1852
m.1790, East Stour, Dorset

John Thompson 1771>1841 = Sarah Rolt? ?-?
m.1804, Stepney, London

John Hann Sr. [GS] 1800-1857 = Mary Ann [Matilda] Thompson [GS] 1816-1882
transported & arrived Sydney on the "Guildford" 5 March 1824
m.1835, Parramatta, NSW
transported & arrived Sydney on the "Fanny" 2 February 1833

Children of John Hann Sr. & Mary Ann Thompson:

Jane Hann 1835-1889 m.1854 William Olive 1822-1894
- Sarah J. Olive (1855-1906)
- Edwin W. Olive (1856-1911)
- Elizabeth M.A. Olive (1858-?)
- Louisa G. Olive (1859-?)
- Joseph J. Olive (1861-1927)
- Emma E. Olive (1862-1927)
- Fanny Olive (1864-1948)
- Susan A. Olive (1865-?)
- Charles G. Olive (1867-1889)
- Lucy M. Olive (1869-?)
- Janet M. Olive (1871-?)
- Frederick J. Olive (1873-?)
- David J.S. Olive (1874-1949)
- Archibald C. Olive (1877-1890)
- Thomas Olive (1880-1948)

Joseph Hann 1836-1909 m.1859 Margaretha Strauss 1841-1921
- John G. Hann (1860-1893)
- Joseph Hann (1862-1929)
- Jane Hann (1864-1896)
- Emily G.E. Hann (1866-1941)
- Hannah C. Hann (1868-?)
- Henry O. Hann (1870-1954)
- Robert C. Hann (1872-?)
- Aubrey Hann (1874-?)
- Mary M.M. Hann (1875-?)
- Oliver O. Hann (1877-1899)
- Hamilton H. Hann (1878-1909)
- Ivy B.S. Hann (1880-?)
- Clara M.L. Hann (1883-?)

John Hann Jr. 1838-1909 m.1863 Rebecca Priestly 1844-1909
- Male Hann (1863-1863)
- Ellen E. Hann (1864-1864)

Sarah Hann 1842-1901 m.1858 James Rodgers 1827-1899
- Mary J. Rodgers (1860-1940)
- Sarah A. Rodgers (1861-1915)
- Jane Hann (1863-1954)
- George A. Rodgers (1864-1945)
- James M. Rodgers (1865-1936)
- Joseph C. Rodgers (1867-1915)
- Emily R. Rodgers (1868-?)
- Lucy E. Rodgers (1870-1945)
- Arthur H. Rodgers (1872-1874)
- Arthur H. Rodgers (1874-?)
- Andrew E. Rodgers (1875-1900)
- Alice E. Rodgers (1879-1879)

Mary A. Hann 1843-1919 m.1873 Hamlet Dalby 1843-1913
- Ethel M. Dalby (1873-1959)
- Horatio G. Dalby (1875-1954)
- Evelyn L. Dalby (1877-?)
- Norma L. Dalby (1879-1936)
- Morvere Dalby (1883-?)
- Alethea G. Dalby (1886-?)

Lucy Hann 1845-1917 m.1864 Percival C. Greaves 1833-1924
- Eleanor M.M. Greaves (1865-1944)
- Charles F.W. Greaves (1866-1942)
- Christabella L.L. Greaves (1871-1929)
- Georgana A. Greaves (1873-1942)
- Percival C. Greaves (1879-1942)
- Barbara C. Greaves (1880-1880)
- Frederick W.B. Greaves (1886-1916)

George Hann 1847-1921 m.1869 Jeanette Laird 1849-1933
- Henry J. Hann (1869-?)
- Julianna A. Hann (1871-?)
- Mary M. Hann (1873-?)
- George J. Hann (1876-1953)
- Jeanette C. Hann (1878-?)
- Ida J. Hann (1880-1963)
- William J. Hann (1883-?)
- Hamlet C.Hann (1885-1959)

Emily Hann 1851-1867 m.1866 William J. Starling 1841-1920 d.s.p.

William Hann 1854-1891 m.1874 Matilda J. Page 1853-1941
- Mary A.A. Hann (1874-?)
- Hamlet H.H. Hann (1876-1971)
- Percival W. Hann (1878-1879)
- William H. Hann (1880-1908)
- Lurline M. Hann (1882-?)
- Ernest W. Hann (1884-1957)
- Winifred S. Hann (1886-1923)
- Eustace G. C. Hann (1889-?)
- Rockleagh E. Hann (1890-1967)
- Charles R. Hann (1891-1918)

William A. Hayes c.1875>1902 d.s.p. = Mabel Susan Shoveller 1878-1945 = Samuel West 1876-1928
1m.1902, Sydney, NSW / 2m.1903, Sydney, NSW

Clarence John Hann Shoveller 1880-1940 = Mary Elizabeth White 1892-1951
m.1904, Sydney, NSW

Patrick Joseph Mulroy ?-1961 = Goldie Alathea O'Sullivan 1905-1982
m.1927, Sydney, NSW

Reginald S. West 1904-1952 1m.1934 Irene Hildreach 1906-1986 2m.1940? Daisy E. Strong 1910-1967

Sibyl Susan West 1905-1987 m.1925 John Hugh McBride 1901-1971

Sadie Mabel West 1906-1987 m.1929 William N. Coy 1904-1981

Thomas E. Shoveller 1905-1961 m.1927 Doris M.A. Keough 1906-?

Susan Hann Shoveller 1907-1978 m.1936 Garnet W. Eggins 1905-1976

John W. Shoveller 1909-1978 m.1938 Edna T. Brown

Russell L. Shoveller ▲ 1916-1993 m.1953 Edith May Patmore 1907-1960 d.s.p.

Leslie John Mulroy ? Sr.? -2010 = ... 1938-1999 m.1958 Judith Clancey

Ellen West 1934-?

Anne Marie West 1936-2014 m.1955 John S. Brennan

Reginald W. West 1942-2010

Joyce E. McBride 1925-1996 m.1944 Robert W. Curry

Margaret D. McBride 1927-2010 m.1947 Jack E. McKeown

Beryl K. McBride 1937 m.1963 Arthur C. Peace

John Coy 1926-? m.1946 Irene E. Jane

Dulcie V. Coy 1932-2010 m.1956 Gerald K.

Sibyl J. F. Coy 1942-2010 m.1956 Wilkinson

Keith Coy 1937-1937 Infant

Sadie E. Coy 1950 m.1969 Neil R. Wallace

Marie L. Coy ?-? m? Ray Underwood

Thomas James Shoveller 1926-? [UV] ▲

George S. Shoveller 1931-2016 m.1947 Beryl G. Marshall 1930-2013

Kevin R. Shoveller c.1945-1988 m.1968 Betty S. Rogers

Clarence W. Eggins 1944 m.1967 Pamela M. Lawrence

Helen M. Shoveller c.1940 m.1964 John E. Squire

Leslie Alan Mulroy ? m? ?

? Brennan

? Brennan

John C. McBride 1931-2010 m.1952 Lillian M. Smith

George T. McBride 1934-2018

Betty Coy 1931-2017 m.1949 John A. Darwent 1929-1999

Phyllis Coy 1934-? m.1957 Kevin T. Mangan 1934-2011

Raymond J. Coy 1936-2002 m.1957 Margaret A. Angove

Marilyn S. Coy 1949 m?

Leigh Coy 1951 m? Mr. Adan

Jean Shoveller c.1929-1933 Child

Frank E. Shoveller 1941-2010 m.1968 Cheryl A. Lugton

William Eggins 1944-1944 Infant

Chris Shoveller c.1942

Lionel R. Mulroy Jr. m? Anne

Leslie Alan Mulroy m? ?

Margaret Curry ? m. David F. Wise

Lynette J. Curry 1949-2002 m. Michael D. Soutar

? McBride

Jack McKeown Jr.

Patricia McKeown

Brian A. Peace 1967 m. Elizabeth A. Bate

Julie Mangan

Paul Mangan

Trevor G. Shoveller

Moira H. Shoveller

Kevin Patrick Shoveller

Robert Eggins

Michael Eggins

Barbara J. Curry ?

Robert Curry ?

Zela McBride c.1953 m.1987 David Power

Joan McKeown ?

Michelle McKeown ?

Sharon G. Peace 1972 m. Donald Cross

Mulroy (?)

Michelle Mulroy (?)

Karyn Mulroy (?)

Emily Peace (?)
Rebecca Peace (?)

Kailyn Cross (?)
Nathan Cross (?)

Documents of Thomas Charles Shoveller

Sad and Fatal Accident

"We are this week called upon to chronicle a chapter of fatal and melancholy accidents. Two quiet and much respected lads in the bloom of youth, being suddenly removed from our midst, by accident. We append a resume of the evidence taken at the inquests, which will best explain how each came by his death:-

The first inquest was held at the Royal Hotel, Grafton, on Tuesday last, before Mr. A. Lardner, J. P., Coroner, and a jury of twelve, touching the cause of the death of Thomas Charles Shoveller, who had met his death by drowning, as reported in our last issue.

The first witness examined was James Kinnear, who deposed: He knew Thomas Charles Shoveller: witness and deceased accompanied the Presbyterian Sunday School children on Monday in the steamer "Settler's Friend", to Clarenza Gardens, where they arrived between ten and eleven o'clock; immediately after landing, witness, deceased and some ten others went a short distance up the river and then went in to bathe; several swam across the river; witness and some others with deceased, who could not swim much, remained where they went in; witness had swam out a little, when he heard a cry that deceased was drowning; witness turned back and caught hold of him, when deceased clung to his arm and pulled him under, when witness let go of him and went ashore; they were not more than three or four yards from the bank; the other lads present could not swim; deceased sank when witness let go of him, and he ran to the people fifty yards off, for assistance; the Rev. C. R. Currey, Messrs. Hewitt and Brownhill went into the river almost immediately and endeavoured to recover the body, but did not succeed; the river was dragged during the afternoon, but unsuccessfully; when the alarm was given, witness was about fifteen yards out in the river, and there was no one else close to the deceased when he sank.

James Turnbull stated that the deceased was playing about on the rocks, on the edge of the river, when he suddenly slipped off into deep water, and sank; deceased came up again, and called out Jim to witness, throwing up his hands, and then went down again, going farther out; witness called out, and James Kinnear swam back and caught hold of dthe eceased as he was sinking, when he pulled Kinnear under and never rose after; witness could not swim, but was calling out all the time for help.

James Davies, a constable, stationed at Grafton, proved that he was assisting to drag for the body, which was recovered about one o'clock, in about twenty feet of water, and about thirty yards below the spot pointed out to witness where he sank, and about ten yards from the shore; there were no marks of injuries on the body, except by those caused by the grappling irons; deceased was about twelve years of age.

The jury found, "That Thomas Charles Shoveller was on the 30th of November, accidentally drowned in the Clarence River, whilst bathing." The deceased was a smart, well-behaved, intelligent lad, and a special favourite. His remains were interred in the Grafton Cemetery on Wednesday last, the Public School children, following in the procession, and the greatest sympathy was shown to the parents under the sudden and unexpected heavy domestic bereavement, which had befallen them."

Clarence & Richmond Examiner, Undated, 1891

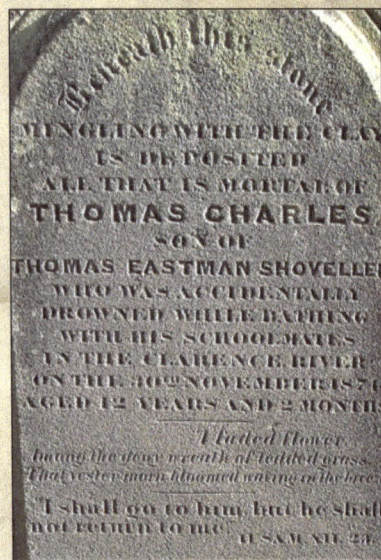

GRAFTON.
Tuesday.

A lad named Thomas Charles, eldest son of Thomas Shoveller, about 13, accompanied the Presbyterian Sunday School on an excursion to the Upper Clarence yesterday, when, with a number of others, immediately on landing, he went for a bathe. Getting beyond his depth, he was drowned. His body was recovered to-day.

FUNERAL NOTICE.
Wed 2-12-1874

The friends of Mr. THOMAS SHOVELLER are requested to attend the funeral of his late son—THOMAS CHARLES—to move from the residence of MRS. HANN, Bacon-street, THIS MORNING, at 10 o'clock.

MACKNEY AND TOMBS, Undertakers.

SHOVELLER.—On the 30th November, by accidental drowning, THOMAS CHARLES SHOVELLER, aged twelve years and two months. With him are gone the hopes of a fond mother, and the cherished expectations of an indulgent father.

▲TOP: Grafton Cemetery, resting place of Thomas Charles Shoveller, painted by Dewhurst (2013). ABOVE (Left): Thomas Charles Shoveller - Death notice (Aust Town & Country Journal, 5 Dec 1874, p.6). (Right): Funeral notice for Thomas Charles Shoveller (Argus, 2 Dec 1874). ◄Memorial headstone for Thomas Charles Shoveller at Grafton Cemetery. BELOW: Thomas Charles Shoveller - Death notice (Clarence & Richmond Examiner, 8 Dec 1874).

3. Thomas Charles Shoveller (1862-1874)

Thomas Charles was the eldest son of Thomas and Susan Shoveller and as such was no doubt being groomed to eventually take over his father's holdings. Thomas Charles was born on the 6th October 1862, and baptised on the 21st December in Grafton.[13] He lived out 12 fun-filled years growing up in the expanding city of Grafton.

Unfortunately, his life was tragically cut short when he accidentally drowned on the

20th November 1874, while swimming with friends in the swollen waters of the Clarence River.[14,15] The death and funeral notices for Thomas Charles Shoveller were recorded in the local newspapers.[16,17,18,19]

His tombstone at Grafton Cemetery was particularly descriptive even for the austere times. So tragic was this event that in 1891, the Clarence and Richmond Examiner re-ran the story as part of a series of 'Historic Events' that occurred since the paper's inception.[20]

4. Leonora Shoveller (1866-1945)

Leonora was the fourth child of Thomas and Susan Shoveller who arrived on the 13th November 1866, and was baptised on the 3rd February 1867 in Grafton.[21]

Lenore grew up in Grafton, and loved the freedom of being raised in the country. She kept a diverse collection of pets that included magpies, kangaroos and horses. With her parents, she occasionally sailed on the coastal steamships to Sydney. Lenore was married

20.2 Descendants of Lenore Shoveller, John H. Mackie & Humphrey J. O'Sullivan [56]

Lenore Shoveller (1866-1945), married firstly in 1890 at Grafton NSW to John Henry MACKIE (1868-1894), with issue:

1. Valteveredo Calceolaria Mackie (1891-1974), married firstly in 1909 at Sydney, NSW to Edmond W. MALINS (1885-1912), with issue:

1.1 Ronald Guildford MALINS (1910-1975) married 1945 to Bernice Walsh, with issue:
a. Kaye Malins (1946) married 1967 to Gerald HEASLIP.
a1. Emma Heaslip (1970), married ??, issue unknown
a2. Kate Heaslip (1974), issue unknown.

1.2 Alwyn Wooldridge MALINS (1912-1997), d.s.p.

After the death of her first husband, Valtie Malins married secondly in 1923 at Sydney, NSW to John William CHISHOLM (1893-1963), with issue:

1.3 Valtie Minlena Chisholm (1926-2003), married in 1944 at Sydney, NSW to Frank HAMMOND (1911-2007), d.s.p.

After the death of her first husband, Lenore Mackie married secondly in 1900 at Sydney, NSW to Humphrey Joseph Vincent O'SULLIVAN (1871-1905), with issue:

2. Melecca O'Sullivan (1901-1901),* d.s.p.

3. Octavia Corelli O'Sullivan (1902-1976), married in 1926 at Glebe, NSW to Robert Archibald ROCKWELL (1904-1966), with issue:

3.1 Joy Corelli Rockwell (1927-2018), married in 1966 at St Cuthbert's Church, Naremburn, NSW to William HYDE (1925-2000), with issue:
a. Robert William HYDE (1967-2016), born on the 21st February 1967, but died suddenly on the 4th April 2016. He was in a de facto relationship with Sharon Marsen (1965), with issue:
a1. Ashleigh Maree Hyde (1996)
a2. Kelsey Ann Hyde (1999)

3.2 Robert Hunter ROCKWELL (1929-1984), married in 1954 at Sydney, NSW to Betty Jean Wardle (1935-1996), with issue:
a. Tracy Paul ROCKWELL (1955), married firstly in 1980 at Portland, Oregon, USA to Jane Sule (1957), daughter of Dr Dwayne Richard Paulson & Corinne Domina Sule. (Div. 1998), with issue:
a1. James Barrett ROCKWELL (1981)
a2. Olivia Hansen Rockwell (1983)
a3. Laura Eastman Rockwell (1985), married in 2014 at Portland, Oregon to Jacob EBLING (1976), with issue:
a3.1 Sydney Elizabeth Ebling (2014)
a3.2 Thomas Daniel EBLING (2016)
Tracy married secondly in 2002 at Sydney, NSW to Lamia Lily (1972), daughter of Joseph Yammine & Berta Maroun (Div. 2014), no issue.
Tracy has been with Marie Rose Barbour (1968) since May 2012, no issue.
b. Robert Wayne ROCKWELL (1959-1963),* born on the 10th Aug 1959 at Crown St. Womens Hospital, Surry Hills, NSW, but tragically died of pnuemonia on the 14th July 1963 at Royal Alexandra Hospital for Children, Camperdown, NSW, d.s.p.
c. Sandra Kay Rockwell (1964), married firstly in 1985 at Sydney,

NSW to Lawrence AGIUS (1957), (Div. 2007), with issue:
c1. Jack Lawrence AGIUS (20th Nov 1987), with issue:
c1.1 Harvey Scott AGIUS (2013)
c2. Kathryn Elizabeth Agius (10th Mar 1990) married to Troy FIELDING in 2015 at Coogee, with issue:
c2.1 Georgia Fielding (2022)
c3. Caroline Mary Agius (11th Oct 1993), was with Theron Carl RICHARDS, with issue:
c3.1 Benjamin Xavier RICHARDS (2015)
c3.2 Bonnie Michelle Richards (2018)
c4. Margaret Bernadette Agius (8th Apr 1995), was with Craig Ernest McMURRICH (seperated), with issue:
c4.1 Mack Clem McMURRICH (2017)
c4.2 Dustin Laurence McMURRICH (2019)
Kay Agius (nee Rockwell) married secondly in 2006 to Mark PLUMMER at Grey's Point (Div. 2012), no issue.

3.3 Elwood Lorraine ROCKWELL (1933-1987), was a companion to Mary ?, no issue.

3.4 Lindsay Archibald ROCKWELL (1937), married in 1957 at St Cuthbert's Church, Naremburn, NSW to Lynette Ellen (1939-2006) daughter of Hugh Airlie Watson and Alice, with issue:
a. Rhonda Janine Rockwell (1960), married 20th July 1984 at the Carrington Hotel, Katoomba to David Edward CROSSLEY (1956), with issue:
a1. Sarah Alice Crossley (1983) married 3rd Sept 2011 at St. Aloysius College, Kirribilli to Marcus LOOMES (1981), with issue:
a1.1 Harrison Stephen LOOMES (2015)
a1.2 Norah Catherine Loomes (2018)
a2. Matthew Charles CROSSLEY (1986) with Catherine Heenan.
b. Glen Lindsay ROCKWELL (1962), married firstly in 1987 to Jennette May Musson (1956), Separated 2003, with issue:
b1. Kirsty Lee Rockwell (24/12/1988), with Waylon CAESAR (1990- 2021) with issue:
b1.1 Kassius Leon CAESAR (2020)
b2. Shani Ann Rockwell (12/7/1991), with Paul GIBSON (?), with issue:
b2.1 Crysta Kirsty Gibson (11/3/2011)
Following his divorce, Glen was with Rebecca Louise Smith (1977) from about 2004, Separated 2018, with issue:
b3. Alice Lynette Rockwell (30/10/2007)
b4. Warren Glen ROCKWELL (13/9/2009)
b5. Edward Louis ROCKWELL (19/12/2011).

3.5 Ronie Malcolm ROCKWELL (1943-2000), 1961 to Coral Joy (1942-1981), the daughter of George Stretton and Winifred Brooker, with issue:

a. Brett Anthony ROCKWELL (1961) born on the 30th Sep 1961, he married in 1982 to Julie Denyer, with issue:
a1. Matthew ROCKWELL (1983)
a2. Daniel ROCKWELL (1985)
a3. Stephen ROCKWELL (1989)
b. Mark Malcolm ROCKWELL (1962) born on the 20th Sep 1962, he married firstly c.1980 to Joyce Moore, with issue:
b1. Adam ROCKWELL (c.1977)
b2. Sarah Rockwell (c.1978)
b3. David ROCKWELL (c.1980)
Mark married secondly c.1982 to Michele Thomas, with issue:
b4. Mark ROCKWELL (c.1982)
b5. Simone Rockwell (c.1983)
b6. Ben ROCKWELL (c.1984)

Mark married thirdly in 1999 to Lara Musjuk, and reverted to his mothers maiden name of STRETTON, with issue:
b7. Larissa Valentina Stretton (2006)
c. Paul Steven ROCKWELL (1965) born on the 9th Sep 1965, and with Christine Brown (1969), with issue:
c1. Coen ROCKWELL (1996)
c2. Kayne ROCKWELL (2000)
After his divorce, Ronie resided with Cheryl Joy (1945-2013), the daughter of Arthur William Pooley and Molly Jeanne Graham, in a de facto relationship for a number of years, and married in 1981 in Sydney, with issue:
d. Samuel Joshua ROCKWELL (1974), d.s.p.
e. Jessica Molly Rockwell (1977), d.s.p.

3.6 Janet Lenore Rockwell (1946), married firstly in 1965 at St Cuthbert's Church, Naremburn, NSW to Roland Lawrence Whiting (c.1945-1982), with issue:
a. Michelle Lena Whiting (1965), born on the 10th Dec 1965, was with Heath Wilson (seperated), with issue:
a1. Haden Wilson-Whiting (2007).
b. Stephen Hunter WHITING (1968), born on the 20th Aug 1968, and married to Malini Jivan in 2014, d.s.p.
c. Adam Roger WHITING (1971), born on the 18th Sep 1971, and is with Steven Burns, no issue.
Janet married secondly in 1981 at Burra Station, NSW, to Gordon Carr, but after separating moved to Wellington, New Zealand, no issue. Janet married thirdly in 1987 to at Wellington, New Zealand to Ilya Sippen, but later separated, no issue.

4. Sylvia Veronica O'Sullivan (1903-1914),* died age 11, d.s.p.

5. Goldie Alathea O'Sullivan (1905-1982), married in 1927 at Sydney, NSW to Patrick Joseph MULROY (1903-1961), with issue:

5.1 Lionel Raymond MULROY (1928-2010), was a companion to Shirley ?, no issue.

5.2 Lesley John MULROY (1938-c.1999), married in 1958 to Judith Anne Clancey in Sydney (#15130), with issue:
a. Lionel Raymond MULROY (1959) married to Anne ?, with issue:
a1. Stella Mulroy (c.1995)
a2. Unknown Mulroy
b. Leslie Allan MULROY (c.1962) married, with issue:

* Died before adulthood - d.s.p.
(Some names not listed in the index).

twice, firstly at the age of 24 on the 22nd March 1890 in Grafton to Tasmanian born John Henry Mackie (1868–1894), the son of Charles Mackie (convict) and Honora Ann Meade.[22] Very soon after their wedding, the young couple had a daughter in Valtieveredo Calceolaria Mackie, who arrived on the 25th of March 1891.[23] Unfortunately, John Mackie proved not to be a good husband and, perhaps fortuitously for Lenore, he suddenly passed away and the age of just 26, in 1894.[24]

Lenore, who was also given the nickname of 'Luddie', remarried six years later on the 11th July 1900 to Humphrey Joseph Vincent O'Sullivan (1871-1905) at St. Mary's Cathedral in Sydney.[25] Humphrey was the son of James Mahony O'Sullivan, an Irish immigrant, and Ellen Frawley, who like Lenore's mother Susan, was also a pioneer of the bush and the first

Grafton Transport Milestones

1838	"Susan" & "Eliza" - First Sailing Ships	1905	Opening of Railway to Tweed Heads	1948	Arrival of Commercial Flying Boats
1844	"William IV" - First Paddle Steamer	1923	Opening of Railway to Sydney	1958	Road sealed from Sydney to Brisbane
1865	1st Propeller Steamships	1932	Opening of Grafton Road/Rail Bridge	2020	Freeway from Sydney to Brisbane

▲TOP (Left): The "SS Australian" in 1900. (Right): The Railway Wharf with the "SS Induna" awaiting a train, 1925. MID (Left): In 1925, the "SS Induna" was converted to carry railway carriages across the Clarence River, linking north and south rail junctions at Grafton. (Right): In 1932 the double decker Grafton bridge opened with a superimposed flypast by Kingsford Smith. ABOVE (Left): Prince St. Grafton in 1939 showing the increasing number of motor cars in the main street. (Right): During World War II, seaplanes made regular stops at Grafton, and commercial flights gained popularity from the late 1940s.

Documents of Lenore Shoveller & Family

MARRIAGE.
MACKIE—SHOVELLER.—On the 3rd March inst., by the Ven. the Archdeacon, in Christ Church Cathedral, Grafton, JOHN HENRY MACKIE, of Auckland, New Zealand, to LEONORA, daughter of Thomas Shoveller, of Grafton.

Leonora Mackie v John Henry Mackie.—Proceedings taken for an order for maintenance.
Complainant deposed that her husband contributed scarcely anything to her support since she married him about two years ago. For the past eight months she received nothing from him. She has one child.

John Henry Mackie was summoned for disobeying an order of the Court enjoining him to pay towards the maintenance of his wife, Leonore Mackie. An order was given for the arrest of defendant.

M U S I C.

MRS. MACKIE is prepared to receive PUPILS for the Piano. References to present pupils and their parents. REDUCED TERMS.
LENORE MACKIE, Fitzroy-street, Grafton, opposite the Church of England Schoolroom.

13th January 1894
To the woman I love,
Mrs. Mackie,
    My Own Darling. Allow me who loves you more than my very life to say a few brief words to you, yes to you my little darling, who is just about beginning a new life, yes you have chosen me before all other men. For better or worse, chosen me to make your sad and unfortunate life happy. You have made me my "Darling" the happiest of all men by your promise to be mine. And as God is to be my judge I shall fulfil my promise to you ..... ?.
From your future husband
Humphrey J.V. O'Sullivan

Bowden's Hotel
Sydney May 23/95

Received from Mrs Lenore Mackie The sum of £400 and £55 ?/- at 6 ?? from date in full payment of purchase money for Lease Licence Furniture Goodwill & Effects of Bowden's Hotel, Elizabeth St, City as per arrangement.—
E S Ellworth
?? ??

BOWDEN'S FAMILY HOTEL.
ELIZABETH-STREET (one door from Hunter-st,)
SYDNEY.

Affords country visitors the best accommodation in Sydney
For COMFORT, RESPECTABILITY,
ITS CENTRAL POSITION, AND
MODERATE CHARGES

Hot and cold water baths.
Telephone for the use of visitors.
LENORE MACKIE, Proprietress.

News reached town yesterday of the death of Mr. Humphrey O'Sullivan, which took place in Sydney from pneumonia. He leaves a widow and three children, and a number of his relatives are resident on the Clarence and in the vicinity of Coff's Harbour.

O'SULLIVAN.—July 21 1945 at hospital, Lenore, late of Eden Street, North Sydney, aged 70 years.

▲TOP (Left): 1-John Henry Mackie & Lenore Shoveller - Marriage notice (C&RE, March 22nd, 1890, p4); 2-Court proceedings against John Henry Mackie (C&RE, 18th June 1892, p3); (Centre): 1-Summons for John Henry Mackie (C&RE, 16th Aug 1892, p3); 2-Lenore Mackie was an accomplished pianist and advertised for music pupils (C&RE, 8th July 1893, p5); (Right): Part transcription of Humphrey Joseph O'Sullivan's letter of January 1894. MID (Left): Lenore Mackie's receipt for Bowden's Hotel, 23rd May 1895. (Right): Advertisement for Lenore Mackie's 'Bowden's Hotel' (C&RE, 21st September 1895, p8). ABOVE: Photograph of Lenore O'Sullivan (nee Shoveller), circa 1940. (Left): Humphrey Joseph O'Sullivan - Death notice (C&RE, 1 July 1905, p5). (Right): Lenore O'Sullivan - Death notice (SMH, 23 July 1945, p.12).

white child born on the far South Coast of New South Wales. The first daughter for Lenore and Humphrey was Melecca L. M. O'Sullivan who arrived in 1901, but she sadly died four weeks later.[26,27] The regally named Octavia Corelli Susan O'Sullivan arrived next on the 1st of February 1902.[28] The third daughter born to Lenore and Humphrey O'Sullivan was Sylvia Veronica O'Sullivan in 1903, but she unfortunately passed away in 1914 at the tender age of just 11.[29,30] The fourth and final child to arrive was yet another daughter in

▲TOP: The mighty 'The Big River,' renamed the Clarence River by the NSW Government in 1840. (Photo by Tracy Rockwell, 2021). ABOVE: 1900 Postcard of the Grafton wharf, with Susan Island in the background.

Goldie Alathea O'Sullivan, who was born on the 22nd of February 1905.[31]

Lenore produced five girls, but although only three survived to adulthood, their numerous descendants continue today (*see 20.2 Descendants of Lenore Shoveller, John Henry Mackie & Humphrey Joseph O'Sullivan*). The life, events and descendants of Lenore Shoveller and her two husbands John Henry Mackie and Humphrey Joseph Vincent O'Sullivan, are covered in more detail in the volume 8 of the Rockwell Genealogies, entitled 'Nostalgia for Naremburn.'

▲ The paddlesteamer "Shamrock" making a run down river.

5. Janet E. A. Shoveller (1869-1870)

Janet E. A. Shoveller was the next child born to Thomas and Susan Shoveller, and she arrived on the 6th December 1869, but she sadly died the very next year adding to the high infant mortality of these pioneering regions.[32,33]

6. George Lorraine Shoveller (1873-1946)

George Lorraine was their next born and came along in 1873 in Grafton.[34] He was the second son of Thomas and Susan Shoveller and became the eldest son following the death of his brother Thomas Charles, who drowned in the Clarence River in 1874. George likely attended the National School in Grafton, and was later registered on the electoral roll as a grazier. However, it is questionable as to whether he ever actually managed a herd or flock, or was perhaps labelled with that occupation by his father, as a means of legitimising his land purchases.

Documents of Mabel Susan Shoveller & Family

KEEPING IT DARK.

A Romantic Marriage.

A CLERK'S PETITION.

William Albert Hayes asked for a divorce from Mabel Sylvia Hayes, formerly Shoveller, on the ground of her adultery with Samuel West, who was joined as co-respondent.

The parties were married at an agency in Bent-street in November, 1902.

The petitioner, who is a clerk in the Tramway Office, said he became engaged to his wife in January, 1901, it being understood that they were to be engaged for three years before marriage.

In November, 1902, respondent was reading a book, and she suggested that he should read it also. He asked what it was about. She said it was about two young people who were engaged. Other people were trying to make mischief amongst them, so they decided to get married, on the understanding that when it suited them they should celebrate it publicly. She suggested they should do the same. The result was they got married privately, and they kept it a secret.

His Honor: That is how you account for going to the agency?—Yes.

Continuing, petitioner said they never lived together, and marital relations never existed between them. Respondent went over to her brother's place at North Sydney, where she told him West was boarding. Petitioner's mother told him something in 1903.

Dr. Sharfstein gave evidence that he attended the respondent as Mrs. West during her confinement.

Petitioner's mother stated that respondent had told her she was Mrs. West.

A decree nisi was granted, returnable in three months.

WEST.—The Relatives and Friends of the late Mabel West are invited to attend her Funeral; to leave her late residence, 63 Morehead Street, Waterloo, This Afternoon, at 1 o'clock, for Crematorium, Rookwood. Labor Motor Funerals, Ltd., 24 Enmore Road, Newtown. Phones, LA2777 (4 lines).

In Memory of

A LOVING HUSBAND & FATHER

RECINALD S. WEST

DIED 10TH DEC. 1951

R · I · P

POWER — McBRIDE. — John and Lilian McBride, of Warrawee, joyfully announce the engagement of their younger daughter, Zela, to David, youngest son of John and Joan Power, of Bardwell Park.

DARWENT, John Albert (Jack). — Beloved son-in-law of Sadie Coy (deceased), loved brother-in-law of Dulcie and James (deceased) Wilkinson, Fay and Gerald (Pud) McCallum, Phyllis and Kevin Mangan, Ray (Mick) and Margaret Coy (Vic), Marie and Ray Underwood, Sadie and Neil Wallace and Leigh (Maz) Adan (W.A.). Loved and respected uncle and great-uncle to all his nieces, nephews, great-nieces and great-nephews.
Precious memories
will keep him near.

COY, Sadie Mabel. — March 11 1987, late of Padstow, beloved mother of John, Betty, Dulcie, Phyllis, Faye, Ray, Marie, Sadie and Leigh, dear mother-in-law and grandmother and great-grandmother of their families.
Aged 80 years.
Privately cremated March 12, 1987.

McKEOWN, Jack. — July 10, 1999, of Minto, beloved husband of Margaret, loving father of Jack, Joan, Patricia and Michelle, loved father-in-law of Allan and cherished grandfather, loved and sadly missed by his family and friends.
Aged 72 years.

JACK's relatives and friends are invited to attend his funeral service, to be held at Forest Lawn Crematorium, Leppington, on Wednesday (July 14, 1999), commencing at 12.30 p.m.
BUTLER FUNERALS,
A.F.D.A.
Camden.   (02) 4655 8265
Campbelltown. (02) 4625 1854
Narellan.   (02) 4647 5968

▲TOP: Sibyl Susan West & John Hugh McBride - Marriage certificate (St. John's Church, Glebe, Parish Register). LEFT COLUMN: 1-Mabel S. Hayes (nee Shoveller) & Samuel West - Keeping It Dark (The Australian Star, 17 March 1904, p.7). 2-Mabel S. West - Funeral notice (SMH, 5th July 1945). CENTRE COLUMN: 1-Reginald Searle West - Memorial at Guyra General Cemetery, NSW; 2-Zela McBride & David Power - Engagement notice (SMH, 30 July 1986, p.23); 3-Jack Albert Darwent - Death notice (SMH, 9 June, 1999, p.20); 4- Sadie Mabel Coy (nee West) - Death notice (SMH, 12 March 1987). RIGHT COLUMN: 1-Photograph of Mabel Susan Shoveller at her wedding to William A. Hayes, 1902; 2-Jack Edward McKeown - Death notice (SMH, 13 July 1999, p.21).

Following the death of his father in 1908, George moved to Sydney where he worked as a labourer and resided in Glebe. It was while at his home at 123 Mitchell St, Glebe that George was joined by his mother Susan, who moved from Grafton to be closer to her children and grandchildren, with all of them now living in Sydney. George married in 1918 at Rockdale to Mary (1873-1952), the daughter of John Luney and Bridget Hoare.[35] Following his mother's death in 1919, George and Mary Shoveller relocated north, where they moved into 32 Grafton Avenue, Naremburn then 165 Alexander Street, Crows Nest from 1933, before finally ending up at 5 Eden St, North Sydney. No further details or occupations of George and Mary Shoveller have come to light. He died on the 14th August 1946 and was buried at Macquarie Park Cemetery (*RC, M11, 0022*), without issue.[36] His wife Mary died some 20 years later in 1967 in Newcastle, NSW.[37]

7. Mabel Susan Shoveller (1878-1945)

Mabel Susan Shoveller was born in Grafton on the 3rd June 1878 and baptised on the 24th August, becoming the youngest daughter of Thomas and Susan Shoveller.[38] Mabel likely also attended the National School in Grafton. She married firstly in secret in 1902 at Sydney to William Andrew Hayes (c.1875>1902),[39] but the marriage was brief and ended in divorce.[40] Mabel remarried a year later, this time to a half-caste aboriginal by the name of Samuel West (1876-1928) at Sydney.[41]

SHOVELLER.—The Relatives and Friends of Mrs. Mary Shoveller are invited to attend the Funeral of her dearly beloved Husband, George; which will leave St. Mary's Church, Ridge Street, North Sydney, This Day, Friday, at 10.30 a.m., for the Catholic Cemetery, Northern Suburbs. Whelan and Glacken A.F.D.A., 263 Miller Street, North Sydney. XB1510

Luney

20.3 Descendants of Mabel Susan Shoveller & Samuel West [56]

West | Shoveller

Mabel Susan Shoveller (1878-1945), married firstly in 1902 at Sydney, NSW to William Albert HAYES (c.1875>1902), without issue:
Following her divorce, Mabel married secondly in 1903 at Sydney, NSW to Samuel WEST (1876-1928), with issue:

1. Reginald Searle WEST (1904-1951), married firstly in 1934 at Charlestown, NSW to Irene Hildreach (1906-1986), with issue:

1.1 Ellen West (1934-?), issue unknown.

1.2 Anne Marie West (1936-2014), married in 1955 to John Stanley BRENNAN (1933-2014), with issue:
a. Private Brennan (?)
b. Private Brennan (?)
Anne married secondly in 1972 to Len JUSTO (?-2013), no issue.

1.3 Reginald W. WEST (1942-2010), d.s.p.

Reginald married secondly in 1940 at Lismore, NSW to Daisy Edna Strong (1910-1967), no issue.

2. Sibyl Susan West (1905-1987), married in 1925 at Lavender Bay Christ Church, North Sydney, NSW to John Hugh McBRIDE (1901-1971), with issue:

2.1 Joyce Elizabeth May McBride (1925-1996), married 1944 at Millers Point, Sydney, NSW to Robert Wellington CURRY (1923-2004), with issue:
a. Margaret Lorraine Curry (?), married David Francis WISE (?), issue unknown.
b. Barbara Jessica Curry (?), issue unknown.
c. Lynette Joy Curry (1949-2002), married Michael David SOUTAR (?), issue unknown.
d. Robert CURRY (?), issue unknown.

2.2 Margaret Doreen McBride (1927-2010), married Jack Edward McKEOWN (1926-1999, NX180194▲), with issue:
a. Jack MCKEOWN (?)
b. Joan McKeown (?)
c. Patricia McKeown (?)
d. Michelle McKeown (?)

2.3 John Charles McBRIDE (1931-2015), married in 1952 to Lilian Muriel Smith (?), with issue:
a. Female McBride
b. Zela McBride (c.1953), married in 1987 to David POWER, issue unknown.

2.4 George Thomas McBRIDE (1934-2018), married 1957 to Patricia R. Steptoe, with issue:
a. Private McBride (?)
b. Private McBride (?)
c. Private McBride (?)
d. Private McBride (?)

2.5 Beryl Katherine McBride (c.1937), married 1963 to Arthur Conrad PEACE, with issue:
a. Brian Arthur PEACE (1967), married c.1963 to Elizabeth Anne Bate (1988), with issue:
a1. Emily Cathryn Peace
a2. Rebecca Elizabeth Peace
b. Sharon Gaye Peace (1972), married 1997 to Donald

CROSS, with issue:
b1. Kailyn Cross
b2. Nathan CROSS

3. Sadie Mabel West (1906-1987), married in 1929 at Surry Hills, NSW to William Nelson COY (1904-1981), with issue:

3.1 John COY (1926-?), married in 1946 at Auburn to Irene Elizabeth Jane (?-?), issue unknown.

3.2 Betty T. Coy (1931-2017), married in 1949 to John Albert (Jack) DARWENT (1929-1999), with issue:
a. Private (?)
b. Private (?)
c. Private (?)

3.3 Dulcie Valerie Coy (1932-2010), married James WILKINSON (?-?), issue unknown.

3.4 Phyllis Coy (1934), married in 1957 at Campsie, NSW to Kevin Thomas MANGAN (1934-2011), with issue:
a. Julie Mangan (?), issue unknown.
b. Paul MANGAN (?), issue unknown.

3.5 Sibyl Judith Faye Coy (1935), married in 1956 at Sydney, NSW, to Gerald Keith 'Pud' McCALLUM, issue unknown.

3.6 Nelson changed to Raymond James COY (1936-2002), married Margaret Anne Angove (?), issue unknown.

3.7 Keith COY (1937-1937),* died an infant, d.s.p.

3.8 Marilyn Susan Coy (1949), issue unknown.

3.9 Sadie Coy (1950), married in 1969 at Hornsby, NSW to Neil WALLACE (?), issue unknown.

3.10 Leigh Coy (1951), married Mr. ADAN, issue unknown.

3.11 Marie Lucy Coy (?), married Ray UNDERWOOD (?), issue unknown.

* Died before adulthood - d.s.p.
(Some names not listed in the index)

▲TOP: George Lorraine Shoveller - Funeral notice (SMH, 16th Aug 1946, p.16), with a blazon for his wife, Mary Luney.

Very soon afterwards, the newlyweds had a son in Reginald Searle West (1904-1951), who was born in 1904, his middle name honouring the world champion sculler from Grafton - Henry Ernest Searle (1866-1889).[42] The next year Samuel and Mabel had a daughter in Sibyl Susan West (1905-1987),[43] and 1906 brought their final child in Sadie

Documents of Clarence John Hann Shoveller & Family

▲TOP: Thomas Eastman Shoveller & Doris Mary Agnes Keough - Marriage certificate (St. John's Church, Glebe, Parish Register). MID: George Stanley Shoveller & Beryl Gertrude Marshall - Marriage certificate (St. Mark's Church, Darling Point, Parish Register). ABOVE (Left): Clarence John Hann Shoveller - Funeral notice (SMH, 19 Jul 1940, p.6). (Right): Jane Patmore - Death notice (SMH, 16th Jan 1953).

20.4 Descendants of Clarence John Hann Shoveller & Mary E. White [56]

Clarence John Hann SHOVELLER (1880-1940), married in 1904 at Sydney, NSW to Mary Elizabeth White (1883-1952), with issue:

1. Thomas Eastman Shoveller (1905-1961), a wharf labourer, married in 1927 at St Johns Church, Glebe, NSW to Doris Mary Agnes Keough (1906-?), with issue:

1.1 Thomas James SHOVELLER (1926-?) ▲, enlisted in the AIF (# N481611), marriage & issue unknown [UV].

1.2 Jean Shoveller (c. 1929-1933),* died young, d.s.p.

1.3 George Stanley SHOVELLER (1931-2016), married in 1947 at Sydney, NSW to Beryl Gertrude Marshall (1930-2013), with issue:
a. Trevor George SHOVELLER (c.1948)
b. Moira Helen Shoveller (c.1950)

1.4 Frank Edward SHOVELLER(1941-2010), married 1968 to Cheryl Ann Lugton (?), issue unknown.

1.5 Kevin Richard SHOVELLER (?-1988), married 1968 to Betty

Shoveller | White

Shirley Rogers (?), with issue:
a. Kevin Patrick SHOVELLER (?), issue unknown?

2. Susan Hann Shoveller (1907-1978), married in 1936 at Hurstville, NSW, to Garnet Wesley EGGINS (1905-1976),

with issue:

2.1 William EGGINS (1944-1944),* died an infant, d.s.p.

2.2 Clarence Wesley EGGINS (1944-?), married 1967 at Sydney, NSW to Pamela May Lawrence (?), with issue:
a. Robert EGGINS (c.1968)
b. Michael EGGINS (c.1970)

3. John Woodford SHOVELLER (1909-1978), married 1938 to Edna Tranter Brown (1905-?), with issue:

3.1 Helen Margaret Shoveller (c.1940), married in 1964 at Rockdale to John Edward SQUIRE (?), issue unknown.

3.2 Chris SHOVELLER (c.1942)

4. Russell Lorraine SHOVELLER (1916-1993) ▲, married in 1953 at Sydney, NSW to Edith May Patmore (?-1960). He was buried at Field of Mars Cemetery, East Ryde, NSW, without issue.

* Died before adulthood - d.s.p.
(Some names not listed in the index.)

#NX204180 Capt. Lloyd Meally Carr (1922 - 1992)

By nature Lloyd Carr was a very private person, the great great grandson of John Shoveller LLD and Elizabeth Eastman. Lloyd Carr was one of five brothers, born at Bega on the south coast of New South Wales, although the family later moved to Sydney. He graduated Bachelor of Dental Surgery from the University of Sydney in 1944, and joined the Australian Army Dental Corps with the rank of Captain.

After discharge, he practised privately for a short time at Grafton, New South Wales. His Masters degree was awarded by the University of Sydney in 1953; and he received his Diploma of Public Health Dentistry from St. Andrews University in 1959. In 1960 Lloyd joined the recently formed Australian Capital Territory School Dental Service and as its Director, established its format and the protocols which were the foundation of a successful organization and public facility.

World War Two Service

CAPTAIN
LLOYD MEALLY CARR
NX204180

SERVICE	AUSTRALIAN ARMY
DATE OF BIRTH	11 AUGUST 1922
PLACE OF BIRTH	BEGA, NSW
LOCALITY ON ENLISTMENT	KINGSFORD, NSW
NEXT OF KIN	CARR, RAY
DATE OF DISCHARGE	19 DECEMBER 1946
POSTING AT DISCHARGE	60 DENTAL UNIT

Australian Government
Department of Veterans' Affairs

In 1973 he was seconded to the Commonwealth Department of Health as Assistant Director-General of Health (Dental Services). Then, working through the Australian Dental Services Advisory Council, Lloyd established the Australian School Dental Service which served as a model for extension of the service throughout Australia under the auspices of the Commonwealth Government. The development and co-ordination of the Australian School Dental Service was a huge undertaking which involved the provision of the physical facilities as well as the engagement of staff from a number of disciplines and the establishment of training facilities. Clinical auxiliaries were trained in all of the Australian States and in New Zealand.

During this time, Lloyd made a substantial contribution to the long-term advocacy and controversy that led ultimately to the fluoridation of Canberra's water supply in 1964. Lloyd was a member of the ACT Dental Board from 1961-75. He later wrote a series of articles in the Australian Dental Journal in the 1970s and 1980s chronicling the decline in dental caries experience during this period. The reports culminated in the publication of Dental Health of Children in Australia 1977-86 which records one of the great triumphs in the conquest of disease this century. It was Lloyd's vocation to be actively involved in all aspects of this triumph in Australia and his knowledge of the subject was respected widely here and throughout the world. He was also a member and secretary of the NHMRC's Dental Health Committee for various periods from 1965 to 1987 and Chairman of the Dental Public Health Sub-committee in 1985-87 as well as Chairman of the NHMRC Working Party on Fluorides in the Control of Dental Caries in 1985. He had a prime role in the policy, planning and implementation of the National Oral Health Survey. He was a member of the World Health Organization's Expert Panel on Oral Health 1982-88, and a Consultant to the FDI Commissions on Public Dental Health Services and Oral Health Research and Epidemiology. During the period 1953-66 he published some 14 papers. In 1965 he became an Inaugural Fellow of the Australian College of Dental Surgeons (now the Royal Australasian College of Dental Surgeons), and in 1972 was elected a Fellow of the International College of Dentists.

On his retirement in 1986, Lloyd was appointed as Dental Consultant to the Commonwealth Department of Health. He also took a new and equally demanding path as he became closely involved and identified with the Federal Office of the Australian Dental Association where he had previously advised and assisted on a number of issues such as workforce studies. He was elected to the ADA Dental Health Services Committee in 1979, and in 1986 was appointed an Assistant Editor to the Australian Dental Journal and a member of the Journal Editorial Board. He continued to pursue his interests in athletics, tennis and sailing, and he enjoyed music, particularly opera. (Written by R.G.W., (1993) Lloyd Meally Carr - Obituary (Australian Dental Journal, 1993, Vol-38, No.1).

#N181715 Sgt. Russell Lorraine Shoveller (1916 - 1993)

Russell Lorraine Shoveller was He initially enlisted in the AIF on the 12th August 1940 at Miller's Point, NSW, but was classified 'Fit for Class IIA - Defective Eyesight' after medical examination. He registered himself as being 23 years of age, was single and working as a 'Salesman', and gave his address as 13 Wright's Road, Drummoyne, NSW. He was 5' 8" tall, and blue eyes, medium complexion with brown hair, was a C of E, and his next of kin was listed as Mary Elizabeth Shoveller (mother), and he was a great great grandson of John Shoveller LLD and Elizabeth Eastman. He was taken up on the 28th May 1942 and assigned to the base Postal Unit. He was promoted to the rank of Corporal on the 29th December 1943, and then to Sergeant on the 10th October 1945. In July 1946 he was posted to the 1st Australian Book Depot. His 1930 days of active service were spent on home soil due to his medical classification. Russell was discharged from the AMF on the 8th September 1947 and awarded the General Service Badge.

World War Two Service

SERGEANT
RUSSELL LORRAINE SHOVELLER
N181715

SERVICE	AUSTRALIAN ARMY
DATE OF BIRTH	12 SEPTEMBER 1916
PLACE OF BIRTH	SYDNEY, NSW
DATE OF ENLISTMENT	12 AUGUST 1940
LOCALITY ON ENLISTMENT	DRUMMOYNE, NSW
PLACE OF ENLISTMENT	MILLERS POINT, NSW
NEXT OF KIN	SHOVELLER, MARY
DATE OF DISCHARGE	8 SEPTEMBER 1947
POSTING AT DISCHARGE	AMF WING RGH

Australian Government
Department of Veterans' Affairs

#N481611 Thomas James Shoveller (1926 - ?)

Thomas James Shoveller enlisted in the AIF on the 5th March 1945 at Victoria Barracks, Paddington, NSW, just two months prior to the end of the war in Europe. He registered himself as being 18 years and 2 mths old, was single and unemployed, but had worked previously as a 'process worker', and gave his address as 72 Darghan Street, Glebe, NSW. He was 5' 8" tall, and blue eyes, fair complexion with light brown hair, was a Roman Catholic, and his next of kin was listed as George Thomas Shoveller (father), and he may have been a great grandson of Thomas & Susan Shoveller of Grafton, NSW (unverified). He was taken in on the 5th March 1945 and initially assigned to train in artillery, but after September he was appointed to Unit 113 at Concord Military Hospital (Staff). His 794 days of active service were spent on home soil due to the fact that the war came to an end. Thomas was discharged from the AMF on the 7th May 1947 and awarded the General Service Badge. He was a great great grandson of John Shoveller LLD and Eastman.

World War Two Service

PRIVATE
THOMAS JAMES SHOVELLER
N481611

SERVICE	AUSTRALIAN ARMY
DATE OF BIRTH	28 DECEMBER 1926
PLACE OF BIRTH	CANTERBURY, NSW
DATE OF ENLISTMENT	5 MARCH 1945
LOCALITY ON ENLISTMENT	GLEBE, NSW
PLACE OF ENLISTMENT	PADDINGTON, NSW
NEXT OF KIN	SHOVELLER, GEORGE
DATE OF DISCHARGE	7 MAY 1947
POSTING AT DISCHARGE	113 C MH

Australian Government
Department of Veterans' Affairs

SHOVELLER, Thomas Eastman (1827-1908)
Born 1827, London, England. Occupation hotel keeper, store keeper.
Died 21 May 1908, Grafton. Buried 22 May 1908 Grafton cemetery.
Married 6 Mar 1856, C of E church, Grafton.
HANN, Susan (1840-1919)
Born 29 Dec 1840, Clarence River. Daughter of John and Mary Ann (nee Thompson).
Died 23 Feb 1919, Glebe.
Issue:
1. Susan Teresa, b.1858.
   d.1858.
2. Susan Eva, b.24 Aug 1859, Grafton.
   m. E. Meally.
3. Eva Rose Jane, b.1861, Grafton.
   d.25 Dec 1862, Grafton.
4. Thomas Charles, b.6 Oct 1862, Grafton.
   d.30 Nov 1874, Grafton.
5. Lenora, b.13 Nov 1866, Grafton.
   m.3 Mar 1890, John Henry Mackie, Grafton.
6. Janet E., b.1870.
   d.1870.
7. George Lorraine, b.1873.
   m.1918, Mary Luney, Rockdale.
8. Mabel, b.3 Jun 1878, Grafton.
   m.1903, Samuel West, Sydney.
9. Clarence John Hann, b.19 Aug 1880, Grafton.
   m.1904, Mary White, Sydney.
Thomas was the proprietor of the "Clarence River Stores", corner of Prince and Bacon Streets, Grafton. He also owned the "Flying Horse Hotel" at the Cross Roads in 1862. One of the first alderman on the City Council. First Postmaster of Grafton. This was the first marriage celebrated in the old C of E Church when it stood on the corner of Duke and Victoria Streets, Grafton. Was a committee member of the School of Arts in 1857. (10)

MEMORIAL TO THE CUB SCOUTS ACCIDENTALLY DROWNED 11-12-1943

THIS MEMORIAL OVERLOOKS THE SCENE OF PROBABLY THE WORST RIVER TRAGEDY ON THE CLARENCE SINCE EUROPEANS ARRIVED IN 1838.

LATE ON THE AFTERNOON OF SATURDAY DECEMBER 11, 1943, THIRTEEN MEMBERS OF THE 1ST GRAFTON CUB PACK DROWNED WHEN THEIR PUNT WAS SWAMPED WHILE RETURNING FROM A BREAK-UP PICNIC ON SUSAN ISLAND.

THE THIRTEEN WOLF CUBS – FOUR FROM GRAFTON & NINE FROM SOUTH GRAFTON WERE AGED FROM EIGHT TO TEN YEARS. THEY WERE AMONG A PARTY OF THIRTY ONE ON THE PUNT.

A COLONIAL ENQUIRY ON FEBRUARY 1 & 2 1944, RETURNED A FINDING OF ACCIDENTAL DROWNING.

THIS MEMORIAL WAS ERECTED BY THE CITIZENS OF GRAFTON & DISTRICT TO MARK THE 50TH ANNIVERSARY OF WHAT THE STATE COMMISSIONER FOR CUBS DESCRIBED IN 1943, AS THE WORST TRAGEDY IN THE HISTORY OF THE BOY SCOUTS ASSOCIATION IN NSW.

▲TOP: Jacaranda Avenue, now the focus of the city's annual Jacaranda Festival, was first planted in Grafton in 1907, just one year prior to the death of Thomas Eastman Shoveller. ABOVE (Left): Listing for Thomas Eastman Shoveller in the Grafton Pioneer Register ('Pre-1900 Clarence River Pioneer Register,' Clarence River Historical Society, p.198). (Right): Memorial plaque erected in 1993, to commemorate the 50th anniversary of the drowning of 13 cub scouts that occurred on the Clarence River at Grafton, on the 11th December 1943.

Mabel West (1906-1987).[44]

Mabel became a single mother when Samuel West left her about 1917 to marry Sarah Ward.[45] Mabel resided thereafter at 63 Moorehead Street at Redfern, and died aged 67 in 1945.[46] Mabel produced a son and two daughters, all from her second husband Samuel West, with all three surviving into adulthood, and their numerous and known descendants continue today, each possessing some indigenous heritage (*see 20.3 Descendants of Mabel Susan Shoveller & Samuel West*).

8. Clarence John Hann Shoveller (1880-1940)

Named in honour of his maternal grandfather, Clarence John Hann Shoveller (aka John) was born in Grafton on the 19th August 1880, and baptised on the 14th November.[47] He was the youngest son and the last child of Thomas and Susan Shoveller, and he too likely attended the National School in Grafton. John moved to Sydney as a young man and married Mary Elizabeth (1892-1952), the daughter of Michael and Helen White at Paddington in 1904.[48] Their first son was born in Sydney in 1905, and was named in honour of his paternal grandfather Thomas Eastman Shoveller (1905-1961).[49] Two years later they honoured John's mother by naming their daughter Susan Hann Shoveller (1907-1978).[50] Another son arrived in John Woodford Shoveller (1909-1978),[51] and their last child was Russell Lorraine Shoveller (1916-1993) who completed the family on his birth in 1916.[52]

Clarence worked as a painter, then storeman and packer, and resided at 133 Kent St, Sydney before moving to Victoria Road then 23 Tavistock St in Drummoyne. He died aged 60 at Balmain on the 17th July 1940, and was buried at the Field of Mars Cemetery, East Ryde, NSW (*Ang; K; 381*).[53,54] His wife Mary Elizabeth Shoveller passed away some 11 years later in 1952 also at the age of 60, and was buried alongside Clarence.[55] While no further details of Clarence and Mary have come to light, they produced three sons and a daughter with all four surviving into adulthood, and their known descendants continue today (*see 20.4 Descendants of Clarence John Hann Shoveller & Mary E. White*).

Summary

While this genealogy is dedicated to the memory of Thomas Eastman Shoveller and his wife Susan Hann, the research honours all of the ancestors that went before them. And it doesn't end there as undoubtedly, the lineage of Shoveller, Bignell, Eastman and Sabine families continue today, and the blood of these ancestors survives in the bodies of their descendants, all immensely proud and thankful for their foresight and courage. Indeed, this genealogy extends further in following the path of one daughter Lenore Shoveller, through her life, marriages and descendants, which is available in Volume 8 of the Rockwell Genealogies entitled... 'Nostalgia for Naremburn.'

While much of the detailed history of the ancestors in these pages shall remain buried forever in the sands of time, I hope to have shone some light upon the fascinating lives of a few, for its the past that tells us who we are. It is my sincere hope that the lovingly collected material contained in these pages is of benefit to those who are passionate about these families, the people, the historic events they experienced and their many captivating stories and anecdotes.

References

1. NSW Dept of BDM. (1859). Birth & Baptism Certificate for Susan Eva Shoveller, 24th August 1859 (#258/7801).
2. NSW Dept of BDM. (1858). Death Certificate for Susan Therese Shoveller, 1858 (#3660/122).
3. NSW Dept of BDM. (1859). Birth & Baptism Certificate for Susan Eva Shoveller, 24th August 1859 (#258/7801).
4. NSW Dept of BDM. (1879). Marriage Certificate for Susan Eva Shoveller & Edward Meally at Grafton, 1879 (#3246/1879).
5. NSW Dept of BDM. (1879). Birth Certificate for Charles Edward Meally, 1879 (#14355/1879).
6. NSW Dept of BDM. (1882). Birth Certificate for Latona S. Meally, 1882 (#16837/1882).
7. NSW Dept of BDM. (1900). Death Certificate for Latona S. Meally, 1900 (#8937/1900).
8. NSW Dept of BDM. (1885). Birth Certificate for Eva Nathalia Meally, 1885 (#20444/1885).
9. NSW Dept of BDM. (1910). Marriage Certificate for Edward Charles Meally & Nellie M. Ford, 1910 (#12137/1910).
10. Eva Meally & Frederick Della Ca - Wedding announcement (Grafton Argus 16th Oct 1912).
11. Mrs Susan Eva Meally [nee Shoveller] - Death notice (Clarence & Richmond Examiner, 30th Aug 1913).
12. NSW Dept of BDM. (1936). Death Certificate for Edward Meally, 1936 (#17947/1936).
13. NSW Dept of BDM. (1862). Birth & Baptism Certificate for Thomas Charles Shoveller, 6th October 1862 (#8141/1862).
14. NSW Dept of BDM. (1874). Death Certificate for Thomas Charles Shoveller, 1874 (#05065/1974).
15. Thomas Charles Shoveller - Fatal and Melancholy Accident (Clarence & Richmond Examiner,, 1st December 1874).
16. Thomas Charles Shoveller - Funeral notice (Argus, 2nd Dec 1874).
17. Thomas Charles Shoveller - Death notice (Aust Town & Country Journal, 5th Dec 1874, p.6).
18. Thomas Charles Shoveller - Death notice (Clarence & Richmond Examiner, 8th December 1874).
19. Thomas Charles Shoveller - Drowning (Aust Town & Country Journal, 12th Dec 1874, p.21).
20. Inquest into death of Thomas Charles Shoveller - 30 Nov 1874 (reprinted in Clarence & Richmond Examiner, Undated, 1891).
21. NSW Dept of BDM. (1866). Birth Certificate for Leonora Shweller [sic. Shoveller], 13 Nov 1866 (#9029/1866).
22. NSW Dept of BDM. (1890). Marriage Certificate for John Henry Mackie & Lenore Shoveller, 3 March 1890 (#3797/1890).
23. NSW Dept of BDM. (1891). Birth Certificate for Valteveredo Calceolaria Mackie, 25 March 1891 (#14676/1891).
24. NSW Dept of BDM. (1894). Death Certificate for John Henry Mackie, 1894 (#3418/1894).
25. NSW Dept of BDM. (1900). Marriage Certificate for Lenore Mackie (nee Shoveller) & Humphrey Joseph O'Sullivan, 11th July 1900 (#5186/1900).
26. NSW Dept of BDM. (1901). Birth Certificate for Melecca O'Sullivan (#7223/1901).
27. NSW Dept of BDM. (1901). Death Certificate for Melecca O'Sullivan (#3017/1901).
28. NSW Dept of BDM. (1902). Birth Certificate for Octavia Corelli Susan O'Sullivan (#4112/1902).
29. NSW Dept of BDM. (1903). Birth Certificate for Sylvia Veronica O'Sullivan (#11867/1903).
30. NSW Dept of BDM. (1914). Death Certificate for Sylvia Veronica O'Sullivan (#9782/1914).
31. NSW Dept of BDM. (1905). Birth Certificate for Goldie Alathea O'Sullivan (#12992/1905).
32. NSW Dept of BDM. (1869). Birth Certificate for Janet E. A. Shoveller, 6th December 1869 (#10165/1869).
33. NSW Dept of BDM. (1870). Death Certificate for Janet E. A. Shoveller, 1870 (#1446/1870).
34. NSW Dept of BDM. (1873). Birth Certificate for George Lorraine Shoveller, 1873 (#11288/1873).
35. NSW Dept of BDM. (1918). Marriage Certificate for George Lorraine Shoveller & Mary Luney, 1918 (#8020/1918).
36. NSW Dept of BDM. (1946). Death Certificate for George Lorraine Shoveller, 14th August 1946 (#20194/1946).
37. NSW Dept of BDM. (1967). Death Certificate for Mary Shoveller (nee Luney), 1967 (#23962/1967).
38. NSW Dept of BDM. (1878). Birth Certificate for Mabel Susan Shoveller - 3 June 1878 (#13336/1878).
39. NSW Dept of BDM. (1902). Marriage Certificate for Mabel Shoveller & William Hayes, 1902 (#8434/1902).
40. Mabel Hayes (nee Shoveller) & Samuel West - Keeping It Dark (The Australian Star, 17 March 1904, p.7).
41. NSW Dept of BDM. (1903). Marriage Certificate for Mabel Hayes (nee Shoveller) & Samuel West, 1903 (#7665/1903).
42. NSW Dept of BDM. (1904). Birth Certificate for Reginald Searle West (#6986/1904).
43. NSW Dept of BDM. (1905). Birth Certificate for Sibyl Susan West (#25396/1905).
44. NSW Dept of BDM. (1906). Birth Certificate for Sadie Mabel West (#20451/1906).
45. Samuel West - Charged with Abduction (Northern Star, 30 Aug 1917, p.3).
46. NSW Dept of BDM. (1945). Death Certificate for Mabel Susan West (nee Shoveller), 1945 (#20451/1945).
47. NSW Dept of BDM. (1880). Birth Certificate for Clarence John Hann Shoveller - 19 Aug 1880 (#15169/1880).
48. NSW Dept of BDM. (1904). Marriage Certificate for Clarence John Hann Shoveller & Mary Elizabeth White, 1904 (#34/1904).
49. NSW Dept of BDM. (1905). Birth Certificate for Thomas Eastman Shoveller, 1905 (#156/1906).
50. NSW Dept of BDM. (1907). Birth Certificate for Susan Hann Shoveller, 1907 (#20541/1907).
51. NSW Dept of BDM. (1909). Birth Certificate for John Woodford Shoveller, 1909 (#33246/1909).
52. NSW Dept of BDM. (1916). Birth Certificate for Russell Lorraine Shoveller, 1916 (#33249/1916).
53. NSW Dept of BDM. (1940). Death Certificate for Clarence John Hann Shoveller, 1940 (#18255/1940).
54. Clarence John Hann Shoveller - Funeral notice (SMH, 19 Jul 1940, p.6).
55. NSW Dept of BDM. (1952). Death Certificate for Mary Elizabeth Shoveller (nee White), 19452(#21348/1952).
56. Ancestry, (2022). Descendant data from Ancestry.com.au.

Appendices

Roll of Arms for the Direct Ancestors of

THOMAS EASTMAN SHOVELLER

APPENDIX A

A History of Portsmouth

From… 'Local Histories - Tim's History of British Towns, Cities and So Much More' [https://localhistories.org/a-history-of-portsmouth/].

Portsmouth in the Middle Ages

Portsmouth was founded about 1180 when a merchant called Jean De Gisors founded a little town in the South-West corner of Portsea Island. Jean De Gisors was a merchant who owned a fleet of ships. He was also a landowner who owned land on Portsea Island. In the Southwest of the island was a small inlet from the sea called the Camber. It was a sheltered place for ships to land and De Gisors decided it was an ideal place to start a town.

De Gisors divided up the land into plots for building houses and he started a market. Craftsmen and merchants came to live in the new settlement.

In 1188 a parish church was dedicated to St Thomas (in the 20th century it became Portsmouth Cathedral). In 1194 King Richard I gave Portsmouth a charter. (A document granting the townspeople certain rights).

By the early 13th century Portsmouth was described as 'one of our most important ports'. However, the population of Portsmouth was probably only about 1,200 people. The main exports from Medieval Portsmouth were wool and grain. The main imports were wine, woad for dyeing, wax for candles, and iron.

In 1212 a building called the Domus Dei (house of God) was built at Portsmouth. It was a hospice for pilgrims. There was also a hostel for lepers outside the town.

Portsmouth was, at first, run by a man called a reeve assisted by bailiffs. By the 14th century, Portsmouth had a mayor elected by the merchants. There were also constables responsible for arresting wrongdoers.

In 1369 a military governor was appointed who was responsible for the defense of the town.

However, Portsmouth was burned down 4 times during the 14th century during a period of almost continuous warfare between England and France. The French burned Portsmouth in 1338, 1369, 1377, and 1380, (This was easy as most of the buildings were of wood with thatched roofs. On the other hand they could be easily rebuilt).

Portsmouth was not fortified till after the last attack in 1380. It was given wooden walls. Then about 1418, a tower was erected at the entrance of Portsmouth Harbour called the Round Tower. Cannons on it could fire at any enemy ship attempting to enter the harbour.

In the 16th century, a giant chain was stretched across the mouth of the harbour. The winch was by the Round Tower. The chain could be lowered to let in friendly ships but raised to prevent enemy ones from entering the harbour.

In 1450 the Bishop of Chichester was murdered in Portsmouth. Sailors in the town had not been paid for a long time. According to one account, the bishop brought some money but not enough to pay the sailors all they were owed. When the sailors found out they were enraged. The Bishop was in the Domus Dei (the 'hospital' for poor and sick people). A mob dragged him out and stabbed him to death.

For this crime, the whole town of Portsmouth was placed under an interdict. This meant that mass could not be heard in the town and no other sacraments could be performed. This lasted until 1508.

In 1494 Henry VII strengthened the town's fortifications by building the square tower. Henry also changed the destiny of Portsmouth when he built a dockyard in 1495. The dockyard was a place where royal warships could be built or repaired. From then on Portsmouth became a naval port. The dockyard was built a short distance north of the town. At first, it consisted of a single dry dock.

Portsmouth in the 16th century

In 1527 Henry VIII enlarged Portsmouth dockyard. In 1540 Henry closed the Domus Dei. It was turned into an armory. Later it became part of the military governor's residence.

Henry also built a castle, east of Portsmouth, overlooking the sea. Southsea Castle, as it is called, was built in 1544. Then in 1545, Henry VIII watched as his warship Mary Rose sank in the Solent.

However, in the late 16th century Portsmouth declined in importance. Other dockyards were opened on the Thames. They took business away from Portsmouth. In the late 16th century and early 17th century, ships were repaired at Portsmouth but none were actually built.

Portsmouth also suffered an outbreak of plague in 1563. About 300 people died, which was a significant number in a town of perhaps 2,000 people.

Nevertheless, the population of Tudor Portsmouth continued to grow and it might have reached about 2,500 by 1600. In the Elizabethan period, people began to build houses on the little peninsula called Point.

Portsmouth in the 17th century

Early in the 17th century Portsmouth was described as a poor and beggarly town. In 1625 there was another outbreak of plague. But under Charles I (1625-49) Portsmouth began to regain some of its former importance.

In 1628 one of the king's advisers, the Duke of Buckingham was assassinated in the town. He was stabbed to death by a sailor called John Felton in a house on High Street. Felton was hanged for the crime and his body was hanged in chains on land east of the town until it decomposed as a warning to others.

Then in 1642 came civil war between king and parliament. Most of the people in Portsmouth, including the mayor supported parliament. But the military governor of the town, Colonel Goring supported the king and he commanded the soldiers in Portsmouth.

The navy sided with parliament and Portsmouth was blockaded by sea. Parliament sent men to besiege Portsmouth by land. Southsea Castle was taken after only token resistance. The guns of Southsea castle were then used to fire at the town of Portsmouth. On the other side of Portsmouth, the town of Gosport joined the parliamentary side. Here too, guns were set up and were fired at Portsmouth.

Besieged by land and sea and with no support in the town Goring realized the situation was hopeless. He decided to surrender but he obtained good terms. He threatened to explode a gunpowder magazine and wreck the town unless he was allowed to escape from Portsmouth unharmed. He was duly allowed to escape with his few supporters.

Then in 1662 King Charles II married a Portuguese woman named Catherine of Braganza in Portsmouth.

Following the end of the civil war in 1646 Portsmouth prospered. In 1650 a ship called the Portsmouth was launched in the Dockyard. It was the first ship to be built in the town for over 100 years. Between 1650 and 1660 12 ships were built in Portsmouth and the town was very busy. Its population had probably grown to over 3,000.

In the late 17th century Portsmouth dockyard (and the town) continued to grow. In 1663 a new wharf was built for the exclusive use of the navy and the dockyard. In 1665 a mast pond was dug (masts were soaked in it for years to season them). As the dockyard lay north of the town surrounded by fields it was easy for it to expand.

In 1667-85 the fortifications around the town were rebuilt. New walls were built with many bastions (triangular towers). Two moats were dug outside the walls separated by a strip of land. Afterward, Portsmouth was one of the most heavily fortified towns in Europe.

Portsmouth in the 18th century

At the end of the 17th century and the beginning of the 18th century, Portsmouth Dockyard continued to expand. New docks and warehouses were built. A church dedicated to St Anne was built in 1704. Rows of houses were built in the dockyard for senior officers who needed to be close to their work. A naval academy for training naval officers was opened in the dockyard in 1733.

Meanwhile, the town of Portsmouth had reached the bursting point by the end of the 17th century. So people began to build houses north of the town on the area known as the Common, near the dockyard. The first houses were built there about 1690.

But the governor of the dockyard was alarmed by this new development. He feared that if houses were built near the dockyard they would provide cover for advancing enemy troops. In 1703 he threatened to fire his cannons at any new houses. (The dockyard had its own guns).

The dockyard workers appealed to Prince George the husband of Queen Anne, who was visiting Portsmouth at the time. In 1704 royal permission was given for people to build houses near the dockyard. So a new suburb called Portsmouth Common grew. In 1792 it changed its name to Portsea.

This new suburb soon outgrew the original town, which became known as Old Portsmouth. In 1801 Portsea had a population of about 24,000 while Old Portsmouth had less than 8,000. Nevertheless, it was not until the 1770s that the town walls were extended to include the new suburb.

In 1764 a body of men called the Improvement Commissioners was set up in Portsea. They had the power to pave and clean the streets. They also appointed a man called a scavenger who collected rubbish, with a cart, once a week. In 1768 a similar body was set up in Old Portsmouth. In 1776 they were given the power to light the streets with oil lamps and from 1783 they appointed night watchmen to patrol the streets.

In 1733 a rich man left land in his will. The land was to be rented and the money used to provide a free school. Portsmouth Grammar School opened in Penny Street in 1750. Despite its founder's intention it later became a fee-paying school.

Portsmouth in the 19th century

In 1811 Portsmouth gained its first piped water supply, but you had to pay to be connected and only the rich and middle class could afford it. In 1820 the Portsea Improvement Commissioners installed gas street lighting. Old Portsmouth followed in 1823.

In the 18th century Portsmouth was limited to the South West corner of Portsea Island. During the 19th century, it spread across the whole island. By the 1790s a new suburb was growing up around Commercial Road and Charlotte Street. It became known as Landport after the Landport gate.

As Portsmouth grew it reached the village of Buckland. By the 1860s this village had been 'swallowed up'. By 1871 the population of Portsmouth had grown to 100,000. In the late 1870s and 1880s, Stamshaw was built up. At the same time, the village of Fratton was also 'swallowed up' by the growing city.

In 1809 a new suburb began to grow. It became known as Southsea after the castle. The first houses were built for skilled workers in the 'mineral' streets (Silver Street, Nickel Street, etc).

Slightly later middle class houses were built in Kings Terrace and Hampshire Terrace. But the new suburb remained small until 1835. Then it surged eastwards. By the 1860s the suburb of Southsea had grown along Clarendon Road as far as Granada Road.

In 1857 Southsea gained its own Improvement Commissioners responsible for paving, cleaning, and lighting the streets. Meanwhile, another suburb was growing. This one was working class. About 1820 some houses were built west of Green Road on land belonging to Mr. Somers. The new suburb was named Somerstown. By the late 1880s growth had spread to Fawcett Road and Lawrence Road.

Meanwhile further south in the 1860s and 1870s growth spread along Albert Road. The roads around Festing Road were built in the 1880s.

South of Southsea were two marshes. One, the Little Morass stood near Old Portsmouth. It was drained in 1820-23. Another larger marsh, the Great Morass, existed south of Albert Road. It was not drained till the late 19th century.

Clarence Esplanade was built by convict labour in 1848. Clarence Pier opened in 1861. Both are named after Lord FitzClarence who was once military governor of Portsmouth.

Milton became built up in the late 19th century and Eastney became built up between 1890-1905. North End began to grow after 1881 when a horse-drawn tram began to operate between Portsmouth and the village of Cosham, north of Portsea Island. By 1910 the area was built up.

By 1900 the population of Portsmouth was 190,000 about the same as it is today.

Like all cities in the 19th century, Portsmouth was dirty and unhealthy. In 1848-49 more than 800 people died in a cholera epidemic.

However, things improved later in the century. In 1865-70 the council built sewers. In 1875 a bylaw stated that any house within 100 feet of the main sewer must be connected to it. Portsmouth had a water supply as early as 1811. In 1858 the council purchased the company and improved the supply. Despite these improvements in public health, 514 people died in a smallpox epidemic in 1872.

There were other improvements in amenities in Portsmouth during the 19th century. In 1836 Portsmouth gained its first modern police force. In 1878 the first public park, Victoria Park, opened. In 1883 Portsmouth gained its first public library. In 1885 the first telephone exchange opened. In 1894-96 streetlights in Portsmouth were converted from gas to electricity.

In 1849 Portsmouth gained its first modern hospital, The Royal Portsmouth Hospital. (It closed in 1979). In 1879 St James hospital, a lunatic asylum opened near the village of Milton in the South East of Portsea Island. In 1884 an infectious diseases hospital opened near the village. St Mary's hospital opened at Milton in 1898.

There were also improvements in transport in the 19th century. In 1840 the first horse-drawn buses began running in Portsmouth. They were followed, in 1865 by horse-drawn trams. In 1847 the railway reached Portsmouth.

In 1818-22 a canal was built across Portsea Island. The Portsmouth to Arundel canal began just outside the town where Arundel Street is today (hence its name). It ran along the site of the railway between Portsmouth and Fratton. It then ran along the site of Goldsmith Avenue to Milton then ran south of Locksway Road to locks on the southeastern shore of Portsea Island. The barges were towed by steam tugs across the sea into Chichester Harbour where the canal began again. The canal closed in 1838.

The fortifications around Portsmouth were rebuilt. The old walls around the town were now obsolete. They were demolished in the 1860s. The millpond between Old Portsmouth and Portsea was filled in the year 1876.

In 1862-68 a chain of forts was built along Portsdown Hill, which overlooks the town. Since the 18th century, there had been an earth rampart across the north of Portsea Island manned by marines. This was rebuilt in the 1860s. In 1867 a Marine Barracks was built in the hamlet of Eastney.

Portsmouth in the 20th century

After 1900 Portsmouth continued to grow. By 1910 the village of Copnor had been engulfed by the expanding city. Growth also spread north to Hilsea.

In 1920 the boundaries of Portsmouth were extended to include the village of Cosham north of Portsea Island and in 1932 to include Drayton and Farlington to the northeast. This area was growing rapidly and soon all these villages became suburbs of the growing city. In 1934-36 Highbury estate was built south of Cosham.

The first council houses were built in 1911 in Portsea in Curzon Howe Road. In the 1920's more council houses were built at Wymering, west of Cosham. Other council houses were built at Hilsea Crescent Hilsea and at Henderson Road Eastney. In the 1930's many more council houses were built at Wymering. They were needed as slum clearance was taking place in Portsea. By 1939 the population of Portsmouth reached 260,000.

The old horse-drawn trams were replaced by electric ones in 1901-03. But the electric trams were replaced closed in 1935-36. The first motor buses in Portsmouth began running in 1919. Other facilities continued to improve. Queen Alexandra hospital opened on the slopes of Portsdown Hill in 1908.

Six cinemas opened in 1910. By 1939 there were more than 30 cinemas in Portsmouth. A golf course opened at Great Salterns on the northeast of Portsea Island in 1926. In 1928, Cumberland House, Eastney was opened as a museum and art gallery. In 1922 the council purchased Southsea Common, a stretch of land by the sea, and laid it out with gardens, bowling greens, and tennis courts.

During the Second World War Portsmouth was an obvious target for German bombing because it was a major naval base. Altogether 930 people were killed in Portsmouth by bombing. There were 67 air raids on Portsmouth between July 1940 and May 1944. The worst was on 24 August 1940 when 125 people were killed, on 10 January 1941 when 171 people were killed and on 27 April 1941 when 102 people were killed. Furthermore, on 15 July 1944, a V1 flying bomb hit Newcomen Road in Stamshaw, killing 15 people. Also, 6,625 houses were destroyed and a further 6,549 were severely damaged.

After the war, the most pressing need was for new housing. At first Portsmouth council erected prefabs (houses made in sections in factories that could be fitted together in a few days). Some were erected on bomb sites. Others were erected on Portsdown hill above Cosham. More than 700 prefab houses were built in 1945-47.

In February 1946 the council began to build more permanent houses, most of them off Portsea Island. A new estate was built at Paulsgrove, northwest of the city. The first houses were built there in 1946. The estate was completed by 1953. The population of Paulsgrove now stands at 15,000.

Another estate was built at Leigh Park about 10 miles Northeast of Portsmouth. The first houses were ready in 1949 but the building went on till 1974. By then the population of Leigh Park had risen to 40,000. n Apart from wartime bombing another reason for building new houses was slum clearance. In 1955 a survey showed that 7,000 houses in Portsmouth were unfit for human habitation.

In the 1960s and early 1970s a whole section of central Portsmouth was rebuilt including Landport, Somerstown and Buckland. As well as demolishing slums the council gave people grants to improve their homes.

Several new council estates were built in the early 1970s. Portsdown Park was a mixture of flats and houses built on Portsdown Hill above Cosham. But Portsdown Park soon began to suffer damp. Efforts to cure the damp failed and in 1987 the estate was demolished. It was replaced by private housing.

Other council houses were built some miles north of Portsmouth at Crookhorn and Wecock Farm.

From the late 1970s, many new private houses were built in Portsmouth. In the late 1970s, an estate was built at Gatcombe Park in Hilsea. In the 1980s another estate was built at Anchorage Park on the North East corner of Portsea Island. In the 1990s a new estate and marina were built at Port Solent North West of Portsea Island.

In the 1980s shopping malls were built, the Bridge Centre in Fratton and the Cascades in Commercial Road.

In the early 20th century the main employer in Portsmouth was the dockyard. It employed 8,000 men in 1900. During the First World War, the number rose to 23,000 but it fell to 9,000 when the war ended. From the 1930's the threat of another war led to an expansion of the dockyard workforce.

Meanwhile, other industries like brewing and corset making prospered. A new employer was the Airspeed factory, which made parts for aircraft. It opened in the North East of Portsea Island.

After World War II the city council tried to diversify industry in Portsmouth. An industrial estate was built in Fratton in 1946-48. Other industrial estates were built in the 1950s at Paulsgrove and Farlington. In the 1960s a new industrial estate began at Hilsea north of Burrfields Road. In the 1980s new industrial estates were built at Cosham and at Hilsea.

The pattern of employment in Portsmouth changed rapidly. The dockyard workforce was drastically reduced.

Traditional industries like brewing and corset making vanished but electrical and electronic engineering became a major employer. There was also a large increase in the number of jobs in service industries. In 1968

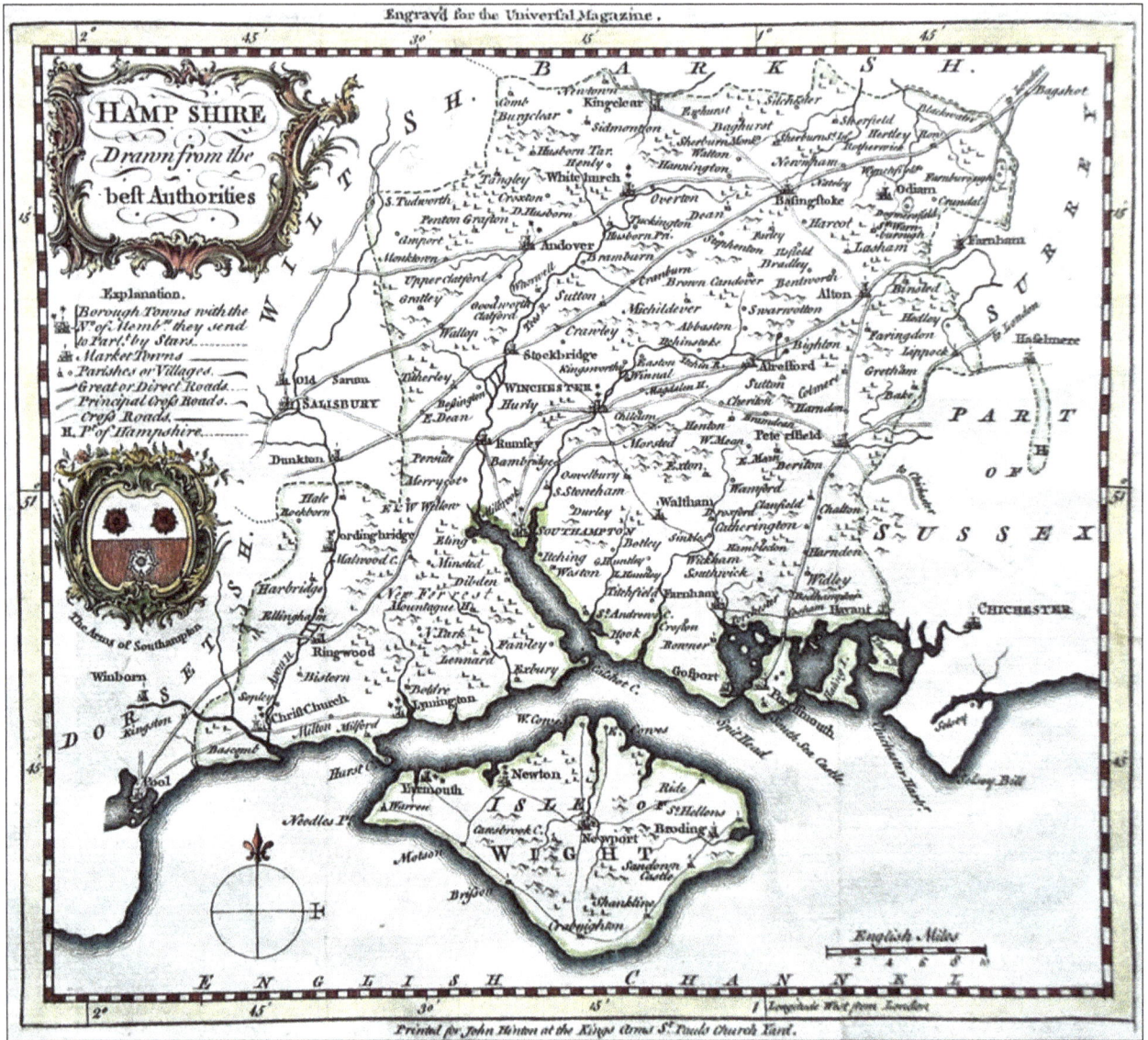

▲Old map of the County of Hampshire on the south coast of England, showing Portsmouth, Titchfield and Warnford.

Zurich insurance moved its headquarters to Portsmouth. In 1979 IBM UK moved its headquarters to the city.

Tourism also became a major industry in Portsmouth. Mary Rose, the Tudor warship was raised from the seabed in 1982 and became a museum. The D Day museum opened in 1984 and in 1987 HMS Warrior, Britain's first iron warship was moved to Portsmouth. Meanwhile, The Cascades shopping mall opened in 1989.

Portsmouth in the 21st century

In the early 21st century Portsmouth has become a thriving city and tourism is flourishing. In 2001 a new shopping centre opened at the Gunwharf. Also in 2001 the Millennium Promenade opened, and the Pompey Centre was built in 2003. The Spinnaker Tower opened in 2005. By 2018 the population of Portsmouth was 205,000.

APPENDIX B

'Robert Bowyer (1758-1834), Artist, Publisher & Preacher'

By K.R. Manley, in 'Baptist Quarterly,' Vol. 23:1, 1969, pp.32-46.

Robert Bowyer (1758-1834)

Artist, Publisher and Preacher

ROBERT BOWYER must be unique in the history of Baptists. As officially-appointed miniature painter to King George III he often moved freely in the world of the Court and the fashionable; yet throughout all his adult life he retained an active membership of Baptist churches. Indeed in his later years he served as pastor to a small cause he had helped to begin. Certain features of his public life have been traced,[1] but the need for a fuller outline with due attention to his religious activities seems long overdue.

Bowyer came originally from Portsmouth.[2] He had at least one brother, Amos, and two sisters, Susannah and another known later as Mrs. Leeks.[3] Unfortunately the only sources for the beginnings of his career as an artist are family and personal reminiscences.[4] The romantic version of these is that Bowyer was offered, whilst still a youth, an opportunity to migrate to America. His heart already belonged to one Mary Shoveller, also of Portsmouth, and Bowyer determined to offer her, as a keepsake, a self-portrait attempted with the aid of a looking-glass. A gentleman saw the result, pressed Bowyer to attempt the same for him, and Bowyer's career was launched. Rather than go to America, he went to seek his fame in London.[5] The other more prosaic version was that Bowyer was already in London and began painting miniatures after observing some in a shop in Newgate Street.[6] All that appears certain is that Bowyer came from an unpromising background, and unlike many other fashionable artists of the day, his success was due largely to his own initiative and the skilful use of his native gift.

Bowyer was a member of the Baptist Church at Meeting-House Alley, Portsmouth, whence he was dismissed to the Carter Lane Church, Southwark, on 10 March 1776.[7] Mrs. Mary Bowyer (presumably the former Miss Shoveller) was also received at Carter Lane in the October of the following year,[8] and the young couple set up home in Tower Street.[9] Their pastor was the youthful John Rippon (1751-1836), destined to achieve fame not only as a distinguished pastor but as a hymnologist and editor of the *Baptist Annual Register* (1790-1802).[10] Rippon and Bowyer became good friends, as will be shown, but Bowyer does not figure prominently in the records of the Carter Lane Church.

In order to underline the distinction Bowyer brought to contemporary Baptists, it is proposed first to trace his career as an artist and publisher before noting further details of his private and religious life.

Bowyer achieved considerable prominence as a portrait miniaturist. From about the middle of the eighteenth century the popularity and patronage of portrait miniature had greatly increased, and the number of miniaturists working at any one time comes to be reckoned in scores.[11] Bowyer was not destined to be one of the greatest, such as Crossway, Crosse or Smart,[12] but nevertheless was honoured and well-known by his contemporaries. He was supposed to have been a pupil of John Smart (1741-1811) who was reputed to be a pious member of the strict religious sect of Glassites, or Sandemanians,[13] although one contemporary thought him vulgar, sensual, and greedy for money.[14]

The Royal Academy, founded by George III in 1768, sought to raise the status of painting, drawing, engraving, sculpture, and architecture by giving tuition to students and arranging an annual exhibition. Between 1783 and 1828 Bowyer had thirty-two portraits exhibited at the Royal Academy,[15] and in 1782 one at the exhibition of the Free Society of Artists.[16] This kind of recognition meant that when Meyer died, Bowyer was in 1789 appointed miniature painter to the King.[17] The manner of these appointments is uncertain, and was not necessarily expressive of the King's own choice. "Bowyer! Who is Bowyer? He is no painter! I never heard of him," said the King on learning of his appointment.[18] The King had preferred Richard Collins who in fact received much of his patronage. Bowyer did however make "an extraordinary miniature of George III, with a flat diamond over it half an inch square"[19] and another portrait of him by Bowyer is reproduced as a plate for Hume's *History of England* which Bowyer published in 1797. Bowyer is also known to have painted portraits of George IV, and William IV.[20] There is another story told that towards the end of George III's life, when he was closely confined because of his insanity, Bowyer sat in the Royal Chapel at Windsor and took a likeness of the King on his thumbnail. Then as quickly as possible afterwards he made a sketch and took it to the Prince Regent. The latter was supposed to have been so affected that he could not allow it to be published (it was such a remarkable likeness), and told Bowyer to name his own price. One version says this was fifty guineas,[21] but this in another place became one hundred and five pounds.[22] The motives for the Regent's action are of course open to several interpretations.

Bowyer received much fashionable patronage. His portrait of Sir Edward Hughes "was described as a wonderful performance, and the Prince of Wales said it was one of the best miniatures he ever beheld."[23] By the Queen's desire, Dr. Francis Willis, physician for treatment of insanity who attended George III from 1788 to 1807, sat to Bowyer for the portrait which Fittler engraved in 1789.[24] Other subjects included the Dukes of Clarence and of York, Lord Sandwich, Earl Russell, Charles Fox the famous M.P., Lord Nelson, and four British Admirals.[25] Contemporary Dissenters painted by Bowyer included the Baptists John Rippon, Andrew Fuller, and Samuel Pearce[26] as well as the eccentric Antinomian, William Huntington, 'S.S.' (= 'Sinner Saved').[27]

Unfortunately few original portraits by Bowyer have been traced. There is a miniature portrait of Warren Hastings in the collection of the Duke of Buccleuch which is attributed to Bowyer.[28] There was also a miniature of Nelson, attributed to Bowyer on the grounds that it was a reduction of a full-scale portrait in oils by Bowyer, once in the Royal Library at Windsor Castle but not now there.[29] Modern experts are not as fulsome as Bowyer's contemporaries in their estimates of his work. G. C. Williamson in 1904 had found "three examples of his work at Christie's auction rooms which were catalogued as early works by Smart. They bear considerable resemblances, especially in the colour schemes, to the works of Smart, but are not nearly so well painted as regards the faces or hands. His work is looser and not so enamel-like as is the finest of Smart, and there is a yellowness in the faces which marks a striking divergence from his master."[30] Similarly, Basil S. Long in 1929 described a miniature of Sir John Webb signed "R B / 1786" which was a copy of a miniature painted by Smart in 1784 and concluded, "it is not particularly good, but imitates with partial success the manner of Smart. The initials are finely written, like Smart's."[31] More recently, one of Long's successors at the Victoria and Albert Museum, Mr. Graham Reynolds, wrote that Bowyer "hardly seems in the two or three works known to be by him to have deserved his high contemporary reputation."[32]

Deserved or not, of that "high contemporary reputation" there can be no doubt. His fame as an artist was supplemented by his labours as a publisher of lavishly illustrated works. The high quality of English engravings in the late eighteenth century encouraged the publication of ornately illustrated editions of major works. Boydell specialized in Shakespeare,[33] Thomas Macklin in the Poets and the Bible, whilst Bowyer turned his endeavours to historical pictures.[34] His first undertaking was an extensive and expensive task. In 1792 he issued a prospectus for a 'superbly embellished' edition of David Hume's *History of England* (first published in an unadorned edition, 1754-61). Bowyer had arranged with David Williams (1738-1816) to superintend the edition and write a continuation, but the letter's supposed Republican sympathies meant that the agreement had to be broken since the privilege of dedication to the Crown was likely to be withdrawn.[35] Accordingly in 1793 Bowyer issued, *An Elucidation of Mr. Bowyer's Plans for a magnificent edition of Hume's History of England with a Continuation by C. Gregory.* (In fact, no continuation was ever published.) The aim of the illustrations was defined as being "to rouse the passions, to fire the mind with emulation of heroic deeds, or to inspire it with detestation of criminal actions." Bowyer commissioned leading artists, including Henry Tresham, Robert Smirke, John Opie, P. J. De Loutherbourg, and spared no expense in obtaining the finest engravings, many by Bartolozzi. By 1806 five parts in nine folio volumes had been published, and the paintings had been exhibited in Bowyer's 'Historic Gallery' housed in Shomberg House in Pall Mall.[36] Unfortunately a "series of unpropitious times and circumstances respecting the Fine Arts" (the country was at war) meant that the project was a financial failure and Bowyer suffered a severe loss.[37] Following the example of John Boydell, Bowyer applied to Parliament for permission to dispose of his valuable collection of paintings, drawings, and engravings by means of a lottery. This was granted on 11 April 1805 (45 Geo III c. xxiv), and the period extended in 1807 (47 Geo III c. i). Bowyer's own moral character was unimpeached,[38] but what his Baptist friends thought of the lottery is unknown. The scheme was that 22,000 tickets of three guineas each were offered, there were 1,451 "capital prizes" and "every adventurer" received "in warranted fine impressions of works . . . the full and intrinsic value of his stake of three guineas."[39] Perhaps these conditions eased any taint of gambling from the tender consciences of his fellow-Baptists. The lottery cannot have been a great success because the 'Historic Gallery' was sold by Coxe on 29 and 30 May 1807.[40]

This was the same year that Wilberforce's campaign to abolish the Slave Trade reached a decisive moment: on 23 February the House had declared, by 283 votes to 16, that the Slave Trade was illegal. Despite his own set-back Bowyer immediately issued a prospectus for a new work, "intended to commemorate the final triumph of Humanity in the cause of the Natives of Africa,"[41] *A Tribute of the Fine Arts, in Honour of the Abolition of the Slave Trade.* Although no copy of this work has been located, it was evidently published in 1810, for on 16 February Bowyer wrote to George III and asked him to accept a copy: "The kind attentions which I have repeatedly been honored with from your Majesty, demand & will ever receive my most grateful & dutiful acknowledgments—Having just completed a most beautifully embellished Volume of Poems (which have been written expressly for the occasion) on the Abolition of the Slave trade, . . . I would most humbly flatter myself with the hope that your Majesty will deign to accept a Copy of this my new publication. . . ."[42] This publication was presumably the basis of the description of Bowyer as a supporter of the Anti-Slavery movement.[43]

Bowyer again built up his business as a dealer in prints and publisher of expensively illustrated volumes. There are several accounts from Bowyer to the Prince Regent, and in one of these is listed a set of small views to illustrate the Bible which were sold to the Prince Regent on 30 September 1812.[44] In 1816 he published, *An Illustrated Record of Important Events in the Annals of Europe, during the last Four Years; comprising a series of Views of the Principal Places, Battles, etc., etc., etc. Connected with those events;* . . . This was an unwieldy volume of thirty pages, adorned with large prints of foreign cities such as Moscow and Berlin. It was reprinted in 1817. In 1823 he published *An Impartial Historical Narrative of those Momentous Events which have taken place in this Country During the Period from the year 1816 to 1823. Illustrated with Engravings by the first artists.* The illustrations reproduced in colour included the trial of Queen Caroline and the Coronation of George IV. Another work known to be published by Bowyer was *Fac-similes of Water Colour Drawings*, 1825. Not without reason did the *Gentleman's Magazine* in its obituary of Bowyer describe him as "the spirited publisher of the embellished History of England, which bears his name, and of various splendid popular works."[45]

But Bowyer's *magnum opus*, the famous 'Bowyer's Bible,'[46] was never published though this was his intention. As early as 1791 (not 1802, as Earland suggested)[47] Bowyer had begun advertising his scheme. His pastor, John Rippon, active in writing to American friends in connection with his *Baptist Register,* enclosed brochures about the "Unique Cabinet Bible, by Mr. Bowyer" to Rev. Jedidiah Morse of Boston[48] and Rev. James Manning, President of Rhode Island College, Providence.[49] With the latter was enclosed a brochure for the President of the United States, which Bowyer hoped Manning, once a member of Congress, might deliver for him. Rippon commented, "Bowyer and Fittler are likely to get several Thousand Pounds by this publication."[50] Later, in August 1796, Rippon advertised the "curious and beautiful edition of the Bible by Bowyer" on the cover of Number xiii of his *Register.*[51]

What Bowyer set out to do was to produce the most fully and beautifully illustrated edition of the Bible ever seen. He sought to acquire all the engravings, etchings, and original drawings related in any way to the Bible that he could locate. Illustrations were obtained from many parts of Europe. Bowyer was evidently in Paris during the brief peace of 1802 and at some time obtained personal permission from Napoleon to engage in his collection of prints. The family treasured the following autograph letter:

> "Let Mr. Boywer refer this matter to the French Consul, Mr. Otto, and if he sees no objection, let a passport be granted to Mr. Bowyer's agent. Buonaparte."[52]

But Bowyer kept adding to the Bible without actually publishing anything. After more than thirty years' work the 'Bowyer Bible' was an extraordinary and unique production. The text was taken from an 1800 edition of Macklin's Bible, which was then the most lavishly illustrated available. Bowyer printed his own title-page dated 1826 and by the addition of more than six thousand engravings expanded the Macklin Bible of seven volumes into no less than forty-five volumes. Illustrations of every subject in any way connected with the Scriptures were included: trees, plants, flowers, quadrupeds, birds, fish, insects, fossils, Scripture atlases, astronomical and architectural plates not to mention the illustrations of the narrative events. One hundred and thirteen original drawings by P. J. de Loutherbourg at a cost of £1,158,[53] were included as 'vignette embellishments.' The work of more than six hundred engravers was included. The artists represented range from 'Michael Angelo and Raffaelle' to Reynolds and West: Rembrandt, Dürer, Titian, and Rubens were all included. Two people, for more than four years, were fully employed in mounting the engravings and ruling the edges.[54] The Bible almost defies description and statistics must suffice: the Old Testament filled 23 volumes with 2,315 engravings, the Apocrypha had 3 volumes and 959 engravings whilst the New Testament had 19 volumes and 3,019 engravings.[55] The whole set was housed in a magnificently ornate oak book-case measuring eight feet six inches square.

But such a mammoth Bible had long since passed beyond the possibility of being commercially published. Bowyer had compiled, at a cost estimated at about £4,000 this "last and greatest example of inserted Biblical illustration."[56] But his problem was, what was he to do with it? A scheme was proposed in 1829 whereby the Bible would be bought by public subscription and given to the Bodleian Library.[57] The printed prospectus, with the support of the Archbishop of Canterbury, Lord Granville, Lord Eldon, the Duke of Newcastle, William Wilberforce and others commended the project to all sons of Oxford. Bowyer was prepared to sell the Bible for £2,500. He penned a letter to Dr. Bliss of the Library in which, with a certain lack of modesty, he wrote:

> ". . . I flatter myself that my Rank as an Artist, & the splendid works which have issued from my Gallery during the last 40 years after an expenditure of more than three hundred thousand pounds in the advancement of the British Schools of painting & Engraving would be a perfect guarantee that this magnificent Bible is equal to every expectation that can be formed, & superior to any description that can be given of it:—I cannot therefore avoid presuming to anticipate that you will feel a gratification in uniting to fix the destiny of this inestimable work in the principal Library of the first University in Europe. . . ."[58]

But despite such flatteries the Librarian was unimpressed, and as insufficient subscriptions were obtained the project failed.[59]

After Bowyer's death, his cherished Bible suffered the ignominy in 1844 of being won in a lottery by a haberdasher.[60] This means of disposing of the Bible was devised by a certain Mrs. Parkes, whose exact relation to the Bowyers is uncertain.[61] The subsequent history of the Bible was traced in a useful monograph by Archibald Sparke.[62] It is now kept in the Central Library, Bolton, to which it was given in 1948, although it had been there on extended loan since 1917.[63]

Thus in brief the public career of Bowyer has been reviewed. Considering the vast sum of £300,000 he claimed to have expended in the cause of British art he died on 4 June 1834,[64] aged seventy-six, a comparatively poor man. Although his will[65] spoke of giving all to his wife and £1,000 to 'my friend' Catherine Andras,[66] the probate granted was for only £1,000.

As to Bowyer's domestic and religious life, there are several points of interest. Robert and Mary Bowyer had one daughter, Harriet, who unhappily died at the age of nineteen on 4 August 1796.[67] Or to be more precise, died happily: as a detailed account of her death, in the manner of the religious periodicals of the day, reveals. This harrowing detail was published by her 'dear Uncle and friend Dr. Rippon' in his *Baptist Register*,[68] and was in fact the substance of the funeral sermon preached by Rippon.[69] The interest of this account is twofold for present purposes. First is the piety of the family as revealed in Harriet, a sweet and delicate young woman, pious and bravely resigned to her fatal illness. The second interest is the concern of Rippon to secure a 'dying testimony' from Harriet. Because of her sickness she had been removed to Portsmouth and the Isle of Wight, and on 19 July 1796 Rippon wrote her a 'pastoral' letter. After affectionately listing Scriptures and some verses of hymns, he proposed a series of questions:

> "Do you *feel* that you are a sinner, a great sinner, in the sight of God? Is sin a trouble, a burden to your soul? And do you hate it, on account of its exceeding sinfulness? if so, write only the word 'yes,' on this line, for which I leave room.
>
> "Do you clearly see your need of Christ to save you from the guilt of sin, and of the Holy Spirit to deliver you from the pollution of it? If so, write 'yes.' . . ."[70]

Six questions were thus proposed, and all answered in the affirmative. They shed an interesting light on both Rippon's pronounced evangelical spirit and his pastoral methods.

Some time after this the Bowyers befriended a young woman of about the same age as Harriet who came from Bristol in order to have some wax models engraved by Bowyer. Catherine Andras was adopted as a daughter. She became wax modeller to Queen Charlotte and supplied the wax effigy of Nelson which was used at his funeral and is now in Westminster Abbey.[71] Later the Bowyers also adopted another girl, niece to Mrs. Bowyer,[72] this was most probably the Mary Shoveller who was received into the Carter Lane Church on 3 May 1812 and whose address was 'Brother Bowyer's Byfleet.'[73] Bowyer had moved to Byfleet in Surrey in about 1802.[74]

John Opie, who after his second marriage became more intimate with the Bowyers painted portraits of Robert Bowyer, Mary Bowyer, and Catherine Andras.[75] To judge from this portrait Robert Bowyer was dark-haired with bushy eye-brows, wore no wig, and had a brooding, penetrating look. His wife appears as sweet-faced and pleasant, and is nursing a small dog.

A further indication of Bowyer's earnestness in religion is found in the *Baptist Register's* article entitled, 'The Happy End of Mrs. Leeks, in her thirty-second year: And a Letter, which was the Instrument of her Conversion.'[76] This letter was written by Bowyer to his sister.[77] Whilst in health, Mrs. Leeks had preferred the company of 'the gay and dissipated' to that of her 'professing relatives.' Stricken with 'an internal cancerous complaint,' she was moved to a home near London where Bowyer called to see her. During the conversation she told him that "She did not recollect that she had done any body any harm, and therefore she hoped she should do very well when she came to die." To any devout evangelical, this was like a red rag to a bull. Bowyer returned home and wrote a long letter, kindly and affectionate, but nonetheless a serious and firm call to repentance. He began by frankly admitting to her that she was dying and this added urgency and necessity upon him to write. He insisted that her hope for eternity could not be "more false", and suggested she should "take a survey of your past life, and see how things have stood between God and your soul." She had given no thought to God, had not kept the Sabbaths holy, had taken His name in vain, what was to be the End? "Why, if these sins are not repented of and forgiven while you live, you must be shut up in Hell with devils and damned spirits for ever: don't my dear sister, think that I am harsh, and want to alarm you more than is necessary: I felt a wish to speak it in milder terms; but God who knows what I am writing at this moment, and my own conscience, forbid me to palliate with you. . . ." Bowyer movingly added, "You are now on a death-bed, a very little while, and *certainly* the last day—the last hour—the last moment will arrive—." Then he proceeded warmly and simply to invite her to place her faith in Christ. This would cause the angels to rejoice, and also "your dear niece, who is now in glory, will rejoice. I think she would address her glorious companions in such language as this—'Oh, blessed, blessed be God! My poor, dear aunt, who has all her life been totally regardless of her soul, in having set at nought the kind invitations of salvation, has this day become a sincere penitent;' and if anything could add to your dear niece's felicity, it would be, if she could add—'And the instrument which the Lord has been pleased to make use of on this happy occasion, has been a letter which my dear father has written to my aunt, respecting her soul'." The letter concluded by Bowyer representing Jesus as saying, "*I came into the world to save sinners, even the very chief of sinners; don't let the magnitude of your crimes prevent you; it is not even yet too late; come to me, and be happy for ever.*"

Bowyer's appeal had the desired effect, and at considerable length another death-bed repentance was proclaimed through the *Register*. What is significant for our understanding of Bowyer is that he was obviously one of those moderate Calvinists—like Andrew Fuller and his own pastor—who directed appeals to the consciences of their hearers. His own honesty in writing had happy results. Rippon in fact also published 'The Happy End' as a separate pamphlet, describing it as "A Present for an afflicted Friend, not likely to recover."[78]

Bowyer was a supporter of the Baptist Missionary Society. His name appears among the first published subscribers' list (1798-99), and he gave one guinea each year until his death.[79] When the first parts of Carey's translation of the Bible into Bengalee arrived in England, in about 1802, Bowyer was requested by the B.M.S. Committee to present a copy to King George III. Proceeding to Windsor, Bowyer wrote a long letter of 'three pages of Post Paper closely written'[80] which detailed the origin and progress of the Mission. This was read by the King 'with the most minute attention,' who, after receiving the book said, "You will be good enough to inform the Gentlemen of the Baptist Mission, that I receive the Book with great pleasure, and return them my best thanks, wishing them every possible success." This story was often repeated by Baptists as an indication of the monarch's piety and his sympathy with their work.[81]

Bowyer was on friendly terms with some of the Mission leaders. William Ward took to India, at the request of Bowyer, a quantity of prints for a firm in Calcutta.[82] Andrew Fuller, the secretary of the B.M.S., sat to Bowyer for a portrait. Either this original, or a print from the engraving, was given to Mrs. Fuller, who at her husband's request sent it to the Serampore missionaries.[83] But Bowyer's closest friend among the B.M.S. leaders was evidently the 'seraphic' Samuel Pearce, minister at Birmingham and devoted worker for the Mission. There are extracts of five letters from Pearce to Bowyer in Fuller's memoir for Pearce.[84] These suggest a warm friendship, for Pearce could write, "not a day has hurried by, since I parted with my dear friends in Pall Mall, but they have been in my affectionate remembrance."[85] Pearce wrote to his wife from Portsmouth on 29 January 1798, "I am most kindly entertained here by Mr. and Mrs. Shoveller . . . *They* have attended *seven* children to the gloomy tomb. . . ."[86] These hosts were presumably Mrs. Mary Bowyer's parents.[87] Bowyer sent to Pearce a print of C. F. Schwartz (1724-98), the famous missionary to Malabar. Pearce thanked Bowyer for the likeness of of a "man whom I have long been in the habit of loving and revering," and added that "the friendship it was intended to express, add to its worth."[88]

But Bowyer was a member of the Carter Lane Church in Southwark. His activities led him far afield, and his prestige presumably brought a certain lustre to a congregation which did however include a number of prosperous merchants, such as William Burls, treasurer of the Church and active in denominational affairs.[89] How was Bowyer regarded in the Church? Were they suspicious of his dealings with the nobility? Or were they proud of his social position—which included the employment of a footman—[90] and did this bring him special consideration? Little is known, but one instance suggests that Rippon at least was anxious not to offend Bowyer in any way, and to retain him in the membership of his Church.

The background of the incident must be briefly sketched. Following a few incidents of church members taking it upon themselves to preach in other churches without due recognition by Carter Lane of their preaching gifts, Rippon in 1788 had led the Church to agree to very strict rules about this matter.[91] These laid down correct procedure for calling members as 'public teachers,' including no preaching prior to the Church's approval, and warned that failure to comply with these rules would lead to exclusion from the fellowship. The rules were strictly observed, and two members were excluded in 1800 and 1801 for irregular preaching.[92]

But Bowyer, after his removal to Byfleet, had begun preaching to some of his neighbours. When he learnt that some members were displeased with this, Bowyer wrote a most illuminating letter to Rippon, which because of its interest is here given in full.[93]

"Byfleet Cobham Surry
6 Jany 1810

My dear Sir

Understanding that it is your opinion as well as that of several members of the Church that I ought not in a *public* manner to have addressed my poor neighbours in a way which is usually denominated preaching, without having first submitted my pretensions to this important office to the judgment of the Church, that they might have determined whether or not my abilities were sufficient for such an honourable and distinguished employment:— I must request my dear Sir that you will have the goodness at the next Church meeting to communicate to the Church the following statement.

That when I commenced these exercises I was really not conscious that I was acting in any way at variance with the orders & regulations of your Church, of which I am a member— If I had, I should probably have requested that my name might be withdrawn from its Books, because I do conceive such regulations (however beneficial its effects may be) not exactly accordant to the Word of God— but it is perfectly unnecessary here to enter at all into that question.— With regard to the Church & myself, tho' I am obliged to say that I think you have been rather remiss in not calling me to account before; if I have been acting in opposition to its laws; yet I cannot but feel pain in mentioning this, because my vanity will not let me account for the remission in any other way than supposing it must proceed from *personal regard* & for which I cannot but sincerely love you— at the same time for the honor of the Church I cannot consent that any personal respect you may feel for me, shall cause either you to bestow or me to accept any indulgence which wd not be granted to any other member.—

I have now been engaged between 4 & 5 years in speaking on a Sabbath day to my poor Neighbours & I am not without hope that the Lord has been pleased to own my labours— at any rate I am meeting with such encouragement to pursue my exertions that I do hope & trust if the Lord is pleased to enable me, that I shall never cease to promulgate his Gospel but with the termination of my life— now my dear Sir, let me appeal to you & my dear Brethren & Sisters of the Church— what would be the consequences if I was to comply with your present wishes— I should stand up there to address you from a text of scripture & for what purpose?— that you may determine whether I have proper gifts for speaking in a public manner to my fellow sinners— Now by this very act I should of course not only acknowledge that you had a right to decide that I was not qualified, but that I ought to be bound by your decision— it would therefore be impossible for me to comply with the wishes of the Church & presume a consistency of conduct.

It may perhaps be proper to notice that a very dear friend, a brother of the Church did mention the matter to me twice, & that my reply was, that I had no particular personal objection to speaking before the Church; but I most candidly acknowledge to you that I had not then digested the matter as I have since done— & that at that time neither its adoption or rejection appeared to me of any great importance;— but I am now fully persuaded that in complying with your wishes, not only the character of the Church but my own would be implicated— I therefore am convinced that the proper line of duty for myself is to request, (& the mode which will be most for the honor of the Church to adopt will be), that I may be permitted to withdraw my name from its Books, in making which request I have only to intreat my Dear Sir that you will believe that my affection for my dear Pastor, the Deacons, & every individual member of the Church has never to the present hour been in the least degree diminished, & that you & them will ever share not only in my most sincere regard but in my prayers at the throne of Grace that you may ever flourish as a Church of Christ of his own right hand planting & that when you are all seated around the Table at the marriage Supper of the Lamb you may there have to recognize

Your very affect Brother in Christ
R. Bowyer"

This letter was a credit to Bowyer: he was courteous, intelligent, and did not seek preferential treatment. It further confirms his genuine evangelical spirit and concern to spread the Gospel. He was now a man in his fifties, and his theological and personal reasons for not submitting to the Church's estimate of his abilities are understandable. However, the fact that Bowyer claimed not to know about the rules is surprising: he was a member when they were introduced, thirteen men had already submitted to extensive 'trials,' whilst a further two had been excluded for irregularity.[94] Does this imply that Bowyer's activity in the life of the Church was minimal? Bowyer's conclusion that the only honourable procedure was to withdraw his name from the membership seems both honest and valid.

What was Rippon's reaction? The Churchbook contains no indication that the contents of Bowyer's letter were ever brought before the Church. Not until eighteen months later, on 27 July 1811 did Rippon raise the matter; and then with consummate tact, as follows:[95]

> "Our Pastor reported, that he, the Deacons, and other Members of the Church, had, for a considerable time, noticed the laudable efforts of our Brother Robert Bowyer of Byfleet near Weybridge Surry, who at his own expence, had erected a place on his Estate, for the establishement of a Sunday School, and in which he had also been successfully instructing his neighbours in the way of Salvation.
>
> "The report appearing to give satisfaction. He proceeded to observe, That we have a standing rule which requires such persons who are inclined to the work of the Ministry to submit their gifts to the decision of the Church. But as our Brother Bowyer has been a Church Member upwards of Thirty Years, and is a person of acknowledged talents, by those who have heard him in his own house; and as his situation in life raises him above the influence of pecuniary considerations in the Ministerial work, he recommended it to the Church, in this extraordinary case to dispense with the standing rule; and without delay to encourage our Brother to go forward in the sacred work of the Ministry.
>
> "It was then moved by an unanimous shew of hands of the Brethren & Sisters resolved
>
> "That we cordially agree in the name of the great head of the Church to desire our Brother Robt Bowyer to preach the Gospel wherever God in his providence may call him to do it— humbly praying that the Lord may crown his endeavors with success.
>
> "Our Pastor then informed the Church that he would cheerfully transmit to our Brother a Copy of the pleasing transactions of the Church in this important business."

Thus the spirit of the law rather than the letter prevailed and common-sense saved the day. But Bowyer was the only member, out of twenty who were called to the ministry during Rippon's pastorate, to be exempted a preaching 'trial.' It seems highly probable that his 'extraordinary case' was the direct result of his 'situation in life,' but the ethics of the procedure are questionable. It is a tribute to the respect in which Bowyer was held that Rippon's diplomatic approach was unanimously adopted. Bowyer's relations with the Carter Lane Church remained cordial. On 23 October 1815 Mr. and Mrs. Bowyer, with Sister Shoveller, were dismissed "to assist in forming a Church in the neighbourhood of Byfleet Surry."[96] In an undated letter to Rippon, presumably from about this period, Bowyer forwarded details of four converts under his ministry who were coming up to Carter Lane for baptism, and noted that the new Church was to be styled, "The Church of Christ of the baptist denom meeting at the United Villages of Weybridge & Addlestone in the County of Surrey."[97] This Church was officially dated from 1815. From 1825 R. Grace was the pastor at Addlestone alone,[98] but Bowyer seems to have continued at Weybridge until near his death for his name appears in a list of churches and pastors published in 1831.[99]

Bowyer does not seem to have received much recognition from his fellow-Baptists, his death was unrecorded in the *Baptist Magazine* although the *Gentleman's Magazine* noted it.[100] He does not seem to have entered very fully into the main stream of Baptist corporate life, but retained all his life Baptist convictions. His artistic and publishing work is known only to a few experts in those fields, even the remarkable 'Bowyer's Bible' is comparatively unknown. Often the history of Baptist churches is confined to the work of pastors; the story of Robert Bowyer is a reminder that many of those who spent many years in the pew have a life worthy of recall from comparative oblivion.

NOTES

[1] Cf. *Dictionary of National Biography*, *s.v.*
[2] Carter Lane Churchbook, 10 March 1776.
[3] J. Rippon (ed.), *Baptist Annual Register*, iv, 1802, p. 762.
[4] i. A. Earland, *John Opie and his Circle*, 1911, incorporated family reminiscences 'taken down by Mrs. Asquith, from the reminiscences of Mrs. Stratton, Mrs. Bowyer's niece and adopted daughter, and used by kind permission of Miss Alice M. Westerdale, grand-daughter of Mrs. Stratton' (p. 71, note 2).
ii. B.(enjamin) (B.(ensley), son of Thomas Bensley who printed many of Bowyer's works, wrote some recollections of Bowyer in *Notes and Queries*, v, 1852, pp. 350 f.
[5] A. Earland, *op. cit.*, pp. 68 f.
[6] *Notes and Queries*, v, 1852, p. 350.
[7] Carter Lane Churchbook, 10 March 1776.
[8] *Ibid.*, 5 October 1777.
[9] *Ibid.*
[10] For Rippon, cf. *D.N.B.*, *s.v.*, although this is quite inadequate.
[11] G. Reynolds, *English Portrait Miniatures*, 1952, p. vi.
[12] For a review of these and other artists of the period, cf. G. Reynolds, *op. cit.*
[13] *Ibid.*, p. 151.
[14] *Memoirs of Thomas Jones* (Walpole Society, vol. 32), quoted by G. Reynolds, *op. cit.*, p. vii.
[15] A. Graves, *The Royal Academy of Arts. A Complete Dictionary of Contributors and their work from its foundation in 1769 to 1904*, 1905, i, *s.v.* 'Bowyer.'
[16] A. Graves, *A Dictionary of Artists who have exhibited Works in the Principal London exhibitions from 1760 to 1893*, 1895, p. 32.
[17] *Gentleman's Magazine*, lix, 1789, p. 281.
[18] G. Reynolds, *op. cit.*, p. 173.
[19] B. S. Long, *British Miniaturists*, 1929, p. 45.
[20] H. M. Hake, *Catalogue of Engraved British Portraits preserved in the Department of Prints and Drawings in the British Museum*, vi, 1925, p. 461.
[21] A. Earland, *op. cit.*, p. 71.
[22] *Notes and Queries*, v. 1852, p. 351.
[23] B. S. Long, *op. cit.*, p. 45.
[24] *Ibid.*
[25] Cp. H. M. Hake, *op. cit.*, p. 461; A. Graves, *The Royal Academy of Arts . . .*, *s.v.* 'Bowyer.'
[26] The print of Rippon was published by Bowyer in 1786, a copy was issued in J. Rippon, *A Selection of Hymns . . .*, 2nd ed., n.d., opp. title-page and in *Christian's Magazine*, i, 1790, opp. p. 435; H. Hake lists the print of Fuller as in the British Museum; and Pearce's portrait was published in *Baptist Register*, iii, 1798-1801, opp. title-page.
[27] H. Hake, *op. cit.*, p. 461. For Huntington (1745-1813), cf. *D.N.B.*, *s.v.*
[28] Information kindly supplied by Mr. J. H. Mayne, Deputy Keeper, Department of Paintings, Victoria & Albert Museum.
[29] Information supplied by Mr. Mayne and the Librarian, Windsor Castle (Mr. R. Mackworth-Young).
[30] G. C. Williamson, *The History of Portrait Miniatures*, i, 1904, p. 184.
[31] *Op. cit.*, p. 45.
[32] *Op. cit.*, p. 173.
[33] Cf. *Journal of the Warburg and Courtauld Institutes*, x, 1948, p. 83.
[34] T. S. R. Boase, 'Macklin and Bowyer,' *Journal of the Warburg and Courtauld Institutes* xxvi, 1963, pp. 148-77.
[35] *Gentleman's Magazine*, lxxxvi, 1816, ii, p. 88. For Williams, founder of the Royal Literary Fund, cf. *D.N.B.*, *s.v.*
[36] H. B. Wheatley, *Round about Piccadilly and Pall Mall . . .*, 1870, p. 335.
[37] *Gentleman's Magazine*, lxxvi, 1806, p. 431.
[38] *Ibid.*
[39] *Ibid.*
[40] Cp. T. S. R. Boase, *op. cit.*, p. 170.
[41] *Gentleman's Magazine*, lxxvii, 1807, p. 655.
[42] Royal Archives, Windsor Castle, Geo. 12946. (Extract supplied by the Librarian.)
[43] A. Earland, *op. cit.*, p. 70.
[44] Royal Archives, Windsor Castle, Geo. 26930.
[45] *Gentleman's Magazine*, n.s., ii, 1834, p. 221.
[46] Cf. A. Sparke, *The Bowyer Bible*, Bolton, 1920.
[47] *Op. cit.*, p. 70.
[48] J. Rippon to J. Morse, London 30 June 1791: original ms. in possession of the Historical Society of Pennsylvania, Philadelphia. For Morse (1761-1826), a leading Congregational minister, cf. *Dictionary of American Biography*, xiii, New York, 1934, pp. 245-47.
[49] J. Rippon to J. Manning, London 28 June 1791: original ms. in Brown University, Providence, R.I. For Manning (1738-91), cf. R. A. Guild, *Life, Times, and Correspondence of James Manning . . .*, 1864; *Dictionary of American Biography*, xii, 1834, pp. 249-51.
[50] James Fittler (1758-1835), marine engraver to George III, engraved much of Bowyer's work. Cf. *D.N.B.*, *s.v.*
[51] The original cover is preserved in the Angus Library, Regent's Park College, Oxford.
[52] A. Earland, *op. cit.*, p. 70.
[53] Proposed Accession to the Bodleian Library, in the Bodleian Library.
[54] *Ibid.*
[55] A. Sparke, *op. cit.*, p. 10.
[56] T. S. R. Boase, *op. cit.*, p. 168.
[57] Prospectus in the Bodleian Library.
[58] Ms. letter bound up with the prospectus.
[59] Ms. note added to the prospectus.
[60] A. Sparke, *op. cit.*, p. 7.
[61] Cf. *Ibid.*, pp. 6f. Sparke supposed that an examination of Bowyer's will would clarify her position: but examination of this has shown that she was not mentioned in it.
[62] *Op. cit.*, pp. 7-9.
[63] Information supplied by the Chief Librarian of the Central Library, Bolton (Mr. T. Ashworth).
[64] *Gentleman's Magazine*, n.s., ii, 1834, p. 221.
[65] In Somerset House, London. (Copy)
[66] For whom, c.f. *infra*.
[67] *Baptist Register*, iii, 1798-1801, p. 100.
[68] *Ibid.*, pp. 96-101.
[69] *Ibid.*, p. 101.
[70] *Ibid.*, p. 98.
[71] A. Earland, *op. cit.*, pp. 69 f.
[72] *Ibid.*, p. 70.
[73] Carter Lane Churchbook, 3 May 1812.
[74] A. Earland, *op. cit.*, p. 70.
[75] *Ibid.* The portraits are reproduced opp. pp. 68, 70, 78.
[76] *Op. cit.*, iv, 1802, pp. 753-63.
[77] Although only the initials are given in the body of the *Baptist Register*, Bowyer's name as author is given in the Index to the volume.
[78] Advertisement in T. Walker, *Second Appendix to Dr. Rippon's Selection of Tunes, consisting chiefly of originals*, n.d.
[79] Baptist Missionary Society *Periodical Accounts*.
[80] *Baptist Magazine*, v, 1813, p. 217.
[81] A. Fuller to W. Ward, Kettering, 31 December 1802, typescript copy in Angus Library (of original in the B.M.S. archives) described the event. Cp. *Baptist Magazine*, v, 1813, p. 217; R. Bowyer, *An Impartial Historical Narrative . . .*, 1823, p. 8; J. Ivimey, *History of the English Baptists*, iv, 1830, p. 106.
[82] A. Fuller to W. Ward, London, 8 May 1802, typescript copy in the Angus Library.
[83] *Ibid.*
[84] A. Fuller, *Memoirs of the late Rev. Samuel Pearce*, 1800, pp. 182, 186, 207, 235f.
[85] *Ibid.*, p. 186.
[86] *Ibid.*, p. 185.
[87] In addition to the two Mary Shovellers already noted in this study, there was a Rev. John Shoveller, who was minister at various times both at Portsea and Newport, Isle of Wight, and who was named as an executor in Robert Bowyer's will. Clearly these were all related, but full details are not known.
[88] A. Fuller, *op. cit.*, p. 236.
[89] For Burls (1763-1837), cf. E. A. Payne, *The Excellent Mr. Burls*, 1943.
[90] Reference in a letter from Rippon to Manning (see note 49 *supra*).
[91] These rules are given in S. J. Price, 'Brother Giles becomes a Recognized Minister,' *Baptist Quarterly*, v, 1930-31, pp. 37-41; H. Davies, *Worship and Theology in England, From Watts and Wesley to Maurice, 1690-1850*, 1961, pp. 137-39.
[92] Carter Lane Churchbook, 17 November 1800 and 20 April 1801.
[93] British Museum Additional Mss, 25386, f. 116.
[94] Details from a study of the Carter Lane Churchbook.
[95] *Ibid.*, 27 July, 1811.
[96] *Ibid.*, 23 October 1815.
[97] British Museum Additional Mss, 25386, f. 65.
[98] W. T. Whitley, *Baptists of London*, 1928, p. 147.
[99] *Baptist Magazine*, xxiii, 1831, p. 591.
[100] *Gentleman's Magazine*, n.s., ii, 1834, p. 221.

K. R. Manley.

APPENDIX C

The Goldsmiths' Company

Email reply from The Goldsmiths' Company.

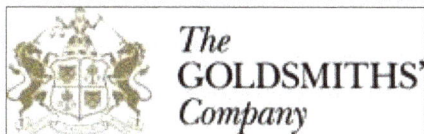

The
GOLDSMITHS'
Company

Company × Craft × Charity
Goldsmiths' Hall, Foster Lane, London
EC2V 6BN, United Kingdom
Tel: +44 (0)20 7606 7010/Fax: +44 (0)20 7606 1511

23 June 2022

Dear Tracy,

Thank you for your enquiry which has been forwarded to the library.

I am afraid that I have not been able to find a reference to William Shoveller in our index of freemen and apprentices, and his name also does not appear in our assay office records for this period. I have also checked a database of 18th century material relating to our missing marks period (largeworkers in the period c. 1758-1773; and smallworkers in the period c.1739-1758.) but with no success.

Sorry to be unable to help you further.

Kind regards,

Deborah Roberts

Library Administrator,
Hallmarking and Genealogical Research Officer
T: +44 (0)20 7606 7010 ex2192
E: Deborah.Roberts@thegoldsmiths.co.uk

APPENDIX D

The Surname Sabin(e): Its Origin & Development From Circa 1200

From... 'The Surname Sabin(e) - Its Origin and Development from circa 1200' by William Henry Waldo Sabine of London (in Roberts, G.B.,1985)

THE SURNAME SABIN(E)
ITS ORIGIN AND DEVELOPMENT FROM CIRCA 1200
Contributed by WILLIAM HENRY WALDO SABINE OF LONDON, ENGLAND

Various surmises have been made from time to time as to the origin of the surname Sabin(e), the most popular being that it is a name of Huguenot origin. Thus in *The New England Historical and Genealogical Register*, 1882, vol. xxxvi, p. 52, the Rev. Anson Titus published an article on "The Sabin Family in America," founded by a William Sabin who appeared at Rehoboth, Mass., in 1643, and who had 20 children by two wives. The author asserted that traditionally William was a Huguenot who had found refuge in England before coming to America.

Again, the "Encyclopaedia Britannica" (11th ed.) stated of General Sir Edward Sabine, the astronomer, that he was descended from a family believed to be of Italian origin. An Oxfordshire vicar, however, assured the contributor that all Sabines must have been Flemish weavers; while quite a few people are confident that they are descended from the Romans on the female side!

True, the Huguenot origin ascribed to William Sabin by Mr. Titus was immediately questioned (*The Register*, vol. xxxvii, p. 37) by Judge A. W. Savery, M.A., who pointed out the danger of accepting these unfounded but all too prevalent family traditions, and cited some mediaeval instances of the name to show that not only was the Huguenot theory baseless but quite unnecessary. Despite his admirably judicial confutation, and a capable note to a similar effect from W. P. A. Phillimore, M.A., B.C.L., of London (p. 311), the Huguenot theory still flourishes, as may be seen in the "Dict. of Am. Biog." under Wallace Sabine. Elsewhere it has been boldly printed that William Sabin came from La Rochelle (vol. iv of the "Compendium of American Genealogy"). The same work more recently claims (vol. vii, 1942, p. 878) that William Sabin was a "mem. of Huguenot family which sought refuge in England, came from Co. Hampshire, Eng., ca. 1640, settled at Rehoboth etc."

It will be observed that no evidence is advanced for thus continuing a mere tradition which Judge Savery and Mr. Phillimore had adequately and rightly dismissed 60 years before.

In order to give the Huguenot theory every possible chance to justify itself the author made extensive researches in England (his native country), spending much time at the British Museum examining printed lists of refugees. He also communicated with the Huguenot Society of London, but neither they nor he could find the slightest trace of any Huguenot at any time bearing the name Sabin(e) or one resembling it. Finally researches took the author to the Public Record Office, where he made a close study of the Subsidy Rolls (MS tax lists) of all aliens residing in England during

Researches carried on at the same time in the public records of England led to several instances of Englishmen named William Sabin(e) who were living at the beginning of the 17th century. Since the patriarch of Rehoboth was already the father of two children when he arrived at that town in 1643, and since he died about 1686, we may conclude that his birth date lies in the first 20 years of the century.

The author's opinion is that he was a member of the strongly Puritan family of Sabin(e)s who flourished at and near the village of Titchfield, Hampshire, in the 17th and 18th centuries. The Puritan vicar of Titchfield, the Rev. Urian Oakes, became pastor of the Church at Cambridge, Mass., and, in 1676, president of the College. It is possible that the following entry in the parish register of Titchfield, examined a few months ago, relates to the founder of the Rehoboth family: —

"October 1609. Baptized. William Sabin the xi daye."

Richard Sabine had married Mary Bushe on 29th October 1608, and these were probably William's parents. Naturally, until a positive link is found it will not be possible to say finally whether the Rehoboth Sabin came from Titchfield, or from Northamptonshire or Kent, to name the two other principal Sabin(e) centres, or from elsewhere. The date of the Titchfield William's birth, and the known Puritanism of his family, do however constitute some presumptive evidence in favour of identifying him with William of Rehoboth. Zachariah Sabin(e) of Titchfield (1593–1670), the author's own direct ancestor, was a patriarch comparable to William of Rehoboth, and it is interesting to compare his first name with the Nehemiahs, Hezekiahs, etc. which Mr. Titus recorded were imposed by William on his children.

One final word may be added to what has been said on the Huguenot theory. Difficult as it is to "prove a negative," the Subsidy Roll for Titchfield in 1525 (P.R.O.–E179/173/181), a

photostat which the author possesses, may be said to do it. It commences thus, giving name, assessment, and tax: —

John Dare shomaker	xx s		iiij	d
Thoms spayle laborer	xx s		iiij	d
John Jonson		xx s	iiij	d
Matthew Fussyn Frenchma	xl s		l	s
John Sabbyn	xx s		iiij	d

Thus it continues, all the villagers being assessed at 20s., and paying 4d. tax except the Frenchman who, as an alien, is doubly assessed and pays three times the tax. Comment is hardly needed.

It is, with complete confidence that the author asserts that, wherever the precise locality of his birth may have been, William Sabin of Rehoboth was an Englishman by origin.

At the present time there are in the United States a very considerable number of Sabin(e)s, most of whom, no doubt, can trace their origin to England, whether it be through the above William or another. A large number have for ancestor the Rev. James Sabine, of the Titchfield family, who arrived at Boston in 1818 (see "Family and Descendants of the Rev. J. Sabine", by John Dickinson Sabine, 1904); while others may be able to trace descent from that Robert Sabyn who was recorded among the inhabitants of Virginia in 1622–25 (Hotten's "Original Lists of Emigrants").

To all it will be of interest to consider some examples of the name, culled from the public records of England, and illustrating not only the antiquity of Sabin(e) as a surname, but also its development from a baptismal name, as indicated by Bardsley in his admirable "Dictionary of English and Welsh Surnames." It is easy to understand how the classical story of the seizure of the Sabine women by the Romans appealed with immense zest to the popular mind, and became almost as famous as the history of Alexander the Great. But the name of the Greek hero, being chiefly given to boys, has survived in greater numbers than Sabin(e), which naturally enough was more frequently used for girls. The masculine use of this name may be sometimes explained by clerks entering as "Sabinus" men with similar sounding Saxon or Norman names. Savin or Sawin is of frequent occurrence in Domesday Book and on coins of the period. One silver penny of Aethelred II in the author's collection was made by a moneyer called Sibwine of London. Other Saxon names which may have been precursors of Sabin(e) were Sbern, Sebbi, Sibbi, and Saba, the latter a diminutive of Saebeorht or Saberct. But in the century following the Norman Conquest, Saxon names rapidly died out, and were replaced by Norman and French forms.

The Great Rolls of the Pipe for Norfolk and Suffolk record in the year 1157, "And in payment of Sabine who was claimant through the death of her lord, 10s." Under date 1199 in the Rotuli Curiae Regis are named "Sabine daughter of Ralph" and "Ralph son of Sabin," both of Kent, while "Sabine wife of Sewal" is given under Essex.

In 1219, in a dower claim before the Bishop of Bath and Glastonbury, William de Leigh assigned to his wife "the foreign service of John Sabinesman and his belongings." The records of the Monastery of Glastonbury refer to the lands of "Dame Sabine (Domine Sabine)," and to "William son of Sabine." In this century hereditary surnames were gradually coming into use, and the words "son of" began to be left out.

In 1238 John Sabine, a priest, and many other persons were held in prison on a charge of breaking into the houses of the Jews at Norwich, and robbing them. The defendants were found not guilty (Close Rolls). Another scandal occurred in Cambridgeshire in 1261 when a pardon, issued from the Tower of London, was granted to Nicholas, son of William Sabine, for the death of Nicholas, son of John le Tunhirde, on testimony before the king that he killed him by misadventure (Cal. Patent Rolls).

The most shocking incident of all, according to the notions of the times, must have been the excommunication by the Archbishop of York in 1281 of Richard Sabine and other men of Beverley for the offence of appealing to Canterbury against his judgement. The excommunicated men were defiant, and became the centre of a political struggle of the first magnitude. The King intervened and ordered the Archbishop not to arrest them, whereupon the Pope (Martin IV) came to the aid of the Archbishop, confirming the excommunications (*Register of Archbp. Wichwane*).

The Hundred Rolls or Feudal Aids of Edward I (1272–1307) record numerous instances of the names, e.g. John Sabyn in Herefordshire, Mathilda Sabine in Buckinghamshire, Alicia Sabyn in Kent; while the variation Imbert' de Sabines is recorded in Sussex.

In the 14th century the occurrence of the name becomes so frequent that it is possible to cite only a few of the more interesting. In 1314, at York, on complaint by the Prior of the Holy Trinity, Robert Sabyn and upwards of 16 other persons were fined 20s for breaking into the houses of the Prior's manor of Leeds, carrying away his goods, and assaulting a monk and others (Cal. Patent Rolls).

Sabyncroft was the pleasant name of a place in Kent in 1319, while the Subsidy Rolls of 1327 refer to Sabineland in the parish of Chiddingley, Sussex. These Rolls name many individual Sabin(e)s, chiefly in Suffolk.

The killing of Roger Sabyn and two other men in Staffordshire in 1334 resulted in the outlawry and pursuit of about 20 persons, several of them knights, but pardons were subsequently granted to at least several of them. Pardons for slaying were not difficult to come by, and under 1361 we read, "Pardon to Henry son of Alan del Clyf of the king's suit for the death of Adam son of Roger Sabyn, as the king has learned by the record of William de Skipwith and his fellows, justices appointed to deliver the goal of York castle, that he killed him in self-defence."

In 1320 Richard Sabyn was elected to Parliament for Stafford borough; 1338 Walter Sabyne was "tenant at will" for 1 messuage and 1 bovate of land in Ravenglas, Cumberland; 1341 William, son of Sabina of Thornham, Norfolk, and William Sabbissone of Thornham were accused of assaulting the King's wool collector; 1345 Simon Sabyn and Roger Sabyn were charged, with others, on complaint of the Abbot of Ramsay with assaulting his servants "so that their life was despaired of;" 1355 John Sabyn, goldsmith, of Leicester, was before the mayor for allowing pigs to stray in the streets of the city at night; 1364 William Sabin was rector of Cranford, Middlesex; 1377 John Sabyne was presented to the living of St. Mary, Totnes; 1379 Robert Sabynson occurs in the Poll Tax for the West Riding of Yorkshire; 1381 Richard Sabyn was presented to the vicarage of Walberton, Chichester; 1385 a pardon was granted to Nicholas Blakhalle, parker, for the deaths of Richard Fisshere and Richard Sabyn of Woodstock; 1397 John Sabyn was a dyer in the City of London.

Sabynplace was recorded in the Calendar of Close Rolls, 1417, as the name of a messuage in the manor of Cudworth, Yorks. The Calendar of Patent Rolls in this century yields the following cases: in 1422 a pardon was granted to John Sabyne of Shorne, Kent, "bocher", for not appearing before Richard Norton and his fellows, late justices of the Bench, to answer the Abbot of St. Mary, Boxle, touching a debt of 4£; likewise in 1424 Robert Sabyn, parson of Bremhill, Wilts., clerk, received a pardon for not appearing touching a debt of 20£; in 1443 occurred a curious case in which William Sabyn, alias William Taylour, of Knebworth, taylour, and several other prisoners were said to have broken out of Hertford gaol by fictitious means. In 1447 there was a grant to John Cassons, esquire, of 9£. 6s. 4d. wherein William Hert of Lincoln stands charged in the Exchequer, of the price of divers goods of William Sabine, late of Saxby, co. Lincoln, "husbondman," forfeit by him for divers felonies. In 1450 Thomas Sabyne of Boughton Aluph, and Richard Sabyn, constable of Maidstone, Kent, took part in the popular insurrection under Jack Cade, later being included in a General Pardon which mentioned that they "in great numbers in divers places of the realm and specially in Kent and the places adjacent of their own presumption gathered together against the statutes of the realm."

Other instances, which must be briefly noted, are mainly from *Early Chancery Proceedings* (P.R.O.): 1454 Adam Sabyn, vicar of Arkesley, Essex; 1457 Isabel Sabyn, land in Boxley, Kent; ca. 1470 Symon Sabyn, land in Canterbury; 1460 William Sabyn, late of Fincham, co. Norfolk, pardoned for non-appearance; 1464 William Sabyn and Joan his wife tenants in Chedescy, Somerset; 1473 John Sabyn, notary, attested the will of John Pynnock, Burford, Oxon., because Pynnock's seal "is unknown to many"; 1481 William Sabin, bailiff, Northampton.

In the course of the 16th century the Sabin(e)s continued to be strongly marked in Northamptonshire and Kent, and in the counties adjoining. About 1520 they began to appear or to be recorded in various places in Hampshire, where their numbers became considerable. At the same time the name was becoming less marked in Suffolk where in the 14th century it was especially strong.

One Suffolk Sabin(e), who left no children, attained some note in the service of Cardinal Wolsey and Henry VIII. He was William Sabyn of Ipswich, who was captain of his own ship, "The Sabyn", in the war against France in 1512–13, and later became "Sergeant in the Army of Our Lord the King," a rank much more distinguished than it is to-day. He was granted a coat-of-arms which appears on his gravestone in the Church of St. Mary at the Key, Ipswich. A letter on the conduct of the war at sea, written by Sabyn to Cardinal Wolsey, is quoted in vol. x of the *Publications of the Navy Records Society*, where likewise appear full details of the ship "The Sabyne." In 1516, his father, John Sabyn, received a pension of 12d. a day for being "in arms in the King's service." William Sabyn benefited by the dissolution of the monasteries, and Henry granted him the site of the Black Friar's Monastery at Ipswich.

A loser by the Dissolution was Robert Sabyn (alias Bongay), prior of Sibton Abbey, Suffolk, who in 1536 found himself with only "a dispensation from his obedience without changing his habit." The *MSS of the Dean and Chapter of Wells* recorded, ca. 1557: —

John Sabyn, thus named in the will of Margaret Soper of Taunton, dated Jan. 24, 1545: — "To Sir John Sabyn, 20 markes to sing and celebrate masses for me for 2 years." A man of some substance must have been that Thomas Saben of Cornwall who in 1553 preferred to pay a composition or fine rather than accept a knighthood.

Only a selection of the early recorded instances of Sabin(e) is given above, while from the middle of this century onwards the examples in parish registers, probate registry indexes, and so forth, are as numerous as they are mostly of a very everyday character. Enough has been presented to establish that the Sabin(e) name is both ancient and widespread in England. Akin to it are such variants as Sabb and Sabey (son of Sabine), but we gladly disown that sad fellow William Sabbes who, when the fateful Spanish Armada was approaching England in 1588, is alleged in the *Acts of the Privy Council*, to have "diswaded and discounselled" the people of Wells and other coast towns (Norfolk) from contributing ships to her Majesties Navy.

APPENDIX E

Genealogy for the Sabine's of Patrixbourne & Canterbury, Kent, England

Compiled from... Tyler Index to Wills, 1460-1882 [Kent, England]

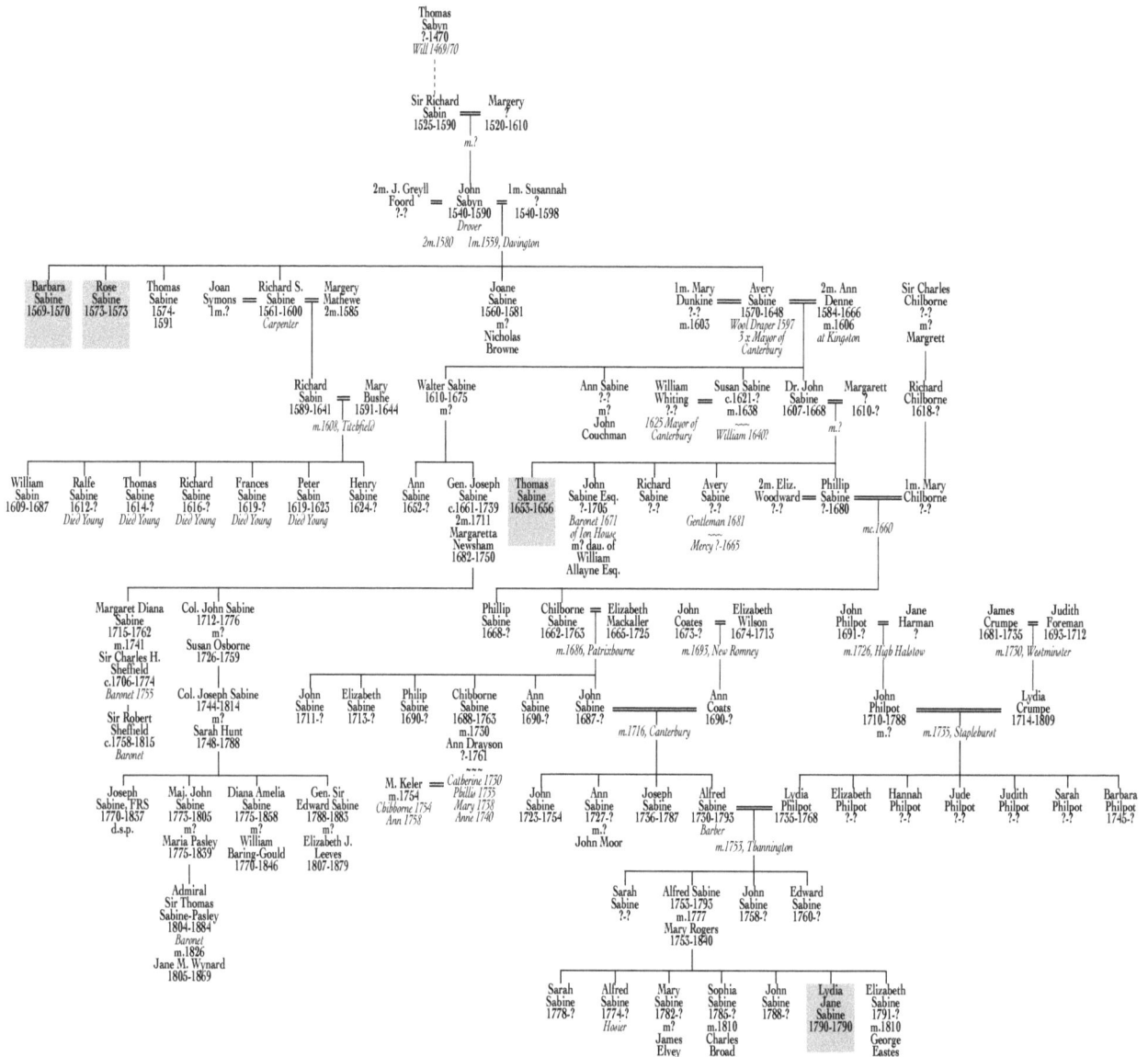

Thomas
Sabyn
?-1470
Will 1469/70

Sir Richard
Sabin
1525-1590 — Margery
1520-1610
m.?

2m. J. Greyll
Foord
?-? — John
Sabyn
1540-1590
Drover — 1m. Susannah
?
1540-1598

2m.1580   *1m.1559, Davington*

Barbara
Sabine
1569-1570

Rose
Sabine
1573-1573

Thomas
Sabine
1574-1591

Joan
Symons
1m.? — Richard S.
Sabine
1561-1600
Carpenter — Margery
Mathewe
2m.1585

Joane
Sabine
1560-1581
m?
Nicholas
Browne

1m. Mary
Dunkine
?-?
m.1603 — Avery
Sabine
1570-1648
Wool Draper 1597
3 x Mayor of Canterbury — 2m. Ann
Denne
1584-1666
m.1606
at Kingston

Sir Charles
Chilborne
?-?
m?
Margrett

Richard
Sabin
1589-1641
m.1608, Titchfield — Mary
Bushe
1591-1644

Walter Sabine
1610-1675
m?

Ann Sabine
?-?
m?
John
Couchman

William
Whiting
?-?

Susan Sabine
c.1621-?
m.1638
~~~
*William 1640?*
*1625 Mayor of Canterbury* — Dr. John
Sabine
1607-1668

Margarett
?
1610-?
*m.?*

Richard
Chilborne
1618-?

William
Sabin
1609-1687

Ralfe
Sabine
1612-?
*Died Young*

Thomas
Sabine
1614-?
*Died Young*

Richard
Sabine
1616-?
*Died Young*

Frances
Sabine
1619-?
*Died Young*

Peter
Sabin
1619-1623
*Died Young*

Henry
Sabine
1624-?

Ann
Sabine
1652-?

Gen. Joseph
Sabine
c.1661-1739
*2m.1711*
Margaretta
Newsham
1682-1750

Thomas
Sabine
1653-1656

John
Sabine Esq.
?-1705
*Baronet 1671*
*of Ten House,*
*m? dau. of*
*William*
*Allayne Esq.*

Richard
Sabine
?-?

Avery
Sabine
?-?
*Gentleman 1681*
~~~
Mercy ?-1665 — 2m. Eliz.
Woodward
?-?

Phillip
Sabine
?-1680

1m. Mary
Chilborne
?-?
mc.1660

Margaret Diana
Sabine
1715-1762
m.1741
Sir Charles H.
Sheffield
c.1706-1774
Baronet 1755

Sir Robert
Sheffield
c.1758-1815
Baronet

Col. John Sabine
1712-1776
m?
Susan Osborne
1726-1759

Col. Joseph Sabine
1744-1814
m?
Sarah Hunt
1748-1788

Phillip
Sabine
1668-?

Chilborne
Sabine
1662-1763 — Elizabeth
Mackaller
1665-1725
m.1686, Patrixbourne

John
Coates
1673-? — Elizabeth
Wilson
1674-1713
m.1693, New Romney

John
Philpot
1691-? — Jane
Harman
?
m.1726, Hugh Halstow

James
Crumpe
1681-1735 — Judith
Foreman
1693-1712
m.1730, Westminster

John
Sabine
1711-?

Elizabeth
Sabine
1713-?

Philip
Sabine
1690-?

Chilborne
Sabine
1688-1763
m.1730
Ann Drayson
?-1761

Ann
Sabine
1690-?

John
Sabine
1687-? — Ann
Coats
1690-?
m.1716, Canterbury

John
Philpot
1710-1788
m.? — Lydia
Crumpe
1714-1809
m.1755, Stapleburst

Joseph
Sabine, FRS
1770-1857
d.s.p.

Maj. John
Sabine
1773-1805
m?
Maria Pasley
1775-1839'

Diana Amelia
Sabine
1775-1858
m?
William
Baring-Gould
1770-1846

Gen. Sir
Edward Sabine
1788-1883
m?
Elizabeth J.
Leeves
1807-1879

Admiral
Sir Thomas
Sabine-Pasley
1804-1884
Baronet
m.1826
Jane M. Wynard
1805-1869

M. Keler
m.1754
Chilborne 1754
Ann 1758 — Catherine 1750
Phillis 1755
Mary 1738
Anne 1740

John
Sabine
1723-1754

Ann
Sabine
1727-?
m?
John Moor

Joseph
Sabine
1736-1787

Alfred
Sabine
1730-1793
Barber
m.1753, Thannington

Lydia
Philpot
1735-1768

Elizabeth
Philpot
?-?

Hannah
Philpot
?-?

Jude
Philpot
?-?

Judith
Philpot
?-?

Sarah
Philpot
?-?

Barbara
Philpot
1745-?

Sarah
Sabine
?-?

Alfred Sabine
1753-1793
m.1777
Mary Rogers
1753-1840

John
Sabine
1758-?

Edward
Sabine
1760-?

Sarah
Sabine
1778-?

Alfred
Sabine
1774-?
Hosier

Mary
Sabine
1782-?
m?
James
Elvey

Sophia
Sabine
1785-?
m.1810
Charles
Broad

John
Sabine
1788-?

Lydia
Jane
Sabine
1790-1790

Elizabeth
Sabine
1791-?
m.1810
George
Eastes

APPENDIX F

Oxford University Archives
Email reply from Oxford University Archives.

Oxford University Archives
Bodleian Library, Oxford OX1 3BG
+44 (0)1865 277145
www.bodleian.ox.ac.uk/oua

16th June 2022

Dear Tracy

Thank you for your enquiry about John Shoveller.

Joseph Foster used original records held by the University Archives to compile his Alumni Oxonienses. As you know, the entry for John Shoveller reads that he matriculated on 16 December 1817 from St Alban Hall. Matriculation was the process by which a student was admitted to the University, so Shoveller became a member of the University and began his University career on that date in 1817.

There are no dates of degrees recorded in Foster's entry for Shoveller and the University recorded degrees in Law as BCL (Bachelor in Civil Law) or DCL (Doctor in Civil Law) and would not have recorded it LL.D (Legum Doctor). I would interpret this that Shoveller already had this degree from elsewhere. There were very few Universities in the early nineteenth century and only Oxford and Cambridge in England at this date. (There were universities in Scotland and elsewhere in Europe). It is possible that Shoveller studied at Cambridge before coming to Oxford. However, it appears from his entry in Foster that Shoveller was not awarded a degree from Oxford.

St Alban Hall no longer exists as an academic hall as it was incorporated into Merton College in 1881. There are some surviving records of St Albans Hall held by Merton College. The following information appears on the Merton College Archives web site:

'St Alban Hall existed as an academic hall before the foundation of Merton College, and belonged to the convent of Littlemore. Merton purchased the hall in 1548 following the dissolution of the convent and exerted a strong influence over it, although in principle it remained an independent academic institution. The hall was finally annexed to Merton in 1881, when the remaining eighteen students were absorbed into the college. The buildings were largely rebuilt as St. Alban Quad between 1905 and 1910, although the Elizabethan entrance onto Merton Street still survives. Noteworthy members of St Alban Hall include Cardinal John Henry Newman (Vice-Principal 1825) and George FitzErnest (c.1815-17) natural son of Ernest, Duke of Cumberland and King of Hanover.

As an academic hall, St Alban Hall had no fellows or estates. Surviving records include the admission register, 1856-77, with retrospective lists of members from 1661; account books, 1856-79; and an incomplete series of buttery books, 1758-1847.'

Should you wish to contact the Archivist at Merton College, please see their web site at https://www.merton.ox.ac.uk/library-and-archives/college-archives

I have been unable to find other records relating to John Shoveller within a quick search of the catalogues held by the University Archives. You may of course wish to check other sources such as the Bodleian Archives and Manuscripts catalogue at https://archives.bodleian.ox.ac.uk/.

I am sure you may be aware of this or even have contributed to it, but there is other research on the Shoveller family available online at https://diaryofayounggenealogist.wordpress.com/2017/08/15/william-and-john-shoveller/

I hope this is of interest
Best wishes
Anna

Anna Petre
Assistant Keeper of the University Archives (Wed-Fri).

APPENDIX G

Clarence River & Grafton Timeline

From... Clarence River Historical Society - Timeline [www.clarencehistory.org.au/html/timeline.html].

Clarence River-Grafton Timeline 1830-1907

1830 Richard Craig escapes from Moreton Bay Penal colony.

1835 Craig pardoned, and tells his story of the 'Big River'.

1838 John Small sails to the Clarence on board the "Susan."
Cedar-getters arrive on the river.
Captain Butcher draws the first map of the Clarence River.

1839 Ship building yard and timber business established by Phillips & Cole.
The Big River was renamed the 'Clarence River.'
'Eatonswill Station' established by the Mylne Brothers.

1840 Route from the Tablelands made 'Craig's Line.'
'Ramornie Station' established by Dr. Dobie.
Post Office opened 1st October - Arthur Price postmaster.
'Yulgilbar' taken up by E.D.S. Ogilvie.
Susan Hann, first white child born in the Clarence River District.

1841 First store on Grafton side near the mouth of Alumny Creek established by Robert Bentley.

1842 'Clarence Settler's Arms' opened near Christopher Creek - Proprietor Durno.
Rev. J. McConnell appointed 1st Anglican clergyman of Grafton and the Clarence.

1843 First marriage recorded... Henry Wall & Bridget Connel?
Baptism of Mary Ann, daughter of Samuel and Arabella Avery.

1847 First Court held at Grafton, 5th April.
Court House built on river bank on Victoria Street.
Surveyor, W. W. Darke, surveyed the town of Grafton.

1850 Rev. John Gibson appointed Presbyterian Minister.

1851 Grafton gazetted as a town. First sale of town blocks.

1852 Government assisted school opened, although other private schools operated beforehand.

1854 Anglican Church built in Duke Street with A. E. Selwyn (minister).
Five acres granted on river to Grafton Steam Navigation Co.

1856 Grafton School of Arts formed.
First marriage in the new Anglican Church between Thomas Shoveller & Susan Hann.
Arrival of 182 German immigrants in March.

1857 First RC church on Nth. Coast opened at South Grafton.

1859 Clarence & Richmond Examiner first printed in Grafton June 28th.
First race meeting officially held.
German Club formed.
Grafton proclaimed a Municipality 28th July. J. E. Chapman, elected first Mayor.

1860 Volunteer Rifle Corps formed.
First Catholic School opened in Church at South Grafton.
Township of Copmanhurst gazetted.

1861 Methodist Church commenced in April at cnr. Prince and Fry Streets.
Baths built on the river bank.
Henry Kendall engaged as solicitor's clerk in Grafton.
Hand powered punt used for river crossing.
Branch of Ancient Order of Royal Foresters formed.
New Court House opened at cnr. Duke and Victoria Streets.

1862 Grafton Hospital Foundation Stone laid.

1863 Telegraph Station opened.
Grafton Hospital opened.
Father Murphy appointed resident priest.
Clarence River Jockey Club formed in August.
Gaol opened in Victoria Street.
Disastrous flood recorded in February (7.05m).
First harbour works at Clarence Heads.

1864 Branch of the 'Oddfellows Lodge' first opened.

1866 Formation of Clarence Pastoral and Agricultural Society.
Foundation Stone of St. Marys Church laid.
Post Office in South Grafton opened.
Ramornie Meat Works opened with Joseph Page as manager.

1867 Bishop Dr. William Collinson Sawyer appointed Anglican Bishop of Grafton.
St. Marys Church opened.
South Grafton School opened as a private school.

1868 Bishop Sawyer is drowned in a boating accident.
First steam punt at Dobie St. was commissioned.
Catholic School opened in Grafton.

1869 The Earl & Countess of Belmore visit the Clarence District.
Belmore Sugar Mill at Ulmarra opened.
Free Presbyterian Church commenced.
Royal Theatre erected in Pound Street, Grafton.

1870 Solferino & Dalmorton Goldfields opened up.

1871 Tannery established cnr. Prince and Hoof Streets.
Grafton Grammar School established by Frederick Newton.
Public School Buildings opened at cnr. Queen and Bacon Streets.

1872 Clarence and New England Railway League formed.

1874 Foundation stone of the Cathedral is laid.
Grafton Argus Newspaper established.
Council adopts a 'Tree Planting Policy'.
Post Office foundation stone laid.
Bawden Bridge opened (April).

1875 Lutheran Church established.

1876 Memorial Park at the Boulevarde dedicated.
Lutheran Church built at cnr. Alice and Oliver Streets.
Baptist Church established with the Minister being the Rev. Richard Fane Becher.

1878 Grafton Grammar School new building opened in Mary Street.
Post Office building on present site opened.
Shares offered in Grafton Gas Lighting Co.

1879 Commercial Bank of Sydney constructed cnr. Prince and Fitzroy Streets.
Volunteer Fire Brigade commenced.

1880 Court House constructed on present site.

1882 Wreck of "SS New England."

1883 Grafton Gaslight Co. formed.

1884 Christ Church Cathedral dedicated.
Salvation Army commenced.
Arrival of Sisters of Mercy.

1885 Grafton proclaimed a city.
Grafton Volunteer Water Brigade founded.
Baptist Church opened in March.

1886 St. Andrews Presbyterian Church opened.
Grafton Club in Fitzroy Street opened.

1888 Criterion Hall opened.

1889 Zietsch's Cordial Factory commenced.
First milk separator in district demonstrated at Grafton Show.

1890 Largest recorded flood in March (8.13m).

1891 District Cricket Association formed.

1892 Grafton Dairy Company began operations.
Grafton Cycle Club formed.

1893 Gaol opened on present site.
Floods in February (7.95m) & June (7.45m).

1897 South Grafton Municipal Council formed.
Town Hall & Council Chambers erected in Prince Street.

1899 McKittrick Park dedicated.
Grafton Clarion Newspaper established at South Grafton.

1900 Reticulated water supply for laying of dust in Prince Street.

1901 Golf Club formed - course now Westlawn Services Golf course.
Turning of first sod Grafton-Casino Railway.

1902 Experiment Farm established.

1903 Grafton Telephone Exchange opened New Years day.
Carrs Creek School of Arts formed.
First railway line to Grafton opened via Casino and Lismore.

1904 Coldstream Bridge opened.

1906 Showground moved to present site in Prince street.
McFarlane Bridge at Maclean opened.

1907 Jacaranda Avenue created.

APPENDIX H

Shoveller
Descendants That Served In Australian Military Forces

Roll of Honour
Shoveller

Descendants That Served In

Australian Military Forces

Name	Lifespan	Conflict	Reg. No.	Rank	Unit	Page
Carr, Lloyd Meally	1922-1992	WWII	#NX204180	Captain	60 Dental Unit	323
Shoveller, Alfred William	1894-1974	WWI	?	Private	File Unopened	227
Shoveller, Alfred John R.	1918-1975	WWII	#NX92938	Private	Inf. Pool	227
Shoveller, John Alfred	?-?	WWII	?	?	?	228
Shoveller, John Harold	1899-1973	WWI	#N96101	Horse Driver	Not Assigned	227
Shoveller, John Harold Jr.	1919-?	WWII	#NX68566	Private	2/4th AIF Battalion	228
Shoveller, Roy Drew	1920-1956	WWII	#NX69452	Private	2/4th AIF Battalion	228
Shoveller, Russell Lorraine	1916-1993	WWII	#N181715	Sergeant	AMF Wing RGH	323
Shoveller, Thomas James	1926-?	WWII	#N481611	Private	113 CMH	323

* - Died On Active Duty
pow - Prisoner of War

APPENDIX I

Shoveller Ancestors - UK Database by Event & Year (1735-1931)

Event	Year	Father	Mother	Surname	First	BMD Date	Bp./Bur. Date	Event Place	County	Death Age	Spouse	Sex	Birth Vol.	Birth Page
Birth & Bap	1737	?	?	Shoveller	John	-	-	?	?	?	-	-		
Birth & Bap	1738	Thomas	?	Shoveller	Mary	-	19 Sep 1736	St. Mary's, Portsea, Hampshire, ENG.	Hampshire	?	-	-		
Birth & Bap	1738	Thomas	?	Shoveller	Thomas	-	-	?	?	?	-	-		
Birth & Bap	1740	Thomas	?	Shoveller	Richard	-	24 Jan 1740	Portsea, Hampshire, England	Hampshire	?	-	-		
Birth & Bap	1741	Thomas	?	Shoveller	William	-	-	?	?	?	-	-		
Birth & Bap	1756	John	Mary	Shoveller	Mary	-	25 Apr 1756	St. Mary's, Portsea, Hampshire, ENG.	Hampshire	?	-	-		
Birth & Bap	1757	John	Mary	Shoveller	Elizabeth	-	04 Dec 1757	St. Mary's, Portsea, Hampshire, ENG.	Hampshire	3	-	-		
Birth & Bap	1760	John	Mary	Shoveller	John	-	06 Apr 1760	St. Mary's, Portsea, Hampshire, ENG.	Hampshire	?	-	-		
Birth & Bap	1762	John	Mary	Shoveller	Elizabeth	-	02 May 1762	St. Mary's, Portsea, Hampshire, ENG.	Hampshire	?	-	-		
Birth & Bap	1764	John	Mary	Shoveller	William	-	22 Apr 1764	St. Mary's, Portsea, Hampshire, ENG.	Hampshire	?	-	-		
Birth & Bap	1764	John	Mary	Shoveller	Francis (m)	-	16 Sep 1764	St. Mary's, Portsea, Hampshire, ENG.	Hampshire	?	-	-		
Birth & Bap	1766	William	Elizabeth	Shoveller	Elizabeth	-	19 Oct 1766	St. Mary's, Portsea, Hampshire, ENG.	Hampshire	?	-	-		
Birth & Bap	1766	John	Mary	Shoveller	Thomas	-	02 Mar 1766	St. Mary's, Portsea, Hampshire, ENG.	Hampshire	?	-	-		
Birth & Bap	1769	William	Elizabeth	Shoveller	Elizabeth	-	08 Oct 1769	St. Mary's, Portsea, Hampshire, ENG.	Hampshire	?	-	-		
Birth & Bap	1771	William	Elizabeth	Shoveller	Anne	-	23 Jun 1771	St. Mary's, Portsea, Hampshire, ENG.	Hampshire	?	-	-		
Birth & Bap	1775	Thomas	Ann	Shoveller	Nanny	-	07 May 1775	St. Mary's, Portsea, Hampshire, ENG.	Hampshire	?	-	-		
Birth & Bap	1775	Thomas	Ann	Shoveller	Daniel	-	15 Oct 1775	St. Mary's, Portsea, Hampshire, ENG.	Hampshire	?	-	-		
Birth & Bap	1777	William	Elizabeth	Shoveller	Sally	-	07 Sep 1777	St. Mary's, Portsea, Hampshire, ENG.	Hampshire	?	-	-		
Birth & Bap	1783	Thomas	Ann	Shoveller	Nancy	-	04 May 1783	Portsea, Southampton, Hampshire, England	Hampshire	?	-	-		
Birth & Bap	1785	Thomas	Ann	Shoveller	Harriet	-	08 Aug 1785	St. Mary's, Portsea, Hampshire, ENG.	Hampshire	?	-	-		
Birth & Bap	1789	William	Mary	Shoveller	John	21 Oct 1789	06 Nov 1789	Skinner St. Independent, Poole, Dorset, ENG.	Dorset	?	-	-		
Birth & Bap	1791	William	Mary	Shoveller	William	05 Mar 1791	26 Mar 1791	Orange St. now King St. Independent, Portsea, Hampshire, ENG.	Hampshire	?	-	-		
Birth & Bap	1794	William	Mary	Shoveller	Mary	05 Feb 1794	14 Oct 1794	Orange St. now King St. Independent, Portsea, Hampshire, ENG.	Hampshire	?	-	-		
Birth & Bap	1796	William	Mary	Shoveller	Jane	09 Mar 1796	13 Apr 1796	Orange St. now King St. Independent, Portsea, Hampshire, ENG.	Hampshire	?	-	-		
Birth & Bap	1798	William	Mary	Shoveller	Elizabeth	20 Mar 1798	-	Portsea, Hampshire, England	Hampshire	?	-	-	RG4_0867	
Birth & Bap	1801	William	Ann	Shoveller	Eliza	-	19 Jun 1801	St. Mary's, Portsea, Hampshire, ENG.	Hampshire	?	-	-		
Birth & Bap	1806	Thomas	Ann	Shoveller	James Thomas	03 Sep 1806	14 Dec 1806	St. Thomas, Portsmouth, Hampshire, ENG.	Hampshire	?	-	-		
Birth & Bap	1808	Thomas	Ann	Shoveller	Ann	03 Feb 1808	02 Mar 1808	St. Thomas, Portsmouth, Hampshire, ENG.	Hampshire	?	-	-		
Birth & Bap	1809	Thomas	Ann	Shoveller	Eliza	-	01 Mar 1809	St. Thomas, Portsmouth, Hampshire, ENG.	Hampshire	?	-	-		
Birth & Bap	1812	Mr. John (LLD)	Elizabeth	Shoveller	Sarah Sabine	21 Dec 1812	30 Jan 1813	Orange St. now King St. Independent, Portsea, Hampshire, ENG.	Hampshire	?	-	-		
Birth & Bap	1813	Mr. John (LLD)	Elizabeth	Shoveller	Mary Elizabeth	07 Dec 1813	13 Feb 1814	Orange St. now King St. Independent, Portsea, Hampshire, ENG.	Hampshire	?	-	-		
Birth & Bap	1813	Thomas	Ann	Shoveller	Thos. Sheppard	-	07 Jul 1813	St. Thomas, Portsmouth, Hampshire, ENG.	Hampshire	?	-	-		
Birth & Bap	1814	Mr. John (LLD)	Elizabeth	Shoveller	Jane Allen	22 Oct 1814	27 Dec 1814	Orange St. now King St. Independent, Portsea, Hampshire, ENG.	Hampshire	59	-	-	3a	100
Birth & Bap	1816	Mr. John (LLD)	Elizabeth	Shoveller	Sarah Sabine	19 Jul 1816	17 Sep 1816	Orange St. now King St. Independent, Portsea, Hampshire, ENG.	Hampshire	?	-	-	RG4_4675	
Birth & Bap	1816	William	Elizabeth	Shoveller	William	16 May 1816	-	21 Lisle St., Cripplegate, London, ENG.	London	?	-	-		
Birth & Bap	1818	Dr. John (LLD)	Elizabeth	Shoveller	John	10 Jun 1818	14 Jul 1818	Orange St. now King St. Independent, Portsea, Hampshire, ENG.	Hampshire	?	-	-	RG4_4675	
Birth & Bap	1818	William	Elizabeth	Shoveller	John	19 Jun 1818	19 Jun 1818	21 Lisle St., Cripplegate, London, ENG.	London	?	-	-		
Birth & Bap	1819	Wiggins	?	Shoveller	Hannah	09 Nov 1819	-	Christchurch, Hampshire, ENG.	Hampshire	72	-	-	2b	419
Birth & Bap	1819	William	Elizabeth	Shoveller	Robert	-	-	21 Lisle St., Cripplegate, London, ENG.	London	?	-	-		
Birth & Bap	1820	Dr. John (LLD)	Elizabeth	Shoveller	Thomas Eastman	11 Apr 1820	01 Sep 1820	Orange St. now King St. Independent, Portsea, Hampshire, ENG.	Hampshire	?	-	-	RG4_4675	
Birth & Bap	1821	William	Elizabeth	Shoveller	Elizabeth Meta	14 Dec 1821	-	Kentiot Town, Middlesex, England	London	?	-	-		
Birth & Bap	1822	Dr. John (LLD)	Elizabeth	Shoveller	Mary Elizabeth	14 Mar 1822	07 Jun 1822	Orange St. now King St. Independent, Portsea, Hampshire, ENG.	Hampshire	?	-	-		
Birth & Bap	1824	Dr. John (LLD)	Elizabeth	Shoveller	William Henry	30 Apr 1824	31 Dec 1824	Orange St. now King St. Independent, Portsea, Hampshire, ENG.	Hampshire	?	-	-		
Birth & Bap	1826	Dr. John	Elizabeth	Shoveller	Martha	26 Apr 1826	09 Jun 1826	Orange St. now King St. Independent, Portsea, Hampshire, ENG.	Hampshire	?	-	-		
Birth & Bap	1827	Dr. John	Elizabeth	Shoveller	Thomas Eastman	25 May 1827	11 Jul 1827	Orange St. now King St. Independent, Portsea, Hampshire, ENG.	Hampshire	?	-	-		
Birth & Bap	1827	William	Elizabeth	Shoveller	Hannah Mary	14 Aug 1827	-	Lisle St., Middlesex, England	London	?	-	-		
Birth & Bap	1832	William	Elizabeth	Shoveller	Samuel	23 Mar 1832	-	No 21 Lisle Street, --, Middlesex	London	?	-	-		
Birth & Bap	1848	John Hampden	Hannah	Shoveller	Hannah Mary	-	-	St. Luke	London	?	-	-	RG5_152	306
Birth & Bap	1850	John Hampden	Hannah	Shoveller	Helen Elizabeth	-	-	Haverstock Terrace, Hampstead, London, ENG.	London	?	-	-	2	230
Birth & Bap	1851	John Hampden	Hannah	Shoveller	John Hampden	-	-	Hampstead, London, ENG.	London	?	-	-	3	69
Birth & Bap	1851	William Henry	Mary Anne	Shoveller	Ellen	-	-	St. Giles	London	?	-	-	III, 251, 31	1
Birth & Bap	1853	John Hampden	Hannah	Shoveller	Harriet Jessie	-	-	Hampstead, London, ENG.	London	?	-	-	1a	437
Birth & Bap	1854	William Henry	Mary Anne	Shoveller	William Henry	-	-	St. Pancras	London	?	-	-	1b	8
Birth & Bap	1855	John Hampden	Hannah	Shoveller	Alice Frances	-	-	Hampstead, London, ENG.	London	?	-	-	1a	437
Birth & Bap	1856	William Henry	Mary Anne	Shoveller	Ada Mary	-	-	Kensington	London	19	-	-	1a	3

Event	Year	Father	Mother	Surname	First	BMD Date	Bp./Bur. Date	Event Place	County	Death Age	Spouse	Sex	Birth Vol.	Birth Page
Birth & Bap	1857	John Hampden	Hannah	Shoveller	Sidney Howard	-	-	Hampstead, London, ENG.	London	?	-	-	1a	476
Birth & Bap	1860	John Hampden	Hannah	Shoveller	Edith Florence	-	-	Hampstead, London, ENG.	London	?	-	-	1a	536
Birth & Bap	1862	John Hampden	Hannah	Shoveller	Alfred Russell	-	-	Hampstead, London, ENG.	London	?	-	-	1a	544
Birth & Bap	1862	William Henry	Mary Anne	Shoveller	Eva Rosa Jane	-	-	Hendon	London	?	-	-	3a	90
Birth & Bap	1877	John Hampden	Marion	Shoveller	John Sydney	-	-	Kingston, Surrey, ENG.	Surrey	?	-	-	2A, 288	
Birth & Bap	1879	John Hampden	Marion	Shoveller	Marion Winifred	11 May 1879	-	Park Rd Villa, Norbiton, Kingston, Surrey, ENG.	Surrey	?	-	F	2a	312
Birth & Bap	1881	John Hampden	Marion	Shoveller	Stanley Howard	-	-	Kingston, Surrey, ENG.	Surrey	?	-		2a	329
Marriages	1735	?	?	Shoveller	Thomas (of Portsea)	-	16 Nov 1735	Alverstoke, Hampshire, ENG.	Hampshire	?	Mary Benson (of Portsea)			
Marriages	1755	?	?	Shoveller	John	-	13 Jul 1755	Wymering, Hampshire, ENG.	Hampshire	?	Mary ?			
Marriages	1760	?	?	Shoveller	William	-	10 Nov 1760	St. Mary's, Portsea, Hampshire, ENG.	Hampshire	?	Elizabeth Hall			
Marriages	1777	John	Mary	Shoveller	Mary	-	14 Jul 1777	St. Thomas, Portsmouth, Hampshire, ENG.	Hampshire	?	Robert Bowyer	M		
Marriages	1783	?	?	Shoveller	John	-	04 Feb 1783	St. Mary's, Portsea, Hampshire, ENG.	Hampshire	?	Susanna Horsey	F		
Marriages	1789	?	?	Shoveller	William	-	05 Jan 1789	Warnford, Hampshire, England	Hampshire	?	Mary Bignell	F		
Marriages	1790	William	?	Shoveller	Francis (m)	-	30 May 1790	Gosport, Southampton, England	Hampshire	?	Susannah Wood	F		
Occupation	1816	?	?	Shoveller	Mr John (Schoolmaster)	-	8 Jul 1816	King's House Academy, King's Terrace, nr. Portsmouth	Hampshire	?	-	M		
Marriages	1803	?	?	Shoveller (of Portsea)	Susanna	-	01 Nov 1803	St. Mary's, Portsea, Hampshire, ENG.	Hampshire	?	William Ellis Jnr (of Portsea)	F		
Marriages	1805	?	?	Shoveller	Thos. (bro to Eliz.)	-	17 Nov 1805	Portsea, Southampton, ENG.	Hampshire	S	Ann Paffard	M		
Marriages	1805	Thomas	?	Shoveller	Elizabeth (sis to Thos.)	-	20 Nov 1805	St. Thomas, Portsmouth, Hampshire, ENG.	Hampshire	?	Joseph Paffard	F		
Marriages	1806	Thomas	Mary	Shoveller	Anne	-	03 Oct 1806	Wymering, Hampshire, ENG.	Hampshire	?	John Squibb	F		
Marriages	1812	William	Mary	Shoveller	John	-	26 Mar 1812	St. Mary's, Portsea, Hampshire, ENG.	Hampshire	?	Elizabeth Eastman	M		
Marriages	1815	?	?	Shoveller	William	-	13 May 1815	St. Martin In The Fields, Westminster, London, ENG.	London	?	Elizabeth Dunt	F		
Marriages	1819	?	?	Shoveller	Rev. John	-	13 Apr 1819	Melksham, Wiltshire, ENG.	Wiltshire	?	Eliza Horsey (of Taunton)	F		
Marriages	1821	William	Mary	Shoveller	Mary	-	23 May 1821	St. Mary's, Portsea, Hampshire, ENG.	Hampshire	?	Thomas Stratton	M		
Marriages	1822	William	Mary	Shoveller	Eliza	-	26 Jun 1822	St. Mary's, Portsea, Hampshire, ENG.	Hampshire	S	James Roberton	M		
Marriages	1826	?	?	Shoveller (of Portsea)	John	-	13 Jul 1826	Melksham, Wiltshire, ENG.	Wiltshire	?	Sarah Hook (of Melksham)	F		
Marriages	1832	?	?	Shoveller	Eliza	-	31 Jul 1832	Portsmouth, Hampshire, England	Hampshire	?	James Smith	M		
Marriages	1837	William	Elizabeth	Shoveller	William	-	-	?	?	?	Elizabeth Bailey	M	16	10
Marriages	1846	Dr. John (LLD)	Elizabeth	Shoveller	Mary Elizabeth	1846	-	Banbury, Oxfordshire, ENG.	Oxford	?	James Roberton	M	2	101
Marriages	1847	Dr. John (LLD)	Elizabeth	Shoveller	John	18 May 1847	-	St. Andrew By The Wardrobe And St. Ann Blackfriars, London, ENG.	London	?	Hannah Wiggins (F= William Wiggins)	F	1b	233
Marriages	1854	Dr. John (LLD)	Elizabeth	Shoveller	William Henry	1854	-	St. Pancras	London	?	Mary Ann Smith	F	1b	568
Marriages	1854	Thomas	?	Shoveller	John	1854	-	St. Giles	London	?	Mary Ann Rudkin	F	1b	291a
Marriages	1870	John Hampden	Hannah	Shoveller	Hannah Mary	12 May 1870	-	At Maitland Park, Pancras	London	?	William Langley	M	1b	764
Marriages	1873	?	?	Shoveller	Ellen	1873	-	Portsea, Hampshire, England	Hampshire	?	James Shirvell	M	2b	186
Marriages	1873	John Hampden	Hannah	Shoveller	Hannah Mary	1873	-	Pancras	London	?	James Roberton	F	2a	425
Marriages	1876	John Hampden	Hannah	Shoveller	John Hampden	29 Jun 1876	-	At Christchurch, New Malden, Kingston, Surrey, ENG.	Surrey	?	Marion C. Page	M	2a	271
Marriages	1881	John Hampden	Hannah	Shoveller	Harriet Jessie (of Westmeon, New Barnet)	11 May 1881	-	At New Barnet	Hampshire	?	Alfred William Ostler	M	3a	295
Marriages	1883	John Hampden	Hannah	Shoveller	Edith Florence	6 Sept 1883	-	Congregational Church, New Barnet	London	?	Percy Johnson	M	3a	
Marriages	1903	John Hampden	?	Shoveller	Marion Winifred (May)	8 Oct 1903	-	St Lukes Church, Kingston-on-Thames	Hampshire	?	Bartram Waller Attlee (related to PM)			
Deaths	1798	?	Ann	Shoveller	John (East St)	08 Jun 1798	-	Portsea, Southampton, ENG.	?	0	-			
Deaths	1808	Thomas	Ann	Shoveller	Ann	30 Sep 1808	-	?	?	0	-			
Deaths	1813	Mr. John (LLD)	Elizabeth	Shoveller	Sarah Sabine	21 Jan 1813	-	Orange St, now King St. Independent, Portsea, Hampshire, ENG.	Hampshire	0	-			
Deaths	1814	Mr. John (LLD)	Elizabeth	Shoveller	Mary Elizabeth	6 May 1814	-	Orange St, now King St. Independent, Portsea, Hampshire, ENG.	Hampshire	0	-			
Deaths	1814	Thomas	Ann	Shoveller	Thos. Sheppard	13 Jan 1814	-	?	?	?	-			
Deaths	1816	Rev. Joseph Horsey	?	Shoveller	Mrs (wife of Rev. John Shoveller)	15 Feb 1816	-	?	Hampshire	?	-			
Deaths	1818	?	?	Shoveller	Mrs (mother of Dr. John Shoveller, of Poole)	?? Jan 1818	-	?	Dorset	?	-			
Deaths	1825	Dr. John (LLD)	Elizabeth	Shoveller	Sarah Sabine	06 Jan 1825	-	Orange St, now King St. Independent, Portsea, Hampshire, ENG.	Hampshire	8	-			
Deaths	1825	Dr. John (LLD)	Elizabeth	Shoveller	Thomas Eastman	18 Jun 1825	-	Orange St, now King St. Independent, Portsea, Hampshire, ENG.	Hampshire	5	-			
Deaths	1826	Rev. R. Horsey	?	Shoveller	Eliza (wife of Rev. J. Shoveller Jnr)	1826	-	Bridgnorth	Midlands	30	-			
Deaths	1826	Dr. John	Elizabeth	Shoveller	Martha	01 Apr 1827	-	Orange St, now King St. Independent, Portsea, Hampshire, ENG.	Hampshire	1	-			
Deaths	1831	Rev. John	Elizabeth	Shoveller	Rev. John (of Portsea)	6 Dec 1831	-	Kingston, Jamaica (w Baptist Missionary Society)	Jamaica	?	-			
Deaths	1846	William?	?	Shoveller	William	1846	-	Strand	London	?	-	M	1	281
Deaths	1848	William?	Mary?	Shoveller	Jane	1848	-	Portsea, Hampshire, England	Hampshire	78	-	F	7	109
Deaths	1849	William	?	Shoveller	Thomas	1849	-	Kings Terrace, Southsea, Portsea	Hampshire	?	-	F	7	111
Deaths	1850	?	?	Shoveller	John	1850	-	Portsea, Hampshire, England	Hampshire	?	-	F	7, 139	
Deaths	1852	?	?	Shoveller	Elizabeth (wife of Rev. John Shoveller, LL.D.)	22 July 1852	-	Ealing, Brentford	London	68	-		3a	38
Deaths	1871	Dr. John (LLD)	Elizabeth	Shoveller	John	1871	-	St. Saviour Southwark, London, ENG.	London	53	-	M	1D, 101, 175	
Deaths	1874	Dr. John (LLD)	Elizabeth	Shoveller	Jane Allen	1874	-	Herdon	London	59	-	M	3a	100
Deaths	1874	?	?	Shoveller	Elizabeth Meta	1874	-	Thanet	Kent	52	-	M	2a	478
Deaths	1875	William Henry	Mary Anne	Shoveller	Ada Mary	1875	-	Kensington	London	19	-	F	1a	3
Deaths	1891	William	?	Shoveller	Hannah	1891	-	Christchurch, Hampshire, ENG.	Hampshire	72	-	M	2b	419
Deaths	1899	Dr. John (LLD)	Elizabeth	Shoveller	John	1899	-	Christchurch, Hampshire, ENG.	Hampshire	81	-	M	2B, 545, 143	
Deaths	1931	?	?	Shoveller	John H.	1931	-	Kingston, Surrey, ENG.	Surrey	79	-	M	2A, 582, 41	

APPENDIX J

Unknown Shovellers - UK Database by Event & Year (1696-1913)

Event	Year	Father	Mother	Surname	First	BMD Date	Bp./Bur. Date	Event Place	County	Death Age	Spouse	Sex	Birth Vol.	Birth Page
Birth & Bap	1696	James	Ann	Shoveller	Jane		24 May 1696	Wingham, Kent, England	Kent					
Birth & Bap	1697	?	?	Shoveller	John		?	?	?					
Birth & Bap	1698	James	Ann	Shoveller	Elizabeth		29 Jun 1698	Wingham, Kent, England	Kent					
Birth & Bap	1700	James	Ann	Shoveller	Martha		05 Mar 1700	Wingham, Kent, England	Kent					
Birth & Bap	1702	James	Ann	Shoveller	Grace		21 Feb 1702	Wingham, Kent, England	Kent					
Birth & Bap	1753	John	Mary	Shoveller	Mary		02 Dec 1753	Hythe, Kent, England	Kent					
Birth & Bap	1755	John	Mary	Shoveller	Thur Clousley	15 Jun 1755	06 Jul 1755	St. Thomas-in-the-Cliffs, Lewes, Sussex, England	Sussex					
Birth & Bap	1756	Sturges	Susannah	Shoveller	Ann		25 Jan 1756	St. Martin, Canterbury, Kent, England	Kent					
Birth & Bap	1757	Sturges	Susannah	Shoveller	Margaret		13 Mar 1757	St. Martin, Canterbury, Kent, England	Kent					
Birth & Bap	1759	Sturges	Susannah	Shoveller	Mary		25 Feb 1759	St. Martin, Canterbury, Kent, England	Kent					
Birth & Bap	1771	John	Mary	Shoveller	Sarah		10 Feb 1771	St. Thomas, Portsmouth, Hampshire, ENG.	Hampshire					
Birth & Bap	1774	?	?	Shoveller	William	1774	bd. Ovingdean 1840		Sussex	66	Mrs Ann		2b	274
Birth & Bap	1777	?	?	Shoveller	Sarah		?	Portsea	Hampshire	93				
Birth & Bap	1779	Daniel	Jenny	Shoveller	Burges Charles	1779		?	?					
Birth & Bap	1786	?	?	Shoveller	Charles		21 May 1786	St. Mary's, Portsea, Hampshire, ENG.	Hampshire				2b	315
Birth & Bap	1786	?	?	Shoveller	Mary A		?	Portsea	Hampshire	80				
Birth & Bap	1789	William	Ann	Shoveller	Eliz'Th		19 Apr 1789	St. Mary's, Portsea, Hampshire, ENG.	Hampshire					
Birth & Bap	1789	William	Frances	Shoveller	Harriet		x	St. Mary's, Portsea, Hampshire, ENG.	Hampshire					
Birth & Bap	1792	William	Frances	Shoveller	Eliz'Th		03 Apr 1792	St. Mary's, Portsea, Hampshire, ENG.	Hampshire					
Birth & Bap	1792	?	?	Shoveller	Ann			Guildford	Surrey	74			2a	46
Birth & Bap	1793	William	Ann	Shoveller	Ann		28 Apr 1793	Wymering, Hampshire, ENG.	Hampshire					
Birth & Bap	1794	?	?	Shoveller	Elizabeth			Battle	Sussex	91			2b	36
Birth & Bap	1795	George	Mary	Shoveller	Elizabeth		21 Jun 1795	Chatham, Kent, ENG.	Kent					
Birth & Bap	1797	William	Mary	Shoveller	John	10 Dec 1797	24 Dec 1797	Gillingham, Kent, ENG.	Kent					
Birth & Bap	1800	William	Ann	Shoveller	Henry		19 Oct 1800	Wymering, Hampshire, ENG.	Hampshire	87				
Birth & Bap	1801	?	?	Shoveller	Ellen			Portsea	Hampshire				2b	342
Birth & Bap	1803	William	Ann	Shoveller	Elizabeth Mary		25 Dec 1803	Wymering, Hampshire, ENG.	Hampshire					
Birth & Bap	1807	Charles	Mary	Shoveller	William	01 Mar 1807	19 Jul 1807	St. Mary's, Portsea, Hampshire, ENG.	Hampshire					
Birth & Bap	1807	?	Sarah Ann	Shoveller	William		13 Apr 1807	St. Mary's, Portsea, Hampshire, ENG.	Hampshire					
Birth & Bap	1807	?	?	Shoveller	Caroline			Canterbury, Kent, ENG.	Kent	61			2a	369
Birth & Bap	1809	William	Sarah Ann	Shoveller	William King		14 Jun 1809	Holy Trinity, Gosport, Hampshire, ENG.	Hampshire					
Birth & Bap	1809	John	Jane	Shoveller	John Carter		?	Portsea, Hampshire, England	Hampshire	83			2b	327
Birth & Bap	1809	?	?	Shoveller	James		?	Portsea, Hampshire, England	Hampshire	76			2b	318
Birth & Bap	1809	?	?	Shoveller	Mary		?	Bridge, Kent, ENG.	Kent	74			2a	493
Birth & Bap	1810	?	?	Shoveller	Ann		?	Portsea	Hampshire	76			2b	385
Birth & Bap	1812	Charles	Mary	Shoveller	James	28 Sep 1812		St. Mary's, Portsea, Hampshire, ENG.	Hampshire					
Birth & Bap	1817	?	?	Shoveller	William		?	St. Saviour	London	66			1d	104
Birth & Bap	1818	?	?	Shoveller	John		?	Christchurch, Hampshire, ENG.	Hampshire	81			2b	545
Birth & Bap	1818	?	?	Shoveller	John		?	Leicester Sq, London, ENG?	London	53			1d	101
Birth & Bap	1820	?	?	Shoveller	Henry		?	St. Saviour	London	77			2a	519
Birth & Bap	1820	John	Eliza	Shoveller	John Ebenezer	13 Nov 1820		Blean, Kent, ENG.	Kent					
Birth & Bap	1822	John	Eliza	Shoveller	Eliza		02 Jul 1822	Baptist Church, Meiksham, Wiltshire, ENG.	Wiltshire					
Birth & Bap	1823	?	?	Shoveller	Charlotte			Baptist Church, Melksham, Wiltshire, ENG.	Wiltshire					
Birth & Bap	1828	?	?	Shoveller	Abel			Blean, Kent, ENG.	Kent	63			2a	600
Birth & Bap	1828	William	Ann	Shoveller	William Henry			Bedfordshire	Bed'shire					
Birth & Bap	1830	?	Caroline	Shoveller	Louisa		31 Aug 1830	St. Mary's, Portsea, Hampshire, ENG.	Hampshire					
Birth & Bap	1832	?	?	Shoveller	Daniel		15 Feb 1830	Canterbury, Kent, ENG.	Kent					
Birth & Bap	1836	?	?	Shoveller	Robert		?	Meopham, Kent, ENG.	Kent					
Birth & Bap	1839	Samuel Hook	?	Shoveller	Ada		?	Blean, Kent, ENG.	Kent	36			2a	408
Birth & Bap	1839	William	Elizabeth	Shoveller	Frank		?	St. George South'k	London				4	415
Birth & Bap	1840	?	?	Shoveller	Kezia		?	Wandsworth	London				1d	419
Birth & Bap	1841	William	Elizabeth	Shoveller	Alice		?	St. George South'k	London	50			4	438
Birth & Bap	1844	?	?	Shoveller	Charles		?	Portsea	Hampshire				7	140
Birth & Bap	1845	?	?	Shoveller	Hannah Mary		?	St. George South'k	London				4	449
Birth & Bap	1845	?	?	Shoveller	Julia		?	Warminster	Hampshire				8	431
Birth & Bap	1848	?	?	Shoveller	John		?	Portsea Island, Hampshire, ENG.	Hampshire				7,168,40	
Birth & Bap	1848	?	?	Shoveller	William		?	St. George South'k	London				4	457
Birth & Bap	1849	John C	Ellen	Shoveller	John		?	St. George South'k	London					
Birth & Bap	1849	?	?	Shoveller	Elizabeth Hills		?	Canterbury, Kent, ENG.	Kent				5	77

Event	Year	Father	Mother	Surname	Given Name	Date		Place		Region	No.	Ref	Page
Birth & Bap	1849	?	?	Shoveller	Mary Anne De Kingey		?	Guildford	?	Surrey		4	201
Birth & Bap	1850	John C	Ellen	Shoveller	Ellen		?	Portsea	?	Hampshire		7	191
Birth & Bap	1850	?	?	Shoveller	George		?	Portsea	?	Hampshire		7	181
Birth & Bap	1850	?	?	Shoveller	Sarah		?	Blean, Kent, ENG.	?	Kent		5	27
Birth & Bap	1852	?	?	Shoveller	Jane		?	Gravesend	?	Kent		2a	241
Birth & Bap	1852	?	?	Shoveller	John H.		?	?	?	?		2A, 486, 27	
Birth & Bap	1852	?	?	Shoveller	Stephen John		?	Blean, Kent, ENG.	?	Kent		2a	279
Birth & Bap	1853	?	?	Shoveller	Caroline		?	Medway, Kent, ENG.	?	Kent		2b	353
Birth & Bap	1853	?	?	Shoveller	Jane Ann		?	Portsea	?	Hampshire		2a	468
Birth & Bap	1853	?	?	Shoveller	Olivet		?	Canterbury, Kent, ENG.	?	Kent		2b	
Birth & Bap	1854	Shoveler (R.M.)	Capt	Shoveller	Daughter	4 Feb 1854		Ballymaeaaw, County Waterford		Ireland			
Birth & Bap	1854	?	?	Shoveller	Henry		?	Blean, Kent, ENG.	?	Kent		2a	518
Birth & Bap	1855	?	?	Shoveller	Ernest		?	Strand	?	London		1b	364
Birth & Bap	1856	John	Mary Ann	Shoveller	Charles William		?	Blean, Kent, ENG.	?	Kent		2a	563
Birth & Bap	1856	?	?	Shoveller	Ernest		?	Leicester Sq, London, ENG.	?	London	16	1d	88
Birth & Bap	1856	John C	Ellen	Shoveller	Henry		?	St. Saviour	?	London		2b	260
Birth & Bap	1857	Daniel	Charlotte	Shoveller	Henry		?	Havant	?	Hampshire	23	2b	385
Birth & Bap	1857	?	?	Shoveller	Rosa		?	Portsea	?	Hampshire		1b	392
Birth & Bap	1857	?	?	Shoveller	Mary Jane		?	Shorne, Kent, ENG.	?	Kent		2a	505
Birth & Bap	1858	?	Mary Ann	Shoveller	Caroline		?	Strand	?	London			
Birth & Bap	1858	John	Charlotte	Shoveller	Mary Jane		?	Blean, Kent, ENG.	?	Kent		2a	538
Birth & Bap	1859	Daniel	Harriet	Shoveller	Daniel		?	Leicester Sq, London, ENG.	?	London		2a	547
Birth & Bap	1859	William	?	Shoveller	Catherine		?	Shorne, Kent, ENG.	?	Kent			
Birth & Bap	1860	?	?	Shoveller	Henry		?	Whitstable, Kent, ENG.	?	Kent			
Birth & Bap	1860	?	Charlotte	Shoveller	John Henry		?	Blean, Kent, ENG.	?	Kent		2a	453
Birth & Bap	1860	Daniel	Harriet	Shoveller	William Henry		?	Strand	?	London		1B, 429	175
Birth & Bap	1861	William	Mary Ann	Shoveller	Sarah		?	Blean, Kent, ENG.	?	Kent		2a	
Birth & Bap	1861	John	Mary	Shoveller	William		?	Shorne, Kent, ENG.	?	Kent			
Birth & Bap	1861	Robert	?	Shoveller	John Henry		?	Whitstable, Kent, ENG.	?	Kent		1b	
Birth & Bap	1862	?	Charlotte	Shoveller	George		?	Leicester Sq, London, ENG.	?	London		8c	
Birth & Bap	1862	Daniel	Harriet	Shoveller	Emma Alice		?	Herne, Kent, ENG.	?	Kent		2a	644
Birth & Bap	1862	William	Mary Ann	Shoveller	James		?	St. Giles	?	London		2a	643
Birth & Bap	1863	John	Mary	Shoveller	Charlotte		?	Leigh	?	Manchester			
Birth & Bap	1863	Daniel	?	Shoveller	Harriet		?	Shorne, Kent, ENG.	?	Kent		2a	675
Birth & Bap	1863	William	Robert	Shoveller	Emma		?	Whitstable, Kent, ENG.	?	Kent			
Birth & Bap	1864	?	Mary	Shoveller	Harriett Frances		?	Soho, London, ENG.	?	London			
Birth & Bap	1864	Robert	Harriet	Shoveller	Edward		?	Blean, Kent, ENG.	?	Kent		2a	454
Birth & Bap	1866	Robert	?	Shoveller	Albert Edward Robert		?	Herne, Kent, ENG.	?	Kent		2a	694
Birth & Bap	1866	William	Charlotte	Shoveller	Henry		?	Blean, Kent, ENG.	?	Kent			
Birth & Bap	1866	Daniel	Harriet	Shoveller	Elizabeth		?	Whitstable, Kent, ENG.	?	Kent		2a	696
Birth & Bap	1867	William	?	Shoveller	Henry J.T.		?	Blean, Kent, ENG.	?	Kent			
Birth & Bap	1867	?	?	Shoveller	William		?	Shorne, Kent, ENG.	?	Kent			
Birth & Bap	1868	William	?	Shoveller	Eliza		?	Rochester, Kent, ENG.	?	Kent		2b	442
Birth & Bap	1869	?	?	Shoveller	Albert Newman H		?	Portsea	?	Hampshire	1	2a, 694	738
Birth & Bap	1870	Robert	Harriet	Shoveller	James Albert		?	Blean, Kent, ENG.	?	Kent		2A, 705	433
Birth & Bap	1871	?	?	Shoveller	John Harden		?	Blean, Kent, ENG.	?	Kent		2a	52
Birth & Bap	1871	Daniel	Charlotte	Shoveller	James		?	Herne, Kent, ENG.	?	Kent		2a	82
Birth & Bap	1871	Robert	Mary	Shoveller	John Harden		?	Blean, Kent, ENG.	?	Kent			
Birth & Bap	1873	William	Harriet	Shoveller	Jabez		?	Shorne, Kent, ENG.	?	Kent	3	1d	737
Birth & Bap	1873	?	?	Shoveller	John		?	Herne, Kent, ENG.	?	Kent	0	1d	772
Birth & Bap	1874	?	?	Shoveller	Jane		?	St. Saviour	?	London		1d	532
Birth & Bap	1875	?	?	Shoveller	Charlotte Ann L		?	St. Saviour	?	London		2a	810
Birth & Bap	1878	?	?	Shoveller	John Harden		?	St. Saviour	?	London		2a	903
Birth & Bap	1879	?	?	Shoveller	Sarah Jane		?	Blean, Kent, ENG.	?	Kent		2b	342
Birth & Bap	1880	William	Harriet	Shoveller	Walter John		?	Blean, Kent, ENG.	?	Kent			
Birth & Bap	1881	?	?	Shoveller	William		?	Faversham	?	Kent		2a	871
Birth & Bap	1882	?	?	Shoveller	William		?	Portsea, Hampshire, England	?	Hampshire		2B, 451	
Birth & Bap	1884	?	?	Shoveller	Florence Kezia		?	Milton	?	Hampshire		2a	
Birth & Bap	1888	?	?	Shoveller	Susannah		?	Kingston, Surrey, ENG.	?	Surrey		2a	
Birth & Bap		?	?	Shoveller	Patience		?	Milton	?	Kent		2a	
Birth & Bap		?	?	Shoveller	Louie Emmeline		?		?				
Birth & Bap		?	?	Shoveller	Arthur		?		?				
Birth & Bap		?	?	Shoveller	John Henry R.	8 Oct 1884	?		?				
Birth & Bap		?	?	Shoveller	Bessie Louise		?		?				
Birth & Bap		?	?	Shoveller	Harold Langley		?		?				
Birth & Bap		?	?	Shoveller	Albert James		?		?				

Event	Year	Father	Mother	Surname	First	BMD Date	Bp./Bur. Date	Event Place	County	Death Age	Spouse	Sex	Birth Vol.	Birth Page
Birth & Bap	1888	?	?	Shoveller	William Henry		?	? (charged & imprisoned for theft in 1910)	?				2a	896
Birth & Bap	1890	?	?	Shoveller	Alfred William		?	Milton	Kent				2a	910
Birth & Bap	1892	?	?	Shoveller	Florence Sarah		?	Sheppey	London				2a	882
Birth & Bap	1892	?	?	Shoveller	Valley Amelia		?	Milton	Kent				1d	735
Birth & Bap	1894	?	?	Shoveller	Margery Georgiana		?	Wandsworth	London	4				
Birth & Bap	1895	?	?	Shoveller	Harold John		?	Milton	Kent				2a	903
Marriages	1701	?	?	Shoveller	Richard	23 Jul 1701		St. Thomas, Portsmouth, Hampshire, ENG.	Hampshire		Elizabeth Bellinger	F		
Marriages	1727	?	?	Shoveller	John	18 Jan 1727		Holy Trinity, Gosport, Hampshire, England	Hampshire		Catharine Harmsworth	F		
Marriages	1729	James	Ann	Shoveller	Jane	6 Jul 1729		Romsey, Hampshire, England	Hampshire		John Jacob	M		
Marriages	1735	?	?	Shoveller	Mary	26 Sep 1735		Fleet Prison And Rules Of The Fleet, London, England	London		Thoms. Lekey	M		
Marriages	1744	?	?	Shoveller	John	24 Jan 1744		St. Paul's, Canterbury, Kent, England	Kent		Elizabeth Dodd	F		
Marriages	1747	?	?	Shoveller	George	22 Apr 1747		Canterbury, Kent, ENG.	Kent		Ann Salmon	F		
Marriages	1752	?	?	Shoveller	John	01 Aug 1752		Frostenden, Suffolk, England	Suffolk		Mary Ravens	M		
Marriages	1771	?	?	Shoveller	Mary	06 Jan 1771		Womenswould, Kent, England	Kent		Edward Whitnal	F		
Marriages	1784	?	?	Shoveller	William	03 Oct 1784		Fareham, Hampshire, ENG.	Hampshire		Ann Slade	M		
Marriages	1786	?	?	Shoveller	John	25 Dec 1786		St. Mary's, Portsea, Hampshire, ENG.	Hampshire		Elizabeth Young	W: Richard Young & Richard Gudge		
Marriages	1786	?	?	Shoveller	John	25 Dec 1786		Portsea/Portsmouth	Hampshire		Elizabeth Young (made an 'X')	F		
Marriages	1787	?	?	Shoveller	William	25 Jul 1787		St. Paul, Deptford, Kent, England	Kent		Mary Newitt	F		
Marriages	1789	?	?	Shoveller	John (Thos.?)	29 Jan 1789		St. Mary's, Portsea, Hampshire, ENG.	Hampshire		Mary Barfoot	F		
Marriages	1789	John	?	Shoveller	Thomas (widower)	29 Jan 1789		St Marys, Portsmouth	Hampshire		Mary Barfoot	W: John & Susanna Shoveller		
Marriages	1790	John	Mary	Shoveller	Sarah	12 Jul 1790		St. Martin In The Fields, Westminster, London, ENG.	London		Robert Gilchrist	F		
Marriages	1794	?	Mary	Shoveller	George	19 Jul 1794		Chatham, Kent, ENG.	Kent		Mary Cutbush	M		
Marriages	1795	John	Mary	Shoveller	Elizabeth	28 Nov 1795		Alverstoke, Hampshire, ENG.	Hampshire		John Carter	F		
Marriages	1796	?	?	Shoveller	William	31 Aug 1796		St. Mary's, Portsea, Hampshire, ENG.	Hampshire		Frances Hall	F		
Marriages	1805	?	?	Shoveller	Charles	22 Dec 1805		Portsea, Southampton, ENG.	Hampshire	S	Mary Ann Winsor	M		
Marriages	1806	?	?	Shoveller	William (Surgeon RN)	1806		Titchfield, Hampshire, England	Hampshire		Sarah Ann King	M		
Marriages	1807	?	?	Shoveller	Sarah	05 May 1807		St. Thomas, Portsmouth, Hampshire, ENG.	Hampshire		John Hopkins	F		
Marriages	1809	?	?	Shoveller	John	12 Mar 1809		St. Mary's, Portsea, Hampshire, ENG.	Hampshire		Jane Hatchard	F		
Marriages	1809	?	?	Shoveller	Sarah	08 Mar 1809		Alverstoke, Hampshire, ENG.	Hampshire	S	Robert Ladbrook	M		
Marriages	1812	?	?	Shoveller	William (Surgeon RN)	24 Jun 1812		HMS Conqueror (Alverstoke, Hampshire, ENG).	Hampshire		Ann Marshall	F		
Marriages	1820	?	?	Shoveller	Elizabeth	18 Jun 1820		Alverstoke, Hampshire, ENG.	Hampshire		Edwin Howell	F		
Marriages	1823	William	Mary	Shoveller	Elizabeth	03 Apr 1823		St. Mary's, Portsea, Hampshire, ENG.	Hampshire		John King	M		
Marriages	1829	?	?	Shoveller (of Penzance)	Rev. John	06 Apr 1829		St. Sidwell, Exeter, Devon, ENG.	Devon		Dorothy Toms (of St. Sidwells)	M		
Marriages	1830	?	?	Shoveller	James	07 Sep 1830		Alverstoke, Hampshire, ENG.	Hampshire		Louisa Baker	F		
Marriages	1832	?	?	Shoveller	John Carter	06 May 1832		Alverstoke, Hampshire, ENG.	Hampshire		Eliza Hammond	F		
Marriages	1834	?	?	Shoveller	Francis (m)	1 Dec 1834		St Peter's Church, Canterbury	Kent		Mrs Lake (nee De Lamotte)	F		
Marriages	1836	?	?	Shoveller (of Canterbury)	Mr. F.	??. June 1836		St. George's in the East			Miss Grey (of London)	F		
Marriages	1840	?	?	Shoveller (or King)	Elizabeth	29 Jul 1840		St. Mary's, Portsea, Hampshire, ENG.	Hampshire		Daniel Ford	M		
Marriages	1843	?	?	Shoveller	James	1843		Southampton	Hampshire		Ellen	M	7	262
Marriages	1843	John Shoveler (of Rochester)	?	Shoveller	Eliza	22 Oct 1843		Cliffe (both of Chatham)	Kent		John Newman	M		
Marriages	1844	?	?	Shoveller	Lt. M. K. (Royal Marines)	30 Dec 1844		Wexford	Ireland		Lucinda De Rinzy	F		
Marriages	1847	?	?	Shoveller	John Carter	07 Feb 1847		St. Mary's, Portsea, Hampshire, ENG.	Hampshire		Ellen Dimmick	F	7	167
Marriages	1849	?	?	Shoveller	William	1849		?	?		Harriet ?	F		
Marriages	1856	?	?	Shoveller	Daniel	1856		Shorne, Kent, ENG.	Kent		Mrs Charlotte ?	F		
Marriages	1858	William?	Ann?	Shoveller	William	1858		Portsea, Hampshire, England	Hampshire		Mary Ann Taylor	F	2b	515
Marriages	1860	?	?	Shoveller	Robert	1860		Blean, Kent, ENG.	Kent		Mary Brown Warner	F	2a	1099
Marriages	1860	?	?	Shoveler (of Seasalter)	Thomas	28 Aug 1860		Blean, Kent, ENG.	Kent		Rosa Follwell (of Canterbury)	F	2a	853
Marriages	1866	?	Caroli	Shoveller	Charles	4 Mar 1866		Portsea, Hampshire, England	Hampshire		Clara King	M	2b	537
Marriages	1867	?	?	Shoveller	Louisa	1867		Chichester	Sussex		David Richardson	F	2b	582
Marriages	1869	William	?	Shoveller	Alice	1869		Newington	Surrey		George Robertson	M	1d	281
Marriages	1869	?	?	Shoveller	William	1869		St. George South'k	London		Kezia West	F	1d	175
Marriages	1877	?	?	Shoveller	Ellen	1877		Kensington	London		George Whitaker	M	1a	182
Marriages	1878	John Carter	?	Shoveller	John (of Portsmouth, corn merchant)	13 Jun 1878		Blandford Church, Dorset, ENG.	Dorset	S	Emma Louisa Reed	F	5a	426
Marriages	1881	?	?	Shoveller	William Henry	1881		Faversham	Kent		Fanny Wise	F	2a	1254
Marriages	1883	?	?	Shoveller	Eliza Ann	1883		Faversham	Kent		John Thomas Moon	M	2a	1537
Marriages	1885	?	?	Shoveller	Elizabeth Ellen	1885		Milton	Kent		George Frid OR Thomas Johnson	F	2a	987
Marriages	1888	?	?	Shoveller	James Albert	1888		Milton	Kent		Emma Ware	M	2a	1296
Marriages	1892	?	?	Shoveller	Sarah Jane	1892		Milton	Kent		George Edward Mantle	F	2a	1738
Marriages	1892	?	?	Shoveller	William	1892		Wandsworth	London		Georgiana Overton	F	1d	1201
Marriages	1893	?	?	Shoveller	Albert Newman H	1893		Southampton	Hampshire		Elizabeth Weymouth	M	2c	47
Marriages	1895	?	?	Shoveller	Susannah	1895		Milton	Kent		Amos Glandville	F	2a	1539
Marriages	1896	?	?	Shoveller	Patience	1896		Milton	Kent		John Wm. Horton/John Edwin Saxby	M	2a	1747
Marriages	1902	John Croad (Builder)	?	Croad	William	16 Sep 1902		Him (4 Lion Terrace) / Her (28 Union St) in Portsea	Hampshire		Louie? Emmeline Shoveller	F: John Shoveller (corn Factory)		
Occupation	1814	?	?	Shoveller	William (Surgeon RN)	14 Nov 1814		Appointed to HMS Cornwallis						
Occupation	1816	?	?	Shoveller	Mr	1. Jan 1816		Grocer, Oyster St. Portsmouth	Hampshire					

Occupation	1817	?	?	Shoveller	William (Surgeon RN)	8 Dec 1817		Appointed to HMS Sybille						
Occupation	1820	?	?	Shoveller	William (Surgeon RN)	23 May 1820		Appointed to HMS Creole						
Witness	1788	?	?	Young	Richard	24 Dec 1788		Portsea/Portsmouth	Hampshire		Elizabeth White (made an 'x')	John Shoveller & Thomas Gudge		
Witness	1795	?	?	Lavender	Joseph	20 Nov 1785		Portsea/Portsmouth	Hampshire		Hannah Penn	William Shoveller & Richard Gudge		
Deaths	1787	?	?	Shoveler	John		23 May 1787	St. Peter's, Canterbury, ENG.	Kent	90				
Deaths	1791	?	?	Shoveller	John		07 Dec 1791	Bunhill Fields, London, ENG.	London	?				
Deaths	1793	?	?	Shoveller	John		21 Jul 1793	Portsea, Southampton, ENG.	Hampshire	?				
Deaths	1798	William	Mary	Shoveler	John		16 Jan 1798	?	?	?				
Deaths	1812	?	?	Shoveller	John		25 Dec 1812	Elham, Kent, ENG.	Kent	74				
Deaths	1825	?	?	Shoveller	Mrs Mary (wife of William Shoveller Esq. & mother of Dr. Shoveller)			?	Hampshire	?				
Deaths	1831	?	?	Shoveller (Toms)	Dorothy (wife of Rev. John Shoveller)		1831	Henley-Upon-Thames	London	23				
Deaths	1840	?	?	Shoveller	William (Surgeon RN)		3 Oct 1840	Ovingdean, Brighton	Sussex	66			7	171
Deaths	1840	?	?	Shoveller	Mary		1840	Blean, Kent, ENG.	Kent	?			5	13
Deaths	1840	?	?	Shoveller	Mary		1840	Blean, Kent, ENG.	Kent	?			5	15
Deaths	1842	?	?	Shoveller	Mrs Fanny	2 April 1842	5 Apr 1842	Westgate, Chichester (Bd. St Bartholemews Church)	Sussex	45			7	205
Deaths	1843	Samuel Hook	?	Shoveller	Ada		1843	Stroud, Gloucestershire	London	4				
Deaths	1845	?	?	Shoveller	Hannah Mary		1845	St. George South'k	London	?			4	323
Deaths	1846	?	?	Shoveller	Eliza		1846	Fareham, Hampshire, ENG.	Hampshire	?			7	58
Deaths	1846	?	?	Shoveller	Harriett Jane		1846	Canterbury, Kent, ENG.	Kent	?			5	46
Deaths	1847	?	?	Shoveller	John		1847	Banbury, Oxfordshire, ENG.	Oxford	57			16, 1, 101	
Deaths	1847	?	?	Shoveller	John		1847	Banbury, Oxfordshire, ENG.	Oxford	?			16	1
Deaths	1849	?	?	Shoveler	John		29 Jul 1849	Minster, Kent, ENG.	Kent	?				
Deaths	1850	?	?	Shoveller	John		1850	Portsea, Hampshire, England	Hampshire	?			7	139
Deaths	1850	?	?	Shoveller	Sarah		1850	Blean, Kent, ENG.	Kent	?			5	13
Deaths	1850	?	?	Shoveller	William		1850	Portsea, Hampshire, England	Hampshire	?			7	111
Deaths	1851	?	?	Shoveller	George		1851	Portsea, Hampshire, England	Hampshire	?			7	114
Deaths	1851	?	?	Shoveller	John		1851	Portsea Island, Hampshire, ENG.	Hampshire	?			7, 115, 4	
Deaths	1851	?	?	Shoveller	John		1851	Portsea Island, Hampshire, ENG.	Hampshire	?			7, 139, 101	
Deaths	1851	?	?	Shoveller	John		1851	Portsea, Hampshire, England	Hampshire	?			7	115
Deaths	1852	?	?	Shoveller	Jane		1852	Gravesend	Kent	?			2a	146
Deaths	1852	?	?	Shoveller	Mary		1852	Portsea, Hampshire, England	Hampshire	?			2b	222
Deaths	1854	?	?	Shoveller	Harriet		1854	Canterbury, Kent, ENG.	Kent	?			2a	304
Deaths	1854	?	?	Shoveller	Henry		1854	Blean, Kent, ENG.	Kent	?			2a	352
Deaths	1855	?	?	Shoveller	Jane Ann		1855	Portsea, Hampshire, England	Hampshire	?			2b	214
Deaths	1855	?	?	Shoveler	John		26 Jun 1855	Bishopsbourne, Kent, ENG.	Kent	?				
Deaths	1855	?	?	Shoveler	John		1855	Bridge, Kent, ENG.	Kent	?			2A, 347, 1	
Deaths	1859	?	?	Shoveller	Frank		1859	St. George South'k	London	?			1d	118
Deaths	1859	?	?	Shoveller	George Richard		1859	Poplar	London	?			1c	349
Deaths	1860	?	?	Shoveller	Henry		1860	Blean, Kent, ENG.	Kent	?			2a	340
Deaths	1862	?	?	Shoveller	William		20 Jun 1862	St Bartholemews Church, Chichester, Sussex, ENG.	Sussex	61			2b	207
Deaths	1863	?	?	Shoveller	John		1863	Medway, Kent, ENG.	Kent	?			2A, 235, 5	
Deaths	1865	?	?	Shoveller	Charles		1865	Portsea, Hampshire, England	Hampshire	?			2b	292
Deaths	1865	?	?	Shoveller	Mrs Ann		7 Dec 1865	m. William Shoveller (R.N.)	?					
Deaths	1866	?	?	Shoveller	Mrs Ann (Wife of William Shoveller, R.N.)		1 Feb, 1866	Farncourt(comb), Guildford, Surrey	Surrey	74			2a	46
Deaths	1866	?	?	Shoveller	Mrs Mary Ann		6 Mar 1866	Sackville St, Southsea Portsea	Hampshire	80			2b	315
Deaths	1868	?	?	Shoveller	Caroline		1868	Canterbury, Kent, ENG.	Kent	61			2a	369
Deaths	1869	?	?	Shoveller	John Harden		13 Mar 1869	Blean/Herne, Kent, ENG.	Kent	?			2A, 460,257	
Deaths	1870	?	?	Shoveller	Mrs Sarah (relict of Rev. John Shoveller)		20 Jul 1870	Portsea, Hampshire, England	Hampshire	93			2b	274
Deaths	1872	?	?	Shoveller	Robert		1872	Blean, Kent, ENG.	Kent	36			2a	408
Deaths	1872	?	?	Shoveller	Ernest		1872	St. Saviour	London	16			1d	88
Deaths	1872	?	?	Shoveller	John Harden		1872	Blean, Kent, ENG.	Kent	1			2a	442
Deaths	1872	?	?	Shoveller	John Harden		11 Feb 1872	Blean/Herne, Kent, ENG.	Kent	1			2A, 442,113	
Deaths	1873	?	?	Shoveller	William		1873	St. Saviour	London	0			1d	52
Deaths	1876	?	?	Shovlar	John		1876	North Aylesford, Kent, ENG.	Kent	?			2A, 258, 31	
Deaths	1876	?	?	Shoveller	Walter John		1876	Blean, Kent, ENG.	Kent	3			2A, 433, 301	
Deaths	1877	William	?	Shoveller (Robertson)	Alice		1877	Carter St, Walworth	London	36				
Deaths	1880	?	?	Shoveller	Henry		1880	Havant	Hampshire	23			2b	260
Deaths	1883	?	?	Shoveller	William		1883	St. Saviour	London	66			1d	104
Deaths	1883	?	?	Shoveller	Mary		1883	Bridge, Kent, ENG.	Kent	74			2a	493
Deaths	1885	?	?	Shoveller	Elizabeth		1885	Battle	Sussex	91			2b	36
Deaths	1885	?	?	Shoveller	James		1885	Portsea, Hampshire, England	Hampshire	76			2b	318
Deaths	1886	?	?	Shoveller	Charlotte		1886	Blean, Kent, ENG.	Kent	63			2a	600
Deaths	1886	?	?	Shoveller	Mrs Ann		5 Jan 1886	8 York St, Portsea	Hampshire	76			2b	385
Deaths	1888	?	?	Shoveller	Ellen		1888	Portsea, Hampshire, England	Hampshire	87			2b	342
Deaths	1890	?	?	Shoveller	Kezia		1890	Wandsworth	London	50			1d	419
Deaths	1892	?	?	Shoveller	John Carter		1892	Lorne Rd, Southsea, Portsea Island, Hampshire, ENG.	Hampshire	83			2B, 327, 24	
Deaths	1892	James Shervell	Ellen	Shoveller	Dorothy Grace		9 Jun 1892	Lorn Rd, Southsea	Hampshire	2				

APPENDIX K

Shovellers – NSW Birth, Marriage & Death Registrations (1856-1991)

BIRTHS 1856-1921

Surname	Firstname	Given	Reg #	Father	Mother	Name(S)/District
Shoveller	Norman	H	21044/1911	Alfred E.	Gertrude	Sydney
Shoveller	Eileen	D	19958/1910	Alfred E.	Constance G.	Manly
Shoveller	Alfred	E	18771/1908	Alfred E.	Gertrude	Rockdale
Shoveller	Dorothy	B	41987/1916	Alfred E.	Constance G.	Sydney
Shoveller	Mervyn	R	19761/1914	Alfred R.	Georgina M.	Grafton
Shoveller	John	W	47321/1900	Alfred R.	Georgina M.	Sydney
Shoveller	Alfred	W	01022/1894	Alfred W.	Ruby	Sydney
Shoveller	Thelma	J	27355/1927	Clarence J.	Mary E.	Sydney
Shoveller	Russell	E	156/1905	Clarence J.	Mary E.	Canterbury
Shoveller	Susan	L	33249/1916	Clarence J.	Mary E.	Newtown
Shoveller	John	H	20541/1907	Clarence J. H.	Mary E.	Sutherland
Shoveller	Janet	W	33246/1909	Clarence J. H.	Mary E.	Sydney
Shoveller	Mabel	E.A.	10165/1870	Thomas	Susan	Sydney
Shoveller	George	Lorraine	13336/1878	Thomas	Susan	Waverley
Shoveller	(Female)		11288/1873	Thomas E.	Susan	Hurstville
Shoveller	(Female)		7416/1858	Thomas E.	Susan	Grafton
Shoveller	Thomas	C	7801/1859	Thomas E.	Susan	Bankstown
Shoveller	Clarence	John H.	8141/1862	Thomas H.	Susan	Newtown
Shoveller	William	H	15169/1880	Thomas H.	Phoebe M.	Marrickville
Shoveller	Thomas		20956/1911	Thomas H.	Phoebe M.	Tumut
Shoveller	Jack	S	51961/1917	Thomas H.	Phoebe M.	
Shoveller	Edward		30191/1914	Thomas H.	Phoebe M.	
Shoveller	Unnamed	Male	24344/1916	Thomas H.	Phoebe M.	
Shoveller	Ernest	T	30250/1909	Thomas H.	Elsie C.	
Shoveller	Edna	F	59/1913missing	William E.		

DEATHS 1856-1991

Surname	Firstname	Given	Reg #	Father	Mother	Name/S/Distd
Shoveller	Mary	A	18042/1925	78 Years		St Peters
Shoveller	Susannah	T	10979/1930	78 Yrs		State Hosp. Auburn
Shoveller	Stephen		16398/1931	79 Years		St Peters
Shoveller	Brett	Alfred	5653/1968	Alfred Drew	Rhonda Leslie	Sydney
Shoveller	Glory		18826/1926	Alfred E.	Constant G.	St Peters
Shoveller	Eileen	D	7129/1910	Alfred E.	Constant G.	St Peters
Shoveller	Norman		24143/1981	Alfred, Ernest	Constance Gertrude	
Shoveller	John	Harold	6142/1973	Alfred, Russell	Georgine Maria	Tumut
Shoveller	Alfred	John Russell	25076/1975	Alfred William	Ruby	
Shoveller	Mina	Olive C.	31071/1967	Andrew	Caroline	Sydney
Shoveller	Doris	Mary A.	3759/1946	Charles	Mary Maria	Newtown
Shoveller	Catherine		20359(4)/1990	Charles	Emma Lydia	Marrickville
Shoveller	Gladys		32856/1959	Elsie Caroline	Lucy Elizabeth	Sutherland
Shoveller	Veronica		12655/1955	Henry	Ada	Sutherland
Shoveller	Constance Gertrude		2575/1969	Horace Cleveland	Annie	Sydney
Shoveller	Mary		4631/1978	James	Agnes	
Shoveller	Mary		23962/1967	James	Elizabeth	Hamilton
Shoveller	Georgina	M	1916/1905	John	Bridget	Manly
Shoveller	Alfred	Russell	5123/1937	John	Anna M.	Manly
Shoveller	Thomas	E	5484/1908	John	Elizabeth	Grafton
Shoveller	Mary		16392/1931	John	Mary	Manly
Shoveller	Linda		10494/1956	John D.	Olive	Manly
Shoveller	Roy	Drew	18946/1963	John Harold	Linda	Sydney
Shoveller	Mary	Josephine	14928/1953	John Henry	Ruby Maud	Sydney
Shoveller	Phoebe		10205/1990	Lawrence	Susan	Sydney
Shoveller	John		21348/1952	Mervyn Robert	Mary Josephine	Sutherland
Shoveller	Mary	Elizabeth	27521/1956	Michael	Helen	Hurstville
Shoveller	Dorothy	May	11461/1976	Percival	Violet	Manly
Shoveller	Betty	Edward	19926/1959	Samuel	Blanche	
Shoveller	William	Ernest	17438/1963	Stephen Thomas	Mary Ann	Marrickville
Shoveller	Alfred	T.	3660/1858	Thomas	Susan	Rockdale
Shoveller	Susan	E.A.	14461/1870	Thomas	Susan	Sydney
Shoveller	Janet	C.	50651/1874	Thomas	Susan	Grafton
Shoveller	Thomas		18255/1940	Thomas Eastman	Susan	Grafton
Shoveller	Clarence	John	20194/1946	Thomas Eastman	Susan	Balmain
Shoveller	George	Lorraine	10988(2)/1988	Thomas Eastman	Doris	North Sydney
Shoveller	Kevin	Richard	2713/1927	Thomas Eastman	Phoebe M.	Sutherland
Shoveller	Keith	L	13672/1914	Thomas	Phoebe M.	Sydney
Shoveller	Edward		11244/1933	Thomas H.	Phoebe M.	St Peters
Shoveller	Jean		20414/1928	Thomas E.	Doris M. A.	Sydney
Shoveller	Claude		11351/1915	Thomas H.	Margaret	Sydney
Shoveller	Thomas		22926/1956	Thomas H.	Phoebe M.	Tumut
Shoveller	William		1722/1977	Thomas Henry	Phoebe Margaret	Newtown
Shoveller	Ernest	Henry	1390/1988	Thomas Henry	Phoebe Margaret	St Peters
Shoveller	Maureen	Hazel	14237/1959	Thomas Patrick	Ellen Mary	Newtown
Shoveller	Thomas	Henry	53594/1974	Thomas Stephen	Mary Annh	Sutherland
Shoveller	Alfred	William	15277/1960	Unknown	Georgina Maria	Ursville
Shoveller	Edith		3766/1862	William	Jane	Newtown
Shoveller	Eva		9614/1988	William H.	Mary A.	Grafton
Shoveller	Eleanor		9379/1956	William Shortis	Ettie	Campsie
Shoveller	Ruby	-			Caroline	

MARRIAGES 1856-1971

Shoveller Males

Groom's Surname	Groom's Firstname	Bride's Surname	Bride's Firstname	Reg #	Name(S)/District
Shoveller	Alfred Drew	Osborne	Rhonda Leslie	6347/1963	North Sydney
Shoveller	Alfred E.	Shorts	Eleanor M.	13922/1930	Redfern
Shoveller	Alfred	Shaw	Gertrude	9743/1907	Sydney
Shoveller	Alfred John Russell	Beahen	Marguerite Ellen	25288/1942	Rozelle
Shoveller	Alfred R	Ford	Georgina M.	22371/1899	Sydney
Shoveller	Alfred Russell Sadler	Evelyn	Laura Alberta	16429/1936	Manly
Shoveller	Alfred W	Edwards	Ruby	12326/1917	Mosman
Shoveller	Alfred William	Gallaher	Gladys	1464/1961	Sydney
Shoveller	Clarence J.	White	Mary E.	34/1904	Sydney
Shoveller	Colin Raymond	Johnson	Kerrie-Anne	7948/1966	Waverley
Shoveller	Ernest Thomas	Taggart	Veronica Mary	20789/1940	Sydney
Shoveller	Frank Edward	Lugton	Cheryl Ann	9279/1968	Mosman
Shoveller	Frederick Arthur	Atkinson	Gwendolyne Lorraine	39601/1953	Rockdale
Shoveller	George L.	Luney	Mary	80230/1918	Woolahra
Shoveller	George Stanley	Marshall	Beryl Gertrude	14466/1947	Tumut
Shoveller	Harold Trevor	Roberts	Pauline Ann	24238/1970	Mosman
Shoveller	John Alfred	MacConnell	Betty	5244/1950	Sydney
Shoveller	John H.	Morrison	Linda M.	45051/1922	Mosman
Shoveller	John Harold	Nursey	Mavis Kathleen	3970/1940	Sydney
Shoveller	Keith John	Lockwood	Muriel Annie	28791/1971	Sydney
Shoveller	Keith John	Wilcomes	Marie	10165/1954	Paddington
Shoveller	Kerrie Raymond	Ryan	Maureen Hazel	1155/1965	Sydney
Shoveller	Kevin Richard	Rogers	Betty Shirley	70731/1968	Sydney
Shoveller	Mervyn Robert	Kemsley	Margaret Betty	2468/1964	Canterbury
Shoveller	Mervyn Robert	Lynn	Mary Josephine	1605/1937	Sydney
Shoveller	Mervyn Robert	Vella	Margaret Betty	2468/1964	Marrickville
Shoveller	Michael Alfred E.	Carter	Fay	893/1932	Canterbury
Shoveller	Norman H.	Scott	Una	23885/1964	Hurstville
Shoveller	Ronald Ernest	Whytcross	Phyllis Beryl	14998/1948	Sydney
Shoveller	Roy Drew	Nye	Dorothy May	1421/1953	Sydney
Shoveller	Russell Lorraine	Patmore	Edith May	36809/1928	St Peters
Shoveller	Stephen T.	Moore	Catherine	22621/1898	Sydney
Shoveller	Sydney H.	Niner	Susannah T.	4091/1909	Sydney
Shoveller	Thomas	Dargan	Phoebe M.	7420/1927	Glebe
Shoveller	Thomas H.	Keough	Doris M.A.	36812/1969	St Peters
Shoveller	Warren James	Heyen	Michelle Anne	9925/1910	Newtown
Shoveller	William E.	Treble	Elsie C.	31911/1942	Sutherland
Shoveller	William Edward	MacNamara	Mary		
Shoveller	William Henry	Miller	Elizabeth Janet Thomson	25148/1940	

Shoveller Females

Groom's Surname	Groom's Firstname	Bride's Surname	Bride's Firstname	Reg #	Name(S)/District
Meadows	Richard Terence	Shoveller	Carole Suzanne	6020/1968	Sydney
Banks	Ashley Bede Neil	Shoveller	Caroline May	1915/1968	Newtown
Shaw	John L.	Shoveller	Dorothy B.	1549/21934	Redfern
Hamer	John J.	Shoveller	Edna F. C.	7338/1931	Waverley

INDEX

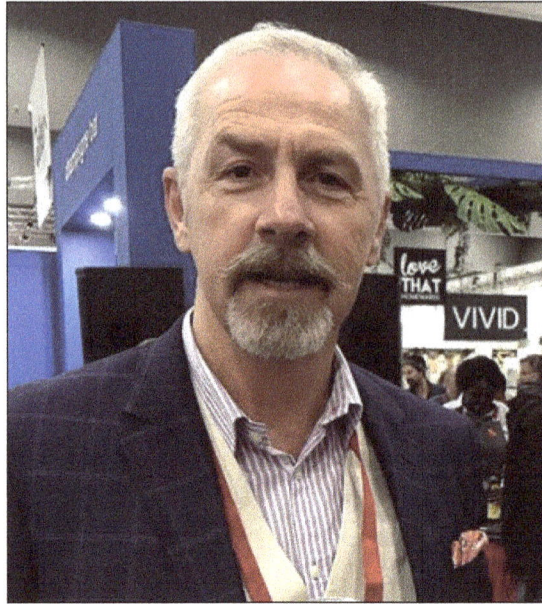

THE AUTHOR

Dr Tracy Rockwell originally taught in both primary and high schools and was later appointed as a lecturer in Human Movement at the Faculty of Education at Sydney University, where he spent 25 years, ahead of launching out on his own as a sports writer, photographer, artist, author and scholar. As a sportman he was a swimmer, surf life saver, rugby player, a NSW representative water polo player and in 2021 was Oceanic Indoor Rowing champion for his age group. With a penchant for history he published 'Water Warriors: Chronicle of Australian Water Polo' in 2009, and received the 'Harry Quittner Medal' for his contribution to Australian Water Polo. He is also an avid genealogist and begins his 'Rockwell Genealogies' with this publication. Other books and illustrated journals by Dr. Rockwell are available through Pegasus Publishing:

TITLE	ISBN	GENRE	FORMAT	PUB.	DATE	PAGES
Water Warriors: Chronicle of Australian Water Polo	978-0-646488-61-5	Sports History	Hardback	2009	597
The Complete Guide to Rugby World Cup (2015)	978-0-994201-42-3	Sports History	Ebook	2015	161
Play Water Polo: An Interactive Instructional Sports Guide	978-0-994201-40-9	Sports Development	Ebook [interactive]	2016	94
The Unknown Journey (Editor)	978-0-994201-48-5	Autobiography	Ebook	2016	136
The Unknown Journey: Surviving Hodgkin's Lymphoma (Editor)	978-0-994201-49-2	Autobiography	Paperback	2016	136
How to Play Water Polo: The Complete Guide to Mastering the Game	978-0-994201-41-6	Sports Development	Paperback	2018	215
Juega Polo Acuático: Guía Interactiva de Deportes de Instrucción	978-0-994201-43-0	Sports Development	Ebook	2018	96
Love Never Lets You Go: Aphorisms about Love Journal [illust.]	978-0-994201-46-1	Sociology	Paperback	2018	216
One Day at a Time: Aphorisms about Life Journal [illust.]	978-0-994201-47-8	Sociology	Paperback	2018	218
Journal of Life's Lessons: With Vintage Images and Aphorisms [illust.]	978-0-994201-44-7	Sociology	Hardback	2019	218
Who's There? Worlds Funniest A-Z Book of 737 Knock Knock Jokes	978-0-994201-45-4	Childrens-Fiction	Paperback	2019	107
Who's There? Worlds Funniest A-Z Book of 737 Knock Knock Jokes	978-1-925909-28-9	Childrens-Fiction	Ebook	2019	107
Australian Seascapes Journal [illust.]	978-1-925909-05-0	Sociology	Paperback	2019	128
Australian Landscapes Journal [illust.]	978-1-925909-06-7	Sociology	Paperback	2019	128
The Complete Guide to Rugby World Cup (2019)	978-1-925909-07-4	Sports History	Paperback	2019	198
My Handy Cruise Journal [illust.]	978-1-925909-10-4	Sociology	Paperback	2019	130
My Handy Travel Journal [illust.]	978-1-925909-11-1	Sociology	Paperback	2019	130
A History of the Ancestors of James Mahoney O'Sullivan and Ellen Frawley	978-1-925909-00-5	Genealogy	Paperback	2020	584
Australian Animals: Through the Looking Glass	978-1-925909-01-2	Childrens-Animals	Paperback	2020	68
Bush Dreaming and Other Plays (Editor)	978-1-925909-02-9	Literature-Drama	Paperback	2020	212
The Spirit of Bronte: A History of Bronte Amateur Water Polo Club 1943-1975	978-1-925909-03-6	Sports History	Paperback	2020	329
Tracy Rockwell: Catalogue Raisonné 2000-2020	978-1-925909-12-8	Art	Paperback	2021	342
Mystery at Melon Flats (Editor)	978-1-925909-04-3	Literature-Novel	Paperback	2022	192
Mystery at Melon Flats (Editor)	978-1-925909-09-8	Literature-Novel	Ebook	2022	192
The Long Road To Grafton: A Genealogy of Thomas Eastman Shoveller	978-1-925909-08-1	Genealogy	Paperback	2022	362

www.ingramcontent.com/pod-product-compliance
Lightning Source LLC
Chambersburg PA
CBHW042337030426
42335CB00030B/3380